Short-Lived Television Series,
1948–1978

Short-Lived Television Series, 1948–1978

Thirty Years of More Than 1,000 Flops

WESLEY HYATT

McFarland & Company, Inc., Publishers

Jefferson, North Carolina, and London

All photographs from Photofest unless otherwise specified.

Library of Congress Cataloguing-in-Publication Data

Hyatt, Wesley.
Short-lived television series, 1948–1978 : thirty years of more than
1,000 flops / Wesley Hyatt.
p.   cm.
Includes bibliographical references and index.

ISBN 0-7864-1420-0 (softcover : 50# alkaline paper) ∞

1. Television programs— United States— Catalogs.   I. Title.
PN1992.3.U5H95   2003   791.45'75'0973 — dc21   2002013334

British Library cataloguing data are available

Cover photograph (left to right): Joe E. Ross, Jack Mullaney,
Mike Mazurki, Pat Cardi, Mary Grace, Cliff Norton, Frank Aletter
and Imogene Coca from the show *It's About Time*

Manufactured in the United States of America

*McFarland & Company, Inc., Publishers
Box 611, Jefferson, North Carolina 28640
www.mcfarlandpub.com*

To the memory of my late cousins
Joey Eshelman and Debbie Swaim.
You are not forgotten.

ACKNOWLEDGMENTS

Asking people to discuss experiences generally considered "failures" is not the easiest task for a writer. A considerable number of potential subjects contacted for interviews for this book refused to talk to me. Perhaps the most polite brushoff came from a producer who wrote, "While I wish you all good fortune with your new book, and would like to be helpful, tearing off the scabs of old wounds would not be a very rewarding experience for me. I hope you understand."

I certainly understood, but respectfully, I couldn't disagree more. Almost everyone with a significant career in television has had a series run a year or less, and in some cases these efforts are more fascinating than many long-running successes. To be a part of them and not want to share your story to later generations, no matter how painful the memories are, is to me being short-sighted. Why should several histories be written about such dubious properties as *The Brady Bunch* and *Gilligan's Island* while "failures" such as the Emmy winner *My World ... and Welcome to It* (Best Comedy Series in 1970) get relatively little ink?

Fortunately, there were a sizable number of people who concurred with my opinion, and their memories—funny, sad, angry, indifferent — are captured within these pages. These people lent their knowledge and opinions to more than entries in this book. So please take note of the following actors, ac-

tresses, writers, directors and producers who took time out of their busy schedules to look back and reveal part of their lives (the list is alphabetical by last name, with the interview date listed afterward):

Norman Alden (July 23, 2001); Dayton Allen (May 12, 2001); Paul Alter (Oct. 22, 2001); William Asher (Nov. 13, 2001); Jeanne Baird (June 25, 2001); Dave Barnhizer (Oct. 20, 2001); William Beaudine Jr. (June 27, 2001); Ted Beniades (June 11, 2001); Bert Berdis (July 16, 2001); Cherney Berg (Sept. 27, 2001); Lyle Bettger (letter dated Sept. 19, 2001); Bradley Bolke (May 5, 2001); Oscar Brand (July 8, 2001); Irving Brecher (Sept. 17, 2001); David Brenner (July 16, 2001); Bruce Brownfield (July 8, 2001); George Burditt (Jan. 18, 2002); Kitty Carlisle Hart (July 4, 2001); Angel Casey (May 3, 2001); Mel Casson (May 7, 2001); Marge Champion (Aug. 23, 2001); Tony Charmoli (July 31, 2001); Stanley Cherry (June 27, 2001); Blair Chotzinoff (Oct. 23, 2001); Jane Connell (Aug. 6, 2001); Robert Courtleigh (June 25, 2001); Pat Cranshaw (July 30, 2001); Chase Crosley (June 2, 2001); Perry Cross (Oct. 25, 2001); Dick Darley (June 11, 2001); Hal Davis (Sept. 17, 2001); Leo De Lyon (July 17, 2001); Sam Denoff (June 7, 2001); Tom Donovan (June 8, 2001); Charles S. Dubin (Oct. 11, 2001); Ruth Duskin Feldman (July 10, 2001); Alix Elias (July 27, 2001); Richard Erdman (May 29, 2001); Howard Erskine (July 4, 2001); Frank Fazakas (May 5,

vii

2001); Norman Felton (letter dated Sept. 25, 2001); Mel Ferber (June 20, 2001); Bob Finkel (Oct. 10, 2001); Olga Ford (July 30, 2001); Bill Foster (Oct. 29, 2001); Jerry Freedman (June 1, 2001); Devery Freeman (letter dated Dec. 1, 2001); Helen Gallagher (Aug. 14, 2001); Mike Gargiulo (Oct. 17, 2001); Greg Garrison (Nov. 21, 2001); Richard Goggin (Sept. 25, 2001); Marty Gold (Aug. 23, 2001); Bruce Gordon (Aug. 11, 2001); Alex Grasshoff (June 4, 2001); Lloyd Gross (June 18, 2001 and Oct. 20, 2001); Argus Hamilton (July 28, 2001); Jeanne Harrison (Oct. 16, 2001); Chris Hayward (Jan. 14, 2002); Dwight Hemion (Oct. 22, 2001); Martin Hoade (Sept. 20, 2001); Celeste Holm (Aug. 1, 2001); Roy Huggins (Nov. 26, 2001); Peter H. Hunt (June 19, 2001); Bill Idelson (Oct. 12, 2001); Coleman Jacoby (Oct. 3, 2001); Frank Jacoby (Oct. 8, 2001); Art James (Oct. 18, 2001); Gerald Jann (Aug. 9, 2001); Clark Jones (June 20, 2001); Buck Kartalian (May 17, 2001); Lee H. Katzin (Nov. 17, 2001); Don Keefer (June 11, 2001); Noah Keen (June 18, 2001); Edward Kemmer (June 28, 2001); Lynwood King (Oct. 8, 2001); Ernest Kinoy (Nov. 12, 2001); Don Kranze (Oct. 29, 2001); Bernie Kukoff (Nov. 13, 2001); Perry Lafferty (Sept. 29, 2001); Arnold Laven (May 28, 2001); Cherylene Lee (July 30, 2001); George Lefferts (Oct. 29, 2001); Ralph Levy (June 30, 2001); Grey Lockwood (Sept. 25, 2001); Salem Ludwig (May 2, 2001); Jim Malinda (May 4, 2001); Martin Manulis (Nov. 2, 2001); Leslie Martinson (May 31, 2001); Don Meier (Oct. 3, 2001); Lee Mendelson (Oct. 10, 2001); Kraig Metzinger (e-mailed Aug. 29, 2001); Robert Ellis Miller (Nov. 13, 2001); Bruce Minnix (Oct. 31, 2001); Kate Murtagh (July 10, 2001); Cliff Norton (July 31, 2001); Fred O'Neill (Oct. 4, 2001); George Pentecost (Aug. 21, 2001); Cynthia Pepper (Dec. 18, 2001); Fern Persons (May 6, 2001); John Peyser (May 30, 2001); Stuart W. Phelps (Sept. 18, 2001); Remo Pisani (July 23, 2001); Seymour Robbie (June 11, 2001); Robert Rockwell (Aug. 21, 2001); Joel Rogosin (May 5, 2001); Sol Saks (Nov. 2, 2001); Jay Sandrich (Nov. 26, 2001); William Self (June 1, 2001); Melville Shavelson (Nov. 14, 2001); Ira Skutch (Sept. 10, 2001); Jeremy Slate (June 15, 2001); Sidney Smith (Oct. 11, 2001); Leonard B. Stern (July 17, 2001); Gil Stratton Jr. (June 4, 2001); Lela Swift (June 11, 2001); Hal Tulchin (June 25, 2001); Kip Walton (e-mailed June 24, 2001); Lisl Weil (May 14, 2001); Jorn Winther (Oct. 10, 2001); Florian Zabach (Aug. 15, 2001); Carmen Zapata (Aug. 15, 2001).

To all of them I say again thank you, and I just wish I had more space to include your often fascinating tales.

To buttress people's stories (and cross-check them for facts), I consulted many sources that I have listed in the bibliography. As for the photos herein, unless otherwise noted, they are from the generous and pleasant people at Photofest in New York City. I tip my hat yet another time to Ronald Mandelbaum and his top-notch research staff, especially Derek Davidson, who found what I was looking for, and Rick Goeren, who gave me contact information on actress Cynthia Pepper (and who must boast the most impressive collection of *Margie* memorabilia on the planet!).

I should thank as always my family, especially my mom, Gayle Hyatt, and father, Ron Hyatt, who supported me diligently and unconditionally once again on a book project. I also owe a huge debt of gratitude for my superiors at Divers Alert Network in Durham, N.C., where I regularly work between devouring bits of entertainment history, so thank you founder, president and CEO Dr. Peter B. Bennett, and executive vice president and chief operating officer Dan Orr. I want to say a very special thanks to my immediate boss, Renée Duncan Westerfield, who offered unprecedented allowances of time and much encouragement for me to do this book. Everyone else should be as lucky to have someone as intelligent and professional to deal with on a daily basis.

Wesley Hyatt
Fall 2002

TABLE OF CONTENTS

THE SEASONS

PREFACE

Benjamin Franklin once noted that "in this world nothing is certain but death and taxes." Americans who have grown up in the latter half of the 20th century and the start of the 21st century might amend that saying to include "and cancellation of TV shows."

After more than 50 years of national telecasting, viewers in the United States have seen thousands of series go on and off, most lasting a year or less. It's just become a fact of life, and those shows typically have disappeared despite protest from hardy fans, with little fanfare apart from some press releases, reviews in publications and maybe an article or two.

For years television historians have relied primarily on mentions in the print media to recall the medium's flops, especially since many of the series from the 1940s through 1970s were unavailable to be seen after their initial run.

I wanted to know more about these series, and I felt they deserved more attention, so I went to the people involved with them to get the stories behind many of the shows. Most information in this book comes from my interviews with them on the genesis, life and death of their programs.

The Scope of the Book

Documented within these pages are all commercial network series which lasted a year or less from the 1948-1949 season through the 1977-1978 season, with a few exceptions to be given shortly. There were short-lived shows before 1948 and after 1978, of course, but I have limited it to this period for specific reasons. The 1948-49 season included the first full nighttime (and some daytime) lineups for the American Broadcasting Company (ABC), the Columbia Broadcasting System (CBS) and the National Broadcasting Company (NBC), as well as the DuMont network, which folded in 1955 after a valiant struggle to keep up with the three major networks. DuMont and NBC had been involved extensively in TV broadcasts in the early to mid 1940s, save for the middle years of World War II, which severely limited air time. By the time the war ended, they both presented a rather large variety of shows which, starting mainly in late 1946, began to be transmitted to a few other East Coast cities beyond New York City, the main city involved in telecasting at the time. Most of the programs were short-lived, but also because they were mostly experimental with hardly any sponsors to back them, they were not supposed to run long anyway.

After years of sitting out of TV due to various concerns, CBS and ABC began their telecasting efforts in depth in 1948, and it was possible at that time in a few cities to have a choice between shows on four networks. Only 1 percent of American households had a TV in 1948, but that came out to several million viewers. And those who didn't have the newfangled machine definitely anticipated getting one in their area, with the result that TV ownership kept growing and growing.

Fast forward to the 1977–1978 season. By that time, only some 3 percent of homes in America did *not* have TVs, and the atmosphere for getting viewers had become more intense over the past few years. When CBS programming president Fred Silverman left the network for ABC in 1975, he led that company to its first seasonal win among the networks in 1975–76. Executives at both CBS and NBC were shaken. Ever since ABC began in 1943 on radio as a spinoff of one of NBC's networks as a result of anti-trust regulations, it always had been #3 overall each season while CBS and NBC often duked it out for the top spot (NBC won through the mid–1950s, but then CBS stayed #1 for 18 years straight, albeit sometimes with just a sliver of a ratings point margin of victory over NBC).

The change in the programming world led to a new unsteadiness in the industry and quicker cancellations than the typical 13 weeks generally given to new programs to prove themselves. Suddenly NBC canned a David Brenner sitcom named *Snip* in 1976 so late into the upcoming season that the annual "Fall Preview" section of *TV Guide* carried a photo and story on the show (the magazine's main listings, which had a later deadline, informed viewers that despite what they had read, *Snip* was not going on the air).

All that was nothing compared to the 1978–1979 season, however. When Silverman left ABC to go to NBC, havoc hit the network suites to see who could be #1, and cancellation fever ran rampant in efforts to have hits as quickly as possible. As with *Snip*, another series failed to make it to the air that season, but on a tighter deadline— CBS canned *Mr. Dugan* just four days before it was to make its debut. There was also a show that lasted just one episode. *Co-Ed Fever*, a ripoff of the movie *Animal House* that unnerved CBS when its viewership following the TV premiere of the hit film *Rocky II* on February 4, 1979, lost 16 shares of the latter's audience. And then there were several other series which lasted only four episodes or fewer (*Apple Pie*, *Flatbush*, *W.E.B.* and even *Mary*, a variety show starring one of TV's favorites, Mary Tyler Moore).

For so many shows to end so early in a season was unprecedented. Unfortunately for those working on series, it became standard operating practice thereafter, with the networks giving producers orders for only six shows to air before making a decision on them rather than the customary 13 weekly episodes as before.

This new programming strategy led to a higher rate of earlier cancellations than ever before, and because of the rise of videocassette recorders and the cable industry at the same time, 1978 provides a nice stopping point to end this survey. The days of network telecasting clearly had peaked after thirty years of steady growth.

Criteria for Inclusion in the Book

The sheer number of possible candidates forced me to set up some restrictions. I deal only with entertainment; no news, documentaries, public affairs, sports or theatrical movie series are in these pages.

Neither are syndicated shows, ones which were sold individually to stations rather than over the networks, because many of them ran only one season, and to include them would easily double the size of this work.

Getting pickier, I excluded some genres of programs, with a few exceptions. I focused on shows with recurring characters, so I've omitted dozens of variety shows with no recurring cast members and anthology series that had only a single host as their returning element on screen each week. But I did allow anthology series to creep in if the host played a character, such as on *Ghost Story*.

Many cartoons such as *Top Cat* and *The Jetsons* were in production only one year yet aired in reruns for years on the network; rather than trying to determine if they belonged, I made the easier decision to drop animated series from consideration altogether.

Summer series generally were replacements for vacationing series and designed not to run long, so I did not include them unless they returned in the regular season and, of course, flopped. It's odd, but it happened several times.

Those sound like pretty big restrictions, yet they still left around 950 series eligible for the book, even being strict about the series starting and ending in a 12-month period (a few entries, such as *The Clear Horizon* and *Science All-Stars*, ran 12 months or less in several stints over a year-long period).

Death or ill health among the participants, plus sheer logistics, left me unable to interview at least one person for each show, so for some entries I've just summarized them within each season's writeup. Nevertheless, I have interviewed enough people to cover 230 shows, or more than a quarter of all the eligible entries, in more depth.

The Book's Arrangement

The series herein are listed chronologically by the September through August seasons in which they debuted. The one exception is the 1975-76 season, where CBS aired *Big Eddie* and *Beacon Hill* in "sneak previews" in August 1975 before their "official" September debuts; I've included them in 1975-76 rather than 1974-75 because of their odd designation. Within most seasons, series are listed in order of their debuts. The exceptions to this arrangement are the 1948-49, 1949-50, and 1950-51 seasons. Nearly a quarter of all the series eligible for this book appeared in those three seasons, but television broadcasting was spotty in those days—there was no cable hookup from the East Coast to the West until 1952 — and consistent information is hard to come by. For each of these three seasons I first cover the profiled shows (i.e., those for which I was able to find and interview personnel), in order of their debut; the remaining shows for each season are listed by title only, in alphabetical order.

The abbreviations used in all entries are C for cast, W for writer, P for producer, EP for executive producer, AP for associate producer and D for director.

I have tried to be as complete as possible, but information regarding writers, producers and directors is sketchy for many early series, and in later ones there were new writers and directors with every episode, whom in the interest of space I've declined to record. Still, this is the most extensive record of these shows' personnel ever put in a reference book (and I used several to help me).

For all but the first five seasons I've listed the time slots in which the series ran and the shows airing opposite them on the other networks (Eastern time zone for both), so the reader can decide how much the competition may have played a part in giving a show an early boot. What surprised me is how infrequently my interviewees blamed their programs' demise on ratings. Generally they felt their failures had more to do with some intrinsic flaws in the presentations instead.

The special arrangement of the first three seasons has already been explained. For the 1951-52 through 1953-54 seasons, I have not listed all the time slots for the nighttime shows, as there was much jockeying between ABC and DuMont over which network would be the third major network to survive, and often their shows ran outside major markets at other time periods, and sometimes on television stations sharing affiliations with more than one network. In the 1954-55 season DuMont faded away and ABC came to prominence.

Entries for series that are covered in depth will enlighten and surprise you with forgotten or unknown facts. You'll learn the links between the 1949 game show *Draw Me a Laugh* and Clifford Irving, the forger of an alleged autobiography by Howard Hughes; the Cannes Film Festival and the 1974 Saturday morning prehistoric adventure series *Korg: 70,000 B.C.*; and much more. You'll learn why 1961's *You're in the Picture* and 1969's *Turn On* lasted only one episode. You'll find out what it was like to be involved with infamous creations like *My Mother the Car* and *The Man from Atlantis*.

Keep in mind that some memories are more vivid than others, particularly among directors and writers used to freelancing on most shows from the late 1950s through 1970s. Allen Reisner, who directed episodes of *Leave It to Larry* and *Going My Way*, told me those shows were so long ago in a career filled with hundreds of TV episodes that he couldn't recall anything specific for me. In some instances, a participant spouted off a fountain of memories of one series while coming up dry with another. Given that we're dealing with properties that existed about a quarter to a half a century ago or more, these limitations are understandable.

My goal is to appreciate people who attempted to entertain America and came up short despite their best efforts. They may have suffered disappointment at the time, but their work was worthwhile. I only hope I have adequately conveyed the feelings they have about their show or shows, and that people in succeeding generations will enjoy these stories concerning the most pervasive medium of our time.

THE SEASONS

1948-49

For Your Pleasure

Musical Variety. Ran on NBC Thursdays 8–8:15 P.M. April 15–June 1948, opposite *Hollywood Screen Test* on ABC, then NBC Wednesdays 8–8:15 P.M. July–September 1948, opposite *The Gay Nineties Revue* on ABC, and then NBC Saturdays 8:30–9 P.M. July–Sept. 10, 1949, opposite *Spin the Picture* on DuMont. C: Kyle MacDonnell, Norman Paris Trio, Jack and Jill (April–June 1948), Blaire and Deane (June–September 1948), Earl Shelton Orchestra (1949). P/D: Fred Coe.

The year 1948 saw the debut of several notable personalities who would be the leading lights of early television — Milton Berle, Arthur Godfrey, Ed Sullivan. But for every one of them there were several like Kyle MacDonnell, who wanted to make the big time but did not do so for various reasons. Her first effort toward TV stardom was a starring regular role on *For Your Pleasure*.

Though he had nothing to do with the series, director Ira Skutch was instrumental in getting MacDonnell and her series on the air. "It was put on because John Royal saw Kyle MacDonnell in *Make Mine Manhattan* on Broadway and called Warren Wade and said he wanted to see her on TV," said Skutch. Royal was NBC's vice president of new developments (TV was considered a new development when the department was formed in the 1940s), and Wade was executive producer of NBC Television and Skutch's boss.

Following Wade's edict, Skutch set up a TV audition for MacDonnell at NBC's New York station one evening at 7:30 P.M., singing two songs for seven minutes. "John Royal saw it at home, watched the show, and then we shut down until 8," he said. The station typically began broadcasting at 8 P.M. weeknights in 1948.

Royal was impressed with MacDonnell, so Skutch allowed her to guest a couple of times on a series Skutch directed called *Musical Merry-Go-Round* (originally titled *Disc Magic*), which ran on NBC weekly from July 24, 1947, to March 11, 1949. Those appearances led to her getting her own series. *For Your Pleasure* teamed her with the Norman Paris Trio, an instrumental combo led by Paris on piano, and the dancing team of Jack and Jill, replaced after three months by the similarly forgotten dancing duo of Blair and Deane. It fared well enough that it found a sponsor in the fall of 1948 and become a bigger production starring MacDonnell called *Girl About Town* (see that title in this chapter for more information).

But *Girl About Town* did not pan out as expected, so after its run in the summer *For Your Pleasure* returned without dancers but with an orchestra and an expanded 30-minute format like *Girl About Town* rather than its previous 15-minute length. The revival proved to be not for the pleasure of many. It lasted just two more months before NBC replaced it with two 15-minute series from Chicago, *Chicago Jazz* and *Stud's Place*.

America Song

Musical Variety. Ran on NBC Wednesdays 8–8:15 P.M. April 21–July 1948, then NBC Tuesdays 7:30–7:50 P.M. July–September 1948, opposite news on CBS and news on DuMont, then NBC Mondays 7:30–7:50 P.M. October 1948–February 1949, opposite *Kiernan's Corner* on ABC, news on CBS and news on DuMont, and then various 15-minute slots NBC evenings March–April 25, 1949. C: Paul Arnold, Nellie Fisher, Ray Harrison. D: Ira Skutch.

The names Paul Arnold, Nelle Fisher and Ray Harrison meant little to most people even when they were regulars on *America Song*, but despite their lack of fame the show's director, Ira Skutch, credited them with pioneering TV's presentation of music and dance. Using selections of American folk music (hence the title) sung by Arnold and danced by Fisher and Harrison, Skutch worked with them and his crew to show numbers as best as they could with three cameras live from New York in the early days of TV.

"As I recall, we used to work three to four days each show, but not all day," said Skutch. "We — the four of us — would pick the material, and Nellie would do the choreography. We would rehearse about three hours the day of the show."

Concerning the regulars, Fisher, who Skutch called "a very good dancer and an excellent choreographer," had the most impressive performing background, having been in the cast of the 1940s Broadway hit musicals *One Touch of Venus* and *On the Town*. She and Harrison worked together in the Broadway revue *Make Mine Manhattan*, which opened on Jan. 15, 1948, before they left to do the TV series. As for Arnold, who strummed the guitar as well as sang, he never had even an entry on any of the pop or country music charts.

Skutch thought the planning he did with the trio paid off in a fine if short, and short-lived, series. "It was excellent," he said. "Whatever criticism we got was all very good. It was really a lovely show, too good for today's market."

However, he did acknowledge the folk music presented may not have been the grab-ber for early TV audiences either. Regarding fan mail for the show (about the best gauge at the time, since there were no ratings), he said, "We got very little."

And advertisers were not arguing over the right to sell their wares on the program either. "We never had a sponsor, at least when I left the network in October 1948," Skutch said. He freelanced for six months, then thrived when he joined the regular directing staff of the prestigious *Philco TV Playhouse* in January 1949 and stayed with that show until it ended in 1955, then joined the staff of the Mark Goodson-Bill Todman game show production company for nearly 30 years.

The on-air cast was nowhere nearly as fortunate as Skutch on TV. Harrison never had another regular TV job. Arnold had the short-lived *Paul Arnold Show* in 1949-50 (q.v.), then disappeared. And Fisher worked on the first two years of the hit *Your Show of Shows* from 1950 to 1952, only to get only one other regular role on the low-budget 1954 summer music series *Melody Tour*.

Places Please (a/k/a Backstage with Barry Wood)

Talent/Variety. Ran on CBS Mondays, Wednesdays and Fridays 7:15–7:30 P.M. Aug. 16, 1948–Feb. 25, 1949 opposite *Doorway to Fame* (Mondays), *Birthday Party* (Wednesdays) and *Key to the Missing* (Fridays) on DuMont and *Kukla, Fran and Ollie* on NBC (except for *Story of the Week* on Wednesdays November 1948–Jan. 5, 1949), then CBS Tuesdays 10–10:15 P.M. March 1–May 24, 1949, opposite boxing on ABC and NBC. C/P: Barry Wood. D: Ralph Levy, Kingman T. Moore.

After a regular stint as a singer on radio's *Your Hit Parade* from 1939 to 1940, Barry Wood spent most of the 1940s in unsuccessful radio series and on the pop music chart with a few minor hit records. With his career not going full throttle, he entered the new medium of TV as host and producer of *Places Please*, a variety show spotlighting newcomers.

"It wasn't amateurs," remembered director Ralph Levy. He remembered some of the talent who appeared included Bob Fosse and his then-wife, Mary Ann Niles, who were a dance team at the time; comic Jack Sterling; and choreographer John Butler. Fosse, Niles and Sterling worked together as regulars a few months later on *The 54th Street Revue* (q.v.).

Places Please ran thrice weekly before the CBS news for six months, then Wood took his act into a weekly later slot under the title *Backstage with Barry Wood*, thanks to getting a sponsor with Household Finance Corp. (*Places Please* had no commercials). Kingman T. Moore replaced Levy as director for the show, and Charles Speer signed on as its writer. That version ran only two months.

Levy had fond memories of the host of the show. "Barry was a very nice person," he said. "He was a great singer." Wood also was quite a busy guy that season. He produced a similar show that replaced *Places Please* on its thrice nightly slot, *Manhattan Showcase* (q.v.), and another 1948-49 variety series *Kobbs Korner* (q.v.). By the 1950s Wood dropped his on-camera duties and just became a TV producer, including a long run on *The Bell Telephone Hour*. He died in 1970 at age 61.

Girl About Town

Musical Variety. Ran on NBC Wednesdays 8–8:30 P.M. Sept. 8, 1948–January 1949, opposite *The Gay Nineties Revue* on ABC, *Kobbs Korner* on CBS and *Photographic Horizons* on DuMont, then NBC Sundays 10–10:30 P.M. February–June 11, 1949, opposite *Action Autographs* and *Bowling Headliners* on ABC and news on CBS. C: Kyle MacDonnell, Johnny Downs (1948), Earl Wrightson (1948–49), the Norman Paris Trio. P: Fred Coe. D: Ira Skutch. W: Joyce Sentner.

When the Bates Fabric Company, maker of items for beds such as pillow sheets, decided to advertise on NBC, the series the network sold them on was a modified version of *For Your Pleasure* (q.v.). Taken from that show were star Kyle MacDonnell and the Norman Paris Trio as musicmakers. Added was former movie musical star Johnny Downs, playing MacDonnell's press agent, and a new director and writer to give the half-hour show a storyline.

"It had this gimmick of Kyle running about town, and we had 16mm film on it," director Ira Skutch said. The film was silent, with live voiceovers on the show, and included scenes of Kyle appearing at various landmarks in New York City where Downs supposedly had her booked as a performer. Otherwise, the show was done live in a studio from New York City with a few numbers by MacDonnell.

Downs left the show by October to be replaced by Earl Wrightson. Skutch also left the show, but not on his own free will. Once he made a mistake in timing the program, resulting in Bates' final commercial not getting on air, and he was fired.

Yet despite Skutch's contributions and that of others, he would be the first to say that *Girl About Town* definitely was MacDonnell's show all the way, and that she had moderate talent as a performer. "She was a pop singer," said Skutch. "She was pretty good. Barbra Streisand she wasn't." MacDonnell did not have a hit record despite her considerable TV work.

Skutch said this show and its predecessor gave McDonnell the aura of being TV's top female personality for a time in the late 1940s, but it faded quickly as she did not distinguish herself from others coming into the medium. "She was the biggest star on television at the time, on *Life* magazine and so on, but it's hard to sustain that if nothing else comes along," he said.

When *Girl About Town* went off after nine months (the last three under the title *Around the Town*), MacDonnell went back to the old *For Your Pleasure* series in the summer of 1949. She became a regular in the next season on another short-lived effort, *Hold That Camera* (q.v.), then was a panelist on the game show *Celebrity Time* from 1950 to 1951 (in the same time slot *Girl About Town* had in 1949, only on CBS rather than NBC). She virtually vanished from TV after that, and following a role in the national touring company of the play *Twin Beds* in 1953, she has not been heard from since.

Kobbs Korner

Music Variety. Ran on CBS Wednesdays 8–8:30 P.M. Sept. 29, 1948–January 1949, opposite *The Gay Nineties Revue* on ABC, *Girl About Town* on NBC and *Photographic Horizons* on DuMont, then CBS Thursdays 8–8:30 P.M. January–February 1949, opposite *American Minstrels of 1949* on ABC, *Operation Success* on DuMont and *The Arrow Show* on NBC, and then CBS Wednesdays 9:30–10 P.M. March–June 15, 1949, opposite *Kraft Television Theatre* on NBC. C: Hope Emerson (as Maw Shufflebottom), Jo Hurt (as Josiebelle Shufflebottom), Stan Fritts and the Korn Kobblers, Betty Garde (1949). P: Barry Wood. D: Kingman T. Moore. W: Charles Speer.

People who think CBS began to exploit rural-based comedies in the 1960s with *The Andy Griffith Show* and *The Beverly Hillbillies*,

Stan Fritts (in the middle on trombone, in front of pianist Marty Gold) whoops it up with the rest of the Korn Kobblers in this 1949 photo for *Kobbs Korner*. Note the "Tune in CBS *Kobbs Korner*" sign on the wall under the clock, the painted background of country store goods, and the ladder behind the set in the upper right-hand corner, which hopefully was not seen by home viewers.

among others, obviously have forgotten *Kobbs Korner*. This rustic variety show stood out among all the network's other cosmopolitan fare like *The Ed Sullivan Show* in the fall of 1948. Here the setting of this live New York–based show was a country store where Maw Shufflebottom, her daughter Josiebelle and her husband invited viewers to listen to the music of the Korn Kobblers, a combo led by Stan Fritts with pianist Marty Gold, bassist Charles Koenig and trumpeter Nels Laakso.

Six-foot-two Hope Emerson, who would get a supporting Oscar nomination playing a really tough prison matron in the 1950 film *Caged*, played Maw Shufflebottom. "She was in character as Stan Fritts' wife," said Marty Gold, the only surviving member of the Korn Kobblers. "Stan Fritts was up front as our trombone player." Gold said Emerson did not sing

on the show, and likewise Fritts did not act, only play his instrument and other wilder creations like a washboard outfitted with horns, a bell, a whistle, a siren and more.

Gold traced his involvement with the Korn Kobblers back to 1938, when he was offered a place in a band called Schnickelfritz. He liked many of his cohorts there except one. "Freddie Fisher, the leader of the group, was pretty obnoxious and self-serving," Gold said. By 1939 he couldn't take Fisher anymore.

"We got to a point where I was going to leave," he said. "Then the rest of the group [Fritts, Koenig and Laakso] decided they were going to leave him too. We stayed together, and I named our group the Korn Kobblers." Gold said there was no particular reason why he came up with that name, but it appealed to the rest of the group given their style of music.

"They were all good musicians," Gold said. "It was a good Dixieland band. Their premise of comedy was intertwined with a Dixieland feel." The Korn Kobblers also wore funny hats and outfits to augment their humor, which offered a visual appeal that TV could exploit.

Regarding their entry into television via *Kobbs Korner*, Gold said, "I guess we were working somewhere in New Jersey, and we were approached by somebody about it." He frankly was unimpressed by the final result. "It was just a little entry into TV, and I don't think it was very interesting. There was nothing much there. It was really kind of an amateur approach."

After the show ended, the Korn Kobblers remained in operation until 1954. Gold became an arranger and producer for RCA Records for such artists as Peter Nero, John Gary and Della Reese. "I did a variety of work, from children's choruses on up," he said. He retired in 2000, long after *Kobbs Korner* had become just a memory.

The Adventures of Oky Doky

Puppet Show. Ran on DuMont Thursdays 7–7:30 P.M. Nov. 15, 1948–March 1949 opposite the news and *Wren's Nest* (from Jan. 13) on ABC and *Kukla, Fran and Ollie* and *Paris Cavalcade of Fashions* (from Nov. 11, 1948–Jan. 20, 1949) on NBC, then DuMont Tuesdays and Thursdays 6:45–7 P.M. March–May 26, 1949. C: Wendy Barrie, Burt Hilber, Pat Barnard, the Mellodaires, Dayton Allen. P/D: Frank Bunetta. W: Ben Zavin.

AUTHOR: "What was it like to work with Wendy Barrie?"
DAYTON ALLEN: "She spoke well of you. What was your name? Phil?"
AUTHOR: "No, it's Wesley."
ALLEN: "I knew it was. Good, you got a good memory. I always liked that about you."

That conversation is a sample of how my interview went with Dayton Allen. Imagine Groucho Marx reborn as an 82-year-old Florida retiree spouting puns and tangential, off-color jokes over half an hour and you've got a good sense of how my discussion went. I somehow gleaned a few facts about *The Adventures of Oky Doky* through the mayhem.

Oky Doky was a 2½-foot tall puppet first seen on a 1947 series on WABD New York City called *Tots, Tweens and Teens*. A year later that station broadcast a weekly show over the DuMont network with the puppet as a cowboy at a dude ranch. *The Adventures of Oky Doky*, done live at Wanamaker's department store in New York City, employed Dayton Allen as the voice and puppeteer for Oky Doky, while former film starlet Wendy Barrie served as the show's primary hostess.

In one of his few serious moments in our interview, Allen recalled Oky as being "a great puppet" but also a difficult one to maneuver. "It was so big, it was clumsy," he said. "I almost got a hernia lifting it. It was designed for someone who had muscles in his stomach."

As to how Allen got involved in the show, he mentioned its producer/director Frank Bunetta, who later directed *The Jackie Gleason Show*. "I don't know if he got me onto the show," Allen said. But before going any further, he was off spouting jokes not appropriate for me to recount to young readers of this book.

Believe me, I tried to rein in Allen, but there was no stopping him. When I asked how he and Wendy Barrie were involved in the production, he replied, "I was too young at that time to get involved with her. She was a lot older. She did her last film in 1726." And on and on and on....

Allen did let it slip that he joined *Howdy Doody* on May 17, 1949, shortly before his old show ended and had a great time there as both a puppeteer and actor until he and others were fired in 1952 for wanting more money. He also said cartoon producer Joseph Barbera tried to lure him to Hollywood in 1960 to do a voice for *The Flintstones* but he stayed in New York instead and did *Deputy Dawg*, other cartoons, and a regular role on *The Steve Allen Show* from 1958 to 1961.

By the way, Dayton Allen was no relation to Steve Allen. His real name is Dayton Allen Bolke. I talked to his brother Bradley Bolke about the latter's series *Ozmoe* (q.v.). It was a much saner experience for me than with Dayton, but I'm sure you already knew that.

Eddie Condon's Floor Show

Musical Variety. Ran on NBC Saturdays 8:30–9 P.M. Jan. 1–July 1949 opposite *Draw Me a Laugh* (from Jan. 15 to Feb. 5) and *Think Fast* (from March 26 to April) on ABC and sports and movies on CBS, then NBC Saturdays 9:30–10 P.M. July–September 1949, opposite *Paul Whiteman's TV Teen Club* on ABC, movies on CBS and *Cavalcade of Stars* on DuMont, and then CBS Saturdays 7:30–8 P.M. May 13–June 24, 1950, opposite *Hollywood Screen Test* on ABC, *Captain Video and His Video Rangers* on DuMont and on NBC. C: Eddie Condon, Carl Reiner (1950). D: Clark Jones.

By the time *Eddie Condon's Floor Show* debuted at the start of 1949, the star already had been on television five years earlier. A jazz guitarist, Condon did not have any hit records to his name but was an influential presence in his field, playing on many artists' records and publicizing the field via a series of jazz concerts on ABC in 1944-45. He was so respected he managed to release his autobiography, *We Called It Music*, in 1947, when he was in his earlier forties.

According to director Clark Jones, Condon had an appeal among jazz musicians beyond just being a proponent of their music. "He was a wit," recalled Jones. "The Dorothy Parker of jazz." Because of that reputation, Jones said, jazz talent such as Jack Teagarden and Ella Fitzgerald made early plunges into TV via his show as guests. "They came out for nothing, maybe $40," Jones said.

Though Condon's TV series actually started on NBC's New York City affiliate in 1944, then called WNBT, it did not gain the attention of Robert Sarnoff, son of NBC's founder David Sarnoff, until it ran on WPIX, an independent station in New York City. "Bobby Sarnoff was a big fan of the show and got it from WPIX," Jones said. But the show lasted only seven months in two time slots on the network. Nearly a year later, CBS tried Condon Saturdays in the early evenings, this time augmented by Carl Reiner as a co-host, but it lasted only seven weeks.

Jones felt the series did not make it on the networks due to what it had that probably appealed to cosmopolitan New Yorkers who had TV sets at the time — its music. "It was a very limited audience, jazz, and there was a minority of people who liked it," he said. CBS replaced it with a show designed to bring in the masses— the kiddie circus show *Big Top*, which ran on Saturday nights for six months before moving to Saturdays at noon from 1951 to 1957.

Condon did not have another network series after 1950, as the medium generally pre-ferred more commercial, pop-oriented acts to spotlight. He died in 1973 at the age of 67.

Stand By for Crime

Crime Drama. Ran on ABC Saturdays 9:30–10 P.M. Jan. 11–April 1949, opposite sports on CBS, films on DuMont and basketball (through March) and *Saturday Night Jamboree* (from April) on NBC, then ABC Saturdays 8–8:30 P.M. May–Aug. 27, 1949, opposite *Spin the Picture* (from June 18) on DuMont and *The U.S. Marine Band* (from July 9) on NBC. C: Boris Aplon (as Inspector Webb; through April), Mike Wallace, billed as "Myron Wallace" (as Lt. Anthony Kidd; from May), George Cisar (as Sgt. Kramer; from May). P/D: Greg Garrison. W: Nancy Goodwin, Jane Ashman.

His greatest fame has been as the top inquisitor of the CBS newsmagazine *60 Minutes* since 1968, but reporter Mike Wallace made his first TV appearance on *Stand By for Crime*, a mystery series wherein he played a lieutenant from a homicide squad. The story of the show and how he got involved with it is no mystery, however, thanks to the vivid memory of its producer and director Greg Garrison.

Garrison's relationship with Wallace went back to when Garrison was a copyboy for the news department at a radio station in Chicago. "The key announcer there was Mike Wallace," Garrison said. "I was a kid 17 years old, going to Northwestern [University], and he was my idol." But World War II interrupted their jobs, and Wallace served in the Navy while Garrison went to the Army. The two men lost touch.

After the war, Wallace returned to Chicago while Garrison became a director in Philadelphia. An ABC executive offered Garrison the chance to direct for the network either from New York or Chicago. Garrison picked the latter, not only because of having spent time there earlier but because of its burgeoning programming that offered him a variety of opportunities, including creating series. One of them was *Stand By for Crime*.

"It was the old *Ellery Queen* radio show," Garrison said of the series. "At the end of the show people would call to guess who the murderer was or guests would give their ideas."

That element worked fine, and *Stand By for Crime* had the honor of being the first show from Chicago transmitted to New York via the opening of a coaxial cable linking the East and

Midwest networks. But there was a problem with its original lead.

"Boris Aplon was a radio actor," Garrison said. "A very nice guy. A very wonderful guy. But he couldn't remember his name without a script. In one show, I think he was looking for a dead body that didn't exist."

Aplon got worse every week until there was one show where, according to Garrison, "He had it so fouled up I couldn't stand it, and I even ripped the card crediting me as director for that show. I told him, 'Boris, I love you, but you're fired.' I turned to one of the script girls and said, 'Get Mike Wallace.'"

Wallace was surprised when he was contacted. He had no idea Garrison was back in Chicago. The two men shared a warm reunion, but Wallace said he was a radio personality who worried about how he would look on television. Garrison convinced him that his fears were unfounded and that he could do the job.

Billed under his given name Myron Wallace, he did the show with George Cisar as his aide Sgt. Kramer. *Stand By for Crime* lasted through the summer of 1949 until ABC replaced it with *Paul Whiteman's TV Teen Club*, which ran until 1954, while Wallace and Garrison moved on to bigger and better TV jobs through the 21st century.

Draw Me a Laugh

Game Show. Ran on ABC Saturdays 8:30–9 P.M. Jan. 15–Feb. 5, 1949, opposite *Eddie Condon's Floor Show* on NBC and sports on CBS. C: Patricia Bright, Walter Hurley, Mel Casson, Jay Irving, Oscar Brand. P: Milton E. Krents. D: Howard Cordery.

Cartoonists Mel Casson (then drawing the *Jeff Crockett* comic strip for the *New York Herald-Tribune* newspaper) and Jay Irving ("He did cartoons of fat cops in *Collier's* magazine," said Casson) created *Draw Me a Laugh*. As Casson recalls, "Television had just reared its ugly head, and we as cartoonists felt this was the medium of the future and went to get our feet wet." They sold their idea of various cartoon-related games (e.g., Irving drawing a character while blindfolded) to ABC executive Ward Byron. "They were desperate for ideas at that time," noted Casson. "He was intrigued by it because it involved drawing."

Producer Milton E. Krents found the cast

and crew, including Patricia Bright, who was dropped as hostess almost immediately in favor of Walter Hurley ("I don't think Milton liked her," Casson said), and folk singer Oscar Brand, who played the show's theme song plus improvised tunes about the cartoons. Two guest cartoonists joined the show each week and received gifts instead of money for payment. "Krents got very expensive watches for them," Casson said.

In the main game, viewers sent in ideas to do cartoons for Casson and a guest cartoonist, and members of the studio audience voted on which was funnier. "I think we paid $100 for the cartoon ideas we selected," Casson said. But one submission cost a viewer more than that. "It seems as though one time someone sent in an idea, and he had deserted his wife. She picked up on him, and she tracked him down with the police," Casson said.

Despite a good review from *Variety*, *Draw Me a Laugh* lasted less than a month. "It just wasn't picking up a big enough audience, according to Ward Byron," said Casson. He was not surprised, saying the execution of his and Irving's idea fell short of what they had envisioned. "I knew from the early stages *Draw Me a Laugh* wouldn't go."

Casson and Irving then created a local New York program called *Judge for Yourself* (not the Fred Allen series of the same name from 1953 to 1954). After it ran just 15 weeks, they left TV to concentrate on cartooning. "*Jeff Crockett* went on for eight years," said Casson. He then did other daily comic strips syndicated to various newspapers. "I've been doing *Redeye* for more than 10 years," he said.

Irving died in 1970, but his son arguably got the fame *Draw Me a Laugh* might have given him if it was a hit. Clifford Irving went to prison for 17 months after being convicted of forging an autobiography of Howard Hughes which Irving claimed he had ghostwritten. Casson, who considered Clifford "a very nice kid growing up," was glad his cartoonist buddy wasn't around to witness his son's situation, for as he put it, "That would've just killed the guy."

Draw Me a Laugh came from New York. If they had done it in Chicago, occasional writer Casson might have been on the show following his in 1949, *Stump the Authors*.

Stump the Authors

Talk. Ran on ABC Saturdays 9–9:30 P.M. Jan. 15–April 2, 1949 opposite basketball on NBC and sports on CBS. C: Syd Breeze, Angel Casey, Dorothy Day, Jack Payne, Lou Zara.

Stump the Authors began on Chicago TV station WBKB in September 1946 with storytellers Dorothy Day, Jack Payne and Lou Zara and host Sydney Mason. The program, also heard on Chicago radio, simply gave Day, Payne and Zara items for which they had to improvise tales, with each trying to outdo the others' concoctions. Day was a Catholic pacifist who wrote her autobiography *From Union Square to Rome* in 1938; Zara wrote several novels, including *This Land Is Ours* (1940) and *Against This Rock* (1943); and Payne was a short story writer.

Less than three years later, *Stump the Authors* came onto ABC as one of its first network shows from Chicago. Syd Breeze replaced Sydney Mason as host (or "editor," as he was called), while actress Angel Casey joined him as co-hostess, not as one of the authors as most books claim. As she noted about her limited extent as a scribe, "I had written some kids' songs, but I had never pushed them much to get them done."

Yet ironically, her stage name came from a book. As she explained, "When I was a junior in college, I dated a boy working with the *Cincinnati Inquirer* (newspaper). The people there wanted me to write book reviews, so I did. One day I went in to get my books and they were tied in a ribbon. And on top was a book called *Angel Casey*. And the boy I was dating was named Bob Casey." She also noticed that the picture on the book looked remarkably like her.

Angel Casey did not impress its namesake ("I thought it was a terrible book, very shallow," she said), but the name stayed with her after she married Bob Casey. And when she went to audition with one director, she found that her married name of Lorraine Casey would not get her into the door, but "Angel Casey" would, so she stuck with it as a professional name. (She later remarried and became Mrs. Lorraine Meinecke in private life.)

Casey had been on television before doing *Stump the Authors*. "I was called in and was told what the idea was, and all I had to do was be the hostess as if I was at home," she said. "Everything was so impromptu. I only had to greet the people."

She is not certain why it ended on ABC after less than three months, although she did note that "Perhaps they didn't promote it properly." Nevertheless, she said, "It was a most enjoyable show to do."

Casey returned to ABC as the assistant on the children's show *Hail the Champ* from 1952 to 1953 and continued to act in Chicago into her eighties. "Last year (in 2000) I did a diabetes commercial," she said. "I would still like to have a show. I'm not doing as much as I'd like to do." As for the rest of her castmates' whereabouts, Day died in 1980, and the others—well, let's just say this author is stumped.

Admiral Broadway Revue

Variety. Ran on NBC and DuMont Fridays 8–9 P.M. Jan. 28–June 3, 1949, opposite *Vaudeo Varieties* (through April 15) and movies and *Ladies Be Seated* (from April 22) on ABC and *Adventures in Jazz* on CBS. C: Sid Caesar, Imogene Coca, Mary McCarty, Marge and Gower Champion, Tom Avera, Ronnie Cunningham, Judson Laire, Estelle Loring, Loren Welch, the Charles Sanford Orchestra. P/D: Max Leibman. W: Mel Tolkin, Lucille Kallen, Ray Carter.

Admiral Broadway Revue was the trial run from the critical and commercial hit series *Your Show of Shows*, which ran on NBC from 1950 to 1954. Both shared much the same personnel and format of music, dance and comic skits, but *Admiral Broadway Revue* went off quickly for an odd reason—it was too successful. The sponsor, Admiral, advertised its appliances on the show, and the audience was so large and responsive (understandable, given that it aired on two networks at the same time, virtually the only series to do so) that the company was unable to keep up with the demand and sponsor a TV show, so the latter had to go.

"I heard that they couldn't make enough refrigerators and freezers," confirmed Marge Champion, who danced on the show with her then-husband, Gower Champion. "They had no idea it would sell so many."

Champion said her ex-husband worked previously with one cast member before *Admiral Broadway Revue* began. "Gower had been in a show during the war, a Coast Guard show called *Tars and Spars*. Sid Caesar was in it. They played in it about a year." After World War II, Gower married Marge, whom he knew since she was 12 years old, and they did early television in New York as a dancing duo.

"In 1947 we went on a [TV] show on NBC," said Champion. The two also married later that year and guested on *The Milton Berle Show* in 1948 before getting the regular job on *Admiral Broadway Revue*.

"Usually we did a duet of our own," she said of their role on the series. "Quite often we did another number with utility dancers, always being spotlighted. If [choreographer] Jimmy Starbuck needed something that was not a straight hoofing number, he'd use us."

The downside in the show's setup was that the Champions did not get to see the early comedy routines of Caesar and Imogene Coca that would make them stars on *Your Show of Shows*. "We were kind of separated until the day we were shot, and don't forget, it was live," she said. Between rehearsals and frenetic costume changes between numbers, the dancers rarely had a chance to see the sketches like home viewers could.

The success of *Admiral Broadway Revue* was not lost on Pat Weaver, NBC's vice president in charge of television, who a year after it ended brought back much of the cast and crew to do *Your Show of Shows* with the new idea at the time of having multiple sponsors for the show, therefore not causing the show to end if its sole advertiser pulled out. "We did not go to *Your Show of Shows* because by that time we did Broadway shows on our own," Champion said. "We had very well-paying gigs. Originally it [TV] didn't pay very much."

Of course, TV soon would pay nicely, and in the Champions did several specials and their own short-lived series; see *The Marge and Gower Champion Show* in 1956-57.

These Are My Children

Soap Opera. Ran on NBC Mondays through Fridays 5–5:15 P.M. Jan. 31–Feb. 25, 1949. C: Alma Platts (as Mrs. Henehan), George Kluge (as John Henehan), Joan Arlt (as Jean Henehan), Jane Brooksmith (as Patricia Henehan), Martha McClain (as Penny Henehan), Margaret Heneghan (as Aunt Kitty Henehan), Eloise Kummer (as Katherine Carter). P/D: Norman Felton. W: Irna Phillips.

Writer Irna Phillips was arguably the "mother" of the soap opera genre; she undoubtedly was the most successful in her field to triumph on both radio and television. Her crowning jewel was *(The) Guiding Light*, which she created and started on radio in 1937 and celebrated its 65th anniversary in 2002 as a daily TV attraction on CBS. First entering radio as an actress, she became a writer when she sold *Painted Dreams* as a daily show for WGN radio in Chicago in 1930. Apparently the first serialized radio drama, *Painted Dreams* stood out as well because Phillips not only wrote the show but played its lead, Mother Moynihan.

When WGN refused to let the show become a network attraction, Phillips left the station and sold NBC on *Today's Children*, which used the same basic characters just slightly altered. Here Phillips played Mother Moran. That show ended in 1937, when Phillips' mother, the inspiration for the main character on *Today's Children*, died, and Phillips lost inspiration for her series. She revived the property in 1943, without acting on it, and it ran until 1950, at one point sharing characters and plotlines with *The Guiding Light* to serve Phillips' interests. Before the second run ended, Phillips adapted *Today's Children* for what would become the first network daily soap opera, *These Are My Children*.

These Are My Children featured another matriarch, this time named Henehan, running a boarding house that had mostly members of her family as tenants. Conflict came from Mrs. Henehan's egocentric daughter Patricia and henpecked son John, whose wife, Jean, was more enamored with money than love. Airing from Chicago over the just-opened coaxial cable between the East and Midwest networks, *These Are My Children* kicked off NBC's broadcasting weekdays for 15 minutes followed by the obscure *Western Balladeer* (which started on Jan. 31, 1949, too and ran with virtually no note of its content) and then the hit *Howdy Doody*.

In a letter to me, the show's producer and director, Norman Felton, recalled that "We used two cameras and one boom mike [microphone] and, with skill from all participants, cast and crew, we received glowing mail from viewers, despite New York saying, 'It will never be like radio, for how could housewives watch television and do the housework?'" It was apparently that concern that led a doubting NBC to can the show within a month, replacing it with an expanded *Western Balladeer* for twice and then thrice a week before it collapsed on July 15, 1949.

The cast of *These Are My Children* did no other network series save for Eloise Kummer, who showed up in another flop soap, *The Bennetts* (q.v.). Felton would go onto several other TV series through the 1970s, both hits and misses. Phillips had the most success of all in daytime, having hits after her initial effort with *The Brighter Day* (1954–1962), *As the World Turns* (1956–present), *Young Dr. Malone* (1958–1963) and *Another World* (1964–1999). She died in 1973.

Manhattan Showcase

Talent/Variety. Ran on CBS Mondays, Wednesdays and Fridays 7:15–7:30 P.M. (later various three to four times a week in the same slot) Feb. 28–June 16, 1949, opposite *The Earl Wrightson Show* (Mondays; through April), *Child's World* (Wednesdays; through April) and *Wren's Nest* (Thursdays/Fridays; through April) on ABC, *The Wendy Barrie Show* on DuMont and *Kukla, Fran and Ollie* on NBC. C: Johnny Downs, Helen Gallagher, Virginia Gorski (April–June 1949), Evelyn Ward (June 1949), Tony Mottola Trio. P: Barry Wood. D: Franklin Heller.

Following her success playing a supporting role in the hit 1947 Broadway musical *High Button Shoes*, actress/singer Helen Gallagher ventured into TV to be the co-host of *Manhattan Showcase*, a combination musical variety show with performances by up-and-coming talent.

"It was supposed to be like a tryout for people," she said. "Johnny Downs and I would do an opening number, and we'd alternate doing a solo singing spot on each show." Gallagher said Mindy Carson, an actress/singer who was a regular on *Ford Star Revue* (q.v.) and *Club Embassy* (q.v.), made her TV debut on *Manhattan Showcase*. Getting paid just $125 per show as a regular, Gallagher recalled she and other women on the show had to wear black lipstick so that their lips would show better on the primitive black-and-white cameras of the time.

But Gallagher's biggest frustration came when it was announced that the show would

start running four times a week rather than three in April. She balked at having to work for no extra pay, then suggested her pal Virginia Gorski help out with the extra load. "We ended up splitting the number of shows we did each week," she said. The program went back to just three times a week in May, but the two stayed on until June when Evelyn Ward (the first wife of actor Jack Cassidy; their son was actor/singer David Cassidy) replaced them both. Gallagher believed she left because she had a job doing a summer stock production, and stage work was more lucrative and prestigious than TV jobs were at the time. *Manhattan Showcase* ended only a few weeks after Gallagher left, with CBS replacing it with the nightly *Ted Steele Show* in the summer of 1949.

Gallagher honed her craft mainly in Broadway musicals the next quarter century, winning Tonys in 1952 for her supporting role in a revival of *Pal Joey* and in 1971 for a revival of *No, No, Nanette*, while putting TV appearances on the back burner. "I did a lot of commercials," she said. "I never did a series again until *Ryan's Hope*." The daytime soap opera, which debuted on ABC in 1975, featured Gallagher as matriarch Maeve Ryan. While admitting that she took the show because she thought the storylines would emphasize her character — then learned the actors playing her children would be doing the bulk of the stories— Gallagher appreciated doing the show and her new base of fans.

"I think it filled a gap in people's lives," she said. "It wasn't saccharine, it was real people. We had good actors, and Claire Labine was an incredible writer." Both Labine, the show's head writer, and Gallagher earned multiple Emmys for *Ryan's Hope*.

While *Ryan's Hope* went off in 1989, Gallagher said more than a decade later she still gets recognized from her role on the serial. As for whether anyone recalls her for *Manhattan Showcase*, Gallagher laughed and said, "Who remembers *that*?"

Children's Sketch Book

Children's Show. Ran on NBC Saturdays 5:30–6 P.M. March 12–Dec. 31, 1949, then NBC Saturdays 7–7:30 P.M. Jan. 7–Feb. 4, 1950 opposite *Lucky Pup* on CBS. C: Edith Skinner, Lisl Weil, Merrill E. Joels. P/D: Barry Bernard.

The name Lisl Weil, *Contemporary Authors* informs us, rhymes with "easel style." But this illustrator needed no easel for her large canvases which she drew on TV and other venues. She typically used 20-foot panels to create her artwork, which could be easily seen on early tiny TV screens because, as she noted, "I only drew chalks, and very thick."

Weil had done considerable television work in the 1940s in her early twenties before she received the offer of being the featured artist on *Children's Sketch Book*. While Edith Skinner told youngsters a story, assisted by some background noises made by Merrill E. Joels for atmosphere, Weil illustrated certain events, bouncing around at a speedy rate. She marvelled as she recalled her job in 2001.

"It needed a very young person," she said. "I was a very good jumping lady, and I enjoyed it. Nobody could draw as fast as I did. I was extremely fast, as I remember."

Regarding the tales she dramatized, Weil said, "A lot of them were my own stories and stories I chose." Sometimes she was the one who narrated a story as well.

Children's Sketch Book was popular enough for a few months to attract many new fans for Weil. She appreciated the attention but did not think her talent encouraged juveniles to become artists. "You're either going to do it or not," she said. "Only those with an active interest in art do it." She does not see artistry as necessarily a genetic trait either. "It was just something I could do."

Weil said the show ended because she tired of the grind and no one could find a replacement for her. "I just had done it for a certain time, had enough of doing it, and when I left, no one else could do it," she said. She continued making illustrations before stopping more than a decade ago (she didn't remember exactly when) because she felt her skills were lagging, or as she put it, "I do everything 150 percent or nothing at all."

She definitely felt she gave her all and more to *Children's Sketch Book*. "It was a great show," she said. "It was really a high point in my life."

Campus Corner

Music Variety. Ran on CBS Mondays and Fridays 7:45–8 P.M. March 18–April 11, 1949 opposite *Russ Hodges' Scoreboard* on DuMont and news on NBC. C: Beverly Fite, Bob Burkhardt, Dean Campbell, Buzz Davis, Frank Stevens, Burt Taylor. P/D: Ralph Levy.

"That was back when we had two cameras on CBS," director Ralph Levy recalled about *Campus Corner*, also called (though he didn't recall why) *The Quadrangle*. The 15-minute review aired in the early evenings on the starting and ending days of the work week. With no time for sketches, Levy said the show had just time for setups for songs for each show. And with just two cameras, it limited the amount of shots available on the performers as well. "One was a closeup, one a little wider," Levy said.

The show's hostess was aspiring actress Beverly Fite. Joining her were four men plus pianist Buzz Davis. "He was the pianist and composer for a lot of Broadway shows," Levy said. As Buster Davis, he did vocal arrangements for such musicals as *Bells Are Ringing* and *Funny Girl* before he died in 1987. The others had rather minor careers before and after *Campus Corner*. Fite reportedly was still acting as of the 1990s and living in Long Island, New York.

Levy did not recall why *Campus Corner* lasted just a month. That cancellation he forgot easily due to his next job, directing the more prestigious *Ed Wynn Show* (q.v.). As Levy recalled, "Harry Ackerman, who was the vice president of CBS, came to New York and had me go out to Hollywood." He would never direct a New York series again, finding himself more involved with such series as *The Jack Benny Program* and *The George Burns and Gracie Allen Show*, and a few others.

Judy Splinters

Children. Ran on NBC Mondays through Fridays 7–7:15 P.M. June 13–Aug. 5, 1949, opposite *Your Sports Special* on CBS and *Captain Video and His Video Rangers* (off Wednesdays; from June 27) on DuMont, then NBC Mondays through Fridays 5:15–5:30 P.M. Oct. 3, 1949–June 30, 1950, opposite *The Ted Steele Show* (through Dec. 9) and *The Chuck Wagon* (from Dec. 12) on CBS. C/W: Shirley Dinsdale. P/D: Norman Felton (in Chicago June–August 1949); P: Roger Muir. D: Al Howard. (Muir and Howard in New York 1949–50).

Before Shari Lewis made her name as TV's top female ventriloquist in the in the 1960s, there was Shirley Dinsdale and her dummy Judy Splinters. Shirley had just celebrated her 16th birthday when national radio audiences heard her and Judy do their routines on *The Eddie Cantor Show* from 1942 to 1943. She was just in her early 20s when she made her TV debut in 1947 on Los Angeles station KTLA and hosted a regular local Thursday night series there called *Kiddie Party*. That exposure won her the first Emmy for a performer, in 1948 for Outstanding Personality (Emmys at the time were awarded locally in Los Angeles), and led NBC executives to draft her for a network show.

"She was a hit on the West Coast, so NBC wanted it to move to New York," recalled producer/director Norman Felton in a letter to me. "It stopped in Chicago on the way, where I had a set built overnight, and organized a group to meet it at the railroad station." Her series there took the billing of her puppet, as it would in New York.

Felton was able to have her for two months in Chicago for an early evening show before she moved onward to New York to do a series airing right ahead of that ratings juggernaut of early children's programming, *Howdy Doody*. In fact, the producer of *Howdy Doody*, Roger Muir, also did the same honors for *Judy Splinters*. On the latter show for 15 minutes daily Shirley and Judy bantered about various topics, including Judy encouraging Shirley to find a man and settle down (despite all my research, I've never been able to figure it if Judy offered this advice due to personal experience, or if she just wanted to stop having Shirley around her in a polite manner). Judy also cut loose on a few tunes.

Unfortunately for Shirley, what she really needed was strong backing from a sponsor to stay on the air. By 1950 NBC's daytime lineup started to get sold out all the way up to a 3 P.M. start with *The Kate Smith Hour* and ending with *Howdy Doody*. When Dinsdale took off for a summer vacation from *Judy Splinters*, it turned into being a permanent absence from the network. Quaker Oats was ready to sponsor the Chicago children's show *Panhandle Pete and Jennifer* (see 1950-51) and its more successful followup *The Gabby Hayes Show* (1950-54) in the *Judy Splinters* time slot, and apparently no other sponsors thought the act was worth continued exposure on the network level.

Dinsdale didn't work with Judy much longer after their daily show ended. She married in 1953 and retired from performing. The ventriloquist died on May 3, 1999, at the age of 72.

Mixed Doubles

Sitcom. Ran on NBC Fridays 9–9:30 P.M. Aug. 5–September 1949, opposite *Break the Bank* on ABC, *This Is Show Business* on CBS and *Key to the Missing* on DuMont, then NBC Saturdays 8:30–9 P.M. September–Oct. 29, 1949, opposite *Paul Whiteman's TV Teen Club* on ABC and *Spin the Picture* on DuMont. C: Billy Idelson (as Bill Abbott), Ada Friedman (as Ada Abbott), Eddy Firestone (as Eddy Coleman), Rhoda Williams (as Elaine Coleman; through Aug. 12), Bonnie Baken (as Elaine Coleman; from Aug. 19). P/D/W: Carlton E. Morse.

Billy Idelson had made his name on radio as Rush, the adopted son on the classic comedy *Vic and Sade* from 1932 to 1946. Carlton E. Morse was an even bigger presence in that medium, having created and written *One Man's Family* (1932–59) and *I Love a Mystery* (1939–52). Both hoped to conquer the new medium of television. But while Idelson later found fortune as a producer with *Love, American Style* and other shows, Morse floundered with his efforts, beginning with this initial try.

"The original title of that was *Slice of Life*," Idelson said. "It was on KFI, which was a local Los Angeles station. We did it there for about six months. The show at the time was 20 minutes long and ran three times a week. We did two of them by script and one improv [each week]. It had a certain 'whatever' and NBC asked Carlton to take it to New York."

Along with the move came a title change, to *Mixed Doubles*. "I think they just thought it was a better title," Idelson said. There also were no more improvised episodes, just scripts from Morse concerning events in the lives of the Abbotts and the Colemans, young couples who lived next door to each other in meager apartments while their husbands worked as copywriters with an ad agency. Idelson said he knows of no specific inspiration for Morse for the idea of the show.

Although the couples' exploits were serialized, Idelson said, "It essentially was a comedy, but Carlton E. Morse was not a comedy writer, so the comedy was weak." It was like a serial in that one of its leads left the show and was replaced by another actress without comment, but Idelson said he doesn't recall Rhoda Williams leaving the show, much less Bonnie Baken replacing her.

Idelson was similarly clueless about whether the show ever had a sponsor or exactly why it went off within three months on the network. However, he did think it failed as entertainment due to how Morse ran the series. "He had no idea how visual comedy or drama would work," he said. "He was strictly radio. He had no concept of television." For example, Idelson said Morse thought the actors should stand in one place and not move rather than let the boom mike follow them and absorb their voices.

Following the cancellation of *Mixed Doubles*, the entire cast save Idelson disappeared from view and never were regulars on another network TV series. Idelson went back to Hollywood (as he put it, "I didn't want to know New York"). Morse brought *One Man's Family* to TV a week after *Mixed Doubles* ended, which may have been his ultimate plan for television rather than continue the alleged comedy. It had a modest run from 1949 to 1952, then an indifferently received revival in daytime in 1954-55. After flopping in 1958 with another daytime soap, *Kitty Foyle* (q.v.), Morse mostly ended his unproductive association with the boob tube.

ALSO IN 1948-49

ABC Barn Dance	The Growing Paynes	Playtime
Adventures in Jazz	The Hartmans	Quizzing the News
The Alice Pearce Show	Here's Archer	Rehearsal Call
Amanda	Hold It Please	Ruth Winchell
American Minstrels of 1949	I'd Like to See	Ruthie on the Telephone
And Everything Nice	Identify	Saturday Night Jamboree
The Arrow Show	Inside Photoplay	School House
The Black Robe	Jack Leonard	Scrapbook Junior Edition
Broadway Spotlight	The Jacques Fray Music Room	Sing-Co-Pation
Buzzy Wuzzy	Kiernan's Corner	The Skip Farrell Show
Captain Billy's Showboat	Ladies Be Seated	Sonny Kendis
Champagne and Orchids	Ladies' Day	Sparring Partners with Walter
Child's World	The Laytons	Kiernan
Classified Column	Maggi's Private Wire	Spin the Picture
The Cliff Edwards Show	Mary Margaret McBride	The Stan Shaw Show
The Eyes Have It	Masters of Magic	That Reminds Me
Face the Music	The Missus Goes A-Shopping	That's O'Toole
The Fashion Story	Movieland Quiz	Through the Crystal Ball
Fashions on Parade	Music in Velvet	Treasure Quest
The 54th Street Revue	Musical Almanac	Welcome Aboard
Flight to Rhythm (a/k/a De-	Off the Record	Wesley
lora Bueno Show)	Paris Cavalcade of Fashions	A Woman to Remember
Fun for the Money	Photographic Horizons	Wren's Nest
The Gay Nineties Revue	Picture This	

1949–50

The Little Revue

Music. Ran on ABC Sundays 8:30–9 P.M. Sept. 4, 1949–March 1950, opposite *The Ed Sullivan Show* on CBS, films (through November) on DuMont, and *Colgate Theatre* on NBC, then ABC Fridays 9:30–10 P.M. March–April 21, 1950, opposite *Actor's Studio* alternating with *Ford Theatre* on

CBS and *The Big Story* alternating with *Life Begins at Eighty* on NBC. C: Nancy Evans, Dick Larkin, Bill Sherry, Gloria Van, Billy Johnson, Nancy Doran and Dick France, the Bill Weber Marionettes, the Rex Maupin Orchestra. P/D: Greg Garrison. W: Dan Schuffman.

"It was the most fun I ever had," producer/director Greg Garrison said of *The Little Revue*. Considering that Garrison's extensive TV credits include *The Dean Martin Show* and Martin's freewheeling "celebrity roast" specials of the 1970s, that show must have been festive beyond belief.

Garrison explained that its appeal was being a music show, pure and simple. "There was no audiences, no dialogue. There were music segues all the way through. Nobody spoke. All you heard were the lyrics."

The regulars of *The Little Revue* were little-known vocalists then as well as now, although Nancy Doran and Dick France were a dance duo. The only singers to have any other network series credits beyond this show were Nancy Evans and Gloria Van. Evans sang concurrently on a series featuring a mellow bandleader, *Wayne King*, a job she held from 1949 to 1951, while Van took over her spot on that same show until it ended on June 26, 1952. Like *The Little Revue*, *Wayne King* was a show originating from Chicago. Van also did two other short-lived network TV series in 1949-50, *Windy City Jamboree* and the successor to *The Little Revue*, *Tin Pan Alley TV* (see "Also in 1949–50" for both).

More successful than the artists was Garrison himself. ABC's Chicago station was a top provider of series on the network in the fall of 1949, offering at least seven hours of programming. As one of its top directors in that city, he often worked several shows at the same time that appeared nationally rather than locally. For example, while *The Little Revue* aired, Garrison also helmed a panel show called *Majority Rules* (q.v.).

Garrison said the hectic schedule never bothered him. "I just went in and did them," he recalled. "In 1949, I probably did a minimum of six shows a week, anywhere from 15 minutes to a half hour." His busiest period network-wise had to have been a few months before *The Little Revue* debuted. In late April and May 1949, Garrison directed the mystery series *Stand By for Crime*, the game shows *Identify*, *Treasure Quest*, and *Ladies Be Seated* (see 1948-49 for details on them), and the kiddie show *Super Circus*, among other credits.

Super Circus was the only big hit for Garrison while in Chicago, as ABC was struggling to establish its TV network, but his efforts got him noticed by NBC, who hired him away for bigger projects. He went to New York in 1950 to direct *The Kate Smith Hour* and other programs, including *The Milton Berle Show*. At the same time, ABC cut back on most of its programming from the Windy City, and by 1955, when it moved *Super Circus* to New York City, network shows from Chicago became a rarity.

The Life of Riley

Sitcom. Ran on NBC Tuesdays 9:30–10 P.M. Oct. 4, 1949–March 28, 1950, opposite *Suspense* on CBS and movies (through Jan. 10) and *Cavalcade of Bonds* (from Jan. 17) on DuMont. C: Jackie Gleason (as Chester A. Riley), Rosemary DeCamp (as Peg Riley), Lanny Rees (as Junior Riley), Gloria Winters (as Babs Riley), Sid Tomack (as Jim Gillis), John Brown (as Digby "Digger" O'Dell). P/D/W: Irving Brecher.

Producer Irving Brecher debuted *The Life of Riley* on radio in 1944. William Bendix played dim-witted Chester A. Riley, who stumbled through life amid well-intentioned but weak support from his wife, Peg, and children Junior and Babs, and dubious help from co-worker Jim Gillis and undertaker "Digger" O'Dell. It became a hit, but Bendix nixed doing a TV rendition in 1949.

"He was under contract to [movie producer] Hal Roach, and Bendix thought it [TV] would blow over," Brecher said. "I went and got Gleason because my sponsor on radio wanted to get into television." Gleason was Jackie Gleason, a relative unknown at the time who needed the work.

Sponsor Pabst Blue Ribbon Beer had wanted the show live from New York, but Brecher couldn't do that and produce the radio show in Hollywood at the same time. He met with NBC President Niles Trammell to discuss what to do. "He overrode them [Pabst] if I would pay the cost of filming them," Brecher said. "It cost me $2,000 per episode for 26 weeks, so I was out $52,000."

Brecher saved some money by using his

Jackie Gleason reads an eye-popping script for television's first version of *The Life of Riley*.

radio scripts for all 26 shows and directing them too. He planned to do more than 26 TV shows, but smelled something fishy about the total amount of episodes Pabst wanted to sponsor that season.

"The reason it didn't go any further is I refused to have the sponsor renew it another six weeks, because I would have only 32 rather than [the then-standard] 39 weeks on air," Brecher said. "They had only really put on *The Life of Riley* to hold the time slot for boxing in October. Thanks, Pabst." (Actually, Pabst's boxing series *Blue Ribbon Bouts* was on CBS Wednesdays at 10 P.M. that fall.)

The Life of Riley ended on radio in 1951. "In 1952 NBC came to me and said Bendix is now looking to do TV," Brecher said. Brecher licensed the show to NBC, and that version ran on TV from 1953 to 1958.

But Brecher had not forgotten the Gleason series. "When we parted company as friends, I said, 'Someday, we'll rerun those shows, Jackie, and because you've been so good in this venture, I'll give you 10 percent of the residuals,'" said Brecher. The producer later rued that decision.

"In '67 I decided to buy back the negatives of the series. I alerted Gleason I was going to put the Gleason shows back on. I said, 'I want to put them on with an introduction by you.' He flatly refused." He declined to let the shows be repeated as part owner too.

"I then had to sue him for what they call 'declamatory relief,'" said Brecher. He won the lawsuit, but by that time of the ruling, the interest in rerunning black and white series faded too, and TV's first *The Life of Riley* did not appear in repeats until the TV Land cable channel used them in 1997 — nearly 50 years after they first ran. To paraphrase Riley's own famous catch phrase, what a revoltin' development that was for the series.

The Crisis

Drama. Ran on NBC Wednesdays 8–8:30 P.M. Oct. 5–Dec. 28, 1949, opposite *The Wendy Barrie Show* on ABC, *Arthur Godfrey and His Friends* on CBS and movies on DuMont. C: Adrian Spies (as the interviewer), Arthur Peterson (as "the director"; October), Bob Cunningham (as "the director"; November–December). P/D: Norman Felton.

The Crisis emerged from a collaboration of its creators, Norman Felton and Adrian Spies. Felton, who previously produced and directed in 1949 *These Are My Children* (q.v.) and *Judy Splinters* (q.v.), described Spies in a letter to me as an "ex–New York City cub reporter" who joined him on this live show from Chicago as a regular on camera as well as off.

Each week Spies would talk to a person about his life, but it was not a standard interview show, as once the interviewee described a trying time he had faced, actors guided by an on-stage "director" would take over playing

that person and the circumstances of the personal tribulation in an effort to surmise how the problem was resolved. Felton described the series as "partially written, with ordinary people telling an account of a 'crisis' in their lives, but we stopped before they told what happened after [the event]. My actors ad-libbed what they thought was a 'guessed' ending." After the players' improvised conclusion played out, Spies talked with a guest to determine how correct the playlet was in reflecting what actually happened.

This half-talk show/half-drama combination was unlike anything else on TV at the time, but Felton did not think the unusual format nor the formidable competition of *Arthur Godfrey and His Friends* were necessarily the reasons for its disappearance after 13 weeks. Instead, Felton mentioned that the actors may have been too good in portraying the hardships the participants described, at least from what he heard from network executives. "New York called me in Chicago and, since people started sending us money to give the 'people' on the show, they got frightened! Took us off! (Sound like TV in 2001?)"

Felton and Spies went on to greater success on television. Felton became a producer and director for *Robert Montgomery Presents* (1950–1957) and created and produced several other series. Spies would write for TV through the 1970s for various series (*Dr. Kildare, Star Trek*) and TV-movies (e.g., *The Failing of Raymond*). And while "director" Bob Cunningham never did much else of consequence in the entertainment world, fellow "director" Arthur Peterson did go to Hollywood and score an odd hit as the senile Major on the nighttime sitcom *Soap* from 1977 to 1981.

The Ed Wynn Show

Comedy Variety. Ran on CBS Thursdays 9–9:30 P.M. Oct. 6, 1949–Dec. 1949 opposite *Crusade in Europe* (through Oct. 27) and *Starring Boris Karloff* (from November) on ABC, *The Morey Amsterdam Show* on DuMont and *Fireball Fun-for-All* (through Oct. 27) and *Kay Kyser's Kollege of Musical Knowledge* (from Dec. 1) on NBC, then CBS Saturdays 9–9:30 P.M. Jan. 7–March 1950 opposite *Roller Derby* on ABC, *Cavalcade of Stars* on DuMont and *Your Show of Shows* (from Feb. 25) on NBC, and then CBS Tuesdays 9–9:30 P.M. April–July 4, 1950, opposite *Cavalcade of Bands* on DuMont and *Fireside Theater* on NBC. C: Ed Wynn, Lud Gluskin Orchestra. P: Harlan Thompson. D: Ralph Levy. W: Hal Kanter, Leo Solomon, Seaman Jacobs.

The silly, giggling "Perfect Fool" of 1930s radio fame came to TV amid considerable hoopla in 1949. "That was the first West Coast show seen in the East," recalled its director Ralph Levy. Due to technical limitations of the time, the series did not air live to the East Coast, but rather viewers there watched *The Ed Wynn Show* on kinescopes—films made by aiming a camera on a studio monitor to record the live shows for non-connected stations. Kinescopes often were grainy, and Levy thinks that they hurt the show's potential to be a hit. "I think that was one of the drawbacks of it, the quality of them."

In contrast, Levy found his star to be a top performer for the show. "Ed Wynn was a great talent," he said. "He wasn't a big name commercially at the time. Probably one of the great comedians of the country. A clown is what you'd describe him."

But Levy acknowledged that being a clown on a nighttime TV variety series wears down the audience fast. As to how Wynn fit the medium, Levy said, "He adapted fine, but I don't think there is a great Ed Wynn audience."

Nevertheless, there were plenty of reasons to watch the show. Top radio comedy writer Hal Kanter made his debut working in TV on this show and took a pay cut to do so, even though his rate of $750 per week supposedly was the most anyone made writing for TV at the time. And then there were the guests that appeared, some making their earliest network TV appearances, especially Lucille Ball and Desi Arnaz a year and a half before *I Love Lucy*. Regarding the film and radio stars who tested the waters of TV through this show, Levy said, "I don't know to what extent they wanted to get on, but it was the only show networked from Hollywood, and they didn't want to go to New York to do it."

Ed usually finished second to his NBC competition on the East Coast during his show's run, and no sponsor picked it up to return another year. Nevertheless, he did win Emmys for his work in January 1950 for Best Live Show and Most Outstanding Live Personality (the Emmys were based around programming in Los Angeles at the time). He became an alternating host of *All-Star Revue* from 1950 to 1952, then had one last series in 1958 which also was named *The Ed Wynn Show* (q.v.).

Mysteries of Chinatown

Police Drama. Ran on ABC Sundays 9:30–10 P.M. Dec. 4, 1949–May 1950, opposite *The Fred Waring Show* on CBS, *They Stand Accused* (through March) and *Windy City Jamboree* (from March 19) on DuMont, and *Philco TV Playhouse* on NBC, then ABC Sundays 9–9:30 P.M. May–September 1950, opposite *The Fred Waring Show* (through July 9) and *The Robert Q. Lewis Show* and movies (from July 16) on CBS, *Windy City Jamboree* (through June 18) and *They Stand Accused* (from June 25) on DuMont, and *Philco TV Playhouse* (through July 16) and *Masterpiece Playhouse* (from July 23) on NBC, then various time slots through Oct. 23, 1950. C: Robert Bice (as Dr. Yat Fu), Gloria Saunders (as Ah Toy). P/W: Ray Buffum. D: Richard Goggin, Bob Finkel.

"Strictly pedestrian stuff" is how director Richard Goggin characterized the action on *Mysteries of Chinatown*, a melodrama that aired live in Hollywood and on kinescope for the rest of the country on ABC. The show related the adventures of Dr. Yat Fu, a shop owner who investigated crimes as well in San Francisco's Chinatown district.

The real mystery to the show is its cast. Though several sources credit actor Marvin Miller as playing Dr. Fu, "Miller was never a part of it," insisted Goggin. He said the little-known Robert Bice was the lead, with Gloria Saunders playing his niece ("not much of an actress, but a great build," opined Goggin). He could not recall who played the other character he said was a regular, Dr. Fu's nephew, "a squirrelly type."

There were two standing sets for the series. One was a room said to be the residence of where Dr. Fu and his kin stayed. The other was an antique shop that Dr. Fu ran where tourists came by. "There were three or four main characters, and the rest was 'fill-in,'" Goggin said in describing each episode's cast. Beside his regulars, one or two guest actors, the technical crew and writer Ray Buffum, that was about all the people involved in the unsponsored show along with Goggin.

"I know we had to pay Buffum $150 a script," Goggin said. "I did casting and everything else." Goggin added that the writer worked very well with him as they went through rehearsals on the show. "Buffum was pretty good about this. I'd look at him, and if I had any problems, I told him, and he'd rewrite them."

Goggin acknowledged it was a challenging job directing a live show for half an hour without any advertisements. "You had no commercials to break away from, so you had to improvise getting away from scenes," he said. "It was very tight to do. It was very much like summer stock."

The lack of a sponsor for the show is what Goggin believed led to its cancellation. He left the program before it ended; in fact, he left broadcasting entirely for a period when he gave up *Mysteries of Chinatown*. "I took a leave of absence in 1950, and I'd been teaching part-time at UCLA in the theater arts department, and I decided to go there," he said. He later was a station manager for the public television station in St. Louis, then taught at New York University. Though still listed in the Directors Guild of America member handbook in 2001, Goggin admits that "I spent more years away from directing in broadcasting than doing it." No crime in that — not even in Chinatown.

Easy Aces

Comedy. Ran on DuMont Wednesdays 7:45–8 P.M. Dec. 14, 1949–June 14, 1950, opposite *The Earl Wrightson Show* on CBS and news on NBC. C: Goodman Ace, Jane Ace, Betty Garde. P: Ziv Television Programs. D: Jeanne Harrison. W: Goodman Ace.

Frederic W. Ziv is credited with pioneering the idea of syndicating recorded programs to individual radio stations in the 1930s, thus bypassing the networks' method of distributing series live to member affiliates. One of his leading assistants was Jeanne Harrison. "I directed and produced all their shows," Harrison said, noting among her credits the Ziv productions *Boston Blackie* and *The Cisco Kid*. "I did 35 shows a week at one time."

When Ziv entered TV production in 1948, Harrison did the same too. However, even though the property she handled in 1949 was syndicated by Ziv on radio from 1945 to 1947, those were transcriptions of the *Easy Aces* radio show done from 1932 to 1943 on CBS and NBC, and had not involved Harrison. Never-

theless, she got along fine with the show's creator/writer/star, Goodman Ace, when they started on the video effort. "He was wonderful to work with," she said.

Filmed in New York City, the TV *Easy Aces* featured Goodman and his real-life wife Jane Ace as a married duo with the same name living in a suburban home. Jane was the mistress of malaprops, normally spouting off phrases like "Time wounds all heels." Her banter with her husband formed the crux of each show. Betty Garde played Jane's friend Dorothy.

Harrison remembered the beginning for *Easy Aces* better than specific jokes and plots. "The opening shot was sort of cute. I designed it. Jane was sitting and reading a book called *Brain Surgery — Self-Taught.*"

Between the Aces' routines, Harrison used stock footage to fill out the show. One bit took considerably more effort than she realized at first glance. "I had done one show, and I had picked up some footage of pygmies," she said. "The network rejected it because their little 'kazookies' were hanging out." Harrison sent the film to a lab where technicians painted out the exposed male anatomy in each individual frame to comply with Dumont's wishes and let the show air.

Airing in what was on every other weeknight the time slot for bandleader Vincent Lopez, *Easy Aces* died a hard death in the summer of 1950. "It was not a very well received show," said Harrison. It was the only Ziv series to air on DuMont, though like almost all other Ziv shows it was syndicated to local TV stations too, most of whom dropped it by the time DuMont did.

Goodman later went on to success on TV writing for Milton Berle and Perry Como, but he also made clear often that he did not like much of the programming by the networks. Asked whether Mr. Ace was comfortable with the medium, Harrison said. "He was not at all. Not at all. He thought all the game shows were dumb." As for Jane, she more or less stayed out of the public eye after the TV series before dying in 1974, eight years before her husband passed away.

Life with Snarky Parker

Puppet. Ran on CBS Mon/Tue/Thu/Fri 7:45–8 P.M. Jan. 9–March 1950, then Mon–Fri 6:15–6:30

P.M. April–Aug. 30, 1950 opposite *Small Fry Club* on DuMont, then Sept. 11–Oct. 13, 1950 Mon–Fri 5:15–5:30 P.M. opposite *Lois and Looie* on ABC and *NBC Comics* on NBC. C: Bil Baird, Cora Baird, Frank Fazakas, Frank Sullivan. P/D: Yul Brynner. W: Bil Baird, Tom Murray, Paul Peterson.

Television in the 1950s had three popular puppet troupes—the *Howdy Doody* gang, *Kukla, Fran and Ollie*, and the team led by the husband and wife duo of Bil and Cora Baird. The Bairds had two full-time employees in their act, Frank Fazakas and Frank Sullivan, and the two Franks worked with them on their TV series, none of which surprisingly lasted more than a year despite the group's critical acclaim and general popularity. Their first series was *Life with Snarky Parker*.

The title character was a deputy sheriff in the 19th-century western town of Hot Rock. Bil Baird voiced Snarky. "Snarky Parker was Bil's alter ego," said Fazakas, who elaborated about the character with a laugh. "Actually, he was a little creep!"

Other characters were Ronald Rodent, the recurring varmint; Miss Butterball, the school marm who was Snarky's love interest; Paw, her father; and Slugger Ryan, the piano player in the Bent Elbow Saloon who narrated each story. Slugger would reappear in the Bairds' later series *The Whistling Wizard* and *The Bil Baird Show*.

"My part was the best part — Heathcliff the horse, a 2-year-old horse who sat in bed and read poetry," Fazakas said. "The writers loved him." When not reading, Heathcliff served as Snarky's faithful steed.

Supervising the tempo of the show was producer/director Yul Brynner, the same Brynner who would achieve fame five months after *Life with Snarky Parker* ended as the lead in the Broadway musical *The King and I*. Fazakas described Brynner as "first class, and a gentleman." The show aired live from New York at three studios CBS built over the visiting room of Grand Central Station. Fazakas said that *Lucky Pup*, another puppet show which either ran directly before or after *Life with Snarky Parker* for most of its run, also performed at those studios.

The show ended after the company did not get a renewal from the network to continue, without much of a reason, as Fazakas recalled. He did know that "All the contracts were made in 13-week increments at the time," and after the third 13-week cycle, CBS dropped its interest on the show. Its replacement was an odd one indeed—*The United Nations General Assembly Sessions*, which ran until Dec. 15, 1950 (CBS had been airing the sessions earlier in the afternoons since Nov. 7, 1949). The Bairds returned to CBS in 1951-52 with *The Whistling Wizard* (q.v.).

Answer Yes or No

Game Show. Ran on NBC Sundays 10:30–11 P.M. April 30–June 23, 1950, opposite *Youth on the March* on ABC and news on CBS. C: Moss Hart, Arlene Francis. P: Wayne Wirth, West Hooker. D: Joe Cavalier, Doug Rodgers.

Moss Hart is remembered as a leading light of New York's theater scene from the 1930s through 1950s (for the uninitiated, he co-wrote the Pulitzer Prize–winning Broadway hit *You Can't Take It with You* in 1936 along with George S. Kaufman and directed the original production of *My Fair Lady* in 1956, among other accomplishments). In that light, it may seem odd for him to have taken a go at hosting an early game show on TV. But his widow, Kitty Carlisle Hart, said the job was just an extension of his activities in show business.

"It wasn't outlandish or strange," Hart said. "Moss liked to act. He was originally an actor and turned into a playwright when acting didn't pan out." She also reminded the author that George S. Kaufman was a regular in the variety panel show *This Is Show Business* from 1949 to 1954.

The format for the show had a celebrity panel ask two guests questions (guess what kind) to determine how and why the guests would react to a situation read by Moss Hart. Viewers submitted ideas for the program and received $5 if they made it on the show. That was all to it.

The only regular panelist was Arlene Francis. Ironically, she and Mrs. Hart often got confused in later years due to their regular presence on Goodson-Todman game shows (Francis was on *What's My Line?* and Hart did *To Tell the Truth*). "They didn't like to mix us up [doing the same shows]," Mrs. Hart said of Goodson-Todman. "They thought Arlene and I were too much alike." In fact, when Francis died in 2001, some people actually called Hart to see if she was the one who passed away!

Apart from remembering that Truman Capote was a guest on the show, Mrs. Hart admits her memories of *Answer Yes or No* are fuzzy, although she did state that "It was a good show." Producers Hooker and West did another short-lived game show, *Say It with Acting* (q.v.) in 1951 before leaving the field, but Moss Hart did not do another regular TV job after the two-month run of *Answer Yes or No.*

"He wasn't going to have time for it," Mrs. Hart said. "He didn't have the time or the interest. He was doing plays." Moss Hart died in 1961 at the age of 57.

By the way, the answer to the question "Doesn't Moss Hart mention this show in his best-selling, still in print 1959 autobiography *Act One?*" is "No."

ALSO IN 1949-50

Abe Burrows' Almanac
Acrobat Ranch
Alkali Ike
The Amazing Polgar
Animal Clinic
Art Ford on Broadway
Auction-Aire
The Ben Grauer Show
Buck Rogers
The Carolyn Gilbert Show
Chicago Jazz
Chicagoland Mystery Players
Cities Service Band of America
Country Style
A Couple of Joes

Ford Star Revue
The Front Page
The Girls
Glamour-Go-Round
Hold That Camera
In the Morgan Manner
Inside U.S.A. with Chevrolet
Joey Faye's Frolics
Kuda Bux, Hindu Mystic
Majority Rules
Mama Rosa
The Marshal of Gunsight Pass
Melody, Harmony and Rhythm
Mr. Black
Mr. Magic and J.J.

The O'Neills
The Paul Arnold Show
Photocrime
The Pinky Lee Show
Ranger Ranch Roundup
The Ransom Sherman Show
Shoppers Matinee
Starlit Time
Strictly for Laughs
Sugar Hill Times
Sunday at the Zoo
That Wonderful Guy
Tin Pan Alley TV
Toni Twin Time
Windy City Jamboree

1950-51

The Joe DiMaggio Show

Children's. Ran on NBC Saturdays 5:30–5:45 P.M. Sept. 23–Dec. 16, 1950. C: Joe DiMaggio, Jack Barry. P: Jack Barry, Dan Enright. D: Grey Lockwood. W: Mike Oppenheimer.

One of the all-time favorite baseball players for the New York Yankees, "Joltin' Joe" DiMaggio came to TV following a spectacular career on the diamond in the 1940s, making a name as one of the best players at bat. He was still active on the team when he moved onto TV just a month after his similarly named radio show ended a year-long run. That show, with an odd format of game show and drama playlets, had Jack Barry as host and Dan En-

right as director; for the TV effort Barry and Enright were producers, with Barry still introducing DiMaggio on each show.

Taking Enright's role on TV was Grey Lockwood. "I had just been directing the old *March of Time* newsreels," he said. "I went to NBC, and right away they put me on NBC, and I did half of them. This was the first filmed show for NBC."

Lockwood was surprised at how swiftly he got a job on the TV network. "I didn't know anybody at NBC really," he said. He was even more taken aback when he learned his first series would be to direct DiMaggio, a celebrity he admired.

"I was a big baseball fan, but nobody knew

that when they assigned me," he said. "We got along like bugs in a rug. Some said he was difficult, but I didn't find him that way. He was a hell of a nice guy.

"But he was a terrible actor or host. He was wooden." Lockwood speculated it was that awkwardness on the air that led the show to run only three months, although he admitted he was not sure because he was not with the program through the end.

"I started off and went halfway through the 13 shows, and then I was doing another thing called *Lights Out*, a half-hour nighttime drama, and I couldn't do both of them," he said. He added it had nothing to do with Barry and Enright: "They were fun. They were professional."

The TV *Joe DiMaggio Show* had "the Yankee Clipper" talk with around 10 kids on a clubhouse set; they in turn got to interview a weekly guest athlete on the show. DiMaggio also introduced clips of sport events. Theoretically, filming all this for just a 15-minute slot should have been little problem, but Lockwood said the results were so unimpressive he didn't mind going to do live TV with *Lights Out*. "I used to see it at a bar, and I made sure I had four [drinks] on the way," he said.

There's little chance anyone will ever see the shows again despite them being filmed, for DiMaggio's contract called for all the prints to be destroyed once they ran on TV in order to enhance his appeal to do movies. That film career never happened, nor did any further TV series, as DiMaggio preferred to shun the media spotlight from the 1950s onward. He died on March 8, 1999, at the age of 84.

Two Girls Named Smith

Sitcom. Ran on ABC Saturdays Noon–12:30 P.M. Jan. 20–Oct. 13, 1951, opposite *Big Top* on CBS and *Rootie Kazootie* (Oct. 13 only) on NBC. C: Peggy Ann Garner (as Babs Smith; through Sept. 22), Marcia Henderson (as Babs Smith; from Sept. 29), Peggy French (as Peggy Smith), Joseph Buloff, Adelaide Klein. P: Richard Lewis. D: Charles S. Dubin. W: Peter Barry.

New York theatergoers who tuned into *Two Girls Named Smith* in 1951 might have had the feeling they were watching something which reminded them of a Broadway show a decade earlier. Let's see: a pair of young sisters

aspiring to make it in New York, with some wacky fellow tenants visiting them ... hmm, it sounds an awful lot like, umm...

"It was based, kind of, on *My Sister Eileen*," confirmed director Charles S. Dubin. "They were trying to be like that show. I think that's what might have led it to be cancelled." Lawyers who held the rights to *My Sister Eileen*, which actually began as a series of stories in *The New Yorker* magazine, threatened a lawsuit for copyright infringement that led to a quick decision to end the series rather than fight the charge.

Prior to that maneuver, *Two Girls Named Smith* was one of the highest-rated daytime weekend TV series on the air, and managed an impressive distribution rate of being on 53 stations, making it one of the easiest shows to see in America in 1951. Done live from New York without a studio audience, it took the cast six working days to get the show together.

"We had a reading of the script, as I recall, on a Monday," he said. He and the crew then practiced staging the show before the big Saturday productions, which took a considerable toll on the backstage personnel.

"We went in even earlier than the cast, at dawn on Saturday mornings, 5 A.M.," Dubin said. "We used stand-ins so that the actors didn't have to come in until 8." Despite the grueling schedule, Dubin said, "It was a fun show."

Starring originally was former child film actress Peggy Ann Garner, who won a special Oscar for her sensitive work in the 1945 film *A Tree Grows in Brooklyn* but found fewer satisfying job offers in Hollywood in the late 1940s, thus precipitating her move to New York City. Other, better-paying job offers resulted in her departure, and Marcia Henderson replaced her as Babs on the last three shows.

Besides those ladies and Peggy French as their sister, the show also featured Adelaide Klein as their landlady plus a few guest actors. Esteemed theatrical actor Joseph Buloff was a regular too. "In the original *My Sister Eileen* there was a superintendent of the apartment house," Dubin said. "They had him in the series in the guise of being a poet. He had come out of playing Ali Hakim in *Oklahoma!* in a five-year run."

Dubin's comment points out again the reason the show ended so quickly due to being an obvious *My Sister Eileen* ripoff. But here's the kicker: in the 1960-61 season CBS brought an official TV series version of *My Sister Eileen* onto its nighttime lineup, and guess what? It lasted a month less than the run of *Two Girls Named Smith*.

The Victor Borge Show

Comedy Variety. Ran on NBC Saturdays 7–7:30 P.M. Feb. 3–June 30, 1951, opposite *Hollywood Theatre Time* on ABC and *The Sam Levenson Show* on CBS. C: Victor Borge, the Phil Ingalls Orchestra. D: Perry Lafferty. W: Victor Borge, Eddie Lawrence, Max Wilk.

"He was probably as talented a person as I worked with in my life," said director Perry Lafferty about comic pianist Victor Borge. That's high praise indeed, considering Lafferty's resume involves such prestigious shows as *Robert Montgomery Presents* and *The Twilight Zone*. But paradoxically, Borge's unique abilities also were what Lafferty felt hurt the series, which came on as a midseason replacement for the unlamented *Hank McCune Show* (q.v.). His comic routines with a piano never were matched by any other comedian, and were well known by the time his series debuted in 1951, but beyond that area, Borge did virtually nothing in his act.

"Nobody stopped to think it through at the time, but he's so special with what he does on the piano with music, that it's not something you sit down with writers," Lafferty explained. "Nobody might have thought that — including me — that television would burn his act up. Now, you had to think, 'What do you do with him? He doesn't do acting, he just plays the piano.' It was the hardest thing in my career."

Somehow writers Eddie Lawrence (a comedian in his own right who had a minor hit record with his "The Old Philosopher" routine in 1956) and Max Wilk came up with new routines for the show, though Lafferty groused that "Victor Borge fought everything we wanted to do. You go write for him when you've got a month." One that sounds odd enough to make you want to see it was a takeoff on *Your Hit Parade* doing the late 1950 hit "Orange Colored Sky" in German.

Another bit had Victor trying in vain to pound out a song properly on the piano. Dur-

ing the course of his struggle, other people entered and perfectly played the tune on his piano, including to his consternation (and the audience's amusement) a 10-year-old girl. Other up-and-coming talent did the show too, including an early appearance by actor/comedian Louis Nye, according to Lafferty.

Yet it all was not enough to drag in a large audience, even in spite of weak competition. After running nearly five months, *The Victor Borge Show* left the schedule in the summer of 1951 and never returned. Nevertheless, the "Great Dane" (Borge was born in Copenhagen, Denmark) remained a popular guest on other variety series and specials until his death on Dec. 23, 2000, nearly a week shy of his 92nd birthday.

A Guest in Your House

Poetry/Variety. Ran on NBC Mondays through Fridays 3:15–3:30 P.M. March 5–March 30, 1951, opposite *Bride and Groom* on CBS Tuesdays and Thursdays. C: Edgar Guest, Rachel Stevenson. D: Frank Jacoby.

"That was hilarious," recalled director Frank Jacoby of *A Guest in Your House*. The series ran on NBC daytime for just four weeks and lasted only 15 minutes, yet Jacoby could vividly draw on memories about it 50 years later simply because it was so different from anything done on daytime then or now.

Basically, *A Guest in Your House* had Edgar Guest spewing his verses to any housewives watching the show, along with imparting a few words of wisdom. Joining him as his aide was Rachel Stevenson, who often found herself moved by what Guest said. That was about all it offered, with no studio audience to supply any reactions other than Stevenson.

Let's let Jacoby elaborate on the show's background here. "I joined NBC in 1949," he said. "I think that was the first show they gave to me." (It was an in-house network production, hence no producer credit.) He was familiar with its star, noting that "Edgar Guest was known as the poet laureate of America." Guest even once made up a limerick for Jacoby when he came to eat with him during the show's run.

As for what Jacoby knew about Stevenson, he said, "Only that she worked for him. But she would do nothing on the show!" Jacoby later corrected himself when he said he typically started each show with a shot of both Guest and Stevenson, then moved the camera to cover just Guest when he read his poetry until Stevenson indicated she was overcome with emotion from his words, resulting in the camera retreating to show her in tears. "She could cry at the drop of a hat," marveled Jacoby.

This hardly scintillating format attracted no sponsors, which Jacoby thinks was its undoing and the reason why NBC replaced it with a travelogue titled *Vacation Wonderland*. Jacoby said Guest tried to woo the Ford Company to advertise on it, but despite the fact that Guest and company founder Henry Ford were old friends from Detroit (and both anti–Semites, according to Jacoby), Guest couldn't get the Ford account.

So with no sponsor and a setup with limited appeal at best, why did NBC try *A Guest in Your House* at all? "Number one, it was very inexpensive," Jacoby said. "Number two, we were trying everything in those days." But Jacoby admitted that "It was awful."

Once NBC evicted *A Guest in Your House* from its lineup, "Edgar and Rachel went back to Detroit," Jacoby said, with Guest dying in 1959 two weeks before what would have been his 78th birthday. But he was not forgotten in TV land; Edith Bunker, the "dingbat" wife on the sitcom *All in the Family* in the 1970s, referred to him as her favorite poet on one show. Now if she had been a guest on *A Guest in Your House*, that might have been a TV show worth watching!

Ozmoe

Children's Show. Ran on ABC Tuesdays and Thursdays 5–5:15 P.M. March 6–April 12, 1951, opposite *NBC Comics* (through March 30) and *Hawkins Falls* (from April 3) on NBC and *Lucky Pup* on CBS. C: Bradley Bolke, Jan Kindler, Eleanor Russell, Alan Stapleton, Jack Urbant. P: Henry Banks. D: Carl Shain, Richard Ward. W: Skip Weshner.

Alternating daily with *The Mary Hartline Show*, *Ozmoe* was a live New York kids' show with a unique twist. "The characters were stationary," says Bradley Bolke. "They couldn't move too much. Rods moved their heads and mouths. It was not a marionettes or puppets show."

Bolke did not manipulate the characters.

He just provided his voice. "I was Poe the crow," Bolke notes. "He liked to think of himself in more romantic terms as a raven." He does not recall who in the cast provided the voices of the other characters, which included Ozmoe the monkey, his pal leprechaun Roderick Dhon't, and more interacting in ABC's fictional sub-subbasement Studio Z.

But Bolke does know how he got onto the show. "My recollection of it was the people that created this, they all had kind of backed a fellow named Henry Banks," he says. "They had an office on 42nd Street, and they would have auditions. And they had me on retainer."

Bolke enjoyed doing Banks' program. "I was young, I was new in the business, and everybody I worked with was very nice," he says. He even overlooked an element that might have infuriated another struggling actor. "This was just when television was being unionized," he says. "They just ran short of cash, and some weeks they paid me IOUs." Bolke still has the papers—and still has not received the money due to him for his work.

The situation mattered little in the long

Perhaps the homeliest puppet ever made for television had to be the title character for *Ozmoe*. Can you imagine any kid wanting to bring this home as a toy?

run for Bolke, as *Ozmoe* ended after a month on air. Bolke thinks its early end may have been due to preemptions from Sen. Estes Kefauver's hearings on organized crime, which all the networks carried for a period in daytime hours. However, he also notes too that "There was some sort of network background shenanigans there too," without specifying what they were. In any event, *Ozmoe* was replaced by daily installments of *The Mary Hartline Show* (q.v.).

After *Ozmoe*, Bolke had the most productive TV career of its cast, going on to do the voice of Chumley the walrus on *Tennessee Tuxedo and His Tales* from 1963 to 1966. "Right now, I'm resting on my laurels," he says, adding that the same is true for his brother who also had a TV career with a short-lived show — Dayton Allen (see *The Adventures of Oky Doky*).

Kreisler Bandstand

Musical Variety. Ran on ABC Wednesdays 8:30–9 P.M. March 21–June 13, 1951, opposite *Arthur Godfrey and His Friends* on CBS and *All-Star Revue* on NBC. C: Fred Robbins. P: Dick Gordon, George Foley. D: Perry Lafferty.

Like many shows of its period, *Kreisler Bandstand* took its name from its sponsor, in this case Jacques Kreisler watches. "They made watchbands too," said director Perry Lafferty. "The idea of the show was to take a big-name band of the time and have a guest star with them, including Ella [Fitzgerald] and Benny Goodman."

Hosting the live affair from New York was former radio disk jockey Fred Robbins. But his role on the show was basically just to introduce the guests, and Lafferty said he could barely recall working with him, since the emphasis was on the bands and singers.

Lafferty added, "That was a pretty straight half hour of music. In those days, you could sort of get away with filming a band, with closeups of lips and band members and so on." But Lafferty majored in music in college, and he acknowledged that his background prodded him to do a little more than the standard operating procedure at the time.

"There was no chance of rehearsal at all, so I'd listen to the records [by each band] and make notes on camera shots for them," he said. "Sometimes I had to have them sing the arrangement through the phone to me!"

Even with such difficulties, Lafferty was in awe of the talent he got to deal with during the short run of *Kreisler Bandstand*, including Cab Calloway and Duke Ellington. "It was just a little show, and we got to have these major bands," he said.

Unfortunately, the public was not as impressed, easily favoring the show's competition of *Arthur Godfrey and His Friends*. The constant turnover with a new band every week may have disappointed viewers who preferred a consistent sound. For his part, Lafferty thought its speedy end was due to Kreisler running out of cash to subsidize the cost of the show. "They probably had just enough money for 13 weeks," he said.

For whatever reason, ABC replaced the show (and moved its lead-in, the sitcom *The Ruggles*, to a different time slot) with a movie series curiously titled *Northwest Patrol*. *The Paul Dixon Show* then assumed that slot on Aug. 8, 1951, and stayed on ABC a year, followed by three years on daytime on DuMont. As for Robbins, this was the last of four consecutive network flops he had from 1949 to 1951, including his earlier show this season *The Robbins Nest* (q.v.). He finally got a hit in 1953 hosting *Coke Time with Eddie Fisher*, which ran until 1957.

The Jerry Colonna Show

Comedy Variety. Ran on ABC Mondays 8–8:30 P.M. May 28–June 1951, opposite *Lux Video Theatre* on CBS, and *The Paul Winchell–Jerry Mahoney Show* on NBC, then ABC Fridays 8–8:30 P.M. June–August 1951, opposite *Mama* on CBS and *Quiz Kids* on NBC, then ABC Thursdays 10–10:30 P.M. August–September 1951, opposite *Racket Squad* on CBS and *The Bigelow Theatre* on DuMont, and finally ABC Saturdays 7:30–8 P.M. October–Nov. 17, 1951, opposite *Beat the Clock* on CBS and *One Man's Family* on NBC. C: Jerry Colonna, Barbara Ruick, Gordon Polk, Cookie Fairchild's Band. P: Joe Bigelow. D: Stuart Phelps. W: Joe Bigelow, Ray Brenner, Frank Goldberg.

Jerry Colonna was one of the most recognizable "second bananas" on radio. Projecting a loud voice, he injected a note of insanity into Bob Hope's radio show from 1938 to 1948, playing a character who drove Hope and crew crazy by his odd pronouncements. With his bushy walrus mustache and bulging eyes, he seemed to be a natural to do even better in TV's

Jerry Colonna appears to be looking for his pal Bob Hope through the camera used for *The Jerry Colonna Show.* The accompanying press release for this photograph read as follows: "Maestro Colonna will not only clown his way through the program but will bust loose with an occasional roof-shattering aria guaranteed to swell the membership of noise abatement societies the land over."

visual medium, but *The Jerry Colonna Show* did not have the appeal needed to carry it beyond a six-month run.

According to director Stuart Phelps, Colonna in person was nothing at all like the whacked-out character he created. "He was very quiet, very reasonable, very organized, very concerned about his performance," Phelps said. "He wanted the show to succeed very badly and tried to do everything he could to make it work."

Colonna basically did the same job Hope did on his TV specials, according to Phelps. "He would tell jokes and do skits." Most of the rest of the cast was obscure, with the exception of actress Barbara Ruick, who showed up in several 1950s variety series, including earlier this season on *The College Bowl*. Though supposedly a singer as well as actress, Phelps recalled that "She was an actress probably in some skits we'd put together. I don't think she sang."

The Jerry Colonna Show came from Hollywood, where it aired live at a different time than listed above, but appeared in the East and Midwest on kinescope. "Anything that came out of Hollywood that early was," noted Phelps. Kinescoping was filming a show off a TV studio monitor and usually resulted in poor-quality copies to watch. Phelps thought that fact may have affected the show's popularity outside Los Angeles.

Then there was the reality that Colonna's fame came from being a supporting comic, and viewers may not have wanted to accept him as a star on his own show. "I suppose that was part of it," Phelps said. "They knew him as one character, and now he was fronting a band."

A final factor may have been the constant rescheduling ABC did to the series. The show aired on four different nights over less than half a year, making it difficult for an audience to keep up with it.

Whatever the reason(s), *The Jerry Colonna Show* was history before the end of 1951. Colonna went back to being a frequent guest on Bob Hope's TV specials through the early 1960s, though he did serve as ringmaster on the last season of the Sunday afternoon series *Super Circus* in 1955-56. A stroke in 1966 left him mostly inactive from show business until he died in 1986 at the age of 82.

The Freddy Martin Show

Musical Variety. Ran on NBC Thursdays 10–10:30 P.M. July 12–August 1951, opposite *Roller Derby* on ABC and *Racket Squad* on CBS, then NBC Wednesdays 10:30–11 P.M. September–Nov. 28, 1951, opposite *Celanese Theatre* alternating with *King's Crossroads* on ABC and *Pabst Blue Ribbon Bouts* and *Sports Spot* on CBS. C: Freddy Martin and His Orchestra, Merv Griffin, Murray Arnold, the Martin Men. P/D: Perry Lafferty. W: Irving Taylor.

"Mr. Silvertone" Freddy Martin had been leading his own orchestra for nearly two decades before coming to television as a regular attraction. Popular with the public but rather disdained by the critics as being "square," Freddy Martin and His Orchestra had tried several short-lived radio shows from 1933 to 1942 before making the plunge into television.

The orchestra also had compiled more than 80 charted records when their TV show debuted. In fact, the band was having success with "My Truly, Truly Fair" as the series started, sung by Merv Griffin.

"Merv Griffin was the boy singer with the band," recalled producer/director Perry Lafferty. "The show had some elements of *Your Hit Parade* in that you would dramatize the song. There was a little comedy back and forth between the regulars too." The show's script writer, Irving Taylor, also supplied some songs used.

Beside Griffin, other featured regulars on the show were pianist/singer Murray Arnold and five singers who billed themselves as the Martin Men. "We did it from the Center Theater in New York, one of the biggest theaters in New York," Lafferty said.

The show's official title was *The Hazel Bishop Show* in honor of its sponsor. Lafferty said an embarrassing event happened on one live commercial for the cosmetics company. "They made a thing called Hazel Bishop No Smear Lipstick, where a girl would dab a handkerchief on her mouth and show it did not come off on it. Well, one night, the lipstick came off on the handkerchief, and it was the end of the world."

Despite everyone's best efforts, and the band's continuing popularity, *The Freddy Martin Show* did not fare well after its summer run. The show faltered considerably behind the ratings earned by its competition, *Pabst Blue Rib-*

bon Bouts, whose boxing contests had a head start against the program by starting a half hour earlier. The top 20 series dealt a final blow to *The Freddy Martin Show* after just two months of head-to-head competition.

The show ended around the same time Martin's record "Down Yonder," with a vocal by Murray Arnold, left the music charts. Freddy Martin and His Orchestra would make the charts just twice thereafter, in 1953 and 1954, before being drowned out of the airwaves by rock and roll, though they would continue to perform more than two decades later. Martin died in 1983, while Griffin, who left the band shortly after the series ended, went on to TV fame as a talk show host from 1965 to 1986 and producer of such hits as *Jeopardy!* and *Wheel of Fortune.*

Crime with Father

Comedy. Ran on ABC Fridays 9–9:30 P.M. Aug. 31, 1951–Jan. 18, 1952, opposite *Down You Go* on Du-Mont, *Schlitz Playhouse of Stars* on CBS and *The Big Story* on NBC. C: Rusty Lane (as Capt. Jim Riland), Peggy Lobbin (as Chris Riland). P: Wilbur Stark. D: Charles S. Dubin. W: Larry Menkin.

Though *The Complete Directory to Prime Time Network and Cable TV Shows* and *Encyclopedia of Television: Series, Pilots and Specials* both describe *Crime with Father* as a crime drama, the show's director, Charles S. Dubin, claims it was more than that. "It was a combination of comedy as well as crime detective," he said.

The regular cast was small, as befitted its low budget. Capt. Jim Riland of the New York Police Department enlisted the assistance of his teenage daughter Chris in solving murders. She was smart but also had the stereotypical female adolescent foibles of the time about becoming a woman, like boundless enthusiasm, that made her efforts a mixed blessing with her veteran cop father. "Pop thought she was a help, but he liked to kid her a lot about being a hindrance," Dubin said.

The show aired live in the East from New York — studios at 7 West 66th Street, to be precise. Dubin got the assignment because he was on staff at ABC at the time. "The show had two standing sets — the father's apartment and the office they both used," Dubin said. The limited funding for the show prevented much else in the way of many other sets and scenery or major guest stars, and naturally did not help in gaining much of an audience.

Crime with Father faced the charge of cancellation in less than five months on the air. "I think the sponsor, whoever it was, did not think it had enough ratings to merit going on," said Dubin. Its time slot, which it inherited when *The Jerry Colonna Show* (q.v.) moved to Saturdays, had as its replacement an undistinguished filmed anthology series from Hollywood called *Rebound,* which was replaced by another anthology series in the summer of 1952 titled *Encore Playhouse.* ABC then ran news — a full hour of it, no less — in the slot for the first half of the 1952-53 season. As these programming moves show, the network clearly was in desperate straits for having decent series with paltry budgets in the early 1950s.

As for what happened to the stars of *Crime with Father,* actress Peggy Lobbin appears to be one of those performers who comes and goes on television without much else to show on her show business resume beside this series. Rusty Lane turned out relatively better, getting three more regular series roles after the series left, though none of the programs were a hit. They were on *Jimmy Hughes, Rookie Cop* (see 1952-53), the 1953 summer science fiction series *Operation Neptune,* and *The Clear Horizon* (see 1959-60). He died in 1986 at age 87.

ALSO IN 1950-51

All Around the Town	Chester the Pup	For Your Information
Andy and Della Russell	The College Bowl	Front Page Detective
The Better Home Show	Cowboys and Injuns	Fun Fair
Buck Bradley's Rodeo	Day Dreaming with Laraine	Going Places with Betty Betz
The Buffalo Billy Show	Day (a/k/a The Laraine Day	The Hank McCune Show
Can You Top This?	Show)	Henry Morgan's Great Talent
The Carmel Myers Show	Fashion Magic	Hunt

Hold 'Er Newt
The Horace Heidt Show
I Cover Times Square
It's Fun to Know
It's in the Bag
Jimmy Blaine's Junior Edition
The Johnny Johnston Show
Look Your Best
Major Dell Conway of the Flying Tigers
The Mary Hartline Show
Miss Susan
The Most Important People
The Nick Kenny Show
Not for Publication

Oh, Kay!
Once Upon a Tune
Paddy the Pelican
Panhandle Pete and Jennifer
Party Time at Club Roma
The Patricia Bowman Show
Penthouse Party
The Peter Lind Hayes Show
Q.E.D.
Remember This Date
Rhythm Rodeo
The Robbins Nest
S.S. Telecruise
Sandy Strong
Sawyer Views Hollywood
Say It with Acting

Seven at Eleven
Shadow of the Cloak
Sheilah Graham in Hollywood
Sing It Again
Stage Entrance
Star Time
Susan Raye
Tag the Gag
Take a Chance
The Ted Mack Family Hour
Who's Whose
With This Ring
Young Mr. Bobbin
Your Pet Parade

1951-52

The Egg and I

Soap Opera. Ran on CBS Mondays through Fridays Noon–12:15 P.M. Sept. 3, 1951–Aug. 1, 1952, opposite *The Frances Langford–Don Ameche Show* (from Sept. 10–March 15) on ABC, *For Your Information* (through Nov. 16) and *The Women's Club* (from Dec. 24) on DuMont and *Ruth Lyons' 50 Club* (from Oct. 1) on NBC. C: Pat Kirkland (as Betty MacDonald; through March 7), Betty Lynn (as Betty MacDonald; from March 10), John Craven (as Bob MacDonald), Doris Rich (as Ma Kettle), Frank Twedell (as Pa Kettle), Grady Sutton (as Jed Simmons), Ingeborg Theek (as Lisa Schumacher), Karen Hale (as Paula French). P: Montgomery Ford. D: Jack Gage. W: Manya Starr, Robert Soderberg.

The Gallery of Mme. Lui-Tsong

Crime Drama. Ran on DuMont various nighttime slots Sept. 3–Nov. 21, 1951. C: Anna May Wong (as Mme. Lui-Tsong). D: William Marceau. W: Ira Marion.

The Frances Langford–
Don Ameche Show

Variety. Ran on ABC Mondays through Fridays Noon–1 P.M. Sept. 10, 1951–March 14, 1952, opposite *The Egg and I*, *Midday News* (through Sept. 21), *Love of Life* (from Sept. 24), *Search for Tomorrow*

and *The Steve Allen Show* (through Feb. 22) on CBS, *For Your Information* (through Nov. 16) and *The Women's Club* (from Dec. 24) on DuMont and *Ruth Lyons' 50 Club* (from Oct. 1), *The Bunch* (from Jan. 7–Feb. 22) and *It's a Problem* (from Feb. 25–March 7) on NBC. C: Frances Langford, Don Ameche, Neil Hamilton, Fran Lee (as Mrs. Fix-It), Tony Romano and His Orchestra. P: Ward Byron. D: Robert Massell.

The Bill Goodwin Show

Variety. Ran on NBC Tuesdays and Thursdays 3:30–4 P.M. Sept. 11, 1951–March 27, 1952, opposite *Meet Your Cover Girl* (Thursdays through Nov. 1) and *The Mel Torme Show* (Tuesdays and Thursdays from Nov. 5) on CBS. C: Bill Goodwin, Eileen Barton, Roger Dann, the Joe Bushkin Trio. P/D: Sherman Marks. W: Bob Quigley.

The Dell O'Dell Show

Magic. Ran on ABC Fridays 10–10:30 P.M. Sept. 14–Dec. 14, 1951. C: Dell O'Dell. P/W: Wally Sherwin.

The Mel Torme Show

Musical Variety. Ran on CBS Mondays through Fridays 4:30–5 P.M. Sept. 17–Oct. 26, 1951, opposite *The Kate Smith Hour* on NBC, then CBS Mondays through Fridays 3:30–4 P.M. Nov. 5, 1951–Jan. 11, 1952, opposite the alternating *Bert*

Parks Show and *Bill Goodwin Show* on NBC, and then CBS Tuesdays and Thursdays 3:30–4 P.M. Jan. 14–Aug. 21, 1952, opposite *The Ralph Edwards Show* (through May 16) and *The Johnny Dugan Show* (from May 19) on NBC. C: Mel Torme, Kaye Ballard, Al Pellegrini, Peggy King (1951), Ellen Martin (1951), The Red Norvo Trio (1951), The Terry Gibbs Combo (November 1951–1952). P: Bob Bach. D: Lloyd Gross, Ben Magnes.

Jazz/pop vocalist Mel Torme had been a fairly active presence in movies, radio and music since the mid–1940s before making a plunge as a regular attraction on TV in 1951. He hosted the summer nighttime replacement series *TV's Top Tunes* along with singer Peggy Lee in July and August before moving into daytime with *The Mel Torme Show*.

Joining Mel on the latter was his musical

The star of *The Mel Torme Show* grins off-camera while tickling the ivories in this 1952 photograph from the set.

conductor, Al Pellegrini, actress/singer Kaye Ballard, singer Ellen Martin and dancer Peggy King. As expected, the emphasis on the series was on singing. "It was a daily show, and we had to come up with a lot of stuff involving music," recalled director Lloyd Gross.

One segment Gross remembered especially well was "The Tenement Symphony," where the live show went out on the streets of New York City and provided music amid a backdrop of the alleys and buildings in Manhattan. They did the segment in the fall, then delayed trying it during the winter due to cold, unpleasant weather. When they resumed the segment, a bit of serendipity landed on the show. "We repeated it in the spring on a day when it rained, stopped, and then there was a beautiful snowstorm coming down," Gross said.

Gross also recalled Torme had a nice guest list of musicians. "A lot of Mel's friends showed up — Buddy Rich, Nat 'King' Cole," he said. "It was fun."

The Mel Torme Show ran in color for its first two months, or rather CBS's version of color, which the network pushed unsuccessfully with the FCC. "There were originally two directors who went down to the FCC for the color tests," Gross said. "I was one of them." For more details on the CBS color system, see *The Whistling Wizard*.

After the experiment with color, *The Mel Torme Show* took a week off before returning in a new time slot in black and white with some shakeups in its cast. King and Martin were gone, and Pellegrini now conducted the Terry Gibbs Combo rather than the Red Norvo Trio (both Norvo and Gibbs are noted names in the jazz field). Two months under the new setup, CBS had it alternate daily with *The Bert Parks Show*, which had been its competition on NBC before switching networks.

Even though the show appeared less often, Gross said *The Mel Torme Show* went off the air due to production costs and not ratings. "It got a little expensive for its time," he said. "It should've gone on indefinitely, as it got better." Gross added that Torme wanted to go to Hollywood to continue his career. He appeared regularly on two short-lived summer TV series, the 1953 variety show *Summertime U.S.A.* and the 1971 nostalgia documentary *It Was a Very Good Year*, as well as a considerable num-

ber of guest appearances from the 1950s through 1990s before he died in 1999.

The Dennis James Show

Variety. Ran on ABC Mondays through Fridays 11:30 A.M.–Noon Sept. 24, 1951–Feb. 15, 1952, opposite *Strike It Rich* on CBS and *Dave and Charley* and *Richard Harkness News Review* (both from Jan. 7) on NBC. C: Dennis James, Julia Meade. P: Aaron Steiner. D: Lou Sposa. W: Elizabeth Pierce.

The Amazing Mr. Malone

Crime Drama. Ran on ABC Mondays 8–8:30 P.M. Sept. 24, 1951–March 10, 1952. C: Lee Tracy (as John J. Malone). P/D: Edgar Peterson. W: Alvin Boretz.

This Is Music

Music. Ran on DuMont various nighttime slots Nov. 29, 1951–Oct. 9, 1952. C: Alexander Gray, Nancy Carr, Bruce Foote, Lucille Reed, Bill Snary, Jackie Van (1952), Jacqueline James (1952), the Robert Trendler Orchestra. P: Jay Faraghan, Bob Stebbins. D: Barry McKinley. W: Fran Coughlin.

Ruth Lyons' 50 Club

Variety. Ran on NBC Mondays through Fridays Noon–12:30 P.M. Oct. 1, 1952–Sept. 5, 1952, opposite *The Frances Langford–Don Ameche Show* (through March 15) on ABC, *The Egg and I* and *Love of Life* on CBS, and *For Your Information* (through Nov. 16) and *The Women's Club* (from Dec. 24) on DuMont. C: Ruth Lyons, Willie Thall, Dick Noel, the Bert Farber Orchestra. P/D: Gene Walz.

Mr. District Attorney

Crime Drama. Ran on ABC Mondays 8–8:30 P.M. Oct. 1, 1951–June 23, 1952. C: Jay Jostyn (as District Attorney Paul Garrett), Len Doyle (as Harrington), Vicki Vola (as Miss Miller). P/D: Edward C. Byron. W: Robert J. Shaw.

Here's Looking at You

Informational. Ran on NBC Mondays through Fridays 3:15–3:30 P.M. Oct. 8–Dec. 28, 1951, opposite *Bride and Groom* (through Nov. 1) and *Mike and Buff* (from Nov. 5) on CBS. C/P: Richard Willis.

Chesterfield Sound Off Time

Variety. Ran on NBC Sundays 7–7:30 P.M. Oct. 14, 1951–Jan. 6, 1952, with the following rotating stars and their production staffs: Bob Hope P: Al Capstaff, Ed Sobel, Glen Wheaton. W: Larry Marks, Larry Gelbart. Jerry Lester P: Monroe Hack. D: Warren Jacober. W: Lou Meltzer, Artie Phillips, Manny Manheim. Fred Allen P: Ezra Stone. D: Warren Jacober. W: George Oppenheimer, Bob Weiskopf, Phil Sharp, Jack Creamer, Eva Wolas, George Moxel.

The Whistling Wizard

Puppet. Ran on CBS Mondays through Fridays 5:30–5:45 P.M. Oct. 15–Oct. 26, 1951, opposite *Howdy Doody* on NBC and Saturdays 11–11:30 A.M. Nov. 3, 1951–Sept. 20, 1952, opposite *Foodini the Great*, *Personal Appearance Theater* and *Space Patrol* on ABC and *Kids and Company* on DuMont. C: Bil Baird, Cora Baird, Frank Fazakas, Ray Hedge, Frank Sullivan. W: Andy Russell, Alan Stern. P: Bil and Cora Baird. D: Frances Buss, Richard Saunders.

When asked to compare *The Whistling Wizard* to the Baird company's previous series *Life With Snarky Parker* (q.v.), Frank Fazakas said it was "More sophisticated, (had) better writers. Andy Russell wrote several shows." Russell later was the head writer for Jackie Gleason's *The Honeymooners* series.

What really distinguished the show to TV historians was it was one of the few series telecast by CBS using its mechanical color system, which the network hoped would win approval by the Federal Communications Commission over NBC's color system. "The color in CBS color was absolutely stunning," Fazakas said. "But unreliable." It also was non-compatible with the black-and-white TV sets already in use, and as few sponsors wanted to use it and an FCC panel deciding in late September against it being the industry standard due to its incompatibility with existing sets, CBS phased out using the system at the end of October for black and white, just two weeks into it being used on *The Whistling Wizard*.

In spite of its quick use, Fazakas did recall that "The color took five times as much lighting than normal." Luckily for the performers, it was their puppet characters who felt the increased heat for the telecasts. They included a leprechaun named Dooley, the Whistling Wizard, Charlemane the lion and Ting-a-Ling the firefly (all voiced by Bil Baird), and J.P. the boy and the evil Spider Lady (both voiced by Cora Baird). As on *Life With Snarky Parker*, Fazakas voiced Heathcliff the talking horse. All took part in assorted fantasies based on famous tales or historic events.

After CBS ended its color experiment, *The Whistling Wizard* became a Saturday morning entry. Fazakas did not recall the exact reason why it went off less than a year later. But its disappearance did not mean a long absence from series TV for the Bairds and crew. They returned a year later on *The Bil Baird Show* (q.v.).

Byline (a/k/a News Gal)

Drama. Ran on ABC Saturdays Noon–12:30 P.M. Oct. 20 and 27, 1951, opposite *Big Top* on CBS and *Rootie Kazootie* on NBC, then ABC Sundays 7:30–8 P.M. Nov. 4–Dec. 9, 1951, opposite *This is Show Business* on CBS and *Young Mr. Bobbin* on NBC. C: Betty Furness (as Harriet Hildebrand). P: Hal Davis. D: Cort Steen, Don Medford. W: Hal Davis, George Quint.

The Gayelord Hauser Show

Interview. Ran on ABC Wednesdays and Fridays 1–1:15 P.M. Oct. 31, 1951–April 25, 1952, opposite *The Steve Allen Show* (through Feb. 22) on CBS. C: Gayelord Hauser, Ona Munson. P: Sherman H. Dryer. D: Robert Massell.

Fairmeadows, U.S.A.

Soap Opera. Ran on NBC Sundays 3–3:30 P.M. Nov. 4, 1951–April 27, 1952, opposite *The U.N. in Action* (from Nov. 11–Jan. 6) and *The Quiz Kids* (from Jan. 20–April 13) on CBS and pro football (through Nov. 25) on DuMont. C: Howard St. John (as John Olcott), Ruth Matteson (as Alice Olcott), Mimi Strongin (as Evie Olcott). P: Ezra McIntosh. D: Allan Rhone. W: Agnes Ridgeway.

The Women's Club

Informational. Ran on DuMont Mondays through Fridays Noon–12:15 P.M. Dec. 24, 1951–Aug. 1, 1952, opposite *The Frances Langford–Don Ameche Show* (through March 15) on ABC, *The Egg and I* on CBS and *Ruth Lyons' 50 Club* on NBC. C: Julann Caffrey.

Those Endearing Young Charms

Sitcom. Ran on NBC Sundays 5:30–6 P.M. Dec. 30, 1951–Jan. 6, 1952, opposite *Super Circus* on ABC and *Lamp Unto My Feet* on CBS, then NBC Sundays 6:30–7 P.M. March 30–April 6, 1952, and then NBC Tuesdays and Thursdays 7:15–7:30 P.M. May–June 17, 1952, opposite *Captain Video* on DuMont. C: Maurice Copeland (as Ralph Charm); Betty Arnold (as Abbe Charm; replaced by Fern Persons); Gerald Garvey (as Clem Charm); Pat Matthews (as Connie Charm; replaced by Charon Follett); Clarence Hartzell (as Uncle Duff). P/D: Ben Park. W: Bill Barrett.

Those Endearing Young Charms, done live in Chicago, had none-too-endearing erratic scheduling over NBC for six months. It first ran for two weeks in the late afternoon, temporarily displacing *Sky King*, then another two weeks on early Sunday evenings before being replaced by *Once Upon a Fence* (q.v.) and finally ended as a replacement for *Bob and Ray* alternating nightly with *The Goldbergs*. Between the first two network slots, there were replacements in the cast with sister Connie Charm and mom Abbe Charm. Taking over the latter role was Fern Persons.

Persons, a longtime Chicago radio actress, said she joined the show because she was under contract with the NBC network and officials drafted her for it. "I don't know why I didn't audition, and I don't know why Betty Arnold left," she said.

Recalling *Those Endearing Young Charms*, Persons noted, "It was a family show. It was light. We played in a studio, at the Studebaker Theater. I don't think it ever had a sponsor." The series itself was a standard issue sitcom set with a family with a father (Ralph), mother, son, daughter and a wacky uncle.

Some radio performers had a difficult time adapting to the needs of television. Persons said she was not one of those and felt at home doing the sitcom. "I had been trained for the theater, and knew how to use my body," she said. "To me, radio was the adjustment." She also was familiar with filling a part formerly done by another actress, noting that when she did the early 1940s radio soap opera *Helpmate*, "I took the lead role from Arlene Francis."

Those Endearing Young Charms was Persons' only network series role. She downplayed acting for a time but resumed her profession in the late 1960s doing plays and radio commercials after her husband died "because it was very therapeutic for me." She was still active in 2001, taping a role on the Chicago dramatic radio series *Unshackled*.

As for *Those Endearing Young Charms*, it somewhat surprisingly was the last sitcom done in Chicago for nearly 50 years until the spring of 2001 when ABC debuted *What About Joan?*, starring Windy City native Joan Cusack. TV network executives in 1952 became more enamored with doing shows in Hollywood than Chicago, and by the 1960s only rarely did network shows emanate from the city. Some natives were upset by this dropoff of national exposure, but others were like Persons, who told me, "I didn't really miss it."

Battle of the Ages

Game. Ran on DuMont Tuesdays 9–9:30 P.M. Jan. 1–June 17, 1952, then CBS Saturdays 10:30–11 P.M. Sept. 6–Nov. 29, 1952. C: John Reed King (DuMont), Morey Amsterdam (CBS). P: Norman S. Livingston. D: Andrew McCullough, Frank Bunetta, Mondo Brown.

Claudia, the Story of a Marriage

Comedy/Drama. Ran on NBC Sundays 6:30–7:30 Jan. 6–March 23, 1952, then CBS Mondays 9:30–10 P.M. March 31–June 30, 1952. C: Joan McCracken (as Claudia Naughton), Hugh Reilly (as David Naughton), Margaret Wycherly (as Mrs. Brown), Lilia Skala (as Bertha), Faith Brook (as Julia Naughton), Alex Clark (as Harley Naughton), Paul Andor (as Fritz), Mercer McCloud (as Roger). P: Carol Irwin. W: Dougherty Brown.

Breakfast Party

Variety. Ran on NBC Mondays through Fridays 10–10:30 A.M. Jan. 7–May 23, 1952, opposite *Morning News* and *Arthur Godfrey Time* (Mondays through Thursdays only) on CBS. C: Mel Martin, Eileen Martin, the Bel-Aires (Bruce Brownfield, accordion; Larry Downs, guitar; Mel Horner, bass).

A local show on WLW-TV in Cincinnati in 1951, *Breakfast Party* came onto NBC's morning lineup a week before *Today*, but unlike that show ran far less than 50 years. Its competition from *Arthur Godfrey Time*, then the #1 daytime show, no doubt hastened its disappearance from NBC after four months.

The show's musical director, Bruce Brownfield, did not recall the involvement with NBC. However, he did remember other facts. He organized and led the Bel-Aires musical trio, a name that came from the sounds of the men's first names—Bruce, Mel, and Larry. "They stuck that name on us," he said of WLW management. "A pain in the ass, but they did it." Moreover, he was younger than Larry Downs and Mel Horner, and according to Brownfield, they resented taking directions from someone who was their junior. "We didn't get along the greatest," he said.

Nevertheless, the Bel-Aires provided music with little controversy on air to the show's regulars, which included its host Mel Martin and the unrelated Eileen Martin. "Eileen was a singer from Ft. Thomas, Kentucky," Brownfield said. "Mel Martin was a handsome guy and had been on the road a little bit and decided to settle down and do a TV show."

The format was variety, which meant pretty much anything went. "The group did two planned numbers, and maybe the vocalists would do two," Brownfield said. There also was the game "Waving Time," where the camera panned the studio audience while the Bel-Aires played and when the music ended the person seen on camera got a prize. There were sketches too. "We got mixed up in it quite a bit, and they needed anybody with a warm body on air," Brownfield said.

The program remained a local favorite in Cincinnati almost a year after the network cancellation. Then came a major event on air on April 10, 1953. As Brownfield recalled, "The show went on, and Mel Martin went on the air and said he was going to be a religious preacher. He said, 'As of now, I'm out of here,' and he walked off the show. And then we all thought, 'What do we do?'" The announcer Jim Wood substituted as host, but no Mel Martin meant the *Breakfast Party* was over for most viewers, and the show ended quickly thereafter.

Brownfield said Martin is still an evangelist living near Cincinnati, while he has lost touch with the other regulars. The other Bel-Aires are now dead, though they stayed with him into the 1960s to do Ruth Lyons' shows and radio and club spots. (Brownfield said out-

side work was needed, since he and others joked that the call letters for WLW stood for "World's Lowest Wages.") After Lyons retired in 1967, Brownfield became the bandleader for *The Paul Dixon Show* until that entertainer's death in 1974. That program was syndicated nationally in 1973, making it the only other time since *Breakfast Party* that Brownfield appeared on TV outside Cincinnati.

The Bunch

Musical Variety. Ran on NBC Mondays through Fridays 12:30–1 P.M. Jan. 7–Feb. 22, 1952, opposite *The Frances Langford–Don Ameche Show* on ABC and *Search for Tomorrow* and *The Steve Allen Show* on CBS. C: Hugh Downs, Bette Chapel, the Art Van Damme Orchestra, the Joseph Gallichio Orchestra. P: Ben Park, Don Meier. D: Lynwood King. W: Marvin David.

The Bunch was a network version of a 1951 Chicago series titled *Coffee And* that had Hugh Downs and Nancy Wright mostly singing (that's right — the future low-key host of *20/20* was singing!). "Believe it or not, it was done in Studio D, which was the *Kukla, Fran and Ollie* stage — the smallest stage in the NBC Merchandise Mart," said director Lynwood King.

When NBC decided to carry it, Wright was dropped in favor of Bette Chapel. "When we went to the full network routine, I think it behooved them to go to 'name value,'" King said. "Bette Chapel was the most popular member of *Garroway at Large* [the 1949–51 nighttime series starring Dave Garroway before he hosted *Today* from 1952 to 1961]. She was more popular than Dave Garroway. She was a girl-next-door perky type."

King said the format was simple, with a little twist. "For a half hour, we'd do four or five songs, and the rest would be gimmicky or schtick." For example, once Downs babbled with polysyllabic words about the universe as members of Art Van Damme's band peeled off with Chapel to perform "How High the Moon" on a different part of the set. "When we came back on to Hugh after the song, he was still pontificating. It was that kind of humor."

Extending the fun would be the appearance of the Joseph Gallichio Orchestra on Fridays, when Downs would sit in with the band and play a kazoo. The group, and the rest of the regulars, did the job mainly because they enjoyed it, for as King noted, "We had no money and no budget. It was a very small operation."

And although a writer was credited for the show, King indicated there was not much of a script to go by other than the list of songs for that day's show. "We would rehearse the Van Damme numbers the day before, but it was really basically ad lib."

The Bunch lasted less than two months without a sponsor. King believed NBC executives made little effort to sell the show in order to force it to be cancelled as the network's daytime lineup began to be sold out on other series. "New York didn't like the attention Chicago was getting," he said. "I've since learned years later that New York killed [network programming from] Chicago because they didn't want competition from it." As with Downs, King himself would be one of those people having to relocate to New York to get jobs with the network, though in King's case, it happened after he did another Chicago-based network show, *The Breakfast Club* (see 1953-54).

Dave and Charley

Comedy. Ran on NBC Mondays through Fridays 11:30–11:45 A.M. Jan. 7–March 28, 1952, opposite *The Dennis James Show* on ABC (through Feb. 15) and *Strike It Rich* on CBS. C/P/W: Cliff Arquette (as Charley Weaver), Dave Willock. D: John B. Lyman III.

The Public Life of Cliff Norton

Comedy. Ran on NBC Mondays through Fridays 11:10–11:15 P.M. Jan. 7–Feb. 29, 1952 opposite *Chronoscope* (Mondays, Wednesdays and Fridays only) on CBS. C: Cliff Norton.

Don't tell Cliff Norton this series flopped. "It originated in Chicago, and it was anything but a failure," said. "I was on three years locally." The problem was when NBC put it on nationally after most of its affiliates' 10-minute late evening newscasts. Then, Norton said, "We shot it on film in New York, and it lost the spontaneity it had before. And the producers didn't have much of a sense of humor, and we did. It was no longer bright and funny and appealing."

Norton, a Chicago native, debuted on TV in 1946 on the city's only station on air then,

WBKB. By 1950 *The Public Life of Cliff Norton* basically kicked off the evening schedule on that channel by running live from 5:30–5:35 P.M. daily, followed by a news program and then *Kukla, Fran and Ollie* at 6 P.M. (the latter aired over NBC live in the Midwest and East Coast from 1949 to 1951, then live on the West Coast as well by 1951). Norton also was a regular on Dave Garroway's variety show *Garroway at Large*, which ran on NBC from 1949 to 1951 on Sunday evenings.

"It was exhilarating," Norton said of his TV schedule at the time. "I was very young, very ambitious. I never stopped being creative." He added that for one 20-week stretch he not only did both TV series but also headlined two shows a night every evening of the week at a club in Chicago, with shows starting at 8 P.M. and 11:30 P.M. or midnight.

Regarding his series, Norton said it was an intimate affair with hardly any guests, just himself doing comedy for the camera. "It was a one-man show. I used a dummy, outrageously, badly wardrobed both as a male and female. Sometimes I would spoof interview shows, and I would do terrible things to the dummy."

Norton admits that *The Public Life of Cliff Norton* got a great assist from its writer, Paul Rhymer, who had written the humorous daily radio serial *Vic and Sade* from 1932 to 1946. "He would come up with all these marvelous ideas. We'd put 'em through, and then he'd go home and write them." The only time Norton said he didn't do shows were during the hiatus in the summer months. "I don't think we ever repeated a show — maybe only a couple of times by request," he said.

NBC brought Norton to its late night lineup a week before Dave Garroway hosted the debut of *Today*, the 7–9 A.M. daily informational show that is still running as of this writing. While Garroway flourished, Norton's program vanished in less than two months. NBC aired no other network show after 11 P.M. until *The Tonight Show* debuted in the fall of 1954. Norton continued as an actor and comedian in New York and Hollywood until his retirement in 1998, compiling two other failed series on the way (see *What's Going On?* in 1954-55 and *It's About Time* in 1966-67).

The U.S. Royal Showcase

Comedy Variety. Ran on NBC Sundays 7–7:30 P.M. Jan. 13–June 29, 1952. C: George Abbott (host through April 6), Jack Carson (host from April 13). P: Joe Bigelow. D: George Abbott.

The Ralph Edwards Show

Game/Variety. Ran on NBC Mondays, Wednesdays and Fridays 3:30–4 P.M. Jan. 14–May 16, 1952, opposite *The Bert Parks Show* on CBS. C: Ralph Edwards, Steve Reeves, Sara Berner, Carole Richards, the Varieteers. P: Ralph Edwards. D: Cal Howard. W: Paul Edwards, Tom Adair, Mort Lachman.

Metropolitan Opera Auditions of the Air

Opera Talent. Ran on ABC Tuesdays 8:30–9 P.M. Jan. 15–April 1, 1952. C: Milton J. Cross. P: William Marshall. D: Herman Liveright.

Quick on the Draw

Game. Ran on DuMont Tuesdays 9:30–10 P.M. Jan. 15–Dec. 9, 1952. C: Robin Chandler, Bob Dunn. P: Kermit Schafer. D: Bill Warwick, David Lowe.

The Continental

Women's Interest. Ran on CBS Tuesdays and Thursdays 11:15–11:30 P.M. Jan. 22–April 17, 1952, then ABC Tuesdays and Fridays 11–11:15 P.M. Oct. 11, 1952–Jan. 6, 1953. C/P/W: Renzo Cesana. D: Ed Leftwich.

The Al Pearce Show

Variety. Ran on CBS Mondays through Fridays 10:45–11 A.M. Feb. 11–April 1, 1952, opposite *Winner Take All* (from Feb. 27) on NBC, then CBS Mondays through Fridays 11–11:30 A.M. April 4–May 9, 1952, and then CBS Mondays through Thursdays 10:45–11 A.M. and Fridays 10:30–11 A.M. June 30–Sept. 26, 1952. C: Al Pearce. P: Stefan Hatos. D: Bill Sterling. W: Jack Harvey, Howard Blake, Carl Gass.

Rendezvous

Drama. Ran on ABC Wednesdays 9:30–10 P.M. Feb. 13–March 5, 1952. C: Ilona Massey (as Nikki Angell), David McKay. D: Seymour Robbie. W: Harry and Gail Ingram.

It's a Problem

Discussion. Ran on NBC Mondays through Fridays 12:30–1 P.M. Feb. 25–March 7, 1952, opposite *Search for Tomorrow* on CBS, then NBC Mondays through Fridays 11:30 A.M.–Noon March 10–Oct. 13, 1952, opposite *Strike It Rich* on CBS. C: Ben Grauer, Fannie Hurst, Helen Parkhurst (through August), Alice Thompson (from August). P: Phyllis Adams. D: Howard Davis.

Junior Hi-Jinx

Children's. Ran on CBS Sundays 12:15–12:30 P.M. March 2–May 25, 1952, opposite *Tootsie Hippodrome* on ABC. C: Warren Wright. P: Charles Vanda. D: Fred O'Neill.

Junior Hi-Jinx began on TV as a daily local offering in Philadelphia in 1950. The program featured the adventures of puppet Willie the Worm, operated by Warren Wright. "It was a very popular show for kids," said director Fred O'Neill.

Though O'Neill wasn't sure, it probably was its viewership in the "City of Brotherly Love" that convinced CBS executives to add the show to the network lineup. It aired early Sunday afternoons following another 15-minute show from Philadelphia, *Ranger Joe* (which had been on ABC since Dec. 3, 1950, before moving over to CBS the same day *Junior Hi-Jinx* debuted), while the local show continued Mondays through Fridays. "We did the same kind of show on CBS," O'Neill said.

Wright operated Willie using his right arm. Recalling the creation of the worm, O'Neill said, "He had this puppet which he made out of accordion-type exhaust pipe and big glasses." Wright was the only puppeteer on the show, although O'Neill recalled there was at least one scenario involving seahorses that required one of the show's assistant directors to get involved.

The seahorses came about in an elaborate story line that may or may not have been seen on the network. O'Neill didn't know for sure, but he did recall the crew having to create a diving bell to carry Willie underwater in a fish tank background. "I had piano wires coming left and right behind the fish tank and the bell," he said. "And one night the fish tank developed a leak, and we had to keep the ADs [assistant directors] up all night to fill it with water."

O'Neill worked with Wright to come up

with general situations to use involving Willie for each show. "We concocted as many situations as we could to interest young tots," he said. "One time he was a coal miner and went deep down in a hole. And he also had an unseen friend named Newton who was always getting him in trouble."

Through it all, O'Neill said Wright had a respect and love for his puppet. Once the two men were on a tour promoting the series when they stopped to eat lunch at a restaurant. "We sat down and he suddenly ran out and grabbed Willie and brought him inside. He said, 'Oh, my God, what if somebody stole Willie?'"

Despite their efforts, or maybe because of the competition, *Junior Hi-Jinx* did not cut as a CBS show and ended in less than three months after failing to get a sponsor. O'Neill stayed with the local program through 1954 before going to work in Washington, D.C., for a period. "It did run maybe four years, possibly five," he said. "We did change the name in the latter years to *Willie the Worm*." (O'Neill also had no knowledge of why it originally was called *Junior Hi-Jinx*.) Wright vanished from view thereafter, never having another national TV series.

It's a Business?

Sitcom. Ran on DuMont Wednesdays 9–9:30 P.M. March 19–May 21, 1952, opposite *The Ruggles* (through April) and *The Adventures of Ellery Queen* (from April) on ABC, *Strike It Rich* on CBS and *Kraft Television Theatre* on NBC. C: Leo De Lyon, Bob Haymes, Dorothy Loudon. P: Paul Rosen. D: Frank Bunetta. W: Bob Weiskopf.

"My real name is Irving Levine," said Leo De Lyon. "And I was a pianist originally doing funny hand things. And then I did *Arthur Godfrey's Talent Scouts* in 1947. I won that by doing one of my musical numbers, almost like Spike Jones, and that started me off as Leo De Lyon."

Actually, that started him off professionally. The punny moniker came earlier. "I was working off–Broadway at the Sawdust Trail as a piano player. I started to build a little following and the boss said, 'You can't call yourself Irving Levine. You ought to call yourself Lee Vine.'" Then everyone called him Lee, and because he did roaring sounds in his act, he modified it to Leo De Lyon, a la comedy actor Billy DeWolfe (which was the latter's real name).

De Lyon's first regular TV role was on *It's a Business?*, a sitcom set at the Broadway Music Publishing Company circa 1917. "What it was was a bunch of song pluggers in a music house," he said. In non–show business parlance, that meant aspiring songwriters tried to encourage De Lyon and partner Bob Haymes to listen to their tunes and agree to publish them (in the show's time period, the sheet music industry was bigger than recording songs).

"Bob Haymes' voice was very similar to his brother's (big band singer Dick Haymes), a rich baritone sound. Dorothy Loudon was the nice, innocent secretary. And there were big artists who came in to sing their songs," De Lyon said. (He, Haymes and Loudon had character names, but De Lyon did not recall them and no published accounts have listed them.) Most of the guests were character actors, not singers, he claimed.

"We used live music with no lip syncing," De Lyon said, with Mort Lindsey as the show's musical director. A comic storyline filled out the tuneful interludes. "It was a tremendous amount of work, but we loved doing it," he said. "And it was live. Everything was out on a net."

So why didn't *It's a Business?* have the business to be a hit? "Unfortunately, it was done on the DuMont network, with a limited number of outlets," De Lyon said. "And we did it in a theater, but no audience, and I've always you need laughter on a comedy. Unfortunately, when people would view it at home with two or three people in a room, it wouldn't be as funny."

De Lyon survived the series to go on and provide the voices of the felines Spook and The Brain on the 1960s cartoon series *Top Cat*. "Back in the early 1970s I did around four years with Phil Silvers," he said. "I was his conductor, arranger, and did bits with him. The happiest four years of my life." The experience led him to believe that "In my heart, I knew I was a musician," so he became an arranger for aspiring singers — not too far from the same role he had on *It's a Business?*

Give and Take

Game. Ran on CBS Thursdays 3:30–4 P.M. March 20–June 12, 1952, opposite *The Johnny Dugan Show* (from May 19) on NBC. C: Bill Cullen. P:

Jack Carney. D: Frank Satenstein. W: Bill Cullen, Jack Roche, Mark Humboldt.

Dagmar's Canteen

Variety. Ran on NBC Saturdays 12:15–12:45 A.M. March 22–June 14, 1952. C: Dagmar, Jennie Lewis, Ray Malone, Tim Herbert, Milton DeLugg and His Orchestra. P: Hal Friedman. D: Alan Neuman. W: Lou Meltzer, Allan Walker.

Once Upon a Fence

Children's. Ran on NBC Sundays 6:30–7 P.M. April 13–July 20, 1952. C: Dave Kaigler, Katherine Heger.

Draw to Win

Game. Ran on CBS Tuesdays 8:30–9 P.M. April 22–June 10, 1952. C: Henry Morgan, Bill Holman,

Abner Dean. P: Winston O'Keefe, Joel O'Brien, Marlo Lewis. D: Joel O'Brien.

Your Surprise Store

Game. Ran on CBS Mondays through Thursdays 10:45–11:15 A.M. and Fridays 10:30–11 A.M. May 12–May 23, 1952, then CBS Mondays through Thursdays 10:30–11:15 A.M. and Fridays 10:30–11 A.M. May 12–May 23, 1952. C: Lew Parker, Jacqueline Susann. P: Hal Fimberg. D: Frank Satenstein. W: Elroy Schwartz, Harry Grossweiner, Stan Hart.

Pud's Prize Party

Children's. Ran on ABC Saturdays 11:30 A.M.– Noon June 21–Dec. 20, 1952, opposite *Smilin' Ed McConnell and His Buster Brown Gang* on CBS and *Kids and Company* (from Aug. 9) on DuMont. C: Todd Russell. D: George Webber.

1952-53

Happy's Party

Children's. Ran on DuMont Saturdays 11–11:30 A.M. Sept. 6, 1952–May 9, 1953, opposite *Space Patrol* on ABC and *There's One in Every Family* (from Nov. 10 to Feb. 7, 1953) on CBS. C: Ida Mae Maher.

Stage a Number

Talent. Ran on DuMont various nighttime slots Sept. 17, 1952–May 20, 1953. C: Bill Wendell. P: Roger Gerry.

Life with Luigi

Sitcom. Ran on CBS Mondays 9:30–10 P.M. Sept. 22–Dec. 29, 1952, then CBS Thursdays April 9–June 4, 1953. C: J. Carrol Naish (as Luigi Basco; 1952), Vitto Scotti (as Luigi Basco; 1953), Alan Reed (as Pasquale; 1952), Thomas Gomez (as Pasquale; 1953), Jody Gilbert (as Rosa; 1952), Muriel Landers (as Rosa; 1953), Mary Shipp (as Miss Spaulding), Sig Rumann (as Schultz), Ken Peters (as Olson), Joe Forte (as Horwitz). P: Cy Howard. D: Mac Benoff. W: Mac Benoff, Lou Derman.

There's One in Every Family

Game. Ran on CBS Mondays through Fridays 11–11:30 A.M. Sept. 29–Nov. 7, 1952, then CBS Mondays through Saturdays 11–11:30 A.M. Nov. 10, 1952–June 12, 1953 (Thursdays off starting Feb. 12), opposite *Space Patrol* (Saturdays) on ABC and *Happy's Party* (Saturdays through May 9) on DuMont. C: John Reed King (through March 6), Mike Wallace (through March 7), Dean Miller (from March 9). P: Richard Lewine. D: James Sheldon, Rai Purdy (New York). P/D: Stefan Hatos (Los Angeles).

Heaven for Betsy

Sitcom. Ran on CBS Tuesdays and Thursdays 7:45–8 P.M. Sept. 30–Dec. 23, 1952. C: Jack Lemmon (as Pete Bell), Cynthia Stone (as Betsy Bell). D: Richard Linkroum. W: Russ Beggs.

Doc Corkle

Sitcom. Ran on NBC Oct. 5–19, 1952, opposite *The Hot Seat* on ABC and *This Is Show Business* on CBS. C: Eddie Mayehoff (as Doc Corkle), Billie Burke (as Melinda), Arnold Stang (as Winfield

Dill), Hope Emerson (as Nellie Corkle), Connie Marshall (as Laurie Corkle), Chester Conklin (as Pop Corkle). P/D: Lou Place. W: Alan Lipscott, Devery Freeman, Bob Fisher.

There had been a handful of short-lived TV series prior to the 1952-53 to run three episodes or less, but none of them debuted at the start of the fall season when most new shows were unveiled. *Doc Corkle* had the dubious honor of being the shortest-lived fall series until the autumn of 1963 when *100 Grand* tied it with a grand total of just three weeks on the air.

Doc Corkle starred comic Eddie Mayehoff as the title character, a dentist strapped for money (already a dubious premise, given the number of customers going to dentists at the time who paid hefty fees for the service). His nurse and assistant in cash-raising schemes was Melinda. The name may have been a play on actress Billie Burke's best-known acting role, as Glinda the Good Witch in the 1939 classic *The Wizard of Oz*.

Also showing up were Doc's towering sister Nellie, his daughter Laurie, and Laurie's meek boyfriend, Winfield Dill, a millionaire. The walrus-mustached silent film comedian Chester Conklin appeared as Doc's dad. As with co-star Billie Burke, this would be his only regular TV series credit.

"*Doc Corkle* had too short a run for the charisma of its star to take hold," opined writer Devery Freeman in a letter to me. "Likewise the cast. Eddie Mayehoff was a good comedian, a great second banana, but essentially untested.

"The writing was professional, but it seems to have been indecisive about direction — whether to make it a high comedy farce or a warm family show. I see those things in retrospect."

All that sponsor Reynolds Metals saw on *Doc Corkle* at the time was a disappointing show. The advertiser made an unprecedented decision at the time and canned the program after a trio of showings, even though since it was filmed in Hollywood there had to have been at least a few more waiting to be shown. Rather than run those episodes off, Reynolds Metals decided instead to bring back a 1952 summer series that aired live from New York immediately in place of *Doc Corkle*.

Mr. Peepers originally ran in a different time slot in the summer of 1952 — Thursdays from 9:30–10 P.M., replacing the variety show *Ford Festival* (April 5, 1951–June 26, 1952) — but it did well enough in its new period replacing *Doc Corkle* to last there until its cancellation on June 12, 1955. The show starred Wally Cox as the lead, a mild-mannered teacher, and it definitely was a warm family show, unlike the uncertain *Doc Corkle*.

Mayehoff had another shot at TV series stardom a year and a half after *Doc Corkle* went off, but it bombed as well (see *That's My Boy* in 1953-54). In fact, the only cast member to survive this fiasco and have a hit on TV was Arnold Stang, who provided the title voice for the 1960s cartoon *Top Cat*, among other regular and guest roles.

Everywhere I Go

Talk. Ran on CBS Tuesdays and Thursdays 2–2:30 P.M. Oct. 7, 1952–Jan. 6, 1953. C: Dan Seymour, the Sammy Spear Orchestra. P: Irving Gitlin. D: Lloyd Gross. W: Charles Romine, David Moore.

The Buick Circus Hour

Variety/Drama. Ran on NBC Tuesdays 8–9 P.M. Oct. 7, 1952–June 16, 1953. C: Joe E. Brown (as the clown), John Raitt (as Bill Sothern), Dolores Gray (as Kim O'Neill), Frank Gallop (as the ringmaster). P/Stage Director: John C. Wilson. D: Frank Burns. W: Anita Loos, Jerry Seelen.

Club Embassy

Variety. Ran on NBC Tuesdays 10:30–10:45 P.M. Oct. 7, 1952–June 23, 1953, opposite *The Name's the Same* (from December) on ABC. C: 1952 — Bob Elliott, Ray Goulding, Audrey Meadows, Florian Zabach, Julia Meade; 1953 — Mindy Carson, Danny Hoctor, Connie Russell, the Embassy Quartet. P/D: Fred Heider.

The comedy duo of Bob (Elliott) and Ray (Goulding) prospered on Boston radio from 1946 to 1951 before NBC signed them to do both network radio and TV series. They glowed on radio but missed on TV, with their witty, often improvised wordplay coming across poorly on a medium not known for sophistication. Their first effort, *Bob and Ray*, ran from 1951 to 1952 with Audrey Meadows and later Cloris Leachman as a female regular before they joined a more elaborate series the next season called *Club Embassy*.

Joining the men on *Club Embassy* was Florian Zabach, a violinist who shared a manager with Bob and Ray. He came to fame in 1951 with a million-selling instrumental called "The Hot Canary." "Everything was predicated by 'The Hot Canary,'" Zabach said. "I did it on Milton Berle's show and others. It got so that certain people thought, 'Gee, the kid only knows one tune.'"

Eager to show he could do more, Zabach signed onto the TV series to play music between Bob and Ray's routines with Audrey Meadows. "They couldn't sustain Bob and Ray for a full time period," noted Zabach of his job. "They went from skit to skit and weren't cohesive."

Zabach said he basically stayed just the "glue" between comedy pieces on *Club Embassy*. "I got into skits very little, usually as a voice or small part. They came prepared with what they did, which was nothing what I had to do." Julia Meade played a cigarette girl seen sashaying amid the title nightclub setting.

The ensemble did not reach a big audience, however, so NBC jettisoned them for an all-music lineup featuring vocalist Mindy Carson (replaced by Connie Russell on May 19) and dancer Danny Hoctor. It bombed, petering out against the weak competition of the game show *The Name's the Same* while a revival of the *Bob and Ray* show lasted just from April–Sept. 28, 1953. Ironically, Bob and Ray would host *The Name's the Same* in 1955 shortly before it ended.

Zabach went on to score a minor hit in 1953 ("Red Canary"), then in 1954 filmed the syndicated *Florian Zabach Show* in Hollywood. "I think we worked every three days on shows," he said. "I'd conduct and interview guests. It really opened up the world for me." It led to Zabach being invited to conduct various concerts around the world, including one in 2001 with the Singapore Symphony Orchestra.

Try as he might, though, Zabach admits he can't rid himself of "The Hot Canary," which people still remember and ask him to play more than a half century later. "I still have to play it," he said. "I try to sneak it in somewhere in my concerts." Regarding *Club Embassy*, his final comment was that even though it wasn't a success, "It was a very pleasurable thing."

Scott Music Hall

Musical Variety. Ran on NBC Wednesdays 8:30–9 P.M. Oct. 8, 1952–Aug. 26, 1953. C: Patti Page, Frank Fontaine, Mary Ellen Terry, the Carl Hoff Orchestra. P: Harry Herrmann. D: Buzz Kulick. W: Bob Weiskopf, Jack Huston, Charles Spaulding.

Ladies Date

Game. Ran on DuMont Mondays through Fridays 1–1:30 P.M. Oct. 13, 1952–July 31, 1953. C: Bruce Meyer, Bob Hund. P: Sandy Howard. D: Jim Saunders.

Leave It to Larry

Sitcom. Ran on CBS Tuesdays 8–8:30 P.M. Oct. 14–Dec. 23, 1952. C: Eddie Albert (as Larry Tucker), Ed Begley (as Mr. Koppel), Betty Kean (as Amy Tucker), Glenn Walken (as Stevie Tucker), Lydia Schaefer (as Harriet Tucker). P: Leo Solomon. D: Mervyn Nelson, Allen Reisner. W: Leo Solomon, Vinnie Bogert, Billy Friedberg.

Balance Your Budget

Game. Ran on CBS Saturdays 10–10:30 P.M. Oct. 18, 1952–May 2, 1953. C: Bert Parks. P: Peter Arnell. D: Sherman Marks.

All Aboard

Children's. Ran on CBS Sundays 12:15–12:30 P.M. Oct. 19, 1952–Jan. 11, 1953, opposite *Tootsie Hippodrome* on ABC. C: Skeets Minton, Junie Keegan. P: Lester Lewis. D: Frederick A. Carr. W: Mort Lewis, Lawrence Markes.

Steve Randall (a/k/a Hollywood Off Beat)

Adventure. Ran on DuMont Fridays 8–8:30 P.M. Nov. 7, 1952–Jan. 30, 1953. C: Melvyn Douglas (as Steve Randall). P/D: Marion Parsonnet. W: Rip von Runkle.

My Hero

Sitcom. Ran on NBC Saturdays various nighttime slots Nov. 8, 1952–Aug. 1, 1953. C: Bob Cummings (as Bob Beanblossom), Julie Bishop (as Julie Marshall), John Litel (as Willis Thackery). P: Mort Green. D: Harold Daniels. W: Norman Paul, Jack Elinson, Bob Cummings.

Biff Baker U.S.A.

Adventure. Ran on CBS Thursdays 9–9:30 P.M. Nov. 13, 1952–March 26, 1953. C: Alan Hale, Jr. (as Biff Baker), Randy Stuart (as Louise Baker). P: Alan Miller. D: Richard Irving. W: Frank Burt, Fenton Earnaham.

Junior Rodeo

Children's. Ran on ABC Saturdays 11:30 A.M.– Noon Nov. 15–Dec. 13, 1952, opposite *Smilin' Ed McConnell and His Buster Brown Gang* on CBS and *Kids and Company* on DuMont. C: Bob Atcher, Valerie Alberts. D: Grover Allen. W: Bill Adams.

The Greatest Man on Earth

Game. Ran on ABC Thursdays 8–8:30 P.M. Dec. 3, 1952–Feb. 19, 1952. C: Ted Brown (through Jan. 15), Vera Vague (from Jan. 22), Pat Conway. P: Walt Framer. D: Bob Doyle.

The Big Idea

Informational. Ran on DuMont Mondays 9–9:30 P.M. Dec. 15, 1952–May 1953, opposite *Perspective* (from Jan.–April 6) on ABC, *I Love Lucy* on CBS and *Hollywood Opening Night* (through March 23) and *Eye Witness* (from March 30) on NBC, then DuMont Thursdays 10–10:30 P.M. May–Oct. 15, 1953, opposite *My Little Margie* (through July 10), *Pentagon U.S.A.* (from Aug. 6– Sept. 24), and *Philip Morris Playhouse* (from Oct. 8) on CBS and *Martin Kane, Private Eye* on NBC. C: Donn Bennett, Ray Wood.

Wisdom of the Ages

Discussion. Ran on DuMont Tuesdays 9:30–10 P.M. Dec. 16, 1952–June 30, 1953, opposite boxing on ABC, *Suspense* on CBS and *Armstrong Circle Theatre* on NBC. C: Jack Barry, Ronnie Mulluzzo, Marcia Van Dyke, Leo Cherne, Mrs. H.V. Kaltenborn, Thomas Clark. P: Jack Barry, Dan Enright. D: David Lowe.

Valentino

Romance. Ran on ABC Thursdays 9:30–10 P.M. Dec. 18, 1952–March 5, 1953, opposite *Big Town* on CBS, *What's The Story?* on DuMont, and *Ford Theatre* on NBC. C: Barry Valentino.

Meet Betty Furness

Interview. Ran on CBS Fridays 10:45–11 A.M. Jan. 2–June 25, 1953. C: Betty Furness. P: Lester Lewis. D: Ted Huston. W: Priscilla Kent.

Meet Me at the Zoo

Informational. Ran on CBS Saturdays 1–1:30 P.M. Jan. 10–May 30, 1953, opposite baseball on ABC (May 30 only). C: Jack Whitaker, Freeman Shelly, Roger Connant. P: Charles Vanda. D: Glen Bernard. W: Arnold Rabin.

Why?

Game. Ran on ABC Mondays 10–10:30 P.M. Jan. 12–April 20, 1953, opposite *Studio One* on CBS, boxing on DuMont and *Robert Montgomery Presents* on NBC. C: John Reed King, Bill Cullen. P: Bill Cullen. D: Roger Sharpe.

Action in the Afternoon

Western, live from Philadelphia. Ran on CBS Mondays through Fridays 4–4:30 P.M. Feb. 2– May 8, 1953, opposite *The Kate Smith Hour* on NBC, then CBS Mondays through Fridays 3:30–4 P.M. May 11–Sept. 11, 1953, opposite *Welcome Travelers* on NBC, then CBS Mondays through Fridays 4–4:30 P.M. Sept. 14, 1953–Jan. 29, 1954, opposite *Turn to a Friend* (from Oct. 5–Dec. 31) on ABC and *Welcome Travelers* on NBC. C: Barry Cassell (as Ace Bancroft), Jack Valentine (as himself), Harris Forrest (as Ozzie Matthews), Mary Elaine Watts (as Kate), John Zacherly (as the coroner), Chris Keegan, Sam Kressen, Creighton Stewart, Blake Ritter, the Tommy Ferguson Trio. P: Charles Vanda. D: William Bode, John Ullrich, Merrill Brockway. W: Don Pringle, Paul Pierce.

The Bill Cullen Show

Variety. Ran on CBS Thursdays 11:15–11:30 A.M. Feb. 12–May 14, 1953. C: Bill Cullen, Betty Brewer, the Milton DeLugg Trio.

What's Your Bid?

Auction. Ran on ABC Saturdays 7:30–8 P.M. Feb. 14–April 11, 1953, opposite *Beat the Clock* on CBS, *The Pet Shop* (through March 14) and *Johnny Jupiter* (from March 21) on DuMont and *My Hero* on NBC, then DuMont Sundays 10–10:30 P.M. May 3–July 5, 1953, opposite *Hour of Decision* on ABC, *The Web* on CBS and *The Doctor* on NBC. C: Leonard Rosen (through April 11), Robert Alda (from May 3), John Reed King (through April 11),

Dick Shepard (from May 3), Roslyn Woods (through April 11). P: Frank Bunetta, Leonard Rosen, Charles Kasher. D: Frank Bunetta, Bob Doyle, Sonny Diskin. (Doyle on ABC, Bunetta on DuMont)

The Eddie Albert Show

Variety. Ran on CBS Mondays through Fridays 3:30–4 P.M. March 2–May 8, 1953, opposite *Welcome Travelers* on NBC. C: Eddie Albert, Ellen Hanley, the Norman Paris Trio. P: Franklin Heller. D: James Sheldon. W: Jack Woods, Charles Romine, Leslie Lieber.

Freedom Rings

Game. Ran on CBS Tuesdays and Thursdays 2–2:30 P.M. March 2–Aug. 27, 1953. C: John Beal, Rex Marshall, Malcolm Broderick, Alice Ghostley, Joy Hilton, Chuck Taylor, Ted Tiller, the Ben Ludlow Orchestra. P: Richard Linkroum. D: Lloyd Gross, Don Appell.

Freedom Rings is one of the more notorious examples of how much sponsors could — and did — influence their TV shows in the 1950s, when they controlled much of the content. It was nothing more than an elaborate infomercial, before that word came into vogue in the 1990s, designed to pitch advertiser Westinghouse Electric's products to housewives. The games involved a household setting, prizes included Westinghouse merchandise and there was a home game viewers could play only if they got cards from their participating Westinghouse dealers.

The setup unimpressed Lloyd Gross, one of the show's directors. "It was kind of dull. They'd have contests like making a bed," he said. Gross previously directed *Everywhere I Go* (q.v.), which like *Freedom Rings* alternated daily with the game show *Double or Nothing*.

What really appalled Gross was Westinghouse's approach to the commercials. "They insisted on doing their live commercials on the stage," he said. "They'd bring out all of their items on a dolly, and it became a horrendous thing to move and set up." Most other live series then had live commercials too, but Gross thought Westinghouse crowded the stage of the regular show unnecessarily in order to pitch their merchandise.

Hosting initially was character actor John Beal, who enacted playlets with other regulars, including Alice Ghostley as his wife. "She was a very funny girl," Gross said of Ghostley, who later had success as a frequent comic support on such series as *Bewitched* and *Designing Women*. "A very nice person to work with." Gross said Beal was pleasant to direct as well, but the actor left the series within three months to be replaced by Rex Marshall, formerly the show's announcer.

In the end, *Freedom Rings* evidently did not bring in the business Westinghouse had wanted. The company already had a substantial investment with the Monday night dramatic anthology series *Studio One*, and officials decided their daytime TV resources would be better spent on professional football on DuMont in September 1953. With the advertiser out, the show's reason for being went too, and it ended in less than six months. Gross summed up his feelings as "I didn't really miss it."

Having directed this game show plus talk (*Everywhere I Go*) and variety (*The Mel Torme Show*; q.v.) in daytime, Gross expanded himself further in 1954 by directing the daily soap opera *Portia Faces Life*. That series just barely missed inclusion in this book (it ran April 5, 1954–July 1, 1955), and Gross said it could and should have run longer if the network had not fired its producer, Beverly Smith. "I got along with Bev and, not knowing any better, I said, 'Well, if you're going to go, I am too,'" Gross said. The new producer also fired some of the cast as well, including Frances Reid as the title character, and Gross thinks that led to its fall. Gross resurfaced in daytime again in yet another different format — the 1961 children's game show *On Your Mark* (q.v.).

Quick as a Flash

Game. Ran on ABC various nighttime slots March 12, 1953–Feb. 25, 1954. C: Bobby Sherwood (through May), Bud Collyer (from May), Jimmy Nelson, Faye Emerson. P: Dick Lewis, Charles Moss. D: Ed Nugent (March–July), Harold Loeb (September 1953–February 1954).

Personality Puzzle

Game. Ran on ABC Thursdays 10:30–11 P.M. March 19–June 25, 1953. C: Robert Alda, Lisa Ferraday. P: Alan Pottash. D: Eddie Nugent.

Johnny Jupiter

Puppet. Ran on DuMont Saturdays 7:30–8 P.M. March 21–June 13, 1953. C: Vaughn Taylor (as Ernest P. Duckweather), Gilbert Mack (as his boss), Carl Harms. D: Frank Bunetta. W: Jerry Coopersmith.

Jimmy Hughes, Rookie Cop

Crime Drama. Ran on DuMont Fridays 8:30–9 P.M. May 8–July 3, 1953. C: William Redfield (as Jimmy Hughes, early episodes), Conrad Janis (as Jimmy Hughes, later episodes), Rusty Lane (as Inspector Ferguson), Wendy Drew (as Betty Hughes). P: Wilbur Stark, Jerry Layton. D: Barry Shear. W: William C. Crane, Bob Corcoran.

Music from the Meadowbrook

Music. Ran on ABC Saturdays 7–8 P.M. May 23–September 1953, opposite *The Stork Club* and *Beat the Clock* on CBS and *Mr. Wizard* and *Ethel and Albert* (through June) and *My Son Jeep* (from July 4) on NBC, then ABC Saturdays 8:30–9 P.M. Oct.–Dec. 26, 1953, opposite *The Jackie Gleason Show* on CBS, NFL football on DuMont and *The Original Amateur Hour* on NBC, and then ABC Thursdays 10–10:30 P.M. Jan. 26–April 19, 1956, opposite *The Johnny Carson Show* (through March 29) and *The Arthur Murray Party* (from April 5) on CBS and *Lux Video Theatre* on NBC. C: Frank Dailey, Jimmy Blaine, the Ralph Marterie Orchestra (1953), the Ralph Flanagan Orchestra (1956). P/D: Eddie Nugent (1953). D: Hal Davis (1956). W: Ed Brainard (1956).

"It was after the era of the big bands, and it wasn't quite the same thing," said director Hal Davis of *Music from the Meadowbrook*. ABC drafted Davis, a staff director at the network, to helm the second of two short-lived efforts in the 1950s to make this series work, but both times combined barely amounted to one year on the air.

The Meadowbrook was a popular nightclub in Cedar Grove, New Jersey, operated by Frank Dailey. "It's not the size of Roseland [a famous New York City ballroom]," said Davis. "I would guess it held probably 100 couples." Many big bands made the stop there to do radio remotes in the 1930s and 1940s, and it even had its own radio show Saturday afternoons in 1941 called *Matinee at Meadowbrook* before coming to TV.

Davis acknowledged that showing band music on TV with its visual aspect was more elaborate to do than the earlier radio remotes. "It does present some challenges," he said. "We overcame it by planning, which is the secret of live television. I'd rehearse so I'd know where the cameras would be and edit bar by bar of each piece of music."

The main people shown on TV were band members, but Davis noted, "There was a side balcony in this dance hall. I put an emcee up there, which gave me a good cover shot if needed on the dance floor." The emcee was Jimmy Blaine, who Davis said also did a few interviews with guests to fill out the show and give the musicians a rest.

The regular orchestra in 1956 was led by Ralph Flanagan. "He was an arranger for Glenn Miller," Davis said. A few other bands sometime dropped by, but as Davis noted earlier, most were past their heyday of the "big band" sound of the 1930s and 1940s.

David said as for the dancers on the show, all were non-professionals. "It mostly drew young people — high school seniors and so on," he said. "This was a 'dressy' affair." He recalled some having big birthday cakes at their tables for a few shows.

Most sources list operator Frank Dailey as dropping in on the show some. Davis said that while he recalled seeing him on the series, "I don't think he had much to do with it. He had a reputation as being a very genial person, kind of a Jersey City person." (Actually, it's understandable that Davis did not recall Dailey, for the latter died a month into the show's run on Feb. 27, 1956, at age 54.)

In the end, though, the combination of Dailey, Blaine, the music and the dancers never attracted a sponsor outside the U.S. Army, which put on some promotional spots to recruit young men for the military. Davis allowed that the advent of rock 'n' roll in 1956, which the bands definitely did not play, might have been a factor in why the second go-round failed, but he admitted that ultimately "I don't have any strong theory why it didn't sustain itself."

The Orchid Award

Testimonial/Variety. Ran on ABC Sundays 6:45–7 P.M. May 24–July 1953, opposite *See It Now* (through June 21) and *Adventure* (from June 28) on CBS, *New York Times Youth Forum* on DuMont and *The Roy Rogers Show* on NBC, then ABC Sundays 9:15–9:30 P.M. July 1953–Jan. 24, 1954, opposite *General Electric Theater* (alternating with *The Fred Waring Show* from September) on CBS, *Rocky King, Inside Detective* on DuMont and *Goodyear TV Playhouse* alternating with *Philco Television Playhouse* on NBC. C: Bert Lytell (May–July 1953), Ronald Reagan (July 1953–1954), Donald Woods (July 1953–1954), the Paul Weston Orchestra. P: Harold Romm. D: Bob Finkel, Greg Garrison. W: Gordon Auchincloss.

"*The Orchid Award* is such an old show that I don't have it on my bio!" laughed director Bob Finkel. He and Greg Garrison split directing honors for the live show, for after its first two months with Bert Lytell as host, it alternated hosts weekly with Ronald Reagan doing the honors in Hollywood and Donald Woods doing the same in New York. Garrison directed Woods' efforts while Finkel handled the Reagan shows.

"I must tell you, he was so bad," Finkel said of Reagan. "He didn't have what was needed for that kind of show, which was a testimonial tribute." (Reagan would do much better a few months after *The Orchid Award* ended by hosting from the fall of 1954 until 1962 *General Electric Theater*, which ironically aired opposite *The Orchid Award* for most of the latter's run.)

Finkel clarified that *The Orchid Award* was a celebration of the living and not of those who passed away. "It wasn't as we what now know of as a biographical tribute, because the people were active at the moment. It was more an acknowledgment of a performer. It was a tribute to somebody important at the moment." Those honored did receive an actual orchid from the host as well as a recounting of their careers and a chance to perform.

The guests were mostly celebrities, some of considerable note not associated with television (Rex Harrison, Lauritz Melchior). So how did *The Orchid Award* manage to snare them to do a mere 15-minute show with the promise of getting just a snazzy flower? Finkel said it probably had to do with the fact that the show was a production from the MCA talent agency, and the company encouraged (or forced) their clients to appear. "Those performers were doing us a favor," he acknowledged. "The money they were getting was a pittance."

Finkel said it took just two days to rehearse and then do the program, by his recollection. "I would imagine the first day was setting up and getting the cameras together," he said. "There were no production numbers involved, just somebody standing or singing."

As to why *The Orchid Award* did not bloom into a longer-running series, Finkel attributed it to its 15-minute format, one which was dying on nighttime network TV in 1954 save for the news and early weeknight music shows before 8 P.M. Few other 15-minute shows were being made to fill out a half hour, and apparently those involved with the show did not think it merited an expansion to 30 minutes. "That was certainly the only objection I remember," Finkel said. ABC replaced it with the equally short-lived *Jane Pickens Show* (see 1953-54).

Anyone Can Win

Game. Ran on CBS Tuesdays 9–9:30 P.M. June 14–Sept. 1, 1953. C: Al Capp. EP: Everett Rosenthal. P/D: Sylvia Taplinger.

TV General Store

Auction. Ran on ABC Sundays 11 A.M.–Noon June 14–July 12, 1953. C/P: Dave and Judy Clark.

Atom Squad

Science Fiction. Ran on NBC Mondays through Fridays 5–5:15 P.M. July 6, 1953–Jan. 22, 1954. C: Bob Hastings (as Steve Elliot), Bob Courtleigh (as Dave), Bram Nossem (as the Chief). EP: Adrian Samish. W: Paul Monash.

Roughly a half century after its debut *Atom Squad* has been nearly forgotten by most TV viewers—and by its leading man, Bob Courtleigh. The brother of actor Steven Courtleigh ("I played a young [George] Washington and he was an older Washington on an anthology show"), he joined with another Bob (Hastings, to be exact) to do a daily serial for the kiddies. The two Bobs made up the Atom Squad, an agency battling foreign spies, usually Communists, who attempted to invade the good old U.S.A.

Courtleigh admitted he was short on memories about the show, other than it was "nerve-tingling live" and had scenarios that might have made lesser adult actors cringe. "I don't remember too many fights, but there

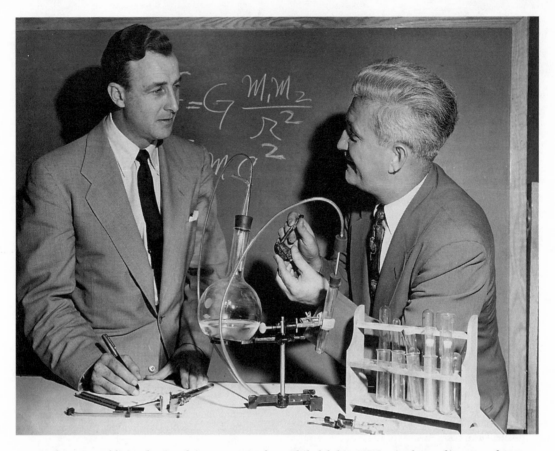

In this 1953 publicity shot involving two series from Philadelphia, NBC paired one of its stars of *Atom Squad*, Bob Courtleigh (left), with Dr. Roy K. Marshall, host of the same network's science series *The Nature of Things*. The latter went off NBC a year later after a five-year run after Dr. Marshall pleaded no contest to charges of sending obscene literature through the mails to teenage girls.

were some moments you could laugh about on live TV," he said, although he could not recall any specific incidents.

The show emanated from NBC's affiliate WPTZ in Philadelphia and replaced *Hawkins Falls*, an adult soap opera which had held the time slot for more than two years until NBC moved it into the mornings and tried this show as a presumably more compatible lead-in to *The Gabby Hayes Show* at 5:15. Despite its city of origin, Courtleigh said, "All the New York actors of the time came and went there" as guest stars, though again he could not recall any particular one of them.

Courtleigh did not recall the reasons for the cancellation of *Atom Squad* either. After it ended, he had a regular role on another, more adult serial also produced by Adrian Samish and airing from Philadelphia called *First Love*

(July 5, 1954–Dec. 30, 1955). He then moved to Hollywood to act but never had another regular TV role. Though he had no mementos and few memories of *Atom Squad*, he still said he liked doing the show. "It was a fun time," he noted.

Faring better than Courtleigh was Hastings, who like Courtleigh had an actor brother (Don Hastings, a regular as Bob Hughes on *As the World Turns* since 1960). Bob Hastings went to Hollywood too and hit with *McHale's Navy* from 1962 to 1966 (as Lt. Carpenter), *All in the Family* from 1973 to 1977 (as bartender Tommy Kelsey) and *General Hospital* from 1979 to 1986 (as Capt. Burt Ramsey). Even Samish made the trek to Hollywood too, and scored his biggest success as a producer on the crime drama *Cannon* in the 1970s.

Glamour Girl

Game. Ran on NBC Mondays through Fridays 10:30–11 A.M. July 6, 1953–Jan. 8, 1954, opposite *Arthur Godfrey Time* (Mondays through Thursdays) and *Wheel of Fortune* (Fridays through Dec. 25) and *The Jack Paar Show* (Fridays from Nov. 13) on CBS. C: Harry Babbitt (through Oct. 5), Jack McCoy (from Oct. 8), Gaylord Carter. EP: Jack McCoy. P: Don Ross. D: Bill Bennington.

The Bennetts

Soap Opera. Ran on NBC Mondays through Fridays 11:15–11:30 A.M. July 6, 1953–Jan. 8, 1954, opposite *I'll Buy That* and *The Bil Baird Show* (Tuesdays and Thursdays from Aug. 4–Oct. 29) on CBS. C: Don Gibson (as Wayne Bennett), Paula Huston (as Nancy Bennett, early episodes), Eloise Kummer (as Nancy Bennett, later episodes), Jack Lester (as Blaney Cobb), Beverly Younger (as Meg Cobb), Viola Berwick (as Speedy Winters). P: Ben Park. D: John Hinsey. W: Bill Barrett.

Follow Your Heart

Soap Opera. Ran on NBC Mondays through Fridays 11:45 A.M.–Noon Aug. 3, 1953–Jan. 8, 1954, opposite *Strike It Rich* on CBS. C: Sallie Brophy (as Julie Fielding); Grant Richards (as Peter Davis); John Seymour (as Samuel Tilden Fielding); Nancy Sheridan (as Mrs. Fielding); Laura Weber (as Jocelyn Fielding); Howard Erskine (as Harry Phillips). P: Adrian Samish. D: Norman Morgan. W: Elaine Carrington.

Atom Squad was set in New York but aired from Philadelphia. At the same time a few hours earlier on the same network, *Follow Your Heart* was set in Philadelphia but aired from New York. Yet while the former aimed for kids, the latter was a romantic drama set squarely for housewives. Its creator and writer, Elaine Carrington, used her 1939–58 radio series, *When a Girl Marries,* as the basis for the soap and centered stories around 19-year-old Julie Fielding who lived with her mom, dad and sister Jocelyn. Her central dilemma involved whether to stay engaged to her next-door neighbor Harry Phillips or go after her father's new assistant Peter Davis.

Portraying Julie's fiancé was Howard Erskine, who coincidentally had acted opposite Sallie Brophy in stock productions before *Follow Your Heart.* "I played it for several weeks, and at that time I became a Broadway pro-

ducer," he said of his role. His play *Late Love* was in tryouts in Hartford, Conn., when Erskine notified the staff he would have to leave the series if and when the play made it to New York City. Officials listened and nodded without heeding his words, even as he kept reminding them of his situation every week.

Then, a few days before the play opened on Broadway on Oct. 13, 1953, the production staff realized Erskine really was going to vacate his part. Given the choice of whether to recast the character or write him out, they did the latter. "They quickly made a scene where Sallie Brophy and I had an argument and broke our engagement off," Erskine said. "And you never heard of me again."

Three months after Erskine dropped out, so did the series from the NBC schedule. Erskine said he didn't know why, though he joked that "I wish I could say that it was because I left it." His play *Late Love* was not a hit (it ended Jan. 2, 1954, after 95 performances), but it did give Erskine the entrée he needed into producing for Broadway. He won a Tony in 1955 for co-producing *The Desperate Hours* and remains an active producer to this day, while occasionally acting in Woody Allen's films (he has done six at present).

As for Erskine's former co-star, he said Sallie Brophy is living in Princeton, New Jersey. "She has a business which coaches senior executives on speaking," he said. In effect, you could say both he and she followed their hearts and left acting for new ventures. Sadly, Elaine Carrington, one of the pre-eminent soap opera writers in radio, never had another chance to do a TV serial following *Follow Your Heart* before she died in 1958 at age 66.

The Bil Baird Show

Puppet. Ran on CBS Tuesdays and Thursdays 11:15–11:30 A.M. Aug. 4–Oct. 29, 1953, opposite *The Bennetts* on NBC. C: Bil Baird, Cora Baird, Frank Fazakas, Frank Sullivan. EP: Marlo Lewis. P: Richard Lewine, Burt Shevelove. D: Burt Shevelove. W: Bil Baird.

Despite its title, puppeteer Frank Fazakas credits the co-producer and director of *The Bil Baird Show* as its creator and leading light. "Burt Shevelove put that together, and he was more or less the mentor to us after that," Fazakas said.

The storyline of *The Bil Baird Show* featured a rabbit named Groovy Gus who served as a disk jockey while other puppets "danced" to songs he played. Also joining in the fun were pianist Slugger Ryan. Fazakas provided the voice of the puppet but, he recalled, "He took two people to operate. Someone played the piano while another one would operate the head." Fazakas generally played the piano, while Bil Baird handled the head.

The Bil Baird Show had an odd schedule of appearing twice a week on CBS. On Mondays and Wednesdays *Arthur Godfrey Time* ran 90 minutes and took over the program's slot, while on Fridays its lead-in *I'll Buy That* expanded from 15 to 30 minutes. That setup may have hastened the show's cancellation after 13 weeks. In any event, the Baird bunch went on to do other series in the 1950s, including *The Jack Paar Show*, but as the 1960s progressed they found themselves less in demand. Fazakas blamed their downturn on a general lack of appreciation of puppetry in the United States. "Somehow or another, it doesn't seem to be an American art," he said.

In 1969 Fazakas left Bil Baird (Cora died in 1967) after 22 years with the puppeteer after the two had a falling out over matters Fazakas would not specify. However, he did note that regard to the act, "I saw it wasn't going any place." Baird did theater productions in New York, but none of them reached the acclaim he had for his work in the 1950s, while Fazakas went on to join a troupe he felt did have plenty of potential, Jim Henson and his Muppets. The octogenarian is now retired.

Fazakas did allow despite his doubts that his puppetry did have some impact on television during their heyday. "Bil Baird and the company and myself were the focus of puppets in America at the time," he said. They had one more short-lived series credit in the 1950s; see *Washington Square.*

Judge for Yourself

Game. Ran on NBC Tuesdays 10–10:30 P.M. Aug. 18, 1953–May 11, 1954. C: Fred Allen, Dennis James, Bob Carroll (1954), the Skylarks (1954), Kitty Kallen (1954), Judy Johnson (1954), Milton DeLugg and His Orchestra. P: Mark Goodson, Bill Todman. AP: Arnold Peyser. D: Jerry Schnur.

1953-54

On Your Way

Game. Ran on DuMont Wednesdays 9:30–10 P.M. Sept. 9, 1953–Jan. 20, 1954, then ABC Saturdays 7–7:30 P.M. Jan. 23–April 17, 1954. C: Bud Collyer (through Jan. 20), Kathy Godfrey (from Jan. 23), John Reed King (from Jan. 23). EP: Lawrence White. P: Bud Collyer (through Jan. 20), Mike Dutton (from Jan. 23). D: Martin Magner (through Jan. 20), Richard DePew (from Jan. 23).

Bonino

Sitcom. Ran on NBC Saturdays 8–8:30 P.M. Sept. 12–Dec. 26, 1953. C: Ezio Pinza (as Babbo Bonino), Mary Wickes (as Martha), David Opatoshu (as Walter Rogers) Conrad Janis (as Edward), Lenka Peterson (as Doris), Chet Allen (as Jerry; through Nov. 11), Donald Harris (as Jerry; from Nov. 18), Oliver Andes (as Carlo), Gaye Huston (as Francesco), Van Dyke Parks (as Andrew), Fred (Anthony) Eisley (as John Clinton). EP: Fred Coe. P/D: Gordon Duff. W: Robert Alan Aurthur, David Shaw.

The George Jessel Show

Testimonial. Ran on ABC Sundays 6:30–7 P.M. Sept. 13, 1953–April 11, 1954, opposite *You Are There* on CBS, *Meet Your Congress* on DuMont and *The Roy Rogers Show* on NBC. C: George Jessel. P/W: Manny Manheim. D: Stuart W. Phelps. W: George Jessel, Sam Carlton.

Because he specialized in vaudeville and live performances, did only a handful of movies, and made most of his TV appearances on talk and variety shows and specials that never were repeated, the name of George Jessel is not often recalled by members of today's generation as being among the leading comics of the first half of the 20th century, which he was. About the only reference made to him nowadays is Robin Williams' sneering impersonation of Jessel's nasal speaking voice and clipped delivery. But in his time, particularly in the 1920s through 1940s, he was at the top.

Jessel attempted to keep his celebrity going on television in the 1950s as a regular. In the 1952-53 season he was a rotating host of *All Star Revue* on NBC, then went to ABC the next season to really push himself. Beside hosting *The George Jessel Show*, he also presided over the short-lived *The Comeback Story* (q.v.) on Friday nights and even did a Thursday night radio series called *George Jessel Salutes*, which was off the air quicker than his concurrent TV series. (Jessel never had a hit radio series, but as with television he was a popular guest star.)

"He was the cigar-chomping, kind of big mouth guy," recalled director Stuart W. Phelps of his one-time boss. "Fun, charming, used to get angry a lot. He was brash and from New York."

The setup for *The George Jessel Show* was the same as that which later became popular as the "celebrity roasts" on *The Dean Martin Show* in the 1970s. Jessel, who always billed himself as the "Toastmaster General of the United States," gave a humorous tribute to a guest of honor each week. As indicated by the writing credits, these comments were not spontaneous nor created by Jessel alone.

In fact, there was a rehearsal for the guest of honor on what to do as well, even though this was a live show and supposedly extemporaneous. According to Phelps, "We'd have the guest. We'd have a couple of walk-throughs without them and then bring them in, and tell them, 'You go here, and then you go here.'"

Phelps thought the reason for the show's short run was that the testimonial format hurt it, being too much of a novelty and too limited to sustain a weekly audience. Whatever the case may have been, Jessel was off by the spring of 1954.

Jessel did not get another regular TV shot until a decade later, on *Jackie Gleason and the American Scene Magazine* in 1965-66. He tried the weekly testimonial format again in 1968 hosting the syndicated series *Here Come the Stars*, but it found just as few viewers as *The George Jessel Show* did 15 years earlier and went off quickly. He died in 1981 at the age of 83.

The Peter Potter Show

Music. Ran on ABC Sundays 9:30–10:30 P.M. (just 9:30–10 P.M. by Jan. 31) Sept. 13, 1953–March 28, 1954. C/P: Peter Potter. D: Richard Gottleib.

Marge and Jeff

Sitcom. Ran on DuMont Mondays through Fridays 7:15–7:30 P.M. Sept. 21, 1953–Sept. 24, 1954, opposite news on ABC. C: Marge Greene, Jess (Jeff) Cain. P: Ernest Walling. D: Leonard Valenta. W: Marge Greene.

Melody Street

Music. Ran on DuMont Wednesdays 8:30–9 P.M. Sept. 23–Oct. 28, 1953, then DuMont Fridays 8:30–9 P.M. Nov. 8, 1953–Feb. 5, 1954. C: Allan Brown (1953), Elliot Lawrence (1953), Tony Mottola (1954), Lyn Gibbs, Joe Buwen, Roberta McDonald. P: Roger Gerry. D: Barry Shear. W: Bill Dalzell.

The Jerry Lester Show

Comedy Variety. Ran on ABC Mondays through Fridays 3–4 P.M. Sept. 28, 1953–May 14, 1954, opposite *The Big Payoff* and *The Bob Crosby Show* on CBS and *The Kate Smith Hour* on NBC. C: Jerry Lester, Leon Belasco, Kathy Collins, Lorenzo Fuller, Ellie Russell, the Buddy Weed Orchestra. P: Vernon Becker, Milton Stanson. D: Bill Dodson.

The Comeback Story

Interview. Ran on ABC Fridays 9:30–10 P.M. Oct. 2, 1953–Feb. 5, 1954, opposite *Our Miss Brooks* on CBS, *Nine Thirty Curtain* (from Oct. 23–Jan. 1) on DuMont and *Campbell TV Soundstage* on NBC. C: George Jessel (through January), Arlene Francis (from January). EP/D: Sherman Marks.

The Pride of the Family

Sitcom. Ran on ABC Fridays 9–9:30 P.M. Oct. 2, 1953–Sept. 24, 1954, opposite *Schlitz Playhouse of Stars* on CBS, *Life Begins at 80* (through June 18) and *The Stranger* (from June 25) on DuMont and *The Big Story* (through July 9) and *The Best in Mystery* (from July 16) on NBC. C: Paul Hartman (as Albie Morrison), Fay Wray (as Catherine Morrison), Natalie Wood (as Ann Morrison), Bobby Hyatt (as Junior Morrison). P/D: Bob Finkel. W: Paul Schneider, Clint Comerford.

In 1952 the talent agency MCA (Music Corporation of America) received an unusual

In the midst of their long and celebrated careers, Fay Wray (top), Natalie Wood (right) and Paul Hartman (middle) found time to do the sitcom *Pride of the Family*. Joining them was the now-forgotten Bobby Hyatt (no apparent relation to the author) at left.

waiver from the Screen Actors Guild allowing it to produce TV shows as well. One of their first recruits was director Bob Finkel, who previously did only live series such as *The Orchid Award* (see 1952-53).

"I remember being called in by Lew Wasserman, Jennings Lang and others because I was an MCA client," said Finkel. "They brought me in and said they were getting into filmed TV extensively, and they told me to go into it. And I did, and I was very excited." To prepare himself, Finkel enlisted the advice of a veteran studio cameraman who gave him a crash course on how to film a half-hour show in just two days, per MCA's schedule.

The property Finkel received to direct was *The Pride of the Family*, a standard 1950s sitcom featuring a sometimes bumbling father who worked in advertising at a small town newspaper, his devoted wife, Catherine, and his enthusiastic teenage daughter, Ann, and son Junior. What was most memorable about it was its cast. Paul Hartman previously starred on stage with his wife, Grace Hartman, doing comic dance routines, then found new fame in the late 1960s playing Emmett Clark on *The Andy Griffith Show* and its followup, *Mayberry, R.F.D.* Fay Wray ("An adorable lady," noted Finkel) always will be remembered as the ingénue clutched by a giant ape in the 1933 screen classic *King Kong*. And then there was Natalie Wood.

"Natalie Wood was just beginning to grow out of being a child actor, and I believe it was her agent, Jerry Zeitman, who pushed for her to do the show," Finkel said. "She was brilliant even then, I remember. She lifted the scenes in which she was in. She was kind of like a catalyst."

Finkel recalled one scenario showing Wood's approach to her craft. "It was a hackneyed plot in which she was to go to a school dance and her date fell through. So her dad took her. But when she was told her boyfriend wouldn't take her, she had to cry. She wouldn't do it in rehearsal, and I asked her why. She told me, 'Mr. Finkel, when that red light on the camera goes on [indicating filming], then I cry.'"

The Pride of the Family ended after just a season because it was not a huge hit that had sponsors flocking to it, according to Finkel. "If anybody would make something profitable and viable, MCA would've," he said. "I don't think anybody was going to buy a half-hour sitcom unless it was very, very successful."

CBS reran the series Sundays 7–7:30 P.M. June–July 10, 1955, as a temporary summer replacement for *Lassie*. By that time, Wood was on her way to being a movie star after her lead role in *Rebel Without a Cause*. She rarely acted on television thereafter until a few TV-movies in the 1970s before her accidental drowning death in 1981 at age 43.

Turn to a Friend

Game. Ran on ABC Mondays through Fridays 4–4:30 P.M. Oct. 5–Dec. 31, 1953, opposite *Action in the Afternoon* on CBS and *Welcome Travelers* on NBC. C: Dennis James. P: Drexel Hines. D: Lou Sposa.

Colonel Humphrey Flack

Sitcom. Ran on DuMont various nighttime slots Oct. 7, 1953–July 2, 1954. C: Alan Mowbray (as Col. Humphrey Flack), Frank Jenks (as Uthas P. Garvey). P: Wilbur Stark, Jerry Layton. D: Lester Vail. W: Ed Jurist.

Back That Fact

Game. Ran on ABC Thursdays 9–9:30 P.M. Oct. 22–Nov. 26, 1953. C: Joey Adams, Al Kelly, Hope Lange, Carl Caruso. P: Jack Barry, Dan Enright, Ed Friendly, Jack Farren. D: Mickey Trenner.

The Igor Cassini Show

Interview. Ran on DuMont Sundays 6–6:30 P.M. Oct. 25, 1953–March 3, 1954 (6:15–6:30 P.M. by January), opposite *Meet the Press* on NBC. C: Igor Cassini. P: Geoffrey Jones. D: Wes Harris. W: Gene Hurley.

Stars on Parade

Musical Variety. Ran on DuMont various nighttime slots Nov. 4, 1953–June 30, 1954. C: Don Russell (Nov. 4 and 11), Bobby Sherwood (from Nov. 18), Elliot Lawrence.

Take It from Me

Sitcom. Ran on ABC Wednesdays 9–9:30 P.M. Nov. 4, 1953–Jan. 20, 1954, opposite *Strike It Rich* on CBS, *Colonel Humphrey Flack* (through Dec. 31) and *Chicago Symphony* (from Jan. 6) on DuMont, and *Kraft Television Theatre* on NBC. C: Jean Carroll, Alan Carney, Lynn Loring. P/D: Alan Dinehart. W: Coleman Jacoby, Arnie Rosen.

Nightclub performer Jean Carroll made her bid to be TV's new favorite comedienne in 1953, but this predecessor to Phyllis Diller and Joan Rivers lasted only slightly more than two months with her series. Her entertainment career prior to *Take It from Me* was very minor. Her only regular radio role was when she was the hostess of *The Sealtest Village Store* during the summer of 1945, substituting for Joan

Davis. Seven years later, she spent two weeks at the RKO Palace Theater in New York as one of nine acts on the bill, where she was dubbed "America's First Lady of Laughs."

"We did material for her a couple of years, long before she did the show," writer Coleman Jacoby said. By "we," Jacoby meant himself and his partner Arnie Rosen. However, he was not certain whether the men got the job to write for the series because of their previous work or because they were part of the same talent agency that packaged the program.

The show's setup was akin to *The Jack Benny Program*, with Carroll addressing the audience at the start of each show before going into a plot involving her husband, Herbie, played by Alan Carney, and her daughter in a New York City apartment setting. Jacoby recalled Carroll used a verbal comic style in her monologues, but he did not remember the sitcom storyline, although he allowed that "She may have done some acting that I don't remember."

Jacoby also said he didn't know why the show went off the air so quickly, though he suspected that it was because it was not like the other sitcoms on at the time such as *The Adventures of Ozzie and Harriet*. "It was the age of family shows, and though she had one kid and her husband, it wasn't the same," he said.

There also is the strong possibility that ABC simply did not have enough money to afford keeping *Take It from Me* on the air. Beset with money woes and horrible ratings (not a single nighttime series on ABC cracked the top 30 this season), it basically was fighting against DuMont to be the surviving network to compete against CBS and NBC. When *Take It from Me* left the air, the network filled the time through the fall of 1954 with *The Big Picture*, a syndicated military documentary provided for free by the U.S. Army.

Whatever the reason was, *Take It from Me* was the last major professional hurrah on a national scale for Carroll. She died in relative obscurity in 1972 at the age of 63. Her TV husband, Alan Carney, also did no other series and died in 1973 at the age of 61. Their TV daughter, Lynn Loring, fared considerably better than both of them, continuing to act in TV on a few other series (*Search for Tomorrow*, *The F.B.I.*) before going into movie and TV production work by the 1980s.

Your Chevrolet Showroom

Variety. Ran on ABC Fridays 10–11 P.M. Nov. 20, 1953–Feb. 12, 1954, opposite *My Friend Irma* and *Person to Person* on CBS, *Chance of a Lifetime* and *Down You Go* on DuMont, and boxing on NBC. C: Cesar Romero. P/D: Perry Lafferty. W: Bob Quigley.

Cesar Romero was one of the most durable TV personalities, appearing in scores of shows of all types from the 1950s until shortly before his death in 1994. His first regular role was his shortest-lived one on the medium, however. *Your Chevrolet Showroom* ran on ABC less than three months, although it actually started locally in New York on Oct. 25, 1953.

The Latin star lived in Los Angeles even while he hosted the live show from the Big Apple. "Cesar Romero would fly in from Hollywood every week," said producer/director Perry Lafferty. That was an unusual and expensive perk to do, but Chevrolet wanted him as host strong enough to agree to the condition, even though Romero was known as an actor and not an emcee.

"Usually those things were the result of talking to the agency and the client," Lafferty said of the selection of Romero. "He was quite a well-known star. He was a wonderful man, 6-foot-4, gorgeous, built, suave and sophisticated." It was that cosmopolitan image that Chevrolet wanted to project to entice the public to buy their automobiles.

Unfortunately for all involved, *Your Chevrolet Showroom* suffered from a lack of decent acts to showcase, with the bigger names appearing on the more lavishly budgeted efforts on Ed Sullivan, Milton Berle, Jackie Gleason, *The Colgate Comedy Hour* and *Your Show of Shows*, just to name a few other variety shows on at the time. Romero's name alone was not enough to attract audiences, and the competition against it performed considerably better, with boxing on NBC being a top 20 show that season. Lafferty declined to speculate on the reason why the show ended quickly, but he suspected that Chevrolet had a 13-week contract to do the show and opted not to continue as the ratings fell short of what the company had hoped.

Romero later spent a year (1955-56) starring in the syndicated adventure series *Passport to Danger*, followed by two years as a panelist on the nighttime game show *Take a Good Look* (1959–61) and hosting his own syndicated travelogue, *Cesar's World*, in 1968. His last regular role was as Jane Wyman's husband on *Falcon Crest* from 1985 to 1987, although he had plenty of guest roles before and after each of his series. His sponsor Chevrolet went on to back another variety show with no regulars, *The Chevy Show* from 1955 to 1956, before hitting the jackpot with *The Dinah Shore Chevy Show* from 1956 to 1961, with the Southern singer of the title belting out the memorable theme song "See the U.S.A. in Your Chevrolet" each week.

The New Revue

Variety. Ran on CBS Fridays 5:30–6 P.M. Jan. 8–June 18, 1954, opposite *Howdy Doody* on NBC. C: Mike Wallace, Helene Ellis, Harrison Muller, Toni Southern, the Honeydreamers, the Norman Paris Trio.

Opera Cameos

Ran on DuMont Sundays 7:30–8 P.M. Jan. 10–Nov. 21, 1954 (off the summer). C: Giovanni Martinelli, Maestro Guiseppe Bamboschek. P: Carlo Vinto.

The Mask

Mystery. Ran on ABC Sundays 8–9 P.M. Jan. 10–May 16, 1954 (repeated on some stations Tuesdays and Wednesdays 8–9 P.M. in March and April). C: Gary Merrill (as Walter Guilfoyle), William Prince (as Peter Guilfoyle). P: Robert Stevens, Hallsted Welles. D: Robert Stevens. W: Hallsted Welles.

Breakfast in Hollywood

Interview. Ran on NBC Mondays through Fridays 10:30–11 A.M. Jan. 11–Feb. 5, 1954, opposite *Arthur Godfrey Time* (Mondays through Thursdays) and *The Jack Paar Show* (Fridays) on CBS. C: Johnny Dugan, Jeff Donnell. P: William Kayden. D: John B. Lyman III.

The Jane Pickens Show

Music. Ran on ABC various nighttime slots Jan. 31–Sept. 12, 1954. C: Jane Pickens, the Vikings. P: Ardien Rodner, Jr. D: Lee Davis. W: Bob Claver.

Woman with a Past

Soap Opera. Ran on CBS Mondays through Fridays 4–4:15 P.M. Feb. 1–July 2, 1954, opposite *Welcome Travelers* on NBC. C: Constance Ford (as Lynn Sherwood), Felice Camargo (as Diane Sherwood, early episodes), Barbara Myers (as Diane Sherwood, later episodes), Gene Lyons (as Steve Rockwell), Mary Sinclair (as Sylvia Rockwell; through May), Geraldine Brooks (as Sylvia Rockwell; from May), Jean Stapleton (as Gwen), Ann Hegira (as Pegs). P: Richard Bill. D: Marcella Cisney. W: Mona Kent.

The Betty White Show

Variety. Ran on NBC Mondays through Fridays 12:30–1 P.M. Feb. 8–July 2, 1954, opposite *Search for Tomorrow* and *Guiding Light* on CBS, then NBC Mondays through Fridays 4:30–5 P.M. July 5–Sept. 10, 1954, opposite *On Your Account* on CBS, and then NBC Mondays through Fridays Noon–12:30 P.M. Sept. 13–Dec. 31, 1954, opposite *Valiant Lady* and *Love of Life* on CBS. C: Betty White, the Four Jokers, the Frank DeVol Orchestra. P: Fred Henry. D: Bill Bennington.

Who's the Boss?

Game. Ran on ABC Fridays 9:30–10 P.M. Feb. 19–June 25, 1954, opposite *Our Miss Brooks* on CBS and *Campbell TV Soundstage* on NBC, then ABC Fridays 8:30–9 P.M. July 2–Aug. 20, 1954, opposite *Topper* on CBS. C: Walter Kiernan (through July 9), Mike Wallace (from July 16), Dick Kollmar, Sylvia Lyons, Peggy McCay, Horace Sutton. P: Lester Lewis. D: Charles S. Dubin.

An obvious knockoff of *What's My Line?*, *Who's the Boss?* featured a panel of four celebrities trying to guess the correct employer of the secretaries who were contestants on the show. After receiving the customary inquisition from the regulars, the secretaries won $100 for each panelist they fooled into giving an incorrect answer regarding their boss.

Hosting the festivities initially was reporter Walter Kiernan. "He was a very good commentator," said director Charles S. Dubin. He also was an experienced TV game show host, having done the honors for NBC's *Who Said That?* since 1951 through the end of his run on *Who's the Boss?* His replacement was Mike Wallace — yes, the *60 Minutes* veteran reporter Mike Wallace — who also had hosted a few TV game shows such as *There's One in Every Family* (see 1952-53).

The regulars on the show included actress Peggy McCay, who at the time was starring on the CBS daytime soap opera *Love of Life*, and Horace Sutton, the travel editor for the *Saturday Review* periodical. Sylvia Lyons was the wife of Leonard Lyons, a columnist with *The New York Post* tabloid. Coincidentally (or not?), Dick Kollmar was the husband of the *New York Journal-American* newspaper columnist Dorothy Kilgallen, a regular panelist at the same time on *What's My Line?*

The show itself was easy for all to do, since it basically just required the panel to appear in time to make the start of the show, and only a basic rehearsal each week for it by Dubin. "It was really a format rehearsal with stand-ins, and get the lady on her marks," he noted. But because it was a live show from New York, a few mistakes crept in anyway.

Dubin recalled an unintentionally humorous commercial for the show's sponsor, Gruen wristwatches. "They had frozen a Gruen watch in a huge cake of ice. They couldn't cut into it in one minute, and I had to stop it in two. Kiernan said at the end of the show, 'It's still running in there!'" laughed Dubin.

But there wasn't much amusement in *Who's the Boss?* being regularly beaten handily in the ratings by *Our Miss Brooks*. The program moved up an hour earlier in the summer of 1954, but that didn't attract new viewers either, and after six months on the air, it vanished.

Dubin thought its similarity to others in the same genre hurt it. "A lot of panel shows came into existence at the time," he said, and indeed beside the ones previously mentioned, there also was *Down You Go*, *I've Got a Secret*, *Judge for Yourself*, *The Name's the Same*, and *Twenty Questions*, among other shows, on the air during that period. Producer Lester Lewis later modified the show into a summer series seen in 1959 called *Who Pays?* with Mike Wallace again as host.

The Breakfast Club

Variety. Ran on ABC Mondays through Fridays 9–10 A.M. Feb. 22, 1954–Feb. 25, 1955. C: Don McNeill, Fran Allison, Sam Cowling, Johnny Desmond, Eileen Parker, the Eddie Ballantine Orchestra. P: Cliff Petersen. D: Lynwood King. W: Eddie McKean.

It would be harder to find a longer-running network radio show to flop so completely on television as *The Breakfast Club*. The series ran on network radio successfully for more than 35 years (1933–68), while on TV it barely lasted one year. At least one participant felt part of its failure was due to the perspective of its host, Don McNeill. "Don never really changed for television," said director Lynwood King of the video version of *The Breakfast Club*. "It was static."

King had no involvement with the radio show. However, he had directed McNeill when the latter promoted his sponsor Philco's TV products during the 1952 Republican convention. "I guess I did a good enough job, because I got the call from McNeill's office and went over and did the interview and left NBC after five years for the TV show," King said.

As indicated earlier, few concessions were made when it was decided to broadcast *The Breakfast Club* on TV the same time it was on radio. "I would get up at five in the morning and would go over with the radio people what would happen, because nothing would change for television," said King of his preparations. "We were in the basement of the Morrison Hotel, and I had a fourth camera to shoot the audience." Otherwise, the show pretty much was just the radio show with moving pictures, with interaction between McNeill and his audience, songs from Eileen Parker and Johnny Desmond and comedy from Sam Cowling and Fran Allison (the latter as gossip "Aunt Fanny"). The exception was the commercials, as there were different sponsors for radio and TV.

McNeill would say a key word in his script that cued a radio engineer to play a commercial he recorded earlier. While that ran, McNeill did a live commercial for his TV sponsor. To prevent the possibility of problems coming back to the main show from the different commercials, the Eddie Ballantine Orchestra played music to bridge the gap. King and the rest of the staff had a two-week dry run to practice the process before the show's TV debut. "It was very tricky, but Don was very good at it," he said.

The TV sponsorship was another area that King thought hurt the series. The show locked in Philco to sponsor three days every week and the Swift meat company to advertise the other two days. According to King, contracts with these companies were set up in a manner that

"There was no way they [ABC] could make money on it." If the show had allowed for multiple sponsors, King thought it might have been profitable for the network.

Prior to this series, McNeill had a Wednesday night ABC series called *The Don McNeill TV Club* from Sept. 13, 1950–Dec. 19, 1951. Apart from hosting a game show called *Take Two* (see 1962-63), he did relatively little other TV work.

It's About Time

Game. Ran on ABC Thursdays 8–8:30 P.M. March 4–March 25, 1954, opposite *The Ray Milland Show* on CBS, *Madison Square Garden Highlights* on DuMont and *You Bet Your Life* on NBC, and then Sundays 7:30–8 P.M. April 25–May 2, 1954, opposite the alternating *Jack Benny Program* and *Private Secretary* on CBS, *Opera Cameos* on DuMont and *Mr. Peepers* on NBC. C: Dr. Bergen Evans, Fran Allison, Ruthie Duskin, Vin Gottschalk, Robert Pollack, Sherl Stern. P: Rachel Stevenson, Jay Sheridan, John Lewellen. D: Dan Schuffman.

A rare graduate of *The Quiz Kids* 1940s radio show who continued to work in broadcasting was Ruth Duskin. "I had graduated from the program at age 16 in 1950," Duskin said. "Lou Cowan and John Lewellen had been the producers on *Quiz Kids* [actually, Lewellen had packaged the series as well as *It's About Time*] and said I should be on this show."

It's About Time featured Duskin as a regular panelist along with four others in Chicago, where the show emanated — Fran Allison, the Fran of *Kukla, Fran and Ollie*; Vin Gottschalk, a deejay; Robert Pollack, a drama critic; and Sherl Stern, a housewife. They answered questions about historical events read by host Dr. Bergen Evans, an English professor at Northwestern University.

Prior to *It's About Time*, Dr. Evans hosted the game show *Super Ghost* in the summers of 1952 and 1953 on NBC with Pollack and Stern as regulars, Lewellen as producer and Cowan as packager. Duskin guested a few times there, but primarily she attended Northwestern (and got married in 1953). She was more available for *It's About Time*, but she faced more scrutiny than anticipated for the way she appeared on TV in her new role (she obviously didn't have that problem with *The Quiz Kids* being a radio show).

"Somebody didn't like the way I looked," she said. "They thought I had a rather wide face and didn't photograph well." The powers that were also felt that her clothing accentuated what they did not like, so a fashion consultant gave her a wardrobe which Duskin was not wild about but did not resist as she tried to please the higher-ups. It failed, though: "On the fourth show, they canned me because of my appearance." Lewellen apologized for having to ax her. As it turned out, the show only lasted two more months anyway.

Duskin blamed the failure of *It's About Time* on the novelty of quiz shows wearing off on television as more of the public became college educated and less impressed by the parlor-type displays of wisdom being shown on the games with panels. "The times changed, and quiz shows themselves, they were big time or they were out," she said, pointing to the success of *The $64,000 Question* in 1955 as what she meant. (Ironically, Cowan packaged that game and fell from grace once it was revealed how rigged the game was for certain contestants.) She also thought the general public never quite took to Dr. Evans as a TV host. "Maybe due to his high-pitched voice, which seemed very effete," she said.

Whatever the reason, there was only one other network game show from Chicago after *It's About Time*—*Take Two* (q.v.). Duskin, now under her married name of Ruth Duskin Feldman, became a freelance writer for magazine and college textbooks and wrote *Whatever Happened to the Quiz Kids?*, first published in 1982 and reissued in 2000. While not craving publicity, the Chicago resident admits that "Writing books is a way of keeping your name in the limelights."

That's My Boy

Sitcom. Ran on CBS Saturdays 10–10:30 P.M. April 10, 1954–Jan. 1, 1955, opposite *Your Show of Shows* (through June 5), *Saturday Night Revue* (from June 12–Sept. 18) and *The George Gobel Show* (from Oct. 2,) on NBC, *On Guard* (through May 29), *Travel Corner* (from June–Sept. 4) and *The Stork Club* (from Sept. 11) on ABC, and *Colonel Humphrey Flack* (through May), NFL football (from Oct. 2–Nov. 20), and wrestling (from Nov. 27) on DuMont: C: Eddie Mayehoff (as "Jarring" Jack Jackson); Gil Stratton, Jr. (as Junior Jackson); Rochelle Hudson (as Alice Jackson); Mabel Albertson (as Henrietta Patterson); John Smith (as Bill Baker). P: Cy Howard.

Gil Stratton, Jr., played Junior, the owlish son of ex–college football star "Jarrin' Jack" Jackson, played by Eddie Mayehoff, on *That's My Boy!* Offstage the two actors were nowhere near as close as this picture suggests.

The 1951 film *That's My Boy* starred Jerry Lewis in his fourth theatrical flick as a weak-willed, gawky son to an ex–college football star who wished his offspring would follow in his macho footsteps. Three years later, it became a series done before a studio audience at CBS Television City in Hollywood which aired live on the East Coast. Gil Stratton, Jr., took the lead because he was an actor under contract with CBS, and they agreed to pay him the salary he would have received in his then-regular summer job as an umpire if he would do the show. Although Stratton had seen the film, he was under no pressure to act as manically as Lewis did in it, nor did he want to do so.

However, one element from the movie that did arrive intact was Eddie Mayehoff as the brash father. Stratton found him overbearing onstage and off. "I was a professional baseball umpire for nine years with no health problems," Stratton said. "[Then] I worked for six months with Eddie Mayehoff and got an ulcer. It was not a happy experience."

Stratton summed up Mayehoff thusly: "He was crazy." How crazy? Well, according to Stratton, once the president of Plymouth cars, the show's sponsor, visited the set. "At that time, Plymouth's biggest competitor was Buick. What do you think he [Mayehoff] drives into CBS Television City brand new?" (Hint: It rhymes with "oo-wick.") And at the office Christmas party, Mayehoff decided the perfect gift for his co-workers would be bottles of booze — in half-pint containers.

Stratton had nicer memories of Rochelle Hudson, who played his mom caught in the middle of the two men in her life, but really did not get to know Mabel Albertson, who played the wife of Mayehoff's boss. Rounding out the cast was John Smith as Stratton's pal (the same role Dean Martin played in the 1951 film).

That's My Boy had a decent audience until the fall of 1954, when the hot new variety series *The George Gobel Show* went against it in the same time slot. "We were doing fine for 26 weeks, and all of a sudden they went on, and we were like a balloon shot down," Stratton said. He even watched George Gobel later that evening on the West Coast while the kinescope of his own show aired opposite it! (The Gobel connection still endures; Stratton has lunch every other Wednesday with Hal Kanter, the writer/producer of *The George Gobel Show*.)

Gobel hastened the cancellation of *That's My Boy*. Stratton moved into sportscasting and noted, "I worked 43 years for CBS, did the Los Angeles Rams play-by-play" and other jobs before retiring. CBS reran *That's My Boy* Sundays 7:30–8 from June–Sept. 13, 1959 as a summer replacement for *The Jack Benny Program*. Irony of ironies: When *The Jack Benny Program* returned, it moved to Sundays 10–10:30 P.M. alternating with — *The George Gobel Show*!

But Stratton didn't care to watch his old show. When I told him, "I take it *That's My Boy* is something that took part in your life that you could either take or leave," he snapped back, "You got that right!"

The Martha Wright Show

Music. Ran on ABC Sundays 9:15–9:30 April 18–Dec. 5, 1954 (off July–September). C: Martha Wright, Norman Paris, Bobby Hackett and His Band. P: A.S. Fallace (April–July), Matt Hartlib (September–December). D: Cort Steen (April–July), Matt Hartlib (September–December). W: Fred Heider.

The Stranger

Crime Drama. Ran on DuMont Fridays 9–9:30 P.M. June 25, 1954–Feb. 11, 1955. C: Robert Carroll (as the Stranger). P/D: Frank Telford. W: Nelson Gidding, Carey Wilbur.

A Time to Live

Soap Opera. Ran on NBC Mondays through Fridays 10:30–10:45 A.M. July 5–Dec. 31, 1954, opposite *Arthur Godfrey Time* (Mondays through Thursdays) and *The Garry Moore Show* (Fridays) on CBS. C: Pat Sully (as Julie Byron), Larry Kerr (as Don Richard, early episodes), John Himes (as Don Richard, later episodes), Len Wayland (as Chick Buchanan), Viola Berwick (as Madge Byron), Zohra Alton (as Greta Powers, early episodes), Jeanne Jerrens (as Greta Powers, later episodes), Barbara Foley (as Lenore Eustice), Zachary Charles (as Rudy Marion), Dort Clark (as Lt. Miles Dow), Muriel Monsel (as Donna Sims). P/D: Alan Beaumont. W: Bill Barrett.

The Bob Smith Show

Variety. Ran on NBC Mondays through Fridays Noon–12:30 P.M. July 5–Sept. 10, 1954, opposite *Valiant Lady* and *Love of Life* on CBS, then NBC Mondays through Fridays 4–4:30 P.M. Sept. 10–Oct. 1, 1954, opposite *On Your Account* on CBS. C: Bob Smith (through Sept. 3), Skitch Henderson (from Sept. 8), Clark Dennis, the Honeydreamers, the Bob Nicholson Orchestra. P: Roger Muir.

The Seeking Heart

Soap Opera. Ran on CBS Mondays through Fridays 1:15–1:30 P.M. July 5–Dec. 10, 1954. C: Scott Forbes (as Dr. John Adams), Dorothy Lovett (as Grace Adams), Flora Campbell (as Dr. Robinson

McKay), Christopher Plummer, Les Damon, Judith Braun, Robert Webber. P: Minerva Ellis. D: James Yarborough. W: Welbourn Kelley.

Golden Windows

Soap Opera. Ran on NBC Mondays through Fridays 3:15–3:30 P.M. July 5, 1954–April 1, 1955, opposite *The Big Payoff* on CBS. C: Leila Martin (as Juliet Goodwin), Eric Dressler (as Charles Goodwin), Grant Sullivan (as John Brandon; 1954), Herbert Patterson (as Tom Anderson), Sonny Adams (as Ann Summers; 1954), Harriet MacGibbon (as Ruth Brandon; 1954), Millicent Brower (as Ellen Stockwell; 1954), Barbara Cook (as Hazel; 1954), Joe DeSantis (as Carl Grant; 1955), Martin Kosleck (as Otto; 1955), Philip Pine (as Dr. Paul Anderson; 1955). P: Mary Harris. D: Dan Levin. W: John M. Young.

Concerning Miss Marlowe

Soap Opera. Ran on NBC Mondays through Fridays 3:45–4 P.M. July 5, 1954–July 1, 1955, opposite *The Bob Crosby Show* on CBS. C: Louise Allbritton (as Margaret "Maggie" Marlowe; 1954–55), Helen Shields (as Margaret "Maggie" Marlowe; by April 1955), Efrem Zimbalist, Jr. (as Jim Gavin), Sarah Burton (as Barbara Gavin), Kathleen Comegys (as Mrs. Gavin, a/k/a Belle Mere), Jane Seymour (as Harriet the Hat), Chris White (as Kit Christy), David Buka (as Ralph; 1954), Ross Martin (as Bojalian), Byron Sanders (as Mike Donovan). P: Tom McDermott. D: Larry White. W: John Pickard, Frank Provo.

One Minute Please

Game. Ran on DuMont various nighttime slots July 6, 1954–Feb. 17, 1955. C: John K.M. McCaffery (through Nov. 12), Allyn Edwards (from Nov. 19), Hermione Gingold, Alice Pearce, Cleveland Amory, Ernie Kovacs, Marc Connelly. P/D: David Lowe.

Out on the Farm with Eddy Arnold

Informational. Ran on NBC Sundays 5–6 P.M. July 11–Aug. 29, 1954, opposite *Super Circus* on ABC and *Adventure* on CBS, then NBC Sundays 4–4:30 P.M. Oct. 3–Nov. 21, 1954, opposite pro football on ABC and DuMont and *The American Week* on CBS. C: Eddy Arnold (through Aug. 29), Clint Youle, William Landmeier, Lloyd Burlingham (through Aug. 29), the Mid-States Four (through Aug. 29). P: Ben Park. D: Don Meier. W: Marvin David, Dorothy Ruddell.

Having a TV crew at your home might have daunted many people in 1954, but not so with the Landmeier family of Cloverdale, Illinois. Spotlighted every Sunday on *Out on the Farm with Eddy Arnold*, the clan allowed the famous country singer of the title as well as some other on-air personalities, a director and more to have more or less full run of the 160-acre Landmeier farm in an effort to let the public know of the concerns in agricultural parts of America.

"They were awfully nice people," remembered director Don Meier, who added that for those who wanted directions, "Cloverdale's pretty much straight out of Chicago, about 15–20 miles." The family would take the cameras with them to shoot at pheasant on the grounds. The two daughters would tell of activities they did in their 4-H club. Most impressively, Meier recalled how they once dynamited their pond to clean it out.

Most of the camera time was spent with the father, William Landmeier, though Meier said William's wife, Martha, did show up considerably. "Fran Allison [star of *Kukla, Fran and Ollie*], she did some work with Martha Landmeier in the kitchen — cooking, sewing — when she did the show," he said.

But the real attraction to viewers initially had to be host Eddy Arnold, who lent his vocal talents between segments talking to the Landmeiers. "He was great," Meier said. "He used to get up in the barn and sing his songs." Others on the show were Chicago weathercaster Clint Youle, who according to Meier did more than just deliver forecasts, although the director couldn't remember specifically what other tasks Youle performed; agriculture expert Lloyd Burlingham ("He usually gave a farm report"); and even a barbershop quartet called the Mid-States Four.

What sparked Meier's interest in the program was its potential difficulties. As he noted, "This was the first time that they were exploring TV shows from a remote location. It was really quite primitive in those days. The people in Chicago at the time, they were really pioneers in those areas."

The live show did well enough during its summer run to return in October. But it was now stripped of a half hour, as well as its star Arnold and most other regulars. As just *Out on the Farm*, it featured only Mr. Landmeier and Youle, and went off within two months.

Meier didn't know why or how Arnold left, nor the reason for a shorter time period, but did make a stab as to why it went off so quickly. "My suspicion is it never gained the audience it needed. It wasn't just for agricultural audiences either, but it didn't get the wider audience."

The director did get a bigger audience, and a chance to work in even more remote locations, when he handled the Marlin Perkins exotic outdoors program *Wild Kingdom* before retiring. Arnold would return to NBC to do another agriculture-oriented series; see *Today on the Farm* in 1960-61.

Time Will Tell

Game. Ran on DuMont Fridays 10:30–11 P.M. Aug. 20–Oct. 15, 1954. C: Ernie Kovacs. P: Bob Adams. D: Harry Coyle.

The Greatest Gift

Soap Opera. Ran on NBC Mondays through Fridays 3–3:15 P.M. Aug. 30, 1954–April 1, 1955, opposite *The Big Payoff* on CBS, then NBC Mondays through Fridays 3:30–3:45 P.M. April 4–July 1, 1955, opposite *The Bob Crosby Show* on CBS. C: Anne Burr (as Dr. Eve Allen), Philip Foster (as Dr. Phil Stone), Athena Lorde (as Betty Matthews), Martin Balsam (as Harold "Hal" Matthews, early episodes), Will Hare (as Harold "Hal" Matthews, later episodes), Jack Klugman (as Jim Hanson; 1954), Marian Russell (as Lee Connor; 1954), Ward Costello (as Ned Blackman; 1955), Gene Peterson (as Ned Blackman after Costello; 1955), Janet Ward (as Fran Allen; 1955), Anne Meara (as Harriet; 1955). P: Al Morgan. D: Joe Behar. W: James P. Cavanaugh.

1954-55

The Mickey Rooney Show (a/k/a Hey Mulligan)

Sitcom. Ran on NBC Saturdays 8–8:30 P.M. Sept. 4, 1954–June 4, 1955, opposite *The Dotty Mack Show* on ABC and *The Jackie Gleason Show* on CBS. C: Mickey Rooney (as Mickey Mulligan), Claire Carleton (as Mrs. Mulligan), Regis Toomey (as Mr. Mulligan), Carla Balenda (as Pat), John Hubbard (as Mr. Brown), Joey Forman (as Freddie), Alan Mowbray (as the drama teacher). P: Joseph Santley. D: Leslie Martinson. W: John Fenton Murray, Benedict Freeman.

Let's Dance

Musical Variety. Ran on ABC Saturdays 8–9 P.M. Sept. 11–Oct. 16, 1954, opposite *The Jackie Gleason Show* on CBS, pro football (from Oct. 2) on DuMont, and *The Mickey Rooney Show* and *Place the Face* on NBC. C: Julius LaRosa, Martha Wright, Fran Allison, June Valli, the Ralph Flanagan Orchestra, the Art Mooney Orchestra. P: Alan Dinehart.

Willy

Sitcom. Ran on CBS Saturdays 10:30–11 P.M. Sept. 18, 1954–March 1955, opposite pro football (through Nov. 20) and wrestling (from Nov. 27–March 5) and *Your Hit Parade* on NBC, then CBS Thursdays 10:30–11 P.M. April–July 7, 1955, opposite *Lux Video Theatre* on NBC. C: June Havoc (as Willa Dodger), Danny Richards, Jr. (as Franklin Sanders), Mary Treen (as Emily Dodger), Lloyd Corrigan (as Papa Dodger), Whitfield Connor (as Charlie Bush), Hal Peary (as Mr. Perry Bannister; from March), Sterling Holloway (as Harvey Evelyn; from March). P/W: William Spier. D: William Asher. W: Louis Pelletier.

Come Closer

Game. Ran on ABC Mondays 8–8:30 P.M. Sept. 20–Dec. 13, 1954, opposite *The George Burns and Gracie Allen Show* on CBS, *The Ilona Massey Show* (from Nov. 1) on DuMont and *Caesar's Hour* (from Sept. 27) on NBC. C: Jimmy Nelson. P: Herbert Moss. D: Lou Sposa.

The Imogene Coca Show

Comedy Variety. Ran on NBC Saturdays 9–9:30 P.M. Oct. 2, 1954–June 25, 1955, opposite boxing (through Jan. 15) and *Ozark Jubilee* (from Jan. 22) on ABC, *Two for the Money* on CBS and pro football (through Nov. 20) on DuMont. C: Imogene Coca, Bibi Osterwald (as Helen Milliken; 1955), Hal March (as Jerry Crane; 1955), David Burns (as Harry Milliken; 1955), the Carl Hoff Orchestra. P/D: Ernest D. Glucksman, Marc Daniels. W: Lucille Kallen, Ernest Kinoy, Mel Brooks, Max Wilk.

Ernest Kinoy's TV fame comes from his socially conscious dramatic scripts, including Emmy wins in 1964 for *The Defenders* and in 1977 for the miniseries *Roots*. Even he admits he's surprised and unsure how he got involved writing comedy for *The Imogene Coca Show*.

"I had no history whatsoever [of writing comedy]," he said. "I think there must have been some finagling at the agency, and I don't know who did it." "The agency" was William Morris, which packaged *The Imogene Coca Show* with its clients and apparently thought Kinoy, a NBC radio staff writer at the time, had what it took to do a live TV variety program.

Kinoy soon realized he was out of his element on the show. "You were locked in a room with six or seven writers all day all week. Lucille Kallen was the headwriter, and after a short time Mel Brooks showed up. It was a very strange experience for me, because you got there and shouted at each other with ideas. The least paid writer in the group took notes to create workable sketches.

"Somewhere toward the end of the week, you read the script to [Coca] at her home. You had to laugh at your own material. It was a very odd experience."

The process had been used on *Your Show of Shows*, which ran from 1950 to 1954 starring Coca and Sid Caesar before the show dissolved and the time slot was inherited by *The Imogene Coca Show*. Kallen and Brooks had done the earlier show and were accustomed to it; Kinoy was not.

"At one point I brought in a portable typewriter, and everybody looked at me strangely," he said. On the other hand, the lunacy of Brooks was in full bloom, always arriving late with a weird declaration. "He would come in holding his hand to his sternum saying, 'Send out for chicken soup!'"

After a few weeks, Kinoy had it with the show. "I called my agent and said, 'Get me out of it!' And I quit. This was not my experience, and I couldn't take it anymore."

Most of America couldn't take the show either. After four low-rated months, the show dropped the variety format for a sitcom with Coca playing newlywed Betty Crane interacting with another married couple, the Millikens. It didn't help; *Two For the Money* easily outrated it, and *The Imogene Coca Show* left the air four months later.

Was Coca just not right to host a show alone? Said Kinoy: "She was a very funny performer. Whether she was up to carrying the main force of a show, I don't know. I suspect some of the problems were trying to be *The Sid Caesar Show* without Sid Caesar."

The latter's own show, *Caesar's Hour*, ran from 1954 to 1957. He and Coca reteamed the next season in a bomb (see *Sid Caesar Invites You* in 1957-58), then Coca did one more disastrous regular TV series (see *Grindl* in 1963-64) before doing occasional TV work into the 1980s. She died in 2001 at age 92.

The Donald O'Connor Texaco Show

Sitcom. Ran on NBC Saturdays 9:30–10 P.M. Oct. 9, 1954–Sept. 10, 1955, opposite boxing (through Jan. 15), *Ozark Jubilee* (from Jan. 22 to June 25) and *The Lawrence Welk Show* (from July 2) on ABC, *My Favorite Husband* (through June 4) and *Down You Go* (from June 18) on CBS and pro football (through Nov. 20) and wrestling (from Nov. 27 to March 5) on DuMont. C: Donald O'Connor (as himself), Sid Miller (as himself), Joyce Smight (as Doreen). P/D: Donald O'Connor. W/D: Sidney Miller. W: Hal Fimberg, Eddie Maxwell.

Honestly, Celeste!

Sitcom. Ran on CBS Sundays 9:30–10 P.M. Oct. 10–Dec. 5, 1954, opposite *Talent Patrol* (through Nov. 21) and *What's Going On?* (from Nov. 28) on ABC, *Life Begins at Eighty* on DuMont and *Goodyear TV Playhouse/Philco TV Playhouse* on NBC. C: Celeste Holm (as Celeste Anders), Scott McKay (as Bob Wallace), Mike Kellin (as Marty Gordon), Geoffrey Lumb (as Mr. Wallace), Mary Finney (as Mary). P/D: Joseph Scibetta. W: Larry Gelbart, Hal Collins, Norman Lear.

Celeste Holm first triumphed on Broadway, where she debuted in 1938 and scored a hit playing Ado Annie in the original 1943 production of the musical *Oklahoma*. Moving to movies in 1946, she won the Oscar for Best Supporting Actress in 1947 for her third picture, *Gentlemen's Agreement*, followed by nominations in the same category in 1949 for *Come to the Stable* and 1950 for *All About Eve*. Her next stop was television, but this medium would not be as conducive to her initially as the other venues of entertainment had been.

Still considered a hot property in the 1950s, Holm decided to appear regularly in the medium in a sitcom property she chose. "I thought this was one I could have some control over in the writing," she said. With Larry Gelbart, later headwriter of the TV version of *M*A*S*H*, in charge of scripts, Holm thought she would not have to worry about that department, but that belief proved to be wrong.

Holm played a Minnesotan college journalism teacher who left her job to pursue an actual career reporting in Manhattan for the fictional *New York Express* newspaper. (In reality, Holm was born and bred in New York City.) Mr. Wallace was her boss, and his son Bob was her friend. (Asked if he was more than that, Holm said, "He was going to be." Obviously, the show's short run allowed them only to be platonic pals.) Marty the cabbie helped Celeste in pursuit of her stories. Mary was Mr. Wallace's secretary. The show was filmed in Hollywood.

Despite having a nice lead-in program, *General Electric Theater*, which finished in the top 20 the 1954-55 season, *Honestly, Celeste!* was honestly unpopular. "I don't think it was interesting," Holm explained frankly. "The writing wasn't that good, nor the concept." Norman Lear, later the creator of *All in the Family* (and who would later cast Holm in three episodes of that series' successor, *Archie Bunker's Place*) joined the writing staff to help out, but Holm felt her character was too dull for anyone to really create any audience appeal with her.

"I've played so many different parts," she noted. "It didn't allow me much scope as an actress." Apparently the viewing audience agreed, and after just nine shows *Honestly, Celeste!* was off the air, replaced by the obscure anthology series *Stage 7*, which ran until Sept. 25, 1955.

Holm said the cast was not a problem on the show and said they were a fine group to

Scott McKay takes a gander at Celeste Holm as she lets him listen in on one of her conversations on *Honestly, Celeste!* McKay also was seen on Broadway in *The Teahouse of the August Moon* in 1954.

work with. She would outlive the rest of them, being the only one still alive in the 21st century. She would go on to do a summer game show called *Who Pays?* in 1959 followed by another sitcom with a brief life span in 1970-71 called *Nancy* (q.v.).

All About Baby

Informational. Ran on DuMont Fridays 2–2:15 P.M. Oct. 15, 1954–Jan. 7, 1955, opposite *The Robert Q. Lewis Show* on CBS, then DuMont Thursdays and Fridays 2–2:15 P.M. Jan. 13–April 8, 1955, opposite *The Robert Q. Lewis Show* on CBS, and then DuMont Thursdays and Fridays 1:45–2 P.M. April 14–July 1, 1955, opposite *Welcome Travelers* on CBS. C: Ruth Crowley, R.N.

The Halls of Ivy

Sitcom. Ran on CBS Tuesdays 8:30–9 P.M. Oct. 19, 1954–July 1955, opposite *Twenty Questions* (through May 3) and *Who Said That?* (from May 10) on ABC, *Studio 57* on DuMont and *The Milton Berle Show* alternating with *The Martha Raye Show* (through June 21) and *The Arthur Murray Party* (from June 28) on NBC, then CBS Thursdays 10:30–11 P.M. July–Sept. 29, 1955, opposite *Lux Video Theatre* on NBC. C: Ronald Colman (as Dr. William Todhunter Hall), Benita Hume (as Victoria "Vicky" Hall), Mary Wickes (as Alice), Herb Butterfield (as Clarence Wellman), Ray Collins (as Dr. Merriweather; 1954), James Todd (as Dr. Merriweather; 1954–55). P: William Frye. D: Norman Z. McLeod, William Cameron Menzies. W: Don Quinn, Barbara Merlin.

The Ilona Massey Show

Music. Ran on DuMont Mondays 8–8:30 P.M. Nov. 1, 1954–Jan. 3, 1955, opposite *Come Closer* (through Dec. 13) on ABC, *The George Burns and Gracie Allen Show* on CBS and *Caesar's Hour* on NBC. C: Ilona Massey, the Irving Fields Trio. P/W: George Paley. D: Pat Fay.

Edgar Bergen had Charlie McCarthy and Paul Winchell had Jerry Mahoney, but it was ventriloquist Jimmy Weldon who sported a baseball cap with his dummy partner Webster Webfoot for the children's game show *Funny Boners.*

Funny Boners

Children's Game. Ran on NBC Saturdays 11–11:30 A.M. Nov. 20, 1954–July 9, 1955, opposite *Space Patrol* (through Feb. 26) on ABC and *Captain Midnight* (through Feb. 26) and *Winky Dink and You* (from March 5) on CBS. C: Jimmy Weldon. EP: Ralph Edwards. P: Leslie Raddatz. D: Stuart Phelps. W: Leslie Raddatz, Gil Howard.

It took a certain amount of guts for ventriloquist Jimmy Weldon to agree to follow another, better-known ventriloquist act on the NBC Saturday morning schedule in 1954-55. *The Paul Winchell–Jerry Mahoney Show* preceded *Funny Boners*, and even Weldon's director, Stuart Phelps, conceded that Weldon, while talented, was not quite in the same league as Winchell. After mentioning the other top ventriloquist of the time, Edgar Bergen, Phelps noted that "If you put the three of them in a row, [Weldon] would be last." Ouch.

Phelps described Weldon as having borrowed considerably from Bergen, with his two main dummies heavily influenced by Bergen's counterparts. The first one children saw every show was Webster Webfoot, a duck who was a braggart. "That was his Charlie McCarthy," Phelps said. "And he had a guy named Easy Marvin who was his Mortimer Snerd." For those unfamiliar with them, McCarthy was a witty bon vivant with a monocle, while Mortimer was a dopey looking and acting stooge.

Every program had a set order involving what Weldon did when on the show, starting with repartee with Webster Webfoot. According to Phelps, "He would do a whole routine with him, and then he had his 'announcer,' Easy Marvin, out to do a sketch, and then he played the game."

"The game" was a group of silly stunts involving children from the studio audience. If that sounds an awful lot like executive producer Ralph Edwards was imitating his long-running nighttime game show *Truth or Consequences*, well — guilty as charged. "It was a cheap version of it, a kids' version," allowed Phelps, who concurrently directed the latter game show during its run from May 18, 1954–Sept. 28, 1956. (After several sporadic nighttime runs, *Truth or Consequences* had its most successful TV run on daytime from Dec. 31, 1956–Sept. 24, 1965, followed by nine years in syndication from 1966 to 1975.)

The reason why *Funny Boners* went off the air seems to have disappeared over the years. It outlasted its ABC competition (ABC, suffering major financial hurdles in the mid–1950s, scaled back Saturday morning programming entirely until the early 1960s), and CBS switched its series against it too, usually a sign that meant the other network was losing the ratings war. Phelps admitted he didn't know why *Funny Boners* stopped cracking after a little more than seven months on the air. But end it did, replaced by *Commando Cody* (q.v.).

Ironically, Weldon would have success with children later as a voice in cartoons, as would Winchell on a larger scale. Weldon was the voice of Yakky Doodle, a wisecracking duck (again!) seen as a segment on the syndicated, and much repeated, 1961 series *Yogi Bear*. Where is he nowadays? According to Phelps, "He does invitational speaking. He's very good."

Happy Felton's Spotlight Gang

Children's. Ran on NBC Saturdays 10–10:30 A.M. Nov. 20, 1954–Feb. 26, 1955. C: Happy Felton. P/D: Craig Allen. W: Charles Speer.

What's Going On?

Game Show. Ran on ABC Sundays 9:30–10 P.M. Nov. 28–Dec. 26, 1954, opposite *Honestly, Celeste!* (through Dec. 5) and *Stage 7* (from Dec. 12) on CBS, *Life Begins at Eighty* on DuMont and *Goodyear TV Playhouse/Philco TV Playhouse* on NBC. C: Lee Bowman, Kitty Carlisle Hart, Hy Gardner, Audrey Meadows, Cliff Norton, Gene Raymond, Susan Oakland. EP: Allan Sherman. D: Jerome Schnur.

The shortest-lived series ever to come from the prolific game show production company of Mark Goodson and Bill Todman was *What's Going On?* "It was very unsuccessful," ruefully admitted panelist Kitty Carlisle Hart.

Only five shows ran, and the ones that did felt like an eternity for the participants.

Six celebrities made up the panel, with actor Lee Bowman as host. Each week three of them stayed in the Elysee Theater in New York and tried to ascertain where the other three were and what they were doing by using yes-or-no questions. Typically two were in the New York City area and another was in Chicago. The problem was that this was done live, and technical snafus bedeviled its effectiveness.

"It was supposed to be very elaborate," Hart said. "We were supposed to talk to each other from the studio and on location. But the technology was not all there. Nobody could hear anybody."

Fellow panelist Cliff Norton concurred with Hart. "I remember on the show I was in a pen with a bunch of sheep in Chicago in the stockyards," he said. "Right at the beginning of my spot, one of the animals stepped on the cable and cut me off." The technical crew had to scramble to fix the disaster while Norton's segment was delayed.

With the audio difficulties, it became difficult to determine "what's going on" for both the panelists and home viewers. ABC replaced it with the more reliable and less complex to telecast *Pantomime Quiz* on Jan. 2, 1955, where it ran for three months.

Luckily, all was not lost for Hart on TV. Two years after *What's Going On?* ended, Goodson-Todman Productions installed her as a regular panelist on *To Tell the Truth*, which ran on CBS in the nighttime and daytime from 1956 to 1968, then became a syndicated series from 1969 to 1978 and 1980–81, plus a daytime series on NBC from 1990 to 1991. Hart showed up on all of them, though she was a regular panelist only on CBS and the 1969–78 versions.

"They were the best," Hart said of Godson-Todman Productions. "They never left anything to chance. [Well, maybe with *What's Going On?*, but Hart charitably did not say so.] Mark Goodman was a pro."

As for the others on *What's Going On?*, Hart said there were no personality clashes she could recall. "I liked everybody I worked with," she said. "We got along very well. Except for Henry Morgan [when she guested a few times on *I've Got a Secret*, where the caustic comedian was a regular from 1952 to 1967; oddly, the executive producer of *What's Going On?*, Allan

Sherman, also was the same for that game]. I don't think he spoke to me." Hy Gardner joined Hart on *To Tell the Truth* from 1957 to 1959, while Lee Bowman and Audrey Meadows were regulars guessing disguised celebrities on *Masquerade Party* from 1958 to 1960. Cliff Norton and Gene Raymond went back to acting, while little-known Susan Oakland disappeared as mysteriously as she had shown up on the show.

The Road of Life

Soap Opera. Ran on CBS Mondays through Fridays 1:15–1:30 P.M. Dec. 13, 1954–July 1, 1955. C: Don McLaughlin (as Dr. Jim Brent), Virginia Dwyer (as Jocelyn McLeod Brent), Bill Lipton (as John "Butch" Brent), Harry Holcombe (as Malcolm Overton), Barbara Becker (as Sybil Overton Fuller), Charles Dingle (as Conrad Overton), Dorothy Sands (as Aunt Reggie Ellis), Elizabeth Lawrence (as Francie Brent), Elspeth Eric (as Lil Monet), Michael Kane (as Armand Monet), Hollis Irving (as Pearl Snow), Nelson Case (as narrator). P: John Egan. D: Walter Gorman. W: Charles Gussman.

So This Is Hollywood

Sitcom. Ran on NBC Saturdays 8:30–9 P.M. Jan. 1–June 1955, opposite *The Dotty Mack Show* on ABC and *The Jackie Gleason Show* on CBS, then NBC Fridays 10:30–11 P.M. July –Aug. 19, 1955, opposite *Windows* on CBS. C: Mitzi Green (as Queenie Dugan), Virginia Gibson (as Kim Tracy), Jimmy Lydon (as Andy Boone), Gordon Jones (as Hubie Dodd), Peggy Knudson (as April Adams). P/W: Ed Beloin. D: Richard Bare. W: Dean Reisner, Phil Davis, George O'Hanlon, Jimmy O'Hanlon, Charles Stewart.

Hollywood Today with Sheilah Graham

Informational. Ran on NBC Mondays through Fridays 10:45–11 A.M. Jan. 3–Aug. 19, 1955, opposite *Arthur Godfrey Time* (Mondays through Thursdays) and *The Garry Moore Show* (Fridays) on CBS. C: Sheilah Graham.

Norby

Sitcom. Ran on NBC Wednesdays 7–7:30 P.M. Jan. 5–April 6, 1955, opposite *Kukla, Fran and Ollie* and news on ABC and *Captain Video* (through March 29) and news (through March 29) on Du-

Mont. C: David Wayne (as Pearson Norby), Joan Lorring (as Helen Norby), Susan Hallaran (as Diane Norby), Evan Elliott (as Hank Norby), Ralph Dunn (as Mr. Rudge), Janice Mars (as Wahleen Johnson), Carol Veazie (as Mrs. Maude Endles), Jack Warden (as Bobo), Maxine Stuart (as Maureen). P: David Swift. D: Richard Whorf. W: Harvey Otkin, James Lee, David Rayfiel, George Kirgo.

The Swift Show Wagon

Variety. Ran on NBC Saturdays 7:30–8 P.M. Jan. 8–Oct. 1, 1955, opposite *Ozark Jubilee* (from July 9) on ABC and *Beat the Clock* on CBS. C: Horace Heidt. P: Jerry Brown. D: Joseph Cavalier.

Professional Father

Sitcom. Ran on CBS Saturdays 10–10:30 P.M. Jan. 8–July 2, 1955, opposite *The Stork Club* (through March 12) and *Compass* (from March 19) on ABC, wrestling (through March 5) on DuMont and *The George Gobel Show* on NBC. C: Steve Dunne (as Thomas Wilson, M.D.), Barbara Billingsley (as Helen Wilson), Ted Marc (as Thomas "Twig" Wilson, Jr.), Beverly Washburn (as Kathryn "Kit" Wilson), Phyllis Coates (as Madge Allen, R.N.), Ann O'Neal (as Nana). P: Harry Kronman. D: Sherman Marks. W: James O'Hanlon, Robert Ross, David Schwartz.

Jan Murray Time

Variety. Ran on NBC Fridays 10:45–11 P.M. Feb. 11–May 6, 1955, opposite *Person to Person* on CBS and *Down You Go* on NBC. C: Jan Murray, Tina Louise, Fletcher Peck, the Novelties. P/D: Dave Brown.

Ted Mack's Matinee

Variety. Ran on NBC Mondays through Fridays 3–3:30 P.M. April 4–Oct. 28, 1955, opposite *The Big Payoff* on CBS. C: Ted Mack, Dick Lee, Elise Rhodes, the Dreamboaters. P: Louis Graham. D: Lloyd Marx.

It Pays to Be Married

Game. Ran on NBC Mondays through Fridays 3:30–4 P.M. July 4–Oct. 28, 1955, opposite *The Bob Crosby Show* on CBS. C: Bill Goodwin. EP: James L. Saphier. P/D: Stefan Hatos.

Commando Cody

Science Fiction. Ran on NBC Saturdays 11–11:30 A.M. July 16–Oct. 8, 1955, opposite *Winky Dink and You* on CBS. C: Judd Holdren (as Commando Cody), Aline Towne (as Joan Gilbert), William Schallert (as Ted Richards; through July 30), Richard Crane (as Dick Preston; from Aug. 7), Gregory Gay (as the Ruler), Craig Kelly (as Mr. Henderson). P: Mel Tucker. AP: Franklin Adreon. D: Fred C. Brannon, Harry Keller. W: Ronald Davidson, Barry Shipman.

The Children's Corner

Children's. Ran on NBC Saturdays 10:30–11 A.M. Aug. 20–Sept. 10, 1955, then NBC Saturdays 10–10:30 A.M. Dec. 24, 1955–April 28, 1956. C: Fred Rogers, Josie Carey. P: Doris Ann. D: Martin Hoade. W: Fred Rogers.

When he retired in 2001, Fred Rogers left an impressive legacy of teaching generations of American children how to lead their lives and behave with others in his gentle children's series *Mister Rogers' Neighborhood*, which began its run on public television in 1967. Less remembered is the fact that he did basically the same series on network TV more than a decade earlier with *The Children's Corner*.

Director Martin Hoade had a connection to Rogers before the series started. "I worked at NBC in the public affairs department," he said. "My main work was religious programs. In my work, I worked with Fred Rogers. Fred worked with NBC as a stage manager."

Fred left NBC's New York headquarters for its Pittsburgh affiliate WQED in 1953. There, said Hoade, "He developed this program with the puppets and doing all these characters with Josie Carey. Fred did the whole job." It was *The Children's Corner*, and it had Rogers using his voice on imperious King Friday XIII, meek Daniel Striped Tiger and others that would become regular features later on *Mister Rogers' Neighborhood*.

The Children's Corner might have stayed just a local show had it not been for Hoade's boss Davidson Taylor. Taylor sent Hoade to Pittsburgh to persuade Dr. Benjamin Spock to do a TV series for NBC (see *Dr. Spock* in the 1955-56 section). While at the reception room, Hoade saw Rogers' series and told Taylor about it. Hoade said his boss thought that "It was a worthwhile production for public affairs, but there was no place for it." But Taylor soon relented and put it on the air.

When *The Children's Corner* became a network offering live from New York, Hoade said, "Mr. Taylor asked me if I would handle it, and it was a very simple operation. I was asked to do it, and I was glad to do it." After a brief late summer run, it returned in the middle of the 1955-56 season to kick off NBC's Saturday morning schedule, but its audience was not as big as other shows on the lineup, and with no sponsor lined up for the show and Rogers feeling uncertain about doing a network show, it ended four months later.

"I think Fred felt his commitment was in Pittsburgh, because WQED was supportive of him," Hoade said. That station continued airing *The Children's Corner* through 1961 and its quasi-remake *Mister Rogers' Neighborhood* starting in 1965 before the latter aired nationally two years later.

Why did Rogers last so long as a children's host? Here's Hoade's opinion: "There was a purity to the program and a consistency. Fred had a capacity to talk to his audiences. He never allowed compromises in his language and his plotlines. He illuminated a landscape for those children. That's the important thing."

Speaking as one child so "illuminated," let me just add these words: "Thank you and congratulations on a job well done, Fred Rogers."

The World at Home

Informational. Ran on NBC Mondays through Fridays 10:45–11 A.M. Aug. 22–Sept. 9, 1955, opposite *Arthur Godfrey Time* (Mondays through Thursdays) and *The Garry Moore Show* (Fridays) on CBS. C: Arlene Francis. EP: Dick Linkroum. P/D: Norman Frank. W: Harold Azine, Gene Wyckoff, Lee Charell.

1955-56

Warner Brothers Presents *see* Kings Row *and* Casablanca.

It's Always Jan

Sitcom. Ran on CBS Saturdays 9:30–10 P.M. Sept. 10, 1955–June 30, 1956, opposite *The Lawrence Welk Show* on ABC and *The Jimmy Durante Show* on NBC. C: Janis Paige (as Janis Stewart), Patricia Bright (as Pat Murphy), Merry Anders (as Val Marlowe), Jeri Lou James (as Josie Stewart), Arte Johnson (as Stanley Schreiber), Sid Melton (as Harry Cooper). P/W: Arthur Stander. D: Sheldon Leonard.

Kings Row

Drama. Ran on ABC Tuesdays 7:30–8:30 P.M. Sept. 13, 1955–Jan. 17, 1956, opposite *Name That Tune* and *Navy Log* (through Nov. 1) and *The Phil Silvers Show* (from Nov. 8) on CBS and *The Dinah Shore Show*, *NBC News* and *The Milton Berle Show* alternating with *The Martha Raye Show* and *The Chevy Show* on NBC. C: Jack Kelly (as Dr. Parris Mitchell), Nan Leslie (as Randy Monaghan), Robert Horton (as Drake McHugh), Victor Jory (as Dr. Alexander Tower), Lillian Bronson (as Grandma), Robert Burton (as Dr. Gordon). P: Roy Huggins. D: Paul Stewart. W: Jameson Brewer.

Roy Huggins is one of the most successful TV series producers of all time, being the man behind such hits as *Maverick*, *The Virginian*, *The Fugitive* and *The Rockford Files*, to name just a few. But every producer has to start somewhere, and for Huggins it was *Kings Row*, much to his chagrin.

Huggins came to TV by way of a contract with the Columbia movie company. He had only one of several scripts he wrote there made into a movie, 1954's *Hangman's Knot*, which left him unsatisfied creatively. "I decided in 1955 that motion pictures were on their last legs," he said. "I thought television was the wave of the future."

Warner Brothers hired him as a producer and assigned him to *Kings Row*, one of three new series they had rotating weekly under the umbrella title of *Warner Brothers Presents*. It was Warner's initial foray into TV series. "They

had already shot one and produced a couple of scripts," he said of his first peek at the series. "I looked at what was done and thought, 'How do I get out of this?'"

Based on the 1942 movie of the same name nominated for a Best Picture Oscar, *Kings Row* featured Jack Kelly, Nan Leslie and Robert Horton playing the roles done by Bob Cummings, Ann Sheridan and Ronald Reagan in the movie. They lived and worked in the fictional town of Kings Row in the early 1900s, with Kelly playing psychiatrist Dr. Mitchell under the guidance of Dr. Tower. His efforts on and off the job met with much melodrama on the show.

"Everybody, including the network, thought it would be a hit," Huggins recalled. But he knew better than they did. "It was an adult soap opera on at 7:30. It made no sense. It also was a bad soap opera. They had people doing it who did not know what they were doing. They were not writers."

Fortunately for Huggins, the sponsor of *Warner Brothers Presents*, Monsanto, became greatly distressed by the series' poor critical and audience response. They decided the only hope for it was *Cheyenne*, which rotated with *Kings Row* and *Casablanca* (q.v.). "The head of Warner television called me in and said, 'I know you're on *Kings Row*, but we need you badly on *Cheyenne*,'" recalled Huggins. As producer he successfully revamped *Cheyenne* into an "adult" western, and when *Warner Brothers Presents* ended after a year, *Cheyenne* stayed on the air until 1963.

Prior to that, however, *Kings Row* ended its run after four months. Because of the rotation system, it aired only seven shows. The show's lead was not forgotten, however; in 1957, when Huggins produced *Maverick*, Jack Kelly joined that series to co-star with James Garner, and stayed with that show until its cancellation in 1962.

Casablanca

Drama. Ran on ABC Tuesdays 7:30–8:30 P.M. Sept. 27, 1955–April 24, 1956, opposite same competition that was listed for *Kings Row*. C: Charles

McGraw (as Rick Jason), Marcel Dalio (as Capt. Renaud), Dan Seymour (as Ferrari), Michael Fox (as Sasha), Clarence Muse (as Sam), Ludwig Stossel (as Ludwig). P: Jerry Robinson. D: John Peyser.

No amount of money planned for the TV version of *Casablanca* could get that 1942 movie classic's star, Humphrey Bogart, to "play it again, Sam" (the oft-misquoted line from the original film; Bogart actually said to Sam the piano player, "You played it for her, you can play it for me … play it," in reference to the song "As Time Goes By"). But director John Peyser thought he could get a lead for TV that would, if not match Bogart's performance, at least be a serviceable replacement. His plan went awry, however, as did much of the TV *Casablanca*.

"I figured the only guy who could replace the original guy and not be killed would be Tony [Anthony] Quinn," said Peyser. He presented his idea to Warner Brothers president Jack Warner, who said if Quinn agreed to do the program for a salary of $5,000 per show plus two movies for Warner Brothers, he would hire the actor. Quinn's agent liked the idea too but told Peyser he had to run it past John Houseman, who was producing the film Quinn was shooting at the time, *Lust for Life*. Houseman and Dore Schary, president of MGM, both approved of releasing Quinn off the picture by Aug. 1, 1955, to shoot the series. An ecstatic Peyser returned to tell Warner the good news, but when he did Warner suddenly had an attack of prejudice against Quinn. "He said, 'I don't want to pay that greasy Mexican all that money!'" Peyser said.

Taking Quinn's place instead as lead was Charles McGraw, who had just starred in a 1954 syndicated series called *The Adventures of Falcon* but was hardly a household name like Anthony Quinn. "Poor Charlie McGraw," Peyser said. "He couldn't act his way out of a hat." Peyser believes McGraw's inability to convince being an American émigré fighting Nazis, coupled with "unbelievable, incredibly lousy scripts," sealed the show's fate.

Peyser did see a bright spot working with Warner Brothers, which hired him not long after he came to Hollywood from New York City to direct *The Man Behind the Badge* series. "They gave me all the props and sets they could lavish on it," he said. Having served in Europe during World War II, Peyser felt he did a solid job recreating the 1940s atmosphere of Rick's café and its denizens, which beyond Sam included bartender Sasha and police chief Capt. Renaud.

Casablanca rotated weekly under the umbrella title *Warner Brothers Presents* with the series *Kings Row* (q.v.) and *Cheyenne* until it was decided to just air *Cheyenne* after seven months. Nearly 30 years later, NBC aired a revival with a miscast David Soul as Rick which ran just five times, from April 10–April 24, 1983, and from Aug. 27 to Sept. 3, 1983. Regarding that *Casablanca*, Peyser said what many viewers at the time must have felt: "I never heard of it, saw it, or wanted to see it."

Brave Eagle

Western. Ran on CBS Tuesdays 7:30–8 P.M. Sept. 28, 1955–June 6, 1956, opposite *Disneyland* on ABC and *Eddie Fisher Coke Time* and news on NBC. C: Keith Larsen (as Brave Eagle), Neena Nomkeena (as Keena), Kim Winona (as Morning Star), Bert Wheeler (as Smokey Joe). EP: Art Rush, Mike North. P: Jack C. Lacey. D: Paul Landres.

The Adventures of Champion

Western. Ran on CBS Fridays 7:30–8 P.M. Sept. 30, 1955–Feb. 3, 1956, opposite *The Adventures of Rin Tin Tin* on ABC and *Eddie Fisher Coke Time* and news on NBC. C: Barry Curtis (as Ricky North), Jim Bannon (as Uncle Sandy North), Francis McDonald (as Will Calhoun), Ewing Mitchell (as Sheriff Powers). P: Louis Gray. D: George Archainbaud, Ford Beebe.

Dr. Spock

Informational. Ran on NBC Sundays 3–3:30 P.M. Oct. 9, 1955–Aug. 9, 1956, opposite football on ABC and DuMont (both through Dec. 11) and *Talkaround* (through Jan. 1) and *Face the Nation* (from Jan. 8–April 8) on CBS. C: Dr. Benjamin Spock. P: William W. Parish. D: Charles K. Dargan.

Talkaround

Informational. Ran on CBS Sundays 3–3:30 P.M. 1955–Jan. 1, 1956, opposite football on ABC and DuMont (both through Dec. 11) and *Dr. Spock* on NBC. C/P: Katherine Copeland. EP: Irving Gitlin.

Choose Up Sides

Game. Ran on NBC Saturdays Noon–12:30 P.M. Jan. 7–Feb. 25, 1956, then NBC Saturdays 12:30–1 P.M. March 3–March 31, 1956, both times opposite *Big Top* on CBS. C: Gene Rayburn, Tommy Tompkins, Roger Peterson. P: Mark Goodson, Bill Todman. D: Lloyd Gross. W: Frank Wayne, Bob Howard.

When asked whether he would characterize *Choose Up Sides* as a stunt show or a children's show, director Lloyd Gross responded cannily, "I call it a numbers show. They had two teams, and they'd choose up the sides to be on."

Choose Up Sides first appeared on TV on Nov. 2, 1953, as a local show in New York City with Dean Miller as host. A year later Miller was in Hollywood starring in the hit sitcom *December Bride* from 1954 to 1959. He then co-hosted the daily series *Here's Hollywood* from 1960 to 1961, leaving the show about midway through its run to own and operate broadcasting stations in Ohio, something he would still be doing 40 years later.

But back to *Choose Up Sides*. The basic premise had two teams of four kids each having to complete stunts the fastest to win. It resembled a junior version of producers Mark Goodson and Bill Todman's nighttime hit *Beat the Clock*, although here there was no limit for how long the participants could try to accomplish a task. They either finished it first or lost.

On *Choose Up Sides* Gene Rayburn (standing next to the title emblem) described various competitions between the Bronco Busters, represented by the cowboy hat drawing on the left wall, and the Space Pilots, whose leader Roger Peterson is seen here manipulating a pool cue with a ball attached that his blindfolded young partner had to catch with a device in his right hand. If the expressions of the children in the audience are any indication, including the one picking his nose on the lower left row, this activity was somewhat less than scintillating.

When NBC drafted the show as a midseason addition to its Saturday afternoon lineup, the host selected for the job was Gene Rayburn. Rayburn was the announcer on *The Tonight Show* with Steve Allen at the time, a job he had held since 1954, plus done a few game shows as a panelist or host.

"He had been in the entourage of a couple of shows," noted Gross. "Gene was fine. He was a very outgoing individual anyhow. He got along with the kids."

The kids fell into two teams led by adult captains— the "Bronco Busters" under Tommy Tompkins and the "Space Pilots" under Roger Peterson. They also sometimes competed for prizes for home viewers who sent in postcards and had them picked by the players.

But all the competition on every show was put on hold when announcer Don Pardo came out around the middle of each show billed as "Mr. Mischief" and gave a day. The child in the audience whose birthday landed on or nearest that day got to play a game called "Sooper Dooper Doo," where he or she flung 15 playing cards toward a beach ball with a gummy surface and tried to have as many as possible adhere to the ball. The show did not crown a winner in this contest until it had been attempted over four weeks.

According to Gross, the show went off after 13 weeks because the show could not attract a sponsor. NBC replaced it with the long-running children's science series *Watch Mr. Wizard*.

NBC Comedy Hour

Comedy Variety. Ran on NBC Sundays 8–9 P.M. Jan. 8–June 10, 1956, opposite movies on ABC and *The Ed Sullivan Show* on CBS. C: Gale Storm (February through April), Jonathan Winters, Hy Averback, the Al White Dancers, the Tony Charmoli Dancers, the Gordon Jenkins Orchestra, the Al Goodman Orchestra. EP: Sam Fuller. P/D: Ernest D. Glucksman. D: Jim Jordan. W: Robert O'Brien, Irving Elinson, Coleman Jacoby, Arnold Rosen.

The Gordon MacRae Show

Musical Variety. Ran on NBC Mondays 7:30–7:45 P.M. March 5–Aug. 27, 1956 opposite *Twilight Theater* (through July 9) and *Bold Journey* (from July 16) on ABC and *The Adventures of Robin Hood* on

CBS. C: Gordon MacRae, the Cheerleaders, the Van Alexander Orchestra. P/D: Irv Lambrecht. W: Sheila MacRae.

Guy Lombardo's Diamond Jubilee

Musical Variety. Ran on CBS Tuesdays 9–9:30 P.M. March 20–June 19, 1956, opposite *Make Room for Daddy* on ABC and *Fireside Theater* on NBC. C: Guy Lombardo and His Royal Canadians. P/W: Gordon Auchincloss. D: Charles S. Dubin.

Apparently to capitalize on the unexpected TV success of Lawrence Welk, whose summer show on ABC in 1955 became a big hit, CBS decided to bring Canadian bandleader Guy Lombardo onto the network lineup in 1956 as a midseason replacement for the faltering sitcom *Meet Millie* (Oct. 25, 1952–March 6, 1956). Like Welk, Lombardo's rather bland arrangements met with disdain among many professional musicians and critics yet found favor with much of the general public, especially with dozens of hits in the 1930s and 1940s like "Red Sails in the Sunset" and "It's Love-Love-Love."

Guy and his band, dubbed appropriately His Royal Canadians (though not all hailed north of the border), came to TV first in a syndicated series from 1954 to 1955. It was a pivotal time for the group, as 1954 would mark the band's last hit record ("Hernando's Hideaway") and first time doing a TV special to ring in New Year's Eve. Because of the latter, the tune "Auld Lang Syne" became widely associated with the band, even though they never had a hit with it. Anyway, the syndicated show was not a success, but Lombardo's band still had marquee value when the CBS series started in 1956.

Director Charles S. Dubin said he liked working with the band on the show. "They had a vast repertoire," he noted. He added that music made up the bulk of its content, and when it came to what Lombardo had to do, "There was very little banter. He would introduce the number and the guest stars. He was very placid, very calm."

There was more than music, however. The show's theme was a "Song of Your Life" contest wherein up to five guest viewers got to come to New York and receive $1,000 if Guy read their letters about what tune had the most impact on their personal sagas and then led the band in the playing of that tune. Sometimes a guest star turned up too to vocalize, such as Polly Bergen. I had to laugh when Dubin, showing a true director's perspective, recalled her appearance by noting that "She had a great bone structure."

Dubin said that directing the program was relatively easy for him. The Royal Canadians "didn't want to rehearse, and there was very little budget for it too," he said. "I had picked up a technique by then to help me out." What Dubin did was to get copies of the songs to be played and practiced with them by having the cameramen cut to cards on stage indicating where various sections of the band would be sitting — brass, strings, etc.

Still, despite the efforts of Dubin and company, *Guy Lombardo's Diamond Jubilee* was a 14-carat flop, with CBS replacing it with the summer sitcom *Joe and Mabel*. Lombardo's band kept doing New Year's Eve specials on

CBS until his death in 1977. Two offshoots of the group, The Guy Lombardo Big Band and Guy Lombardo's Royal Canadians with Al Pierson, currently still perform.

High Finance

Game. Ran on CBS Saturdays 10:30–11 P.M. July 7–Dec. 15, 1956, opposite *Adventure Theater* (through Sept. 1) and *Your Hit Parade* (from Sept. 8) on NBC. C: Dennis James. P: Peter Arnell. D: Lou Sposa.

NBC Bandstand

Musical Variety. Aired on NBC Mondays through Fridays 10:30–11 A.M. July 30–Nov. 2, 1956, opposite *Arthur Godfrey Time* (Mondays through Thursdays) and *The Garry Moore Show* (Fridays) on CBS. C: Bert Parks.

1956-57

Hey, Jeannie!

Sitcom. Ran on CBS Saturdays 9:30–10 P.M. Sept. 8, 1956–May 4, 1957, opposite *The Lawrence Welk Show* on ABC and *Caesar's Hour* on NBC. C: Jeannie Carson (as Jeannie MacLennon), Allen Jenkins (as Al Murray), Jane Dulo (as Liz Murray). P: Charles Isaacs. D: James V. Kern, Les Goodwins. W: Stanley Shapiro, Fred Fox.

Noah's Ark

Drama. Ran on NBC Tuesdays 8:30–9 P.M. Sept. 18, 1956–Feb. 26, 1957, opposite *The Life and Legend of Wyatt Earp* on ABC and *The Brothers* (from Oct. 2) on CBS. C: Paul Burke (as Dr. Noah McCann), Vic Rodman (as Dr. Sam Rinehart), May Wynn (as Liz Clark). P/D/W: Jack Webb. W: Frank Burt.

The Buccaneers

Adventure. Ran on CBS Saturdays 7:30–8 P.M. Sept. 22, 1956–Sept. 14, 1957, opposite movies (through June 15) and *Flight #7* (from June 22–Aug. 31) on ABC and *People Are Funny* on NBC. C: Robert Shaw (as Captain Dan Tempest),

Peter Hammond (as Lt. Beamish), Edwin Richfield (as crewman Armando), Brian Rawlinson (as crewman Gaff), Paul Hansard (as crewman Taffy), Alex Mango (as crewman Van Brugh), Wilfred Downing (as crewman Dickon). P: Hannah Weinstein, Ralph Smart. D: Robert L. Day, Pennington Richards.

The Adventures of Sir Lancelot

Adventure. Ran on NBC Mondays 8–8:30 P.M. Sept. 24, 1956–June 24, 1957, opposite *The Danny Thomas Show* (through Feb. 4) and *Wire Service* (from Feb. 11) on ABC and *The George Burns and Gracie Allen Show* on CBS. C: William Russell (as Sir Lancelot), Jane Hylton (as Queen Guinevere), Ronald Leigh-Hunt (as King Arthur), Cyril Smith (as Merlin), Peter Bennett (as Leonides), Bobby Scroggins (as Brian). P: Dallas Bower, Hannah Weinstein. D: Ralph Smart, Bernard Knowles, Arthur Crabtree, Anthony Squire.

Stanley

Sitcom. Ran on NBC Mondays 8:30–9 P.M. Sept. 24, 1956–March 11, 1957, opposite *The Voice of Firestone* on ABC and *Arthur Godfrey's Talent*

Scouts on CBS. C: Buddy Hackett (as Stanley Peck), Carol Burnett (as Celia), Paul Lynde (as voice of Horace Fenton), Frederic Tozere (as Mr. George Phillips), Jane Connell (as Jane), Reedy Talton (as Marvin). P/D: Max Leibman. W: Neil Simon, Billy Friedberg.

With the combined comic talents of Buddy Hackett, Carol Burnett and Paul Lynde, one wonders how in retrospect *Stanley* could fail. Although supporting actress Jane Connell said she didn't know why, it would be a safe assumption to bet it was because of its time slot. Its CBS competition, *Arthur Godfrey's Talent Scouts*, was still a top 15 series in the 1956-57 ratings, and its lead-in, *The Adventures of Sir Lancelot* (q.v.), was weak.

Nonetheless, *Stanley* merits attention from TV scholars not just for its stars but also its producer/director. Max Leibman produced *Your Show of Shows* from 1950 to 1954 and *Max Leibman Presents*, a monthly series of specials (called "spectaculars" at the time) from 1954 to 1956. *Stanley* was his first try at a sitcom, and Connell said he made quite an impression with her.

"We used to rehearse over at City Center [in Manhattan]," she said. "I remember a very short man getting all the people together for the shows. He also employed Pat Carroll a lot, and he was admonishing us that we were much too heavy." Overall, Connell said, "He never was anything but very curious in rehearsal."

The live sitcom starred Hackett as a well-meaning but often inadvertently bumbling newsstand operator in the lobby of the plush (and fictional) Sussex-Fenton Hotel in New York City. Burnett played his girlfriend, Celia, who loved him despite his faults and the pressures he received from the hotel manager, Mr. Phillips.

Lynde was the voice of the hotel owner on an intercom, which seems a waste given how much physical comedy the actor might have been able to do on camera. Lynde's work with the others was so distanced that Connell told me she'd almost forgotten about him doing the show. Connell herself played Celia's best friend.

Connell got the job via an off–Broadway production. "I was doing *The Threepenny Opera* at the time in the Village [Greenwich Village]. And I think I had an agent with the William Morris company. I think they relied on them casting it."

She said she became like her character and considered Burnett a friend on the show. "We got along fine. I'd known about Carol when I had been doing revue work in California." She added that the two of them had their costumes done at a store called Altman's at 34th Street and Broadway and "I remember going down in the bus with Carol to get the clothing."

While Connell and most of the rest of the cast went onto other, more successful roles (she played Agnes in the hit Broadway musical *Mame* in 1966, for example), it is odd to report that Hackett never has been a regular on a hit TV series despite appearing frequently in the medium for more than 50 years. Apart from *Stanley*, he spent just a year replacing Art Carney as the foil on *The Jackie Gleason Show* from 1958 to 1959, hosted a wan syndicated revival of *You Bet Your Life* in 1980, lent his voice to the disastrous three-episode nighttime cartoon *Fish Police* in 1992, and flopped once again in 1999 in a supporting role on the sitcom *Action*.

The Jonathan Winters Show

Comedy Variety. Ran on NBC Tuesdays 7:30–7:45 P.M. Oct. 2, 1956–June 25, 1957, opposite *Cheyenne* on ABC and *Name That Tune* on CBS. C: Jonathan Winters, Don Pardo (through March), Wayne Howell (from March), the Eddie Safranski Orchestra. P/D: Norman Frank. W: Jonathan Winters, Jack Douglas, Jim Lehner, George Atkins.

The Brothers

Sitcom. Ran on CBS Tuesdays 8:30–9 P.M. Oct. 2, 1956–Feb. 26, 1957, opposite *The Life and Legend of Wyatt Earp* on ABC and *Noah's Ark* on NBC. C: Gale Gordon (as Harvey Box), Bob Sweeney (as Gilmore Box), Ann Morriss (as Dr. Margaret Kleeb), Frank Orth (as Capt. Sam Box; 1956), Howard McNear (as Capt. Sam Box; 1956–57), Nancy Hadley (as Marilee Dorf), Oliver Blake (as Carl Dorf), Robin Hughes (as Barrington Steel). P: Edward Feldman. D: Hy Averback. W: William Davenport.

The Adventures of Hiram Holliday

Sitcom. Ran on NBC Wednesdays 8–8:30 P.M. Oct. 3, 1956–Feb. 27, 1957, opposite *Walt Disney* on ABC and *Arthur Godfrey and His Friends* on CBS. C: Wally Cox (as Hiram Holliday), Ainslie Pryor (as Joel Smith). P/D/W: Phil Rapp.

Circus Time

Variety. Ran on ABC Thursdays 8–9 P.M. Oct. 4, 1956–June 27, 1957, opposite *The Bob Cummings Show* and *Climax!* on CBS and *You Bet Your Life* and *Dragnet* on NBC. C: Paul Winchell, Betty Ann Grove (1957), the Ralph Herman Orchestra. P: Martin Stone. AP: Leon Newman. D: James Walsh.

Wire Service

Drama/Adventure. Ran on ABC Thursdays 9–10 P.M. Oct. 4–Feb. 7, 1957, opposite *Climax!* and *Playhouse 90* on CBS and *The People's Choice* and *The Tennessee Ernie Ford Show* on NBC, then ABC Mondays 7:30–8:30 P.M. Feb. 14–Sept. 23, 1957, opposite *The Adventures of Robin Hood* and *The George Burns and Gracie Allen Show* on CBS and *The Nat King Cole Show* (through June 24), *Georgia Gibbs and Her Million Record Show* (from July 1–Sept. 2), and news, and *The Adventures of Sir Lancelot* (through June 24) and *The Charlie Farrell Show* reruns (from July 1–Sept. 16) on NBC. C: Dane Clark (as Dan Miller), George Brent (as Dean Evans), Mercedes McCambridge (as Katherine Wells). P: Don Sharpe, Warren Lewis. D: Alvin Ganzer. W: Al C. Ward, Samuel Elkin.

The Ray Anthony Show

Musical Variety. Ran on ABC Fridays 10–11 P.M. Oct. 12, 1956–May 3, 1957, opposite *The Lineup* and *Person to Person* on CBS and boxing and *Red Barber's Corner* on NBC. C: Ray Anthony and His Orchestra, Leroy Anthony, Frank Leahy, Don Durant, Med Flory, Gene Merlino, The Four Freshmen, The Belvederes, The Savoys. P: Art Rowe, Sidney Smith. D: Sidney Smith.

ABC programmed *The Lawrence Welk Show* on July 2, 1955, just as a summer replacement, but to the network's amazement, the show was such a huge hit Saturday nights that it stayed on for the regular 1955-56 season. Enthusiastic with the results, ABC and the sponsor looked to extend the show's popularity in 1956-57. One way was adding a talent show called *Lawrence Welk's Top Tunes and New Talent*, which ran until 1959. The other was to find a musician to do a similar show, and that person was Ray Anthony.

Anthony worked with several big bands including Glenn Miller's before setting up his own orchestra in the late 1940s. His group prospered in the early to mid–1950s with many hits, the biggest of which, 1952's "At Last,"

ironically was a remake of a 1942 Glenn Miller hit. He had his own syndicated show earlier in 1956 before doing his network series.

"It was kind of a big band jazz version of the Welk show," producer/director Sidney Smith said of the network edition. "Dodge sponsored both of them."

Smith said he got involved with the program because "I had kind of developed a method of doing music for television — cutting by the bars and so on — from being on *Your Hit Parade*." He said when he directed *The Ray Anthony Show* live from Hollywood, "I already had in my scripts what the shots would be. We did have a segment where we'd cut to Ray, I guess to provide appeal."

As a host, Smith said Anthony was fine in the job but noted that "He was very much a stickler. He just took care of the music and let me know what he was going to do on stage." When Anthony wasn't hosting or conducting the band, the show featured a sizable number of regulars to perform, including Ray's brother Leroy Anthony ("A great tap dancer," Smith said); male quartet the Four Freshmen, whose biggest hit "Graduation Day" hit the charts a few months before the show's debut; and oddest of all, Frank Leahy giving a brief update on sports events.

Smith had no idea why *The Ray Anthony Show* didn't last longer than a season on ABC, but chances are Dodge was unhappy to be advertising on a show finishing third in its time slot. A month before it ended, the series shrank a half hour and ran from just 10–10:30 P.M. Anthony went on to do two syndicated shows, in 1962 and 1968, but by then his music no longer made the charts, and he and his band made only infrequent appearances on TV thereafter.

Tales of the 77th Bengal Lancers

Adventure. Ran on NBC Sundays 7–7:30 P.M. Oct. 21, 1956–June 2, 1957, opposite *You Asked for It* on ABC and *Lassie* on CBS. C: Philip Carey (as Lt. Michael Rhodes), Warren Stevens (as Lt. William Storm), Patrick Whyte (as Col. Standish). P: Herbert B. Leonard. W/D: Douglas Heyes.

Washington Square

Musical Variety. Ran on NBC Sundays 4–5 P.M. Oct. 21, 1956–April 21, 1957, opposite *College Press Conference* and *Medical Horizons* on ABC and

NFL football and *CBS Sunday News* (both through Dec. 23) and *Odyssey* (from Jan. 6) on CBS. C: Ray Bolger, Elaine Stritch, Rusty Draper, the Three Flames, Jo Wilder, Daniza Illitsch (as Mama Rosa; through Nov.4), Kay Armen (as Mama Rosa; from Nov. 18), Mata and Hari, Arnold Stang (voice only), the Bil and Cora Baird Puppets, the Charles Sanford Orchestra. P: William A. Bacher. D: Greg Garrison. W: Mac Benoff, Al Schwartz, Buddy Arnold.

Ray Bolger starred in *Washington Square* as an agent looking for talent in New York City in this musical revue with a light plot. The format allowed him, the regulars and a guest or two to break into song as he visited them. For example, at the Greenwich Village Inn, Bolger met Broadway belter Elaine Stritch, the hotel's operator; country crooner Rusty Draper; R&B act the Three Flames; and the dance duo of [Ruth] Mata and [Eugene] Hari. It was not all music, however; at the Washington Square Playhouse, actress Jo Wilder did a dramatic scene between acts.

"It was a very expensive show to do, time consuming, but I really enjoyed doing the show," said director Greg Garrison. "We had a great cast."

Beside those already mentioned, opera star Daniza Illitsch played aspiring opera star Mama Rosa, a widow with six kids (pop singer Kay Armen replaced her after two shows). There were also puppets courtesy of Bil and Cora Baird, with one involving a turtle using the voice of Arnold Stang. Garrison added that "The guy who wrote the music was Jerry Herman, who later wrote *Hello, Dolly!*"

The only detriment Garrison recalled about the show involved Ray Bolger's wife, Gwen, who also was his manager. "She wanted to change the name to *The Ray Bolger Show* after a couple of weeks on the air," he said. (Note: Bolger had a sitcom on ABC from 1953 to 1955 titled *The Ray Bolger Show* in its second season.) When he learned about her suggestion, producer William Bacher said he wanted to keep the *Washington Square* title even though only New Yorkers probably knew it referred to an area in Greenwich Village. Also, accepting Gwen's idea could lead to other problems in Bacher's mind in terms of demands from her, such as raising her husband's salary in honor of getting a show named after him. "In which case, if it's called *The Ray Bolger Show*, we don't have any leverage against them, do we?" Bacher asked Garrison rhetorically.

Garrison blamed the show's failure on its scheduling. The program showed up every other week, alternating with *Wide Wide World*. "NBC didn't know what to make of the show, so they put it on opposite football," he said. "Can you imagine a musical comedy at this time slot?" The network did give it four nighttime shots as specials in 1957 after it left Sunday afternoons, but Garrison speculated NBC was just being charitable rather than considering it for an evening run: "They probably had an opening or two."

NBC replaced *Washington Square* with an arguably even more elaborate series, the highclass cultural offering *Omnibus*, which had aired on CBS and ABC at various times since Nov. 8, 1952. It ran in the *Washington Square* time slot through May 10, 1959, alternating with *Wide Wide World* in 1957-58 and *Kaleidoscope* in 1958-59.

Giant Step

Game. Ran on CBS Wednesdays 7:30–8 P.M. Nov. 7, 1956–May 29, 1957, opposite *Disneyland* on ABC and *Eddie Fisher Coke Time* (through Feb. 20) and *The Xavier Cugat Show* (from Feb. 27) and news on NBC. C: Bert Parks. EP: Steve Carlin. P: Ed Jurist. D: Seymour Robbie.

Can Do

Game. Ran on NBC Mondays 9–9:30 P.M. Nov. 26–Dec. 31, 1956, opposite *Life is Worth Living* on ABC and *I Love Lucy* on CBS. C: Robert Alda. P: Thomas Naud. D: Joe Cates.

You're on Your Own

Game. Ran on CBS Saturdays 10:30–11 P.M. Dec. 22, 1956–March 16, 1957, opposite *Ozark Jubilee* (from Dec. 29) on ABC and *Your Hit Parade* on NBC. C: Steve Dunne. EP: Jack Barry, Dan Enright, Robert Noah. P: Tom Donavan. D: Howard Merrill.

Air Time '57

Musical Variety. Ran on ABC Thursdays 10–10:30 P.M. Dec. 27, 1956–April 4, 1957, opposite *Playhouse 90* on CBS and *Lux Video Theater* on NBC. C: Vaughn Monroe, Bobby Hackett, the Elliot Lawrence Orchestra. P: Allan Stanley. D: Hal Davis. W: Harvey Orkin.

Blondie

Sitcom. Ran on NBC Fridays 8–8:30 P.M. Jan. 4–Sept. 27, 1957, opposite *The Adventures of Jim Bowie* on ABC and *West Point* on CBS. C: Arthur Lake (as Dagwood Bumstead), Pamela Britton (as Blondie Bumstead), Florenz Ames (as J.C. Dithers), Stuffy Singer (as Alexander), Ann Barnes (as Cookie), Elvia Allman (as Cora Dithers), Hal Peary (as Herb Woodley), Lucien Littlefield (as Mr. Beasley). P: William Harmon. D: Hal Yates. W: John L. Greene.

The Galen Drake Show

Children's. Ran on ABC Saturdays 7–7:30 P.M. Jan. 12–May 11, 1957, opposite *Beat the Clock* (through Feb. 2) and *The Vincent Lopez Show* (from Feb. 9–March 9) on CBS. C: Galen Drake, Stuart Foster, Rita Ellis.

Hold That Note

Game. Ran on NBC Tuesdays 10:30–11 P.M. Jan. 22–April 2, 1957, opposite *Do You Trust Your Wife?* on CBS. C: Bert Parks, Janice Gilbert, Johnny Olsen, Peter Van Steeden Orchestra. EP: Herb Wolf, Ed Wolf. P: Jack Rubin. D: Lloyd Gross.

Break the Bank debuted on radio three years before coming to TV on Oct. 22, 1948. It was considered the "big money" quiz show of the time, as it offered contestants a top prize of at least $1,000 if they correctly answered a series of questions (with one miss allowed) followed by a right response to the top question in the contestant's chosen category. But it was never as big a hit on television, and in the 1955-56 season when it flopped on ABC against its competition, *I've Got a Secret* on CBS (which had a top prize of just $80), the decision was made to make it more like *The $64,000 Question*, the game show which debuted on June 7, 1955, and soon was the #1 hit on TV.

On Oct. 9, 1956, *Break the $250,000 Bank* debuted on NBC in the time slot following *The $64,000 Question* on CBS. With a top prize amount nearly three times that of the CBS show, *Break the $250,000 Bank* nonetheless faltered because its format was cumbersome and did not allow players much room to get near the titular top dollar amount. During the three months that version ran, noted the show's director Lloyd Gross, "They couldn't get it past $65,000."

Along with little progress being made by contestants came general indifference from the public despite weak competition (ABC had no network show airing at the time, while CBS had the so-so *You Bet Your Life* knockoff *Do You Trust Your Wife?* starring ventriloquist Edgar Bergen and his dummies). "Herb Wolf and his dad, Ed, were the [executive] producers and made a change," Gross said. The result was *Hold That Note*.

Hold That Note was a music identification program involving two players with the object being to name three songs in a row played by the orchestra. There were 25 notes allowed per song, and whatever notes were left over after a song was identified went into a jackpot where each note was worth $50. The champion could play as often as he or she liked, though a loss meant they got only a portion of the jackpot.

Despite the music angle, *Hold That Note* essentially was the same show as *Break the $250,000 Bank*, with the same crew on and off stage (Bert Parks was the host, Ed Wolf's daughter Janice Gilbert his assistant and Johnny Olsen the announcer). But the meager group who liked the latter were not impressed with the revamp, and it attracted even fewer viewers, leading it to end a little over two months. As Gross put it, "Changing a show in the middle of the stream, you just don't do that."

Interestingly, the day before *Hold That Note* ended, CBS debuted *The $64,000 Challenge*, which allowed winners from *The $64,000 Question* to compete for even more money. The big winner there until it and *The $64,000 Question* went off amid scandal in 1958 was Teddy Nadler, who compiled a winning total of $252,000. Hmmm ... what amount does that sound like?

Close-Up

Talk. Ran on NBC Mondays through Fridays 1–1:30 P.M. Feb. 18, 1957–Jan. 31, 1958, opposite *Stand Up and Be Counted* (through Sept. 6) and news on CBS. C: Tex McCrary, Jinx Falkenburg. EP: George Heinemann. D: Marshall Stone. W: Hank Wexler.

Club 60

Musical Variety. Ran on NBC Mondays through Fridays 1:30–2:30 P.M. Feb. 18, 1957–Jan. 10, 1958,

Dennis James and Nancy Wright smile at someone away from the camera on *Club 60*. Apparently neither realized they would do the show for only five months before being canned.

opposite *As the World Turns* and *Our Miss Brooks*
reruns (through Sept. 13) and *Beat the Clock*
(from Sept. 16) on CBS. C: Mort Sahl (2/18–3/10),
Dennis James (3/13–8/16), Howard Miller (8/19–
1/10), Mike Douglas, Nancy Wright (2/18–8/16),
Barbara Becker (8/19–1/10), the Mellolarks, the

Art Van Damme Quartet, the Joseph Gallichio
Orchestra. P: Harry Trigg, Bob Dressler. D: Dave
Barnhizer.

Imagine launching a series and have your
star cancel on you just before its debut. That's

what happened on *Club 60*. Don Sherwood, a San Francisco radio host, was to be the star of the series, based in Chicago. "He was a hot radio disk jockey out there, and we sent a couple of executives out there and checked him out," recalled director Dave Barnhizer. All agreed on him doing the series, but Sherwood apparently was not prepared for what awaited him in Chicago.

When Sherwood arrived for rehearsal, the city was in a blizzard. That unsteadied him, as did the rehearsal. "We were highly organized, knew what we wanted the show to be—fast moving," said Barnhizer. He thought the rehearsal went fine until the next day, when Sherwood called the producers from Phoenix on his way back to San Francisco, saying he quit because the weather and the uptempo pace for the show disturbed him.

Out of desperation to replace Sherwood, razor-sharp satirist Mort Sahl got the nod to be the host. "Mort became the host for four weeks, and that was funny," Barnhizer said. "He was so out of the place, too hip for the ladies. He and I recognized how ludicrous it was."

The show nabbed a more appropriate host with game show veteran Dennis James took over. "He was absolutely just right to do the show, and whatever success it had was due to him," said Barnhizer. "He turned it into an Arthur Godfrey show, talking to the singers and so on." Those vocalists were Mike Douglas, Nancy Wright and the Mellolarks, backed by the Joseph Gallichio Orchestra (or Art Van Damme and his band on Wednesdays, when the orchestra had the day off).

Regarding future talk show host Douglas, Barnhizer said, "He was great. He always wanted to be the host." Barnhizer's assistant director on *Club 60*, Woody Fraser, later worked at a Cleveland station planning to do a talk show hosted by Don Adams before Barnhizer suggested Douglas as host. *The Mike Douglas Show* went on in Cleveland in 1961, then went into syndication in 1963 and had a long run as a daily series until 1982.

While Douglas didn't get to host *Club 60*, another man did, even though Dennis James was doing well—Chicago deejay Howard Miller. "They were trying to find something for Howard to do," Barnhizer said. "I think they were trying to promote him." The show was

retitled *The Howard Miller Show* and Barbara Becker replaced Wright with the change, but network viewers did not cotton to Miller as they had with James, and the show ended four months later.

Barnhizer blamed not Miller for the show's cancellation but rather the network for not getting the show sponsors. "NBC refused to try and sell it, and I think it was part of an effort to get rid of the orchestra," he said. Ironically, Barnhizer and the Joseph Gallichio Orchestra came back on NBC with another series a few years later; see *Patterns in Music* in 1961-62.

The Xavier Cugat Show

Musical Variety. Ran on NBC Wednesdays and Fridays 7:30–7:45 P.M. Feb. 27–May 24, 1957, opposite *Disneyland* (Wednesdays) and *The Adventures of Rin Tin Tin* (Fridays) on ABC and *Giant Step* (Wednesdays) and *Beat the Clock* (Fridays) on CBS . C: Xavier Cugat, Abbe Lane. D: Barry Shear.

The Marge and Gower Champion Show

Sitcom. Ran on CBS Sundays 7:30–8 P.M. March 31–June 9, 1957, opposite movies on ABC and *Circus Boy* on NBC. C: Marge and Gower Champion (as themselves), Jack Whiting (as Marge's dad), Buddy Rich (as Cozy), Peg La Centra (as Amanda), Barbara Perry (as Miss Weatherly), the Richard Pribor Orchestra. P: Joe Connelly, Bob Mosher, Paul Harrison. D: James Sheldon. W: Joe Connelly, Bob Mosher.

"It was a dancing sitcom," said Marge Champion in describing the format of her and her then-husband Gower's TV series, which alternated weekly with *The Jack Benny Program*. The Champions played themselves in the live offering, and other characters included Marge's dad, who was the couple's agent; Cozy, their drummer/accompanist; and Amanda, Marge's friend. There was a storyline for each show, and guest stars such as Dan Dailey, but mostly the emphasis was on the Champions dancing.

"We did a couple of big numbers with other people," Marge noted. "That really just killed us. I was 37 then, almost 38 years old, and I had just had my first child in November. The problems always were you had an eight-hour rehearsal day, and every time we had a lot of people on the show — extras, dancers, etc.—

Gower leaps in the air as Marge looks on in a routine for *The Marge and Gower Champion Show.*

we had to work around them." Given her age and recent birth, she grew weary quickly of the non-stop practices needed for the show.

Yet Ms. Champion did admit she remained very proud of one routine done on a show, danced to the tune of "They Didn't Believe Me." "It just seems to be the essence of that period for a young, married couple," she said. "We were just putting our stuff away for the night and started dancing. It was very simple." It also emphasized what she felt were her and Gower's strong point as a terpsichorean team — the ability to tell a story just by movements.

The Marge and Gower Champion Show aired live from New York City. Although it did not have the same high ratings as its alternate, *The Jack Benny Program*, it certainly was not a bomb against its weak competition, and the fact that it ended after just six shows ran is rather surprising. When asked what the reason was for its cancellation, Marge said, "I don't remember. I think it was too expensive. But I celebrated when it was cancelled." (No doubt by giving herself a rest.)

In the 1960s the Champions became better known as choreographers than a dancing duo. They eventually found themselves growing apart as a couple too and divorced in 1971. Gower died nine years later amid circumstances that sound like the way a showman would want to pass away — just before the Broadway opening of the last musical he directed, *42nd Street*.

Marge remained active as a choreographer and performer and enjoyed a renewed interest at the turn of the century when she participated in a Broadway revival of the musical *Follies*. "When they interview me the last six, seven, eight months, I haven't done anything but [talk about] *Follies*," she noted in mid-2001. She also lectures on dance on cruise ships and other venues.

What does Marge think of dancing nowadays? "All the choreography now seems to have 10 steps when you only need three," she said. As for those interested in her field, she added with the voice of experience, "If you want to still dance in your eighties, you better start early."

Susan's Show

Children's. Ran on CBS Saturdays 11–11:30 A.M. May 4, 1957–Jan. 18, 1958, opposite *Fury* on NBC. C: Susan Heinkel, John Coughlin (as Caesar P. Penguin). P: Frank Atlass. D: Barry McKinley.

Date with the Angels

Sitcom. Ran on ABC Fridays 10–10:30 P.M. May 10–June 28, 1957, opposite *The Lineup* on CBS and boxing on NBC, then ABC Fridays 9:30–10 P.M. July 5–Dec. 27, 1957, opposite *Schlitz Playhouse of Stars* on CBS and *The Big Moment* (through Sept. 13) and *The Thin Man* (from Sept. 20) on NBC, then ABC Wednesdays 9:30–10 P.M. Jan. 1–Jan. 29, 1958, opposite *I've Got a Secret* on CBS and *Kraft Television Theatre* on NBC. C: Betty White (as Vicki Angel), Bill Williams (as Gus Angel), Natalie Masters (as Wilma Clemson), Roy Engel (as George Clemson), Maudie Prickett (as Mr. Cassie Murphy), Richard Reeves (as Mr. Murphy, a/k/a "Murph"), Lillian Bronson (as Mrs. Drake), Gage Clark (as Dr. Gordon), Burt Mustin (as Mr. Finley), Richard Deacon (as Roger Finley), Jimmy Boyd (as Wheeler). P: Don Fedderson. D: James V. Kern. W: George Tibbles.

Popsicle Five-Star Comedy Party

Children's. Ran on ABC Saturdays 5:30–6 P.M. May 18–July 13, 1957. C: Paul Winchell, Ben Blue, Jerry Colonna, Ole Olsen and Chic Johnson, Senor Wences, Anne Martin, Bob Bean. P/D/W: Herb Moss.

The Arlene Francis Show

Variety. Ran on NBC Mondays through Fridays 10–10:30 A.M. Aug. 12, 1957–Feb. 21, 1958, opposite *The Fred Waring Show* (through Aug. 30) and *The Garry Moore Show* (from Sept. 2) on CBS. C: Arlene Francis, Hugh Downs, the Foursome, the Norman Paris Trio. P: Alan Beaumont. D: Ted Nathanson. W: George Kirgo, Mike Morris.

Hotel Cosmopolitan

Soap Opera. Ran on CBS Mondays through Fridays Noon–12:15 P.M. Aug. 19, 1957–April 11, 1958, opposite *Tic Tac Dough* on NBC. C: Donald Woods (as himself), Henderson Forsythe (as the house detective). P: Roy Winsor. D: John Desmond. W: Harold Gast.

1957-58

The Big Record

Musical Variety. Ran on CBS Wednesdays 8–9 P.M.
Sept. 18, 1957–March 19, 1958, opposite *Disneyland* and *Tombstone Territory* on ABC and *Wagon Train* and *Father Knows Best* on NBC, then CBS Wednesdays 8:30–9 P.M. March 26–June 11, 1958, opposite *Tombstone Territory* on ABC and *Father Knows Best* on NBC. C: Patti Page, the Vic Schoen Orchestra. EP: Lester Gottleib. P: Leo Cooley. D: Jerome Shaw.

The Polly Bergen Show

Musical Variety. Ran on NBC Saturdays 9–9:30 P.M. Sept. 21, 1957–May 31, 1958, opposite *The Lawrence Welk Show* on ABC and *The Gale Storm Show* on CBS. C: Polly Bergen, Bill Bergen, the Peter Gennaro Orchestra, the Luther Henderson, Jr., Orchestra. P/D: Bill Colleran; Colleran became just the director and Mel Brooks became producer with the second show. W: Mike Stewart, Phil Minoff, Tom Murray.

Harbourmaster (a/k/a Adventures at Scott Island)

Adventure. Ran on CBS Thursdays 8–8:30 P.M. Sept. 26–Dec. 26, 1957, opposite *Zorro* on ABC and *You Bet Your Life* on NBC, then ABC Sundays 8:30–9 P.M. Jan. 5–June 29, 1958, opposite *The Ed Sullivan Show* on CBS and *The Steve Allen Show* on NBC. C: Barry Sullivan (as Capt. David Scott), Paul Burke (as Jeff Kittridge), Nina Wilcox (as Anna Morrison), Michael Keens (as Cap'n Dan), Evan Elliott (as Danny). P/D: Felix Feist. W: Carey Wilbur.

O.S.S.

Adventure, from London's ATV network. Ran on ABC Thursdays 9:30–10 P.M. Sept. 26, 1957–Jan. 9, 1958, opposite *Playhouse 90* on CBS and *The Tennessee Ernie Ford Show* on NBC, then on ABC Mondays 7:30–8 P.M. Jan. 13–March 17, 1958, opposite *The Adventures of Robin Hood* on CBS and *The Price Is Right* on NBC. C: Ron Randell (as Capt. Frank Hawthorn), Lionel Murton (as the Chief), Robert Gallico (as Sgt. O'Brien). P: Jules Buck. D: Peter Maxwell, Robert Siodmak. W: Paul Dudley.

The Lux Show Starring Rosemary Clooney

Musical Variety. Ran on NBC Thursdays 10–10:30 P.M. Sept. 26, 1957–June 19, 1958, opposite *Navy Log* (through Jan. 23), *Modern Science Theater* (from Jan. 30 to March 13) and *Make Me Laugh* (from March 20) on ABC and *Playhouse 90* on CBS. C: Rosemary Clooney, Paula Kelly and the Modernaires (through March 1958), the Jones Boys (from March 1958), Frank DeVol and His Orchestra. P/D: Dick Darley. P: Joe Shribman. W: Danny Arnold, Howard Leeds, Tom Waldman.

Dick and the Duchess

Sitcom. Ran on CBS Saturdays 8:30–9 P.M. Sept. 28, 1957–March 22, 1958, opposite *Ozark Jubilee* on ABC and *The Perry Como Show* on NBC, then CBS Fridays 7:30–8 P.M. April 4–May 16, 1958, opposite *The Adventures of Rin Tin Tin* on ABC and *Truth or Consequences* on NBC. C: Patrick O'Neal (as Dick Starrett), Hazel Court (as Jane Starrett), Richard Wattis (as Peter Jamison), Michael Shepley (as Inspector Stark), Beatrice Varley (as Mathilda), Ronnie Stevens (as Rodney). P/D: Sheldon Reynolds. W: Harry Kurnitz.

Club Oasis

Variety. Ran on NBC Saturdays 9–9:30 P.M. Sept. 28, 1957–Sept. 6, 1958, opposite *The Lawrence Welk Show* on ABC and *The Gale Storm Show* on CBS. C (all summer of 1958): Spike Jones and His City Slickers, Helen Grayco, Joyce Jameson, Billy Barty. P/D: Greg Garrison. W: Mel Diamond, Sidney Miller.

The Gisele MacKenzie Show

Musical Variety. Ran on NBC Saturdays 9:30–10 P.M. Sept. 28, 1957–March 29, 1958, opposite *The Lawrence Welk Show* on ABC and *Have Gun, Will Travel* on CBS. C: Gisele MacKenzie, Jack Narz (through Jan. 11), Tom Kennedy (from Jan. 18), the Curfew Boys, the Joe Pryor Group, the Axel Stordahl Group. P/W: Charles Isaacs. D: Joe Landis. W: Hugh Wedlock, Howard Snyder, Billy Barnes, Bob Rogers.

Joan Caulfield practices her gestures while Marion Lorne studies a book on the French language in preparation for their globetrotting misadventures on *Sally*.

Sally

Sitcom. Ran on NBC Sundays 7:30–8 P.M. Sept. 15, 1957–March 30, 1958, opposite *Maverick* on ABC and *The Jack Benny Show* alternating with *Bachelor Father* on CBS. C: Joan Caulfield (as Sally Truesdale), Marion Lorne (as Mrs. Myrtle Banford), Gale Gordon (as Bascomb Bleacher; 1958), Johnny Desmond (as Jim Kendall; 1958), Arte Johnson (as Bascomb Bleacher, Jr.; 1958). P: Frank Ross. D: William Asher. W: Phil Shulken.

A top-billed actress in 1940s hit movies like *Blue Skies* and *Welcome Stranger*, Joan Caulfield saw her box-office appeal fade in the early 1950s and turned to television. Her first series effort had her assume the lead in *My Favorite Husband*. But what had been a hit for Lucille Ball on radio only prompted comparisons with Ball's hit performance on *I Love Lucy* on TV, and perhaps because of that *My Favorite Husband* ran less than three years, from Sept. 12, 1953 to Dec. 27, 1955.

Caulfield took another turn at bat with *Sally*. Now Joan played Sally Truesdale, a woman who trekked abroad with wealthy, ditzy Mrs. Myrtle Banford. Their encounters with natives almost always turned into disasters of some sort, but they managed to extricate themselves from them by the end of each show in true sitcom fashion. Caulfield's husband, Frank Ross, served as the show's producer and crafted the concept himself.

"He came to me with this idea," recalled director William Asher. "I included Marion Lorne in the cast, who was a friend. I think the first half of the show was funny, but didn't have a connection to the real life that we live.

"It was a woman traveling around the world and everyone she meets. It just didn't seem to reflect how our society functions. They changed the format, but it was too late." Indeed, the last seven episodes had Sally return to her old job as salesgirl at the Banford-Bleacher Department Store, where she worked directly for co-owner Bascomb Bleacher (whose son Junior tried awkwardly to follow his dad's footsteps) and found romance with co-worker Jim Kendall, an artist in the advertising section of the store.

Asher acknowledged that the misadventures that involved Sally and Myrtle were not unlike those of Lucy and Ethel on *I Love Lucy*, a show which he also directed. But, he emphasized, "*Lucy* at its heart was about a marriage. Everyone relates to that." He also did not fault the cast, noting that "Joan was wonderful. Everybody was good." He remained pals with Lorne, who became a frequent guest as Aunt Clara on *Bewitched* from 1964 until her death in 1968, winning a posthumous Emmy for her work there. Asher produced and directed *Bewitched* while his then-wife, Elizabeth Montgomery, starred in the show.

As for Caulfield, she and Ross divorced in 1960, two years after *Sally* had sunk. She then emphasized working in the theater and rarely on TV (or movies, for that matter). She died in 1991 at age 69.

The Eve Arden Show

Sitcom. Ran on CBS Tuesdays 8:30–9 P.M. Sept. 17, 1957–March 25, 1958, opposite *The Life and Legend of Wyatt Earp* on ABC and *The George Gobel Show* alternating with *The Eddie Fisher Show* on NBC. C: Eve Arden (as Liza Hammond), Allyn Joslyn (as George Howell), Frances Bavier (as Nora), Gail Stone (as Jenny Hammond), Karen Greene (as Mary Hammond). EP: Robert Sparks. P: Julian Claman, Edmund Hartmann. D: Sheldon Leonard, John Rich. W: Sol Saks, Sherman Marks.

Writer Emily Kimbrough (1899–1989) did only one TV series as a regular, the short-lived *Who's Whose* (see 1950-51). However, her 1948 book about her making lectures on tour, *It Gives Me Great Pleasure*, served as the inspiration for Eve Arden's return to television after a year layoff. Previously she had done *Our Miss Brooks* on radio from 1948 to 1957 and on TV from 1952 to 1956; *The Eve Arden Show* was nowhere nearly as prosperous, running just 26 episodes.

Brought in to write the pilot for the series was Sol Saks. "I was working on another show called *Mr. Adams and Eve*, and they wanted me to do the pilot for Eve Arden," Saks recalled, with "they" being CBS executives. "I said I wouldn't, I didn't have the time. And then they stopped production on *Mr. Adams and Eve* to let me do it." (*Mr. Adams and Eve* began as a midseason replacement on CBS on Jan. 4, 1957, and ran until Sept. 23, 1958.)

Saks said his memory about concocting the script was sketchy. "I probably talked to some people," he said. "I think they had the basic premise of the story, that she was a guest speaker." He recalled what he presented to network officials made them happy but added, "Usually, you came in with an idea, and they would accept it. I don't remember too many meetings about the show."

Joining Saks for the pilot was Sheldon Leonard as director, who performed the same task at the time on *The Danny Thomas Show*. "Both Sheldon and I were doing the pilot when the network knew we were not available for the series," Saks said. However, the CBS officials did not inform potential sponsors for the series of that fact, nor apparently Arden either. In her 1985 autobiography, *The Three Phases of Eve*, Arden wrote of her dismay in learning Saks and Leonard were not available beyond the pilot, and blamed the proliferation of writers with their own take on the material as the reason for it failing, even though it followed the hit *The Phil Silvers Show*.

Saks concurred that Arden's assessment was right, and that unlike *Bewitched*, a series where he also wrote just the pilot and no other episodes, the writers did not follow his basic premise for the series. What did continue in the rest of the run were the basic characters, which beside Arden's Liza Hammond were Liza's agent, George Howell, her twin daughters Jenny and Mary, and her mother, Nora, who took care of Liza's daughters and house while the author was on tour.

The sitcom was Arden's second-to-last regular TV series until *The Mothers-in-Law*, which ran from 1967 to 1969. The actress playing her mother, Frances Bavier, went on to play Aunt Bea on *The Andy Griffith Show* from 1960 to 1968 and *Mayberry, R.F.D.* from 1968 to 1971.

The Court of Last Resort

Drama. Ran on NBC Fridays 8–8:30 P.M. Oct. 4, 1957–April 11, 1958, opposite *The Adventures of Jim Bowie* on ABC and *Trackdown* on CBS. C: Lyle Bettger (as Sam Larsen), Paul Birch (as Erle Stanley Gardner). P: Elliott Lewis, Jules Goldstone. D: John M. Lucas. W: Leonard Heideman.

Erle Stanley Gardner was quite a hot property on TV in the fall of 1957. The author saw his series of books featuring sleuthing lawyer Perry Mason start a nine-year run on CBS on Sept. 21 starring Raymond Burr in the title role. Nearly two weeks after that debut, Erle himself became portrayed on TV in a series based another of his creations, the *Court of Last Resort*.

The idea was an extension of the basic appeal of *Perry Mason*: Review the cases of people convicted of crimes who claimed to be innocent. Gardner led a seven-member group of male criminal law experts who investigated people's claims to determine if they were wrongly detained. The Court of Last Resort was not a ruling or legislative body, but if the members found evidence clearing a person, they did

present it to the authorities and actually freed some persons from jail.

Tracking down the leads for the Court on TV was Sam Larsen. Court member themselves paid a rather minor role on most of the shows, with Gardner being seen most frequently to discuss the case. Other than court members and Larsen, the other characters had different names from the real-life men and women whose stories were dramatized, or as *Dragnet* stated in its epilogue, "The names have been changed to protect the innocent."

In a letter from Bettger, the actor prefaced that he had limited memories of doing *The Court of Last Resort*. "It was, after all, 40-some years ago, and my memory is not that good anymore at age 86."

Nevertheless, he was able to remember that regarding its short run, "It was a shock and *great* disappointment to me, and *still* is. I thought it was a damn good show, and was at a loss to explain its failure — except for one reason.

"The network and our producers selected a Friday night at 8 P.M. to run the show — just about the poorest day and time in those days on about all of TV. Timing is very important in TV, then and even now, though it has indeed changed drastically." Whether it was the time slot or some other factor, NBC adjourned *The Court of Last Resort* from its lineup after six months. For some unknown reason, ABC reran the series Wednesday evenings from Aug. 1959 to Feb. 17, 1960.

By the way, Gardner technically could be credited for another TV series in 1957. *The Edge of Night*, a daily soap opera on CBS that started April 2, 1956, was based on the *Perry Mason* daily radio series that ran from 1943 to 1955. But Gardner did not like the melodramatic aspects of that series and denied letting Mason come to TV in that form, so the sponsor modified the radio show and its characters into being *The Edge of Night*. The show ran until Dec. 28, 1984, spending its last nine years on ABC.

The Guy Mitchell Show

Musical Variety. Ran on ABC Mondays 8–8:30 P.M. Oct. 7, 1957–Jan. 13, 1958, opposite *The George Burns and Gracie Allen Show* on CBS and *The Restless Gun* on NBC. C: Guy Mitchell, Dolores Hawkins, The Ted Cappy Dancers, The Van Alexander Orchestra. P: Phil Cohan. D: Kevin Jonson. W: Ben Starr, William Derman.

Keep It in the Family

Game. Ran on ABC Saturdays 7:30–8 P.M. Oct. 12, 1957–Feb. 8, 1958, opposite *Perry Mason* on CBS and *People Are Funny* on NBC. C: Keefe Brasselle (Oct. 12 only), Bill Nimmo (from Oct. 19). P/W: Art Stark. D: Mickey Trenner. W: Leonard Stern.

What's It For?

Game. Ran on NBC Saturdays 10–10:30 P.M. Oct. 12, 1957–Jan. 4, 1958, opposite *Mike Wallace Interviews* on ABC and *Gunsmoke* on CBS. C: Hal March, Abe Burrows, Hans Conried, Betsy Palmer, Toni Gilman (November), Lisa Ferraday (December–January). P: Ed Jurist. D: Seymour Robbie.

The Frank Sinatra Show

Variety/Anthology. Ran on ABC Fridays 9–9:30 P.M. Oct. 18, 1957–June 27, 1958, opposite *Mr. Adams and Eve* (through Feb. 7) and *The Phil Silvers Show* (from Feb. 14) on CBS and *M Squad* on NBC. C: Frank Sinatra, Nelson Riddle and His Orchestra. P/W: Paul Dudley. D: William Self.

Frank Sinatra was his own worst enemy in doing TV series. I make that strong comment after reading reviews and articles on his shows and talking with their directors. "The Voice" regarded early TV casually. Viewers noticed that and ignored him in response. As a result, he never had the long TV runs other singers such as Perry Como and Dinah Shore managed in the 1950s.

The first *Frank Sinatra Show* ran on CBS from Oct. 7, 1950 to April 1, 1952. Watching the Saturday night debut was director John Peyser, who idolized Sinatra but hated the program. "What a disaster, you cannot believe," Peyser said. The next morning Peyser got a call to be the show's director, agreed to do so—and found himself in the midst of chaos.

Sinatra, then living in Los Angeles, would arrive in New York Friday mornings to do his live show the next day, then leave immediately to return home. His inaccessibility for most of the week made it almost impossible to plan songs and sketches for the series.

"We had a new producer every other week, pretty much," Peyser said. "Rehearsal? You

never heard of it." Peyser thought Sinatra's other problems such as declining record sales added to his lack of focus on the series. Tired of a situation which gave him an ulcer, Peyser left after 32 weeks. The show ended one year later.

In 1957 ABC gave Sinatra another series, thinking that his renewed popularity would make this *Frank Sinatra Show* a hit. "I was thrilled when they hired me," director William Self said. "I thought, 'This show is going to be a success.'"

Unfortunately, Sinatra repeated his earlier mistakes, and compounded them. "He didn't want to rehearse any more than he had to, and on the singing numbers, he didn't believe we had to rehearse them," Self said. "It was difficult on our guest stars."

Sinatra now also wanted to alternate variety shows with dramas. "He didn't want to do a show every week that would require a lot of effort," Self said. This was not what Self had expected.

"I came into the show after it was conceived and sold," he said. "At that time, it was going to be Frank in a nightclub with guests." But Sinatra ignored live shows, which were the custom at the time, in favor of quickly shot dramas, some starring and some just hosted by him. With that setup, Self noted, "I think the public didn't know what to expect on the show," and the ratings slumped. By the time Sinatra made changes, it was a lost cause. "I felt he was trying to make it work, but not putting in as much energy as he should have," said Self of the series overall.

Sinatra later had some highly rated and praised 1960s music specials. Had he been as attentive to his TV series as he was with those productions, we might have remembered him as a TV star as well as a top performer in music and movies. Because we don't, he has no one to blame but himself.

The Patrice Munsel Show

Musical Variety. Ran on ABC Fridays 8:30–9 P.M. Oct. 18–Dec. 27, 1957, opposite *Dick Powell's Zane Grey Theater* on CBS and *The Life of Riley* on NBC, then ABC Fridays 9:30–10 P.M. Jan. 3–June 13, 1958, opposite *Schlitz Playhouse of Stars* on CBS and *The Thin Man* on NBC. C: Patrice Munsel, the Martins Quartet (Ralph Blane, Hugh Martin, Phyllis Rogers, Jo-Jean Rogers), the Charles

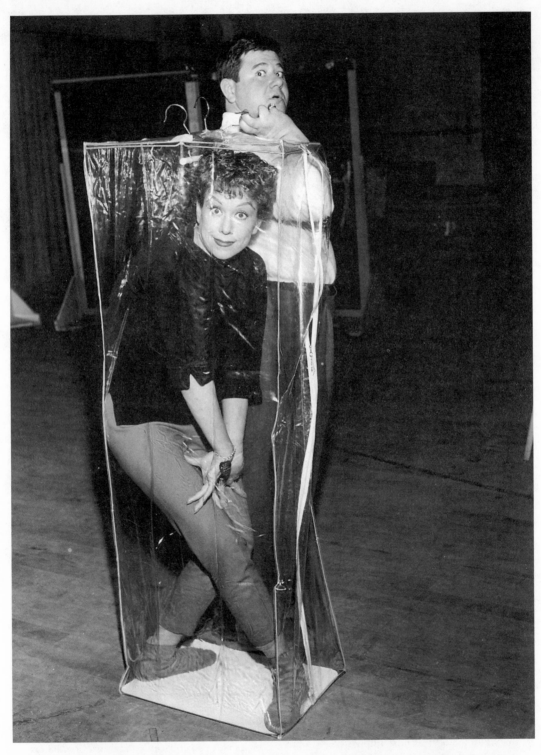

I see it, but I still don't believe it: Buddy Hackett tries to wrap up classy opera vocalist Patrice Munsel in a plastic garment bag during rehearsal for the March 21, 1958, edition of *The Patrice Munsel Show*. Don't try this at home, kids, even if you do leave the zipper open at the top like they did.

Sanford Orchestra. P: Clark Jones, Robert Schuler. D: Clark Jones.

A Metropolitan Opera soprano hosting her own live variety show from New York? Try getting that concept past a network president today. Yet that's what happened back in 1957 with the debut of *The Patrice Munsel Show*.

Moreover, the show's co-producer and director, Clark Jones, said Munsel was not as bad an idea to appeal to the masses as one might think of most opera stars. "She could do anything — opera, musical comedy, ballads — and sang beautifully," he said.

Regarding the format, Jones said, "It was mostly singing, but there was repartee. We also had Buddy Hackett on that show once." A refined songstress doing jokes with a comedian with a slurred Brooklyn dialect — the mind boggles. Jones added that Larry Gelbart, later the head writer of the *M*A*S*H* TV series and many hit comedy movies, was one of the show's writers.

Augmenting the goings-on were the musical foursome the Martins Quartet, composed of sisters Phyllis and Jo-Jean Rogers and singer/songwriters Ralph Blane and Hugh Martin. The group had no hits, but they had been popular on radio, where they were heard on several shows, and could boast that the men wrote such hits as "Buckle Down, Winsocki" and "The Trolley Song" in the 1940s.

With all that going, what went wrong? According to Jones, the show's failure stemmed from the hostess being too talented and not empathetic enough to home viewers. "It was because she was an entertainment athlete," he said. "She was not vulnerable. She did not have the lovability [Judy] Garland had."

ABC tried Munsel both before and after the ill-fated *Frank Sinatra Show* (see next entry), but neither time slot worked. Her TV career thereafter never amounted to much, though she did act in, of all things, *The Wild Wild West* in 1969. But Munsel participated in other venues of entertainment beside TV and opera. She did Broadway (*A Musical Jubilee*, a revue ran 92 performances in 1975 with a cast including Lillian Gish, Tammy Grimes, John Raitt and Dick Shawn) and starred in the 1953 film *Melba*. Her husband, Robert Schuler, co-produced *The Patrice Munsel Show*.

Dotto

Game. Ran on CBS Mondays through Fridays 11:30 A.M.–Noon Jan. 6–Aug. 15, 1958, opposite *Truth or Consequences* on NBC, and NBC Tuesdays 9–9:30 P.M. July 1–Aug. 12, 1958, opposite *Broken Arrow* on ABC and *To Tell the Truth* on CBS. C: Jack Narz. P: Ed Jurist. D: Jerome Schnur.

The End of the Rainbow

Game. Ran on NBC Saturdays 10–10:30 P.M. Jan. 11–Feb. 15, 1958, opposite *Mike Wallace Interviews* on ABC and *Gunsmoke* on CBS. C: Art Baker (through Jan. 25), Bob Barker (from Feb. 1). EP: Ralph Edwards. P: Edwin Bailey. D: Tom Belcher. W: Rick Sanville, Art Jacobson, Henry Hoople.

Love That Jill

Sitcom. Ran on ABC Mondays 8–8:30 P.M. Jan. 20–April 28, 1958, opposite *The George Burns and Gracie Allen Show* on CBS and *The Restless Gun* on NBC. C: Anne Jeffreys (as Jill Johnson), Robert Sterling (as Jack Gibson), James Lydon (as Richard), Betty Lynn (as Pearl), Polly Rose (as Myrtle), Barbara Nichols (as Ginger), Nancy Hadley (as Melody), Kay Elhardt (as Peaches). P/W: Alex Gottleib. D: William Seiter.

Sid Caesar Invites You

Comedy Variety. Ran on ABC Sundays 9–9:30 P.M. Jan. 26–May 25, 1958, opposite *General Electric Theater* on CBS and *The Dinah Shore Chevy Show* on NBC. C: Sid Caesar, Imogene Coca, Carl Reiner, Paul Reed, Milt Kamen, the Bernie Green Orchestra. P: Hal Janis. D: Frank Bunetta. W: Mel Tolkin, Neil Simon, Mel Brooks, Mike Stewart, Danny Simon, Larry Gelbart.

The Betty White Show

Comedy Variety. Ran on ABC Wednesdays 9:30–10 P.M. Feb. 5–April 30, 1958, opposite *I've Got a Secret* on CBS and *Kraft Television Theatre* on NBC. C: Betty White, Johnny Jacobs, Del Moore, Reta Shaw, Frank Nelson, the Frank DeVol Orchestra. P: Don Fedderson. D: James V. Kern. W: George Tibbles, Si Rose, Seaman Jacobs.

Make Me Laugh

Game. Ran on ABC Thursdays 10–10:30 P.M. March 20–June 12, 1958, opposite *Playhouse 90* on CBS and *The Lux Show Starring Rosemary Clooney* on NBC. C: Robert Q. Lewis. P: Mort Green,

George Foster, Pat Weaver, Johnny Stearns. D: Johnny Stearns.

How Do You Rate?

Game. Ran on CBS Mondays through Thursdays 10:30–11 A.M. March 31–June 26, 1958, opposite *Treasure Hunt* on NBC. C: Tom Roddy, Dr. Robert Goldenson. EP: Steve Carlin. P: Ronald N. Durbin. D: Seymour Robbie.

Wingo

Game. Ran on CBS Tuesdays 8:30–9 P.M. April 1–May 6, 1958, opposite *The Life and Legend of Wyatt Earp* on ABC and *The George Gobel Show* alternating with *The Eddie Fisher Show* on NBC. C: Bob Kennedy. P: Dave Brown. D: Kevin Joe Jonson.

Stars of Jazz

Musical Variety, seen locally in Los Angeles two years before going on the network. Ran on ABC Fridays 8:30–9 P.M. April 18–June 6, 1958, opposite *Dick Powell's Zane Grey Theater* on CBS and *The Life of Riley* on NBC, then ABC Mondays 9–9:30 P.M. June 9–Sept. 1, 1958, opposite *The Danny Thomas Show* (through June 30) and *I Love Lucy* reruns (from July 7) on CBS and *Twenty-One* on NBC, then ABC Thursdays 10–10:30 P.M. Sept. 11–Oct. 1958, opposite *Playhouse 90* on CBS and *The Price Is Right* (through Sept. 18) and *You Bet Your Life* (from Sept. 25) on NBC, and then ABC Sundays 9:30–10 P.M. Nov.–Nov. 30, 1958, opposite *Alfred Hitchcock Presents* on CBS and *The Dinah Shore Chevy Show* on NBC. C: Bobby Troup. EP: Peter Robinson. P: Jimmie Baker. D: Hap Weyman.

Jefferson Drum

Western. Ran on NBC Fridays 8–8:30 P.M. April 25–Sept. 5, 1958, opposite *The Adventures of Jim Bowie* on ABC and *Trackdown* on CBS, then NBC Fridays 7:30–8 P.M. Sept. 26–Oct. 10, 1958, opposite *The Adventures of Rin Tin Tin* on ABC and *The Boing Boing Show* (Sept. 26 and Oct. 3) and *Your Hit Parade* (from Oct. 10) on CBS, and then NBC Thursdays 7:30–8 P.M. Oct. 16, 1958–April 23, 1959, opposite *Leave It to Beaver* on ABC and *I Love Lucy* reruns on CBS. C: Jeff Richards (as Jefferson Drum), Cyril Delevanti (as Lucius Coin), Eugene Martin (as Joey Drum), Robert Stevenson (as Big Ed). P: Matthew Rapf. D: Christian Nyby. W: E. Jack Neuman.

This Is Music

Music. Ran on ABC Fridays 8:30–9 P.M. June 13–Sept. 5, 1958, opposite *Dick Powell's Zane Grey Theater* (through July 11) and *Destiny* (from July 18) on CBS and *The Life of Riley* on NBC, then ABC Thursdays 10–10:30 P.M. Nov. 1958–May 21, 1959, opposite *Playhouse 90* on CBS and *You Bet Your Life* on NBC. C: Colin Male, Ramona Burnett, Bud Chase, Lee Fogel, Paula Jane, Gail Johnson, Wanda Lewis, Bob Shreeve, Bob Smith, The O'Neill Dancers.

For Love or Money

Game. Ran on CBS Mondays through Fridays 10–10:30 A.M. June 30, 1958–Jan. 30, 1959, opposite *Dough-Re-Mi* on NBC. C: Bill Nimmo. EP: Walt Framer. P: Bob Wald. D: Ken Whelan.

Haggis Baggis

Game. Ran on NBC Mondays through Fridays 2:30–3 P.M. June 30, 1958–June 19, 1959, opposite *Music Bingo* (from Dec. 5, 1958 to April 10, 1959) and *The Gale Storm Show* reruns (from April 13) on ABC and *Art Linkletter's House Party* on CBS and on NBC Mondays 7:30–8 P.M. June 30–Sept. 29, 1958, opposite *Cowtown Rodeo* (through Sept. 8) on ABC and *The Adventures of Robin Hood* on CBS. C: Jack Linkletter (nighttime), Fred Robbins (through Feb. 6), Dennis James (from Feb. 9). EP: Joe Cates. P: David Brown. D: Ted Nathanson.

Today Is Ours

Soap Opera. Ran on NBC Mondays through Fridays 3–3:30 P.M. June 30–Dec. 26, 1958, opposite *American Bandstand* (through Sept. 26) and *Beat the Clock* (from Oct. 13) on ABC and *The Big Payoff* on CBS. C: Patricia Benoit (as Laura Manning), Patrick O'Neal (as Karl Manning), Ernest Graves (as Glenn Turner), Peter Lazar (as Nick "Nicky" Manning), Joyce Lear (as Leslie Williams Manning), Chase Crosley (as Ellen Wilson), John McGovern (as Peter Hall). P: Robert M. Rehbock. D: Walter Gorman. Creators, W: Julian Funt, David Lesan.

Today Is Ours told the story of a divorcee trying to manage being a working mother. Though she was not its star, the story resonated with actress Chase Crosley, who played a pal of star Patricia Benoit's character Laura Manning. Crosley went through a few personal and professional tribulations over the years, beginning with her joining Today Is Ours.

Crosley acted in several off–Broadway plays in the 1950s before she obtained an agent prior to auditioning for *Today Is Ours*, which proved to be lucky for her. After getting a Mexican divorce, Crosley returned to New York to learn she had won the role, only to be dismayed that her contract called for her to do it three years. Her agent intervened and reduced that requirement, but then she faced a bigger threat to face on the air.

"The third day in, I had done bits and pieces on TV, like *Camera Three* [a Sunday morning dramatic anthology series], but there was a ton of exposition here," she said. "My character was a very neurotic person, and I went up." She had a TelePrompTer device to cue her lines on the live show but couldn't see it, and though she made it through the scene, the incident worried her.

"Several weeks I would have nightmares at night about it," she said. Finally she went to her acting coach, Michael Egan, for help. "He called me in and gave me specific things to do on every line. There are techniques that help out in cases like that."

She also made a key decision regarding her character. "*Today Is Ours* is when I decided I didn't like the idea that people were black and white, good and bad," she said. "I though that people can be nice in some areas and mean in others. I tried to make my villains as sympathetic as possible."

With Crosley pioneering a new kind of not-all-evil foe, along with featuring a divorce heroine, *Today Is Ours* was a soap opera ahead of its time in the conservative 1950s and lasted only six months. Supposedly some of the cast appeared in the early episodes of its successor, *Young Dr. Malone*, but Crosley did not recall it. "I was just so involved in what I was doing that I had no recollection of that," she said. However, she did join *Young Dr. Malone* from 1961 to 1963 as a regular, followed by a steady gig on *Guiding Light* from 1963 to 1968.

She couldn't continue to do soaps in a stressful marriage raising two children in the 1970s, so she became an English teacher in Chappaqua, N.Y. She later became a drama teacher for 12 years in various New York schools, then retired in 1990 to go into acting in community theater. Her return brought her acclaim and a small part on *Guiding Light* again in the 1990s, but she rejected any long-term TV roles.

"It doesn't interest me that much," she said. "I like television, but I love theater." She has overall fond memories of *Today Is Ours* and noted surprisingly in 2001 that "I still have people who remember me from it."

Anybody Can Play

Game. Ran on ABC Sundays 8:30–9 P.M. July 6–Sept. 28, 1958, opposite *The Ed Sullivan Show* on CBS and *The Steve Lawrence–Eydie Gorme Show* (through Aug. 31) on NBC, then ABC Mondays 9:30–10 P.M. Oct. 6–Dec. 8, 1958, opposite *The Ann Sothern Show* on CBS and *The Alcoa-Goodyear Theater* on NBC. C: George Fenneman. P: John Guedel. D: John Alexander. W: Mannie Manheim, Eddie Mills, Marion Pollack.

E.S.P.

Game, then Anthology. Ran on ABC Fridays 9–9:30 P.M. July 11–Aug. 22, 1958, opposite *The Phil Silvers Show* on CBS and *M Squad* on NBC. C: Vincent Price. P: George Wolf, Leo Morgan. D: Lou Sposa.

Kitty Foyle

Soap Opera. Ran on NBC Mondays through Fridays 2:30–3 P.M. Jan. 13–June 27, 1958, opposite *Art Linkletter's House Party* on CBS. C: Kathleen Murray (as Kitty Foyle), Bob Hastings (as Ed Foyle), Larry Robinson (as Mack Foyle), Ralph Dunn (as Pop Foyle), Kay Medford (as Sophie Foyle), Marie Worsham (as Stacylea Balla), Judy Lewis (as Molly Scharf), William Redfield (as Wyn Stafford), Valerie Cossart (as Olivia Stafford), Conard Fowkes (as Flip Martin), Lee Bergere (as Nick Amsted), Les Damon (as Rosie Rittenhouse). EP: Charles Irving. D: Hal Cooper, Gary Simpson. W: Carlton E. Morse.

Lucky Partners

Game. Ran on NBC Mondays through Fridays 2–2:30 P.M. June 30–Aug. 22, 1958, opposite *Beat the Clock* on CBS. C: Carl Cordell. EP: Martin Stone. P: Carl Jampel. D: Dick Schneider.

1958-59

The George Hamilton IV Show

Musical Variety. Ran on CBS Saturdays Noon–1 P.M. Sept. 6–Sept. 27, 1958, opposite *True Story* and *Detective's Diary* on NBC, then ABC Mondays through Fridays Noon–12:30 P.M. April 13–May 29, 1959, opposite *Love of Life* on CBS and *Tic Tac Dough* on NBC. C: George Hamilton, Mary Glick, Jan Crockett (1958), Jo Davis (1958), the Country Lads (1958), the Tennessee Wildcats (1958), Clint Miller (1959), Roy Clark (1959), Buck Ryan (1959), Smitty Idwin (1959), Alec Houston (1959), Jack French (1959). P: Herb Benton (1958), Don Tucker (1959). D: Bill Linden (1958), Tommy Winkler (1959).

Northwest Passage

Adventure. Ran on NBC Sundays 7:30–8 P.M. Sept. 14, 1958–Jan. 4, 1959, opposite *Maverick* on ABC and *The Jack Benny Program* alternating with *Bachelor Father* on CBS, then NBC Fridays 7:30–8 P.M. January–July, 1959, opposite *The Adventures of Rin Tin Tin* on ABC and *Your Hit Parade* (through April 24) and *Rawhide* (from May 1) on CBS, then NBC Tuesdays 7:30–8 P.M. July–Sept. 8, 1959, opposite *Cheyenne* alternating with *Sugarfoot* on ABC and *Stars in Action* on CBS. C: Keith Larsen (as Major Robert Rogers), Buddy Ebsen (as St. Hunk Marriner), Don Burnett (as Ensign Langdon Towne), Philip Tonge (as Gen. Amherst). EP: Samuel Marx. P: Adrian Samish. W: Sloan Nibbley, George Waggner.

County Fair

Game/Variety. Ran on NBC Mondays through Fridays 4:30–5 P.M. Sept. 22, 1958–Sept. 25, 1959, opposite *American Bandstand* on ABC and *The Edge of Night* on CBS. C: Bert Parks, Bill Gale and His Fairgrounds Philharmonic. P: Perry Cross. D: Joe Durand. W: Bob Carmen, Mike Marmer, Larry Miller.

County Fair first opened up as a broadcasting attraction on radio's Blue Network (later to become ABC) on July 10, 1945. Before the end of the year it moved to CBS radio, where it stayed until 1950. It had contestants play carnival games. The format remained intact when two packagers bought the rights to the title and sold it to NBC. The network as-

signed a producer on staff, Perry Cross, to handle the TV series.

But don't tell Cross his version was merely a game show. As he put it, "It was a physical audience participation show. If they did this, they got a prize. But they were always trying to integrate variety elements—people singing songs and so on. Daytime didn't have anything like that on at the time."

Daytime also didn't have anything like what went wrong on the live show from New York on April 7, 1959, involving a competing couple. "A contestant's wife was supposed to be blindfolded and stamp out balloons on the floor," recalled Cross. "If she didn't succeed, they were going to 'bomb him out.' So they gave him a make believe firecracker. There also was a box over his head to cover him with flour too."

The firecracker was supposed to do a simple pop at the same time the flour was dropped, but Cross noted, "Unbeknownst to anyone, there was apparently flour in it [the fake firecracker] too. The flour fused and ignited and became combustible, and there was a flash fire which ignited him too." Viewers saw the man run out of camera view in flames. He survived albeit with burns to his hands and face, while Cross and company got unwanted publicity from the stunt gone wrong. "The newspapers called the show *County Fire*. It was not my greatest moment."

Nevertheless, Cross said the event had no bearing on why *County Fair* ran just a year. He attributed it instead to the show's mix of stunts, singing and other elements that never quite jelled. "It was a bastardized format, and they were trying a new form," he said.

Cross would go on to do *The Tonight Show* hosted by Jack Paar, and then endure the huge bomb *The Jerry Lewis Show* (see 1963-64). *County Fair* host Bert Parks, who had been on TV almost continuously on game shows since *Break the Bank* started in 1948, did this show while hosting *Masquerade Party* on the nighttime schedule. He remained in demand after *County Fair* ended too, as on the Monday after its cancellation (Sept. 28, 1959), he hosted the last four weeks of *The Big Payoff* before it ended its nearly eight-year run on daytime TV.

The Patti Page Oldsmobile Show

Musical Variety. Ran on ABC Wednesdays 9:30–10 P.M. Sept. 24, 1958–November 1958, opposite *I've Got a Secret* on CBS and *Bat Masterson* on NBC, then ABC Mondays 10–10:30 P.M. Dec. 1958–March 16, 1959, opposite *The Westinghouse Desilu Playhouse* on CBS and *The Arthur Murray Party* on NBC. C: Patti Page, Rocky Cole, the Jerry Packer Singers, the Matt Mattox Dancers, the Vic Schoen Orchestra. P: Ted Mills. AP: George Charles. D: David Geisel. W: Sheldon Keller.

The Ed Wynn Show

Sitcom. Ran on NBC Thursdays 8–8:30 P.M. Sept. 25, 1958–Jan. 1, 1959, opposite *Zorro* on ABC and *December Bride* on CBS. C: Ed Wynn (as John Beamer), Jacklyn O'Donnell (as Laurie), Sherry Alberoni (as Midge), Herb Vigran (as Ernest "Ernie" Henshaw), Jesslyn Fax. P: Ben Feiner, Jr. D: William Russell. W: Devery Freeman.

"It wasn't easy to stop the baggy pants, you know, and go legitimate overnight. And it's nice to know that the believability of the new Ed Wynn seems to be a welcome substitute for the funny hats of 'The Perfect Fool.' This kind of believability, ladies and gentlemen, spiced with warmth and wisdom and humor, is the quality that you can expect to find week after week in John Beamer, the man I play in the series"— Ed Wynn in a speech to potential sponsors at the end of the pilot for *The Ed Wynn Show*.

The Ed Wynn of *The Ed Wynn Show* of 1958 was quite a different comedian than the one of the variety show with the same name nine years earlier (see 1949-50 for details on that). The jokester with the funny costumes in outlandish sketches vanished in favor of a more restrained albeit still impish persona in a sitcom filmed in Hollywood with the requisite laugh track. Wynn got the series on the strength of this new image seen in his Emmy-nominated acting on "Requiem for a Heavyweight" on *Playhouse 90* in 1956 and "On Borrowed Time" on *Hallmark Hall of Fame* in 1957. Unfortunately, his sitcom lasted even less time than his earlier series did.

Wynn played John Beamer, a widowed retiree raising two granddaughters in his home.

Laurie was in college, and Midge's dad was on tour of duty in Saudi Arabia while her mother was dead. "It's good for the house, and it's good for me," he noted on the show's pilot about the living arrangement, while failing to address exactly how the two girls were related to each other. The other regular, Ernie Henshaw, was John's friend of 30 years who also was his attorney.

A writer on the show felt the series flopped by what it had Beamer do. "*The Ed Wynn Show* made the fatal mistake of setting itself up as a sort of anthology show," wrote Devery Freeman in a letter to me. "He played a busybody old man helping people with *their* problems. A good family show must turn inward upon itself dealing with its own problems." Indeed, the first show had Wynn's character spend more time with Laurie's college friends than with Midge, and involved them in a boycott of local businesses to protest how his unnamed Midwestern hometown slighted the students—a setup as humorless in execution as it sounds.

Freeman added that apart from that misstep, he respected the cast and crew in the production ("all involved were talented pros"). He previously worked with Wynn in 1957 in a one-hour comedy special called *The Great American Hoax* which won Freeman a Writers Guild of America award.

In contrast, *The Ed Wynn Show* won no awards and was off the air after New Year's Day 1959. NBC replaced it by shifting another short-lived series, *Steve Canyon* (q.v.). Wynn guested often on TV thereafter until his death in 1966.

The Further Adventures of Ellery Queen

Mystery. Ran on NBC Fridays 8–9 P.M. Sept. 26, 1958–Sept. 4, 1959, opposite *Walt Disney* on ABC and *Trackdown* (through Jan. 2) and *The Jackie Gleason Show* (through Jan. 2) and *Rawhide* (from Jan. 9) on CBS. C: George Nader (as Ellery Queen), Lee Philips (as Ellery Queen). EP: Albert McCleery. D: Walter Grauman, Alan Cooke, Livia Granito, Lamont Johnson, Alan Hanson. W: Nicholas E. Baehr.

Behind Closed Doors

Drama. Ran on NBC Thursdays 9–9:30 P.M. Oct. 2, 1958–April 9, 1959, opposite *The Pat Boone–Chevy*

Showroom on ABC and *Dick Powell's Zane Grey Theater* on CBS. C: Bruce Gordon (as Commander Matson). P: Sam Gallu.

The "closed doors" viewers went behind in this series were those of Rear Admiral Ellis M. Zacharias, USN (Ret.). His experiences in office working for naval intelligence over more than two decades provided the basis for the scripts, which usually took incidents and dramatized them in situations involving conflict with Communist governments America had at the time. Star Bruce Gordon characterized them as "Cold War espionage tales."

Gordon, who had been working in Hollywood nearly a decade without much notice, played the show's only continuing role, which surprisingly was not Adm. Zacharias. "I played Cmdr. Matson, his [fictional] assistant," he said. "There was really no reason to have an admiral on the show."

As to how Gordon got involved in the series and what he did on it, he said. "I had to audition and I got it. There were several I acted in. Adm. Zacharias opened the show a couple of times too."

Though many of the stories were set in foreign countries, TV's budgetary restrictions, as well as the legendary cheapness of the studio producing the show, Screen Gems, had most of them filmed in one location. "We shot at the Columbia ranch out of the Santa Fe ranch," Gordon remembered. That area had to make do whether the location was in America or some other nation like Yugoslavia.

Another way Screen Gems saved money was to have Gordon record several of his introductory comments to the different shows in one big batch. Gordon didn't recall exactly how many introductions he filmed at one time but added, "They probably got several in." He also was not sure of how many shows he did where he acted as well as hosted.

With weak lead-ins from three different game shows during the 1958-59 season — the fading *Twenty-One*, which NBC pulled in October after it was under congressional investigation for being rigged; its four-week temporary replacement *Concentration*; and the *This is Your Life* knockoff *It Could Be You—Behind Closed Doors* fell behind its ABC and CBS competition throughout its run. It posed no threat particularly to *Dick Powell's Zane Grey Theater*, which posted its best ratings ever this season by

finishing at #13. As to speculating if ratings were the cause of the cancellation or some other factor was, Gordon said, "I really can't. It wasn't a hands-on relation there. I was just a hired actor."

Gordon didn't have to worry about losing the show for long. He scored a hit from 1959 to 1963 on *The Untouchables* playing mobster Frank Nitti. However, he would have another short-lived show in 1966-67 with *Run, Buddy, Run* (q.v.). Producer Sam Gallu, who Gordon liked, must have had quite a fondness for the U.S. Navy. In addition to this show, he produced both the dramatic anthology *Navy Log* from 1955 to 1958 and the 1960-61 syndicated adventure show *The Blue Angels*, which dealt with the Navy's four-man precision flying team.

Yancy Derringer

Western. Ran on CBS Thursdays 8:30–9 P.M. Oct. 2, 1958–Sept. 24, 1959, opposite *The Real McCoys* on ABC and *Concentration* (through Nov. 20), *It Could Be You* (from Nov. 27 to March), *Oldsmobile Music Theatre* (from March 26 to May 7), *Too Young to Go Steady* (from May 14 to June 25), and *The Lawless Years* (from July) on NBC. C: Jock Mahoney (as Yancy Derringer), X Brands (as Pahoo-Ka-Ta-Wah), Kevin Hagen (as John Colton), Julie Adams (as Amanda Eaton), Frances Bergen (as Madame Francine). EP: Warren Lewis, Don Sharpe. P/W: Richard Sale, Mary Loos. D: Richard Sale.

The Rough Riders

Western. Ran on ABC Thursdays 9:30–10 P.M. Oct. 2, 1958–Sept. 24, 1959, opposite *Playhouse 90* on CBS and *The Tennessee Ernie Ford Show* (through) and *21 Beacon Street* (from July 2) on NBC. C: Kent Taylor (as Capt. Flagg), Jan Merlin (as Lt. Kirby), Peter Whitney (as Sgt. Sinclair). P: Maurice Unger. D: Eddie Davis. W: Brett Hill.

Cimarron City

Western. Ran on NBC Saturdays 9:30–10:30 P.M. Oct. 11, 1958–Sept. 26, 1959, opposite *The Lawrence Welk Show* and *The Sammy Kaye Show* (through February) and *The Big Picture* (from June to August) on ABC and *Have Gun Will Travel* and *Gunsmoke* on CBS. C: George Montgomery (as Matthew Rockford), Audrey Totter (as Beth Purcell), John Smith (as Deputy Sheriff Lane Temple), Stuart Randall (as Art Sampson),

Addison Richards (as Martin Kingsley), Fred Sherman (as Burt Purdy), Claire Carleton (as Alice Purdy), Dan Blocker (as Tiny Budinger), George Dunn (as Jesse Williams), Pete Dunn (as Dody Hamer), Tom Fadden (as Silas Perry), Wally Brown (as Jed Fame). EP: Richard Lewis. P: Felix Jackson. W: Gene L. Coon. D: Jules Bricken.

The Peter Lind Hayes Show

Variety. Ran on ABC Mondays through Fridays 11:30 A.M.–12:30 P.M. Oct. 13, 1958–April 10, 1959, opposite *Top Dollar* and *Love of Life* on CBS and *Concentration* and *Tic Tac Dough* on NBC. C: Peter Lind Hayes, John Bubbles, Don Cherry, the Four Voices, the Bert Farber Orchestra. P: Frank Musiello. D: Robert Bleyer. W: George Hope, Charles Slocum, Chuck Horner.

Mother's Day

Game. Ran on ABC Mondays through Fridays 12:30–1 P.M. Oct. 13, 1958–Jan. 2, 1959, opposite *Search for Tomorrow* and *Guiding Light* on CBS and *It Could Be You* on NBC. C: Dick Van Dyke, Dotty Mack. P: Carl Jampel. D: Alex Leftwich. W: Elroy Schwartz.

The Liberace Show

Musical Variety. Ran on ABC Mondays through Fridays 1–1:30 P.M. Oct. 13, 1958–April 10, 1959. C: Liberace, Dick Roman, Marilyn Lovell, the Gordon Robinson Orchestra. P: Gil Rodin. D: Joe Landis. W: Tom Waldman, Sol Stein.

Chance for Romance

Game. Ran on ABC Mondays through Fridays 2–2:30 P.M. Oct. 13–Dec. 5, 1958, opposite *The Jimmy Dean Show* on CBS and *Truth or Consequences* on NBC. C: John Cameron Swayze. P: Irving Mansfield, Peter Arnell. D: Clay Yurdin.

The George Burns Show

Sitcom. Ran on NBC Tuesdays 9–9:30 P.M. Oct. 21, 1958–April 14, 1959, opposite *The Rifleman* on ABC and *The Arthur Godfrey Show* on CBS. C: George Burns (as himself), Bea Benaderet (as Blanche Morton), Larry Keating (as Harry Morton), Ronnie Burns (as himself), Harry Von Zell (as himself), Lisa Davis (as Miss Jenkins). P/D: Rod Amateau. W: Norman Paul, Keith Fowler, Harvey Helm, William Burns.

The Uncle Al Show

Children's. Ran on ABC Saturdays 11 A.M.–Noon Oct. 25, 1958–April 11, 1959, opposite *Heckle and Jeckle* and *The Adventures of Robin Hood* reruns on CBS and *Fury* and *Circus Boy* reruns on NBC, then ABC Saturdays Noon–1 P.M. April 18–Sept. 19, 1959, opposite *The CBS Saturday News* on CBS and *True Story* and *Detective's Diary* on NBC. C: "Uncle" Al Lewis, Wanda Lewis (as Captain Windy), Janet Greene (as Cinderella), Larry Smith. P/W: Al Lewis. D: Mike Tangi.

The D.A.'s Man

Crime Drama. Ran on NBC Saturdays 10:30–11 P.M. Jan. 3–Aug. 29, 1959, opposite *Markham* on CBS (from May 2). C: John Compton (as Shannon), Ralph Manza (as Al Bonacorsi), Herb Ellis (as Frank LaValle). P: Frank LaTourette. D: Joseph E. Parker. W: James Moser.

The Music Shop

Musical Variety. Ran on NBC Sundays 7:30–8 P.M. Jan. 11–March 8, 1959, opposite *Maverick* on ABC and *The Jack Benny Program* alternating with *Bachelor Father* on CBS. C: Buddy Bregman. P: Maurice Duke. D: Barry Shear.

Oldsmobile Music Theatre

Musical Variety. Ran on NBC Thursdays 8:30–9 P.M. March 26–May 7, 1959, opposite *The Real McCoys* on ABC and *Yancy Derringer* on CBS. C: Florence Henderson, Bill Hayes. P: Jacqueline Babbin. W: Thom Blake.

The Jimmie Rodgers Show

Musical Variety. Ran on NBC Tuesdays 8:30–9 P.M. March 31–Sept. 8, 1959, opposite *The Life and Legend of Wyatt Earp* on ABC and *To Tell the Truth* on CBS. C: Jimmie Rodgers, Connie Francis, the Kirby Stone Four, the Clay Warnick Singers, the Buddy Morrow Orchestra. P: Bob Claver. D: Kevin Joe Johnson.

Pete Kelly's Blues

Crime Drama. Ran on NBC Sundays 8:30–9 P.M. March 31–July 1959, opposite *The Lawman* on ABC and *The Ed Sullivan Show* on CBS, then NBC Fridays 7:30–8 P.M. July–Sept. 4, 1959, opposite *The Adventures of Rin Tin Tin* on ABC and *Rawhide* on CBS. C: William Reynolds (as Pete Kelly), Connee Boswell (as Savannah Brown), Than Wyenn (as George Lupo), Phil Gordon (as

Fred), Fred (Anthony) Eisley (as Johnny Cassiano). P/D/W: Jack Webb. W: Frank LaTourette.

Laugh Line

Game. Ran on NBC Thursdays 9–9:30 P.M. April 16–June 11, 1959, opposite *The Pat Boone–Chevy Showroom* on ABC and *Dick Powell's Zane Grey Theater* on CBS. C: Dick Van Dyke, Dorothy Loudon. P: Frank Wayne, Mace Neufeld. D: Seymour Robbie.

The Sam Levenson Show

Variety. Ran on CBS Mondays through Fridays 10:30–11 A.M. April 27–Sept. 25, 1959, opposite *Treasure Hunt* on NBC. C: Sam Levenson. P: Charles Andrews. D: Clarence Schimmel. W: Ben Jolson, Andy Rooney, Art Baer.

Too Young to Go Steady

Sitcom. Ran on NBC Thursdays 8:30–9 P.M. May 14–June 25, 1959, opposite *The Real McCoys* on ABC and *Yancy Derringer* on CBS. C: Joan Bennett (as Mary Blake), Donald Cook (as Tom Blake), Brigid Bazlen (as Pam Blake), Martin Huston (as Johnny Blake), Lorna Gillam (as Timmy). EP: David Susskind. AP: Murray Susskind. W: Ronald Alexander.

Across the Board

Game. Ran on ABC Mondays through Fridays Noon–12:30 P.M. June 1–Oct. 9, 1959, opposite *Love of Life* on CBS and *Tic Tac Dough* on NBC. C: Ted Brown. EP: Robert Stivers. P: Hal Davis. D: Hal Tulchin.

Director Hal Tulchin said he was the one who developed the concept for a crossword puzzle show which became *Across the Board*. However, he did not have the clout at the time to get it on the air, so he relied on producer Robert Stivers, who Tulchin said was "very in with the right people" along with his partner, Joe Cates, in getting it sold to ABC. "Bob and Joe were in the big league," Tulchin said.

Prior to *Across the Board*, Tulchin had directed a few TV series, including *It's a Hit* (q.v.) and a pioneer in videotaping series, which proved invaluable in getting *Across the Board* on air, as ABC had few videotaped daytime programs at the time. "I was one of the first videotape directors in, I think it was about 1958," he said. "Through a whole strange set of circumstances I became a specialist on videotape as a director and producer." He videotaped many TV ads too and claimed "As a result of doing Revlon commercials, I was I think the first to videotape fashion commercials."

Videotaping *Across the Board* was basically like doing a live show without retakes at the time, Tulchin noted. "You'd have to edit literally with a microscope," he said. So the show's technical aspects took a back seat to its format, which had two players attempt to solve a crossword via visual clues. Contestants earned one point per letter for each answer they knew, and the one with the most points won the game.

"We tried to get outgoing, cockamamie contestants," Tulchin said. Complementing the nuttiness was their host, Ted Brown, a longtime New York announcer and radio deejay. "Ted Brown was lots of fun," Tulchin said. "He had a sense of humor. He was terrific."

The hints were similarly outlandish. "It was kind of *Hellzapoppin*," he said, referring to the 1940s Broadway revue by Olsen and Johnson which stressed wild gags. In fact, one of the planned segments was so far out for ABC censors that they threw out the tape and used a repeat — a rarity for a daytime game show. As Tulchin recalled, "I had a guy in drag. He was for real, and at the end of the show, he revealed himself by taking off his wig. ABC junked the show."

Looking back at the show's run, Tulchin felt the concept was solid. He only was disappointed with one major prop. "The [crossword] board itself was all mechanical. I think it we had had an electronic thing, it would've been more successful." After it ended, Tulchin set up his own independent production company which he still oversees to this day.

The idea of a game show based on crossword puzzles later surfaced with considerably more success in the syndicated entry *The Cross-Wits* from 1975 to 1981. Tulchin was not impressed. "I didn't think it was anywhere as near entertaining as our show," he said. "We were funnier, to be honest."

The Court of Human Relations

Informational. Ran on NBC Mondays through Fridays 2–2:30 P.M. June 22–Aug. 14, 1959, opposite *Art Linkletter's House Party* on CBS and *The Gale Storm Show* reruns on ABC. C/P: A.L. Alexander. D: Ted Nathanson.

Oh, Boy!

Musical Variety. Ran on ABC Wednesdays 7:30–8 P.M. July 16–Sept. 3, 1959, opposite *The Playhouse*

on CBS and *The Californians* on NBC. C: Tony Hall, Lord Rockingham's XI. P: Jack Good. D: Rita Gillespie. W: Trevor Peacock.

1959-60

Tightrope

Police Drama. Ran on CBS Tuesdays 9–9:30 P.M. Sept. 8, 1959–Sept. 13, 1960, opposite *The Rifleman* on ABC and *The Arthur Murray Party* (through Jan. 26), *Startime* (from Feb. 2 to May 31) and *Richard Diamond, Private Detective* (from June 28 to Sept. 6) on NBC. C: Mike Connors (as Nick). P/W: Clarence Greene, Russell Rouse. D: Russell Rouse.

Johnny Staccato (a/k/a Staccato)

Drama. Ran on NBC Thursdays 8:30–9 P.M. Sept. 10, 1959–March 24, 1960, opposite *The Real McCoys* on ABC and *Johnny Ringo* on CBS, then ABC Sundays 10:30–11 P.M. March 27–Sept. 25, 1960, opposite *What's My Line?* on CBS. C: John Cassavetes (as Johnny Staccato), Eduardo Ciannelli (as Waldo). EP: William Frye. P: Everett Chambers. D: Joseph Pevney. W: Richard Berg.

The Troubleshooters

Adventure. Ran on NBC Fridays 8–8:30 P.M. Sept. 11, 1959–June 17, 1960, opposite *Walt Disney* on ABC and *Rawhide* on CBS. C: Keenan Wynn (as Kodiak), Bob Mathias (as Frank Dugan), Bob Fortier (as Scotty), Carey Loftin (as Skinner), Bob Harris (as Jim), Chet Allen (as Slats). EP: Richard Steenberg, John Gibbs. P: Allen Rivkin. D: Robert Altman.

The Man and the Challenge

Adventure. Ran on NBC Saturdays 8:30–9 P.M. Sept. 12, 1959–Sept. 3, 1960, opposite *Leave It to Beaver* on ABC and *Wanted: Dead or Alive* on CBS. C: George Nader (as Dr. Glenn Barton). P: Ivan Tors. D: Andrew Merton. W: Lee Erwin.

Fibber McGee and Molly

Sitcom. Ran on NBC Tuesdays 8:30–9 P.M. Sept. 15, 1959–Jan. 19, 1960, opposite *The Life and Leg-*

end of *Wyatt Earp* on ABC and *The Many Loves of Dobie Gillis* on CBS. C: Bob Sweeney (as Fibber McGee), Cathy Lewis (as Molly McGee), Addison Richards (as Doc Gamble), Harold Peary (as Mayor Charles LaTrivia), Jack Kirkwood (as Fred Nitney), Paul Smith (as Roy Norris), Elisabeth Fraser (as Hazel Norris), Barbara Beaird (as Teeny). P/D: William Asher. W: Bill Davenport.

The last major network radio series to be adapted to television was *Fibber McGee and Molly*. The sitcom arrived as nearly all network radio entertainment programming was dead, and in fact *Fibber McGee and Molly* spent its last two years on radio as four-minute routines on NBC's weekend *Monitor* radio show before ending on Sept. 6, 1959, a little more than a week before the show's TV debut.

The real heyday of *Fibber McGee and Molly* on radio was in the 1940s, when it even was the #1 show in 1943 (it started on NBC April 16, 1935). In 1953, as TV had become the dominant form of broadcasting among American audiences, it converted from a weekly half-hour show to a daily 15-minute program in various slots for three years before being part of *Monitor*. In effect, *Fibber McGee and Molly* was an aged product as television headed into the 1960s, and at least one TV participant thought it was a mistake to try and update it.

"The old radio show was wonderful," said producer/director William Asher. "I think that it was too old hat, though we certainly modernized it."

One of the main transitions was in using a new cast, partly because those who starred in the radio version (the real-life couple of Jim and Marian Jordan) declined all offers to do their show on TV. Asher said their TV replacements were fine: "[Bob] Sweeney was wonderful, and Cathy Lewis, she was great too." Actually, Harold Peary had been in the radio show, but as Throckmorton P. Gildersleeve from 1939 to 1941 before spinning off to star in his own radio series *The Great Gildersleeve* from 1941 to 1957, rather than as argumentative Mayor La Trivia.

Most of the cast played old characters from radio: Fibber, the guy who liked to stretch the truth and look for an angle to benefit himself; Molly, his wife who was weary of his antics; Teeny, the neighborhood girl who irritated Fibber; and Doc Gamble, a friend who also tended to get into verbal volleys with Fibber.

The catch phrases and routines from the radio show popped up too, such as Molly's "Tain't funny, McGee!" when Fibber let loose a weak joke, and the McGees' closet, which when opened on radio sounded like it unleashed a torrent of bric-a-brac. With these similarities, one might think that the TV series recycled everything from the radio series, but Asher clarified that "We used things from the radio, like the closet, but not the scripts."

Still, Asher conceded that "I just think it was a tired idea. The network just didn't feel comfortable with it." Though he insisted that the ratings, while not strong, were good enough that "It could've been renewed," NBC decided instead to end the program and its cute "claymation" opening titles midseason, although oddly they did rerun it briefly daily from 4 to 4:30 P.M. April 18–May 20, 1960 and Aug. 15–23, 1960, before it disappeared completely.

Love and Marriage

Sitcom. Ran on NBC Mondays 8–8:30 P.M. Sept. 21, 1959–Jan. 25, 1960, opposite *Cheyenne* on ABC and *The Texan* on CBS. C: William Demarest (as William Harris), Jeanne Bal (as Pat Baker), Murray Hamilton (as Steve Baker), Stubby Kaye (as Stubby Wilson), Kay Armen (as Sophie), Susan Reilly (as Susan Baker), Jennie Lynn (as Jennie Baker). P: P.J. Wolfson, Louis F. Edelman. D: Bob Sweeney. W: Melville Shavelson.

The title alone of this series gave an indication of where it stood regarding the emergence of rock 'n' roll in the 1950s. *Love and Marriage* did not use the top 10 hit song of the same name, which Frank Sinatra introduced in a production of *Our Town* on *Producers' Showcase* on Sept. 19, 1955. But from the show's setup, it was obvious the powers behind it favored light pop music over the raucous likes of Elvis Presley, whose "A Big Hunk o' Love" was

#1 on the charts shortly before *Love and Marriage* debuted.

Love and Marriage grew out of a previous professional relationship between its producer and writer. "Lou Edelman was the producer," said writer Melville Shavelson. "He wanted to do a series on music. I had done [the 1951 movie] *I'll See You in My Dreams* with Lou, and it was such a successful picture that he felt we could get into a series with music."

After meeting with Edelman about possible ideas, "I knew the kind of characters he wanted," Shavelson said. And here's what they came up with:

The Harris Music Publishing Company, based in Hollywood, faced ruin because founder and operator, William Harris, wanted to avoid handling rock 'n' roll songs. To save his company, and alleviate his stress from the situation, his daughter Pat Baker tried to recruit hit tunes for him in the genre surreptitiously to turn the company around. William never liked that, nor did he care much for Pat's husband, Steve (he had more affection for his granddaughters Susan and Jennie). Making life more bearable for him was his faithful secretary, Sophie, and his song promoter pal, Stubby Wilson, who liked to recall the pre-rock days in the industry to William's enjoyment (and probably to the boredom of any viewer under the age of 20).

Directing the pilot was Bob Sweeney, the same Bob Sweeney who starred that same season in *Fibber McGee and Molly* (q.v.). After that series ended, Sweeney pursued directing full time, including many episodes of *The Andy Griffith Show*.

Some believe that the anti-rock sentiments expressed by *Love and Marriage* limited its audience and made it appear old fashioned and corny in light of the music's popularity. To that notion, Shavelson allowed that "I suppose the audience thought the music was passé." Then again, being up against two top-rated westerns at the time did not help, either.

Shortly after the start of 1960, NBC booted *Love and Marriage* off its schedule as well as its lead-in, *Richard Diamond, Private Detective* (the latter returned in summer reruns in 1960 after three years on the air). Replacing them in the hour block was *Riverboat*, which also started like *Love and Marriage* in September 1959 and did not last too long in its new loca-

William Demarest is grumpy (actually, when wasn't he?) about something involving Jeanne Bal, playing his daugher, and Murray Hamilton, as his son-in-law, on *Love and Marriage*.

tion, going off on Jan. 16, 1961. Incidentally, the title *Love and Marriage* appeared again on another, even shorter-lived sitcom that ran on the Fox network just twice, from Sept. 28 to Oct. 5, 1996.

The Dennis O'Keefe Show

Sitcom. Ran on CBS Tuesdays 8–8:30 P.M. Sept. 22, 1959–June 7, 1960, opposite *Sugarfoot* alternating with *Bronco* on ABC and *Laramie* on NBC.

C: Dennis O'Keefe (as Hal Towne), Hope Emerson (as Amelia "Sarge" Sargent), Rickey Kelman (as Randy Towne), Eloise Hardt (as Karen Hadley), Eddie Ryder (as Eliot). P: Les Hafner. D: Norman Abbott. W: Alan Lipscott, Bob Fisher.

Dick Clark's World of Talent

Variety. Ran on ABC Sundays 10:30–11 P.M. Sept. 27–Dec. 20, 1959, opposite *What's My Line?* on CBS. C: Dick Clark, Jack E. Leonard. P: Irving Mansfield, Peter Arnell. D: Grey Lockwood. W: Larry Markes.

The House on High Street

Dramatic Anthology with Regulars. Ran on NBC Mondays through Fridays 4–4:30 P.M. Sept. 28, 1959–Feb. 5, 1960, opposite *American Bandstand* on ABC and *The Brighter Day* and *The Secret Storm* on CBS. C: Philip Abbott (as John Collier), Dr. Harris B. Peck (as himself), Judge James Gehrig (as himself). P: John Haggart. W: William Kendall Clarke. D: Lela Swift.

Fifteen years before she began directing the daytime soap *Ryan's Hope* (1975–89), and winning several Emmys there, Lela Swift had her first regular daily job with *The House on High Street.* "My agent was part of the package [for the show]," she said. "He got me on it."

The ambitious series, dealing with troubled youths and their treatment by law enforcement officials, drew its playlets from real life. "The cases were based on children's court cases," Swift said. "And the material was so intense, we couldn't do it in a day. We'd rehearse all week and shoot them in half hours in one day." Most cases ran from three to five days.

Regulars on the New York City–based series included only one actor, Philip Abbott, later to play agent Arthur Ward on *The F.B.I.* from 1965 to 1974. He played probation officer John Collier, who interviewed the participants in the dramas. "He was very good in the part, very soul searching," Swift said. "You didn't feel he was acting it."

But who really impressed Swift was psychiatrist Dr. Harris B. Peck, who played himself. "I don't know where he came from, but he was really good," Swift said. Dr. Peck reviewed the scripts, then meet with the actors in a "group therapy session" to give them insights into their characters. "He would take them into the dressing room in which the actors, in their own roles, would answer questions and get motivations from him. He got wonderful responses," Swift said.

In fact, Dr. Peck probed the actors so well that, according to Swift, "I would have to stop them at dress rehearsal. They would get so intense, I was sure they wouldn't have anything left." Apart from his backstage activities, Dr. Peck appeared on camera with another man playing himself, Judge James Gehrig, and Philip Abbott's John Collier to discuss the cases in character.

Yet despite their efforts, *The House on High Street* finished third behind the competing 15-minute soaps on CBS and the first half-hour of *American Bandstand* on ABC. Swift pointed to the format as the culprit for why it lasted just over four months. "On anthologies, people don't watch it the way they do soap operas," she said. "If you missed one episode of our show, you missed a great deal." Swift said even her mother told her that.

NBC tried only one other daytime anthology after *The House on High Street. The Doctors* began on April 1, 1963, telling the daily stories of four alternating hospital staff members, which became five regulars in weekly stories by July 1963. On March 2, 1964, the show became a full-blown soap with continuing melodramatic storylines, a pattern it maintained until it ended on Dec. 31, 1982.

Split Personality

Game. Ran on NBC Mondays through Fridays 4:30–5 P.M. Mondays through Fridays Sept. 28, 1959–Feb. 5, 1960, opposite *American Bandstand* on ABC and *The Edge of Night* on CBS. C: Tom Poston. P: Robert Rowe. D: Paul Alter.

Having won an Emmy for Best Supporting Actor in a Comedy Series in the spring of 1959, Tom Poston was a somewhat unexpected choice to host *Split Personality.* The man who made his name by playing a person so absent-minded he forgot his name on the "man on the street" segments of *The Steve Allen Show* hardly came across as game show emcee material.

But Allen left New York to do his series in Los Angeles in the fall of 1959, and Poston decided to stay put rather than make the move as well, making him a free and hot property. Poston also had become a regular panelist on *To Tell the Truth* in 1958 and showed that the dumb guy routine was indeed just an act. And since Mark Goodson–Bill Todman Productions packaged both *To Tell the Truth* and *Split Personality*, he was a contender to do the latter show when it bowed.

"Tom had done a lot of other stuff, and he's a very humorous guy and a very smart guy," said director Paul Alter, who thought Poston did a fine job as host.

Split Personality had two players face a large blackboard divided between them. Each player selected for his or her opponent a characteristic of the mystery person to be identified each game in a square on the opponent's side of the board. To heighten the suspense, neither player knew exactly what information the other one had as each selected square was revealed. The first player to name the mystery person won a game, and winning two games let that player guess the two celebrities whose images were combined into one. If successful, he or she won merchandise.

Alter said it was a difficult task to do the primary game because of the variables involved. "Believe it or not, there were about 30 or 40 squares that could be lighted," he said. "Each one had its own projector [to light up the answer contained in the square]. That made it expensive."

However, Alter said it was not cost alone that concerned the production crew. They also found the intelligence level of their contestants was not as high as they'd thought (hadn't game show producers already known that?). "The ordinary contestant could not identify famous people beyond celebrities," he said. "We'd show [then–First Lady] Mamie Eisenhower, and no one would get her. We made the assumption that the American public would know that, and they didn't."

Whether it was due to those factors and/or the ratings, NBC had no split decision over *Split Personality* and dropped it a little after four months. The network replaced it for the rest of the 1959-60 season with a collection of reruns of nighttime action series under the umbrella title *Adventure Time*. As for Poston, he never hosted another game show, though he stayed with *To Tell the Truth* until CBS cancelled it in 1967.

Hobby Lobby (a/k/a The Charley Weaver Show)

Talk/Comedy. Ran on ABC Wednesdays 8–8:30 P.M. Sept. 30, 1959–March 23, 1960, opposite *The Lineup* (through Jan. 20) and *Be Our Guest* (from Jan. 27) on CBS and *Wagon Train* on NBC. C: Cliff Arquette (as Charley Weaver). P: Art Stark. D: David Lowe.

Wichita Town

Western. Ran on NBC Wednesdays 10:30–11 P.M. Sept. 30, 1959–April 6, 1960, opposite boxing on ABC and *Armstrong Circle Theater* alternating with *The U.S. Steel Hour* on CBS, then NBC Fridays 8:30–9 P.M. June 24–Sept. 23, 1960, opposite *Man from Blackhawk* on ABC and *Hotel de Paree* on CBS. C: Joel McCrea (as Marshal Mike Dunbar), Jody McCrea (as Ben Matheson), Carlos Romero (as Rico Rodriguez), George Neise (as Dr. Nat Wyndham), Bob Anderson (as Aeneas MacLinahan), Robert Faulk (as Joe Kingston). EP: Frank Baur. D: Jerry Hopper. W: Richard Alan Simmons.

The Betty Hutton Show

Sitcom. Ran on CBS Thursdays 8–8:30 P.M. Oct. 1, 1959–June 30, 1960, opposite *The Donna Reed Show* on ABC and *Bat Masterson* on NBC. C: Betty Hutton (as Goldie Appleby), Gigi Perreau (as Pat Strickland), Richard Miles (as Nicky Strickland), Dennis Joel (as Roy Strickland), Joan Shawlee (as Lorna), Jean Carson (as Rosemary), Tom Conway (as Howard Seaton), Gavin Muir (as Hollister). P/W: Stanley Roberts. D: Edward Ludwig.

Johnny Ringo

Western. Ran on CBS Thursdays 8:30–9 P.M. Oct. 1, 1959–Sept. 29, 1960, opposite *The Real McCoys* on ABC and *Johnny Staccato* (through March 24) and *Producers' Choice* (from March 31) on NBC. C: Don Durant (as Johnny Ringo), Karen Sharpe (as Laura Thomas), Mark Goddard (as Cully), Terence de Marney (as Case Thomas). P/W: Aaron Spelling. D: Howard Koch.

Law of the Plainsman

Western. Ran on NBC Thursdays 7:30–8 P.M. Oct. 1, 1959–Sept. 22, 1960, opposite *The Gale Storm Show* on ABC and *To Tell the Truth* on CBS. C: Michael Ansara (as Deputy U.S. Marshal Sam Buckhart), Dayton Lummis (as Marshal Andy

Morrison), Gina Gillespie (as Tess Logan), Nora Marlowe (as Martha Commager). EP: Jules Levy, Arthur Gardner, Arnold Laven. P: Peter Packer.

The team of producers Jules Levy and Arthur Gardner and producer/director Arnold Laven made a formidable trio in TV production during the late 1950s through mid–1960s. They had three big hits— *The Rifleman*, *The Detectives* and *The Big Valley*. Their only miss was *Law of the Plainsman*, which grew out of *The Rifleman*.

"Michael Ansara had been on one of *The Rifleman* episodes," Laven recalled. "I know Jules in particular had been a fan of Michael Ansara as an actor." Ansara had starred on the ABC series *Broken Arrow* from 1956 to 1958 as Apache Chief Cochise. "Because he played an Indian successfully, the three of us (Levy, Gardner and Laven) barnstormed, as best I can remember, ideas back and forth, and out of that came *Law of the Plainsman*," said Laven.

The main element Laven recalled the trio creating was making Ansara's character, Sam Buckhart, a Harvard-educated Apache, a twist to the usual backgrounds given to Indians on TV westerns. Given the job to refine their concept was Cyril Hume, who had written several episodes of *The Rifleman*. "He developed a pretty good screenplay and, as a result, I made an episode of *The Rifleman* which was intended to be a pilot," said Laven.

The pilot, titled "The Indian," aired Feb. 17, 1959, five months into the first season of *The Rifleman* (the show would run until 1963). ABC, which aired *The Rifleman*, passed on the show, but NBC bought it. Added to the series was Marshal Morrison, Sam's boss in the New Mexico Territory in the 1880s; Martha the boarding house operator; and Tess Logan, Sam's ward. Laven agreed the addition of the young girl clearly was meant to mimic the father-son appeal of the characters Chuck Connors and Johnny Crawford played on *The Rifleman*. Levy had wanted to call the show *The Plainsman*, but Paramount Studios had registered the title for the 1936 Gary Cooper film and would not allow it to be used, so it became *Law of the Plainsman*.

Laven did not direct *Law of the Plainsman* even though he did so for the pilot because he was more involved with *The Detectives*, where due to circumstances he had to serve as its sole producer and story editor for the 1959-60 season. Nevertheless, he kept tabs on *Law of the Plainsman* and believes it failed because it used so many freelance writers for scripts, thus never developing a consistent tone. He recalled no one wrote more than three episodes of *Law of the Plainsman*.

"If we had a Cyril Hume to write every script, we'd had a shot," said Laven. As it stood in the end, he said, "It just wasn't that good a show, I am regretful to say."

After its one-season run, *Law of the Plainsman* returned in repeats from July to September 1962 on ABC. Appropriately, it was a summer replacement for the show which spawned it, *The Rifleman*.

Hotel De Paree

Western. Ran on CBS Fridays 8:30–9 P.M. Oct. 2, 1959–Sept. 23, 1960, opposite *The Man from Blackhawk* on ABC and *The Bell Telephone Hour* (through June) and *Wichita Town* (from June 24) on NBC. C: Earl Holliman (as Sundance), Judi Meredith (as Monique Devereaux), Jeanette Nolan (as Annette Devereaux), Strother Martin (as Aaron Donager). EP: William Self. P: Julian Claman. D: Robert Aldrich. W: Sam Rolfe.

Five Fingers

Espionage Drama. Ran on NBC Saturdays 9:30–10:30 P.M. Oct. 3, 1959–Jan. 9, 1960, opposite *The Lawrence Welk Show* and *Ozark Jubilee* on ABC and *Have Gun Will Travel* and *Gunsmoke* on CBS. C: David Hedison (as Victor Sebastian), Luciana Paluzzi (as Simone Genet), Paul Burke (as Robertson). EP: Martin Manulis. P: Herbert Swope, Jr. D: Robert Stevens. W: Richard Berg.

How did Martin Manulis, an Emmy nominee in 1955 for his role as producer of the live series *Climax!* and a veteran of other major New York anthology series, get involved in the thoroughly Hollywood production of *Five Fingers*? It's a question to which he wondered jokingly whether even he knew the answer before admitting the truth.

"I, at the time, for my sins, became head of production at 20th Century Fox," he said. "I had only done live television, not film." Despite his background, he endeavored to help produce the studio with what he hoped would be a hit.

Enter producer Herbert Swope, Jr. The

latter had been at Fox since at least 1952, when the studio released a movie called *Five Fingers*. It starred James Mason as a British agent purportedly selling spy secrets to the Germans in World War II. Manulis and Swope adapted the idea into making the lead character an American pretending to be a Communist overseas in order to gather secrets on the Reds. The title was his code name with U.S. officials—"Five Fingers."

David Hedison played the lead, while Paul Burke played his main American contact, Robertson. As part of his cover, Hedison's character was a talent agent traveling with his client, singer Simone Genet, who loved him without knowing of his spying activities. Playing Simone was Italian import Luciana Paluzzi.

"This was her first American appearance," recalled Manulis of Paluzzi. "I believe that when she talked to me from Italy, she spoke quite well. When she arrived here, having signed a contract to do this series, you could hardly understand her."

Despite that drawback, Manulis said he felt in general *Five Fingers* "was a good show. It was also a rather complex show. Everybody was playing a spy and different parts, and it was hard to understand."

Perhaps the most noteworthy episode featured ventriloquist Edgar Bergen in one of his first straight acting parts. "He was very good," Manulis said. "We wanted to use him in what he did best. There were some shows like that, that had their own sense of style. Others didn't."

Competition from the #1 and #3 series of the 1959-60 season—*Gunsmoke* and *Have Gun Will Travel*, respectively—led *Five Fingers* to get a thumbs down from viewers and be cancelled after three months. Manulis did not bemoan the decision. "Some shows turned out very well," he said. "But I thought when it went off the air, there was nothing lost finishing up its run."

Both Hedison and Burke fared better on TV in the 1960s, with Hedison starring for four years on *Voyage to the Bottom of the Sea* (1964–68) and Burke staying with *Twelve O'Clock High* from 1964 to 1967. Paluzzi, however, never did another regular American TV series role.

The Alaskans

Adventure. Ran on ABC Sundays 9:30–10:30 P.M. Oct. 4, 1959–Sept. 25, 1960, opposite *Alfred Hitchcock Presents* and *The Jack Benny Show* alternating with *The George Gobel Show* (through June 26) and *I Love Lucy* reruns (from July 3) on CBS and *The Dinah Shore Chevy Show* (through May 22) and *The Chevy Mystery Show* (from May 29). C: Roger Moore (as Silky Harris), Jeff York (as Reno McKee), Ray Danton (as Nifty Cronin), Dorothy Provine (as Rocky Shaw). EP: Bill Orr. P: Harry Tatleman. D: Josef Leytes. W: Lowell Barrington.

Bourbon Street Beat

Detective Drama. Ran on ABC Mondays 8:30–9:30 P.M. Oct. 5, 1959–Sept. 26, 1960, opposite *Father Knows Best* and *The Danny Thomas Show* (through July 18) and *Celebrity Talent Scouts* (from Aug. 1) on CBS and *Tales of Wells Fargo* and *Peter Gunn* on NBC. C: Andrew Duggan (as Cal Calhoun), Richard Long (as Rex Randolph), Arlene Howell (as Melody Lee Mercer), Van Williams (as Kenny Madison), Eddie Cole (as the Baron). EP: William T. Orr. P: Charles Hoffman, Harry Tatleman. D: Leslie H. Martinson, Charles Rondeau, Andre de Toth, Paul Henreid.

In its debut season of 1958-59, *77 Sunset Strip* was not a huge hit but did well enough for ABC on Friday nights to encourage the network to ask for similar series from its production company, Warner Brothers. Warner responded by selling two pilots for the 1959 fall schedule, *Hawaiian Eye* ("*77 Sunset Strip* goes to Honolulu") and *Bourbon Street Beat* ("the New Orleans *77 Sunset Strip*"). *Hawaiian Eye* managed to run four years, but *Bourbon Street Beat* was an underperformer, disappearing after its first season.

Apart from the sultry locale (which was duplicated on studio lots, never on location in Louisiana), *Bourbon Street Beat* was virtually interchangeable with *77 Sunset Strip* on a character-by-character basis. In place of Efrem Zimbalist, Jr.'s, middle-aged detective lead Stuart Bailey from *77 Sunset Strip* was Andrew Duggan's Cal Calhoun on *Bourbon Street Beat*. Roger Smith's handsome younger detective Jeff Spencer from the original show was now suave Richard Long's Rex Randolph. For perky girl sidekick, the equivalent for Suzanne Fabray on *77 Sunset Strip* was Melody Lee Mercer on *Bourbon Street Beat*. Let's not forget the dreamboat aspiring private eye for each — Ed Byrne's immortal "Kookie" and his comb found a kindred spirit with darkly handsome Van Williams' Kenny Madison. And to round out the local color for each series, *Bourbon Street Beat* matched Roscoe the racing nut from *77 Sunset Strip* with the Baron, a local jazz pianist.

The copycat nature of *Bourbon Street Beat* (and *Hawaiian Eye*) drove TV critics furious. They accused Warner Brothers of engaging in assembly line production of TV shows, and indeed during a writers' strike in 1959 the studio began recycling its scripts from one show to another with few problems. But Leslie Martinson, who directed seven episodes, had only hosannas for the series, its actors and its executive producer, William T. Orr.

"Bill Orr, I would say, in my seven and a half years at Warners under Bill Orr, there are not enough words I can say in praise of him," Martinson said. "He built that dynasty up to eight hours a week on television."

As for the cast, he noted. "You couldn't work with two greater pros than Richard Long — great — and Andy Duggan — just money in the bank. And Van Williams — a delight."

Martinson also prided himself on finding new talent for television, and it was on *Bourbon Street Beat* where he scored a major hit. "Richard Chamberlain played a guest role, and in the same picture was Jim Coburn," he said. "They were both in the same episode. It had kind of two guest leads. Anyway, regarding Richard, he had no film credits at the time. I read him and thought he was great for the part."

Martinson blamed the show's cancellation on its time slot, against CBS's top two sitcoms in 1959-60. "It was real tough," he said. But the characters were not forgotten after the show left. The next season Kenny Madison showed up on another Warners clone, *Surfside Six*, which ran until 1962, while Rex Randolph joined *77 Sunset Strip* for the 1960-61 season.

Philip Marlowe

Detective Drama. Ran on ABC Tuesdays 9:30-10 P.M. Oct. 6, 1959–March 29, 1960, opposite *The Red Skelton Show* on CBS and *Startime* (through Jan. 26) and *The Arthur Murray Party* (from Feb. 2) on NBC. C: Philip Carey (as Philip Marlowe). P/W: Gene Wang. D: Robert Ellis Miller.

The Man from Blackhawk

Western. Ran on ABC Fridays 8:30-9 P.M. Oct. 9, 1959–Sept. 23, 1960, opposite *Hotel De Paree* on CBS and *The Bell Telephone Hour* (through April 1) and *Wichita Town* (from June 24) on NBC. C: Robert Rockwell (as Sam Logan). P: Herb Meadow. W: Stirling Silliphant.

"Remember a movie called *Mr. Blandings Builds His Dream House*?" actor Robert Rockwell asked me. (I did, but for the uninitiated, it was a 1948 movie comedy starring Cary Grant.) "Well, they were going to make into a series at Screen Gems. It never became a series, but my agent sold me for *The Man from Blackhawk* instead."

The series was a mixed blessing for Rockwell. On one hand, he was glad to get a regular job and break out of the typecasting he suffered playing the incredibly oblivious teacher Philip Boynton pursued by Eve Arden's lovesick Connie Brooks on the sitcom *Our Miss Brooks* from 1952 to 1956. "It took me over a year to do more than a day's work after *Our Miss Brooks*," he said.

But on the other hand, his agent didn't get him a nice contract with the Screen Gems production company even though he was the only regular on the show. "I wasn't too happy, because he had me get $500 a week," he said. "Screen Gems was a lousy outfit. Cheap."

Still, Rockwell felt the show held promise to stand out amid the glut of westerns on TV in 1959. "It wasn't really a western," he argued. "It was about an insurance investigator running down leads of people shot for insurance money. Some of them were set in New York, some down South. They tried to vary it." The Blackhawk in the title stood for the Blackhawk Insurance Company, a Chicago-based firm which Sam Logan represented in the 1870s.

Rockwell said the series was doing fine in his opinion in its initial episodes. "The only problem was in November, after we did 13 [shows] or so, the writers went on strike," he said. Screen Gems officials responded by recycling old scripts, cutting the program's budget in half, and making more changes to save a buck.

"I came back and found my producer and director had been replaced," he said. "There was not any quality left. It could've been a great show. Stirling Silliphant [an Oscar winner for

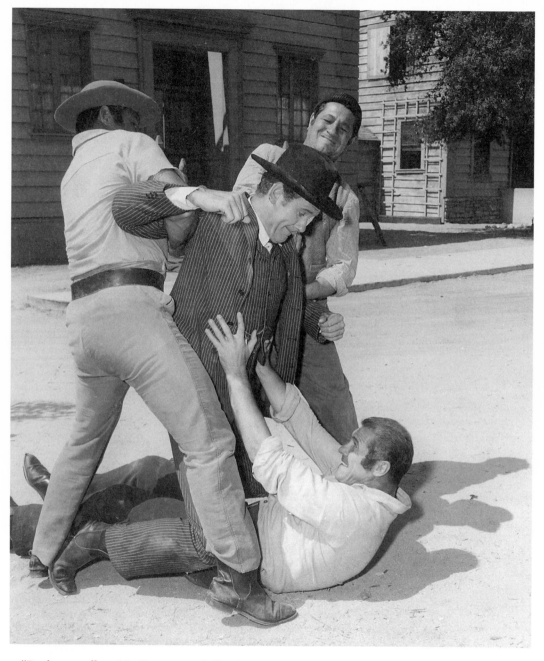

"Don't ever call me Mr. Boynton again!" Robert Rockwell is held back by two men as he gets ready to beat the tar out of Bob Bray in a scene from *The Man from Blckhawk.*

writing *In the Heat of the Night* in 1967] was one of the original writers."

ABC replaced the adult drama with the very successful cartoon *The Flintstones*. Rockwell said *The Man from Blackhawk* didn't even go into reruns in syndication, unlike some other short-lived filmed series of the period. "That was never released again, to my knowledge," he said. "It was just dumped, and that was it."

That was not it for Rockwell, however. Though he did not get another regular TV role, he remained quite active as a guest star in dramas and comedies through the 1990s, when he was seen in commercials for a candy product. Describing his current TV acting activities in 2001, the octogenarian said with a sly voice, "They've sort of retired me."

Mr. Lucky

Adventure. Ran on CBS Saturdays 9–9:30 P.M. Oct. 24, 1959–Sept. 3, 1960, opposite *The Lawrence Welk Show* on ABC and *The Deputy* on NBC. C: John Vivyan (as Mr. Lucky), Ross Martin (as Andamo), Tom Brown (as Lt. Rovacs), Pippa Scott (as Maggie Shank-Rutherford), Joe Scott (as Maitre d'). EP: Gordon Oliver. P: Jack Arnold. D: Blake Edwards. W: Blake Edwards, Arthur Ross.

The Red Rowe Show

Variety. Ran on CBS Mondays through Fridays 10–10:30 A.M. Nov. 16, 1959–July 8, 1960, opposite *Dough Re Mi* on NBC. C: Red Rowe, Bill Cunningham, Peggy Taylor, the Billy Liebert Orchestra. P: Chet Brouwer. D: Jimmy Johnson.

The Kate Smith Show

Musical Variety. Ran on CBS Mondays 7:30–8 P.M. Jan. 25–July 18, 1960, opposite *Cheyenne* on ABC and *Riverboat* on NBC. C: Kate Smith, the Harry Simeone Chorus, Neal Hefti and His Orchestra. EP: Ted Collins. P: Jack Philbin. D: Jerome Shaw.

Be Our Guest

Musical Variety. Ran on CBS Wednesdays 7:30–8:30 P.M. Jan. 27–June 1, 1960, opposite *The Court of Last Resorts* reruns (through Feb. 17) and *Music for a Spring Night* (from Feb. 24) and *Hobby Lobby* (through March 23) on ABC and *Wagon Train* on NBC. C: George De Witt (through March 11), Keefe Brasselle (from March 18), Mary Ann Mobley, Ray McKinley and the Glenn Miller Orchestra. EP: Al Singer. P: Perry Cross. D: Seymour Robbie. W: Poot Pray, Bob Corcoran, Ervin Drake, Sam Dreben.

Man from Interpol

Police Drama from the United Kingdom. Ran on NBC Saturdays 10:30–11 P.M. Jan. 30–Oct. 22, 1960, opposite *Ozark Jubilee* (through Sept. 24) and boxing and *Make That Spare* (from Oct. 8) on ABC. C: Richard Wyler (as Anthony Smith), John Longden (as Superintendent Mercer). P: Edward J. and Harry Lee Danziger. D: Godfrey Grayson. W: Brian Clemons.

The Overland Trail

Western. Ran on NBC Sundays 7–8 P.M. Feb. 7–Sept. 11, 1960, opposite *Colt .45* (through March 27) and *Broken Arrow* reruns (from April 3) and *Maverick* on ABC and *Lassie* and *Dennis the Menace* on CBS. C: William Bendix (as Frederick Thomas Kelly), Doug McClure (as Frank "Flip" Flippen). EP: Nat Holt. P/W: Samuel A. Peeples. D: Virgil W. Vogel.

Happy

Sitcom. Ran on NBC Wednesdays 9–9:30 P.M. June 9–Sept. 28, 1960, opposite *Hawaiian Eye* on ABC and *The Millionaire* on CBS, then NBC Fridays 7:30–8 P.M. Jan. 13–Sept. 8, 1961, opposite *Matty's Funday Funnies* on ABC and *Rawhide* on CBS. C: Ronnie Burns (as Chris Day), Yvonne Lime (as Chris Day), David and Steven Born (as Charles Hapgood "Happy" Day), Leone Ledoux (as voice of Happy), Lloyd Corrigan (as Charlie Dooley), Doris Packer (as Clara Mason). P: Manny Rosenberg. D: Bob Butler (1960), Paul Harrison (1961). W: Frank Gill, Jr. (1960), J. Carleton Brown (1960), Margaret Fitts (1961).

Full Circle

Soap Opera. Ran on CBS Mondays through Fridays 2–2:30 P.M. June 27, 1960–March 10, 1961, opposite *Day in Court* on ABC and *Queen for a Day* (through Sept. 2) and *The Jan Murray Show* (from Sept. 5) on NBC. C: Robert Fortier (as Gary Donovan), Dyan Cannon (as Lisa Linda Crowder), John McNamara (as Loyal Crowder), Jean Byron (as Dr. Kit Aldrich), Michael Ross (as Virgil Denker), Nancy Millard (as Ellen Denker), Andrew Colmar (as Ray Pollard), Bill Lundmark (as David Talton), Ann Daniels (as Chris Talton), Gene Lyons (as Parker Hill; 1960), Byron Foulger (as Carter Talton; 1960), Sam Edwards (as the Deputy; 1960), Amzie Strickland (as Beth Perce; 1960). P: Norman Morgan. D: William Howell, Livia Granito. W: Bill Barrett.

The Clear Horizon

Soap Opera. Ran on CBS Mondays through Fridays 11:30 A.M.–Noon July 11, 1960–March 11, 1961, opposite *Concentration* on NBC and (from Oct. 10) *The Bob Cummings Show* repeats on ABC, and Mondays through Fridays 11:30–11:55 A.M. Feb. 26–June 11, 1962, opposite *Concentration* on NBC and *Yours for a Song* on ABC. C: Edward Kemmer (as Roy Selby), Phyllis Avery (as Anne Selby), Jimmy Carter (as Ricky Selby; 1960–61), Charles Herbert (as Ricky Selby; 1962), Rusty Lane (as Sgt. Harry Moseby), Eve McVeagh (as Frances Moseby), Michael Fox (as Lt. Sig Levy), others. P: Charles Pollacheck. D: Joseph Behar, Hal Cooper. W: Manya Starr.

The Clear Horizon was that rare TV series to be revived after cancellation with much of its cast intact. Canned after eight months on air, the daily serial returned nearly a year later, only to have a shortened comeback of four months. Adding to its novelty is that its star, Edward Kemmer, had starred in the children's TV adventure serial *Space Patrol* from 1950 to 1955 as a military officer and now was playing another man in uniform.

"I played a communications officer," Kemmer said. Specifically, he was an Army Signal Corps officer whose wife became attracted to another man at one point (don't all wives do that on soap operas?). Despite the military backdrop, Kemmer said that initially "There wasn't much of any action scenes, but I remember once this big businessman tried to bribe me."

Kemmer found *The Clear Horizon* less hectic than *Space Patrol*, even though both series aired daily live from Hollywood. One reason was that he had fewer scenes to do per show — only two or three. The other was that he got to use Teleprompters, an invention that put the script off camera in big letters he could read in case he forgot his lines.

Among the people with the show, Kemmer praised writer Manya Starr ("She's a marvelous writer and a wonderful person"), who cast him following a reading, and co-star Phyllis Avery ("She's solid as a rock"). He changed his tune when describing how the show first went off.

"The president of daytime, the whole management changed," Kemmer said (he didn't recall the name of the president, but it wasn't Fred Silverman — he took the job in 1963). "He swept a lot of stuff off of daytime. I think he felt he had to make changes."

Though Kemmer did not recall the details, he believed that support for the show remained strong enough among the network brass that they held out the idea of returning it in case its replacements faltered, which is what happened. "I think there was kind of a tacit thing, someone told me that, 'I hope you're free,'" he said.

For its second go-round *The Clear Horizon* had more plots focusing on adventure and espionage. "I was held hostage in a boat," Kemmer said. "I didn't shave for a few days." But CBS remained dissatisfied with the ratings, so it vanished for good.

Kemmer returned to soaps in 1964 when he moved to New York City to do *The Edge of Night*. "I was supposed to be there for nine months," he said. "Connie [Constance] Ford was going to kill me. As soon as I was killed on this, Proctor and Gamble [the company packaging the series] put me on another show." He was a regular on *The Secret Storm* (1965–66), *As the World Turns* (1966–70 and 1975–78) and *Somerset* (1970–74) before retiring from acting in 1991. He met actress Fran Sharon while doing *As the World Turns*. The two have been married since 1969.

Being remembered as a children's show or soap opera star would irk some celebrities, but not Kemmer. "I'm very grateful," he said. "It's all been very nice. I'm grateful for all the breaks."

1960-61

The Aquanauts

Adventure. Ran on CBS Wednesdays 7:30–8:30 P.M. Sept. 14, 1960–Sept. 27, 1961, opposite *Hong Kong* on ABC and *Wagon Train* on NBC. C: Jeremy Slate (as Larry Lahr); Keith Larsen (as Drake Andrews; 1960–January 1961); Ron Ely (as Mike Madison; 1961); Charles Thompson (as the Captain; 1961). P: Ivan Tors.

Jeremy Slate felt he was fated for his role on *The Aquanauts*. "I was born practically on the Atlantic Ocean," said the actor, who grew up in Margate, New Jersey. At age five he nearly was lost at sea when he floated in an inner tube ("For seven and a half hours I drifted down on the ocean out of sight"), but he somehow made his way back to shore. He became a lifeguard when he grew up and claimed that "I was the first person after World War II to swim Long Island Sound."

With that history of water behind him, Slate felt confident when his agent set up an interview for him with Ivan Tors about that producer's new TV series *The Aquanauts*, even though Slate had just come to Hollywood from New York in July 1960. The interview went so well that Tors nearly forgot to ask him whether he could swim. Slate assured him that he could, so the job was his.

The idea for *The Aquanauts* came from a request of CBS President Jim Aubrey to Tors regarding the latter's hit syndicated series about scuba diving, *Sea Hunt*, starring Lloyd Bridges, which was then moving into its fourth season. "Jim Aubrey went to Ivan and said, 'Do you think you could do an hour-long series like *Sea Hunt*, only with two people?'" Slate said. Tors said yes, and as a result Slate spent half of his work week "either on the water, in the water or under the water."

But the producer also added "educational" dialogue about the professional salvage scuba diving done by Larry Lahr (Slate's character) and Drake Andrews, played by Keith Larsen. Slate considered this a poor move. "I thought it was totally amateurish and totally didactic in teaching people about diving," he said. CBS felt the same way and, amid slumping ratings, Perry Lafferty came on board, replaced Keith Larsen with a character played by Ron Ely starting Jan. 25, 1961, and had the title changed to *Malibu Run* three weeks later.

The format changed so that now, according to Slate, "It showed where we lived, a beautiful hotel with a pool where two bachelors hung out." As to why Larsen was canned, Slate said, "They had seen so much of Keith playing out what Ivan had written for him that they couldn't see him around the pool." Also added was the grizzled Captain, who served as Slate and Ely's contact and pal near the hotel.

Yet all the changes meant little running

opposite what was then the #1 series in America. "We were run down by *Wagon Train*," Slate admitted. Still, *The Aquanauts/Malibu Run* had its followers, much to Slate's surprise. "People still come up to me and mention that show. That's what freaks me out," he said.

Slate went on to spend most of the 1980s acting as Chuck Wilson on the daytime soap *One Life to Live* before retiring. He now lives in Big Sur, California — near the ocean, naturally.

The Tab Hunter Show

Sitcom. Ran on NBC Sundays 8:30–9 P.M. Sept. 18, 1960–Sept. 10, 1961, opposite *The Lawman* on ABC and *The Ed Sullivan Show* on CBS. C: Tab Hunter (as Paul Morgan), Richard Erdman (as Peter Fairfield III), Jerome Cowan (as John Larsen), Reta Shaw (as Thelma). P/D: Norman Tokar. W: Stanley Shapiro, Alex Gottlieb.

The Ray Bolger Show lasted only from 1953 to 1955 on ABC, but it did provide a nice dividend for Richard Erdman, who played Ray's buddy Pete on the sitcom. "One of the writers on that was Stanley Shapiro," Erdman said. "Stanley wrote the pilot for *The Tab Hunter Show* and called me in for it."

Erdman played the best pal to the lead on this show too, but this Pete was more of a swinger than the earlier one. "I was a rich, multimillionaire, spoiled playboy, which was a joy to me," Erdman said. Given the still strong popularity for blond, hunky Hunter ("The show got on the air because of him," Erdman said), whom Erdman previously acted opposite in the 1953 film *The Steel Lady*, the actor thought he might be settling into a successful series.

Unfortunately, Erdman watched *The Tab Hunter Show* go downhill as the season progressed. Despite a strong supporting cast of veterans Jerome Cowan (as Tab's boss) and Reta Shaw (as Tab's maid), there were scripting problems in writing for Hunter, who had guested on TV since the mid to late 1950s but never did a regular series prior to this one. "Tab really wasn't going across. They didn't use him as well as they should," Erdman said. While agreeing that comedy "wasn't his milieu," Erdman thought Tab tried to make the scenarios click. "He did the best he could," Erdman said.

Erdman blames the directing as another

This shot for *The Tab Hunter Show* has Richard Erdman brandishing a hammer to test the reflexes of a justifiably worried unnamed model while star Tab Hunter observes. Between Erdman and Hunter is the workplace where Tab's character drew the immortal cartoon *Bachelor-at-Large*.

aggravating factor. He thought Norman Tokar, who served as the show's initial producer as well, was great, but when he was forced out of the job, a succession of directors took his place to the detriment of the series. "The last few shows we shot were hopeless," he said. Erdman

even offered to direct them himself (an interest he would later fulfill often on TV starting with *The Dick Van Dyke Show*), but Tab's agent convinced the lead actor it would look bad if the supporting actor of a series directed him. (That nowadays is a normal occurrence on many programs.) Erdman didn't think badly of Hunter turning the idea down, though. "He was very considerate to me," he said.

What Erdman and Hunter did agree was that the competition from *The Ed Sullivan Show*, then a top 20 hit, killed them. *The Tab Hunter Show* came on midway during Sullivan's extravaganza, and the weak lead-in of the children's adventure series *National Velvet* did not help matters either. "We beat him once," Erdman said of Sullivan. "It should've been a good spot, and we couldn't beat Sullivan." They couldn't beat *The Lawman* opposite them on ABC either; that show finished in the top 30, well ahead of the third place *Tab Hunter Show*.

Hunter did not get another regular series role until *Mary Hartman, Mary Hartman* in 1976. Erdman got one quicker than that, in 1962, but it ran even shorter than *The Tab Hunter Show* (see *Saints and Sinners*).

Hong Kong

Adventure. Ran on ABC Sept. 21, 1960–Sept. 27, 1961, opposite *The Aquanauts* on CBS and *Wagon Train* on NBC. C: Rod Taylor (as Glenn Evans), Lloyd Bochner (as Police Chief Neil Campbell), Jack Kruschen (as Tully), Harold Fong (as Fong; 1960), Gerald Jann (as Inspector Ling), Mai Tai Sing (as Ching Mei). P: Herbert Hirschman. D: Ida Lupino. W: Robert Buckner.

A Golden Globe winner as one of the best series in 1960, *Hong Kong* employed the setting of that British colony but was not filmed there. As usual for the period, much of the activity took place on Hollywood soundstages instead. But there was a sense of intrigue imparted on each show — and off stage as well, for that matter.

For one thing, actor Gerald Jann told me despite what most references say, his character did not replace Harold Fong playing Rod Taylor's houseboy after Fong left within the first

Glenn Evans (Rod Taylor) listens as club operator Tully (Jack Kruschen) gives him the lowdown of the local action on *Hong Kong*.

month of the show. Instead, he played a detective in a role slated for Victor Sen Yung, later to play Hop Sing on *Bonanza*. Jann didn't even know he taking over that job. "I was there to do a part, and when I got there, the wardrobe man said he'd show me Victor's dressing room," he said.

Jann said his role was as "Inspector Ling of the Hong Kong Police Department. Lloyd Bochner was my superior." The star of the show, however, was Taylor as American reporter Glenn Evans, who found a lot of shady activity in the land he was assigned to cover. "His character was regularly getting into trouble all the time, and Lloyd and I would get him out of it."

Added in the mix was Tully, owner and operator of the Golden Dragon nightclub. "He was a street contact," Jann said. Playing him was stocky character actor Jack Kruschen. "He had just finished doing *The Apartment*," Jann noted, referring to the 1960 comedy movie that earned Kruschen an Oscar nomination for Best Supporting Actor. Coincidentally, Jann played a waiter in one scene of *The Apartment*.

Later in 1960 another regular joined — the alluring Ching Mei, played by Mai Tai Sing. "She was a nightclub owner, and was actually one in San Francisco at the time — the Rickshaw," Jann said of Sing. "She met Rod Taylor at the Chinatown parade. She was a dancer and did a lot of things."

Even with all this, *Hong Kong* never really got any momentum to last more than a year. Jann attributed it to both its top-rated western competition and some backstage disagreements he declined to specify. "*Wagon Train* was number one at the time, and they had kind of a thing going between Roy Huggins [who became vice president in charge of TV production at 20th Century Fox, the show's production company, in late 1960] and Rod Taylor," he said. "A conflict of personality." (Huggins declined to address the situation with me, whatever it was.)

Jann said he had no beef with the cast or crew of the show. "I met a lot of wonderful people," he said. "Lloyd Bochner used to go fishing with me. So did Jack Kruschen." The actor never had another series after *Hong Kong*, but in 2001 he could boast of being an actor for more than 50 years. His most recent work on TV has been mainly in commercials.

Dan Raven

Police Drama. Ran on NBC Fridays 7:30–8:30 P.M. Sept. 23, 1960–Jan. 6, 1961, opposite *Matty's Funday Funnies* and *Harrigan and Son* on ABC and *Rawhide* on CBS. C: Skip Homeier (as Lt. Dan Raven), Dan Barton (as Det. Sgt. Burke), Quinn Redeker (as Perry Levitt). P/W: Lewis Reed, Tony Barrett. D: Joseph M. Newman.

The Tom Ewell Show

Sitcom. Ran on CBS Tuesdays 9–9:30 P.M. Sept. 27, 1960–July 18, 1961, opposite *Stagecoach West* on ABC and *Thriller* on NBC. C: Tom Ewell (as Tom Potter), Marilyn Erskine (as Fran Potter), Mabel Albertson (as Irene Brady), Cindy Robbins (as Carol Potter), Sherry Alberoni (as Debbie Potter), Eileen Chesis (as Sissie Potter). P/D: Hy Averback. AP: Bill Harmon. W: Madelyn Martin, Bob Carroll, Jr.

Guestward Ho!

Sitcom. Ran on ABC Thursdays 7:30–8 P.M. Sept. 29, 1960–Sept. 21, 1961, opposite *The Witness* (through Dec. 15), *The Ann Sothern Show* (from Dec. 22 to March 30) and *Angel* (from Dec. 22 to April 13) and *The Summer Sports Spectacular* (from April 27) on CBS and *The Outlaws* on NBC. C: Joanne Dru (as Babs Hooten), Mark Miller (as Bill Hooten), J. Carrol Naish (as Hawkeye), Flip Mark (as Brook Hooten), Earle Hodgins (as Lonesome), Jolene Brand (as Pink Cloud), Tony Montenaro, Jr. (as Rocky). EP: Cy Howard. P/D: Jerry Thorpe. W: Ronald Alexander.

The Witness

Drama. Ran on CBS Thursdays 7:30–8 P.M. Sept. 29–Dec. 15, 1960, opposite *Guestward Ho!* and *The Donna Reed Show* on ABC and *The Outlaws* on NBC, then CBS Thursdays 9–10 P.M. Dec. 22, 1960–Jan. 26, 1961, opposite *My Three Sons* and *The Untouchables* on ABC and *Bachelor Father* and *The Tennessee Ernie Ford Show* on NBC. C: Verne Collett (as court reporter), William Griffis (as court clerk), and Charles Haydon, Paul McGrath, William Smithers and Frank Milan as committee members. P: Murray Susskind, Jacqueline Babbin. D: William A. Graham. W: Irve Tunick.

The Westerner

Western. Ran on NBC Fridays 8:30–9 P.M. Sept. 30–Dec. 30, 1960, opposite *The Flintstones* on ABC and *Route 66* on CBS. C: Brian Keith (as Dave Blasingame), John Dehner (as Burgundy Smith). P/D: Sam Peckinpah. W: Robert Heverly.

Michael Shayne

Detective Drama. Ran on NBC Fridays 10–11 P.M. Sept. 30, 1960–Sept. 22, 1961, opposite *The Detectives Starring Robert Taylor* and *The Law and Mr. Jones* on ABC and *The Twilight Zone* and *Eyewitness to History* (through June 16) and *Person to Person* (from June 23) on CBS. C: Richard Denning (as Michael Shayne), Jerry Paris (as Tim Rourke), Patricia Donahue (as Lucy Hamilton; 1960–61), Margie Regan (as Lucy Hamilton; 1961), Herbert Rudley (as Lt. Will Gentry), Gary Clarke (as Dick Hamilton). P: Joseph Huffman. D: Robert Florey, Paul Stewart. W: William Link, Richard Levinson.

Today on the Farm

Informational. Ran on NBC Saturdays 7–8 A.M. Oct. 1, 1960–March 11, 1961. C: Eddy Arnold, Alex Dreier, Mal Hansen, Carmelita Pope, Joe Slattery, Slim Wilson. P: Ed Pierce. D: Max Miller. W: Earl Hamner.

The Walter Winchell Show

Variety. Ran on ABC Sundays 10–10:30 P.M. Oct. 2–Nov. 6, 1960, opposite *What's My Line?* on CBS and *This is Your Life* on NBC. C: Walter Winchell. P/D: Alan Handley. W: Walter Winchell (billed with his name backwards as "Retlaw Chellwin"), Milt Rosen, Harvey Bullock, Ray Allen.

The Islanders

Adventure. Ran on ABC Sundays 9:30–10:30 P.M. Oct. 2, 1960–March 28, 1961, opposite *The Jack Benny Program* and *Candid Camera* on CBS and *The Dinah Shore Chevy Show* and *The Loretta Young Show* on NBC. C: William Reynolds (as Sandy Wade), James Philbrook (as Zack Malloy), Diane Brewster (as Wilhelmina Vandeveer), Daria Massey (as Naja), Roy Wright (as Shipwreck Callahan). P/D/W: Richard L. Bare.

Stagecoach West

Western. Ran on ABC Tuesdays 9–10 P.M. Oct. 4, 1960–Sept. 26, 1961, opposite *The Tom Ewell Show* (through July 18) and *The Red Skelton Show* (through July 18) and *Comedy Spotlight* (from July 25) and *Playhouse 90* reruns (from July 25) on CBS and *Thriller* on NBC. C: Wayne Rogers (as Luke Perry), Robert Bray (as Simon Kaye), Richard Eyer (as David Kane). P: Vincent Fennelly. D: Donald McDougall, Thomas Carr, Harry Harris. W: D.D. and Mary M. Beauchamp.

Dante

Adventure. Ran on NBC Mondays 9:30–10 P.M. Oct. 3, 1960–April 10, 1961, opposite *Adventures in Paradise* on ABC and *The Andy Griffith Show* on CBS. C: Howard Duff (as Willie Dante), Alan Mowbray (as Stewart Styles), Tom D'Andrea (as Biff), James Nolan (as Inspector Loper). P: Mike Meshekoff. D: Richard Kinon. W: Harold Jack Bloom.

My Sister Eileen

Sitcom. Ran on CBS Wednesdays 9–9:30 P.M. Oct. 5, 1960–April 12, 1961, opposite *Hawaiian Eye* on ABC and *The Perry Como Show* on NBC. C: Elaine Stritch (as Ruth Sherwood), Shirley Bonne (as Eileen Sherwood), Leon Belasco (as Mr. Appopoplous), Jack Weston (as Chick Adams), Rose Marie (as Bertha), Raymond Bailey (as Mr. D.X. Beaumont), Stubby Kaye (as Marty Scott). P/W: Dick Wesson. D: Oscar Rudolph.

Angel

Sitcom. Ran on CBS Thursdays 9–9:30 P.M. Oct. 6–Dec. 15, 1960, opposite *My Three Sons* on ABC and *Bachelor Father* on NBC, then CBS Thursdays 8–8:30 P.M. Dec. 22, 1960–April 13, 1961, opposite *The Donna Reed Show* on ABC and *The Outlaws* on NBC, and finally CBS Wednesdays 9–9:30 P.M. April 19–Sept. 20, 1961, opposite *Hawaiian Eye* on ABC and *Kraft Mystery Theater* on NBC. C: Annie Farge (as Angel Smith), Marshall Thompson (as John Smith), Doris Singleton (as Susie), Don Keefer (as George). EP: Jess Oppenheimer. P: Edward H. Feldman. D: Lamont Johnson, Ezra Stone.

Veteran TV director Lamont Johnson spent almost all his career behind the camera doing series dramas such as episodes of *The Twilight Zone* and powerful TV-movies such as *Fear on Trial* (1975), so it comes as a surprise to report he was the main director on the fluffy sitcom *Angel*. In fact, it was Johnson who recommended that executive producer Jess Oppenheimer let his old pal Don Keefer play the next-door neighbor on the sitcom, which he did, to Keefer's delight.

There was another bonus for Keefer in doing the show. "My real wife was in the pilot," he said, referring to actress Catherine McLeod. She and actor Herb Vigran played a couple in a few episodes, according to Keefer, but the show mainly involved him and Doris Singleton, as George and his wife Susie, interacting with John Smith and his wife Angel, a French emigrant somewhat befuddled by America and its customs.

"Susie, she sort of took Angel under her wings and also would get in digs at her husband," Keefer said. "It was two cultures against one another. It was just like [*I Love*] *Lucy*, except we had a French girl."

That latter comparison is apt, because Oppenheimer was the producer of *I Love Lucy* from 1951 to 1956. Keefer noted that "CBS was quite high on [*Angel*]. It was the first series Jess had produced after *I Love Lucy*." Like that series, *Angel* was filmed with three cameras before a studio audience, but it fell far short of the earlier program's success.

"It never got high ratings, and you heard complaints Annie Farge, the leading girl, her accent was so thick, the average American couldn't understand her," Keefer said. Beaten initially by *My Three Sons*, CBS tried the show in two other time slots before giving up on it after one season.

Farge, an actual native of France, never did another American TV series. "She went back to her home and had a small child," Keefer said. "She became a very successful producer of rock music. I understand she had something to do with the Paris production of *Hair*." He also heard from former co-star Doris Singleton that she and her husband saw Farge at the Cannes Film Festival around 1990.

As for the rest of the cast of *Angel*, Keefer remains active as an actor. He termed an appearance in the 1997 Jim Carrey film comedy *Liar Liar* "great fun." Marshall Thompson, as Angel's husband John, starred in the hit drama *Daktari* from 1966 to 1969. He died in 1992. And Doris Singleton is now retired but still loved and admired for her occasional appearances as Caroline Appleby on *I Love Lucy*— the show to which *Angel* received unfortunate comparisons.

"You got some 'splaining to do, Lucy!" Oh, wrong sitcom. But doesn't it look like Marshall Thompson and Annie Farge are doing their best to look like the Ricardos in this photograph from *Angel*?

Mr. Garlund (a/k/a The Garlund Touch)

Adventure. Ran on CBS Fridays 9:30–10 P.M. Oct. 7, 1960–Jan. 13, 1961, opposite *77 Sunset Strip* on ABC and *The Bell Telephone Hour* on NBC. C: Charles Quinlivan (as Frank Garlund), Kam Tong (as Kam Chang). P/D/W: Bernard Girard.

Bringing Up Buddy

Sitcom. Ran on CBS Mondays 8:30–9 P.M. Oct. 10, 1960–Sept. 25, 1961, opposite *Surfside Six* on ABC and *Tales of Wells Fargo* on NBC . C: Frank Aletter (as Buddy Flower), Enid Markey (as Aunt Violet Flower), Doro Merande (as Aunt Iris Flower). P: Joe Connelly, Bob Mosher. D: David Butler. W: George Tibbles.

Klondike

Adventure. Ran on NBC Mondays 9–9:30 P.M. Oct. 10, 1960–Feb. 6, 1961, opposite *Surfside Six* on ABC and *The Danny Thomas Show* on CBS. C: Ralph Taegar (as Mike Halliday), James Coburn (as Jeff Durain), Mari Blanchard (as Kathy

O'Hara), Joi Lansing (as Goldie). P/D: William Conrad. W: Sam Peckinpah, Carey Wilbur.

Peter Loves Mary

Sitcom. Ran on NBC Wednesdays 10–10:30 P.M. Oct. 12, 1960–May 31, 1961, opposite *Naked City* on ABC and *The U.S. Steel Hour* alternating with *Armstrong Circle Theatre* on CBS. C: Peter Lind Hayes (as Peter Lindsey), Mary Healy (as Mary Lindsey), Bea Benaderet (as Wilma), Merry Martin (as Leslie Lindsey), Gil Smith (as Steve Lindsey), Alan Reed (as Happy Richman), Howard Smith (as Horace Gibney), Arch Johnson (as Charlie). P/W: Dan Simon. D: Rod Amateau.

Harrigan and Son

Sitcom. Ran on ABC Fridays 8–8:30 P.M. Oct. 14, 1960–Sept. 26, 1961, opposite *Rawhide* on CBS and *Dan Raven* (through Jan. 6), *One Happy Family* (from Jan. 13 to March 10 and May 12 to Sept. 8) and *Five Star Jubilee* (from March 17 to May 5) on NBC. C: Pat O'Brien (as James Harrigan, Sr.), Roger Perry (as James Harrigan, Jr.), Georgine Darcy (as Gypsy), Helen Kleeb (as Miss Claridge). P/W: Cy Howard. D: Walter Grauman.

Saturday Prom

Musical Variety. Ran on NBC Saturdays 5:30–6 P.M. Oct. 15, 1960–April 1, 1961, opposite *All Star Golf* on ABC. C: Merv Griffin, the Saturday Prom Seven, the NBC Orchestra. P: Ed Pierce. D: Lynwood King. W: Hal Hackaday, Don Epstein.

"That went on the air as a live answer to Dick Clark," director Lynwood King said of *Saturday Prom*. The series did not compete directly against Clark's long-running rock music and dancing series *American Bandstand*; that show ran daily from 4 to 5:30 P.M. It also ran nowhere near as long as *Bandstand*, ending April Fools Day 1961 after less than six months on the air.

Nevertheless, *Saturday Prom* is memorable for its on-air personnel. Beyond having future talk show host Merv Griffin introducing bands, the show's house band, the 22-piece NBC Orchestra, had a few notable folks. "Bobby Vinton was the orchestra leader," King said, referring to the singer whose heyday came a few years later with such hits as "Blue Velvet" and "There! I've Said It Again." "He was the saxophone player. I don't even know if he sang. And the first trumpet player was Doc Severinson."

Severinson later became the flamboyantly-dressed bandleader on *The Tonight Show Starring Johnny Carson* from 1967 to 1992.

Of course, Vinton and Severinson were unknown when *Saturday Prom* was on the air. Its host, however, already was a known quantity, as he was hosting the game show *Play Your Hunch* on NBC weekday mornings when the series started. King noted that Griffin was a professional but had an urge to vocalize on the show even though it was geared to play rock music. "Merv wanted to sing, and he always wanted to sing 'When Sunny Gets Blue,'" laughed King.

As with *American Bandstand*, there were a group of high school students who came to dance on the show, with King estimating the number per show being around 30 teenagers. "They were all ladies and gentlemen," he said. "They all had fun, and we loved them. Those kids were so good, they would split [down the runway] for the closeups for the crane [camera]." As for the guest rock singers and groups, there were two staging areas with elevated platforms where they performed.

King termed the show's producer Ed Pierce a "worrywart," since he always considered what could go wrong yet never did with the show. King himself said he had few hassles on the job other than rehearsing with the groups. "I didn't walk in until Friday," he said. "I didn't have anything to do with the bookings."

In fact, King didn't anything to do with rock music either prior to doing this show, but he said he enjoyed the music and the musicians. "I'm very eclectic," he noted. "I've done symphony orchestras all the way down."

NBC apparently was more impressed by the competition than with *Saturday Prom*, as it brought *All Star Golf* over from ABC in 1961 in the same time slot following a summer break. It made no effort to try another weekend *Bandstand* clone thereafter.

The Road to Reality

Soap Opera. Ran on ABC weekdays 2:30–3 P.M. Oct. 17, 1960–March 31, 1961, opposite *Art Linkletter's House Party* on CBS and *The Loretta Young Show* reruns on NBC. C: John Beal (as Dr. Lewis), Robert Drew (as Vic), Judith Braun (as Joan), Salem Ludwig (as Harry), Eugenia Rawls (as Margaret), Robin Howard (as Rosalind, 1960),

James Dimitri (as Lee, 12/15/60–3/31/61), Kay Doubleday (as Chris; 12/20/60–3/31/61). P: Julian Bercovici. D: Paul Nickell. Creator/Editor: John G. Fuller.

Using tapes from group sessions with a real-life New York psychoanalyst as the basis for its melodramas, John Beal starred on this serial as Dr. Lewis, while five or six other actors played his patients who discussed their neuroses and personal lives. These actors mostly were stage veterans, including Salem Ludwig, who played Vic, a man afraid of commitment.

Ludwig said he was not sure who picked him for the show. He had done television but never had a regular role on it prior to that time. "Somebody must have seen me in a play," he recalled. "I was in Chicago in the summer, and when I got home, I got this offer." Given the choice between touring in a play and staying in New York videotaping a daily soap, he picked the latter.

While his memories about his and other characters have faded, Ludwig did remember one event on the program. "It was early videotaping the show in its seventh week," he said. "I couldn't handle it, memorizing 30 minutes of dialogue every day. One day I just went sky high when we were recording and couldn't remember my lines. They wanted memorization, but then they had a TelePrompTer [a device showing one's lines off camera] after that."

Ludwig believed the show met an early demise due to its failure to address openly the mental and emotional problems raised in the discussions, fearing controversy among viewers (it did warn at the start of each show something "shocking" might be discussed). "The trouble with a program like that is, when you get into stuff like that, it gets censorable ahead of time," he said. He feels its watered-down approach to the issues hampered the show's appeal and notes that "Today, they could've gone more with the material than we were allowed." ABC waited two years after it ended before trying another soap opera, this time hitting with the still-running *General Hospital*.

The Road to Reality was the only regular series for Robin Howard, Kay Doubleday and Ludwig. "Series never came my way," Ludwig noted. "On the other hand, my tastes were kind of special anyway." He occupied himself with stage work and occasional movies, working with famed director Elia Kazan in four pro-

ductions alone. The octogenarian remained active on TV too, making guest shots on *Third Watch* and *Law & Order* in the 2000-2001 season. And his name often graced the resumes of actors who studied under him at HB Studios in New York. "I've been teaching for 30 years," he noted proudly.

So while *The Road to Reality* did not lead Ludwig to the pathway of stardom, it did provide him with an overall pleasant detour in his long career with a cast and crew he praised. "We had a great time," he said. "We enjoyed doing the show."

Westinghouse Playhouse

Sitcom. Ran on NBC Fridays 8:30–9 P.M. Jan. 6–July 7, 1961, opposite *The Flintstones* on ABC and *Route 66* on CBS. C: Nanette Fabray (as Nan McGovern), Wendell Corey (as Dan McGovern), Bobby Diamond (as Buddy McGovern), Jacklyn O'Donnell (as Nancy McGovern), Doris Kemper (as Mrs. Harper). P: Larry Berns. D: Herschel Daugherty. W: Ranald MacDougall.

One Happy Family

Sitcom. Ran on NBC Fridays 8–8:30 P.M. Jan. 13–March 10, 1961 and May 12–Sept. 8, 1961, both times opposite *Harrigan and Son* on ABC and *Rawhide* on CBS. C: Dick Sargent (as Dick Cooper), Jody Warner (as Penny Cooper), Chick Chandler (as Barney Hogan), Elizabeth Fraser (as Mildred Hogan), Jack Kirkwood (as Charlie Hackett), Cheerio Meredith (as Lovey Hackett). P/W: Al Lewis, Sid Dorfman. D: Al Lewis.

You're in the Picture

Game. Ran on CBS Fri 9:30–10 P.M. Jan. 20, 1961, opposite *77 Sunset Strip* on ABC and *The Bell Telephone Hour* on NBC. C: Jackie Gleason, Pat Carroll, Pat Harrington, Jr., Jan Sterling, Arthur Treacher. P: Steve Carlin. D: Seymour Robbie.

"I did no creative work on that show," director Seymour Robbie flatly stated about one of TV's biggest bombs ever, *You're in the Picture*. A game show which brought back Jackie Gleason as a regular attraction, it was so bad he spent the following week apologizing for it. *You're in the Picture* thus became a series which lasted just one program.

Given the show's magnitude as a flop, it is understandable that Robbie dissociated himself from it. He came on to direct the show after meeting with its packager, which earlier had hit with *The $64,000 Question.*

"They created the show," Robbie said. (Specifically, Bob Synes and Don Lipp took that credit — or blame, if you prefer.) "They asked me if I wanted to do a show with Jackie Gleason. I said, 'Are you kidding? Jackie Gleason?! Sure!'"

The urge to direct Gleason is understandable; not so is why the star, known for excellent characterizations in his variety shows such as the Poor Soul, Joe the Bartender and of course Ralph Kramden, decided to host a weak panel show wherein a quartet of celebrities stuck their heads in carnival cutouts and tried to guess what scene their surrounding artwork depicted, with all prizes going to charity. Robbie offered that "He was a little lazy at the time and wanted to make a few bucks." But *You're in the Picture* produced more headaches than easy money for Gleason.

The live show debuted messily as Pat Harrington, Jr., flew from Los Angeles to New York City at the last minute to replace an injured Keenan Wynn. Harrington had just finished a season on *The Danny Thomas Show*; his fellow panelist Pat Carroll would join the show in the fall of 1961. Otherwise, there was little to connect the four players involved. The lack of chemistry showed (they yelled out questions and guesses over each other), as did Gleason's uneasiness as host. The result was alternately chaotic and dull. Some viewers thought Gleason was doing something out of *The Twilight Zone*, which is what followed the show.

"The reviews were devastating, and I think Jackie was ashamed of it," Robbie said. "We talked about it in depth. I said, 'Jackie, you have a reputation for being direct and forthright to the people.'" The next Friday, Jan. 27, 1961, Gleason spent the whole half hour to beg forgiveness and explain what went wrong to an appreciative, understanding audience. He then hosted a talk program, *The Jackie Gleason Show*, the rest of the season, but Jackie was a better performer than host and, to use one of Jackie's catch phrases, away it went after March 24, 1961.

Thankfully, Gleason rebounded on TV the next year when he started another variety show. In fact, Robbie noted, "He hired me later in 1962 to do *The American Scene Magazine.*" The series ran eight years, the last four known sim-

ply as *The Jackie Gleason Show*. It ended in 1970, by which time *You're in the Picture* faded from memory for most people.

The Americans

Drama. Ran on NBC Mondays 7:30–8:30 P.M. Jan. 23–Sept. 11, 1961, opposite *Cheyenne, Bronco* and *Sugarfoot* on ABC and *To Tell the Truth* and *Pete and Gladys* on CBS. C: Darryl Hickman (as Ben Canfield), Dick Davalos (as Jeff Canfield). EP: Frank Telford. P: Gordon Kay. D: Douglas Heyes. W: John Gay.

Number Please

Game. Ran on ABC Mondays through Fridays 12:30–1 P.M. Jan. 31–Sept. 29, 1961, opposite *Search for Tomorrow* and *Guiding Light* on CBS and *It Could Be You* and news on NBC, then ABC Mondays through Fridays 2–2:30 P.M. Oct. 2–Dec. 29, 1961, opposite *Password* on CBS and *The Jan Murray Show* on NBC. C: Bud Collyer. P: Jean Kopelman. AP: Helen Marcus, Bill Barry. D: Donald Bohl, Glenn Swanson.

Gunslinger

Western. Ran on CBS Thursdays 9–10 P.M. Feb. 9–Sept. 14, 1961, opposite *My Three Sons* and *The Untouchables* on ABC and *Bachelor Father* and *The Tennessee Ernie Ford Show* (through June 29) and *Great Ghost Tales* (from July 6) on NBC. C: Tony Young (as Cord), Preston Foster (as Capt. Zachary Wingate), Charles Gray (as Pico McGuire), Dee Pollock (as Billy Urchin), Midge Ware (as Amber "Amby" Hollister), John Pickard (as Sgt. Major Murdock). EP: Charles Marquis Warren. P: Seeleg Lester. D: Andrew McLaglen. W: John Dunkel, Louis Vittes.

Acapulco

Adventure. Ran on NBC Mondays 9–9:30 P.M. Feb. 27–April 24, 1961, opposite *Surfside Six* on ABC and *The Danny Thomas Show* on CBS. C: Ralph Taeger (as Patrick Malone), James Coburn (as Gregg Miles), Telly Savalas (as Mr. Carver), Allison Hayes (as Chloe), Bobby Troup (as Bobby), Jason Robards, Sr. (as Max). P: John Robinson. D: John Meredyth Lucas. W: Cy Chermak.

Double Exposure

Game. Ran on CBS Mondays through Fridays 11–11:30 A.M. March 13–Sept. 29, 1961, opposite

Morning Court (through May 12) and *The Gale Storm Show* reruns (from May 15) on ABC and *The Price Is Right* on NBC. C: Steve Dunne. P: Bob Quigley. D: Jerome Shaw.

Your Surprise Package

Game. Ran on CBS Mondays through Fridays 11:30 A.M.–Noon March 13–Sept. 29, 1961, opposite *The Bob Cummings Show* reruns on ABC and *Concentration* on NBC, then CBS Mondays through Fridays 11:30–11:55 A.M. Oct. 2, 1961–Feb. 23, 1962, opposite *The Bob Cummings Show* reruns (through Dec. 1) and *Yours for a Song* (from Dec. 4) on ABC and *Concentration* on NBC. C: George Fenneman. EP: Al Singer. P: Allan Sherman. D: Hal Cooper.

Face the Facts

Game. Ran on CBS Mondays through Fridays 2–2:30 P.M. March 13–Sept. 29, 1961, opposite *Day in Court* on ABC and *The Jan Murray Show* on NBC. C: Red Rowe. P: Irving Mansfield, Peter Arnell. D: Joe Behar. W: Dave Greggory.

Five Star Jubilee

Musical Variety. Ran on NBC Fridays 8–8:30 P.M. March 17–May 5, 1961, opposite *Harrigan and Son*

on ABC and *Rawhide* on CBS, then NBC Fridays 8:30–9 P.M. May 12–Sept. 22, 1961, opposite *The Flintstones* on ABC and *Route 66* on CBS. C: Snooky Lanson, Tex Ritter, Jimmy Wakely, Carl Smith, Rex Allen, the Promenaders, the Wagon Wheelers, the Jubilaires, the Tall Timber Trio, Slim Wilson and His Jubilee Band.

Danger Man

Adventure. Ran on CBS Wednesdays 8:30–9 P.M. April 5–Sept. 13, 1961, opposite *The Adventures of Ozzie and Harriet* on ABC and *The Price Is Right* on NBC. C: Patrick McGoohan (as John Drake). P/D/W: Ralph Smart. W: Brian Clemens, Ian Stuart Black.

Whispering Smith

Western. Ran on NBC Mondays 9–9:30 P.M. May 15–Sept. 18, 1961, opposite *Surfside Six* on ABC and *The Danny Thomas Show* (through July 10) and *The Spike Jones Show* (from July 17). C: Audie Murphy (as Det. Tom "Whispering" Smith), Guy Mitchell (as Det. George Romack), Sam Buffington (as Chief John Richards). EP: Richard Lewis. P: Herbert Coleman, William Willingham.

1961-62

Follow the Sun

Adventure. Ran on ABC Sundays 7:30–8:30 P.M. Sept. 17, 1961–Sept. 8, 1962, opposite *Dennis the Menace* and *The Ed Sullivan Show* on CBS and *Walt Disney* on NBC. C: Barry Coe (as Ben Gregory), Brett Halsey (as Paul Templin), Gary Lockwood (as Eric Jason), Gigi Perreau (as Katherine Ann Richards), Jay Lanin (as Lt. Frank Roper). P: Anthony Wilson. D: Jules Bricken. W: Toby Benjamin, Howard Browne.

Cain's Hundred

Police Drama. Ran on NBC Tuesdays 10–11 P.M. Sept. 19, 1961–Sept. 11, 1962, opposite *Alcoa Premiere* and *Bell and Howell Close-Up* on ABC and *The Garry Moore Show* (through June 26) and

Talent Scouts (from July 3) on CBS. C: Peter Mark Richman (as Nicholas "Nick" Cain). EP/W: Paul Monash. P: Charles Russell. D: Boris Sagal. W: Wallace Ware.

On Your Mark

Children's Game. Ran on ABC Saturdays 11–11:30 A.M. Sept. 23–Dec. 30, 1961, opposite *The Magic Land of Allakazam* on CBS and *Fury* on NBC. C: Sonny Fox. EP: Sonny Fox. P/D: Lloyd Gross.

ABC was still very much the third network in the broadcasting industry in the early 1960s regarding how it programmed Saturday mornings. Spotty, short-lived efforts in the 1950s left the network with little room to build a lineup, with the result being that when *On Your Mark* debuted in 1961, it actually was the first show to appear on ABC Saturday mornings for the 1961-62 season.

On Your Mark was the creation of Sonny Fox, who had survived a disastrous outing hosting the game show *The $64,000 Challenge* in 1956 while faring better doing the children's adventure *Let's Take a Trip* from 1955 to 1958. With *On Your Mark*, he combined both formats.

"Sonny was a nice guy, very pleasant man to work with," said the series' producer and director, Lloyd Gross. "He was doing something on a local basis at the time." That show was the long-running *Wonderama* on WNEW New York, which began in 1955 and aired Sundays from 7 to 11 A.M. (that's right — a four-hour live show). Fox hosted that show from 1959 to 1967.

The program's setup was simple. Three preadolescents or thereabouts (supposedly 9 to 13 year olds) competed in games relating to a featured occupation for that day's show, with the winner getting a prize geared to that career. For example, on the debut the kids competed in contests related to being an astronaut, with the top prize being a trip to the Cape Canaveral rocket launching complex in Florida. "It was a cute kids' show," Gross said. "It was just a typical youngsters' show."

Gross said while the game worked fine, Fox had problems getting support for it from his sponsor (the show had only one advertiser). "He didn't have the client quite nailed down," he said. "It wasn't the greatest client in the world." When the dubious backer left the enterprise, a replacement could not be found, and *On Your Mark* was off its mark after three months.

When *On Your Mark* went off, ABC did not replace it nor its following show, *Magic Ranch* (q.v.), until the fall of 1962. That finally marked a period where ABC built on its Saturday morning lineup to the point where it was #1 in that time part for the 1965-66 season. As for Fox, he returned to Saturday mornings 15 years later with *Way Out Games* (q.v.).

Patterns in Music

Musical Variety. Ran on NBC Sundays 4:30–5 P.M. Sept. 24, 1961–April 8, 1962, opposite pro football on ABC and CBS, then NBC Sundays 5–5:30 P.M.

April 15–May 27, 1962, opposite *ABC's Wide World of Sports* on ABC and *The Original Amateur Hour* on CBS, and then NBC Sundays 5:30–6 P.M. June 17–Sept. 16, 1962, opposite *ABC's Wide World of Sports* on ABC and *The Original Amateur Hour* on CBS. C: John Doremus, the Joseph Gallichio Orchestra. EP: Harry Trigg. P/D/W: Dave Barnhizer.

Patterns in Music was a televised version of a local Chicago radio show of the same title with the selling point being that all the songs performed were connected by a theme via their titles. For example, the show's TV opener was a tribute to the fall season, and host John Doremus presented the Joseph Gallichio (pronounced "gah-LEEK-ee-oh") Orchestra doing such numbers as "September Song" and "Autumn Leaves." The only difference between radio and TV was that viewers on TV not only saw Gallichio and his orchestra play, but also saw film segments edited to match the music. The latter was not part of the original plan, according to the show's producer/direcor/writer Dave Barnhizer.

"We started out shooting the band, and I said, 'This is awfully boring,' and so I started putting pictures with the music and solicited photographers from across the country, plus free film from the government and so on," he said. He was so intent on capturing the right images with the tunes that he had two 16mm projectors running 12 hours a day at the office to determine what could and should be used.

On the show itself, the role of Doremus was rather limited to announcing the next piece. "He had 30 to 45 words to introduce each tune," Barnhizer said. However, he noted that the orchestra's repertoire was anything but limited. "We had a huge library of arrangements, with that orchestra going back to the radio days." He said the orchestra itself numbered somewhere from 30 to 40 pieces. "There was like 12 fiddles, two or three cellos, two or three in the bass section."

Barnhizer also noted that concerning conductor Gallichio's own musical taste, "Joe was never happy with the popular stuff. He wanted to do classical." Unfortunately for him, the format for *Patterns in Music* left him with few chances to indulge his true musical passion.

Patterns in Music original followed pro football games on NBC, and the idea was that the show would be flexible enough so that if a game ran late, the live show could be shrunk to accommodate the overflow and let the following show start on time. "It started out that way, and apparently they got a lot of fan mail and gave it its own [full] time slot," Barnhizer said. "We would start the show and just go on as if it were planned to be a full half hour."

But while the show generated fan mail, it never had an advertiser during its year run. Although Barnhizer said that the series' budget was "Very cheap, we didn't spend any money at all," that still did not placate NBC executives, who he thought were privately not wanting to support network shows from Chicago and thus helped kill *Patterns in Music*. "They refused to sell it, although they apparently were approached by several sponsors," he said. NBC replaced it with, of all things, *The Bullwinkle Show*. Neither Doremus nor the orchestra did any other network shows.

87th Precinct

Police Drama. Ran on NBC Mondays 9–10 P.M. Sept. 25, 1961–Sept. 10, 1962, opposite *Surfside Six* on ABC and *The Danny Thomas Show* (through June 25) and *The Andy Griffith Show* (through June 25) and *The Lucy-Desi Comedy Hour* (from July 2) on CBS. C: Robert Lansing (as Det. Steve Carella), Ron Harper (as Det. Bert King), Gregory Walcott (as Det. Roger Havilland), Norman Fell (as Det. Meyer Meyer), Gena Rowlands (as Teddy Carella). P: Boris Kaplan. D: Herschel Daugherty. W: Winston Miller.

Ichabod and Me

Sitcom. Ran on CBS Tuesdays 9:30–10 P.M. Sept. 26, 1961–Sept. 18, 1962, opposite *The New Breed* (through Nov. 7) and *Yours for a Song* (from Nov. 14) on ABC and *The Dick Powell Show* on NBC. C: Robert Sterling (as Robert Major), George Chandler (as Ichabod Adams), Christine White (as Abigail Adams), Jimmy Mathers (as Benjie Major), Reta Shaw (as Aunt Lavinia), Jimmy Hawkins (as Jonathan Baylor), Guy Raymond (as Martin Perkins), Burt Mustin (as Olaf), Forrest Lewis (as Colby). P/W: Joe Connelly, Bob Mosher. D: Sidney Lanfield.

Father of the Bride

Sitcom. Ran on CBS Fridays 9:30–10 P.M. Sept. 29, 1961–Sept. 14, 1962, opposite *77 Sunset Strip* on ABC and *The Bell Telephone Hour* alternating with *The Dinah Shore Show* (through June 1) and

Purex Summer Specials (from July 6) on NBC. C: Leon Ames (as Stanley Banks), Ruth Warrick (as Ellie Banks), Myrna Fahey (as Kay Banks Dunston), Rickie Sorenson (as Tommy Banks), Burt Metcalfe (as Buckley Dunston), Ransom Sherman (as Herbert Dunston), Lurene Tuttle (as Doris Dunston), Ruby Dandridge (as Delilah). EP: Robert Maxwell. P: Rudy E. Abel. D: Fletcher Markle. W: Dale and Katherine Eunson, Theodore and Matilde Ferro.

Target: The Corruptors

Drama. Ran on ABC Fridays 10–11 P.M. Sept. 29, 1961–Sept. 21, 1962, opposite *The Twilight Zone* and *Eyewitness* on CBS and *The Bell Telephone Hour* alternating with *The Dinah Shore Show* (through June 1) and *Purex Summer Specials* (from July 6) and *Here and Now* (through Dec. 29) and *Chet Huntley Reporting* (from Jan. 12) on NBC. C: Stephen McNally (as Paul Marino), Robert Harland (as Jack Flood). P: John Burrows, Leonard Ackerman. D: Don Medford. W: Chris Knopf.

The Magic Ranch

Children's. Ran on ABC Saturdays 11:30 A.M.–Noon Sept. 30–Dec. 23, 1961, opposite *The Roy Rogers Show* reruns on CBS and *The Danny Thomas Show* reruns on NBC. C: Don Alan. P: George B. Anderson. D: Ted Schulte. W: Myron Golden Anderson.

Bus Stop

Drama. Ran on ABC Sundays 9–10 P.M. Oct. 1, 1961–March 25, 1962, opposite *General Electric Theater* and *The Jack Benny Program* on CBS and *Bonanza* on NBC. C: Marilyn Maxwell (as Grace Sherwood), Rhodes Reason (as Will Mayberry), Joan Freeman (as Elma Gahringer), Richard Anderson (as Glenn Wagner). EP: William Self. P: Robert Blees. D: Stuart Rosenberg. W: Sally Benson.

Window on Main Street

Sitcom. Ran on CBS Mondays 8:30–9 P.M. Oct. 2, 1961–Feb. 12, 1962, opposite *The Rifleman* on ABC and *The Price Is Right* on NBC, then CBS Wednesdays 8–8:30 P.M. Feb. 21–Sept. 12, 1962, opposite *Straightaway* on ABC and *Wagon Train* on NBC. C: Robert Young (as Cameron Garrett Brooks), Constance Moore (as Chris Logan), Ford Rainey (as Lloyd Ramsey), Brad Berwick (as Arny Logan), James Davidson (as Wally Evans), Carol

Byron (as Peggy Evans), Coleen Gray (as Miss Wycliffe), Warner Jones (as Harry McGill), Tim Matheson (as Roddy Miller). P: Eugene B. Rodney. D: Richard Dunlap. W: Roswell Rogers.

The New Breed

Police Drama. Ran on ABC Tuesdays 9–10 P.M. Oct. 3–Nov. 7, 1961, opposite *Ichabod and Me* on CBS and and *The Dick Powell Show* on NBC, then ABC Tuesdays 8:30–9:30 P.M. Nov. 14, 1961–Sept. 25, 1962, opposite *The Many Loves of Dobie Gillis* and *The Red Skelton Show* (through June 26) and *Comedy Spot* (from July 3) on CBS and *Alfred Hitchcock Presents* and *The Dick Powell Show* on NBC. C: Leslie Nielson (as Lt. Price Adams), John Beradino (as Sgt. Vince Cavelli), John Clarke (as Joe Huddleston), Greg Roman (as Pete Garcia), Byron Morrow (as Capt. Keith Gregory). EP: Quinn Martin. P/D: Walter Grauman. W: Hank Searls.

Mrs. G. Goes to College (a/k/a The Gertrude Berg Show)

Sitcom. Ran on CBS Wednesdays 9:30–10 P.M. Oct. 4, 1961–Jan. 4, 1962, opposite *Hawaiian Eye* on ABC and *The Perry Como Show* on NBC, then CBS Thursdays 9:30–10 P.M. Jan. 11–April 5, 1962, opposite *Margie* on ABC and *Hazel* on NBC. C: Gertrude Berg (as Sarah Green), Sir Cedric Hardwicke (as Prof. Crayton), Mary Wickes (as Maxfield), Skip Ward (as Joe Connell), Marion Ross (as Susan Green; 1961), Leo Penn (as Jerry Green; 1961), Paul Smith (as George Howell), Aneta Corsaut (as Irma Howell), Karyn Kupcinet (as Carol). P/D: Hy Averback. D: Robert Butler, Richard Kinon. W: Cherney Berg, Gertrude Berg, James Fritzell, Everett Greenbaum.

After starring as Molly Goldberg in the sitcom *The Goldbergs* on radio from 1929 to 1945 and 1949 to 1950 and on TV from 1949 to 1955, few thought actress Gertrude Berg ever would be able to escape that character. She shocked those people by earning a Tony Award in 1959 starring in the comedy *A Majority of One* opposite Sir Cedric Hardwicke. That pairing led to the creation of a sitcom by her son Cherney Berg.

"Seeing the success of *A Majority of One* with Sir Cedric Hardwicke, I thought they would work well together," said Berg. "I didn't want to repeat the Goldberg business, so I came up with this thing—a lady, widowed, going to college." His mother played Sarah Green, a par-

ent of two living in a boardinghouse run by a woman named Maxfield. She became pals with students Joe Caldwell and Carol and learned English from Prof. Crayton, on exchange from Cambridge University in England. Hardwicke played Crayton.

Though Hardwicke's only previous regular American TV series role was as a panelist on the 1959 summer game show *Who Pays?*, the junior Berg said it wasn't a problem getting the actor for the sitcom, with one caveat. "He just wanted to stay out of California as much as possible. His wife had a court order for him there," Berg said. (Speaking of California, regarding where the series took place, Berg noted that "We never really did say it was UCLA [the University of California at Los Angeles], but we shot it there." Apart from those exteriors, the program was shot on soundstages with one camera and no audiences.)

Berg wrote the pilot and at least five other episodes of the show. He left the show by mid-season because he disliked Los Angeles and preferred to work in New York City. The move was not due to any conflict with his mom, for whom he previously had written on TV with *The Goldbergs*. "I always enjoyed working with Mother," he said. "I was treated like any other writer, except I could go to her house for supper."

His departure was not the only one by the end of 1961. The show dropped Sarah's kids Susan and Jerry from the cast too. "We didn't write them out," noted Berg. "There was just no need for them." A bigger change was a new time slot and title of *The Gertrude Berg Show* to get more people watching. But it didn't happen.

Nevertheless, Berg didn't believe ratings killed the show. "It had to do with Four Star [the show's production company]. It was something with CBS and NBC, and I kept out of it altogether. That whole Four Star was politically motivated." Berg declined to comment specifically on what was the alleged disagreement.

Both Gertrude Berg and Mary Wickes received Emmy nominations as lead and supporting actress respectively for their work on *Mrs. G. Goes to College*. The show marked the last TV series role for both Berg, who died in 1966, and Hardwicke, who died in 1964.

Sir Cedric Hardwicke lectures to his class how *Mrs. G Goes to College* will go to Thursdays from Wednesdays at the same time in January 1962 while beaming student Gertrude Berg blocks the blackboard.

The Bob Cummings Show

Sitcom. Ran on CBS Thursdays 8:30–9 P.M. Oct. 5, 1961–Feb. 1, 1962, opposite *The Real McCoys* on ABC and *Dr. Kildare* on NBC, then CBS Thursdays 7:30–8 P.M. Feb. 8–March 1, 1962, opposite *The Adventures of Ozzie and Harriet* on ABC and *The Outlaws* on NBC. C: Bob Cummings (as Bob Carson), Murvyn Vye (as Lionel), Roberta Shore (as Hank Gogerty). P: Bob Finkel. D: Don Weis. W: Mel Sharp, Mel Diamond.

"The show was originally a heavy drama," producer Bob Finkel said of the ill-fated *Bob Cummings Show*. With its star being associated more with light comedy than heavy drama, it's not surprising to hear Finkel report that "It was a miserable disaster the first two or three shows." The production company told Cummings to make it into a comedy and brought Finkel in to repair the damage.

The series accommodated Cummings' love of aviation, featuring him as a pilot who helped solve crimes with the use of his specially built aerocar, a single-engine plane that could have its wings removed to become an automobile. (Cummings actually owned that vehicle in real life.) The initial focus was on action sequences, but as that didn't pan out, Finkel helped supervise the show's transition to humor, a changeover that led to the production falling behind because of the new emphasis. "I think they dragged the headwriter off to an institution," Finkel joked, referring to the work done by Mel Diamond.

But it wasn't just the rewriting of scripts that held up the completion of episodes. "It was a tough, tough show to do," Finkel said. "We had to fly down to Palm Springs and do it." The locale of the show was in fact an airfield in Palm Springs, California, which required the crew to go on location. Finkel once was late in driving there from Los Angeles, so he had to fly with Cummings to the site in the aerocar. While noting that "Bob was a very fine pilot," Finkel said viewing up close the mountains they had to fly over to get to the desert was not the sort of sightseeing he appreciated. "I was a nervous wreck," he admitted.

Once everyone arrived on the set, they had to rely on Cummings piloting his aerocar to get the proper scenes needed of the craft in air. "He was the only one who could fly it," Finkel noted. And there was one more fly in the ointment.

"Bob had a problem," Finkel said. "He was a compulsive talker. If you said, 'Hi, Bob, how are you doing?' that was it, and he'd hold up production while telling you these stories."

With all these conflicting elements, Finkel was not startled to learn about the show being cancelled within six months. He did love Cummings as a person and thought he had a wonderful sense of humor, and also praised the work of co-stars Murvyn Vye (as Cummings' assistant) and Roberta Shore (as an adolescent who pined for Cummings).

Before the show ended its run, it was retitled *The New Bob Cummings Show* in 1962, apparently so that people wouldn't confuse it with *The Bob Cummings Show* of 1955–59 (which actually was in reruns on ABC daytime in 1961 under the title *Love That Bob*). Only the dimmest of viewers could have possibly confused that bubbly concoction with the 1961-62 show. In any event, Cummings returned to star in another unsuccessful sitcom in 1964-65; see *My Living Doll*.

Straightaway

Adventure. Ran on ABC Fridays 7:30–8 P.M. Oct. 6–Dec. 29, 1961, opposite *Rawhide* on CBS and *International Showtime* on NBC, then ABC Wednesdays 8–8:30 P.M. Jan. 3–July 4, 1962, opposite *Father Knows Best* reruns (through Feb. 14) and *Window on Main Street* (from Feb. 21) on CBS and *Wagon Train* on NBC. C: Brian Kelly (as Scott Ross), John Ashley (as Clipper Hamilton). P: Josef Shaftel. D: William Dario Faralla. W: Tony Barrett.

Frontier Circus

Drama. Ran on CBS Thursdays 7:30–8:30 P.M. Oct. 5, 1961–Feb. 1, 1962, opposite *The Adventures of Ozzie and Harriet* and *The Donna Reed Show* on ABC and *The Outlaws* on NBC, then CBS Thursdays 8–9 P.M. Feb. 8–Sept. 6, 1962, opposite *The Donna Reed Show* and *The Real McCoys* on ABC and *The Outlaws* and *Dr. Kildare* on NBC, and then CBS Thursdays 7:30–8:30 P.M. Sept. 13, 1962, opposite *The Adventures of Ozzie and Harriet* and *The Donna Reed Show* on ABC and *The Outlaws* on NBC. C: Chill Wills (as Col. Casey Thompson), John Derek (as Ben Travis), Richard Jaeckel (as Tony Gentry). P: Richard Irving. W: William Witney. W: Samuel A. Peeples.

The Investigators

Detective Drama. Ran on CBS Thursdays 9–10 P.M. Oct. 5–Dec. 28, 1961, opposite *My Three Sons* and *Margie* on ABC and *Dr. Kildare* and *Hazel* on NBC. C: James Franciscus (as Russ Andrews), James Philbrook (as Steve Banks), Mary Murphy (as Maggie Peters), Al Austin (as Bill Davis). P: Michael Garrison. D: Joseph H. Lewis. W: John Gerard, James Gunn.

1, 2, 3 — Go!

Children's. Ran on NBC Sundays 6:30–7 P.M. Oct. 6, 1961–May 27, 1962, opposite *Maverick* on ABC and *Mr. Ed* on CBS. C: Richard Thomas, Jack Lescoulie. P: Jack Kuney. D: Charles N. Hill. W: James Ambandos.

The Bob Newhart Show

Comedy Variety. Ran on NBC Wednesdays 10–10:30 P.M. Oct. 10, 1961–June 13, 1962, opposite *Naked City* on ABC and *The U.S. Steel Hour* alternating with *Armstrong Circle Theatre* on CBS. C: Bob Newhart, Paul Weston and His Orchestra. P/W: Roland Kibbee. D: Coby Ruskin. W: Bob Newhart, Bob Kaufman, Charles Sherman, Norman Leibman.

Margie

Sitcom. Ran on ABC Thursdays 9:30–10 P.M. Oct. 12, 1961–April 12, 1962, opposite *The Investigators* (through Dec. 28) and *Mrs. G. Goes to College* (from Jan. 11) on CBS and *Hazel* on NBC, then ABC Fridays 7:30–8 P.M. April 20–Aug. 31, 1962, opposite *Rawhide* on CBS and *International Showtime* on NBC. C: Cynthia Pepper (as Margie Clayton), Dave Willock (as Harvey Clayton), Wesley Tackitt (as Nora Clayton), Hollis Irving (as Aunt Phoebe), Penney Parker (as Maybelle Jackson), Tommy Ivo (as Heywood Botts), Richard Gering (as Johnny Green), Johnny Bangert (as Cornell Clayton). P/W: Hal Goodman, Larry Klein. D: Jack Sher.

Six years after Gale Storm's sitcom *My Little Margie* ended its run, a far different *Margie* came to network TV. Based on a 1946 movie of the same name, this *Margie* featured a teenager living it up in the 1920s in the town of Madison in New England with her parents Harvey (a banker) and Nora, kid brother Cornell and Aunt Phoebe. Her best friend was Maybelle Jackson, while she often dated Heywood and Johnny. In keeping with the theme of the decade in which it was set, the sitcom including old-time tinkling piano music accompanying cards with words between scenes, such as "Ladies, Please Remove Your Hats," as would have been done in silent movies.

Playing Margie was actress Cynthia Pepper, who had played Tim Considine's girlfriend the previous season on *My Three Sons*. "The producers saw me on *My Three Sons* and thought I might be right for it," Pepper said. "I tested three or four times and got it."

She beat out some 250 actresses for the part, including future leading ladies Barbara Parkins (later a star on the *Peyton Place* TV series from 1964 to 1969) and Jill Haworth. "None of us was anything like each other," Pepper said. "They wanted someone who wasn't glamorous, a girl-next-door type."

Still, Pepper did have to make a few accommodations after getting the role. "I was married at the time, and they didn't want me to mention it. And I turned 21 when I was doing the show." She wasn't the only one stretching, however. Regarding actress Wesley Tackitt, she noted, "She definitely wasn't old enough to be my mother!"

The period setting also provided a few challenges. "The dresses were fine, but my hair was short, so I had to wear fake braids." The show filmed 26 episodes without a studio audience at the 20th Century Fox studios plus a western lot for outdoor scenes.

Margie aired after the show which gave Pepper her big break, *My Three Sons*, and while it didn't have the latter's high ratings, it still finished a strong second to its initial competition, the top 10 hit sitcom *Hazel* on NBC. Pepper admitted she believed the show was going to run longer than a year. "We had a 20 share a lot," she said. "I think it was some politics. I heard some different stories. I thought we would come back."

Pepper continued to act after *Margie* disappeared, following in the steps of her show business parents (her dad, Jack Pepper, was married to Ginger Rogers from 1929 to 1931 before marrying Cynthia's mother). She's also done some fan conventions, and at one in 2001 she met up with former *Margie* regular Tommy Ivo. "I hadn't seen him in 30 years," she said. And yes, she still has people who recognize her from *Margie*.

Our Five Daughters

Soap Opera. Ran on NBC Mondays through Fridays 3:30–4 P.M. Jan. 6–Sept. 28, 1962, opposite *Who Do You Trust?* on ABC and *The Verdict is Yours* (through June 15) and *To Tell the Truth* (from June 18) and news on CBS. C: Esther Ralston (as Helen Lee), Micheal Keene (as Jim Lee), Wynne Miller (as Mary Lee Weldon), Iris Joyce (as Marjorie "Margie" Lee), Patricia Allison (as Barbara Lee), Nuella Dierking (as Jane Lee), Jacqueline Courtney (as Anne Lee), Ben Hayes (as Don Weldon), William Tabbert (as Bob Purdon), Edward Griffith (as Pat Nichols), Robert W. Stewart (as Uncle Charlie), Joan Anderson (as Cynthia Dodd), Michael Higgins (as Ed Lawson). P: Eugene Barr. D: Paul Lammers. W: Leonard Stadd, Sid Ellis.

Tell It to Groucho

Interview. Ran on CBS Thursdays 9–9:30 P.M. Jan. 11–May 31, 1962, opposite *My Three Sons* on ABC and *Dr. Kildare* on NBC. C: Groucho Marx, Jack Wheeler, Patty Harmon. EP: John Guedel. P: Bernie Smith. D: Robert Dwan.

Room for One More

Sitcom. Ran on ABC Saturdays 8–8:30 P.M. Jan. 27–Sept. 22, 1962, opposite *Perry Mason* on CBS and *Tales of Wells Fargo* on NBC. C: Andrew Duggan (as George Rose), Peggy McCay (as Anna Rose), Ronnie Dapo (as Flip Rose), Carol Nicholson (as Laurie Rose), Anna Carri (as Mary Rose), Timmy Rooney (as Jeff Rose), Jack Albertson (as Walter Burton), Maxine Stuart (as Ruth Burton). EP: William T. Orr. P: Ed Jurist. D: Leslie H. Martinson, Gene Reynolds, Charles Rondeau.

Championship Debate

Game. Ran on NBC Saturdays 12:30–1 P.M. Feb. 3–May 19, 1962, opposite *The Texan* reruns on ABC and *My Friend Flicka* reruns on CBS. C: Dr. James McBath. EP: George Heinemann. P: Blair Chotzinoff. D: Frank Pacelli.

It's tempting to label *Championship Debate*, which featured a pair of students from two different colleges arguing for and against important resolutions of current concerns, a response to FCC Chairman Newton Minow's description of television in 1961 as a "vast wasteland." But that was not the case, according to its producer, Blair Chotzinoff. "*G.E. College Bowl* inspired it," he said, referring to the

show that ran from 1959 to 1970 and featured college students answering difficult questions rapidly.

However, that show had a sponsor — General Electric, hence the "G.E." of the title — and *Championship Debate* did not, and that made the difference, in Chotzinoff's view. "*Championship Debate* was not selling anything," he said. "I don't think it ever had a chance of going beyond a year."

Yet for viewers willing to give it a chance against western repeats on the other networks, *Championship Debate* offered them a contest unlike anything else on TV at the time. The program was the brainchild of NBC public affairs head George Heinemann. "George, who was my boss, assigned it to me," Chotzinoff said.

Though Heinemann had much of the concept already in place for the show before aired, Chotzinoff did make an important contribution. "I designed and built the sets of the show," he said, adding that he put moderator Dr. James McBath between the two teams and had a manual clock installed to make sure neither team went over its allotted time in giving presentations, rebuttals and cross-examinations.

Dr. McBath was host and timer of the show primarily because he was president of the American Forensic Association, which picked the competing teams. "I think he was recommended, but I think we auditioned a couple of other people," Chotzinoff said. Dr. McBath's regular job at the time was as associate professor of speech at the University of Southern California. As for the show's director, Frank Pacelli, Chotzinoff's main memory of him involved his family. "He was a nephew of the Pope during the war years," he said.

The most successful team on *Championship Debate* surprisingly did not hail from a large university. North Texas State emerged as the American winner, earning them a spot on the final show. "All through the year they had the same two people on each show," noted Chotzinoff.

Chotzinoff went to Oxford in England to recruit two players to face North Texas on the finale. "I was terribly impressed with them, much more than with the American teams," he said. "Those people over there could take at a moment's notice a subject and make an argument."

They also could be snappier with the comebacks, and the last show was a shambles as the North Texas team tried to emulate that approach uneasily and the judges—two American, one British—voted for their countrymen in determining a winner. It was a messy end to an otherwise distinguished production. NBC replaced the show with *Exploring*, a children's educational series which ran until 1966.

Oh, Those Bells

Sitcom. Ran on CBS Thursdays 7:30–8 P.M. March 8–May 31, 1962, opposite *The Adventures of Ozzie and Harriet* on ABC and *The Outlaws* on NBC. C: The Wiere Brothers—Herbert, Harry and Sylvester (as Herbert Bell, Harry Bell and Sylvester Bell), Henry Norell (as Henry Slocum), Carol Byron (as Kitty Mathews), Reta Shaw (as Mrs. Stanfield). P: Ben Brady. D: Danny Dare. W: Albert Lewin, Burt Styler.

Window Shopping

Game. Ran on ABC Mondays through Fridays 12:30–1 P.M. April 2–June 29, 1962, opposite *Search for Tomorrow* and *Guiding Light* on CBS and *Truth or Consequences* on NBC. C: Bob Kennedy, Professor William Wood. EP: Herbert Wolf. P: Alan Gilbert. D: Lloyd Gross.

This memory game nearly has been forgotten itself 40 years after it ran. A replacement for another failed game show, *Make a Face* (which ran in 1961-62 as a daily show, then oddly reappeared as a Saturday morning show for kids in the 1962-63 season), *Window Shopping* simply gave three adults 15 seconds to review an image and then take turns recounting an element within it. Any incorrectly given or repeated item by a contestant eliminated him or her from the game. The last player remaining got to convert points they earned from the game into the same number of seconds in the

bonus round, and use that time to look at a window of prizes amounting up to $3,000. The player then named as many items as he or she had seen in the window, and if one they named matched what was listed inside an envelope, he or she earned the whole kit and kaboodle.

Presiding over *Window Shopping* was Bob Kennedy, an actor and announcer who had only one other regular on-air TV credit, as host of the nighttime game show *Wingo* for just six weeks in 1958 (see 1957-58). However, he had been a substitute host on several other game shows before doing *Window Shopping*. "He was a nice individual," said director Lloyd Gross. "He later got involved in a company that handled various clients and their commercials." He also became a personality on a Chicago morning show in the 1970s, and ABC signed him on to do features for their news show *A.M. America* in 1975 before he died of cancer on Nov. 6, 1974. He was just 41 years old.

Also seen on the show as the judge for the contestants' answers was Professor William Wood of the Columbia University School of Journalism. While most other judges on game shows preferred to be off camera, Gross noted that "We had him on the air. He was the voice of authority on all judgments. He did it basically to get himself on air. He was well in command of any situation, determined the proper answer for each situation."

Beyond talking about the principal participants, Gross didn't care much to rehash *Window Shopping*. "It didn't have any great bounce at all," he said. "I was not at all pleased with it." ABC certainly wasn't either, as it put *Window Shopping* out of business after 13 weeks. The network moved the moderately popular *Camouflage* in its place, and that game show stayed there through Nov. 16, 1962, after having started in the time slot preceding *Window Shopping* on Jan. 9, 1961.

1962-63

Sam Benedict

Law Drama. Ran on NBC Saturdays 7:30–8:30 P.M. Sept. 15, 1962–Sept. 7, 1963, opposite *The Roy*

Rogers and Dale Evans Show (through Dec. 22) and *The Gallant Men* (from Dec. 29) on ABC and *The Jackie Gleason Show* (through June 22) and *The Lucy-Desi Comedy Hour* (from June 29) on

CBS. C: Edmond O'Brien (as Sam Benedict), Richard Rust (as Hank Tabor), Joan Tompkins (as Trudy Wagner). EP/W: E. Jack Neuman. P: William Froug. D: Boris Sagal.

It's a Man's World

Comedy/Drama. Ran on NBC Mondays 7:30–8:30 P.M. Sept. 17, 1962–Jan. 28, 1963, opposite *Cheyenne* (through Dec. 31) and *The Dakotas* (from Jan. 7) on ABC and *To Tell the Truth* and *I've Got a Secret* on CBS. C: Glenn Corbett (as Wes Macauley), Mike Burns (as Howie Macauley), Ted Bessell (as Tom-Tom DeWitt), Randy Boone (as Vern Hodges), Harry Harvey (as Houghton Stott), Jan Norris (as Irene Hoff), Kate Murtagh (as Mrs. Iona Dobson), Scott White (as Virgil Dobson), Jeanine Cashell (as Alma Jean Dobson), Anne Schuyler (as Nora). P/D: Peter Tewksbury.

"It was like *The Waltons*. A wonderful show," said actress Kate Murtagh of her series *It's a Man's World*. The title referred to a houseboat in the Ohio River in the town of Cordella where four men resided. Wes Macauley lived with his orphaned kid brother Howie, his fellow college student Tom-Tom and Vern the guitar player. They dealt with girlfriends, employers (Wes worked at a gas station run by Houghton Scott), and friends, including their neighbors the Dobsons.

Murtagh played Mrs. Dobson. "She and her husband ran all kinds of stores, mostly groceries," she said. "She had a daughter, 17, and they'd be in the middle of the stories. [The husband's name was Virgil, the daughter's Alma Jean.] Our store was opposite of where they docked the boat."

The character Murtagh played appealed to her strongly. "The personality of Iona was so much like me, how I reacted, so jolly," she said. She felt after reading the part that she had it.

Typically each episode of *It's a Man's World* had two stories presented, such as Vern taking a vow that he will tell no fibs for 24 hours, and regretting it, while Iona learned how to play Monopoly. Murtagh thought what made it stand out was the touch of its producer/director Peter Tewksbury.

"He was one of the best directors I worked with," she said. "He didn't say how to say one line, but let us think how our characters were feeling."

Murtagh recalled one scene where Iona gave Alma a perm in preparation for the daughter's date and Tewksbury gave her a suggestion after the initial run-through. "He said, 'Right now, you're doing the lines very well, but you're doing stuff like you would do it. You're a small-town woman with a 17-year-old girl, and this 15-year-old boy may get her pregnant.'" With that idea in mind, Murtagh was able to play the scene better to her and Tewksbury's liking.

Unfortunately, *It's a Man's World* was not getting the ratings to the liking of NBC. "It was on at a bad time," Murtagh said. Up opposite two top 20 shows, *To Tell the Truth* and *I've Got a Secret*, and feeling the pressure, the leading men of the cast began a letter-writing campaign to save the show, speaking to the press to encourage viewers to write and show NBC their support.

"We got thousands of letters," Murtagh said. "I myself wrote back to 1,000 letters." But NBC did not change its mind even amid all the mail and canned *It's a Man's World* after four months.

Murtagh would go on to a long career as a character actress without having another series. Perhaps her most famous job was posing as a waitress for the cover of the *Breakfast in America* album for the rock group Supertramp. The multi-million selling record won a Grammy for Best Album Package in 1979 with her beaming face and body on the cover.

"I've had a lot of fun," she said. "Sometime you get good breaks, and sometime you get bad breaks. *It's a Man's World* was a good break for me."

Saints and Sinners

Drama. Ran on NBC Mondays 8:30–9:30 P.M. Sept. 17, 1962–Jan. 28, 1963 opposite *The Rifleman* and *Stoney Burke* on ABC and *The Lucy Show* and *The Danny Thomas Show* on CBS. C: Nick Adams (as Nick Alexander), John Larkin (as Mark Grainger), Barbara Rush (as Lizzie Hogan), Richard Erdman (as Klugie), Robert F. Simon (as Dave Tobak), Sharon Farrell (as Polly), Nicky Blair (as Charlie). P/D: Marc Daniels.

"That was an unfortunate situation," Richard Erdman said of *Saints and Sinners*. What made it "unfortunate," in his view, were several elements, chief of which was its leading man, Nick Adams, playing reporter Nick Alexander for the fictional *New York Bulletin* newspaper.

Glenn Corbett, Jan Norris and Ted Bessell, left to right, rehearse their scenes as college students on the outdoor set of *It's a Man's World*. Two months after this series ended, Corbett replaced George Maharis as Martin Milner's co-star on *Route 66*, a role he held until the show ended on September 18, 1964.

"Nick was a perfectly strange man, really wasn't meant to carry a TV show," Erdman said. "Sort of a lightweight." (In Adams' defense, it should be noted that he starred for two years as the lead of the western *The Rebel* from 1959 to 1961, which aired in reruns on NBC the summer in 1962 before *Saints and Sinners* debuted.)

Erdman also thought there were inconsistent characterizations. He played Klugie, "sort of a mad artist for the newspaper," but felt the character was so ill-defined it was not noticed. In fact, he said, "I left the show halfway for a few weeks in Spain to do a pilot for a children's show, and I don't think anyone missed me."

In the end, Erdman said, *Saints and Sinners* failed because of "No chemistry, and never any real ratings." The latter can be explained by the tough competition against *The Lucy Show* and *The Rifleman*, but the former stuck more in Erdman's mind. He remembered eating lunch with John Larkin, who had left *The Edge of Night* in 1961 to come to Hollywood and get away from that soap opera which made him a daytime matinee idol. Larkin thought *Saints and Sinners* would be his ticket to nighttime success, but soon into filming he realized it would not be the hit he anticipated. "Those were lunches of great despair," notes Erdman.

Erdman had similar initial hopes for *Saints and Sinners* too. The show began as a pilot on *The Dick Powell Show* called "Savage Sunday," telecast on May 1, 1962. Adams and Larkin played the roles they had on the series, while Ann Blyth's part of reporter Lizzie Hogan went to Barbara Rush in the series. Erdman's character was not on the pilot.

When it became a series, Powell thought of his old friend Richard Erdman for the role of Klugie. "He called me and said, 'Would you be interested in this part?'" said Erdman. Unfortunately for him and the show, Powell produced only the pilot and not the series, and the judgments made by the series staff were not what Erdman expected. He vividly recalled how one actress was fired from a guest part after two days because they didn't think she had the talent for the job. Her name was Elizabeth Montgomery, later to have a huge hit starring on *Bewitched* (1964–72).

Not all of *Saints and Sinners* disappointed Erdman. The actor/director thought the show's direction "was pretty good, by and large." And

he also felt the show had its best episode when it scored a coup and featured the last TV acting role of Irene Dunne. The bad part was it was the final time *Saints and Sinners* aired, on Jan. 28, 1963. The next week, NBC replaced it and its lead-in, *It's a Man's World*, with *NBC Monday Night at the Movies*.

The Wide Country

Drama. Ran on NBC Thursdays 7:30–8:30 P.M. Sept. 20, 1962–Sept. 12, 1963, opposite *The Adventures of Ozzie and Harriet* and *The Donna Reed Show* on ABC and *Mr. Ed* (through March 21) and *Fair Exchange* (from March 28) and *Perry Mason* on CBS. C: Earl Holliman (as Mitch Guthrie), Andrew Prine (as Andy Guthrie). P: Frank Telford. D: Alan Crosland, Jr. W: Donald Sanford.

Fair Exchange

Sitcom. Ran on CBS Fridays 9:30–10:30 P.M. Sept. 21–Dec. 28, 1962 opposite *77 Sunset Strip* on ABC and *Don't Call Me Charlie!* and *The Jack Paar Show* on NBC, then CBS Thursdays 7:30–8 P.M. March 28–Sept. 19, 1963, opposite *The Adventures of Ozzie and Harriet* on ABC and *The Wide Country* on CBS. C: Eddie Foy, Jr. (as Eddie Walker), Audrey Christie (as Dorothy Walker), Lynn Loring (as Patty Walker), Flip Mark (as Larry Walker), Victor Maddern (as Tommy Finch), Diana Chesney (as Sybil Finch), Judy Carne (as Heather Finch), Dennis Waterman (as Neville Finch), Maurice Dallimore (as Willie Shorthouse). EP: Cy Howard. P: Ed Feldman. D: Jerry Thorpe, E.W. Swackhamer, Sherman Marks. W: Arthur Julian, William Templeton, Laurence Marks.

Don't Call Me Charlie!

Sitcom. Ran on NBC Fridays 9:30–10 P.M. Sept. 21, 1962–Jan. 25, 1963, opposite *77 Sunset Strip* on ABC and *Fair Exchange* (through Dec. 28) and *The Alfred Hitchcock Hour* (from Jan. 4) on CBS. C: Josh Peine (as Judson McKay), Linda Lawson (as Pat Perry), John Hubbard (as Col. U. Charles Barker), Cully Richards (as First Sgt. Wozniak), Alan Napier (as Gen. Steele), Arte Johnson (as Cpl. Lefkowitz), Louise Glenn (as Selma Yossarian), Penny Santon (as Madame Fatima). P/D/W: Don McGuire.

Magic Midway

Children's. Ran on NBC Saturdays 11:30 A.M.–Noon Sept. 22, 1962–March 16, 1963, opposite *Top Cat* (through Dec. 29) and *Beany and Cecil* (from

Jan. 5) on ABC and *The Roy Rogers Show* reruns on CBS. C: Claude Kirchner, Douglas Anderson (as Mr. Pocus), Bill Bailey (as Boom Boom), Paul Kiley (as Coo Coo), Bonnie Lee Glier, Lou Stein and the Circus 7 Jazz Band. P: Jack Miller. D: Louis Tyrrell. W: Alan Riefe.

The Reading Room

Children's. Ran on CBS Saturdays 12:30–1 P.M. Sept. 22, 1962–March 16, 1963, opposite *The Magic Land of Allakazam* (from Dec. 29) on ABC and *Exploring* on NBC. C: Ned Hoopes. P: Joe Heller. D: John J. Desmond.

Ensign O'Toole

Sitcom. Ran on NBC Sundays 7–7:30 P.M. Sept. 23, 1962–Sept. 15, 1963, opposite *Father Knows Best* reruns (through Dec. 23) on ABC and *Lassie* on CBS. C: Dean Jones (as Ensign O'Toole), Jay

Gary McKeever (Scott Lane) warily eyes over his shoulder his nemesis Col. Blackwell (Allen Joslyn) on *McKeever & the Colonel*. Though not long-lived, the show did inspire a board game called Bamboozled with the actors and a few other regulars seen on the cover.

C. Flippen (as Chief Petty Officer Homer Nelson), Jack Mullaney (as Lt. (jg) Rex St. John), Harvey Lembeck (as seaman Gabby Di Julio), Jack Albertson (as Lt. Cmdr. Virgil Stoner), Beau Bridges (as seaman Howard Spicer), Bob Sorrells (as seaman Claude White). P/D: Hy Averback. W: Bill Davenport, Sheldon Keller, Howard Merrill, James Allardice, Tom Adair.

McKeever & the Colonel

Sitcom. Ran on NBC Sundays 6:30–7 P.M. Sept. 23, 1962–June 16, 1963, opposite *Password* (through March 17) and *Mr. Ed* (from March 24) on CBS and *Winston Churchill — the Valiant Years* (through Dec. 2) on ABC. C: Scott Lane (as Gary McKeever), Allyn Joslyn (as Col. Harvey T. Blackwell), Jackie Coogan (as Sgt. Barnes), Elizabeth Fraser (as Miss Warner), Keith Taylor (as Tubby Anderson), Johnny Eimen (as Monk). P: Tom McKnight, Bill Harmon. D: Stanley Z. Cherry, Don Weis. W: Arthur Marx, Johnny Bradford, Barry Blitzer.

Describing the cast of *McKeever & the Colonel*, its main director, Stanley Z. Cherry, said they were a distinguished lot hoping in vain this would be the hit to put them on the map. "It was a very elegant group of people, all of whom had seen better days," he said. Even the studio where they filmed the show was showing its age, he added.

The veterans Cherry described were Allyn Joslyn, Jackie Coogan and Elizabeth Fraser, all of whom had acted in Hollywood for more than 20 years, usually in comedies. Joslyn played the colonel of the title, a man in charge of the boys' military school, Westfield Academy. Coogan was Joslyn's aide, and Fraser was the school dietician. Bedeviling them were the antics of three young cadets — McKeever, the ostensible leader, and his buddies Tubby and Monk.

Cherry did not blame any of the older actors for the disappointment of *McKeever & the Colonel*, saying they were pros. But the inexperience of the trio of boys on it showed up on screen, he felt. "It just didn't click. Kids are not that funny.

Their timing is not that great." Indeed, the juvenile regulars (Scott Lane, Keith Taylor and Johnny Eimen) did no other network series after *McKeever & the Colonel.*

Another problem Cherry detected with the series was with the scripts. "We didn't have the greatest group of writers writing for the show," he said. The only exception was its headwriter Arthur Marx, son of comedian Groucho Marx, whose material was deemed "too adult" by the powers that be, forcing him to bring it down to a broader level in a failing effort to appeal to children. (Cherry said he, Marx, and co-producer Tom McKnight all wore fedora hats on the set, adding to its classy atmosphere.)

The reason why the show discouraged "too adult" writing was that *McKeever & the Colonel* aired in the same time slot where kid favorite *Mr. Ed,* the sitcom about a talking horse, flourished on CBS the previous season. NBC hoped to capture some of that audience when CBS moved *Mr. Ed* to Thursdays and replaced it with the nighttime edition of the game show *Password.* But adults and children alike favored *Password* over *McKeever,* and by the time *Mr. Ed* returned to the competing time slot in March 1963, NBC had given up hope on *McKeever & the Colonel.*

Cherry's overall memories of the series were favorable despite its defects on the air. "It was the most relaxed set I had been on," he said. "It was a lot of fun." But the merriment did not translate over TV sets, and after nine months on air NBC dropped *McKeever & the Colonel* in favor of news in the summer of 1963.

The New Loretta Young Show

Comedy/Drama. Ran on CBS Mondays 10–10:30 P.M. Sept. 24, 1962–March 18, 1963, opposite *Ben Casey* on ABC and *David Brinkley's Journal* on NBC. C: Loretta Young (as Christine Massey), James Philbrook (as Paul Belzer), Celia Kaye (as Marnie Massey), Beverly Washburn (as Vickie Massey), Sandy Descher (as Judy Massey), Carol Sydes (as Binkie Massey), Dirk Rambo (as Dirk Massey), Dack Rambo (as Dack Massey), Tracy Stratford (as Maria Massey). P: Jerry London. D/W: Paul Crabtree.

Empire

Western. Ran on NBC Tuesdays 8:30–9:30 P.M. Sept. 25, 1962–Sept. 17, 1963, opposite *Hawaiian Eye* on ABC and *The Red Skelton Hour* (through June 25) and *Talent Scouts* (from July 2) on CBS. C: Richard Egan (as Jim Redigo), Terry Moore (as Constance Garret), Anne Seymour (as Lucia Garret), Ryan O'Neal (as Tal Garret), Warren Vanders (as Chuck Davis; 1963), Charles Bronson (as Paul Moreno; 1963). EP: William Sackheim. P: Frank Pierson. D: Arthur Hiller. W: Frank Nugent.

I'm Dickens — He's Fenster

Sitcom. Ran on ABC Fridays 9–9:30 P.M. Sept. 28, 1962–Sept. 13, 1963, opposite *Route 66* on CBS and *Sing Along with Mitch* on NBC. C: John Astin (as Harry Dickens), Marty Ingels (as Arch Fenster), Emmaline Henry (as Kate Dickens), Dave Ketchum (as Mel Warshaw), Henry Beckman (as Mulligan), Frank DeVol (as Myron Bannister). P: Leonard Stern. D: Arthur Hiller. W: Leonard Stern, Don Hinkley.

After writing for such hits as *The Honeymooners,* *The Phil Silvers Show* and *The Steve Allen Show,* Leonard Stern struck out on his own as a TV producer in 1962 and came up with *I'm Dickens — He's Fenster* as his freshman series effort. "That was a personal favorite," Stern said. "I don't think I ever got the reviews as favorable as that."

The program boiled down essentially to a weekly dose of physical gags involving construction workers. Dickens was the more straight arrow of the two, since he had a wife — in fact, a wife who didn't stay at home, virtually a revolutionary idea for a sitcom in 1962. "It was the first wife who worked on a television comedy," Stern said. Bachelor Fenster was more of a numbskull. Not helping them out much whenever they got in trouble on a job site were fellow carpenters Warshaw and Mulligan.

The final cast member was the men's employer, Myron Bannister. "He personified the worst kind of boss one could have — the equivocator," Stern said. The show's premise would seem to indicate it needed to be filmed by one camera to allow for retakes, but somewhat surprisingly Stern said that "It was done in front of a live audience. No sweetening with a laugh track, which I despise."

What made Stern particularly proud were the reviews comparing the antics of Dickens and Fenster to one of Stern's favorite movie comedy teams, Laurel and Hardy. A member of that duo agreed with that assessment, according to Stern. "I even got a fan letter from Stan Laurel. He told Steve Allen it was the only TV show he watched. I got to talk to him on the phone, then eventually got to see him in person."

With the good reviews and Laurel's blessing, what went wrong? Stern saw it this way: "ABC was the poorest of the networks then. They kept hanging on, hanging on, waiting for the numbers to go up, and they did, but they cancelled it anyway." *I'm Dickens — He's Fenster* came on midway after *Route 66* and *Sing Along with Mitch* had started on the other networks, and while its lead-in, *The Flintstones*, came up within range of the ratings of *Route 66* (the leader in the time slot), *I'm Dickens — He's Fenster* fell somewhat shorter of the mark. "That's the case of being at the wrong place in the wrong time," concluded Stern, who felt it could have done better on NBC or CBS.

Nevertheless, some of the show's cast did quite well after it ended in other 1960s sitcoms. John Astin was a memorable Gomez on *The Addams Family* (1964–66), Emmaline Henry played Amanda Bellows on *I Dream of Jeannie* from 1966 to 1970, and Dave Ketchum popped up as Agent 13 on *Get Smart*, a sitcom with Stern as its executive producer.

The Roy Rogers and Dale Evans Show

Variety. Ran on ABC Saturdays 7:30–8:30 P.M. Sept. 29–Dec. 22, 1962, opposite *The Jackie Gleason Show* on CBS and *Sam Benedict* on NBC. C: Roy Rogers, Dale Evans, Pat Brady, the Sons of the Pioneers, Cliff Arquette (as Charley Weaver), Kirby Buchanon, Kathy Taylor, the Ralph Carmichael Orchestra. P/D/W: Bob Henry. W: Borden Chase, Elon Packard, Stan Davis.

Mr. Smith Goes to Washington

Sitcom. Ran on ABC Saturdays 8:30–9 P.M. Sept. 29, 1962–March 30, 1963, opposite *The Defenders* on CBS and *The Joey Bishop Show* on NBC. C: Fess Parker (as Sen. Eugene Smith), Sandra Warner (as Pat Smith), Red Foley (as Uncle Cooter), Stan Irwin (as Arnie), Rita Lynn (as Miss Kelly). P: Hall Stanley. D: Oscar Rudolph. W: Ben Greshman, Milton Pascal.

Stoney Burke

Western. Ran on ABC Mondays 9–10 P.M. Oct. 1, 1962–Sept. 2, 1963, opposite *The Danny Thomas Show* (through July 22) and *The Andy Griffith Show* (through July 22) and *Comedy Hour Special* (from July 29) on CBS and *Saints and Sinners* (through Jan. 28) and *The Price Is Right* (through Jan. 28) and movies (from Feb. 4) and *The Art Linkletter Show* (from Feb. 18) on NBC. C: Jack Lord (as Stoney Burke), Robert Dowdell (as Cody Bristol), Bruce Dern (as E.J. Stocker), Warren Oates (as Ves Painter), Bill Hart (as Red). P/D/W: Leslie Stevens.

Going My Way

Sitcom. Ran on ABC Wednesdays 8:30–9:30 P.M. Oct. 3, 1962–Sept. 11, 1963, opposite *The Many Loves of Dobie Gillis* and *The Beverly Hillbillies* on CBS and *The Virginian* and *The Perry Como Show* (through June 12) and *Kraft Mystery Theater* (from June 19) on NBC. C: Gene Kelly (as Father Chuck O'Malley), Leo G. Carroll (as Father Fitzgibbon), Dick York (as Tom Colwell), Nydia Westman (as Mrs. Featherstone). P: Joe Connelly. D: Joseph Pevney. W: Emmet Lavery.

Our Man Higgins

Sitcom. Ran on ABC Wednesdays 9:30–10 P.M. Oct. 3, 1962–Sept. 11, 1963, opposite *The Dick Van Dyke Show* on CBS and *The Perry Como Show* (through June 12) and *Kraft Mystery Theater* (from June 19) on NBC. C: Stanley Holloway (as Higgins), Audrey Totter (as Alice MacRoberts), Frank Maxwell (as Duncan MacRoberts), Rickey Kelman (as Tommy MacRoberts), K.C. Butts (as Dinghy MacRoberts), Regina Groves (as Joanie MacRoberts). P: Paul Harrison. D/W: Richard Murphy.

The Gallant Men

War Drama. Ran on ABC Fridays 7:30–8:30 P.M. Oct. 5–Dec. 21, 1962, opposite *Rawhide* on CBS and *International Showtime* on NBC, then ABC Saturdays 7:30–8:30 Dec. 29, 1962–Sept. 14, 1963, opposite *The Jackie Gleason Show* (through June 22) and *The Lucy-Desi Comedy Hour* (from June 29) on CBS and *Sam Benedict* on NBC. C: Robert McQueeney (as Conley Wright), William Reynolds (as Capt. Jim Benedict), Robert Ridgely (as Lt. Frank Kimbro), Richard X. Slattery (as First Sgt. John McKenna), Eddie Fontaine (as PFC Pete D'Angelo), Roland Starza (as Private Ernie Lucavich), Robert Gothie (as Private Sam Hansen), Roger Davis (as Private Roger Gibson). P: Richard Bluel. D: Robert Altman. W: Halsted Welles.

The Dakotas

Western. Ran on ABC Mondays 7:30–8:30 P.M. Jan. 7–Sept. 9, 1963, opposite *To Tell the Truth* and *I've Got a Secret* on CBS and *It's a Man's World* (through Jan. 28) and movies (from Feb. 4) on NBC. C: Larry Ward (as Marshal Frank Ragan), Jack Elam (as Deputy J.D. Smith), Chad Everett (as Deputy Del Stark), Mike Greene (as Deputy Vance Porter). P: Anthony Spinner. D: Stuart Heisler. W: Cy Chermak.

The Art Linkletter Show

Game. Ran on NBC Mondays 9:30–10 P.M. Feb. 18–Sept. 16, 1963, opposite *The Andy Griffith Show* (through July 22) and *Comedy Hour Special* (from July 29) on CBS and *Stoney Burke* on ABC. C: Art Linkletter, Carl Reiner (from April 1), Jayne Meadows (from April 1). EP: Wilbur Stark. P: Irvin Atkins. D: Hal Cooper. W: Stan Dreben, Hy Freedman.

Ben Jerrod

Soap Opera. Ran on NBC Mondays through Fridays 2–2:25 P.M. April 1–June 28, 1963, opposite *Day in Court* on ABC and *Password* on CBS. C: Michael M. Ryan (as Ben Jerrod), Addison Richards (as John P. Abbott), Regina Gleason (as Janet Donelli), Lyle Talbot (as Lt. Choates), Jeanne Baird (as Agnes Abbott), John Napier (as D.A. Dan Joplin), Ken Scott (as Jim O'Hara), Peter Hansen (as Pete Morrison), Martine Bartlett (as Lil Morrison). EP: Roy Winsor. P: Joseph Hardy. D: Fred Carney. W: William Kendall Clarke.

This "daytimer" ("We didn't call ourselves soaps, we called ourselves daytimers," noted actress Jeanne Baird) perished in less than 13 weeks despite being the first one of its genre to be telecast regularly in color. The title character and John P. Abbott, Ben's partner in a law firm, spent the series trying to prove Janet Donelli did not murder her late husband nor her lover Pete Morrison. Joining in the search to find the real killer was Abbott's daughter Agnes, played by Baird.

"I was the right-hand secretary and gal Friday to them," recalled Baird. "There was supposed to be a love thing between me and Michael Ryan [who played Ben Jerrod]. We didn't have to do much with the other characters. Our work was mostly contained in the office."

Baird got her part just through a reading with the producers with no camera test. She felt so confident at what she did that she called her agent and told him, "Well, I got it" before receiving official word on whether she was hired. Sure enough, after going on vacation, she said, "I got back from Hawaii and the part was mine." The only problem the stage-trained Baird had doing the show was getting used to the Teleprompters used to cue actors on their lines, which she loathed, finding the device distracting for someone who memorized lines.

The plan was for *Ben Jerrod* to stand out from the rest of the daytime pack by doing limited-run mysteries. "We were going to complete one story every 13 weeks," Baird said. But the series made it only through one story cycle thanks to its competition. "We were opposite a game show that was very popular," sighed Baird. That was *Password*, and it defeated *Ben Jerrod* so thoroughly that NBC replaced it with a game show that turned out to be another loser, *People Will Talk* (q.v.).

The chances of finding any existing episodes of *Ben Jerrod* are slim for the show, which was videotaped in Hollywood. "All of our shows aired, and they reused the tape," Baird said. Though she did not do another soap as a regular, Baird did not rule out the possibility of doing so when interviewed in 2001, as she was still an actress. "I'd love to, sure, if it's a good character," she said.

There is one happy note regarding *Ben Jerrod*. During a rehearsal for the show Baird brought her 1-year-old daughter to the set, and the NBC publicity department put out photos of them which attracted considerable attention. It encouraged Baird to get her child into the business, and a year later her daughter Victoria Page Meyerink was a regular on the nighttime *Danny Kaye Show* from 1964 to 1967. She later retired from show business, according to Baird.

Take Two

Game. Ran on ABC Sundays 4:30–5 P.M. May 5–Aug. 11, 1963, opposite baseball on ABC and CBS. C: Don McNeill. EP: Fred Olson. P: Jim McLaughlin. D: Dale Julian.

People Will Talk

Game. Ran on NBC Mondays through Fridays 2–2:25 P.M. July 1–Dec. 27, 1963, opposite *Day in Court* (through Sept. 6) on ABC and *Password* on CBS. C: Dennis James. EP: Merrill Heatter, Bob Quigley. D: Joe Behar.

1963-64

Harry's Girls

Sitcom. Ran on NBC Fridays 9:30–10 P.M. Sept. 13, 1963–Jan. 3, 1964, opposite *The Farmer's Daughter* (through Nov. 29) and *The Price Is Right* (from Dec. 6) on ABC and *The Twilight Zone* on CBS. C: Larry Blyden (as Harry Burns), Susan Silo (as Rusty), Dawn Nickerson (as Lois), Diahn Williams (as Terry). P: Billy Friedberg. D: Stanley Z. Cherry.

Unlike most American TV series in 1963, *Harry's Girls* was not shot in Hollywood or New York but in France. However, the continental charm the series strove to present was not evident on the program nor during its filming, according to director Stanley Z. Cherry.

Based on the 1957 MGM movie musical *Les Girls*, which in turn was based on a novel by Vera Caspery, *Harry's Girls* told of a trio of show girls who toured as the support for song-and-dance man Harry Burns. Harry also was the group's manager and found himself exasperated monitoring the offstage involvements of the three ladies in his chorus. Rusty was a romantic, while Lois was every bit the unsophisticated innocent that Terry absolutely was not.

Harry's Girls also borrowed a plot from the 1936 Pulitzer Prize–winning comedy *Idiot's Delight* and implied that Burns and the women did not have enough talent to make it in America. This idea hurt the show, in Cherry's opinion. "How are you going to hold the audience's attention with a terrible act?" he said.

Even given that hurdle, Cherry decided to direct the series after being called following a disastrous early production period on location. "They found out it's impossible to shoot on the streets of Paris," he said, mentioning the noise and other problems during filming there. With the show's sponsor, Colgate, in desperate straits, they contacted Cherry and announced the show would now be done inside a studio in southern France. "I was sent over to save the show after they'd done about four shows," he said.

When Cherry arrived, he learned that not filming outside solved only part of the problem of the slow shooting schedule. "It turns out the reason why nothing works is everybody drinks," he said. The studio had a bar in the middle of the stages to allow the crew to imbibe at will. "At noon, you'd be blitzed," Cherry said.

As a result, there were numerous times when the crew shot a scene only to discover afterward there was no film in the camera, or actors couldn't be heard on what film was shot because their microphones were not turned on during shooting. "Every day, 20 percent of the work had to be done over because of alcohol-related events," Cherry said.

The shooting difficulties might have been overlooked had *Harry's Girls* been a hit, but even against weak, aging competition (both *The Twilight Zone* and *The Price Is Right* were canned at the end of the 1963-64 season), the show faltered. Its cancellation was swift and unexpected to Cherry, who noted that "I went to Paris to do a show, and it was cancelled while I was going there." NBC replaced it with the avant-garde satirical series *That Was the Week That Was*, which lasted just a year and a half.

The Lieutenant

Drama. Ran on NBC Saturdays 7:30–8:30 P.M. Sept. 14, 1963–Sept. 5, 1964, opposite *Jackie Gleason and the American Scene Magazine* on CBS and *Hootenanny* on NBC. C: Gary Lockwood (as Lt. Bill Rice), Robert Vaughn (as Capt. Raymond Rambridge), Steve Franken (as Lt. Samwell Panosian; 1963), Don Penny (as Lt. Harris), Carmen Phillips (as Lily), John Milford (as Sgt. Kagey), Chris Noel (as various roles). EP: Norman Felton. P: Gene Roddenberry. D: Don Medford. W: Ed Waters.

Star Trek fans should be grateful forever that *The Lieutenant* ran only one season. Its cancellation meant that its producer, Gene Roddenberry, had time to create his science fiction series (whose basic idea he had floating in his head) and sell it to NBC a year after this show left the air.

The Lieutenant was the first show Roddenberry produced after years of frustration at being a TV writer and seeing how other producers handled his material. Roddenberry had written an unaired pilot for CBS in 1962 titled *APO 923* putting two lieutenants and a captain from different branches of the military in a

Lt. Rice (Gary Lockwood, left) prepares himself to assume command of a major air-sea battle with the help of Lt. Harris (Don Penny) as their commander, Capt. Rambridge, is critically ill in the "Green Water, Green Flag" episode of *The Lieutenant*. This show actually was shot on board the USS *Princeton* aircraft carrier following its return from duty in Asia.

constantly strong evaluations of his performance from Capt. Rambridge. The captain expected much out of the lieutenant because he saw his potential as a top officer in the Marines.

The other lieutenant of *The Lieutenant*, Panosian, departed the series by October, leaving Lt. Rice to have a new comrade in Lt. Harris. Playing Harris was Don Penny, who in the mid–1970s became a public speaking advisor to President Gerald Ford. As far as the other lead actors on the show, *The Lieutenant* represented Gary Lockwood's second short-lived series role after *Follow the Sun* (see 1961-62), while for Robert Vaughn it was the actor's first regular TV series job.

So how and why did *The Lieutenant* get demoted to the category of cancelled program? "We had the best ratings on NBC Saturday night, but pressure from the Pentagon made us take it off (Vietnam was on the horizon?)," wrote executive producer Norman Felton in a letter to me.

Felton shrugged it off and sold NBC a more successful series in 1964 starring one of the former leads of *The Lieutenant*, Robert Vaughn—*The Man from U.N.C.L.E.* NBC replaced the adult-oriented drama with two half-hour entries aimed straight for the kids—*Flipper* and *The Famous Adventures of Mr. Magoo*.

South Pacific setting in World War II, and he modernized and modified that concept for this series.

NBC's press department described *The Lieutenant* as "the dramatic adventures of a young man who chooses as his profession the United States Marine Corps. Against the background of the peacetime service, the maturing of the man is dramatized in experiences both on duty and off, in scenes filmed in the Camp Pendleton Marine Base and in neighboring beach and mountain locales of Southern California." The "young man" was Lt. Bill Rice, an Annapolis graduate who had many friends at Camp Pendleton, including fellow Lt. Panosian, but nevertheless found himself facing

Arrest and Trial

Drama. Ran on ABC Sundays 8:30–10 P.M. Sept. 15, 1963–Sept. 6, 1964, opposite *The Ed Sullivan Show* and *The Judy Garland Show* (through March 29), *Made in America* (from April 5 to May 3) and *Brenner* (from May 10) on CBS and *Grindl* and *Bonanza* on NBC. C: Ben Gazzara (as Det. Sgt. Nick Anderson), Chuck Connors (as Attorney John Egan), John Larch (as Deputy D.A. Jerry Miller), John Kerr (as Asst. Deputy D.A. Barry Pine), Roger Perry (as Det. Sgt. Dan Kirby) Noah

Ben Gazzara points out an item of interest to Chuck Connors on *Arrest and Trial*. Both men rarely saw eye to eye, as Gazzara tracked down the suspects Connors defended.

Keen (as Det. Lt. Bone), Don Galloway (as Mitchell Harris), Joe Higgins (as Jake Shakespeare), Jo Anne Miya (as Janet Okada). EP: Sy Salkowitz. P: Frank P. Rosenberg. D: Lewis Milestone, Jack Smight.

Arrest and Trial was one of the first two non-theatrical nighttime series to run on ABC in the 1963-64 season. The other was *Wagon Train*, which ran only a year in that format before returning to 60 minutes in its last season (1964-65) after being battered by competition from three top CBS sitcoms—*The Lucy Show*, *The Danny Thomas Show* and *The Andy Griffith Show*. *Arrest and Trial* fared worse, getting clobbered at its start by coming on midway through *The Ed Sullivan Show* and then facing *Bonanza* in its last 60 minutes. Those two top 10 titans caused this unusual drama to last only one season.

As actor Noah Keen noted about *Arrest and Trial*, "It was a very curious combination, combining the before and after of the crime, nabbing and arraigning suspects." The first half of each show involved Det. Sgt. Nick Anderson and his partners Det. Lt. Bone and Det. Sgt. Kirby tracking leads to find the accused party or parties, followed by public defender John Egan handling the same people's cases in court opposite Jerry Miller and Barry Pine from the D.A.'s office. The writers found they had to have Anderson track down fugitives from outside Egan's jurisdiction to prevent either one from appearing incapable or wrong in doing their duties.

Keen described his character, Det. Lt. Bone, as the "general factotum" to the others on the "arrest" side. "My dialogue basically was 'What's going on? Why didn't you do that?'" he said. In spite of his limited role, he did have an odd situation arise when he was off work that affected the show.

"I do remember somewhere in there I was playing in an entertainment baseball league and broke my leg," he said. "So I was confined to behind a desk, because they didn't want me to move on crutches."

Some TV observers have claimed that *Law & Order*, which started on NBC on Sept. 13, 1990, and is still running as of this writing, is similar to *Arrest and Trial*—cops get suspect in first half, then in second half suspect goes to court. "I've not seen too much of *Law & Order*, but from what I've seen, there's much more at-

tention to verisimilitude a la Jack Webb on *Dragnet* on it," Keen said. "They focus incredible attention to exact routine which did not take place on *Arrest and Trial*. *Arrest and Trial* was much more a dramatic interpretation." Also on *Law & Order*, the perspective in court is from the D.A.'s office rather than from a public defender.

Arrest and Trial was one of the first jobs Keen's agent nailed for his client when Keen moved to Hollywood, and even though it ran just one year, he was proud to have done it. "I enjoyed it," he said. ABC replaced it at 9 P.M. with movies in 1964, and kept running them there to a record 23 years before ending the practice in 1987.

100 Grand

Game. Ran on ABC Sundays 10–10:30 P.M. Sept. 15–Sept. 29, 1963, opposite *Candid Camera* on CBS and *DuPont Show of the Week* on NBC. C: Jack Clark. EP: Robert Stivers. P: John P. Green. D: Bill Foster, Jerome Shaw.

The series *100 Grand* proved conclusively that no matter how much money a game show offers, if the presentation is deadly, the audience will not show up. This three-week wonder, easily the quickest cancellation of the 1963-64 season, was the creation of Robert Stivers, a man whose previous claim to fame was as the first person to package orange juice into cardboard cartons. He had test runs of his show for ad agencies and network executives more than 100 not-so-grand times before getting a deal.

The premise was that each week a U.S. Chamber of Commerce would pick a professional to represent the chamber's city opposite an amateur in a selected category. Questions for each category would be written by both contestants, with judges reviewing them and authenticating the answers prior to airtime. To win the title sum, an amateur had to defeat a professional for six shows, playing one game per week.

With the rigged big money quiz show scandals of the late 1950s still fresh in people's minds, Stivers pledged in *Newsweek* magazine that "Neither I, nor my staff, nor the sponsors, will know what the questions are one second before they are heard over the air." That included the show's first director, Bill Foster.

Foster got onto the show having known

its producer, John P. Green, when the latter earlier was a vice president at ABC. "I just set up the look and the style and the system for them," he said of his work. "They wanted to get more theatrical than the usual show, to do something wild for them." Foster complied and had a set constructed with a huge transparent dome to encase the players and prevent them from hearing answers being shouted out in place of the traditional soundproof booth.

As for the debut, Foster charitably said he had no memory of it, but anyone who does no doubt remember it as a disaster. Airing live from New York, the initial matchup had "professional" Dr. Joe Coss, chosen by the Downey, Calif., Chamber of Commerce, face off against "amateur" Waterloo, Wisc., resident William Neil on the Civil War. Dr. Coss met his Waterloo by failing to answer any of Neil's questions. Accompanied by a slow drumbeat, Dr. Coss agonizingly used up his maximum 10-second limit to respond on every query, and had to be stopped leaving the stage before it was announced he would get a $500 U.S. Savings Bond, as did every loser of the game (if he won, he and the chamber would have split $1,000). In the other game, the "professional expert" on opera missed all questions too.

Flustered host Jack Clark assured viewers that the professionals really were experts having an off night, but the damage was done. ABC replaced it in October with another quick on-and-off series, *Laughs for Sale* (q.v.). The irony was that the host of *Laughs for Sale* was Hal March, previously the host of the biggest rigged game show of the 1950s, *The $64,000 Question*.

The Travels of Jaimie McPheeters

Western. Ran on ABC Sundays 7:30–8:30 P.M. Sept. 15, 1963–March 15, 1964, opposite *My Favorite Martian* and *The Ed Sullivan Show* on CBS and *Walt Disney* on NBC. C: Dan O'Herlihy (as "Doc" Sardius McPheeters), Kurt Russell (as Jaimie McPheeters), James Westerfield (as John Murrel), Sandy Kenyon (as Shep Baggott), Donna Anderson (as Jenny), Mark Allen (as Matt Kissel), Meg Wyllie (as Mrs. Kissel), the Osmonds (as the Kissel Brothers), Hedley Mattingly (as Henry T. Coe), Vernett Allen III (as Othello), Michael Witney (as Buck Coulter; 1963), Charles Bronson (as Linc Murdock; 1963–64). P: Don Ingalls. D: Boris Sagal, Jack Arnold. W: John Gay.

Breaking Point

Drama. Ran on ABC Mondays 10–11 P.M. Sept. 16, 1963–Sept. 7, 1964, opposite *East Side/West Side* on CBS and *Sing Along With Mitch* on NBC. C: Paul Richards (as Dr. McKinley Thompson), Eduard Franz (as Dr. Edward Raymer). P/W: George Lefferts. D: Sydney Pollack. W: Allen Sloane.

Viewers first met the characters on *Breaking Point* on the Sept. 9, 1963, episode of the hit medical series *Ben Casey*. The following week the latter vacated the Monday night time slot it had ruled for two years to go to Wednesday nights and let *Breaking Point* take over. It was a bad move; *Breaking Point* reached its title destination within a year following poor ratings, while *Ben Casey* sank opposite the huge CBS sitcom hits *The Beverly Hillbillies* and *The Dick Van Dyke Show* (the respective #1 and #3 series in 1963-64).

The inspiration for *Breaking Point* was *The Eleventh Hour*, a drama about psychiatry that aired on NBC Wednesdays 10–11 P.M. Although hardly a blockbuster, it did knock off the competing *Naked City* on ABC after a three-year run and convinced the network it needed a similar show. "I believe it was [program management director] Dan Melnick of ABC who came to me to ask me to do a psychiatric hour to compete with the one on NBC," said producer/writer George Lefferts.

As with *The Eleventh Hour*, *Breaking Point* had two male leads, with the latter using Paul Richards as resident psychiatrist Dr. "Mac" Thompson. "He was not our first choice," Lefferts said. "Our first choice was Robert Redford." Redford, an up-and-coming actor at the time, asked Lefferts to hold the part while he mulled over doing the pilot. "He said he wanted to take a walk on the beach and think things over," Lefferts said. "Three days later I called his agent, and he said he was still on the beach!" Taking a hint, Lefferts gave up on Redford.

But Redford did guest on the series' fourth show as a man who preyed on women in his group therapy sessions. Other notable names to show up, usually as patients, included Lillian Gish, Walter Pidgeon, John Cassavetes and Rip Torn (as a man with multiple personalities). "We tried to pretty much cover everything that went wrong with your mind," Lefferts said. "The stories carried the show."

He added that there was some censorship in telling the stories. "We couldn't use 'crazy,' which was hard to do." As for the scripts themselves, Lefferts said, "I think about half were original, and I rewrote the rest." Beside Dr. Thompson, the other regular character was Thompson's mentor, Dr. Raymer, who directed the psychiatric clinic at the nonexistent York Hospital in Los Angeles.

According to Lefferts, *Breaking Point* reached its limit with ABC executives when the ratings fell off after the first few episodes from what *Ben Casey* had earned. "ABC got hysterical and brought in more sexy stuff," he said. That approach didn't work either, and *Breaking Point* went off in the fall of 1964 — as did *The Eleventh Hour*. In its time slot returned *Ben Casey*, but fewer viewers came back to that once top 10 hit series, and it went off a year and a half after *Breaking Point* ended its run.

Grindl

Sitcom. Ran on NBC Sundays 8:30–9 P.M. Sept. 15, 1963–Sept. 13, 1964, opposite *Arrest and Trial* on ABC and *The Ed Sullivan Show* on CBS. C: Imogene Coca (as Grindl), James Milhollin (as Anson Foster). EP: Harry Ackerman. P: Winston O'Keefe. D/W: David Swift.

The Greatest Show on Earth

Drama. Ran on ABC Tuesdays 9–10 P.M. Sept. 17, 1963–Sept. 8, 1964, opposite *Petticoat Junction* and *The Jack Benny Program* on CBS and *The Richard Boone Show* on NBC. C: Jack Palance (as Johnny Slate), Stu Erwin (as Otto King). P: Stanley Colbert. D: Don Richardson. W: William Wood.

Channing

Drama. Ran on ABC Wednesdays 10–11 P.M. Sept. 18, 1963–April 8, 1964, opposite *The Danny Kaye Show* on CBS and *The Eleventh Hour* on NBC. C: Jason Evers (as Prof. Joseph Howe), Henry Jones (as Dean Fred Baker). P: Jack Laird. D: Harvey Hart. W: Les Pine.

Temple Houston

Western. Ran on NBC Thursdays 7:30–8:30 P.M. Sept. 19, 1963–Sept. 10, 1964, opposite *The Flintstones* and *The Donna Reed Show* on ABC and *Password* and *Rawhide* on CBS. C: Jeffrey Hunter (as Temple Houston), Jack Elam (as George Tag-

gart). P: Joseph Dackow, Richard Bluel, Lawrence Dobkin, James Lydon. D: Leslie H. Martinson, William Conrad, Charles Rondeau, Gerd Oswald, Abner Biberman.

The Jerry Lewis Show

Talk/Variety. Ran on ABC Saturdays 9:30–11:30 P.M. Sept. 21–Dec. 21, 1963, opposite *The Defenders* (through Nov. 9) and *The New Phil Silvers Show* (from Nov. 16) and *Gunsmoke* on CBS and movies on NBC. C: Jerry Lewis, Del Moore, the Lou Brown Orchestra. EP: Ernest D. Glucksman. P: Perry Cross. AP: Mack Bing. D: John Dorsey. W: Jerry Lewis, Dick Cavett, Bob Howard, Bill Richmond.

When Jack Paar left hosting *The Tonight Show* in April 1962, there was a five-month gap before Johnny Carson could host the show due to his contract for his daytime show *Who Do You Trust?* During the interim, producer Perry Cross supervised a stream of weekly guest hosts, one of whom was Jerry Lewis. "He had such a good time, and ratings were up, so he did another week," said Cross. "He was really relaxed and funny."

With ratings and reviews being the best he had on TV since he left Dean Martin in 1956, interest in Lewis doing a series soared among the networks. ABC offered him an incredible contract making him the highest paid TV personality at the time plus giving him an unprecedented two-hour live series from Hollywood. "I got a call sometime after that, when he had made a deal with ABC," Cross said. "He told me we'd do the same thing as on *The Tonight Show* and would I like to do it?" After mulling it over, Cross said yes and moved to California.

For the series, Lewis, Cross and others envisioned something new. "It was a combination never-before-tried format, which was to try a formal comedy variety show with an informal talk show built around Jerry," Cross said. It also was going to use a bigger studio than that of *The Tonight Show* at what was the El Capitan Theatre in Hollywood. "It had to be renovated and built over. The audience was corralled off a large balcony going up a high angle, and you had to watch a screen to see what was going on below."

Unfortunately, that screen for the audience wasn't working during the heavily hyped debut, and there were more gaffes ahead that evening. "There were audio glitches, it was hot, it was a mess," noted Cross. The problems showed up on air with dead spots and flat routines, and critics savaged the show. ABC executives arrived immediately to suggest corrections, but the initial high viewership dropped off quickly, and the show ended before the start of 1964.

Asked if he thought the critics reviewed the star and the show's publicity rather than its content, Cross said, "I think so. There was a lot more pouncing on him than necessary. The marketing campaign mentioned how great it would be, how big it was. We all got blamed. The network wasn't happy with me or with Jerry. Jerry wasn't happy with me."

To Cross, apart from the debut's technical flaws, the failure was in trying to be both a talk and variety series. "It didn't come together," he said. "The format did not work." He went onto many other TV projects before retiring in 1979. Lewis, hurt considerably by the series, had only one other regular TV series, this time a straight comedy variety show also titled *The Jerry Lewis Show*, from 1967 to 1969, but maintained a constant TV presence with his annual Labor Day telethon for muscular dystrophy into the 21st century.

East Side/West Side

Drama. Ran on CBS Mondays 10–11 P.M. Sept. 23, 1963–Sept. 14, 1964, opposite *Breaking Point* on ABC and *Sing Along With Mitch* on NBC. C: George C. Scott (as Neil Brock), Elizabeth Wilson (as Frieda "Hecky" Hechlinger), Cicely Tyson (as Jane Foster). EP: David Susskind. P: Don Kranze. D: Jack Smight, Tom Gries. W: Ed DeBlasio, Arnold Perl.

"It was a good show, but I don't call it a groundbreaker," said producer Don Kranze of *East Side/West Side*. The show earned Emmy nominations for a dramatic series, actor, writer and director (winning the latter category for Tom Gries), but Kranze remembered it better as an ego trip for its star, George C. Scott.

"George C. Scott decided he would open a theater in his hometown of Detroit," Kranze said. "In order to keep that theater going, he borrowed from CBS, and in order to pay them back, he had to agree to do a series." Scott called David Susskind about setting up a deal, and with that announcement, Kranze said, "The thing was sold without a pilot."

Actually, Susskind did create a pilot afterward, which Kranze called "crappy." But a deal was a deal, so the series went into effect with Kranze drafted to supervise the editing and writing. The basic concept of Scott playing a New York City social worker trying to improve the lot of his impoverished clients under the supervision of "Hecky" Hechlinger. Jane Foster was the secretary, a rare non-stereotypical job for the time in that it was played by a black actress. "We were supposed to use Diana Sands, but her agent went crazy, so we had Cicely Tyson," Kranze said.

Kranze soon found that his biggest problem on the show was his star, who was insistent on virtually every point of contention the two had. "There were no compromises made, as far as I was concerned," he said. He cited one example from the show which won Gries the best director Emmy, "Who Do You Kill?" The crew went to Harlem to shoot on location, then Scott turned to him and said, "I want you to speak to CBS and have them clean up the street after we're finished." Kranze said Scott never accepted his explanation that such a request never would be granted by CBS, but somehow he managed to handle it.

Scott's constant anger ("Always under the surface, he's violent," Kranze said) and demands wore out any way that his show could become a success on TV, in Kranze's view. "We were cut off some 20-some stations in the South. We had a black secretary. There was no way they would play it. And there was nothing for young people to want to watch in it." If by some chance it had been renewed, Kranze said that Scott once told him "Next season I'll marry Cicely Tyson." An interracial marriage on TV was unheard of in the mid–1960s— Scott was pushing boundaries he knew he could not break.

At the very least, *East Side/West Side* was a critical hit for Scott. The same could not be said of his other two series, the weak sitcom *Mr. President* (1987–88) and the dreary cop drama *Traps* (1994). He died a month short of his 72nd birthday in 1999, having earned two other Emmy nominations and two Emmy Awards for specials.

Redigo

Western. Ran on NBC Tuesdays 8:30–9 P.M. Sept. 24–Dec. 31, 1963, opposite *McHale's Navy* on ABC and *The Red Skelton Hour* on CBS. C: Richard Egan (as Jim Redigo), Roger Davis (as Mike), Rudy Solari (as Frank Martinez), Elena Verdugo (as Gerry), Mina Martinez (as Linda Martinez). P: Andy White. D: Alan Reisner. W: Charles Hoffman.

Glynis

Sitcom. Ran on CBS Wednesdays 8:30–9 P.M. Sept. 25–Dec. 18, 1963, opposite *The Price Is Right* (through Nov. 27) and *The Farmer's Daughter* (from Dec. 4) and *The Virginian* on NBC. C: Glynis Johns (as Glynis Granville), Keith Andes (as Keith Granville), George Mathews (as Chick Rogers). EP: Jess Oppenheimer. P: Edward H. Feldman. D: Felix Feist. W: Arthur Julian.

The Edie Adams Show

Musical Variety. Ran on ABC Thursdays 10–10:30 P.M. Sept. 26, 1963–March 19, 1964, opposite *The Nurses* on CBS and *Kraft Suspense Theater* on NBC. C: Edie Adams, Don Chastain, Peter Hanley, the Paul Godkin Dancers, the Randy Rayburn Singers, the Peter Matz Orchestra. P/W: John Bradford. D: Joseph Behar. W: Ed Haas.

The New Phil Silvers Show

Sitcom. Ran on CBS Saturdays 8:30–9 P.M. Sept. 28–Nov. 9, 1963, opposite *The Lawrence Welk Show* on ABC and *The Joey Bishop Show* on NBC, then CBS Saturdays 9:30–10 P.M. Nov. 16, 1963–June 27, 1964, opposite *The Jerry Lewis Show* (through Dec. 21) and *The Hollywood Palace* (from Jan. 4) on ABC and movies on NBC. C: Phil Silvers (as Harry Grafton), Stafford Repp (as Mr. Brink), Herbie Faye (as Waluska), Pat Renella (as Roxy), Jim Shane (as Lester), Douglas Dumbrille (as Mr. Osborne), Steve Mitchell (as Fred Starkey), Bob Williams (as Bob), Buddy Lester (as Nick), Norm Grabowski (as Grabowski), Elena Verdugo (as Audrey; 1964), Sandy Descher (as Susan; 1964), Ronnie Dapo (as Andy; 1964). P/D: Rod Amateau. W: A.J. Russell, Lou Soloman.

The Judy Garland Show

Musical Variety. Ran on CBS Sundays 9–10 P.M. Sept. 29, 1963–March 29, 1964, opposite *Arrest and Trial* on ABC and *Bonanza* on NBC. C: Judy Garland, Jerry Van Dyke (1963), Ken Murray (1964), the Mort Lindsey Orchestra, the Ernie Flatt Dancers (1963), the Nick Castle Dancers (1963), the Peter Gennaro Dancers (1963–64). EP: George Schlatter, Norman Jewison. P: Barry

Smith. D: Bill Hobin. W: William Nichols, Bernard Rothman.

The Sid Caesar Show

Comedy Variety. Ran on ABC Thursdays 10–10:30 P.M. Oct. 3, 1963–March 12, 1964, opposite *The Nurses* on CBS and *Kraft Suspense Theater* on NBC. C: Sid Caesar, Joey Forman, Gisele MacKenzie, Marilyn Hannold. P/D: Greg Garrison. W: Goodman Ace, Aaron Ruben, Selma Diamond, Jay Burton, Tony Webster.

Producer/director Greg Garrison's association with Sid Caesar started with the program that established the comic actor's reputation. "I was the director of *Your Show of Shows*," he said. "I loved Sid." But as talented as Caesar was on air, personal demons that included substance abuse disheartened Garrison. "Between booze and drugs, he was half out of it," Garrison said.

Your Show of Shows ran from 1950 to 1954. Next came two more variety series, *Caesar's Hour* from 1954 to 57, followed in the 1957-58 season by the unsuccessful *Sid Caesar Invites You* (q.v.). Then Caesar earned a Tony nomination for playing seven roles in the musical comedy *Little Me* during the 1962-63 season.

Garrison saw *Little Me* and noticed how much his addictions now affected his performance. "There were some nights where the show would finish at 10:55, and others where it finished at 10:25. He would speed up the show sometimes."

Even so, Garrison remained an admirer, and when Sid told him he wanted him to direct his new series, Garrison was willing. "Sid gave me my chance with *Your Show of Shows* in 1950, and I'm many things, and one is a person with a long memory."

Singer/actress Gisele MacKenzie was the Imogene Coca equivalent in sketches, while comic Joey Forman filled the need of what Howard Morris did with Caesar on *Your Show of Shows*— either climb up Caesar or be thrown around by Caesar. For Garrison, the best news was that Sid was staying sober while embarking on his show, which appeared every other week alternating with *The Edie Adams Show* (q.v.).

"The show is very good. Everything is going well until the assassination," Garrison said, referring to President John F. Kennedy's murder on Nov. 22, 1963. "We were in shock. Sid was absolutely wiped out, and we couldn't get together to do any new material, because he went off the wagon. And we didn't feel like doing comedy, either."

To accommodate Caesar, he had the writers dust off old routines from *Your Show of Shows* to act. But his heart wasn't in it, and just five months after it started, *The Sid Caesar Show* was history. "The ratings weren't bad," Garrison said. "Sid just couldn't perform."

Garrison went on to produce and direct *The Dean Martin Show* from 1965 to 1974, while Sid's reputation as an unreliable alcoholic in the industry kept him from having another series, even though he cleaned up his act by the late 1970s. He did do guest shots, however. Garrison remembered when he visited *The Dean Martin Show* that "We had a staff of 10 to 12 writers for Sid, because Sid had to be and was a very special guy. Up until the day of the show, I was murder on the writers to make sure they gave him the right material."

Though mostly inactive lately, Caesar did make a guest appearance improvising jokes on *Whose Line Is It Anyway?* in late 2000. It showed he still had top timing and delivery. Hail Caesar!

Do You Know?

Children's. Ran on CBS Saturdays 12:30–1 P.M. Oct. 12, 1963–April 25, 1964, opposite *The Magic Land of Allakazam* (through Dec. 28) and *American Bandstand* (from Jan. 4) and *The Bullwinkle Show* on NBC. C: Robert Maxwell.

Laughs for Sale

Game. Ran on ABC Sundays 10–10:30 P.M. Oct. 20–Dec. 22, 1963, opposite *Candid Camera* on CBS and *DuPont Show of the Week* on NBC. C: Hal March. P: Louis Hayward. D: Alan Rafkin.

Tell It to the Camera

Comedy. Ran on CBS Wednesdays 8:30–9 P.M. Dec. 25, 1963–March 18, 1964, opposite *The Farmer's Daughter* on ABC and *The Virginian* on NBC. C: Red Rowe. EP: Allen Funt. P: Mel Ferber. D: Bruce Minnix.

Premiering on Christmas Day 1963, *Tell It to the Camera* was anything but a gift to its

original director, Bruce Minnix, who said he does not list the show on his resume, though not because it ran so shortly. Much of his disdain came in fact from dealing with its creator and executive producer, Allen Funt, who alienated everybody he worked with on the series, in Minnix's opinion.

As Minnix explained, "The producer was Mel Ferber. He and I were friends from our days as associate directors. He called me on the first of December and said, 'Would you like to do this?' and I said yes." What "this" was was a variant on Funt's popular *Candid Camera* series, the #7 rated show of the 1963-64 season which Funt hosted and produced. Here, the participants were not surprised to be part of a practical joke and in fact spoke directly into a TV camera while being interviewed about their attitudes.

"It was almost turning *Candid Camera* inside out," Minnix said of the format of *Tell It to the Camera*. "In this case, you were saying 'Be clever. Talk to me.' They always felt strained to me, even though you got some good lines."

Minnix said he didn't recall the show's host, Red Rowe, interviewing the guests on location on the streets of New York City, thinking that Rowe did mostly introductions of the interviews instead. "Seems to me I was feeding the questions that had been prearranged in interviews," he said.

Also prearranged, without Minnix's knowledge, was how Funt ran his production company. "I discovered he had speakers in everybody's office, and he could flip them on and off whenever he wanted," Minnix said. The dismayed director voiced his objections of this practice to Funt. That did not go over well with Funt, nor did he like it when Minnix said he would meet the staff the next day at the Washington Square locale for the shoot rather than go to the office and then ride with them to the site, even though it was quicker for Minnix to go directly to Washington Square.

The final straw, according to Minnix, was when he worked all day on interviews, got what he wanted and called it an early day without going back to Funt's headquarters and staying there until 5 P.M. That apparently angered Funt enough, and he fired Minnix on a Friday, just five days after the director started work on the series.

Minnix still received credit on the debut

outing, but he regretted the connection. "I thought it was a terrible show," he said. Viewers evidently agreed, and within three months *Tell It to the Camera* was told to get off the CBS schedule. Funt never produced another TV series apart from *Candid Camera*.

The Object Is

Game. Ran on ABC Mondays through Fridays 11:30 A.M.–Noon Dec. 30, 1963–March 27, 1964, opposite *Pete and Gladys* reruns on CBS and *Missing Links* on NBC. C: Dick Clark. P: Wilbur Stark. D: Hal Cooper.

Science All-Stars

Children's/Informational. Ran on ABC Sundays 4:30–5 P.M. Jan. 12–April 26, 1964, opposite *One of a Kind* on CBS and *The Wonderful World of Golf* on NBC, then ABC Sundays 5–5:30 P.M. Jan. 10–April 25, 1965, opposite *The Jack Benny Program* reruns on CBS and *Wild Kingdom* on NBC. C: Don Morrow. EP: Steve Carlin. D: Lloyd Gross (1964), Jerome Shaw (1965).

Though educational in nature, anyone who reads the cast and crew list of *Science All-Stars* could easily assume it was a game show, given the participants' resumes. Host Don Morrow had only one regular network TV credit as host of *Camouflage* from 1961 to 1962. Executive producer Steve Carlin had helmed *The $64,000 Question* in the 1950s. And the show's first director, Lloyd Gross, had done the chore for a slew of game shows, including the hits *Masquerade Party* and *Play Your Hunch*, and so too had second director Jerome Shaw for the likes of *Keep Talking* and *Video Village*.

With all these people involved, it makes you wonder if any of the kids who participated felt they at least deserved some parting gifts for doing the program. But no, all the children received were congratulations and national exposure for showing off their contraptions they had entered successfully into the National Science Fair.

ABC reported that more than 4,000 middle or high school students went through interviews to determine which ones would appear on *Science All-Stars*, a number that sound more hyperbole than fact. In any event, three children discussed their projects with Morrow per show, and that was more than enough for Gross to have to deal with as director.

"The problem with that was it was a complicated show," Gross recalled. "It would bring youngsters on with their 'inventions,' so to speak. It had its moments of being an excellent show, I thought.

"But some of the things were difficult to do. We did a thing with a kid and his rat maze and so on, and had to show how they worked." Getting across the details on such concoctions visually and aurally were the main challenge for the show.

Gross added that he did try and keep the show as spontaneous as possible, even though it was taped in New York City. "What we would do, we would have a short rehearsal, and then the kids would bring them on air," he said. He could not recall whether it was his schedule or his experience with the first run of *Science All-Stars* that led him to be replaced by Shaw for the second go-round.

Science All-Stars appeared on the ABC schedule as a winter replacement following the ends of the 1963 and 1964 seasons of the American Football League. ABC lost the rights to the AFL in 1965 to NBC, which may have made the decision to bring back the show again a moot point, although truth be told it usually finished behind its network competition in the ratings in 1964 and 1965. In any event, Gross, Morrow, Carlin and Shaw continued to work on other TV shows afterward, with almost all of them being — you guessed it — game shows.

Destry

Western. Ran on ABC Fridays 7:30–8:30 P.M. Feb. 14–Sept. 11, 1964, opposite *The Great Adventure* on CBS and *International Showtime* on NBC. C: John Gavin (as Harrison Destry). P: Howard Browne. D: Don Siegel. W: Robert Guy Barrons.

Get the Message

Game. Ran on ABC Mondays through Fridays 11–11:30 A.M. March 30–Dec. 25, 1964, opposite reruns on *The Real McCoys* (through Oct. 2) and *The Andy Griffith Show* (from Oct. 5) on CBS and *Concentration* on NBC. C: Frank Buxton (through Sept. 25), Robert Q. Lewis (from Sept. 28). EP: Robert Noah. P: Jack Ferren. D: Michael Gargiulo.

When *Get the Message* premiered, director Michael Gargiulo had been with its production company of Mark Goodson and Bill Todman for several years. The organization's game show empire was humming along quite nicely when *Get the Message* came on board, joining six other daytime entries Goodson-Todman had on the networks—*The Price Is Right* (lead-in for *Get the Message*), *Missing Links* (lead-out for *Get the Message*), *Say When*, *Password*, *To Tell the Truth* and *The Match Game*. It was a veritable cacophony of contestants at the company. "I remember very vividly we would book 29 panelists a week," Gargiulo said.

Adding to the cultivation of players was *Get the Message*, which Gargiulo freely admitted was a *Password* knockoff. But whereas *Password* employed a player and celebrity giving each other one-word clues, *Get the Message* required two guest celebrities to each supply one-word clues to a contestant to identify a word or phrase. If the player guessed right, he or she got a point. The first team to amass three points won $100 and had its player go for more money by giving one of the team's celebrities one-word clues for another mystery word or phrase. A correct initial guess won $100, followed by diminishing amounts until the fourth and last clue allowed won $10 if properly identified. The teams consisted of all women versus all men.

The *Password* connection is significant, for the host of that series, Allen Ludden, had an actress wife he wed in 1963 who was to be involved in the show. In her 1995 autobiography, *Here We Go Again*, Betty White wrote that Mark Goodson wanted her to be the host for *Get the Message*, but network executives did not want a woman as a game show host. Gargiulo confirmed White's story but added, "It was not only ABC that nixed it. That was an idea that was nixed a lot." (White finally hosted a game show nearly 20 years later. *Just Men!* ran just three months— Jan. 3–May 1, 1983 — on NBC

daily at noon, but it did earn her an Emmy Award as Best Host.)

Instead, Goodson-Todman went with Frank Buxton as host. Gargiulo believed it was Buxton's busy schedule with outside projects, including hosting the ABC Sunday afternoon children's show *Discovery* at the same time, that led him to leave the show, and not any pressure from the network or production company regarding the ratings. "I don't remember any animosity," he said.

Replacing Buxton was Robert Q. Lewis, who coincidentally was the host of the first Goodson-Todman show Gargiulo directed, *Play Your Hunch*. Unfortunately, Lewis did not add a bigger audience for the show, so *Get the Message* got the hunch and left the ABC lineup after Christmas Day 1964. The network did not fill the time slot, leaving it open for affiliates to program for nine months until it tried another short-lived effort, *The Young Set* (see 1965-66).

Made in America

Game. Ran on CBS Sundays 9:30–10 P.M. April 5–May 3, 1964, opposite *Arrest and Trial* on ABC and *Bonanza* on NBC. C: Hans Conried, Don Murray, Walter Slezak, Jan Sterling. P: Steve Carlin. D: Jerome Shaw.

On Broadway Tonight

Talent. Ran on CBS Wednesdays 10–11 P.M. July 8–Sept. 16, 1964, opposite *77 Sunset Strip* on ABC and *The Eleventh Hour* on NBC, then CBS Fridays 8:30–9:30 P.M. Jan. 1–March 12, 1965, opposite *The Addams Family* and *Valentine's Day* on ABC and *The Bob Hope Chrysler Theater* on NBC. C: Rudy Vallee. P: Irving Mansfield. D: Dave Geisel (1964), Stan Harris (1965). W: David Gregory, Saul Turtletaub.

1964-65

The Rogues

Adventure. Ran on NBC Sundays 10–11 P.M. Sept. 13, 1964–Sept. 5, 1965, opposite movies on ABC

and *Candid Camera* and *What's My Line?* on CBS. C: David Niven (as Alexander "Alec" Fleming), Charles Boyer (as Marcel St. Clair), Gig Young (as Tony Fleming), Gladys Cooper (as Aunt Margaret

St. Clair), Robert Coote (as Timmy St. Clair), John Williams (as Inspector Briscoe). EP: Tom McDermott. P: Collier Young. D: Robert Ellis Miller, Ida Lupino, Hy Averback, John Newland. W: Lorenzo Semple, Jr., Marion Hargrove, Ivan Goff, Ben Roberts.

Three top suave movie stars—Charles Boyer, David Niven and Gig Young—came to television representing respectively the French, British and American branches of a family of deceptive yet charming conspirators on *The Rogues*. The lineage of the St. Clairs and the Flemings extended back to the late 18th century, with their descendants maintaining the families' practice of bilking rich felons from their ill-gotten gains, and returning the proceeds to the family, naturally. The English head, Alec Fleming, was the top operative before stepping aside to let his American cousin Tony supervise the international flim-flams, but Alec still remained a major player in the top operations. So too did Marcel, the family's top man in France. Assisting them was Aunt Margaret, who cooked up many of the schemes, and her son Timmy, who participated in the plans impersonating various people. Seen occasionally in the schemes, and never able to connect the family members to the assorted fleecings, was Scotland Yard Inspector Briscoe.

Despite the talents involved, *The Rogues* had nowhere near the audience of its lead-in *Bonanza* (the #1 series for the 1964-65 season), and while its competition was not in the top 30 either, the networks continued the other shows in the same slot the next season while *The Rogues* folded. Yet one of its directors, Robert Ellis Miller, maintained that "That was an enormous success, but it didn't continue because I don't think Mr. Boyer and Mr. Niven had the time to do it."

Miller claimed the leads, accustomed to the more leisurely pace of movies, adjusted easily to the quicker demands of doing a weekly one-hour filmed series. "They were great," he said. "I thought there could be temperaments flying. These things were shot in a few days. But they were Johnny-on-the-spot."

He added that he as a director, he scheduled their hours as best he could to accommodate their needs. "You try to preserve their energy by not having one person get the earliest calls or working late." Miller also said that the glamorous locales the show depicted, such as Manhattan and London, were not done on location—they filmed all the episodes on back lots in southern California.

"We had a good cast, good guest stars," Miller concluded. "That to me was a major thing in my life. I got more calls about the style of it. It didn't seem too 'television-y,' but like a little movie."

The lighthearted capers on *The Rogues* stood in sharp contrast to the real-life demise of two of its stars. On Aug. 26, 1978, Boyer killed himself following the death of his wife two days earlier. Young followed him less than two months later, shooting his wife of three weeks and then himself on Oct. 19, 1978. As for Niven, he died of ALS on July 29, 1983.

No Time for Sergeants

Sitcom. Ran on ABC Mondays 8:30–9 P.M. Sept. 14, 1964–Sept. 6, 1965, opposite *The Andy Griffith Show* (through June 21) and *Summer Playhouse* (from June 28) on CBS and *90 Bristol Court* (through Jan. 4) and *The Man from U.N.C.L.E.* (from Jan. 11) on NBC. C: Sammy Jackson (as Airman Will Stockdale), Harry Hickox (as Sgt. King), Kevin O'Neal (as Airman Ben Whitledge), Laurie Sibbald (as Millie Anderson), Paul Smith (as Capt. Martin), Hayden Rorke (as Col. Farnsworth), Andy Clyde (as Grandpa Jim Anderson), Michael McDonald (as Pvt. Jack Longdon), George Murdock (as Capt. Krupnick), Greg Benedict (as Pvt. Blanchard), Joey Tata (as Pvt. Mike Neddick). EP: William T. Orr. D: Richard Crenna, Leslie Martinson. W: Norman Paul, John L. Green, Elon Packard, William Burns.

Wendy and Me

Sitcom. Ran on ABC Mondays 9–9:30 P.M. Sept. 14, 1964–Sept. 6, 1965, opposite *The Lucy Show* (through July 12) and *Glynis* reruns (from July 19) on CBS and *The Andy Williams Show* on NBC. C: George Burns (as himself), Connie Stevens (as Wendy Conway), Ron Harper (as Jeff Conway), James Callahan (as Danny Adams), J. Pat O'Malley (as Mr. Bundy), Bartlett Robinson (as Willard Norton). EP: Herm Saunders. P: George Burns. D: Richard Crenna, Gene Reynolds. W: Norman Paul, Robert O'Brien, Elon Padard, Willy Burns.

The Bing Crosby Show

Sitcom. Ran on ABC Mondays 9:30–10 P.M. Sept. 14, 1964–June 14, 1965, opposite *Many Happy Returns* (through April 12) and *The Danny Thomas*

Show reruns (from April 19) on CBS and *The Andy Williams Show* on NBC. C: Bing Crosby (as Bing Collins), Beverly Garland (as Ellie Collins), Carol Faylen (as Janice Collins), Diane Sherry (as Joyce Collins), Frank McHugh (as Willie Walters). P: Steven Gethers. D: James Sheldon. W: Don Beaumont.

The Tycoon

Sitcom. Ran on ABC Tuesdays 9–9:30 P.M. Sept. 15, 1964–Sept. 7, 1965, opposite *The Red Skelton Hour* (through June 15) and *Hollywood Talent Scouts* (from June 22) on CBS and *The Man from U.N.C.L.E.* (through Dec. 29), *Hullabaloo* (from Jan. 12 to May 11) and *Cloak of Mystery* (from May 25 to Aug. 8) on NBC . C: Walter Brennan (as Walter Andrews), Van Williams (as Pat Burns), Jerome Cowan (as Herbert Wilson), Janet Lake (as Betty Franklin), Pat McNulty (as Martha Keane), Monty Margetts (as Una Fields). P: Charles Isaacs. D: Alvin Ganzer. W: Fred Fox, Iz Elinson.

Mickey

Sitcom. Ran on ABC Wednesdays 9–9:30 P.M. Sept. 16, 1964–Jan. 13, 1965, opposite *The Dick Van Dyke Show* on CBS and movies on NBC. C: Mickey Rooney (as Mickey Grady), Emmaline Henry (as Nora Grady), Sammee Tong (as Sammy Ling), Tim Rooney (as Timmy Grady), Brian Nash (as Buddy Grady), Alan Reed (as Mr. Swidler). EP: Selig J. Seligman. P: Robert Fisher, Arthur Marx. D: Richard Whorf.

Valentine's Day

Sitcom. Ran on ABC Fridays 9–9:30 P.M. Sept. 18, 1964–Sept. 10, 1965, opposite *The Entertainers* (through Dec. 25), *On Broadway Tonight* (from Jan. 1 to March 12), *The Great Adventure* (from March 19 to April 30) and *Our Private World* (from May 7) on CBS and *The Bob Hope Chrysler Theater* on NBC. C: Tony Franciosa (as Valentine Farrow), Jack Soo (as Rockwell "Rocky" Sin), Janet Waldo (as Libby Freeman), Mimi Dillard (as Molly), Jerry Hausner (as O.D. Dunstall), Eddie Quillan (as Grover Cleveland Fipple). P/W: Hal Kanter. D: George Marshal. W: Jack Sher.

Kentucky Jones

Comedy/Drama. Ran on NBC Saturdays 8:30–9 P.M. Sept. 19–Dec. 26, 1964, opposite *The Lawrence Welk Show* on ABC and *Gilligan's Island* on CBS, then NBC Saturdays 8–8:30 P.M. Jan. 2–Sept. 11,

1965, opposite *The King Family Show* on ABC and *The Jackie Gleason Show* on CBS. C: Dennis Weaver (as Kenneth Yarborough "Kentucky" Jones), Ricky Der (as Ike Wong), Harry Morgan (as Seldom Jackson), Cherylene Lee (as Annie Ng), Arthur Wong (as Mr. Ng), Keye Luke (as Thomas Wong), Nancy Rennick (as Edith Thorncraft). P: Albert Beich, Buzz Kulik. D: Ida Lupino.

A largely unheralded pioneer in political correctness, *Kentucky Jones* featured the first predominantly Asian cast on an American TV series. The major exception was its star, Dennis Weaver, who was doing his first series after spending nine years playing Chester Goode on *Gunsmoke*. Weaver had to wait for his next series, *Gentle Ben* (1967–69), to star in a moderate hit.

But most of the cast otherwise were Asian actors. There was Ricky Der as Dwight Eisenhower "Ike" Wong, a Chinese orphan adopted by Weaver's "Kentucky" Jones, whose nickname came from his first and middle names' initials (Kenneth Yarborough, get it?) There also was Keye Luke as the unrelated Thomas Wong, who was a pal of Mr. Jones; Cherylene Lee, who was Annie Ng; and Arthur Wong, who was Annie's father. The only regular Caucasians were Harry Morgan as ranch helper Seldom Jackson, and Nancy Rennick as Edith the social worker in charge of Ike.

Lee was a fourth-generation Chinese American working as a juvenile actress when she got her part. "I was doing *The King and I* in San Francisco, and Ricky Der, who played Dennis Weaver's son, was also cast from San Francisco," she said. "A mutual friend had suggested me for the part of the girlfriend." After a successful reading, Lee worked once again with Luke and Wong after doing previous shows with them.

"When it started out, it was something along the line of *Bachelor Father*—situations that were humorous but had serious moments," Lee said of the show. "I recall one particular script where Ricky Der believed he was dying and I was his girlfriend. It was very touching. I believe Ida Lupino was the director."

The show was set on a 40-acre ranch in Southern California, with Weaver's character said to be a veterinarian whose wife died before their adoption of Ike Wong went through. Lee said they filmed outdoor scenes on location at a ranch in the Santa Monica mountains, which

Harry Morgan holds a bucket as Ricky Der (on ladder) and Dennis Weaver get ready to brush paint on a house on *Kentucky Jones*.

didn't faze her. "I worked on a number of shows where there were horses," she said. "It was a very relaxed set." Away from the set, she and Der spent at least three hours in school every day and noted that "We had the same teacher."

Lee believed the program's distinguishing characteristic of having Asians in non-stereo-typed roles might have been its downfall in the tense mid–1960s. "It was an unusual thing to do, this mixed cast, something that was not done at the time," she said. "I don't know if that turned off the public at the time."

Noting that "My early career as a child performer affected me," Lee now is a playwright as an adult. "I deal a lot in my work with Asian American issues, particularly Chinese American issues," she said. Unlike some former child actors, she did not feel *Kentucky Jones* exploited her and has warm memories of it. "I never felt I was being asked to do anything out of the ordinary," she said.

Broadside

Sitcom. Ran on ABC Sundays 8:30–9 P.M. Sept. 20, 1964–Sept. 5, 1965, opposite *The Ed Sullivan Show* on CBS and *The Bill Dana Show* (through Jan. 17), *Branded* (from Jan. 24 to July 4) and *Buckskin* reruns (from July 11) on NBC. C: Kathy Nolan (as Lt. (jg) Anne Morgan), Edward Andrews (as Cdr. Rogers Adrian), Dick Sargent (as Lt. Maxwell Trotter), Lois Roberts (as Mechanic's Mate Molly McGuire), Sheila James (as Machinist's Mate Selma Kowalski), Joan Staley (as Machinist's Mate Roberta Love), Jimmy Boyd (as Machinist's Mate Marion Botnik), George Furth (as Ensign Beasley), Don Edmonds (as Nicky D'Angelo; 1964); Arnold Stang (as Ship's Cook First Class Stanley Stubbs; 1965). P/D: Edward J. Montagne. W: Si Rose, Barry Blitzer, Ray Brenner, Frank Gill, Jr., G. Carleton Brown.

Many Happy Returns

Sitcom. Ran on CBS Mondays 9:30–10 P.M. Sept. 21, 1964–April 12, 1965, opposite *The Bing Crosby Show* on ABC and *The Andy Williams Show* on NBC. C: John McGiver (as Walter Burnley), Elinor Donahue (as Joan Randall), Richard Collier (as Harry Price), Jesslyn Fax (as Wilma Fritter), Mark Goddard (as Bob Randall), Mickey Manners (as Joe Foley), Elena Verdugo (as Lynn Hall), Andrea Sacino (as Laurie Randall), Russell Collins (as Owen Sharp). P/W: Parke Levy. D: Sherman Marks, Stanley Z. Cherry. W: Norman Paul.

Many Happy Returns created many unhappy memories for its principal director, Stanley Z. Cherry. "That was a mean set," he said. "Every day the producer would come on the set after see-

ing the dailies [the film scenes shot that day] and fire me. Then he'd reconsider the shows I'd already done a few days later and rehire me. This went on and on and on. Very unnerving." Cherry said the only reason he submitted to this behavior was that his first wife was dying of cancer, and he needed the work as a diversion from the tragic situation.

Yet it's not the producer Cherry faulted for the failure of the show, but rather its star, John McGiver. The latter was an imperious, dome-headed, middle-aged actor with a clipped accent having English overtones (even though he was born in New York City) who had done many character roles in movies and TV shows of the late 1950s and early 1960s. Cherry felt McGiver was a second banana whom viewers didn't accept as the lead on the series. "As the

A somewhat disheveled John McGiver dusts off the sign to his complaint department at Krockmeyer's Department Store on *Many Happy Returns.*

producer said, 'They don't like my guy. And if they don't like my guy, they don't like my show,'" Cherry said.

McGiver played the customer services manager for the busy Krockmeyer's department store in Los Angeles, trying to keep shoppers' temperaments down as they complained while his four employees attempted to handle his requests. He sought solace at home with his married daughter Joan and his granddaughter, played by 4-year-old actress Andrea Sacino. Owen Sharp was the store's manager.

Many Happy Returns was such a disappointment that it became the first series ever to follow one of Lucille Ball's shows not to be in the top 15 in the season ratings (it didn't even make the top 30) since 1951-52, when *Claudia, the Story of a Marriage* (q.v.) followed *I Love Lucy*. Many viewers who tuned in to make *The Lucy Show* the #8 rated series of 1964-65 either turned off their sets or changed the channels after it ended to avoid *Many Happy Returns*.

But one person involved with the program, who prefers to remain anonymous, said another reason for the cancellation involved an offscreen situation of McGiver's co-star. "Elinor Donahue was pregnant," said the source. "She got pregnant during the show, and they didn't want to put on any more children."

Regardless what the real reason was, *Many Happy Returns* left by the summer of 1965 to make room for reruns of *The Danny Thomas Show*. CBS moved *Hazel* from NBC to fill the slot in the fall of 1965, but it too lasted one year. The network finally had a hit there in the fall of 1966 with *Family Affair*.

The Cara Williams Show

Sitcom. Ran on CBS Wednesdays 9:30–10 P.M. Sept. 23, 1964–April 21, 1965, opposite *Burke's Law* on ABC and movies on NBC, then CBS Fridays 8:30–9 P.M. May 7–Sept. 10, 1965, opposite *The Addams Family* on ABC and *The Bob Hope Chrysler Theater* on NBC. C: Cara Williams (as Cara Bridges/Wilton), Frank Aletter (as Frank Bridges), Paul Reed (as Damon Burkhardt), Reta Shaw (as Mrs. Burkhardt), Jack Sheldon (as Fletcher Kincaid), Jeanne Arnold (as Mary Hammilmeyer), Audrey Christie (as Agnes). EP: Keefe Brasselle. P: Phil Sharp. D: Gene Reynolds, Alan Rafkin. W: Larry Markes, Michael Morris.

The Baileys of Balboa

Sitcom. Ran on CBS Thursdays 9:30–10 P.M. Sept. 24, 1964–April 1, 1965, opposite *Peyton Place* on ABC and *Hazel* on NBC. C: Paul Ford (as Sam Bailey), Sterling Holloway (as Buck Singleton), Les Brown, Jr. (as Jim Bailey), John Dehner (as Commodore Cecil Wyntoon), Judy Carne (as Barbara Wyntoon), Clint Howard (as Stanley). EP: Keefe Brasselle. P/D: Bob Sweeney. W: Richard Powell.

The Entertainers

Variety. Ran on CBS Fridays 8:30–9:30 P.M. Sept. 25–Dec. 25, 1964, opposite *Valentine's Day* on ABC and *The Bob Hope Chrysler Theater* on NBC, then CBS Saturdays 9–10 P.M. Jan. 2–March 27, 1965, opposite *The Lawrence Welk Show* and *The Hollywood Palace* on ABC and movies on NBC. C: Carol Burnett, Bob Newhart (1964), Caterina Valente, Ruth Buzzi, John Davidson, Dom DeLuise, Tessie O'Shea (1964), Art Buchwald (1964), Don Crichton (1964), the Lee Hale Singers, the Ernie Flatt Dancers (1964), the Peter Gennaro Dancers (1965), the Harry Zimmerman Orchestra. EP: Bob Banner. P: Joe Hamilton. D: Dave Geisel. W: Vincent Bogert, Syd Zelinka, Tony Webster, Phil Green, Pat McCormick, George Atkins, Treva Silverman, David Panich.

The Reporter

Drama. Ran on CBS Fridays 10–11 P.M. Sept. 25–Dec. 18, 1964, opposite *Twelve O'Clock High* on ABC and *The Jack Paar Show* on NBC. C: Harry Guardino (as Danny Taylor), Gary Merrill (as Lou Sheldon), George O'Hanlon (as Artie Burns), Remo Pisani (as Ike Dawson). EP: Keefe Brasselle. P: John Simon. D: Tom Gries.

"By the grace of God, I'm the only one left from the show," noted actor Remo Pisani about *The Reporter* in 2001. He reviewed the deaths of his co-stars Harry Guardino, Gary Merrill and George O'Hanlon, executive producer Keefe Brasselle and director Tom Gries before making the comment. But he was far from melancholy in describing the series despite his circumstance.

Pisani played Ike Dawson, who began each show talking with Guardino's titular character Danny Taylor at the Manhattan watering hole the Press Box. "It was an actual location for people in the press to get together on 24th Street and Madison Avenue," Pisani said. "I was the owner of the Press Box, and Harry had this meeting place. Harry would always be at my restaurant, then the story would start from there."

Assisting Taylor was cabbie Artie Burns, who drove him around town to track stories for the fictional *New York Globe* newspaper. Lou Sheldon was the paper's city editor who oversaw Taylor's progress on investigations. The episodes often were filmed on location.

"It was shot here in New York City in the 20th Century Studios, which would be 11th Avenue and 54th Street," Pisani said. "They did some shooting in Central Park too. We brought in all the stars from Hollywood."

Pisani auditioned for his role against several actors, with Fries and an associate producer and writer picking him to do his first regular TV part. "I had been working for CBS doing live shows starting out since 1948," he said, noting that he often appeared unnoticed in minor parts in sketches and musical numbers on *The Ed Sullivan Show* as well as the dramatic anthologies from New York in the 1950s and 1960s.

He enjoyed his job immensely. "It was like family. There wasn't any friction whatsoever, any pettiness." Of Brasselle, he said, "Everyone was fond of him." Well, maybe on the show, but not at CBS. *The Reporter* was one of three flop series Brasselle sold to CBS in 1964-65 without any pilots (for the others, see *The Baileys of Balboa* and *The Cara Williams Show*). It's rare to get on just one series without a pilot, and as the Federal Communications Commission investigated whether Brasselle had an "insider deal" with then CBS President Jim Aubrey, the latter found himself in bad publicity and fired from his job in 1965. Pisani said he had not heard about any deals but added, "It's very probable. I remember the show was on without a pilot."

That deal did not cause the early cancellation of *The Reporter*, however. Its ratings were poor enough that CBS ended it before the start of 1965. Pisani took it hard. "I was the most disappointed," he admitted. "For an actor having a running part — it's rough finding work like that."

Nevertheless, Pisani persevered in his craft even though he never had another regular TV job. "Old soldiers never die," he said. "I'm 82 years old and still a member of SAG, Actor's Equity, AFTRA." He did add that the drive is not as strong as it once was for parts. "Occasionally an agent will call me from New York, but at 82 years old, I'm not running into auditions," he said.

Mr. Broadway

Drama. Ran on CBS Saturdays 9–9:30 P.M. Sept. 26–Dec. 26, 1964, opposite *The Lawrence Welk Show* and *The Hollywood Palace* on ABC and movies on NBC. C: Craig Stevens (as Mike Bell), Horace McMahon (as Hank McClure), Lani Miyazaki (as Toki). EP: David Susskind, Dan Melnick. D/W: Garson Kanin.

Mister Mayor

Children's. Ran on CBS Saturdays 8–9 A.M. Sept. 26, 1964–Sept. 18, 1965. C: Bob Keeshan (as Mister Mayor), Jane Connell (as Miss Melissa/Aunt Maude/Mother Homan), Bill McCutcheon (as Dudley Dudley/Herman Homan), Cosmo "Gus" Allegretti (as Cornelius the Clown/Rollo the Hippo/Father Homan). W: Tom Whedon.

CBS had been showing a Saturday morning edition of its daily early morning hit *Captain Kangaroo* since Aug. 4, 1956, when a little more than eight years later tots woke up to see that show replaced by another starring the man who played the Captain, Bob Keeshan, as Mr. Mayor. It was a change designed primarily with money in mind and not as a chance to expand Keeshan's creative horizons, although it certainly did so.

"The whole project was started because Bob Keeshan did not own the title *Captain Kangaroo*," noted actress Jane Connell. "He paid one guy a lot of money for it each week." That guy was his agent, Mitchell Hamilburg, who during a protracted dispute with Keeshan threatened to oust his client from playing the Captain. Eager to stay on the air, Keeshan created *Mister Mayor* as a way to survive should he lose his other job.

Like *Captain Kangaroo*, *Mister Mayor* aimed to educate youngsters while using entertainment, this time with Keeshan playing the mayor of an unspecified fantasy town with odd residents. For the series, Keeshan brought along another *Captain Kangaroo* regular, Cosmo "Gus" Allegretti, who had played Dennis the handyman and other characters on the latter show. But here, he and Keeshan portrayed new roles, along with Bill McCutcheon and Connell.

Connell said she got a role on the show because "Tom Whedon, one of the writers, was a fan of mine." She did three main characters—music teacher Miss Melissa ("That gave me a chance to sing some songs"), freewheeling sports addict Aunt Maude ("She was in [the name brand tennis shoes] Keds, old-fashioned Keds") and Mother Homan, head of a family of three that talked and lived life backwards. "Instead of saying 'Hello,' they said 'Goodbye,'" said Connell.

Allegretti played Connell's husband in the Homan sketches, while McCutcheon was their child Herman (McCutcheon's other character was school custodian Dudley Dudley). For his other roles of Cornelius the Clown and Rollo the Hippo, Allegretti had to wear outfits as he did for various parts on *Captain Kangaroo*.

The show was videotaped, not live as some reports said. For the stage-trained Connell, it took a little getting used to Keeshan's approach during tapings. "Bob was a master of reading [cue] cards," she said. "He never memorized lines."

Mister Mayor ended after a year with Keeshan replacing it with *Captain Kangaroo*, which ran in the slot until Sept. 7, 1968. *Captain Kangaroo* stayed a daily series until Sept. 17, 1982, then moved back to Saturdays from Sept. 18, 1982, until it ended on Dec. 8, 1984. Apparently Keeshan decided he would take the risk of fighting to be on *Captain Kangaroo* rather than try to replace it with *Mister Mayor*. "I think he just got cold feet," opined Connell. She said she would have stayed with the show if it lasted beyond a year, but probably not if it had become a daily attraction replacing *Captain Kangaroo*. Keeshan did only one other regular TV series, *CBS Storybreak*, from 1985 to 1995, before retiring.

My Living Doll

Sitcom. Ran on CBS Sundays 9–9:30 P.M. Sept. 27–Dec. 13, 1964, opposite movies on ABC and *Bonanza* on NBC, then CBS Wednesdays 8–8:30 P.M. Dec. 30, 1964–Sept. 8, 1965, opposite *The Patty Duke Show* on ABC and *The Virginian* on NBC. C: Bob Cummings (as Dr. Robert McDonald), Julie Newmar (as Rhoda Miller), Jack Mullaney (as Peter Robinson), Doris Dowling (as Irene Adams). EP: Jack Chertok. P: Howard Leeds. D: Lawrence Dobkin, Ezra Stone. W: Al Martin, Bill Kelsay.

90 Bristol Court (Umbrella title for the following three series)

KAREN

Sitcom. Ran on NBC Mondays 7:30–8 P.M. Oct. 5, 1964–Aug. 30, 1965, opposite *Voyage to the Bottom of the Sea* on ABC and *To Tell the Truth* on CBS. C: Debbie Watson (as Karen Scott), Richard Denning (as Steve Scott), Mary LaRoche (as Barbara Scott), Gina Gillespie (as Mimi Scott), Bernadette Withers (as Janis), Trudi Ames (as Candy), Teddy Quinn (as Peter), Murray MacLeod (as Spider Gibson), Richard Dreyfuss (as David Rowe III). EP/W: Joe Connelly. P/W: Bob Mosher. D: David Alexander.

HARRIS AGAINST THE WORLD

Sitcom. Ran on NBC Mondays 8–8:30 P.M. Oct. 5, 1964–Jan. 4, 1965, opposite *Voyage to the Bottom of the Sea* on ABC and *I've Got a Secret* on CBS. C: Jack Klugman (as Alan Harris), Patricia Barry (as Kate Harris), Claire Wilcox (as Deedee Harris), David Macklin (as Billy Harris), Fay DeWitt (as Helen Miller), Sheldon Allman (as Norm Miller). EP: Joe Connelly. P: Devery Freeman. D: Sidney Lanfield. W: Danny Simon, Milt Rosen.

TOM, DICK AND MARY

Sitcom. Ran on NBC Mondays 8:30–9 P.M. Oct. 5, 1965–Jan. 4, 1965, opposite *No Time for Sergeants* on ABC and *The Andy Griffith Show* on CBS. C: Don Galloway (as Dr. Tom Gentry), Steve Franken (as Dr. Dick Moran), Joyce Bulifant (as Mary Gentry), John Hoyt (as Dr. Krevoy), J. Edward McKinley (as Horace Moran). EP: Joe Connelly. P: Les Colodny. D: E.W. Swackhamer. W: Bill Jacobson.

NBC spent much of the early 1960s floundering on Monday nights as its efforts like *It's a Man's World* and *Saints and Sinners* (see 1962-63) bombed opposite hits on ABC (*Cheyenne*, *The Rifleman*) and CBS (*I've Got a Secret*, *To Tell the Truth*). Even movies failed to beat the competition. However, in the fall of 1964 the network unveiled an innovation that it hoped finally would win them the evening's rating race: the hour-and-a-half sitcom block.

90 Bristol Court (a title whose first letters spelled out "NBC" ... hmmm) was the brainchild of Joe Connelly, who served as executive producer of all three series. It had a trio of sitcoms united by the fact that all the main characters for each program lived at the title address, an apartment complex somewhere in southern California. The idea was that the audience would stay for all three shows with this gimmick, which *90 Bristol Court* enhanced by having Guy Raymond play handyman Cliff Murdock to stop by and do repairs on each element.

The first show in the lineup, *Karen*, was a copycat of *The Patty Duke Show*, only here the conflict came not from twin teenagers but teenage sisters. Karen was the popular blonde daughter of Steve and Barbara Scott with lots of friends, while little sister Mimi was a tomboy. The last one, *Tom, Dick and Mary*, had the young married couple the Gentrys found themselves having to live with Tom's friend and fellow intern at a hospital, Dr. Dick Moran, much to the couple's inconvenience, even though they needed the money. Between them was *Harris Against the World*, where Jack Klugman did his patented grouch act, complaining about the hassles he faced at work as plant superintendent of a movie studio and at home with his wife, Kate, daughter, son and friends the Millers.

"*Harris Against the World* was at the very least a show that knew how to be funny, and Jack Klugman knew how to deliver," wrote producer Devery Freeman in a letter to me. "It also had the gift of Patricia Barry, an outstanding and beautiful actress. Critics in the trade papers judged it the most likely of the trilogy to succeed. Unfortunately, the idea was sold as a trilogy, and that's the way it was cancelled."

Actually, NBC did let *Karen* stay on the rest of the season while replacing the other two series with *The Man from U.N.C.L.E.* With the extension of the run for *Karen* came an extinction of the *90 Bristol Court* title, as well as Cliff Murdock's appearances on the show. In the fall of 1965, NBC replaced *Karen* and *The Man from U.N.C.L.E.* (which moved to Friday nights) with three half-hour shows with virtually nothing in common: the rock music showcase *Hullabaloo*, the sitcom *The John Forsythe Show* (see 1965-66) and the last season of the medical drama *Dr. Kildare*.

What's This Song?

Game. Ran on NBC Mondays through Fridays 10:30–10:55 A.M. Oct. 26, 1964–Sept. 24, 1965, opposite *I Love Lucy* reruns on CBS. C: Wink Martindale. P/D: Stuart Phelps.

"That really is the forerunner of *Name That Tune*," producer/director Stuart Phelps said of his baby *What's This Song?* "It started on radio in the 1930s, in Seattle. A guy named Dud Williamson did it." Its title then was *What's the Name of That Song?* It featured a pianist who played three tunes fast in a row, after which contestants had to identify the numbers. The show aired in spurts on the national Mutual network radio lineup from 1944 to 1948, by which time Bill Gwinn assumed the hosting duties following Williamson's untimely death in 1948.

In 1949 Gwinn and the show came to local TV in Hollywood and added celebrities. "We had everybody in town," Phelps said. "Walter Huston was in it." The screen actor died in 1950, so *What's the Name of That Song?* was one of his first and last TV appearances. The show ebbed and flowed on various TV stations in Hollywood during the 1950s. Then in February 1964, a revival on KTLA Los Angeles came to NBC's attention and prompted the network to add it to its daily lineup.

Two duos competed, each with a contestant and a guest celebrity. Giving the title of a tune was now just part of a team's duty; they had to sing the first four lines of the song correctly as well. The other team could challenge the veracity and vocalize what they thought the actual lyrics were. Teams earned 20 points for the right titles and 20 points for the right lyrics (or the right challenge to the lyrics, as the case was). The first team to amass 100 points played the "Minute Medley" to name 10 titles within 60 seconds and claim a $200 jackpot.

Most of the guest celebrities on *What's This Song?* were not professional singers. That was intentional. "We'd get people who purposely couldn't sing but were great raconteurs," Phelps said. "People would laugh, and the contestants would help them."

Coordinating all the business on stage was host Wink Martindale. He had been mainly a local radio disk jockey in Hollywood at the time; this was the first of many game shows he would host into the 1990s.

Phelps blamed the show's departure after nearly a year due to a shakeup among NBC's daytime executives. "I think that was the time they had a whole change in philosophy and wanted to go with soaps. We were doing pretty well." Indeed, NBC added the melodramas

Morning Star and *Paradise Bay* to its morning lineup in place of game shows in the fall of 1965 and did poorly (see 1965-66).

The show came back in a slightly revamped format in syndication in 1968 as *Win with the Stars*. That ran a year. Phelps admitted he's considered bringing it back one more time, but with another twist. "I thought, 'Let's do it with country music only,' because those people know lyrics and understand lyrics. With today's music, I can't understand it." At press time, however, no such revival currently is planned.

ABC's Nightlife (a/k/a Nightlife, a/k/a The Les Crane Show)

Interview. Ran on ABC Mondays through Fridays 11:15 P.M.–1 A.M. Nov. 9, 1964–Nov. 12, 1965, opposite *The Tonight Show Starring Johnny Carson* on NBC. November 1964–February 1965 credits: C: Les Crane, the Cy Coleman Orchestra. EP: Edward Warren. P: Richard Lewine. D: Stan Harris. February–November 1965 credits: William B. Williams (through June), Les Crane (from June), Nipsey Russell (from February–July), Jimmy Cannon (from July), the Donn Trenner Orchestra (through June), the Elliot Lawrence Orchestra (from June). P: Daryl Duke. D: Win Opie. W: Arnie Kogen, Norman Klenman, Sanford Sheldon.

Moment of Truth

Soap Opera. Ran on NBC Mondays through Fridays 2–2:30 P.M. Jan. 4–Nov. 5, 1965, opposite *Where the Action Is* (from June 28–Sept. 24) and *The Nurses* (from Sept. 27) on ABC and *Password* on CBS. C: Douglass Watson (as Dr. Robert Wallace), Louise King (as Nancy Wallace), Michael Dodds (as Johnny Wallace), Barbara Pierce (as Sheila Wallace), Lynn Gorman (as Wilma Leeds), Robert Goodier (as Walter Leeds), Toby Tarnow (as Carol Williams), Stephen Levy (as Jack Williams), Ivor Barry (as Dr. Russell Wingate), Fernande Giroux (as Monique Wingate), Peter Donat (as Vince Conway), Mira Pawluk (as Barbara Harris), Anna Hogan (as Linda Harris), Sandra Scott (as Lila), Anne Campbell (as Diane), John Horton (as Eric), Chris Wiggins (as Dexter). Also ran on the Canadian Broadcasting System from Dec. 28, 1964–Sept. 26, 1969.

For the People

Drama. Ran on CBS Sundays 9–10 P.M. Jan. 31–May 9, 1965, opposite movies on ABC and *Bonanza* on NBC. C: William Shatner (as David Koster), Howard Da Silva (as Anthony Celese), Lonny Chapman (as Frank Malloy), Jessica Walter (as Phyllis Koster). EP: Herbert Brodkin. P: Arthur Joel Katz. D: David Greene. W: Ernest Kinoy, Albert Sanders.

As *The Defenders* wound down its final season on the air in 1964-65 after having started on Sept. 16, 1961, CBS added a similar series called *For the People* onto its lineup. Close TV watchers no doubt realized that its setup of having an idealistic young lead being counseled by an older mentor in the same field was the same as that of *The Defenders*, only here the focus was on the prosecutor's office and not on a law firm taking clients.

"It was the same group that did *The Defenders*," said writer Ernest Kinoy. "That's how I got to do the pilot. I think the feeling was 'We'll turn it around. We'll have the hero be the D.A.'"

Ironically, the star of *For the People*, William Shatner, portrayed the young attorney in the two-part pilot for *The Defenders* seen on *Studio One* in 1957. A frequent TV guest in the early 1960s, this was his first regular TV role as an assistant district attorney. Howard Da Silva played his boss, Anthony Celese. Detective Frank Malloy assisted their efforts with his investigative efforts.

The one other regular character was Phyllis Koster. Her role was a novel touch, and not just because she played a cellist, but that she was married to the lead, a rather uncommon circumstance on TV at the time. Neither of the leads on *The Defenders*, Lawrence Preston (played by E. G. Marshall) nor his son Kenneth (played by Robert Reed) were married.

New York City served as the setting for both the series' fictional trappings and actual filming. "Everything was done on a little set, almost as if it were live," said Kinoy.

Another shared characteristic of *For the People* with *The Defenders* was the emphasis of scripts examining social questions such as civil rights. "We based them on various issues around then," Kinoy said. "There was very little thought to providing background to the characters. We used to sneak in the personal life." He compared what happened on the show to the "order" section of the hit drama *Law & Order*.

TV audiences in 1965 were in little mood to examine topical concerns, however, and *For the People* was for within four months. The competition admittedly was tough, running opposite *Bonanza*, TV's #1 series in 1964-65. When asked whether these factors or some others prompted the show's failure, Kinoy answered with the comment that "You can never tell why."

The main legacy of *For the People* was that it left Shatner available to do *Star Trek* the following season. After a summer recess, CBS tried another law series in the time slot in the fall of 1965 by moving *Perry Mason*, but the program was on its last legs and also bombed against *Bonanza*. It ended its nine-year run in the fall of 1966.

Call My Bluff

Game. Ran on NBC Mondays through Fridays March 29–Sept. 24, 1965, opposite *The Donna Reed Show* reruns on ABC and *Love of Life* and news on CBS. C: Bill Leyden. EP: Jack Farren. D: Michael Gargiulo.

Before becoming director of *Call My Bluff*, Michael Gargiulo had spent two years doing the same job with *To Tell the Truth*. That series had many elements employed by *Call My Bluff*, and in fact both were productions from the Mark Goodson–Bill Todman game show empire. But Gargiulo readily acknowledged that *Call My Bluff* was compared to *To Tell the Truth* and came off poorly in this view because when it came to *To Tell the Truth*, "The panelists, they were better panelists, the host was a better host, and the contestants were better contestants."

Call My Bluff did have a few variations from *To Tell the Truth*. Rather than have four regular panelists try to determine which of three people was the real person and not an imposter, *Call My Bluff* had a celebrity and two contestants try to guess which of three definitions given by another trio of two contestants and a celebrity was the right one for an obscure word. A right decision by a trio won a point, and two points netted $100 for a team.

The team with $100 then tried to bluff their way for more money by telling three possible facts regarding a visiting guest and mak-

ing the other team guess which one was correct. If the $100 team bluffed correctly, they won money and faced another team in the word game, but if the non–$100 team won they got to return to the regular game again. The result of all this, in Gargiolo's view, was "Nothing very distinctive."

Gargiulo placed none of the blame on the show's host. "Bill Leyden had one eye," he said. "He was in an Army accident in World War II. Probably one of the best emcees I worked with." He had been on daytime game shows close to a decade before *Call My Bluff*, hosting *It Could Be You* from 1956 to 1961 and *Your First Impression* from 1962 to 1964.

But Leyden's abilities were not enough to overcome what Gargiulo believed was an unexciting game, even though he noted that "If a short-lived show was lucky enough to have a great, great emcee, he would circumvent a weak format." (Leyden would host one other game show; see *You're Putting Me On* in 1968-69.)

Gargiulo clearly indicated his high regard for *To Tell the Truth*, crediting it as even an innovator in the game show field. "It was the first game where panelists did not consult with each other," he said. Apparently most people agreed with him that *Call My Bluff* was not a worthy knockoff from it, and it vanished after six months, with NBC moving *Jeopardy!* into its slot and letting that game run there more than eight years. Gargiulo also told me there are tapes of *Call My Bluff* available for viewing at the Museum of Broadcasting in New York, if anyone cares to do so.

I'll Bet

Game. Ran on NBC Mondays through Fridays 12:30–12:55 P.M. March 29–Sept. 24, 1965, opposite *Father Knows Best* reruns on ABC and *Search for Tomorrow* and *Guiding Light* on CBS. C: Jack Narz. EP: Ralph Andrews, Bill Yagemann. P: Tom Cole. D: Dick McDonough.

The Rebus Game

Game. Ran on ABC Mondays through Fridays 1–1:30 P.M. March 29–Sept. 24, 1965. C: Jack Linkletter. EP: Carl Jampel. P: Julian Bercovici. D: Robin Clark.

Our Private World

Soap Opera. Ran on CBS Wednesdays 9:30–10 P.M. opposite *Burke's Law* on ABC and movies on NBC, and Fridays 9–9:30 P.M. opposite *Valentine's Day* on ABC and *Bob Hope Presents the Chrysler Theatre* on NBC, from May 5 to Sept. 10, 1965. C: Eileen Fulton (as Lisa Hughes); Geraldine Fitzgerald (as Helen Eldridge); Nicolas Coster (as John Eldridge); Julienne Moore (as Eve Eldridge); Sam Groom (as Thomas Eldridge); Robert Drivas (as Brad Robinson); David O'Brien (as Dr. Tony Larson); Sandy Smith (as Sandy Larson); Pamela Murphy (as Franny Martin). P: Allen Potter. D: Tom Donovan. W: Robert J. Shaw.

Top daytime soap opera producer Irna Phillips competed against herself when she and William J. Bell created *Our Private World*, a spinoff of her daily hit *As the World Turns*. The latter had just begun its 10th season when *Our Private World* debuted as CBS's answer to ABC's hit nighttime twice-weekly drama *Peyton Place*. The funny thing is Phillips was a consultant to *Peyton Place* too, but she was more involved with *Our Private World*.

Our Private World supposedly centered on *As the World Turns'* "bad girl" Lisa Hughes (née Miller). She left Oakdale, Ohio, after realizing her ex-husband, Bob Hughes, would not remarry her and headed to Chicago. There she got involved in a love triangle with brothers John and Thomas Eldridge, the sons of overbearing, rich Helen Eldridge. Helen's daughter Eve married Brad Robinson after Franny Martin tried to woo him, but Eve soon had the hots for Dr. Tony Larson, who planned to divorce his wife, Sandy, before he was murdered.

Directing the series was Tom Donovan, who had done the acclaimed 1950s anthologies *Studio One* and *Playhouse 90* before Phillips wanted him for her NBC daytime drama *Another World*. "I hope this doesn't insult you, but we're starting a serial and want you," Phillips told Donovan, who added, "She never called them 'soap operas.'" Donovan directed *Another World* almost a year after its debut on May 4, 1964. "I went right from *Another World* to *Our Private World*," he said.

While *As the World Turns* was the #1 daytime program at the time, *Our Private World* did not carry over its parent show's popularity. One problem was a de-emphasis of Lisa in favor of other characters, which was so extensive that Donovan claimed, "I can't even remember her scenes." He recalled working more with Nicolas Coster and Julienne Moore and added, "Geraldine Fitzgerald was very good to work with." (Fred Silverman, then head of daytime programming for CBS, also turned up often at the studio to prod his creation into being a hit, no doubt to score points with the nighttime programmers. "He worked very hard, stayed quite close to it," Donovan said.)

CBS also bungled the show with odd scheduling. Friday's show was on a half hour earlier than Wednesday's, but there was no reason why CBS couldn't have aired it Fridays from 9:30 to 10 P.M., where it probably would have killed *F.D.R.*, ABC's documentary series about the late president. And while *Peyton Place* was filmed, *Our Private World* was taped, giving it a cheaper look than the former.

Our Private World ended in four months, and Eileen Fulton returned to *As the World Turns* as Lisa (a job she still held 36 years later). But the Eldridges were not forgotten; in a 1992 *As the World Turns* storyline, it turned out Lisa had a son with John Eldridge before divorcing him and coming back to Oakdale. When John died, their son Scott Eldridge forged an uneasy truce with his long-gone mother. Nicolas Coster did not play John again for this plot, but he did show up from 1993 to 1995 as Eduardo Grimaldi, Lisa's seventh (!) husband.

1965-66

The Young Set

Interview. Ran on ABC Mondays through Fridays 11 A.M.–Noon Sept. 6–Dec. 17, 1965, opposite *The Andy Griffith Show* reruns and *The Dick Van Dyke Show* reruns on CBS and *Concentration* (through Sept. 24) and *Morning Star* (from Sept. 27) and *Jeopardy!* (through Sept. 24) and *Paradise Bay* (from Sept. 27) on NBC. C: Phyllis Kirk. P: Shirley Bernstein. D: Arnee Nocks.

The Legend of Jesse James

Western. Ran on ABC Mondays 8:30–9 P.M. Sept. 13, 1965–Sept. 5, 1966, opposite *The Lucy Show* (through June 27) and *Vacation Playhouse* (from July 4) and *Dr. Kildare* on NBC. C: Christopher Jones (as Jesse James), Allen Case (as Frank James), John Milford (as Cole Younger), Tim McIntire (as Bob Younger), Robert Wilke (as Marshal Sam Corbett), Ann Doran (as Mrs. James). P: Don Siegel. D: James Clark. W: Anthony Spinner.

A Man Called Shenandoah

Western. Ran on ABC Mondays 9–9:30 P.M. Sept. 13, 1965–Sept. 5, 1966, opposite *The Andy Griffith Show* on CBS and *The Andy Williams Show* (through May 23) and *Kraft Summer Music Hall* (from June 6) on NBC. C: Robert Horton (as Shenandoah). P: Fred Freiberger. D: Paul Wendkos. W: Norman Katkov.

The Steve Lawrence Show

Musical Variety. Ran on CBS Mondays 10–11 P.M. Sept. 13–Dec. 13, 1965, opposite *Ben Casey* on ABC and *Run for Your Life* on NBC. C: Steve Lawrence, Charles Nelson Reilly (through September), Betty Walker (through September), the Ernest Flatt Dancers, the Dick Williams Singers, the Joe Guercio Orchestra. P: George Schlatter. D: Stan Harris. W: Mel Diamond, Gary Belkin, Tony Webster, Syd Zelinka, Saul Turtletaub.

My Mother the Car

Sitcom. Ran on NBC Tuesdays 7:30–8 P.M. Sept. 14, 1965–Sept. 6, 1966, opposite *Combat!* on ABC and *Rawhide* (through Jan. 4) and *Daktari* (from Jan. 11) on CBS. C: Jerry Van Dyke (as Dave Crabtree), Ann Sothern (as voice of mother), Maggie Pierce (as Barbara Crabtree), Cindy Eilbacher (as Cindy Crabtree), Randy Whipple (as Randy Crabtree), Avery Schreiber (as Capt. Manzini). P/D: Rod Amateau. D: David Davis, Tom Montgomery. W: Allen Burns, Chris Hayward, Phil Davis, George Kirgo, Ray Allen, Tom Koch.

One of TV's most notorious bombs due to its title alone, *My Mother the Car* was not what its co-creator Chris Hayward envisioned. What he and his partner Allen Burns came up with could have been called *My Wife the Car*, though he insisted it would not have been as ridiculous as that sounds.

The inspiration for the show came from *Blithe Spirit*. "Basically, it was a Noel Coward movie and a play with Rex Harrison, and his wife died, and he married another lady, and she came back to haunt him," Hayward explained. In Hayward's modification, the wife would return to earth in a car after dying in an auto accident.

"This was sold to United Artists, and United Artists said, 'This is necrophilia!' They're the ones who let it be his mother and not his wife," Hayward said. Then Rod Amateau, named as the show's producer, altered the concept even more by introducing a running character called Capt. Manzini, who wanted to steal the car for his collection because it was a top-condition 1928 Porter, played on the show by a 1927 Pierce Arrow; obviously, realism was not a top priority on the production. (Note: When contacted by the author, Amateau declined to comment on the show.)

The final product had it so that Dave Crabtree was the only one in his family (Barbara was his wife and Cindy and Randy his kids) that could hear the vehicle talk (indicated by a light on the radio) and knew it was his mother, hence his refusal to sell it to anyone else. At this point, much of what Hayward wanted was being ignored, including his idea as to who should be the voice of the car. "I wanted it to be Gypsy Rose Lee as the mother, or even as the wife," he said. "She was salty, irreverent." Instead, Ann Sothern got the job.

When the show debuted, critics immediately picked it as the worst show on the air. Hayward was in agreement with them. "I was never thrilled with it," he said. "The conception was the thing. I couldn't believe it was being made. It was nothing to be proud of." In fact, he tried to write a script for the show after the pilot and was told that he didn't understand its setup.

If that was the case for Hayward, it was the same for the rest of America. It was a bizarre enough concept to attract initially high viewership, but with nowhere to go with its weekly plots, audiences tuned out, and CBS's mid-season competition, *Daktari*, soundly trounced it to end it after a year. Star Jerry Van Dyke would spend years apologizing for the show. Unfortunately for him, it was not his only flop (see *Accidental Family* in 1967-68).

Jerry Van Dyke is ecstatic to learn that his dear old mom talks to him in the vehicle he bought for his family on *My Mother the Car*. (Author's collection)

Gidget

Sitcom. Ran on ABC Wednesdays 8:30–9 P.M. Sept. 15, 1965–Jan. 5, 1966, opposite *The Beverly Hillbillies* on CBS and *The Virginian* on NBC, then ABC Thursdays 8–8:30 P.M. Jan. 13–Sept. 1, 1966, opposite *Gilligan's Island* on CBS and *Daniel Boone* on NBC. C: Sally Field (as Francine "Gidget" Lawrence), Don Porter (as Professor Russ Lawrence), Betty Conner (as Anne Cooper), Peter Deuel (as John Cooper), Lynette Winter (as Larue), Mike Nader (as Peter "Siddo" Stone). EP: Harry Ackerman. P: Bob Claver (pilot only), William Sackheim. D: William Asher, E.W. Swackhamer. W: Joanna Lee, Irma Kalish, Austin Kalish, Bob Claver, Ruth Brooks Flippen, Barbara Avedon.

For Americans today, there has not been a time in their lives without the existence of Gidget the "girl midget." She first appeared in a book of the same name by Frederick Kohner based on the antics of his California surfer girl daughter that became a movie starring Sandra Dee in 1959. Two movie sequels followed (1961's *Gidget Goes Hawaiian* with Deborah Walley and 1963's *Gidget Goes to Rome* with Cindy Carol) before Sally Field made it her first regular TV role — and one that she would successfully leave behind after years of typecasting in the late 1970s winning Emmys and Oscars for her dramatic acting.

Francine Lawrence, nicknamed "Gidget" because she stood only about 5 feet tall, lived in Santa Monica, California, with her widowed father, Russ. Her married older sister Anne acted as her surrogate mother, worried about what Gidget and her pals Larue, Siddo and others did on the beach, but it was all harmless fun. It also had a catchy theme song sung by Johnny Tillotson, "(Wait 'Til You See) My Gidget," but for some reason it was just the B-side to his low-charting single "Our World" in late 1965.

"The cast was great," said director William Asher. He filmed the beach sequences on location, as he did with the movies *Beach Party* (1963) and *Beach Blanket Bingo* (1965), among others. He also was involved with *Bewitched* at the same time *Gidget* ran but found time to direct both shows.

"What I did was during our layoff period on *Bewitched*, I did the pilot and then 10 shows after it sold," Asher said. "I don't believe it interfered with [the production of] *Bewitched*."

Asher directed other series where he realized why they ended early, but he said, "Now, *Gidget*—I didn't understand. It was not that bad a rating. For some strange reason, the network didn't like it." True, its competition beat it, but all shows against it were in the top 30 at the time, and *Gidget* was not too far behind. In fact, ABC received so many letters of complaint about canceling *Gidget* that the show's executive producer, Harry Ackerman, managed to bring Sally Field back on the network with *The Flying Nun*, which ran from Sept. 7, 1967 to Sept. 18, 1970. (And Columbia Pictures, which later owned the *Gidget* series, released several episodes on videotape and put them into syndication in reruns, making it one of the better-known shows in this book.)

Ackerman also tried to revive the property with a TV-movie pilot called *Gidget Gets Married* that aired Jan. 4, 1972, on ABC with

Monie Ellis in the lead role. That didn't fly, nor did an earlier TV-movie pilot called *Gidget Grows Up* on ABC on Dec. 30, 1969, that starred Karen Valentine. But when Ackerman made a syndicated TV-movie pilot in 1985 called *Gidget's Summer Reunion* featuring Caryn Richman, that did the trick, and as *The New Gidget* the series ran from 1986 to 1988. As for the next rendition of Gidget — just wait.

O.K. Crackerby

Sitcom. Ran on ABC Thursdays 8:30–9 P.M. Sept. 16, 1965–Jan. 6, 1966, opposite *My Three Sons* on CBS and *Laredo* on NBC. C: Burl Ives (as O.K. Crackerby), Hal Buckley (as St. John Quincy), Brian Corcoran (as O.K. Jr.), Brooke Adams (as Cynthia Crackerby), Joel Davison (as Hobart Crackerby), Laraine Stephens (as Susan Wentworth), Dick Foran (as Slim), John Indrisano (as the chauffeur). EP: Rod Amateau. P: Norman Henry, Charles Stewart, Elliott Lewis. D: Rod Amateau, Abe Burrows. W: Abe Burrows.

Mona McCluskey

Sitcom. Ran on NBC Thursdays 9:30–10 P.M. Sept. 16, 1965–April 14, 1966, opposite *Peyton Place* on ABC and movies on CBS. C: Juliet Prowse (as Mona Carroll McCluskey), Denny Miller (as Mike McCluskey), Herbert Rudley (as Gen. Crane), Bartlett Robinson (as Frank Caldwell), Robert Strauss (as Sgt. Stan Gruzewsky), Elena Verdugo (as Alice Henderson). P: George Burns. D: Stanley Z. Cherry.

The Long, Hot Summer

Drama. Ran on ABC Thursdays 10–11 P.M. Sept. 16, 1965–Jan. 13, 1966, opposite movies on CBS and *The Dean Martin Show* on NBC, then ABC Wednesdays 10–11 P.M. Jan. 19–July 13, 1966, opposite *The Danny Kaye Show* on CBS and *I Spy* on NBC. C: Edmond O'Brien (as "Boss" Will Varner; 1965), Dan O'Herlihy (as "Boss" Will Varner; 1966), Roy Thinnes (as Ben Quick), Nancy Malone (as Clara Varner), Paul Geary (as Jody Varner), Ruth Roman (as Minnie Littlejohn), Lana Wood (as Eula Harker). P: Frank Glicksman. D: Ralph Senensky. W: Dean Reisner.

Camp Runamuck

Sitcom. Ran on NBC Fridays 7:30–8 P.M. Sept. 17, 1965–Sept. 2, 1966, opposite *The Flintstones* on ABC and *The Wild Wild West* on CBS. C: Dave Ketchum (as Senior Counselor Spiffy), Arch Johnson (as Commander Wivenhoe), Alice Nunn (as Mahala May Gruenecker), Dave Madden (as Pruett), Leonard Stone (as Doc Joslyn), Nina Wayne (as Caprice Yeudleman), Hermoine Baddeley (as Eulalie Divine), Mike Wagner (as Malden), George Dunn (as the sheriff). P/D/W: David Swift.

Hank

Sitcom. Ran on NBC Fridays 8–8:30 P.M. Sept. 17, 1965–Sept. 2, 1966, opposite *Tammy* (through July 15) and *Summer Fun* (from July 22) on ABC and *The Wild, Wild West* on CBS. C: Dick Kallman (as Hank Dearborn), Linda Foster (as Doris Royal), Howard St. John (as Dr. Lewis Royal), Katie Sweet (as Tina Dearborn), Kelly Jean Peters (as Franny), Lloyd Corrigan (as Professor McKillup), Dabbs Greer (as Coach Ossie Weiss), Sheila Bromley (as Mrs. Ethel Weiss), Dorothy Neumann (as Miss Mittleman), Lou Wills, Jr. (as Asst. Coach Gazzari). EP: Hugh Benson. W: Coleman Jacoby, Arnie Rosen.

The idea of a young adult having to raise his baby sister after his parents' death in a car crash hardly seems a top premise for comedy, but that was the basis for *Hank*. The title character decided that to better his and his sister Tina's lot in life, he would attend classes at the fictional Western State University. Trouble was, he had no money to do that, so he crashed a few courses by impersonating other students who were cutting class or sick at the time. (The sitcom obviously cared little about reality, for even if the ruse did work, Hank could not earn any college credits, much less a diploma, without having paid for the courses. He would end up being a prospective employee committing fraud regarding his background — yeah, that's a laugh riot.)

Hank had a few important allies for his cause who helped cover for him — sympathetic Professor McKillup, Tina's caretaker, Franny, and his girlfriend, Doris Royal. Doris was in a sticky situation, however, as her dad, Dr. Lewis Royal, was the college's registrar who heard stories about this non-paying student and desired greatly to find him. Also wanting to find and recruit Hank were Coaches Weiss and Gazzari because of his ability to run to classes and dodge Dr. Royal. Didn't I mention how this series cared little about reality?

Comedy writer Coleman Jacoby co-wrote the pilot with his partner, Arnie Rosen. "I think *Hank* was somebody else's idea, some who worked with Jack Warner, the idea of being a dropout getting a free education," said Jacoby. (Executive producer Hugh Benson received credit as the show's creator.)

All the roles were cast by the time the men wrote the show, and Jacoby thinks it might have suffered because of the relative obscurity of most of the regulars. "They didn't have big-time stars," he said. As far as its star, Dick Kallman, Jacoby said, "I never heard of him before."

Other than that, Jacoby has little recollection of the series, except that it marked the dissolution of his professional partnership with Rosen, which Jacoby insisted had nothing to do with any sort of disagreement, but rather for Jacoby's own desires. "My family was in New York, my home was there, and I just didn't like California," he said. He wrote some for Jackie Gleason before he retired.

Hank was the only regular series for Richard "Dick" Kallman, who mainly concentrated on stage work in the 1950s and 1960s. In the 1970s he became an antique dealer in New York City, and reportedly was quite content in his job. Sadly, he was found shot to death in his home on Feb. 22, 1980, at the age of 46.

Tammy

Sitcom. Ran on ABC Fridays 8–8:30 P.M. Sept. 17, 1965–July 15, 1966, opposite *The Wild Wild West* on CBS and *Hank* on NBC. C: Debbie Watson (as Tammy Tarleton), Denver Pyle (as Grandpa Mordecai Tarleton), Frank McGrath (as Uncle Lucius), Donald Woods (as John Brent), Jay Sheffield (as Steven Brent), Dorothy Green (as Lavinia Tate), Linda Marshall (as Gloria Tate), David Macklin (as Peter Tate), George Furth (as Dwayne Whitt), Dennis Robertson (as Cousin Cletus Tarleton), Doris Packer (as Mrs. Brent). P: Dick Wesson. D: Sidney Miller. W: George Tibbles.

Convoy

War Drama. Ran on NBC Fridays 8:30–9 P.M. Sept. 17–Dec. 10, 1965, opposite *The Addams Family* and *Honey West* on ABC and *Hogan's Heroes* and *Gomer Pyle, U.S.M.C.* on CBS. C: John Gavin (as Cmdr. Dan Talbot), John Larch (as Merchant Capt. Ben Foster), Linden Chiles (as Chief Officer Steve Kirkland), James Callahan (as Lt. Dick O'-Connell). EP: Frank Price. W: Alfred Hayes.

Honey West

Detective Drama. Ran on ABC Fridays 9–9:30 P.M. Sept. 17, 1965–Sept. 2, 1966, opposite *Gomer Pyle, U.S.M.C.* on CBS and *Convoy* (through Dec. 10), *The Sammy Davis Jr. Show* (from Jan. 7 to April 22) and *Sing Along With Mitch* reruns (from April 29). C: Anne Francis (as Honey West), John Ericson (as Sam Bolt), Irene Hervey (as Aunt Meg). EP: Aaron Spelling. P: Richard Newton. D: Paul Wendkos.

Mr. Roberts

Sitcom. Ran on NBC Fridays 9:30–10 P.M. Sept. 17, 1965–Sept. 2, 1966 opposite *Peyton Place* (through Oct. 29) and *The Farmer's Daughter* (from Nov. 5) on ABC and *The Smothers Brothers Show* on CBS. C: Roger Smith (as Lt. Douglas Roberts), Steve Harmon (as Ensign Frank Pulver), Richard X. Slattery (as Captain John Morton),

George Ives (as Doc), Richard Sinatra (as D'Angelo), Ronald Starr (as Mannion), Roy Reese (as Reber). P: James Komack. D: Seymour Robbie, James Komack.

As Jackie Gleason made plans to move his TV show to Miami in 1965, his director Seymour Robbie decided to leave rather than head with his star to Florida. But as he looked around, "I figured out drama in television out of New York City was dead." Joining many others in his guild, Robbie ventured to Hollywood to continue his career. He connected when he met up with an up-and-coming William Morris agent representing Warner Brothers, which was preparing a TV version of its successful 1955 movie *Mr. Roberts*, based on the play of the same name which debuted on Broadway in 1948.

"Barry Diller [later president of the Para-

As well as they tried, the actors on the television version of *Mr. Roberts* (from left to right, George Ives, Roger Smith, Richard X. Slattery and Steve Harmon) suffered poorly in comparison to their equivalents in the movie version (respectively, William Powell, Henry Fonda, James Cagney and Jack Lemmon).

mount and 20th Century–Fox studios] sold me to that show and *F Troop*," Robbie said. He directed at least five shows of each series, though *F Troop* ran one season longer. Both series were comical looks at armed forces in different eras, with *Mr. Roberts* dealing with a naval crew in the South Pacific during World War II. Amid the boredom of working a cargo ship, Lt. Roberts wanted to get into battle activity while Ensign Pulver just looked for entertainment. Both constantly were stymied by Captain Morton.

Robbie claimed Warners was fairly lavish in its budget for doing a one-camera sitcom at the time. "We used the big battleship they shot the movie on," he said. He also remembers Allan Carr hanging around the set. Carr, later a top movie producer (*Grease*), was the manager of the show's star, Roger Smith, at the time and told Robbie, "No one has directed Roger better than you."

Smith and the rest of the cast were fine for Robbie to handle, but the show's producer, James Komack, left something to be desired. "He was a little difficult," Robbie said. "We differed in casting. He was really, really at the time, over his head. He had never produced a series before." A former actor in an earlier military comedy, *Hennessey* (1959–62), Komack would not have a hit as a producer until 1969 with *The Courtship of Eddie's Father*.

As to why the TV rendition of *Mr. Roberts* failed, Robbie did not single out whether the show was too late an adaptation of the story nor if the rather little-known cast paled in contrast with the movie, where Henry Fonda played Roberts, Jack Lemmon was Ensign Pulver, James Cagney was the captain and William Powell was Doc. Instead, Robbie blamed it on the show being too true to its theme. "It was about tedium and apathy [on a ship]. Of course, on television tedium and apathy is very contagious and not appealing to audiences."

Still, despite this flaw, Robbie said, "That was a perfect show. I loved it." But few others did, so NBC replaced it after a year with *T.H.E. Cat* (q.v.).

The Smothers Brothers Show

Sitcom. Ran on CBS Fridays 9:30–10 P.M. Sept. 17, 1965–Sept. 9, 1966, opposite *Peyton Place* (through Oct. 29) and *The Farmer's Daughter* (from Nov. 5)

on ABC and *Mr. Roberts* on NBC. C: Tom and Dick Smothers (as themselves), Roland Winters (as Leonard J. Costello), Harriet MacGibbon (as Mrs. Costello), Ann Elder (as Janet). EP: Aaron Spelling. P/D: Fred De Cordova. D: Don Taylor. W: Alex Gottleib.

The Trials of O'Brien

Law Drama. Ran on CBS Saturdays 8:30–9:30 P.M. Sept. 18–Nov. 27, 1965, opposite *The Lawrence Welk Show* on ABC and *Get Smart* and movies on NBC, then CBS Fridays 10–11 P.M. Dec. 3, 1965–May 27, 1966, opposite *The Jimmy Dean Show* on ABC and *The Man from U.N.C.L.E.* on NBC. C: Peter Falk (as Daniel J. O'Brien), Joanna Barnes (as Katie), David Burns (as the Great McGonigle), Elaine Stritch (as Miss G), Ilka Chase (as Margaret), Dolph Sweet (as Lt. Garrison). EP: Richard Alan Simmons. P/W: Gene Wang. D: Stuart Rosenberg.

The Loner

Western. Ran on CBS Saturdays 9:30–10 P.M. Sept. 18, 1965–April 30, 1966, opposite *The Hollywood Palace* on ABC and movies on NBC. C: Lloyd Bridges (as William Colton). EP: William Dozier. P: Andy White. D: Alex Marsh. W: Rod Serling.

The Wackiest Ship in the Army

Sitcom. Ran on NBC Sundays 10–11 P.M. Sept. 19, 1965–Sept. 4, 1966, opposite movies on ABC and *Candid Camera* and *What's My Line?* on CBS. C: Jack Warden (as Major Simon Butcher), Gary Collins (as Lt. (jg) Richard "Rip" Riddle), Mike Kellin (as Chief Petty Officer Willie Miller), Rudy Solari (as Gunner's Mate Sherman Nagurski), Don Penny (as Ship's Cook Charles Tyler), Mark Slade (as Radioman Patrick Hollis), Fred Smoot (as Machinist's Mate Seymour Trivers), William Zuckert (as Gen. Cross), Charles Irving (as Admiral Vincent Beckett). EP: Harry Ackerman. P: Herbert Hirschman. D/W: Danny Arnold.

Fractured Phrases

Game. Ran on NBC Mondays through Fridays 10–10:30 A.M. Sept. 27–Dec. 31, 1965, opposite *I Love Lucy* reruns on CBS. C: Art James. P: Stu Billet. D: Lloyd Gross.

Fractured Phrases was a game of phonetic puns, with the right inflections leading to the answers. Two pairs of players competed. One member of each team said a series of words that approximately sounded like a familiar slogan, title or person, and the other had to identify it. A right guess the first go-round won the team two points; if wrong, the partner giving the clue (who didn't know the answer) could guess for one point, and if or she was wrong, the other team could win a point with the right answer. The first team to earn at least 10 points played the bonus round where they got $25 for each "fractured name" they identified.

Wish you could have played it? Well, here are some examples of what players had to say (with answers at the end of this entry; no fair peeking ahead!):

1) Dish Hoe Moscow Juan
2) One Shoe Comb Humble Belly
3) Hairy Belly Fond Tea

To say this concept, created by packager Art Baer, did not win over viewers is an understatement. Host Art James recalled two letters the series received. "One of them was 'Dear NBC: I am an invalid, and it is very difficult for me to get out of my chair, but your show made me do it to change the channel.' And one guy wrote that he had not seen a worse show on television than the first show, until he saw the second show!"

James did not view the series nearly so harshly. It brought him back to the NBC daytime lineup after being on the network four years hosting the game show *Say When!!* (Jan. 3, 1961–March 25, 1965), a variant of *The Price Is Right* packaged by the same production company of Mark Goodson and Bill Todman that aired for most of its run in the same time slot as *Fractured Phrases*. However, during the run of *Say When!!*, James also hosted a local New York game show, *It's Academic*, and he worried about new plans to tape it and *Fractured Phrases* at the same time.

"I was told we were going to tape two *Fractured Phrases* a day and two of *It's Academic*, and I said, 'What?! Four shows a day?!' and I quit *It's Academic*," he said. James did not envision that it soon would become standard operating procedure for taping *five* game shows a day to do a week's worth of programming.

It soon became academic that *Fractured Phrases* crumbled easily opposite reruns of *I Love Lucy*. The series replaced the two-contestant pairs with ones having a celebrity and a

contestant starting Nov. 22, but the ratings failed to rise, and the show went off before 1966 began.

The answers to the earlier questions were: 1) The Show Must Go On; 2) Won't You Come Home, Bill Bailey?; and 3) Harry Belafonte. If your first reaction is to groan, you probably wouldn't have watched the show either.

Morning Star

Soap Opera. Ran NBC Mondays through Fridays 11–11:30 A.M. Sept. 27, 1965–July 1, 1966, opposite *The Young Set* (through Dec. 17) and *Supermarket Sweep* (from Dec. 20) on ABC and *The Andy Griffith Show* reruns on CBS. C: Shary Marshall (as Katy Elliot; 1965), Elizabeth Perry (as Katy Elliot; 1966), Edward Mallory (as Bill Riley), Adrienne Ellis (as Jan Elliot), Ed Prentiss (as Ed Elliot), Shelia Bromley (as Aunt Millie Elliot), Betty Lou Gerson (as Joan Mitchell), Nina Roman (as Liz Mitchell), Burt Douglas (as Gregory Ross), Olive Dunbar (as Ann Burton), Norman Burton (as Joe Bernie), Ron Jackson (as Eric Manning), Betsy Jones Moreland (as Dana Manning), John Dehner (as Stan Manning; early episodes), John Stephenson (as Stan Manning; later episodes), Floy Dean (as Eve Blake), William Arvin (as Dr. Tim Blake), Phyllis Hill (as Grace Allison). P: Ted Corday. D: Joe Behar, Lamar Caselli. W: Janet Hackins, Carolyn Weston.

Let's Play Post Office

Game. Ran on NBC Mondays through Fridays 12:30–12:55 P.M. Sept. 27, 1965–July 1, 1966, opposite *Father Knows Best* reruns on ABC and *Search for Tomorrow* and *Guiding Light* on CBS. C: Don Morrow. P: Ron Greenburg. D: Dick Schneider.

Paradise Bay

Soap Opera. Ran on NBC Mondays through Fridays 11:30 A.M.–Noon Sept. 27, 1965–July 1, 1966 opposite *The Young Set* (through Dec. 17) and *The Dating Game* (from Dec. 20) on ABC and *The Dick Van Dyke Show* reruns on CBS. C: Keith Andes (as Jeff Morgan); Marion Ross (as Mary Morgan); Steve Mines (as Fred Morgan); Heather North (as Kitty Morgan); Dennis Cole (as Duke Spaulding); June Dayton (as Lucy Spaulding); Walter Brooke (as Walter Montgomery); Paulle Clark (as Charlotte Baxter); Alice Reinheart (as Carlotta Chavez); K.T. Stevens (as Estelle Kimball); Craig Curtis (as Chuck Lucas); Frank M. Thomas (as Judge Grayson); Mona Bruns (as

Judge Ellis); Lillian Bronson (as Bertha DeKalb). Creators/W: John Monks, Jr., Jerry D. Lewis. P: Oliver Barbour. D: Dick Darley, William Howell.

"Paradise Bay, a small city south of Hollywood and north of the Mexican border, is the setting for NBC-TV's new half-hour daytime serial of the same name. Here, against the contrasting backdrop provided by the holiday season influx of sun-worshipping tourists and the harvest time flood of migrant farm workers, the residents of this restless, growing community wrestle with the complex problems that confront their contemporaries everywhere in America"— From an NBC press kit.

This serial came from John Monks, Jr. (who co-wrote the Broadway hit *Brother Rat*), and Jerry D. Lewis (not the comedian, but the author of scripts for the radio series *This Is Your F.B.I.* for six and a half years). The main family was the Morgans— Jeff, an ex-actor who owned and operated radio station KPPX; his wife, Mary, whose late uncle had owned KPPX; their son Fred, a 17-year-old high school baseball star; and their daughter Kitty, a 15-year-old who is president of the teenage girls' club the Moonglows. Also seen were Bertha DeKalb, her socialite daughter Lucy Spaulding, and Lucy's son Duke, who was charged with murdering his girlfriend, Sally Baxter, and who newspaper editor Walter Montgomery believed (erroneously) was guilty.

Behind the scenes Dick Darley, directing his first soap opera, alternated daily with William Howell. "I didn't care for alternating, because it set up a tendency of competition in the production company," he said. "The reason why they did it was the sheer volume of material."

For example, a considerable number of scenes were shot on location in southern California. "I remember one chase through a park," Darley said. He also found old scripts showing plans for exteriors at the Zuma Beach parking lot, a marina and a beach house. The taping schedule was grueling too—from 6:30 A.M. to noon every day.

Darley said that most of the actors handled the setup well except for Keith Andes, who played the lead. "Keith had a problem because he was coming from films, and memorization was tough," he said. Overall, Darley noted, "The cast was great, and it became a family, as these shows do."

But a weak lead-in by another soap (see *Morning Star)* and new competition in late 1965 by *The Dating Game* crushed any chances of *Paradise Bay* being a success. In the show's 188th and final episode, written by Manya Starr, Duke, nursing a concussion and broken ribs in the hospital, got accepted to State University and planned to marry a Rosita Martinez. Kitty and Mary Morgan visited him at the hospital, but Fred and Jeff Morgan were not seen (Jeff supposedly was on vacation). The final shot was of a patio with these words superimposed: "We of *Paradise Bay*, in saying goodbye, thank you for your visits with us and hope the time spent brought you as much pleasure as your many kind letters brought us."

Darley, who retired as a director in 1989, still has *Paradise Bay* scripts but laughed about the idea of trying to revive or redo the show. "I think *Paradise Bay* has had its best days," he said.

Never Too Young

Soap Opera. Ran on ABC Mondays through Fridays 4–4:30 P.M. Sept. 27, 1965–June 24, 1966, opposite *The Secret Storm* on CBS and *The Match Game* on NBC. C: David Watson (as Alfie), Pat Connolly (as Barbara), Tony Dow (as Chet), John Lupton (as Frank), Tommy Rettig (as Jo-Jo), Robin Grace (as Joy), Patrice Wymore (as Rhoda), Michael Blodgett (as Tad), Dack Rambo (as Tim). EP: Larry Cohen. D: Bruce Minnix. W: Ric Vollaerts.

Nicknamed *Grief a Go Go* by its staff, the Hollywood-based *Never Too Young* told of the travails and romances of adolescents who hung out in a restaurant run by Alfie, a former singer. The exceptions to the demographic were Frank, Susan's dad, and Rhoda, Joy's mom, who had their own off-and-on relationship. There also was a constant stream of musicians who came by to perform — a most unusual development in the 1960s soap opera world.

"It was the idea that a dropout of the rock and roll milieu — he was English, because it was fashionable then — had opened up a rock bar on the Malibu pier," director Bruce Minnix said. "And all these acts would come by to see their old pal Alfie. Three times a week we had to have a rock and roll number that was on the charts."

Though middle-aged Minnix had not

been a rock music fan, he said, "I loved doing it, because I'd never choreographed those things." Most artists gave him little hassle save for the British group the Animals. "I threw them off the show," he said. "They were drunk and so unruly."

Minnix also remembered another band's appearance in connection with a plot involving Tad, a football player who underwent brain surgery after a car accident. To lift his spirits, his pals put a phone to his ear and heard Simon and Garfunkel at Alfie's pier dedicate their performance of "The Sounds of Silence" to him.

The regular actors handled themselves professionally, according to Minnix. "They were good, and they knew what they were doing," he said. The cast included two ex-child stars trying unsuccessfully to continue their careers as adults, Tony Dow (the older brother on *Leave It to Beaver* from 1957 to 1963) and Tommy Rettig (the owner of *Lassie* from 1954 to 1957). Rettig's character Jo-Jo caused a stir by having his parents called by the principal for having long hair, while Dow's character, Chet, faced being drafted in the Vietnam War, an item soon dropped as the network didn't want to take positions pro or con regarding the increasingly controversial conflict.

Minnix said network censorship resulted in such bland plots. "The restrictions were so incredibly funny," he said. "They couldn't smoke, couldn't drink. They could murder and sleep together, but not show their navels!" But he blamed the show's failure on some ABC affiliates airing it in the mornings, thus preventing its intended audience from seeing it because they were in school.

Minnix has five series episodes in his personal collection, including the last show. "Everything worked out perfectly," he said. "Patrice and John [who played Frank and Rhoda] got together. All the kids solved their problems. And I even appeared on camera with my flight tickets in hand." The director did *Never Too Young* as his only TV series in Hollywood; he went back to New Jersey, where he lives to this day — never too young for home, I guess one could say.

The First Look

Children's. Ran on NBC Saturdays Noon–12:30 P.M. Oct. 16, 1965–April 9, 1966, opposite *The Bugs Bunny Show* on ABC and repeats of *Sky King* on CBS. C: Oscar Brand, Neil Jones, Sally Sheffield, Jackie Washington. P: Bob Bendick.

When folksinger Oscar Brand learned that NBC planned an educational program in color based on Jeanne Bendick's book series *The First Book of...*, he was intrigued, but learned about it too late to be its host initially. "I was very disappointed that I was not going to do it, but it would be done instead by my friend Tom Glazer," Brand said.

Then shortly before its debut, producer Bob Bendick, the husband of Jeanne Bendick, called Brand about Glazer. "He said, 'Oscar, we'd like to talk to you about hosting the show. He doesn't want to stay because he's having problems with our director.'" Brand did not feel comfortable at first replacing fellow folksinger Glazer, nor having to do an hour commute into New York City to do the show on top of taping a TV show in Canada, doing his weekly radio show, *The Folk Song Festival*, and raising three kids.

Brand took the challenge to do the show anyway. "I was supposed to write anywhere from five to seven songs a week for it. That didn't bother me as much as memorizing scripts." Rehearsal was every day for the live Saturday show and soon wore out his castmates, dancer Neil Jones and singers Sally Sheffield and Jackie Washington, all of whom were in their early twenties at the time. "They all slept after rehearsal, and they complained they had no time for anything." He got along with all of them, but he did have some arguments with Washington over interpretations of songs.

Along the same time, the show replaced the director who supposedly gave Glazer problems. The new man turned out to upset Brand considerably. "He was small, irascible and pretty tough on us. Everything was so exact, so specific. You couldn't move from this spot to that spot." And there was one other hitch.

"The first day before it was going to be put on air, there were big ads in newspapers all over the country, only with a picture of Tom rather than me," Brand said. Glazer sued Brand, Bob Bendick and the new director for that ad, claiming they used his fame to get the show on the air and then dropped him, and that Brand stole his idea for the show's theme song. Brand's lawyer came out with a settlement amenable to his client and Glazer.

Despite all its difficulties, Brand liked *The First Look*. "I enjoyed the experience. It came out all right because we [in the cast] leaned on each other. It was quite a success." So why did it last less than a year? "I think they [the Bendicks] wanted more money. Then the network said, 'That's it.'"

Most of the show's main staff apart from Brand faded quickly from the scene, with the director being murdered shortly thereafter. Brand continued performing and doing *The Folk Song Festival*, which still is on the air from New York as of this writing. *The First Look* was his last regular network series, though he has done syndicated programs and guest shots on TV.

The Sammy Davis Jr. Show

Musical Variety. Ran on NBC Fridays 8:30–9:30 P.M. Jan. 7–April 22, 1966, opposite *The Addams Family* and *Honey West* on ABC and *Hogan's Heroes* and *Gomer Pyle, U.S.M.C.* on CBS. C: Sammy Davis, Jr., The Lester Wilson Dancers, The George Rhodes Orchestra. EP: Sammy Davis, Jr. P: Joe Hamilton. D: Clark Jones. W: Buz Kohan, Bill Angelos.

"He was an incredible talent," director Clark Jones recalled of Sammy Davis, Jr. But the diminutive dynamo, always a popular guest star on TV from the 1950s until shortly before his death in 1990, never made it as a series star. This series, his first as a regular, ran only three months, destroyed by *Hogan's Heroes* and *Gomer Pyle* opposite it.

Some blamed the show's failure on its CBS competition, both of which were top 10 hits, or the weak lead-in, the failing sitcom *Hank*. Others pointed to the odd situation Davis faced when the series debuted. He did a special with ABC called *Sammy and His Friends* set to run Feb. 1, 1966, and a clause in his contract for it required Davis to not appear on another network three weeks prior and one week after it aired. NBC, rather than delay his series, had Davis appear on the debut, then used Johnny Carson, Sean Connery and Jerry Lewis as substitute hosts before Davis could return on Feb. 11, 1966. Any chance for momentum to build for the series easily ended during those first few weeks.

Nevertheless, Jones blames none of these reasons as to why *The Sammy Davis Jr. Show*

tanked. "I think it was Sammy himself," he said. "He was not vulnerable. He came on a little strong. He pushed himself." Jones believed audiences prefer more relaxed hosts, such as Carol Burnett, who Jones directed in a special prior to the Davis show. It was Jones' work there with Carol's then-husband, producer Joe Hamilton, which led Jones to doing *The Sammy Davis Jr. Show* with Hamilton.

Jones said it was fruitless to tell Davis to tone down his give-'em-all-you-got approach for the series. "He was the executive producer, and he couldn't be denied," Jones said.

Still, Jones had good memories of the series. "We had Judy Garland on one week, and they got along great," he noted. Jones' overall conclusion was "It was a good try. I think we did a good show."

Davis would try being a regular again in 1973 on *The NBC Follies* (q.v.), then starred in a middling syndicated talk/variety series called *Sammy and Company* from 1975 to 1977. He still had his hardworking style in evidence, which could be why neither became a hit. If nothing else, he does hold the record among black entertainers for hosting the most number of TV variety shows (three), but frankly he'll be more remembered for his guest star work and appearances in other venues of show business.

Blue Light

Adventure. Ran on ABC Wednesdays 8:30–9 P.M. Jan. 12–Aug. 31, 1966, opposite *The Beverly Hillbillies* on CBS and *The Virginian* on NBC. C: Robert Goulet (as David March), Christine Carere (as Suzanne Duchard). EP: Walter Grauman. P: Buck Houghton. W: Larry Cohen.

The Double Life of Henry Phyfe

Sitcom. Ran on ABC Thursdays 8:30–9 P.M. Jan. 13–Sept. 1, 1966, opposite *My Three Sons* on CBS and *Laredo* on NBC. C: Red Buttons (as Henry Wadsworth Phyfe), Fred Clark (as Gerald B. Hannahan), Zeme North (as Judy Kimball), Marge Redmond (as Mrs. Florence Kimball), Parley Baer (as Mr. Hamble). EP: David Levy. P: Luther Davis. D: Charles Rondeau. W: Hannibal Coons, Harry Winkler, Phil Leslie.

The Baron

Adventure. Ran on ABC Thursdays 10–11 P.M. Jan. 20–July 14, 1966, opposite movies on CBS and *The*

Dean Martin Show on NBC. C: Steve Forrest (as John Mannering, a/k/a "The Baron"), Sue Lloyd (as Cordelia Winfield), Colin Gordon (as John Alexander Templeton-Green), Paul Ferris (as David Marlowe). P: Monty Berman. D: Leslie Norman. W: Dennis Spooner.

Arlene Dahl's Beauty Spot

Informational. Ran on ABC Mondays through Fridays 4:25–4:30 P.M. March 28–June 24, 1966, opposite *The Secret Storm* on CBS and news on NBC. C: Arlene Dahl. P/D: Richard Gottleib. W: Yseulte James, Jan Miller.

Court-Martial

Drama. Ran on ABC Fridays 10–11 P.M. April 8–Sept. 2, 1966, opposite *The Trials of O'Brian* (through May 27) and *Wayne and Shuster Take an Affectionate Look at…* (from June 17 to July 29) on CBS and *The Man from U.N.C.L.E.* on NBC. C: Bradford Dillman (as Capt. David Young), Peter Graves (as Maj. Frank Whittaker), Kenneth J. Warren (as M/Sgt. John MacCaskey), Diane Clare (as Sgt. Wendy). EP: Richard Irving. P: Bill Hill. D: Harvey Hart. W: John T. Dugan.

Mickie Finn's

Musical Variety. Ran on NBC Thursdays 9:30–10 P.M. April 21–Sept. 1, 1966, opposite *Peyton Place* on ABC and movies on CBS. C: Fred E. Finn, Mickie Finn, the Dapper Dans, Harold "Hoot" Connors, Mickey Manners. P/D: Dean Whitmore.

Chain Letter

Game. Ran on NBC Mondays through Fridays 11–11:30 A.M. July 4–Oct. 14, 1966, opposite *Supermarket Sweep* on ABC and *The Andy Griffith Show* reruns on CBS. C: Jan Murray. EP: Stefan Hatos. D: Joe Behar.

Showdown

Game. Ran on NBC Mondays through Fridays 11:30 A.M.–Noon July 4–Oct. 14, 1966, opposite *The Dating Game* on ABC and *The Dick Van Dyke Show* reruns on CBS. C: Joe Pyne, The Bantams. EP: Merrill Heatter, Bob Quigley. P: Larry Klein. D: Stuart Phelps.

Showdown has the distinction of being the only game show whose host once brandished a gun on live television. Joe Pyne came to prominence nationally shortly after he started a local

TV talk show in Los Angeles and showed a guest black militant during the time of the Watts riots that he was armed. That and other controversial guests led to *The Joe Pyne Show* being syndicated from 1965 to 1967, and during part of that time, he somehow was felt to be qualified to do this game show.

"What a character he was!" marveled director Stuart Phelps. "He was on the radio [locally] on, I think, KLAC. Heatter-Quigley got ahold of him some way. He was an ex–Marine, had his leg shot off. He didn't take any crap from anybody. He was really a tough bastard."

That doesn't exactly sound like your normal friendly game show host, but then *Showdown* wasn't your typical game show anyway. Two three-member teams competed to answer questions correctly using a board displaying four possible responses. Anyone choosing the wrong response not only was eliminated from the game but landed on the floor via the breakaway seats for the contestants.

"Yeah, you went down," Phelps said. "Of course, everybody knew it could happen, so they were on edge." If that wasn't enough, the show also had a rock 'n' roll house band called the Bantams to play a few musical clues. Add all these elements together, and one just wishes beyond hope that TV collectors can unearth a single copy of this oddity and put it out for sale (to my knowledge, no one has done so yet).

To be fair, Phelps said Pyne treated his game show guests better than he did some of his talk show visitors. "He wasn't surly. He didn't put them down necessarily. He did a good job." Still, Phelps allowed that Pyne "was a little different. He said, 'What I really want to do is buy a boat, cruise the world and do whatever I want.'" He never had the chance. The chain smoker died of lung cancer at age 45 less than four years after *Showdown* went off the air.

The good news about the cancellation of *Showdown* was that it gave its executive producers Merrill Heatter and Bob Quigley the chance to introduce their biggest hit, even if it meant sacrificing this show. "It was doing mediocre apparently, and *The Hollywood Squares* came along and had the right format," said Phelps. That series held NBC's daily 11:30 A.M.–noon slot for nearly a decade (Oct. 17, 1966–Oct. 1, 1976), then moved around a few other times before getting cancelled on June 20, 1980, after nearly 14 years on the network.

Roy Clark takes a break from guitar picking to discuss business with Rusty Draper during rehearsal for *Swingin' Country*.

Swingin' Country

Musical Variety. Ran on NBC Mondays through Fridays 12:30–12:55 P.M. July 4–Dec. 30, 1966, opposite *Father Knows Best* reruns on ABC and *Search for Tomorrow* and *Guiding Light* on CBS. C: Rusty Draper, Roy Clark (July–September), Johnny Tillotson (September–December), Molly Bee, the Swinging Countrymen, the Hometown Singers. EP: Rosalind Ross. P: Jack Watson. D:

Jorn Winther. W: Bobby Bell, Larry Miller, Don Sherman.

It seems odd that *Swingin' Country* came from the production company of Dick Clark. After all, the performer/producer had been associated with rock music on television ever since his longest-running series *American Bandstand* started on ABC in 1957. He had done virtually next to nothing of note in the country music field before this series started, yet director John Winther didn't find it such a stretch for his boss.

"He likes all kind of music, and at the time, he was doing daytime shows like *Where the Action Is*," Winther said. "I thought it was a natural thing to do." Winther also added that Clark was a nice leader. "He was great to work with."

The first daytime series Clark Productions sold to NBC, *Swingin' Country* originally featured Rusty Draper as host of the daily shindig, with assists from singer Molly Bee and fiddler Roy Clark. All the solo regulars already had several hits on the country chart, although few of those were big enough to cross over to the pop chart. Midway through the show's run Clark left and was replaced by vocalist Johnny Tillotson.

"The problem we had on that show was Molly Bee," said Winther. "She was very difficult on the show at the time." Winther declined to specify what hardships he thought Bee created on the set, only noting that "It was not so much work-related as what she did in here spare time. But she was a good performer."

Winther and crew taped the show in Hollywood. "I think we taped one a day," he said. (Soon, almost all taped daytime shows would record five shows in one day as standard operating procedures.) Guest stars dropped by too. "People came on because they had recordings out and needed publicity," Winther said.

In fact, not all the guests were country-related either, according to Winther. "We had Dean Martin on, I think. He taped [his night-time TV variety series] nearby."

Swingin' Country came onto the NBC lineup to replace the equally short-lived *Let's Play Post Office* (q.v.). Apparently there were not enough country fans to dislodge the competition for the series, so it departed from the roster within six months. (Winther said he really wasn't sure why it went off.) NBC replaced it by moving the game show *Eye Guess* from 10 to 10:30 A.M., where it started on Jan. 3, 1966, to fill its slot. That series did well enough to last there until Sept. 26, 1969.

1966-67

The Pruitts of Southampton

Sitcom. Ran on ABC Tuesdays 9–9:30 P.M. Sept. 6, 1966–Jan. 3, 1967, opposite *The Red Skelton Hour* on CBS and movies on NBC, then ABC Fridays 9:30–10 P.M. Jan. 13, 1967–Sept. 1, 1967, opposite movies on CBS and *T.H.E. Cat* on NBC. C: Phyllis Diller (as Phyllis Pruitt), Reginald Gardiner (as Uncle Ned Pruitt), Grady Sutton (as Sturgis the butler), Richard Deacon (as Mr. Thomas Baldwin), Pam Freeman (as Stephanie "Steffi" Pruitt), Lisa Loring (as Suzy), Gypsy Rose Lee (as Regina Wentworth; 1966), John Astin (as Rudolph Angus "Rudy" Pruitt; 1967), Marty Ingles (as Norman Krump; 1967), Paul Lynde (as Harvey; 1967), Billy DeWolfe (as Vernon Bradley; 1967). EP: David Levy. P/W: Everett Freeman, Nat

Perrin. D: Gene Nelson, Oscar Rudolph, Stanley Z. Cherry. W: Lawrence J. Cohen, Fred Freeman, Stanley Roberts, Elon Packard, Bart Andrews.

"How d'you do, how d'you do, how d'you do, my dear..."— opening line of the catchy theme for *The Pruitts of Southampton*.

Loosely based on a 1954 novel by Patrick Dennis called *House Party*, *The Pruitts of Southampton* struck everyone who saw it as a converse *Beverly Hillbillies*. An eccentric old money clan in New York found themselves $10 million in the hole to the Internal Revenue Service thanks to the poor bookkeeping of their globetrotting, vigorous 90-year-old Uncle Ned Pruitt. IRS agent Mr. Baldwin confiscated their

60-room mansion with three pools and a polo field to pay off the debt, but since the government worried about how announcing the Pruitts are bankrupt would affect the economy, he generously let them pretend to still be rich while paying off their debt, albeit that they could live in just eight rooms of the mansion, fire the servants, sell their art, have just one car and cook their food. Somehow they managed to keep hold of their ancient butler, Sturgis, in the deal.

Leading the Pruitts' efforts to keep the good life intact on the tight budget was matriarch Phyllis Pruitt, played by comedienne Phyllis Diller in her first regular TV role, replete with her trademark horse laugh and outlandish fashions. She played a widowed mother of two, Steffi (age 22) and Suzy (age 8), who struggled with comic complications like Baldwin installing a phone booth in the mansion to cut back on long distance phone call costs while trying to keep up with her fellow socialite Regina Wentworth.

After four months of finishing third in the ratings, ABC decided to move *The Pruitts of Southampton* to another night with considerable adjustments in hopes of finding a bigger audience. Now titled *The Phyllis Diller Show* without its original theme (aww...), the program now de-emphasized the family in favor of veteran TV comic actors as boarders paying rent to Phyllis Pruitt. Among them were John Astin as brother-in-law Rudy Pruitt and Billy DeWolfe as writer Vernon Bradley. Interestingly, most of these actors were billed as "guest stars" even though they were more or less regulars, as was Richard Deacon as Mr. Baldwin, who nevertheless was dubbed the show's "special guest star." None of it mattered; the show still dragged in the ratings.

Stanley Z. Cherry, who directed a few episodes before being dismissed ("I was fired off the show because the cameraman complained I made him work too hard"), thought that "Phyllis was a delight" to direct, but was wrong in doing the show. "That didn't work from the word go," he said. "When she's acting, she's a different person [than onstage as a comedienne]. The scripts were bad too."

ABC replaced the series with a western, *The Guns of Will Sonnett*. It performed only slightly better, petering out in 1969 after two years. Diller would return as a TV regular by that time (see *The Beautiful Phyllis Diller Show* in 1968-69).

The Rounders

Sitcom. Ran on ABC Tuesdays 8:30–9 P.M. Sept. 6, 1966–Jan. 3, 1967, opposite *The Red Skelton Hour* on CBS and *Occasional Wife* on NBC. C: Ron Hayes (as Ben Jones), Patrick Wayne (as Howdy Lewis), Chill Wills (as Jim Ed Love), Bobbi Jordan (as Ada), Janis Hansen (as Sally), Jason Wingreen (as Shorty Dawes), Walker Edmiston (as Regan), J. Pat O'Malley (as Vince). EP: Ed Adamson. P/D: Burt Kennedy. W: Marion Hargrove.

Love on a Rooftop

Sitcom. Ran on ABC Tuesdays 9:30–10 P.M. Sept. 6, 1966–Jan. 3, 1967, opposite *Petticoat Junction* on CBS and movies on NBC, then ABC Thursdays 9–9:30 P.M. Jan. 12–April 13, 1967, opposite movies on CBS and *Star Trek* on NBC, then ABC Thursdays 9:30–10 P.M. April 27–Aug. 31, 1967, opposite movies on CBS and *Dragnet* on NBC. C: Peter Deuel (as David Willis), Judy Carne (as Julie Willis), Rich Little (as Stan Parker), Barbara Bostock (as Carol Parker), Edith Atwater (as Phyllis Hammond), Herb Voland (as Fred Hammond), Sandy Kenyon (as Jim Lucas). EP: Harry Ackerman. P/D: E.W. Swackhamer. W: Bernard Slade.

The Monroes

Western. Ran on ABC Wednesdays 8–9 P.M. Sept. 7, 1966–Aug. 30, 1967, opposite *Lost in Space* and *The Beverly Hillbillies* on CBS and *The Virginian* on NBC. C: Michael Anderson, Jr. (as Clayt Monroe), Barbara Hershey (as Kathy Monroe), Keith Schultz (as Jefferson Monroe), Kevin Schultz (as Fennimore Monroe), Tammy Locke (as Amy Monroe), Liam Sullivan (as Major Mapoy), Ron Soble (as Dirty Jim), Ben Johnson (as Sleeve), Jim Westmoreland (as Ruel Jaxon), Robert Middleton (as Barney Wales), Buck Taylor (as John "Brad" Bradford). EP: Frederick Brogger. P: Al C. Ward. D: Bernard Kowalski. W: Otis Carney.

The Man Who Never Was

Adventure. Ran on ABC Wednesdays 9–9:30 P.M. Sept. 7, 1966–Jan. 4, 1967, opposite *Green Acres* on CBS and *The Bob Hope Chrysler Theater* on NBC. C: Robert Lansing (as Peter Murphy/Mark Wainwright), Dana Wynter (as Eva Wainwright), Murray Hamilton (as Col. Jack Forbes), Alex Davion (as Roger Barry). EP/D/W: John Newland. P: Ronald L. Jacks. W: Merwin Gerard.

The Tammy Grimes Show

Sitcom. Ran on ABC Thursdays 8:30–9 P.M. Sept. 8–Sept. 29, 1966, opposite *My Three Sons* on CBS and *Star Trek* on NBC. C: Tammy Grimes (as Tamantha Ward), Hiram Sherman (as Uncle Simon), Dick Sargent (as Terrence Ward), Maudie Prickett (as Mrs. Ratchett). EP: William Dozier. P: Richard Whorf, Alex Gottleib. D: Don Taylor. W: Ralph Goodman, Roland Wolpert.

The Hero

Sitcom. Ran on NBC Thursdays 9:30–10 P.M. Sept. 8, 1966–Jan. 5, 1967, opposite *That Girl* on ABC and movies on CBS. C: Richard Mulligan (as Sam Garret), Mariette Hartley (as Ruth Garret), Bobby Horan (as Paul Garret), Victor French (as Fred Gilman), Joey Baio (as Burton Gilman), Marc London (as Dewey). EP: Leonard Stern. P: Jay Sandrich. D: Bruce Bilson, Bill Wiard. W: Robert Ellis Miller.

Hawk

Police Drama. Ran on ABC Thursdays 10–11 P.M. Sept. 8–Dec. 29, 1966, opposite movies on CBS and *The Dean Martin Show* on NBC. C: Burt Reynolds (as Lt. John Hawk), Wayne Grice (as Det. Dan Carter), Bruce Glover (as Asst. D.A. Murray Slaken), Leon Janney (as Asst. D.A. Ed Gorton). EP: Hubbell Robinson. P: William Sackheim. D: Sam Wanamaker. W: Allen Sloane.

The Green Hornet

Adventure. Ran on ABC Fridays 7:30–8 P.M. Sept. 9, 1966–July 14, 1967, opposite *The Wild Wild West* on CBS and *Tarzan* on NBC. C: Van Williams (as Britt Reid/the Green Hornet), Bruce Lee (as Kato), Wende Wagner (as Lenore "Casey" Case), Lloyd Gough (as Mike Axford), Walter Brooks (as District Attorney F.P. Scanlon). EP: William Dozier. P: Richard Bluel. D: Leslie Martinson. W: Ken Pettus.

The Time Tunnel

Science Fiction. Ran on ABC Fridays 8–9 P.M. Sept. 9, 1966–July 14, 1967, opposite *The Wild Wild West* and *Hogan's Heroes* on CBS and *Tarzan* and *The Man from U.N.C.L.E.* on NBC, then ABC Fridays 7:30–8:30 P.M. July 21–Sept. 1, 1967, opposite *The Wild Wild West* on CBS and *Tarzan* on NBC. C: James Darren (as Dr. Tony Newman), Robert Colbert (as Dr. Doug Phillips), Lee Meriwether (as Dr. Ann MacGregor), Whit Bissell (as Gen. Heywood Kirk), John Zaremba (as Dr. Ray-

mond Swain). EP/D: Irwin Allen. AP: Jerry Briskin. D: Sobey Martin, William Hale. W: Harold Jack Bloom, Shimon Wincelberg, William Welch, Carey Wilbur, Robert and Wanda Duncan.

The Milton Berle Show

Comedy Variety. Ran on ABC Fridays 9–10 P.M. Sept. 9, 1966–Jan. 6, 1967, opposite movies on CBS and *The Man from U.N.C.L.E.* and *T.H.E. Cat* on NBC. C: Milton Berle, Donna Loren, Bobby Rydell, Irving Benson (as Sidney Sphritzer), the Mitchell Ayres Orchestra. EP: Nick Vanoff, William Harbach. P: Stan Harris. D: Mark Goode. W: Buddy Arnold, Stan Burns, Mike Marmer, Stanley Davis, Marvin Worth, Howard Leeds, Hal Goodman, Larry Klein.

Shane

Western. Ran on ABC Saturdays 7:30–8:30 P.M. Sept. 10–Dec. 31, 1966, opposite *The Jackie Gleason Show* on CBS and *Flipper* and *Please Don't Eat the Daisies* on NBC. C: David Carradine (as Shane), Jill Ireland (as Marian Starrett), Tom Tully (as Tom Starrett), Christopher Shea (as Joey Starrett), Bert Freed (as Rufe Ryker), Sam Gilman (as Sam Grafton). EP: Herbert Brodkin. P: Denne Petitelero. D: Robert Butler. W: David Shaw.

Hey Landlord!

Sitcom. Ran on NBC Sundays 8:30–9 P.M. Sept. 11, 1966–May 14, 1967, opposite *The Ed Sullivan Show* on CBS and *The F.B.I.* on ABC. C: Will Hutchins (as Woody Banner), Sandy Baron (as Chuck Hookstratton), Pamela Rodgers (as Timothy Morgan), Miko Mayama (as Kyoko Mitsui), Michael Constantine (as Jack Ellenhorn). EP/W: Garry Marshall. P: Lee Rich, Sheldon Leonard, Bruce Johnson. D: John Rich, Jerry Paris. W: James Brooks, Harvey Miller, Chuck Shyer.

It's About Time

Sitcom. Ran on CBS Sundays 7:30–8 P.M. Sept. 11, 1966–Aug. 27, 1967, opposite *Voyage to the Bottom of the Sea* on ABC and *Walt Disney* on NBC. C: Frank Aletter (as Capt. "Mac" MacKenzie), Jack Mullaney (as Lt. Hector Canfield), Imogene Coca (as Shad), Joe E. Ross (as Gronk), Cliff Norton (as Boss; 1966–January 1967), Kathleen Freeman (as Mrs. Boss; 1966–January 1967), Mike Mazurki (as Clon; 1966–January 1967), Mary Grace (as Mlor), Pat Cardi (as Breer), Alan DeWitt (as Mr. Tyler; 1967), Frank Wilcox (as Gen. Morley). EP/W: Sherwood Schwartz. P/D: George

What are these people staring and smiling at? From left, the case of *It's About Time* included Joe E. Ross, Jack Mullaney, Mike Mazurki, Pat Cardi, Mary Grace, Cliff Norton, Frank Aletter and Imogene Coca. (Author's collection)

Cahan. D/W: David P. Harmon. D: Jack Arnold, Jerry Hopper. W: Elroy Schwartz, Alan Dinehart, Brad Radnitz, Joel Kane.

"It was a promising show, and it broke all its promises" is how Cliff Norton views *It's About Time*. His reputation as a comic actor in Hollywood was so strong by 1966 that he was offered a regular role on the sitcom. Reading the pilot written by David P. Harmon, Norton thought the idea of two astronauts, Hector and Mac, going through a time warp in their space capsule and landing in prehistoric Earth, was funny, as was his role of Boss, the head of the cave-dwelling tribe the astronauts met.

"Boss was a bumbling, fumbling guy who thought he was hot stuff," Norton said of his character. Others in the tribe were Gronk, his wife, Shad, and their kids Mlor and Breer, plus Mrs. Boss and Boss's hulking henchman, Clon.

"It was a wonderful cast of actors, and I thought it was going to be a wonderful show," Norton said. But as a series, the scripts let him down greatly. "The only time on my life I was temperamental was that show," he said. "It was the same crap every week."

According to Norton, "The show was purportedly a comedy show. After all, the conflict between present-day astronauts and 1,000,000 B.C. cave dwellers—what else could it be?" However, Norton said executive producer Sherwood Schwartz worried about running against *Walt Disney*, which had finished in the top 20 in the previous season (1965-66).

"Sherwood and his bunch got scared and thought the only way we could compete was to be an adventure show," Norton said. "So they had us cave folk threatening these sophisticated astronauts every week. They played it for adventure, and they put it into the toilet."

Norton said he and Imogene Coca, who

played Shad, made suggestions to Schwartz on how to make the show better. "We came up with ideas that perhaps weren't worthy of putting on screen, but at least being considered," he said. He didn't get even that luxury, and while Norton said he respects Schwartz as a producer (he created *Gilligan's Island* and *The Brady Bunch*), he thought Schwartz missed the boat on this series.

After four months into the series, with poor ratings, Norton, Kathleen Freeman and Mike Mazurki vanished from the show as the astronauts returned to modern America while bringing Gronk's family with them. Norton's reaction upon hearing he was dismissed was "Thank God." The new format included the astronaut's boss, Gen. Morley, and their landlord, Mr. Tyler, but it did not improve the show in Norton's view. "It really didn't," he said. "It was just a bad show."

Norton enjoyed his cast members and even had fun unnerving a director he said had no sense of humor, George Cahan, by pretending he was drunk between doing perfect single takes for his scenes. Overall, however, he felt this was one job he should have passed up. "With *It's About Time*, I took the money and I walked," he said.

Run, Buddy, Run

Sitcom. Ran on CBS Mondays 8–8:30 P.M. Sept. 12, 1966–Jan. 2, 1967, opposite *The Iron Horse* on ABC and *I Dream of Jeannie* on NBC. C: Jack Sheldon (as Buddy Overstreet), Bruce Gordon (as Mr. Devere, a/k/a "Mr. D"), Jim Connell (as Junior), Nick Georgiade (as Wendell), Gregg Palmer (as Harry). P: Leonard Stern, David Susskind, Dan Melnick, Jack Elinson. W: Jack Elinson, Mel Tolkin, Ernest Chambers, Seamon Jacobs.

This sitcom was a humorous takeoff of a hit drama series starring David Janssen from 1963 to 1967 that became an Oscar-nominated movie in 1993. "That was the genesis, *The Fugitive*, someone having to take odd jobs and they bumbled it," said producer Leonard Stern. But rather being chased by the police as a murder suspect, this sitcom had boyish Los Angeles accountant Buddy Overstreet pursued by racketeer "Mr. D" and his henchmen Wendell and Harry after overhearing their plans in a steamroom to kill a man in Chicago. The cops didn't believe Buddy's story — after all, Mr. D ran Devere Enterprises, a respected business, along with his incompetent son Junior — so Buddy ran across America to escape the gangster's clutches.

Starring as Buddy was little-known Jack

A nervous Jack Sheldon, lying on his back, frets about overhearing the nefarious plans Bruce Gordon (center, with legs crossed) discusses with his henchmen on *Rud, Buddy, Run*.

Sheldon, who Stern admitted was not his first choice for the role. "We did want a physical comic comparable to Red Skelton and Dick Van Dyke," he said. "They're in short supply." Bruce Gordon, who played Mr. D, was more blunt in his feelings about Sheldon, saying, "Unfortunately, he wasn't much of an actor."

Gordon had to audition for the role even though he already had portrayed one of TV's most famous gangsters, namely Frank Nitti on *The Untouchables* from 1959 to 1963. He thought *Run, Buddy, Run* was a funny show and liked his fellow players apart from Sheldon ("They were all fine"). Stern thought Gordon and crew did a fine job too, though he noted its one potential main drawback was that "You're always in danger in this series of making the villains too endearing."

Even though it ran less than four months, Gordon said it could have lasted longer had CBS not bungled making a decision. "The show started low-key and really built up over the year," Gordon said. "And then they cancelled it before the November ratings. And then when those ratings came out, they said, 'Oh, don't do anything else for a month.'"

But it was too late. CBS's earlier announcement of ending the show had the production company start loaning other productions the sets and studios in anticipation of *Run, Buddy, Run* ending its run. As a result, the series could not continue creating episodes, and it left the schedule.

CBS replaced *Run, Buddy, Run* with another short-lived sitcom, *Mr. Terrific* (q.v.). Oddly, for some reason the original pilot for the sitcom, titled *Run Jack Run* and having none of the cast members and a different setup, ran on NBC on July 20, 1970, four years after it was produced.

The Roger Miller Show

Musical Variety. Ran on NBC Mondays 8:30–9 P.M. Sept. 12–Dec. 26, 1966, opposite *The Rat Patrol* on ABC and *The Lucy Show* on CBS. C: Roger Miller, the Eddie Karam Orchestra. P: Gary Smith, Dwight Hemion. D: Dwight Hemion. W: Jeff Harris, Bernie Kukoff, Mason Williams.

"Freewheeling" was how producer/director Dwight Hemion categorized *The Roger Miller Show*, and that word is an apt description of its star too. Singer/songwriter Miller bummed

around Nashville for years until a song about a bum, "King of the Road," was a huge country and pop hit that propelled him into stardom in 1965. It also became the theme for his variety series, and Thumbs Carlisle, his guitarist who supplied background snaps for the record, sat in with the band of the show too, according to Hemion.

Following his hit, Miller became a much-in-demand guest on talk and variety shows not only because of that song and others that were biggies at the time (e.g., "England Swings," "Engine Engine #9"), but also due to his laid-back charm and humor. NBC took a shot and gave him his own series, although they appeared to hedge their bet — *The Roger Miller Show* was the only half-hour variety show on network TV in 1966, whereas the others ran a full hour.

"He was quite a character," Hemion said. "We left a lot of that show to Roger to create on the go. It was written, but the way Roger was, he was a fun guy, and it left room for improvisation."

Writer Bernie Kukoff pretty much agreed with Hemion's assessment. "It was the first network show my partner and I actually wrote," he said, referring to Jeff Harris. (The other writer, Mason Williams, would go on to do scripts for *The Smothers Brothers Comedy Hour* plus score a hit on the music charts on his own with the 1968 instrumental "Classical Gas.") "What there were [in terms of scripted dialogue] were funny comedy exchanges with guests. I don't recall any sketches at all, just some repartee with guests." He recalled that one of those guests was Johnny Carson.

Kukoff also remembered that each show had Miller do at least one song on a set with railroad tracks. "He just came out so huge on the scene from Enid, Oklahoma, and we tried to keep that homey feel," he said.

But NBC might have banked too much on his appeal at the time when they slotted him to go against *The Lucy Show*, the #4 rated series of the 1966-67 season. Asked if he thought the scheduling hastened the end of *The Roger Miller Show*, Hemion cracked, "It didn't help, that's for sure!" After 16 low-rated episodes, NBC replaced it with *Captain Nice* (q.v.). Miller would only be an occasional guest on TV thereafter until his death from cancer at age 56 in 1992.

The Road West

Western. Ran on NBC Mondays 9–10 P.M. Sept. 12, 1966–Aug. 28, 1967, opposite *The Felony Squad* and *Peyton Place* on ABC and *The Andy Griffith Show* and *Family Affair* on CBS. C: Barry Sullivan (as Benjamin Pride), Andrew Prine (as Timothy Pride), Brenda Scott (as Midge Pride), Kelly Corcoran (as Kip Pride), Charles Seel (as Grandpa Tom Pride), Glenn Corbett (as Chance Reynolds), Kathryn Hays (as Elizabeth Reynolds). EP: Norman MacDonnell. P: James McAdams. W: Richard Fielder.

The Jean Arthur Show

Sitcom. Ran on CBS Mondays 10–10:30 P.M. Sept. 12–Dec. 5, 1966, opposite *The Big Valley* on ABC and *Run for Your Life* on NBC. C: Jean Arthur (as Patricia Marshall), Ron Harper (as Paul Marshall), Leonard Stone (as Morton), Richard Conte (as Richie Wells). EP: Richard Quine, Jay Richard Kennedy. P: Si Rose. D: Alan Rafkin. W: Steven Gethers.

The Girl from U.N.C.L.E.

Adventure. Ran on NBC Tuesdays Sept. 13, 1966–Aug. 29, 1967, opposite *Combat!* on ABC and *Daktari* on CBS. C: Stefanie Powers (as April Dancer), Noel Harrison (as Mark Slate), Leo G. Carroll (as Alexander Waverly), Randy Kirby (as Randy Kovacs). EP: Norman Felton. P: Douglas Benton, Mark Hodges, George Lear. D: Barry Shear, Leo Penn, Jud Taylor, Richard Sarafian, Herschel Daugherty. W: Tony Barrett.

It was a sign of 1960s sexism that the distaff spinoff from *The Man from U.N.C.L.E.* sported the title *The Girl from U.N.C.L.E.*, not *The Woman from U.N.C.L.E.* The idea was to start another successful franchise from *The Man from U.N.C.L.E.* (which began on Sept. 22, 1964, but did not blossom into a top 15 hit until the 1965-66 season), but the addition wore out the spy-oriented series instead, and after the year-long run of *The Girl from U.N.C.L.E.*, *The Man from U.N.C.L.E.* perished not long thereafter, on Jan. 15, 1968.

"*The Man from U.N.C.L.E.* was so successful that NBC pressured me to film *The Girl from U.N.C.L.E.*, against my wishes," wrote executive producer Norman Felton in a letter to me. (One wonders if network executives made the same requests to the producers of *Bonanza* and *Get Smart*, the only other NBC series rated ahead of *The Man from U.N.C.L.E.* in the 1965-66 season.)

The parent show introduced the main characters for *The Girl from U.N.C.L.E.* in a *Man from U.N.C.L.E.* episode telecast Feb. 25, 1966. "The Moonglow Affair" introduced two new agents for U.N.C.L.E. (an acronym for the United Network Command for Law Enforcement), April Dancer and Mark Slate, who like Napoleon Solo and Ilya Kuryakin from *The Man …* reported to U.N.C.L.E. leader Alexander Waverly.

Playing April and Mark in the episode were, respectively, Mary Ann Mobley and Norman Fell. For the series Stefanie Powers became April, while Noel Harrison, who had nothing in common physically with Norman Fell, played Mark. To explain his British dialect, Harrison's Mark was said to have come to U.N.C.L.E.'s New York headquarters via transfer from London.

Harrison also was the son of esteemed actor Rex Harrison. Another regular who was a scion of an entertainer was Randy Kirby, playing Randy Kovacs, sort of an intern spy. He was the child of Durward Kirby, the sidekick on the daytime and nighttime editions of *The Garry Moore Show* from 1950 to 1964, and coincidentally was on the air the same time as *The Girl from U.N.C.L.E.* in a revival of *The Garry Moore Show* that ran just four months in 1966-67.

Finally, Leo G. Carroll had the honor of being the first actor playing the same character in two series being produced simultaneously. He was Waverly on both *The Man …* and *The Girl…*, a setup that would not exist again until actor Richard Anderson played Oscar Goldman on both *The Six Million Dollar Man* and *The Bionic Woman* from 1976 to 1978.

Felton thought the plots, as well as interference by NBC, sealed the fate for *The Girl from U.N.C.L.E.* "It proved to be silly, when the network would not accept stories in which 'the Girl' was part of the action," wrote Felton. "'Girls must be nice,' I was told."

NBC replaced it in the fall of 1967 by moving *I Dream of Jeannie* to occupy the first half hour, followed by the start of *The Jerry Lewis Show* (a variety series not to be confused with his disastrous 1963-64 show).

Occasional Wife

Sitcom. Ran on NBC Tuesdays 8:30–9 P.M. Sept. 13, 1966–Aug. 29, 1967, opposite *The Rounders* (through Jan. 3) and *The Invaders* (from Jan. 10) on ABC and *The Red Skelton Hour* (through June 27) and *Spotlight* (from July 4) on CBS. C: Michael Callan (as Peter Christopher), Patricia Harty (as Greta Patterson), Jack Collins (as Max Brahms), Joan Tompkins (as Mrs. Brahms), Sara Seegar (as Mrs. Christopher), Bryan O'Byrne (as the man in the middle apartment), Stuart Margolin (as Bernie), Jack Riley (as Wally Frick), Susan Silo (as Vera), Chris Noel (as Marilyn), Vin Scully (as narrator). EP: Harry Ackerman. P: Robert Claver. D: Ernest Pintoff. W: Fred Freeman, Lawrence J. Cohen.

Jericho

War Adventure. Ran on CBS Thursdays 7:30–8:30 P.M. Sept. 15, 1966–Jan. 19, 1967, opposite *Batman* and *F Troop* on ABC and *Daniel Boone* on NBC. C: Don Francks (as Franklin Sheppard), Marino Mase (as Jean-Gaston André), John Leyton (as Nicholas Gage). EP: Norman Felton. P: Stanley Niss. D: Barry Shear. W: Sheldon Stark.

T.H.E. Cat

Adventure. Ran on NBC Fridays 9:30–10 P.M. Sept. 16, 1966–Sept. 1, 1967, opposite *The Milton Berle Show* (through Jan. 6) and *The Pruitts of Southampton* (from Jan. 13) and movies on CBS. C: Robert Loggia (as Thomas Hewitt Edward Cat), R.G. Armstrong (as Capt. MacAllister), Robert Carricart (as Pepe). P/D: Boris Sagal. W: Harry Julian Fink.

Pistols 'n' Petticoats

Sitcom. Ran on CBS Saturdays 8:30–9 P.M. Sept. 17, 1966–Jan. 14, 1967, opposite *The Lawrence Welk Show* on ABC and *Get Smart* on NBC, then CBS Saturdays 9:30–10 P.M. Jan. 21–Aug. 19, 1967, opposite *The Hollywood Palace* on ABC and movies on NBC. C: Ann Sheridan (as Henrietta Hanks), Douglas Fowley (as Grandpa Andrew Hanks), Ruth McDevitt (as Grandma Hanks), Carole Wells (as Lucy Hanks), Gary Vinson (as Sheriff Harold Sikes), Robert Lowery (as Buss Courtney), Lon Chaney, Jr. (as Chief Eagle Shadow), Marc Cavell (as Gray Hawk), Alex Henteloff (as Little Bear). P: Joe Connelly. D: Sid Lanfield. W: Lois Hire.

The Pat Boone Show

Talk. Ran on NBC Mondays through Fridays Oct. 17, 1966–June 30, 1967, opposite *Supermarket Sweep* on ABC and *The Andy Griffith Show* reruns on CBS. C: Pat Boone, Adam Keefe. P: Armand Grant. D: Gordon Rigsby. W: Saul Turtletaub, Sanford Sheldon.

Dream Girl of '67

Game. Ran on ABC Mondays through Fridays 2:30–2:55 P.M. Dec. 19, 1966–Dec. 29, 1967, opposite *Art Linkletter's House Party* on CBS and *The Doctors* on NBC. C: Dick Stewart (through June 23), Wink Martindale (from June 26–September), Paul Peterson (from September). EP: Chuck Barris. P: Gene Banks. D: Bill Howell. W: Ira Barmak.

Reach for the Stars

Game. Ran on NBC Mondays through Fridays 10–10:25 A.M. Jan. 2–March 31, 1967, opposite *Candid Camera* reruns on CBS. C: Bill Mazer. P: Ron Greenberg. D: Gil Cates.

Mr. Terrific

Sitcom. Ran on CBS Mondays 8–8:30 P.M. Jan. 9–Aug. 28, 1967, opposite *The Iron Horse* on ABC and *I Dream of Jeannie* on NBC. C: Stephen Strimpell (as Stanley Beamish/Mr. Terrific), John McGiver (as Barton J. Reed), Dick Gautier (as Hal Walters), Paul Smith (as Harley Trent). P/D: Jack Arnold. W: Harvey Bullock, R.S. Allen, David P. Harmon.

Captain Nice

Sitcom. Ran on NBC Mondays 8:30–9 P.M. Jan. 9–Aug. 28, 1967, opposite *The Lucy Show* (through June 26) and *Vacation Playhouse* (from July 3) on CBS and *The Rat Patrol* on ABC. C: William Daniels (as Carter Nash/Captain Nice), Alice Ghostley (as Mrs. Nash), Ann Prentiss (as Sgt. Candy Kane), Liam Dunn (as Mayor Finney), William Zuckert (as Chief Segal), Byron Foulger (as Mr. Nash). EP/W: Buck Henry. P: Jay Sandrich. D: Jud Taylor.

Rango

Sitcom. Ran on ABC Fridays 9–9:30 P.M. Jan. 13–Sept. 1, 1967, opposite movies on CBS and *The Man from U.N.C.L.E.* on NBC. C: Tim Conway (as Rango), Guy Marks (as Pink Cloud), Norman Alden (as Capt. Horton). EP: Danny Thomas. P: Aaron Spelling.

Rango marked the first series starring Tim Conway following the successful run of *Mc-Hale's Navy* from 1962 to 1966. Unfortunately

Yep, I'm a Texas Ranger. Tim Conway points out that despite what it seems, he is a legitimate lawman, in the comedy *Rango*.

for him, his starring TV shows always were flops like this one. A better memory about *Rango* springs from the fact that it also was one of many TV collaborations between veteran character actor Norman Alden and producer Aaron Spelling.

"I would like it to be known that Aaron is responsible for so much of my career," Alden said. "I grew up with Aaron Spelling in Texas. He's from Dallas and I'm from Ft. Worth. We used to play ball on Sundays."

Cut to the late 1950s. Alden is acting on the Warner Bros. lot. "One day I was in the makeup department and I noticed on one sheet that Aaron Spelling was directing or producing something with Alan Ladd." Alden re-introduced himself to his old boyhood pal and "We became fast friends."

Years later, when Alden's agent secured him a role on *Rango*, Spelling surreptitiously told him to hold out for a certain amount of money to do the part. The actor followed suit. "I said, 'I won't work for less than this,' and gave him the figure Aaron gave me." Alden got the salary and the part.

"I played the captain of the [Texas] Rangers," Alden said of his job. Capt. Horton found his job at the Deep Wells Texas Ranger Station in Gopher Gulch, Texas, in the 1870s compromised by Ranger Rango, a well-meaning simpleton who found an equal at the station with the Indian Pink Cloud. Horton wanted to rid himself of Rango but, noted Alden, "He promised his [Rango's] father he'd take care of his son." With Rango's dad being head of the Rangers, there was little Horton could do.

Alden had high praise for his co-stars. "Conway was so funny," he said. "I thought he was one of the funniest men I ever met. Guy Marks was a brilliant, funny man. He [as Pink Cloud] was doing everything wrong; he'd do a war dance, and it'd rain."

The only thing that vexed Alden about the show was him being stuck pretty much in the role of straight man with no comic lines. "I talked with the writers, and they said, 'If it goes another season, Tim's like rich candy, and we need to use more of you,'" he said.

But, of course, there was no second season. Alden blames it on the show's time slot. "We were a young people's show, should've been on earlier in the evening," he said. "[Executive producer] Danny Thomas went to New York and tried to get the time changed." Against movies and the last half hour of *The Man from U.N.C.L.E.*, *Rango* died.

Still, Alden harbors a warm spot for *Rango*. How much? Well, he named his dog Rango, and as any canine lover can tell you, there's not much a higher tribute you can pay to someone or something than by doing that.

Everybody's Talking

Game. Ran on ABC Mondays through Fridays Noon–12:30 P.M. Feb. 6–Dec. 29, 1967, opposite *Love of Life* on CBS and *Jeopardy* on NBC. C: Lloyd Thaxton. EP: Jerome Schnur. P: Bill Chastain, Jorn Winther. D: Jorn Winther.

When *Everybody's Talking* joined the ABC daytime lineup in early 1967, that network's schedule already included the likes of *The Dating Game* and *The Newlywed Game*— series that basked in double entendres and other hints of naughtiness previously unheard on afternoon game shows. *Everybody's Talking* followed in that same vein.

"It was kind of a dirty show," said producer/director Jorn Winther. "You had an object like a mattress [as the answer], and you interviewed people on the street and big stars like Glenn Ford, and they'd ask questions like 'What do you like about it?' and they'd say 'I like it hard' or 'I like it soft.'"

Winther said the show's staff interviewed an average of about 60 people for each week's worth of shows to get their comments on the mystery noun which three in-studio contestants competed to be the first to identify. The first player to press a button got the chance to solve the puzzle, with the sooner a correct answer was given resulting in a higher point total for a player. That day's winner played a bonus round for more money and returned to face two new contestants for the next show. Before the show went off the air, three celebrities played the game each week for specific home viewers.

About 15 celebrities and ordinary citizens appeared in prerecorded clips each show. "We had probably about 10 or 12 editors for that show," Winther said about the editing of the man-on-the-street clips. He directed those clips as well as the studio part of the show.

Besides the proliferation of interviews, *Everybody's Talking* had the distinction of being the only show on daytime TV in 1967 whose creator, Jack Barry, had no credit on the show. Broadcasters still had not forgotten Barry being involved in the late 1950s quiz show scandals, with several of his productions, most notably *Twenty-One*, being revealed to be rigged. Executives worried that any mention of his name would provoke complaints even nearly a decade later, so his contribution went largely unnoticed except within the industry.

"I only saw him once," Winther said of Barry. He said while *Everybody's Talking* was Barry's idea, he worked mainly under executive producer Jerome Schnur, whom he called "A very smart man." At first Winther served only as the show's director, then halfway through its run he became its co-producer along with Bill Christian. He remained the show's in-studio director at the same time, but he no longer directed the man-on-the-street interviews due to time constraints.

Winther said the reason why *Everybody's Talking* didn't make it into 1968 was production costs, not ratings. "It was too expensive. We had a huge staff." The show, which had replaced reruns of *The Donna Reed Show*, was in

turn replaced by repeats of another ABC nighttime sitcom, *Bewitched*.

Dateline: Hollywood

Informational. Ran on ABC Mondays through Fridays 10:30–10:55 A.M. April 3–Sept. 29, 1967, opposite *The Beverly Hillbillies* reruns on CBS and *Concentration* on NBC. C: Joanna Barnes, Rona Barrett (by September). P: Richard Brill. D: Jonathan Lucas.

One in a Million

Game. Ran on ABC Mondays through Fridays 11:30 A.M.–Noon April 10–June 16, 1967, opposite *The Dick Van Dyke Show* reruns on CBS and *The Hollywood Squares* on NBC. C: Danny O'Neil. P: Stu Billet. D: Garth Dietrick, Alvin Mifelow. W: Don Segall, Roger Swaybill.

The Family Game

Game. Ran on ABC Mondays through Fridays 11:30 A.M.–Noon June 19–Dec. 29, 1967, opposite *The Dick Van Dyke Show* reruns on CBS and *The Hollywood Squares* on NBC. C: Bob Barker. P: Walt Case. D: Bill Carruthers, Seymour Robbie. W: Larry Gottleib.

The Honeymoon Race

Game. Ran on ABC Mondays through Fridays 11–11:30 A.M. July 17–Dec. 1, 1967, opposite *The Andy Griffith Show* reruns on CBS and *Personality* on NBC. C: Bill Malone. P: John Green. D: Lloyd Gross.

The Honeymoon Race grew out of *Supermarket Sweep*, a game show on ABC from Dec. 20, 1965, until this show replaced it. Director Lloyd Gross got involved in the latter show at the behest of its producer Jerome Schnur following the disastrous shooting of its pilot. "It looked like a hodgepodge," Gross recalled. Gross came in facing a daunting obstacle; the show planned to have contestants try and pile as many consumer goods into shopping carts at a different grocery store along the East Coast every week.

"The first one I did was from Stanford, Conn.," Gross said. "You would go into a supermarket Saturday night and set up the show. I used five huge color cameras and lit up the aisles. I was constantly readying shots, and it went over quite well."

Supermarket Sweep was the first show to air on ABC's daytime lineup for a year and a half. "After having gone town to town in the Northeast setting up grandstands, we went south and ended up in Hollywood, Fla.," Gross said. This Hollywood lies between Ft. Lauderdale and Miami. By that time *Supermarket Sweep* had lost one of its main sponsors, and the production company decided to try another game show, this time with a scavenger hunt involving three couples looking for hidden items at a mall. When officials connected with the Hollywood Mall heard about the plan, they offered the crew to use their mall permanently for it, and thus *The Honeymoon Race* was born.

Taped when the mall was not open (naturally), *The Honeymoon Race* superficially resembled *Supermarket Sweep* in giving players a time limit to collect merchandise, only here each time had to find five particular prizes. "They used golf carts to race down the alleys, stop and go into the store and take out the stuff involved. Each show had about 20 stores involved," Gross said. "The couple that won got a check."

Critics hated *Supermarket Sweep* and *The Honeymoon Race* for their base celebration of materialism, rewarding people for their greed rather than knowledge or ability. As far as the reason why he directed it, Gross laughed and said, "It wasn't *What's My Line?*, let's put it that way! They offered me more money, frankly, than I'd been getting."

Let's not forget the show's packager, Talent Associates Ltd., whose head was none other than prestigious TV talk show host and producer David Susskind. While berating much of what the medium offered, Susskind was mostly mum about his connection to the shows. "He quietly picked up the checks and let the show go on," Gross noted.

The Honeymoon Race did not do well against a new game show on NBC, *Personality*, nor the reliable *Andy Griffith Show*, so the format was redone later in 1967 to have the couples do stunts at the stores rather than hunt for missing items. That twist did not help either, so before the end of the year, ABC replaced it with *Temptation* (see 1967-68).

1967-68

Garrison's Gorillas

War Adventure. Ran on ABC Tuesdays 7:30–8:30 P.M. Sept. 5, 1967–Sept. 17, 1968, opposite *Daktari* on CBS and *I Dream of Jeannie* and *The Jerry Lewis Show* (through May 28) and *Showcase '68* (from June 11) on NBC. C: Ron Harper (as Lt. Craig Garrison), Cesare Danova (as Actor), Rudy Solari (as Casino), Christopher Cary (as Goniff), Brendan Boone (as Chief). EP: Selig J. Seligman. P: Richard Caffey. D: Joseph Sargent. W: David Carp.

Good Morning, World

Sitcom. Ran on CBS Tuesdays 9:30–10 P.M. Sept. 5, 1967–Sept. 17, 1968 opposite *N.Y.P.D.* on ABC and movies on NBC. C: Joby Baker (as Dave Lewis), Ronnie Schell (as Larry Clarke), Billy DeWolfe (as Roland B. Hutton, Jr.), Julie Parrish (as Linda Lewis), Goldie Hawn (as Sandy Kramer).

EP: Sheldon Leonard, Carl Reiner. P/W: Bill Persky, Sam Denoff, Bruce Johnson. D: Carl Reiner.

Good Morning, World grew out of the experiences of its creators, Bill Persky and Sam Denoff. "We worked at a radio station seven years before coming out to L.A.," Denoff said. The men were file managers at WNEW New York, where a top deejay was William B. Williams. "He said, 'Good morning, world,' at the start of his show, and he did it on the TV show too as a voiceover," Denoff said.

The series focused on two morning deejays in Los Angeles, "Lewis and Clarke," who reported to persnickety station operator Roland B. Hutton, Jr. Dave Lewis was married while Larry Clarke was a playboy. The contrasts in their personal and professional lives formed the crux of the comedy.

The happy cast of *Good Morning, World* consisted of, clockwise from top left: Billy De Wolfe, Goldie Hawn, Ronnie Schell, Joby Baker and Julie Parrish.

But it was the lowest-billed regular who got the most out of *Good Morning, World*. Goldie Hawn has been a dancer on an Andy Griffith TV special when her representative from the William Morris Agency sent to her to

read for the part of Linda Lewis. "He thought there was something special with her," Denoff remembered. "This little blonde girl showed up at our office with own coffee and coffeepot to read the part." While noting that "She was not a trained actress" and deciding to use Julie Parrish in the role instead, Persky and Denoff did not forget her and cast Hawn as Linda's pal Sandy. "She was just glorious," Denoff said.

When the series was picked up halfway through its run, Denoff and Persky gave Hawn a raise because of her fine work, which stunned her. She was so appreciative that she even invited them to manage her, an offer they declined. Nevertheless, they did make her character into Larry Clarke's steady girlfriend and involved her more in the plots.

But while Goldie shone, lead actor Joby Baker was not as relaxed in his role as the producers felt he could be. He was fine during rehearsals, but something changed when they filmed the shows before a live audience. "He had some terrible flukes on the shooting days," Denoff said. "He would lose his lines. He would have flop sweat." Baker, primarily a comic actor in films, was a regular in one other series, the irregularly scheduled *Six O'Clock Follies* in 1980 (which did not have a studio audience), before becoming a successful artist.

Beyond that, Denoff found little at fault with the show, though he noted that he and Persky could not devote their full time to overseeing it. "We had to divide our attention between that show and *That Girl*," he said, mentioning the other program they produced at the time. The show tested well in preview audiences, but it never carried near the amount of viewers of its lead-in, *The Red Skelton Show*. CBS replaced it with *The Doris Day Show*, which ran until 1973, while Goldie Hawn struck gold in the fall of 1968 by joining *Rowan and Martin's Laugh-In* as its regular dumb blonde, which she left after two years for a top movie career.

Custer

Western. Ran on ABC Wednesdays 7:30–8:30 P.M. Sept. 6–Dec. 27, 1967, opposite *Lost in Space* on CBS and *The Virginian* on NBC. C: Wayne Maunder (as Lt. Col. George A. Custer), Slim Pickens (as California Joe Milner), Peter Palmer (as Sgt. James Bustard), Michael Dante (as Chief Crazy Horse), Robert F. Simon (as Brig. Gen. Alfred Terry), Grant Woods (as Capt. Miles Keogh). P: Robert Jacks. D: Sam Wanamaker. W: Samuel A. Peeples.

He & She

Sitcom. Ran on CBS Wednesdays 9:30–10 P.M. Sept. 6, 1967–Sept. 18, 1968, opposite movies on ABC and *The Kraft Music Hall* on NBC. C: Paula Prentiss (as Paula Hollister), Richard Benjamin (as Dick Hollister), Jack Cassidy (as Oscar North), Kenneth Mars (as Harry Zarakardos), Hamilton Camp (as Andrew Hummel), Harold Gould (as Norman Nugent). EP/D/W: Leonard B. Stern. P: Don Melnick, Arne Sultan. D: Jay Sandrich, Reza S. Badiyi. W: Allan Burns, Chris Hayward.

"[CBS programming president] Mike Dann did say it was the best show I ever cancelled," said *He & She* creator Leonard B. Stern of his brainchild. Comedian Pat Paulsen made the same statement mockingly at the 1968 Emmy awards, where *He & She* won for writing in a comedy (for Allan Burns and Chris Hayward) along with nominations for actors Paula Prentiss, Richard Benjamin and Jack Cassidy — but strangely no nomination for Outstanding Comedy Series.

Regardless of who said or thought what, Stern said that "It was a personal favorite of mine. Across the country, the reviews were incredible."

He & She involved a young couple in New York City. Dick Hollister was a cartoonist whose creation, the superhero Jetman, was played by egotistical actor Oscar North on a TV series. Paula was his exuberant wife. Their neighbor Harry the fireman lived in an apartment where he oddly walked a plank between their windows to visit (it was on the bottom floor, thankfully). Other characters were the apartment handyman, Andrew Hummel, and Dick's boss, Norman Nugent.

Stern got a near-sale when he pitched the show. "Mike Dann said to me, 'Leonard, if you can get Paula Prentiss to commit, you've got a pilot.'" Prentiss was hot at the time in films like *What's New Pussycat?* Stern learned she'd do it only if her real-life husband, Richard Benjamin, costarred.

"Dick had done nothing on film or television or Broadway," Stern said. "By chance my wife had seen him in Chicago in [the stage comedy] *Barefoot in the Park* and told me you'll love him." Stern took his wife's recommendation and signed Benjamin.

But to some the real star of the show was Jack Cassidy as vain Oscar North. "Jack was an especially fond memory," Stern said. "He was

Ken Mars wraps his right arm around Richard Benjamin while Hamilton Camp and Paula Prentiss observe on *He & She*.

probably the first suggested gay to be on television. He did unnerve the network somewhat. He stepped beyond the bounds of what they considered good taste."

With all the talent involved, *He & She* seemed like a shoo-in for success. Stern believes its time slot destroyed that possibility. "It followed *Green Acres*, and it was incompatible with that show," he said. "It was so different in its intentions."

However, Stern noted toward the end of the season the show won its period as people became accustomed to its sophisticated humor. The network had second thoughts about canceling it, but Stern did not push them to do so. As he honestly admitted, "I always felt we had a great year, and maybe would not have as good a second year."

CBS reran *He & She* from June 26 to Sept. 11, 1970. A week after the repeats ended

The Mary Tyler Moore Show debuted with *He & She* writer Allan Burns as co-executive producer. The show received permission from Stern to do a variation on Oscar North to make him the blustery anchorman Ted Baxter on that show (ironically, Jack Cassidy appeared as Ted's brother in one episode). Building on what *He & She* had done, *The Mary Tyler Moore Show* became the commercial and critical hit the former show should have been. Many feel it couldn't have done so without *He & She* paving the way.

Dundee and the Culhane

Western. Ran on CBS Wednesdays 10–11 P.M. Sept. 6–Dec. 13, 1967, opposite movies on ABC and *Run for Your Life* on NBC. C: John Mills (as Dundee), Sean Garrison (as Culhane). P: Sam Rolfe. D: Boris Sagal. W: Ernest Frankel.

Cimarron Strip

Western. Ran on CBS Thursdays 7:30–9 P.M. Sept. 7, 1967–Sept. 19, 1968, opposite *Batman* (through March 14), *The Second Hundred Years* (from March 21), *The Flying Nun* and *Bewitched* on ABC and *Daniel Boone* and *Ironside* on NBC. C: Stuart Whitman (as U.S. Marshal Jim Crown), Percy Herbert (as MacGregor), Randy Boone (as Francis Wilde), Jill Townsend (as Dulcey Coopersmith). EP: Philip Leacock. P: Bernard McEveety. W: Jack Curtis.

Good Company

Interview. Ran on ABC Thursdays 10–10:30 P.M. Sept. 7–Dec. 21, 1967, opposite movies on CBS and *The Dean Martin Show* on NBC. C: F. Lee Bailey. EP: David Susskind. P: John Aaron. D: Jack Murphy.

The Second Hundred Years

Sitcom. Ran on ABC Wednesdays 8:30–9 P.M. Sept. 8, 1967–Feb. 28, 1968, opposite *The Beverly Hillbillies* on CBS and *The Virginian* on NBC, then ABC Thursdays 7:30–8 P.M. March 21–Sept. 19, 1968, opposite *Cimarron Strip* on CBS and *Daniel Boone* on NBC. C: Monte Markham (as Luke and Ken Carpenter), Arthur O'Connell (as Edwin Carpenter), Frank Maxwell (as Col. Garroway), Karen Black (as Marcia Garroway), Bridget Hanley (as Nurse Lucille Anderson). EP: Harry Ackerman. P: Bob Claver. D: Jud Taylor.

Cowboy in Africa

Adventure. Ran on ABC Mondays 7:30–8:30 P.M. Sept. 11, 1967–Sept. 16, 1968, opposite *Gunsmoke* on CBS and *The Monkees* and *The Man from U.N.C.L.E.* (through Jan. 15), *Rowan and Martin's Laugh-In* (from Jan. 22 to May 27) and *The Champions* (from June 10) on NBC. C: Chuck Connors (as Jim Sinclair), Tom Nardini (as John Henry), Ronald Howard (as Wing Comdr. Howard Hayes), Gerald Edwards (as Samson). EP: Andy White. P: George Cahan. D: Andrew Marton.

Hondo

Western. Ran on ABC Fridays 8:30–9:30 P.M. opposite *Gomer Pyle, U.S.M.C.* and movies on CBS and *Star Trek* on NBC. C: Ralph Taeger (as Hondo Lane), Noah Beery, Jr. (as Buffalo Baker), Kathie Browne (as Angie Dow), Buddy Foster (as Johnny Dow), Gary Clarke (as Capt. Richards), Michael Pate (as Chief Vittoro). P/W: Andrew J. Fenady. D: Lee H. Katzin.

Based on the 1953 film of the same name, which originally was released in 3-D, *Hondo* told the tale of a rugged cavalry scout with sideburns trying to maintain peace in 1869 at Fort Lowell in the Arizona Territory. Hondo Lane had been on both sides of the battles between cowboys and Indians, including seeing his fiancée, an Apache woman who was the daughter of Chief Vittoro, being killed by the cavalry, and tried his best to prevent further violence in the area. Giving him support in his mission were his amiable fellow scout Buffalo Baker, pretty widow Angie Dow and her son Johnny, and Hondo's pet pooch, Sam. Capt. Richards was Hondo's superior.

Director Lee H. Katzin became a part of the production due to his connection with its producer and writer, Andrew J. Fenady. "I got into the Directors Guild via him on *The Rebel*," Katzin said, referring to the 1959–61 western series that Fenady created. "Andy had made a deal with Batjac Productions to try *Hondo* as a series, and I loved westerns, so I did it."

Katzin directed the show's two-part pilot that was released in Europe as a theatrical movie under the title *Hondo and the Apaches*, plus a few other episodes. The shows were shot both in Los Angeles studio and on location in Lancaster, Calif., for outdoor scenes.

"There was a big problem with the show. Ralph Taeger was a nitwit, and a big problem at the time. He didn't handle things well at the time." Katzin noted that he approved of all the cast except for Taeger, whom Fenady selected without running him by Katzin first.

"He was a very sweet person, but very ornery too," Katzin added. He pointed to the pre-show publicity which Taeger was to do as an example. Because the series was with John Wayne's Batjac production company, and Wayne had starred in the 1953 *Hondo*, there were plans for the two men to film a promo together to publicize the new show — an old Hondo and a new one, so to speak. Taeger flew to the set where Wayne was filming the movie *The Green Berets*.

"They got down there, and what happens in movies occasionally, they were running late," Katzin said. "They were supposed to do it at noon, then one, then two, and Ralph got tired and left." By not waiting just a little longer, Taeger passed up a chance to do a unique promotion for the show that might have drawn people to give it a look, in Katzin's opinion. (In fairness to Taeger, I contacted him for this book, but he never responded to my offer.)

Actually, even had the promo been done, it would not have changed the fact that *Hondo* was running opposite *Gomer Pyle, U.S.M.C.*, the #3 series in the 1967-68 season. After a losing 17-week run, ABC replaced it with the only slightly longer-running variety series *Operation: Entertainment*.

Accidental Family

Sitcom. Ran on NBC Fridays 9:30–10 P.M. Sept. 15, 1967–Jan. 5, 1968, opposite *The Guns of Will Sonnett* on ABC and movies on CBS. C: Jerry Van Dyke (as Jerry Webster), Lois Nettleton (as Sue Kramer), Teddy Quinn (as Sandy Webster), Susan Benjamin (as Tracy Kramer), Ben Blue (as Ben McGrath), Larry D. Mann (as Marty Warren). EP/D: Sheldon Leonard. P: Sy Gomberg. W: Melville Shavelson.

In a 1968 issue of *Mad* magazine (#121, to be exact!), a parody of *The Flying Nun* ended with "Bishop Fulton J. Showbiz" introducing other new funny religious sitcoms planned to hit the airwaves—*Jungle Rabbi, Frontier Buddhist, Amish Eye* and *My Three Muslims*. Compounding the joke was that each new series starred Jerry Van Dyke, a man who had the worst track record of leading roles in regular series in the 1960s, up to and including *Accidental Family*, which was off the air a few months before the *Mad* issue ran.

Van Dyke's first regular series role was as host of a summer game show called *Picture This* in 1963. The fall of that year, he turned up as a regular sidekick on *The Judy Garland Show* (see 1963-64), but he was gone by the time 1964 arrived. Next came the infamous *My Mother the Car* (see 1965-66), and after a season off he missed the mark for the fourth time with *Accidental Family*, which ran even shorter than did *My Mother the Car*.

The original title for the series was *Everywhere a Chick Chick*. Executive producer and creator Sheldon Leonard called it that because, according to writer Melville Shavelson, "It was the idea of a nightclub performer having a second life at the farm he owned and having to divide his time between the two things."

However, the show became known as *Accidental Family* instead because of the odd circumstances surrounding its principals. Following the death of his wife, comedian Jerry Webster had to be more of a parent to his 8-year-old Sandy, and to that end he and his son moved into a farmhouse Jerry owned in the San Fernando Valley in California. Plans for the two went awry when they learned that his tenants—Sue Kramer, her 8-year-old daughter, and Sue's uncle Ben McGrath—could not be evicted. A compromise was reached where Sue and company could stay without rent provided she act as guardian to Sandy while Jerry was performing and Ben serve as resident handyman. The other regular, Marty Warren, was Jerry's manager.

Shavelson wrote the pilot but not all the episodes. "We had various writers off and on," he said, though he couldn't recall offhand who else was involved. He had no real idea why the show did not catch fire.

However, given that Leonard had also been executive producer of Van Dyke's brother's hit show, *The Dick Van Dyke Show*, some viewers and critics might have expected a sitcom along those lines and found *Accidental Family* coming up short in comparison. To that notion, Shavelson said, "It's tough to evaluate. Talent like Dick Van Dyke comes along not too often."

In any event, NBC replaced the series with a nighttime version of *The Hollywood Squares*. Van Dyke would not do another regular role until 1970-71's *The Headmaster*— yep, another flop. He finally broke the curse in 1989 with *Coach*, which ran until 1997.

Maya

Adventure. Ran on NBC Saturdays 7:30–8:30 P.M. Sept. 16, 1967–Feb. 10, 1968, opposite *The Dating Game* and *The Newlywed Game* on ABC and *The Jackie Gleason Show* on CBS. C: Jay North (as Terry Bowen), Sajid Khan (as Raji). P: Frank and Maurice King. D: Marvin Chomsky. W: Stirling Silliphant.

Temptation

Game. Ran on ABC Mondays through Fridays 11–11:25 A.M. Dec. 4, 1967–March 1, 1968, opposite *The Andy Griffith Show* reruns on CBS and *Personality* on NBC. C: Art James. EP: Merrill Heatter, Bob Quigley. D: Marty Pasetta.

Temptation obviously did not live up to its title in attracting viewers, nor did it particularly appeal to its host, Art James. "It was a miserable show to do," he said. "There were stage displays of prizes for every round. And then we had to strike the set and put a new display up after the round. It took forever. It took until 2 or 3 o'clock in the morning [to finish taping]."

The dubious concept was for three players to view a trio of merchandise items— one low-priced, one moderately valued, and one expensive — and try and pick the one they thought the other would not select so that he or she could win the prize. Five rounds occurred per show, no doubt to James' distress, with a twist being added in the third and fourth rounds in that players got a hint of what two of them (neither identified) had chosen, and with that knowledge in mind could change their initial pick. The winner with the highest total came back as returning champion for the next show. It was sort of a cross between *Let's Make a Deal* and *The Price Is Right*, only without their excitement.

James had been hosting a syndicated game show called *Matches 'n' Mates* when he got the nod to do *Temptation*. Asked how he got onto the latter series, he noted that "Word gets around, and I probably was seduced by my agent." The show's producers, Merrill Heatter and Bob Quigley, were hot at the time with *The Hollywood Squares* (which aired on NBC in the time slot following *Temptation*), but James was not impressed by them.

"They were cruel to their contestants before the show," he said. "They treated them scornfully and sarcastically." James said that Heatter was the main producer for the show (Quigley was a former comedy writer for Victor Borge, among other acts). Despite disdaining the way the duo ran their operation, James would later guest on *The Hollywood Squares* and host another Heatter-Quigley flop (see *The Magnificent Marble Machine* in 1974-75).

After three months, ABC was so unhappy with the ratings of this series as well as its lead-in, reruns of *The Donna Reed Show*, and its lead-out, *How's Your Mother-in-Law?* (q.v.), that it gave the whole 90-minute slot (10:30 A.M.–noon) to Dick Cavett, who later took the show to ABC late night in 1969. That was it for *Temptation*, but oddly several of the show's

personnel, namely James, model Mary Poms and director Marty Pasetta reunited in 1985 to do another game show, a syndicated daily number called *Catch Phrase*. (Poms was billed as "Shana Forman.") James said it was a "happy circumstance" and not something done by design. The show lasted just a few months because its visual word puzzles were said to be too hard for viewers to understand. Sounds like those people must have been the only fans of *Temptation*.

How's Your Mother-in-Law?

Game. Ran on ABC Mondays through Fridays 11:30 A.M.–Noon Dec. 4, 1967–March 1, 1968, opposite *The Dick Van Dyke Show* reruns on CBS and *The Hollywood Squares* on NBC. C: Wink Martindale. P/W: Mike Metzger. D: Gene Law.

Treasure Isle

Game. Ran on ABC Mondays through Fridays 12:30–1 P.M. Dec. 18, 1967–Dec. 27, 1968, opposite *Search for Tomorrow* and *Guiding Light* (through Sept. 6) on CBS and *Eye Guess* on NBC. C: John Bartholomew Tucker. EP/Announcer: Bill Templeton. P/D: Paul Alter. P: Roy Kammerman. D: Peter Calabrasse.

When game shows from the production company of Mark Goodson and Bill Todman "were at a low ebb," as Paul Alter put it, the director took a look at a pilot at an odd show with a transparent board game leading to a destination called Treasure Isle with bikini-clad ladies. "The course to Treasure Isle was charted out like a map, and I said, 'Why don't you build a lagoon?'" Alter basically inspired the production to live up to its name, and for that he got creator credit for the show.

Alter became a partner in the production company as well with John MacArthur, "about the sixth richest millionaire in America," according to the director. Despite that source of revenue, Alter claimed that "We never got enough money from MacArthur to do what we wanted to do. I imagined a lagoon with false monkeys and other things."

What Alter actually got was a lagoon with two miniature islands at MacArthur's Colonnades Beach Hotel property in Palm Beach Shores, Florida. With 50 tons of cement poured for a foundation to withstand 5,000 pounds of water pressure per square inch, the artificial lake could store up to 2 million tons of water. "I fell off of the island before they were finished building it and broke a toe," Alter recalled.

In the main game, two married or engaged couples retrieved puzzle pieces floating in the water which formed an incomprehensible four-line rhyming poem when put on a board on one island. Once the pieces were in place on the board, clues from each line translated one by one until one of the couples named the real or fictional person described by it. That couple then went to the second island where they had two minutes to hunt for hidden boxes containing pieces of paper with various merchandise prizes listed on them for the couple to keep.

That rather benign description belies how wacky a show *Treasure Isle* was to watch. Host John Bartholomew Tucker, billing himself as "JBT on ABC," seemed bewildered at times in calling the action around him, whether it was describing swimsuit-wearing couples struggling to swim to foam puzzle pieces in the lake or, in one memorable show, having to croak a few bars of "Don't Fence Me In" during the bonus round to indicate to a couple the goods were at the fence! Even more bizarre was that the show's executive producer Bill Templeton was its announcer. Billed as "Sage," he spoke in such a low, and low-key, manner that he sounded more like a commentator on a bowling match or round of golf rather than a high-energy game.

Alter viewed his creation differently. "It was before its time," he said. "If you look at *Survivor* or any of those reality shows, that's what you had." However, there are no plans I have heard to resurrect *Treasure Isle* following a network run where for a year it finished in last place against its competition.

The Baby Game

Game. Ran on ABC Mondays through Fridays 2:30–2:55 P.M. Jan. 1–July 12, 1968, opposite *Art Linkletter's House Party* on CBS and *The Doctors* on NBC. C: Richard Hayes. P: Eric Leiber, Bob Synes. D: Mike Garguilo.

Wedding Party

Game. Ran on ABC Mondays through Fridays 1:30–2 P.M. April 1–July 12, 1968, opposite *As the World Turns* on CBS and *Let's Make a Deal* on

NBC. C: Al Hamel. EP: Art Stark. P: Roy Kammerman, Fred Tatashore. D: Michael Gargiulo.

ABC's early afternoon daily lineup in mid–1968 took straight aim at attracting the young housewife, with its game shows emphasizing couples who were just married or about to be. From 1–2:30 P.M. the schedule consisted of *Dream House*, *Wedding Party*, and *The Newlywed Game*. *The Newlywed Game* ran by the far the longest, from 1966 to 1974 followed by numerous revivals. *Dream House*, featuring two newlywed couples vying to win a home, ran from April 1, 1968 to Jan. 2, 1970.

Running between these two entries was the least successful of the bunch. *Wedding Party* featured a couple attempting to make a match on what item one of them picked while the other was off stage and not listening to the partner. It was a process at least one participant felt made it a stupid game. "It was a dreadful show," said director Michael Gargiulo.

Typically the "picker" had the option of three styles of some furniture merchandise to select and hope his or her partner guessed the same. "It's the classic multiple choice — modern, traditional or regency," Gargiulo said. "It was kind of silly, because most of the time the guy didn't care." If they did match, the couple won not only the prize but a vacation for their honeymoon.

Gargiulo did remember one pair set to be married who guested on the show, but not for what they did during the game. "We used to open up with a silhouette of two people kissing. They were one of our couples on the show. One day we had a Hassidic Jewish couple who can't kiss before they got married. We convinced them they could do it with their faces out of alignment."

Hosting the show was Alan Hamel in what was his first American series. Gargiulo recalled that "We brought him down from Canada. He was doing an ersatz *Tonight Show* up there." Actually, Hamel continued to do that Toronto-based series, titled *In Person*, by commuting to New York City Thursdays and Fridays to tape *Wedding Party* before returning home. Hamel later appeared in America hosting two syndicated series, *The Anniversary Game* from 1969 to 1970 and the talk show *Mantrap* in 1971. He is best known today as the husband and one-time manager of his wife, actress Suzanne Somers.

Wedding Party went off after three months to be replaced oddly by a teenage music series from Dick Clark Productions, *It's Happening*, an extension of the Saturday afternoon series *Happening '68*. Both shows were hosted by Paul Revere and the Raiders, who previously hosted the similar daily series *Where the Action Is* from 1965 to 1967. *It's Happening* wasn't happening anymore after Oct. 25, 1968, although the Saturday *Happening* ran for another year. Taking over the time slot for *It's Happening* was an-other short-lived game show, *Funny You Should Ask* (see 1968-69).

Man in a Suitcase

Adventure. Ran on ABC Fridays 8:30–9:30 P.M. May 3–Sept. 20, 1968, opposite *Gomer Pyle, U.S.M.C.* and movies on CBS and *Star Trek* on NBC. C: Richard Bradford (as McGill). P: Sidney Cole. D: Charles Crichton. W: Francis Magahy, Bernie Cooper.

1968-69

The Beautiful Phyllis Diller Show

Comedy Variety. Ran on NBC Sundays 10–11 P.M. Sept. 15–Dec. 22, 1968, opposite movies on ABC and *Mission: Impossible* on CBS. C: Phyllis Diller, Norm Crosby, Rip Taylor, Dave Willock, Bob Jellison, Merryl Joy, the Curtain Calls, the Jack Regas Dancers, the Jack Elliott Orchestra. EP: Bob Finkel. P/W: Saul Turtletaub, Bernie Orenstein. D: Barry Shear. W: Bob Weiskopf, Bob Schiller, George Balzar, Keith Fowler, Stan Dreben, Hart Pomerantz, Lorne Michaels, Gordon Farr.

A year after the failure of her sitcom *The Pruitts of Southampton* (see 1966-67), Phyllis Diller made a second attempt to star in a TV series, but this variety show lasted even less time on the air than her previous effort. Executive producer Bob Finkel did not recall how he came involved with the program other than being asked to do it at the time, but he accepted the assignment because of his respect for Diller. "I had seen her in her very early days at a club called Interlude on the [Sunset] Strip [in Hollywood]," he said. "I fell in love with her comedy."

As Diller was prone to make fun of her looks in act, that became the basis for the show's setup. "We decided to play against her homeliness," Finkel said. "For example, everything on the credits were 'The Beautiful Electrician,' 'The Beautiful Associate Producer,' etc."

There was a hefty supporting crew of comics, dancers and singers (the Curtain Calls) to assist Diller in big production numbers, and Finkel recalled an animated portion of the show between sketches involved a takeoff on the Mount Rushmore monument in South Dakota. "We had the four presidents on the mountain talking to each other," he said. "That was funny."

But not all the plans for the show came off smoothly. The biggest disaster came courtesy of an idea from director Barry Shear. "He had platforms in the audience so they could move around to various places in the studio where the scenes were," Finkel said. "However, that lasted one week. We couldn't stop it once, and the audience went into the wall!" Shear employed the more traditional method of changing sets on a stage while the audience was stationary thereafter.

Other than the platform mishap, Finkel felt the only thing that really hurt *The Beautiful Phyllis Diller Show* was its star. As he put it, "Phyllis was a standup comedienne. Scripted material was not for her. And she was not too good at exchanges with other performers. I don't think she really enjoyed it."

Neither did NBC, apparently. Seeing that the series was unable to carry over the large audience watching *Bonanza* from 9 to 10 p.m., the network replaced it at the end of 1968 with *My Friend Tony* (q.v.). Diller remained a popular guest thereafter, mostly on variety specials and

Many dramatic stars from the 1950s through 1970s found themselves having to appear on comedy variety shows as part of their duties, which explains why Fess Parker made an unlikely appearance sending up his Daniel Boone character (with Phyllis Diller as his frontier wife!) on the Nov. 3, 1968, edition of *The Beautiful Phyllis Diller Show.*

talk shows, but she never had another shot as a regular TV attraction.

The Outsider

Drama. Ran on NBC Wednesdays 10–11 P.M. Sept. 18, 1968–Sept. 3, 1969, opposite movies on ABC and *The Jonathan Winters Show* (through Dec. 18) and *Hawaii Five-O* (from Dec. 25) on CBS. C: Darren McGavin (as David Ross). EP: Roy Huggins. P: Gene Levitt.

Producer Roy Huggins found himself in the bittersweet position of replacing one of his series with another of his own productions in 1968. In this case, the losing series was *Run for Your Life*, which while no blockbuster was still doing OK in the ratings after a three-year run when NBC aired its last episode on Sept. 11, 1968, and filled it the next week with *The Outsider*. According to Huggins, its cancellation became a foregone conclusion because of its setup of having star Ben Gazzara's character being diagnosed as terminally ill, thus leading him to pursue adventures around the world.

"I said in the pilot 'You only have two years to live,' and Paul Klein [a research executive for NBC] told me people believe that literally, so we can't have the show keep running longer than he's supposed to live," Huggins said. Luckily in the face of this rather ridiculous explanation, Huggins had another program idea waiting in the wings.

The Outsider first aired as a TV-movie pilot on Nov. 21, 1967. It was one of the first of its kind, with only TV-movie pilots for *The Iron Horse*, *The Name of the Game* and *Ironside* having aired previously in the 1966-67 season, and all but *The Iron Horse* were productions of Universal Studios. Darren McGavin played David Ross, an atypical TV private eye in that was a paroled ex-convict who had spent a half-dozen years in the hoosegow while innocent of murder charges. That situation, plus his status as a loner on a low budget working in Los Angeles, clearly shows the influence of this show's premise on Huggins' future hit *The Rockford Files* (1974–80).

Huggins wrote and produced the TV-movie, which performed well enough to encourage NBC to try it as a series. McGavin reprised his role in the series, but Huggins disliked him for the part.

"Universal insisted I use an actor that I did not think was right for the role," he said. McGavin was a familiar TV name at the time thanks to two moderately successful series, the syndicated *Mickey Spillane's Mike Hammer* from 1957 to 1959 and the NBC western *Riverboat* from 1959 to 1961. "He was a nice fellow, but my style of acting favors cool, and his style was hot."

Huggins gave it a shot with McGavin doing the premiere episode, but all that did was convince him how wrong McGavin was for what Huggins wanted. "When I saw the first show we did after the pilot, the 'X' factor had to come out of the performance, and it didn't," he said. "I produced only the pilot. I then turned the series over to someone else."

The Outsider did not perform as well as NBC hoped even against rather weak competition (*Hawaii Five-O* did not become a hit at this time during its first season, although it would draw more viewers in 1969-70). NBC replaced it with another short-lived series, *Then Came Bronson* (q.v.).

The Outcasts

Western. Ran on ABC Mondays 9–10 P.M. Sept. 23, 1968–Sept. 15, 1969, opposite *Mayberry R.F.D.* and *Family Affair* on CBS and movies on NBC. C: Don Murray (as Earl Corey), Otis Young (as Jemal David). EP: Hugh Benson. P: Jon Epstein. D: E.W. Swackhamer. W: Leon Tokatyan.

That's Life

Musical Comedy. Ran on ABC Tuesdays 10–11 P.M. Sept. 24, 1968–May 20, 1969, opposite *60 Minutes* on CBS and movies on NBC. C: Robert Morse (as Robert Dickson), E.J. Peaker (as Gloria Quigley Dickson). EP/W: Marvin Marx. P/D: Stan Harris. W: Rod Parker, Bob Ellison, Walter Stone.

Blondie

Sitcom. Ran on CBS Thursdays 7:30–8 P.M. Sept. 26, 1968–Jan. 9, 1969, opposite *The Ugliest Girl in Town* on ABC and *Daniel Boone* on NBC. C: Patricia Harty (as Blondie), Will Hutchins (as Dagwood Bumstead), Jim Backus (as Mr. J.C. Dithers), Peter Robbins (as Alexander), Pamelyn Ferdin (as Cookie), Henny Backus (as Cora Dithers), Bobbi Jordan (as Tootsie Woodley), Bryan O'Byrne (as Mr. Beasley). EP: Al Brodax. P: Joe Connelly. D: Norman Abbott. W: Gary Belkin, George Tibbles.

Funny You Should Ask!!

Game. Ran on ABC Mondays through Fridays 1:30–2 P.M. Oct. 28–Dec. 27, 1968, opposite *As the World Turns* on CBS and *Let's Make a Deal* on NBC, then ABC Mondays through Fridays 12:30–1 P.M. Dec. 30, 1968–June 27, 1969, opposite *Search for Tomorrow* on CBS and *Eye Guess* on NBC. C: Lloyd Thaxton, Stu Gilliam, Jan Murray. EP: Merrill Heatter, Bob Quigley. P/W: Stan Dreben. D: Jorn Winther.

Funny You Should Ask!! was a variant on an earlier game show from executive producers Merrill Heatter and Bob Quigley called *The Celebrity Game*, which ran on CBS nighttime from April 5, 1964 to Sept. 9, 1965. That show asked players to guess whether a panel of celebrities answered yes or no to provocative questions. *Funny You Should Ask!!* had Lloyd Thaxton first ask five celebrities their responses to a question while two players were in a soundproof booth. The players then both had to guess which of each often humorous answer came from which celebrity. Each round had the contestants try to match four answers with celebrities, and anyone who correctly matched a celebrity to his or her answer four times in one round won the "Funny Money" jackpot, which increased $100 per round. Contestants had to go back to the soundproof booths each round to allow Thaxton to ask the celebrities a new question.

"You had Rose Marie, Phyllis Diller, Morey Amsterdam, all the comedians on it," noted the show's director, Jorn Winther, about the celebrities on the panel. The most frequently appearing celebrities were comedians too—Jan Murray, who previously had hosted and produced many game shows of his own, and Stu Gilliam, a black comic who had been a regular on the nighttime summer series *Dean Martin Presents the Golddiggers* in 1968. Gilliam looked to be a promising star but never made it to the top, as his career languished in the 1970s doing mostly voices for cartoons plus a failed sitcom called *Roll Out!* (see 1973-74). Murray and Gilliam typically alternated weeks on which they did the show rather than appear together.

The show's other regular, host Lloyd Thaxton, was reunited in working with director Jorn Winther less than a year after they had collaborated on *Everybody's Talking* (see 1967-68). "He was very easy to work with," Winther

said. "He also came from music." (Thaxton had hosted a syndicated rock music series under his name from 1964 to 1967, plus hosted a summer nighttime musical talent series on NBC in 1968 called *Showcase '68*.)

Winther added about Thaxton, "He was very bright, very good. He acted as the straight man to the stars. The stars came in and respected him. He maybe could've been a little more lively." Even with that caveat, Winther thought the show ran well and had no reason to give about why it didn't appeal to more viewers.

Funny You Should Ask!! was slaughtered in the ratings in its original time slot opposite two of the biggest daytime hits, *As the World Turns* and *Let's Make a Deal*. When the latter moved to ABC at the end of 1968, the network kept it at the same time slot while giving *Funny You Should Ask!!* a reprieve at an earlier time slot, but it came in third there too, so in the summer of 1969 ABC replaced it with reruns of *That Girl*. Thaxton did no other game shows afterward, preferring to move into production instead.

The Ugliest Girl in Town

Sitcom. Ran on ABC Sept. 26, 1968–Jan. 30, 1969, opposite *Blondie* (through Jan. 9) and *The Queen and I* (from Jan. 16) on CBS and *Daniel Boone* on NBC. C: Peter Kastner (as Tim/Timmie Blair), Patricia Brake (as Julie Renfield), Garry Marshall (as Gene Blair), Jenny Till (as Sondra Wolston), Nicholas Parsons (as David Courtney). EP: Harry Ackerman. P: Robert Kaufman, Jerry Bernstein. D: James Frawley. W: Robert Kaufman.

The Don Rickles Show

Comedy Variety. Ran on ABC Fridays 9–9:30 P.M. Sept. 27, 1968–Jan. 31, 1969, opposite movies on CBS and *The Name of the Game* on NBC. C: Don Rickles, Pat McCormick, the Vic Mizzy Orchestra. P: Frank Wayne. D: Dick Carson. W: Pat McCormick, Jack Riley, Eddie Ryder, Frank Ray.

Hidden Faces

Soap Opera. Ran on NBC Mondays through Fridays 1:30–2 P.M. Dec. 30, 1968–June 27, 1969, opposite *Let's Make a Deal* on ABC and *As the World Turns* on CBS. C: Conrad Fowkes (as Arthur Adams), Gretchen Walther (as Dr. Katherine Logan), Louise Shaffer (as Martha Logan),

Stephen Joyce (as Mark Utley), Tony LoBianco (as Nick Capello Turner), Nat Polen (as Earl Harriman), Joseph Daly (as Sen. Robert Jaffe), Rita Gam (as Mimi Jaffe), Linda Blair (as Allyn Jaffe), John Towley (as Wilbur Ensley), Ludi Claire (as Grace Ensley). P: Charles Fisher. D: Norman Hall, Marvin Silbersher. W: Irving Vendig.

The Storybook Squares

Game/Children's Version of *The Hollywood Squares*. Ran on NBC Saturdays Noon–12:30 P.M. Jan. 4–Aug. 30, 1969, opposite *George of the Jungle* on ABC and *Shazzam!* on CBS. C: Peter Marshall. EP: Merrill Heatter, Bob Quigley. P: Jay Redack. D: Jerome Shaw.

My Friend Tony

Detective Drama. Ran on NBC Sundays 10–11 P.M. Jan. 5–Sept. 31, 1969, opposite movies on ABC and *Mission: Impossible* on CBS. C: James Whitmore (as Prof. John Woodruff), Enzo Cerusico (as Tony Novello). EP: Sheldon Leonard. P: Art Seid, Ernest Frankel. D: Chris Nyby. W: Jerry Thomas.

The Queen and I

Sitcom. Ran on CBS Thursdays 7:30–8 P.M. Jan. 16–May 1, 1969, opposite *The Ugliest Girl in Town* (through Jan. 30) and *The Flying Nun* (from Feb. 6) on ABC and *Daniel Boone* on NBC. C: P/D: Edward H. Feldman. W: Laurence Marks, Arthur Julian.

Turn-On

Comedy. Ran on ABC Wednesday 8:30–9 P.M. Feb. 5, 1969, opposite *The Good Guys* on CBS and *The Virginian* on NBC. C: Bonnie Boland, Hamilton Camp, Teresa Graves, Ken Greenwald, Maxine Greene, Carlos Manteca, Chuck McCann, Maura McGiveney, Alma Murphy, Cecile Ozorio, Bob Staats, Mel Stuart. EP: George Schlatter. P: Digby Wolfe. D: Mark Warren. W: Les Pine, Bob Arbogast, Albert Brooks, George Burditt, Ed Hider, Bryan Joseph, Jack Kaplan, Steve Pritzker, Norman Hudis.

George Burditt had one of the roughest introductions to writing for television when the first show he joined ran just one day. That was *Turn-On*, where the cast found out their jobs lasted as long as the show's first and only guest host, Tim Conway. Burditt recalled that a kickoff party for the debut, he had just told his

wife, "Aren't you glad you came out here?" when another writer, Jack Kaplan, told them, "We've just been cancelled in New York!"

Burditt got involved in the show through his friendship with writers Jack Hanrahan and Phil Hahn. They had written greeting cards for a living as Burditt was doing in Cleveland when they went to work for *Rowan and Martin's Laugh-In* and found success. "You've got to come out here," Hanrahan told Burditt. He was skeptical but, Burditt noted, "I was watching *Laugh-In* and said, 'Jesus, I could write that shit.'" So he put together some material and sent it to the show.

Laugh-In producer Digby Wolfe liked Burditt's jokes. "He called me and said he wanted do a new show like *Laugh-In*, only make it faster and funnier," Burditt said. "Well, it was faster."

Burditt moved his family to Los Angeles and wrote with Bryan Joseph on the show, doing mostly blackouts (quick sketches). He thought he had a winner given the ambitious cast and crew, plus the producers of *Laugh-In* behind them. But watching the show at the premiere party dismayed him in seeing what others involved had done.

"A lot of the stuff was political and not too funny," he said. That same night, Wolfe told him that "We want to make the people so goddamned mad [with this show], they cannot wait next week for it."

That certainly happened, but not the way Wolfe expected. Thousands of irate viewers called protesting the show, saying it was bad and/or in bad taste, and many station managers told the network they would not carry the program afterward. The desertions were so high that ABC virtually had to cancel it to pacify its affiliates. Burditt's own assessment of *Turn-On* was "Its intentions were OK, but it didn't work. It had a right to be turned off."

ABC made a 180-degree turn and replaced *Turn-On* on March 12 with a revival of the squeaky clean musical program *The King Family Show*, which did not return the next season. Schlatter saved a copy of the tape and later showed an unfunny clip with a woman trying to get birth control pills from a vending machine, with weird electronic music pumping in the background, on the syndicated talk show *The Wil Shriner Show* in 1988.

And almost 10 years to the day of the

show's debut/cancellation, CBS did the same to a sitcom called *Co-Ed Fever* on Feb. 4, 1979. It was the first show to end after its debut since *Turn-On*. That circumstance is no longer rare in today's world of instant ratings, however; at least five series since the 1990s have ended their runs on day one.

What's It All About, World?

Comedy Variety. Ran on ABC Thursdays 9–10 P.M. Feb. 6–May 1, 1969, opposite movies on CBS and *Ironside* and *Dragnet* on NBC. C: Dean Jones, Dennis Allen, Maureen Arthur, Dick Clair, Alex Dreier, Gerri Granger, Bayn Johnson (as Happy Hollywood), Jenna McMahon, Scoey Mitchell, Ron Prince, the Kevin Carlisle Dancers, the Denny Vaughn Orchestra. P: Paul Ilson, Ernest Chambers. D: Al Schwartz. W: Bob Fisher, Arthur Marx, George Balzer, Sam Perrin, George Bloom, Mike Elias, Frank Shaw, Treva Silverman.

The Generation Gap

Game. Ran on ABC Fridays 8:30–9 P.M. Feb. 7–May 23, 1969, opposite *Gomer Pyle, U.S.M.C.* on CBS and *The Name of the Game* on NBC. C: Dennis Wholey (through April 11), Jack Barry (from April 18). EP: Daniel Melnick. P: Chester Feldman. D: Michael Gargiulo.

People tend to forget today what a powerhouse *Gomer Pyle, U.S.M.C.* was for CBS when it ran from 1964 to 1969. The network's top-rated show for three of those seasons, it was either #2 or #3 each season except for 1966-67, when it finished #10 when moved from Fridays to Wednesdays. It returned to Fridays the following fall and beat everything ABC ran against it, including *The Felony Squad*, a crime show on since Sept. 12, 1966, on Mondays that lasted only four months opposite *Gomer Pyle* at the start of the 1968-69 season. Replacing it was another *Pyle* victim, the game show *The Generation Gap*.

"Chester Feldman was the producer of *I've Got a Secret*," director Michael Gargiulo recalled of the genesis of *The Generation Gap*. "A very good friend of mine, he was very creative. He thought of this idea where there would be three people of one generation versus three people of another generation. They would a question of the people under 30, but they would ask it regarding something familiar to the people over 50. The problem was, the people over 50 didn't know anything about the people under 30, but the kids in their twenties knew what the people over 50 knew."

Apparently those history classes the baby boomers took really paid off for them here. Anyway, teams earned up to 20 points for correct answers by individual members, and at the end of each show the point score for each team was converted into an equivalent amount in dollars for both teams.

Original host Dennis Wholey barely was in his thirties himself. A broadcaster from the Midwest, he lost the job after two months due to corporate pressure, according to Gargiulo. The show was in ratings trouble when ABC executives told its owners, executive producer Daniel Melnick and David Susskind — the same talk show host and producer who gave the world *The Honeymoon Race* (see 1966-67), that "Make some changes, and we'll extend you." Firing Wholey was one of the alterations. He later hosted *PBS Latenight*, a nightly show seen at 11:30 P.M. on public television from 1982 to 1984, from his home base of Detroit.

Replacing Wholey was middle-aged Jack Barry, a risky choice given that he and his partner, Dan Enright, had been banished from TV since 1958 following revelations of rigging their big money quiz shows such as *Twenty-One*. Regarding Barry's selection, Gargiulo said, "There was concern, but Jack was never convicted of anything. Beside, it didn't make much difference." The series aired only five shows with Barry before going off, but the exposure gave Barry credibility and let him return to producing game shows for the networks, including *The Joker's Wild*, which he hosted on CBS from 1972 to 1975.

Gargiulo said if he'd been in charge, he might have screened for more knowing older contestants. Apart from that, he was happy with *The Generation Gap* despite its run of just four months. "It was a fun show to do," he said.

You're Putting Me On

Game. Ran on NBC Mondays through Fridays 1:30–2 P.M. June 30–Dec. 26, 1969, opposite *Let's Make a Deal* on ABC and *As the World Turns* on CBS. C: Bill Leyden, Larry Blyden, Peggy Cass, Bill Cullen. EP: Bob Stewart. P: Anne Marie Schmidt. D: Lou Tedesco.

1969-70

My World ... and Welcome to It

Sitcom. Ran on NBC Mondays 7:30–8 P.M. Sept. 15, 1969–Sept. 7, 1970, opposite *The Music Scene* (through Jan. 12) and *It Takes a Thief* (from Jan. 19) on ABC and *Gunsmoke* on CBS. C: William Windom (as John Monroe), Joan Hotchkis (as Ellen Monroe), Lisa Gerritsen (as Lydia Monroe), Harold J. Stone (as Hamilton Greeley), Henry Morgan (as Philip Jensen). EP: Sheldon Leonard. P: Danny Arnold. D: Alan Rafkin. W: Melville Shavelson, Rick Mittleman.

When doing this book, the one series most interviewees asked me about was *My World ... and Welcome to It*. A whimsical sitcom based on the cartoons and writings of James Thurber, it won Emmys in 1970 for Best Comedy Series and Best Actor in a Comedy Series (for lead William Windom), vindicating the longtime belief in the property by its creator, writer Melville Shavelson.

Shavelson first unveiled Thurber surrogate John Monroe more than a decade before *My World ... and Welcome to It*. "I had an agent, Jules Goldstone," he said. "We had secured the rights for James Thurber's work for television. He came to me and asked me I wanted to do a pilot." With Goldstone producing, their effort aired as an episode of *Goodyear Theatre* on June 8, 1959, with Arthur O'Connell as Monroe. That failed. So did a pilot with Orson Bean in the lead which aired on *The June Allyson Show* on March 20, 1961.

Then, when Shavelson mentioned his idea to producer Danny Arnold, the latter suggested using William Windom. "That really got us off the ground," Shavelson said. "He had a name as well." The pilot sold, and Shavelson was glad, except that Thurber, who consulted with Shavelson about writing the pilot script, had died.

On *My World ... and Welcome to It* cartoonist John Monroe spoke directly to the camera from his drawing board each week, recounting his vicissitudes with wife Ellen, daughter Lydia, boss Hamilton Greeley, buddy Phil Jensen, and others. The camera went to a drawing recreating the start of his recollection, then dissolved into live action, repeating the process several times in each show. The inventive use of animation, witty scripts, Windom's wry performance and the mercifully muted laugh track made *My World* stand far above the other sitcoms in 1969-70.

Shavelson admitted putting cartoons, which also occasionally depicted Monroe's fantasies, into the episodes was time consuming. "We had a lot of trouble in those days," he said. "The animation had to be hand-drawn." Doing the chore was the David DePatie–Friz Freleng production company, which also was doing *The Pink Panther Show* Saturday mornings on NBC at the same time.

With all its attributes, why did *My World* last just a year? "The ratings were quite good, but at the end, the network got a deal to do a half-hour show with Red Skelton, and they canceled us," said Shavelson. But while *My World and Welcome to It* won Emmys, *The Red Skelton Show*, transferred from CBS after 18 years there, fell out of the top 20 seasonal ratings after 15 seasons in a row from 1955 to 1970 and went off in the fall of 1971. Shavelson conceded it was a Pyrrhic victory for his show.

CBS reran *My World and Welcome to It* May 25–Sept. 7, 1972, on Thursday evenings, and according to Shavelson, "The BBC, they've run it three time over there [in the United Kingdom]." And Windom has toured often in a one-man show playing Thurber. Now all we need is some distributor to release 26 episodes on home video or DVD for further appreciation. Any takers?

The Debbie Reynolds Show

Sitcom. Ran on NBC Tuesdays 8–8:30 P.M. Sept. 16, 1969–Sept. 1, 1970, opposite *The Mod Squad* on ABC and *Lancer* (through June 23) and movies (from June 30) on CBS. C: Debbie Reynolds (as Debbie Thompson), Don Chastain (as Jim Thompson), Patricia Smith (as Charlotte Landers), Tom Bosley (as Bob Landers), Bobby Riha (as Bruce Landers). EP/W: Jess Oppenheimer. D: Ezra Stone.

William Windom indicates a sense of distrust to his wife, Joan Hotchkis, daughter Lisa Gerritsen and even a cartoon dog his James Thurber-ish character John Monroe created on *My World ... and Welcome to It.*

Then Came Bronson

Adventure. Ran on NBC Wednesdays 10–11 P.M. Sept. 17, 1969–Sept. 9, 1970, opposite movies (through Jan. 14), *The Engelbert Humperdinck Show* (from Jan. 21 to July 1) and *The Smothers Brothers Summer Show* (from July 8) on ABC and *Hawaii Five-O* on CBS. C: Michael Parks (as Jim Bronson). P: Robert Justman, Robert Sabaroff. D: Marvin Chomsky. W: Lionel E. Siegal.

The Music Scene

Variety. Ran on ABC Mondays 7:30–8:15 P.M. Sept. 22, 1969–Jan. 12, 1970, opposite *Gunsmoke* on CBS and *My World … and Welcome to It* and *Rowan and Martin's Laugh-In* on NBC. C: David Steinberg, Larry Hankin, Christopher Ross, Paul Reid Roman, Chris Bokeno, Lily Tomlin, the Pat Willias Orchestra. P: Ken Fritz, Stan Harris. D: Stan Harris. W: Carl Gottlieb, Tony Hendra, Stan Jacobson, Dick Schaal, David Steinberg.

The New People

Fantasy Drama. Ran on ABC Mondays 8:15–9 P.M. Sept. 22, 1969–Jan. 12, 1970, opposite *Gunsmoke* and *Here's Lucy* on CBS and *Rowan and Martin's Laugh-In* on NBC. C: Tiffany Bolling (as Susan Bradley), Zooey Hall (as Bob Lee), Jill Jaress (as Ginny Loomis), David Moses (as Gene Washington), Dennis Olivieri (as Stanley Gabriel), Peter Ratray (as George Potter). EP: Aaron Spelling, Danny Thomas. D: George McCowan. W: John Phillips.

Mr. Deeds Goes to Town

Sitcom. Ran on ABC Fridays 8:30–9 P.M. Sept. 26, 1969–Jan. 16, 1970, opposite *Hogan's Heroes* on CBS and *The Name of the Game* on NBC. C: Monte Markham (as Longfellow Deeds), Pat Harrington, Jr. (as Tony Lawrence), Herb Voland (as Henry Masterson), Ivor Barry (as George). P: Bob Sweeney. D: E.W. Swackhamer. W: Bernard Slade.

The Leslie Uggams Show

Musical Variety. Ran on CBS Sundays 9–10 P.M. Sept. 26–Dec. 14, 1969, opposite movies on ABC and *Bonanza* on NBC. C: Leslie Uggams, Dennis Allen, Lillian Hayman, Lincoln Kilpatrick, Allison Mills, Johnny Brown, the Howard Roberts Singers, the Donald McKayle Dancers, Nelson Riddle and His Orchestra. P/W: Saul Ilson, Ernest Chambers. D: Tim Kiley. W: John Amos, Larry Markes, Paul Wayne, Michael Elias, Frank Shaw, Jerry Music, Howard Albrecht.

Jimmy Durante Presents the Lennon Sisters

Variety. Aired on ABC Fridays 10–11 P.M. Sept. 26, 1969–Jan. 16, 1970, opposite movies on CBS and *Bracken's World* on NBC, then ABC Saturdays 9:30–10:30 P.M. Feb. 14–July 4, 1970, opposite *Petticoat Junction* and *Mannix* on CBS and movies on NBC. C: Jimmy Durante, the Lennon Sisters (Dianne, Peggy, Kathy and Janet), the Jack Regas Dancers, the George Wyle Orchestra. EP: Harold Cohen. P/W: Bernie Kukoff, Jeff Harris. D: Bill Davis. W: Hugh Wedlock, Jr., Bill Box, Don Reo.

Operation: Entertainment was one of the least successful TV series produced by Chuck Barris, running from just Jan. 5, 1968 to Jan. 31, 1969, on ABC nighttime. (It's not included here because it was a variety show with no regulars.) However, the network did like the job writing partners Bernie Kukoff and Jeff Harris did on the series enough to offer the duo future work after it ended.

"They wanted us to do a special with the Lennon Sisters," recalled Kukoff. The four well-scrubbed blonde lasses had been a fan favorite on *The Lawrence Welk Show* from late 1955 until their amicable departure from the series in 1968 to pursue other interests. With Welk's show still doing incredibly well for a 14-year-old series (it resided in the top 30 of the ratings in 1968-69), ABC felt there was an audience for the vocalizing quartet, even if the Lennon Sisters had but one moderate hit record to their name, 1956's "Tonight You Belong to Me."

"We wanted to pair them with a funny major guest, and somehow we got Jimmy Durante," Kuckoff continued. "Jimmy did the pilot/special, and they liked the combination a lot, the old comedian and the young sisters."

The special, titled *The Lennon Sisters Show*, ran on May 6, 1969. Four months later, the series debuted as *Jimmy Durante Presents the Lennon Sisters* to give star billing to the oldest in the bunch. "It was kind of an unwieldy title, mainly to get Jimmy on," admitted Kukoff. "He was a wonderful man."

Durante did have an advantage over the Lennon Sisters in that he could sing, or rather croak, a few novelty tunes and sentimental favorites, in addition to doing all the comedy sketches. Most of the guests were big-name comedians as well. "We had Jack Benny twice, and Bob Hope," Kukoff noted.

But the promise of top comedy plus middle-of-the-road interludes from the Lennon Sisters did not win over many viewers. It did not get crushed against its middling competition on Friday nights, but when ABC moved it in early 1970 to Saturdays to replace the 6-year-old *The Hollywood Palace* (and follow *The Lawrence Welk Show* on the lineup), it staggered opposite NBC's movies and CBS's *Mannix*.

Asked why he thought the show didn't get a second year, Kukoff said, "Frankly, I don't know why. ABC was the weakest network at the time, and nobody at the network complained about the show. But it had a limited audience."

Durante, who previously had his own hit TV variety shows for a variety of sponsors from 1950 to 1956, did a few more guest shots until a stroke in 1972 left him unable to perform. He died in 1980. The Lennon Sisters had enough clout to appear often on *The Hollywood Squares* during the 1970s, with two pairs of sisters in two different squares no less, but thereafter their music was very much out of style, and they seldom performed on TV.

The Protectors (a/k/a The Law Enforcers)

Crime Drama. Aired on NBC Sundays 10–11 P.M. Sept. 28, 1969–Sept. 6, 1970, opposite movies on ABC and *Mission: Impossible* on CBS. C: Leslie Nielsen (as Deputy Police Chief Sam Danforth), Hari Rhodes (as D.A. William Withers). EP: Jack Laird. P: Jerrold Freedman. D: Daryl Duke, Fernando Lamas.

"We were trying to bring a fresh point of view to television," producer Jerrold Freedman said of *The Protectors,* also known as *The Law Enforcers.* "There hadn't been too many shows with black leads cast in dramas." To correct that injustice, Hari Rhodes, formerly a supporting player as Mike the native on *Daktari* (1966–69), co-starred on this series as the district attorney of an unnamed metropolis along with Leslie Nielsen as a top cop. The two men sparred over their different approaches to fighting crime, with Nielsen favoring traditional by-the-book methods while Rhodes believing in a more liberalized stance.

The series also featured stories which delved into race and class issues. Those features already were in evidence in the series' pilot, the TV-movie *Deadlock,* which aired on NBC Feb. 22, 1969, with Nielsen and Rhodes. Freedman, who had nothing to do with the pilot, primarily developed the scripts for the series.

Freedman said *The Protectors* had another significant difference than the majority of other TV shows in 1969-70. "We went on location more than was done in those days," he said. "We went down to Santa Ana, Calif., to shoot as our base."

The series appeared every three weeks under the umbrella title *The Bold Ones,* alternating with two other programs, *The New Doctors* and *The Lawyers. The Bold Ones* was the first of what would be a fairly popular setup of doing series in the 1970s—the "wheel" concept, wherein three or four series alternated appearing weekly in the same time slot. *The New Doctors* kicked off the overall series on Sept. 14, 1969 and lasted the longest, running through June 23, 1973 (the "new" part of the title presumably existed so it would not be confused with *The Doctors,* a soap opera airing daily on NBC at the same time). *The Lawyers* debuted the following week, on Sept. 21, 1969, and lasted until Sept. 10, 1972.

Despite the scheduling on the network, Freedman said production on *The Protectors* did not have the same breaks for actors. "We did all of our shows back to back," he said.

Unfortunately for *The Protectors,* viewers did not follow the series enough to warrant a second year of stories, even though it did follow *Bonanza,* the #3 series for the 1969-70 season. Universal Studios, the production company for *The Bold Ones,* replaced it with another one-season attraction, *The Senator* (q.v.). Ironically, Freedman and executive producer Jack Laird worked together again on *Night Gallery,* which began in 1970 as part of another Universal "wheel" series *Four in One.*

In 1972 a series titled *The Protectors* starring Robert Vaughn aired in syndication, but it had nothing to do with the earlier program of the same name.

The Name Droppers

Game. Ran on NBC Mondays through Fridays 12:30–12:55 P.M. Sept. 29–Dec. 26, 1969, opposite *That Girl* reruns on ABC and *Search for Tomorrow* on CBS, then NBC Mondays through Fridays 4–4:30 P.M. Dec. 29, 1969–March 27, 1970, opposite *Dark Shadows* on ABC and *Gomer Pyle, U.S.M.C.* reruns on CBS. C: Al Lohman and Roger Barkley. EP: Merrill Heatter, Bob Quigley. P: Art Alisi. D: Jerome Shaw.

Letters to Laugh-In

Game. Ran on NBC Mondays through Fridays 4–4:30 P.M. Sept. 29–Dec. 26, 1969, opposite *Dark Shadows* on ABC and *Gomer Pyle, U.S.M.C.* reruns on CBS. C: Gary Owens. P: Alan Neuman.

D: Alan J. Levi. W: Hal Collins, Jack Kaplan, Harry Morton, Paul Friedman, Edward Morganstern, Stan Dreben.

The Survivors

Soap Opera. Ran on ABC Mondays 9–10 P.M. Sept. 29, 1969–Jan. 12, 1970, opposite *Mayberry R.F.D.* and *The Doris Day Show* on CBS and movies on NBC, then rerun ABC Thursdays 10–11 P.M. June 11–Sept. 17, 1970, opposite movies on CBS and *The Dean Martin Show* (through July 9) and *Dean Martin Presents the Golddiggers in London* (from July 16). C: Lana Turner (as Tracy Carlyle Hastings), George Hamilton (as Duncan Carlyle), Kevin McCarthy (as Philip Hastings), Ralph Bellamy (as Baylor Carlyle), Jan-Michael Vincent (as Jeffrey Hastings), Diana Muldaur (as Belle), Louis Hayward (as Johnathan Carlyle), Louise Sorel (as Jean Vale), Rossano Brazzi (as Antaeus Riakos), Robert Viharo (as Miguel Santerra), Donna Baccala (as Marguerita), Kathy Cannon (as Sheila Riley), Robert Lipton (as Tom Steinberg), Clu Gulager (as Sen. Mark Jennings), Natalie Schafer (as Eleanor Carlyle). EP/D: Walter Doniger. P: Richard Caffey, William Frye, Gordon Oliver. D: John Newland, Michael Ritchie. W: John Wilder, Michael Gleason.

Pre-dating *Dallas*, *Dynasty* and all the other glossy full-hour nighttime soap operas by a decade or thereabouts, *The Survivors* was perhaps ahead of its time in depicting the trials and tribulations of the jet set by top-name stars. Our poor heroine, Tracy Carlyle Hastings, suffered in an unhappy marriage to Philip Hastings, worried that her son Jeffrey would learn that her old boyfriend Antaeus Riakos was his real father, dealt with her father, Baylor, dying, leading to fights over control of his international banking conglomerate, and on and on and on… And I'm not even going to get into Tracy's half-brother Duncan and his dealing with South American revolutionaries.

Concocting the basic scenario was potboiler novelist Harold Robbins, whose 1962 book *Where Love Has Gone* was a *roman a clef* about Lana Turner's trial for murdering her gangster boyfriend Johnny Stompanato in 1958. Turner loathed the book but needed the work, as her days of being a film star were dwindling, so she agreed to star in the series. She and the other principals shot what was an incredibly expensive pilot (more than $1 million) in France with Walter Frye. Universal Studios, the production company for the series, fired Frye for the high cost and looked for a replacement.

"That was an interesting experience," Walter Doniger said. "I was asked to take it over from William Frye. I saw the pilot. It was too much about rich people, and it didn't connect to people. I made 30 pages of what I thought was wrong."

As Doniger prepared to leave the Universal Studios lot after reviewing the pilot, the security guard as the gate told him that Sidney Sheinberg wanted to see him. The studio executive greeted Doniger with the question, "How would you like to take over the show?"

Doniger mulled the idea over. He already survived being a director for four years on *Peyton Place*, which at one time required him to direct three half-hour shows a week, so he said yes. Though the series failed, he did not regret his decision. "It was a good experience."

He added that contrary to some reports, Lana Turner did not give him problems on the production. "She was very good," he said. However, he also noted "Lana Turner was losing her connection with the public," and that might have been a factor in the show's cancellation.

After ABC ran the show, Universal later edited two episodes into a TV-movie for local stations in 1971 called *The Last of the Powerseekers*. Lana would do one other regular TV role on another fancy nighttime soap opera, *Falcon Crest* in 1982-83, where she made headlines feuding with its star Jane Wyman before leaving.

Get It Together

Musical Variety. Ran on ABC Saturdays Noon–12:30 P.M. Jan. 3–Sept. 5, 1970, opposite *The Monkees* on CBS and *Jambo* on NBC. C: Sam Riddle, Cass Elliot. EP: Dick Clark. P/D: Kip Walton.

When ABC affiliates had an extra half hour to fill on Saturdays at the start of 1970, Dick Clark sold the network on the idea of *Get It Together*, which immediately preceded Clark's long-running hit *American Bandstand* (1957–87). Kip Walton, who was the producer and director of *American Bandstand*, held the same job on the new show.

"*Get It Together* was different from *Bandstand* because it didn't feature dancing," Walton said. "It was based on performances and interviews with Cass and guests." Cass was Cass Elliot, the booming former vocalist of the 1960s rock group the Mamas and the Papas who became the show's co-host with Sam Riddle. Riddle, a top rock deejay in Los Angeles at the time who hosted a *Bandstand*-type show on KHJ-TV, was considered not a big enough "name" for viewers outside southern California, hence the hiring of Cass.

"At that time, Cass was on her own, a bit down on her luck, and open to appearing as a regular on a low-budget show," Walton said. "She immediately clicked as a host. She was *so* bright and talented, well-educated, well-versed on most any subject, funny and kind and unpretentious with her fame.

"I remember one time we went to London to pre-tape the famous English acts of the day (she knew them all and they all loved her). When we arrived at the Dorchester five-star hotel in London, we got out of our chauffeur-driven Rolls-Royce. Cass carried her Army duffle bag to the check-in counter, unloaded some clothes, then dumped the rest on the floor and said, 'You got a washing machine in this place?' to the astonished staff. (Not 3 feet away, an embarrassed Charlton Heston shrank out of the lobby.) That was Cass.

"Also another memory. One in the airport in New York, she was approached by IRS agents (she was always in tax trouble) and served a summons. She accepted it graciously, while also granting her autograph for an agent's daughter!"

But while Cass was something else behind the scenes, *Get It Together* was not bringing in the crowds ABC hoped it would get. As Walton remembered, "We were constantly pre-empted or rescheduled for sports programming, and the show really never had a chance to find and build an audience, so it wasn't renewed. But it remains a fond memory because of Cass."

Elliot died far too young, at age 32 in 1974 of a heart ailment. Her one-time co-host Sam Riddle did not do another TV series in front of the cameras but found much work instead as a producer, including doing that job for the hit 1980s syndicated upcoming talent series *Star Search*.

The Engelbert Humperdinck Show

Musical Variety. Ran on ABC Wednesdays 10–11 P.M. Jan. 21–July 1, 1970, opposite *Hawaii Five-O* on CBS and *Then Came Bronson* on NBC, then ABC Saturdays 9:30–10:30 July 11–Sept. 19, 1970, opposite *Petticoat Junction* and *Mannix* on CBS and movies on NBC. C: Engelbert Humperdinck, the Irving Davies Dancers, the Jack Parnell Orchestra. P: Colin Crews. D: Ian Fordyce. W: Sheldon Keller, Bryan Blackburn, Tony Hawes.

Pat Paulsen's Half a Comedy Hour

Comedy Variety. Ran on ABC Thursdays 7:30–8 P.M. Jan. 22–April 16, 1970, opposite *Family Affair* on CBS and *Daniel Boone* on NBC. C: Pat Paulsen, Pepe Brown, Jean Byron, Bob Einstein, Joan Gerber, Sherry Miles, Pedro Regas, Vanetta Rogers, Hal Smith, George Spell, the Denny Vaughn Orchestra. P: Bill Carruthers. D: Mark Goode. W: Steve Martin, Bob Arbogast, Paul Wayen, Micheal Elias, Frank Shaw, Tom Koch, Larry Marks.

Paris 7000

Adventure. Ran on ABC Thursdays 10–11 P.M. Jan. 22–June 4, 1970, opposite movies on CBS and *The Dean Martin Show* on NBC. C: George Hamilton (as Jack Brennan), Gene Raymond (as Robert Stevens), Jacques Aubuchon (as Jules Maurois).

The Tim Conway Show

Sitcom. Ran on CBS Fridays 8–8:30 P.M. Jan. 30–June 19, 1970, opposite *The Brady Bunch* on ABC and *The High Chapparal* on NBC. C: Tim Conway (as Spud Barrett), Joe Flynn (as Herbert T. Kenworth), Anne Seymour (as Mrs. K.J. Crawford), Johnnie Collins III (as Ronnie Crawford), Emily Banks (as Becky Parks), Fabian Dean (as Harry Wetzel), Dennis Robertson (as Sherman Bell). P: Burt Nodella. D: Alan Rafkin, Harry Falk.

The Best of Everything

Soap Opera. Ran on ABC Mondays through Fridays Noon–12:30 P.M. March 30–Sept. 25, 1970, opposite *Where the Heart Is* and news on CBS and *Jeopardy!* on NBC. C: Julie Mannix (as April Morrison; early episodes), Susan Sullivan (as April Morrison; later episodes), Patty McCormack (as Linda Warren), Katherine Glass (as Kim Jordan), Gale Sondergaard (as Amanda Key), Geraldine

Fitzgerald (as Violet Jordan), John Rust (as Joshua Jordan; early episodes), Peter Harris (as Joshua Jordan; later episodes), M'El Dowd (as Kate Farrow/Mrs. Bang), Rochelle Oliver (as Barbara Lamont), Stephen Grover (as Johnny Lamont), Barry Ford (as Ken Lamont), Ginnie Curtis (as Gwen Mitchell), James Davidson (as Dexter Key), Bonnie Bee Buzzard (as Joanna Key), Diane Kagan (as Anne Carter), Jean-Pierre Stewart (as Mike Carter), Victor Arnold (as Dr. Ed Perrone), Ted LePlat (as Randy Wilson). EP: Don Wallace. P: Jacqueline Babbin. D: Jack Wood, Alan Pultz. W: James Lipton.

1970-71

Hot Dog

Children's. Ran on NBC Saturdays Noon–12:30 P.M. Sept. 12, 1970–Sept. 4, 1971, opposite *The Hardy Boys* (through Dec. 26) and *Motor Mouse and Auto Cat* (from Jan. 2) on ABC and *Scooby-Doo, Where Are You?* on CBS. C: Woody Allen, Jonathan Winters, Joanne Worley. EP: Lee Mendelson. P/D/W: Frank Buxton.

Frank Buxton was the host of the ABC children's show *Discovery* from 1962 to 1966. Lee Mendelson was executive producer since 1965 of the *Peanuts* cartoon specials based on the comic strip of the same name by Charles Schulz. So when Buxton visited Mendelson's office one day, it wasn't too surprising that the former had a notion for a program involving children and animation.

"He had this idea that it would be fun to show kids how things would be made, whether it be maple syrup or basketballs or whatever," Mendelson said. "I thought it would be a good idea, but we could sell it only with celebrities."

The two created a special titled *Hot Dog* (Mendelson said they needed something simple to call it, although it is known Buxton called his office by that name as well). It aired as a Saturday morning special on March 28, 1970, with Woody Allen, Joanne Worley and Tom Smothers doing the introductions. NBC decided to make it into a series for that fall, and Jonathan Winters assumed the third place for the series over Smothers.

The signing of Allen was a real coup for the series, as he never had been a regular performer on any nighttime series (a distinction he still held as of this writing). He had just begun having success as a movie star and director when he did the show, with his film *Bananas* coming out in 1971. "Frank Buxton knew his agent," Mendelson said of how he joined the series. "I knew Joanne and Jonathan."

Mendelson said what was done with Allen on the series was the same as with the other hosts—tell funny stories of how they thought something was created before giving them the explanation via video and animation. "What we did, we sat with Woody in his apartment in New York and taped four or five hours. We probably had for 13 shows about 75 categories we covered, and had him do them all at that taping."

The show employed at least two crews out in the field to cover the topics discussed. While Buxton did the bulk of the work, Mendelson said he did help in editing the segments. The animation for the show came from an outfit called the Yellow Bull Workshop in Lexington, Massachusetts, while background music came from the folk-rock group the Youngbloods, who had been all over the radio in 1969 with their hit "Get Together."

Amid all these contributions came the sad reality that children in 1970-71 overwhelmingly preferred the all-animated competition to *Hot Dog* on CBS, *Scooby-Doo, Where Are You?* "It didn't get the ratings," acknowledge Mendelson as to why *Hot Dog* was a cold show after one year. "The thing that made it great were the comedians, but the kids didn't know who they were." NBC replaced it with a revival of the 1951–65 series *Watch Mr. Wizard*, which also lasted just one season.

The Senator

Drama. Ran on NBC Sundays 10–11 P.M. Sept. 13, 1970–Aug. 22, 1971, opposite movies on ABC and *The Tim Conway Comedy Hour* (through Dec. 28), *The Honeymooners* reruns (from Jan. 3 to May 9), *The Ice Palace* (from May 23 to July 25) and *The Six Wives of Henry VIII* (from Aug. 1) on CBS. C: Hal Holbrook (as Sen. Hayes Stowe), Michael Tolan (as Jordan Boyle), Sharon Acker (as Erin Stowe), Cindy Eilbacher (as Norma Stowe). EP: William Sackheim. P: David Levinson. D: Fernando Lamas, Robert Day, Daryl Duke, Jerrold Freedman, John Badham. W: David W. Rintels.

The Don Knotts Show

Comedy Variety. Ran on NBC Tuesdays 7:30–8 P.M. Sept. 15, 1970–Jan. 12, 1971, opposite *The Mod Squad* on ABC and *The Beverly Hillbillies* and *Green Acres* on CBS, then NBC Tuesdays 8–9 P.M. Jan. 19–July 6, 1971, opposite *The Mod Squad* and movies on ABC and *Green Acres* and *Hee Haw* on CBS. C: Don Knotts, Gary Burghoff, Eddie Carroll, Mickey Deems, John Dehner, Elaine Joyce, Kenneth Mars, Frank Welker, Bob Williams, the Nick Perito Orchestra. EP: Nick Vanoff. P: William O. Harbach. D: Norman Abbott. W: George Balzar, Sam Perrin, Roger Price, Elias Davis, David Pollock.

Storefront Lawyers (a/k/a Men at Law)

Drama. Ran on CBS Wednesdays 7:30–8:30 P.M. Sept. 16, 1970–Sept. 1, 1971, opposite *The Courtship of Eddie's Father* and *Make Room for Granddaddy* (through Jan. 13) and *Room 222* (from Jan. 20) on ABC and *The Virginian* on NBC. C: Robert Foxworth (as David Hansen), Sheila Larkin (as Deborah Sullivan), David Arkin (as Gabriel Kaye), A Martinez (as Roberto Alvarez), Pauline Myers (as Gloria Byrd), Gerald S. O'Loughlin (as Devlin McNeil). EP: Bob Stivers. P: Bill Waters, Ronald Kibbee, Dominique Perrin, Harold Gast.

Nancy

Sitcom. Ran on NBC Thursdays 9:30–10 P.M. Sept. 17, 1970–Jan. 7, 1971, opposite *The Odd Couple* on ABC and movies on CBS. C: Renne Jarrett (as Nancy Smith), John Fink (as Dr. Adam Hudson), Celeste Holm (as Abigail Townsend), Robert F. Simon (as Uncle Everett Hudson), Eddie Applegate (as Willie Wilson), Frank Aletter (as Tom Daily). EP: Sidney Sheldon. P: Jerome Courtland.

To hear Celeste Holm tell it, she was an easy catch for the producers of *Nancy* to hire her. "Someone asked me to do it, and I wasn't doing anything else, so why not?" she recalled. But she would regret the decision later when this sitcom let her down in the writing, as what had happened to her in 1954 with her sitcom *Honestly, Celeste!* (q.v.). "The terrible thing is they wrote a lovely pilot, and then made a terrible show," she said.

Nancy hoped the public's fascination with recent romances involving presidential daughters would translate into making the series a hit. Lyndon Johnson saw his little girl Lynda Bird Johnson wed future Virginia Sen. Chuck Robb in the White House on Dec. 9, 1967, for example. The next year, Julie Nixon married David Eisenhower (Dwight's grandson) in advance of Julie's dad, Richard Nixon, becoming the president. Another Nixon daughter, Tricia, would marry on June 12, 1971.

But there already was a sitcom focusing on a politician's daughter, *The Governor and J.J.*, which ran on CBS from 1969 to 1971, so the idea was not exactly fresh. And as for the execution of storylines, well, let Ms. Holm describe her part as the chaperone of Nancy Smith, daughter of President Smith who married veterinarian Dr. Adam Hudson on Nov. 5, 1970, and lived in his hometown of Center City, Iowa.

"I was supposed to be their kind of manager," Holm said. "I was supposed to take care of them. She should've called her father and said, 'Get this hag off my back!'"

Holm's character wasn't the only one interfering with the unreal romance of Nancy and Adam. There also were intrusions from Secret Service agents Turner and Rodriguez, plus Uncle Everett on Adam's side. Willie and Tom were Adam's buddies. Despite all their hijinks and a time slot following *Ironside* (the #4 rated show in 1970-71), *Nancy* was a bomb.

Sidney Sheldon, the creator and producer of *I Dream of Jeannie*, did the same for this show, but as I could only find the writing credits for the pilot, it's not known if he wrote for the following episodes, whose scripts Holm described as "kind of blah" and the reason why she felt it flopped. "You never know when you get on a series how it's going to go," she said. "You can only hope."

The co-stars of *Nancy*, Renne Jarrett and

John Fink, never had another regular nighttime TV role. As for Holm, even though this series gave her another flop on TV, she did not stop trying her hand in series. She was a regular on *Jessie* (1984), *Falcon Crest* (1985), *Christine Cromwell* (1989–90), *Loving* (1991–92) and *Promised Land* (1996–99). Asked if she would consider doing another one, she said, "Only if the writing is good," she said. "The play's the thing." Indeed it is, and it certainly wasn't with *Nancy*.

The Interns

Medical Drama. Ran on CBS Fridays 7:30–8:30 P.M. Sept. 18, 1970–Sept. 10, 1971, opposite *The Brady Bunch* and *Nanny and the Professor* on ABC and *The High Chapparal* on NBC. C: Broderick Crawford (as Dr. Peter Goldstone), Stephen Brooks (as Dr. Greg Pettit), Christopher Stone (as Dr. Pooch Hardin), Hal Frederick (as Dr. Cal Barrin), Sandra Smith (as Dr. Lydia Thorpe), Mike Farrell (as Dr. Sam Marsh), Skip Homeier (as Dr. Hugh Jacoby), Elaine Giftos (as Bobbe Marsh). EP: Bob Claver. P: Charles Larson.

The Headmaster

Drama. Ran on CBS Fridays 8:30–9 P.M. Sept. 18, 1970–Jan. 1, 1971, and June 25–Sept. 10, 1971, both opposite *The Partridge Family* on ABC and *The Name of the Game* on NBC. C: Andy Griffith (as Andy Thompson), Jerry Van Dyke (as Jerry Brownell), Parker Fennelly (as Mr. Purdy), Claudette Nevins (as Margaret Thompson), Lani O'Grady (as Judy). EP: Richard O. Linke. P: Aaron Ruben.

The Young Rebels

Drama. Ran on ABC Sundays 7–8 P.M. Sept. 20, 1970–Jan. 3, 1971, opposite *Lassie* and *Hogan's Heroes* on CBS and *Wild Kingdom* and *The Wonderful World of Disney* on NBC. C: Rick Ely (as Jeremy Larkin), Louis Gossett, Jr. (as Isaak Poole), Alex Henteloff (as Henry Abington), Hilary Thompson (as Elizabeth Coates), Philippe Forquet (as General the Marquis de Lafayette). EP: Aaron Spelling. P: Jon Epstein.

The Tim Conway Comedy Hour

Comedy Variety. Ran on CBS Sundays 10–11 P.M. Sept. 20–Dec. 13, 1970, opposite movies on ABC and *The Bold Ones* on NBC. C: Tim Conway, Bruce Belland and Dave Somerville, Bonnie

Boland, Art Metrano, McLean Stevenson, Sally Struthers, the Jimmy Joyce Singers, the Tom Hansen Dancers, the Nelson Riddle Orchestra. P: Bill Hobin, Ron Clark, Sam Bobrick. D: Bill Hobin. W: Ron Clark, Sam Bobrick, Barry Levinson, Rudy DeLuca, Tim Conway, Fred S. Fox, Seaman Jacobs.

The Young Lawyers

Drama. Ran on ABC Mondays 7:30–8:30 P.M. Sept. 21, 1970–Jan. 11, 1971, opposite *Gunsmoke* on CBS and *The Red Skelton Show* and *Rowan and Martin's Laugh-In* on NBC, then ABC Wednesdays 10–11 P.M. Jan. 20–May 5, 1971, opposite *Hawaii Five-O* on CBS and *Four-in-One* on NBC. C: Lee J. Cobb (as Attorney David Barrett), Zalman King (as Aaron Silverman), Judy Pace (as Pat Walters), Philip Clark (as Chris Blake; 1971). P: Matthew Rapf. AP: Jerry Briskin. D: Jud Taylor, John Newland.

The Silent Force

Adventure. Ran on ABC Mondays 8:30–9 P.M. Sept. 21, 1970–Jan. 11, 1971, opposite *Here's Lucy* on CBS and *Rowan and Martin's Laugh-In* on NBC. C: Ed Nelson (as Ward Fuller), Percy Rodriguez (as Jason Hart), Lynda Day George (as Amelia Cole). EP: Walter Grauman. P: Philip Barry.

Make Room for Granddaddy

Sitcom. Ran on ABC Wednesdays 8–8:30 P.M. Sept. 23, 1970–Jan. 13, 1971, opposite *Storefront Lawyers* on CBS and *Daniel Boone* on NBC, then ABC Thursdays 9–9:30 P.M. Jan. 21–Sept. 2, 1971, opposite movies on CBS and *Ironside* on NBC. C: Danny Thomas (as Danny Williams), Marjorie Lord (as Kathy "Clancey" Williams), Rusty Hamer (as Rusty Williams), Angela Cartwright (as Linda Williams), Hans Conried (as Uncle Tonoose), Sid Melton (as "Uncle Charley" Halper), Roosevelt Grier (as Rosey Robbins), Michael Hughes (as Michael Johnson), Stanley Myron Handleman (as Henry). EP: Danny Thomas. D: Richard Crenna.

Dan August

Crime Drama. Ran on ABC Wednesdays 10–11 P.M. Sept. 23, 1970–Jan. 6, 1971, opposite *Hawaii Five-O* on CBS and *Four-in-One* on NBC, then ABC Thursdays 9:30–10:30 P.M. Jan. 21–Aug. 26, 1971, opposite movies on CBS and *Adam-12* and *The Dean Martin Show* (through July 1) and *The*

Dean Martin Summer Show (from July 8) on NBC. C: Burt Reynolds (as Det. Lt. Dan August), Norman Fell (as Sgt. Charles Wilentz), Ned Romero (as Sgt. Joe Rivera), Richard Anderson (as Chief George Untermeyer), Ena Hartmann (as Katy Grant). EP: Quinn Martin. P: Anthony Spinner. D: Walter Grauman, Ralph Senensky, Virgil W. Vogel, Gerald Mayer.

Matt Lincoln

Medical Drama. Ran on ABC Thursdays 7:30–8:30 P.M. Sept. 24, 1970–Jan. 14, 1971, opposite *Family Affair* and *The Jim Nabors Hour* on CBS and *The Flip Wilson Show* on NBC. C: Vince Edwards (as Dr. Matt Lincoln), Chelsea Brown (as Tag), Michael Larrain (as Kevin), Felton Perry (as Jimmy), June Harding (as Ann). EP: Frank Pierce. P: Irving Elman.

Barefoot in the Park

Sitcom. Ran on ABC Thursdays 9–9:30 P.M. Sept. 24, 1970–Jan. 14, 1971, opposite movies on CBS and *Ironside* on NBC. C: Scoey Mitchell (as Paul Bratter), Tracy Reed (as Corie Bratter), Thelma Carpenter (as Mabel Bates), Nipsey Russell (as Honey Robinson), Harry Holcombe as Mr. Arthur Kendricks), Vito Scotti (as Mr. Velasquez). EP: William P. D'Angelo. P: Robert Williams. D: Jerry Paris, Bruce Bilson, Charles R. Rondeau. W: Jerry Belson, Garry Marshall, Harvey Miller.

The Immortal

Science Fiction/Adventure. Ran on ABC Thursdays 10–11 P.M. Sept. 24, 1970–Jan. 14, 1971, opposite movies on CBS and *The Dean Martin Show* on NBC, then ABC Wednesdays 9:30–10:30 P.M. May 12–Sept. 8, 1971, opposite *Medical Center* and *Hawaii Five-O* on CBS and *Kraft Music Hall* and *Four-in-One* on NBC. C: Christopher George (as Ben Richards), Don Knight (as Fletcher), David Brian (as Arthur Maitland), Carol Lynley (as Sylvia Cartwright). EP: Anthony Wilson. P: Richard Caffey, Howie Horwitz. D: Leslie H. Martinson, Michael Caffey, Robert Douglas. W: Stephen Kandel, Shimon Wincelberg, Robert and Wanda Duncan.

Words and Music

Game. Ran on NBC Mondays through Fridays 1:30–2 P.M. Sept. 28, 1970–Feb. 12, 1971, opposite *Let's Make a Deal* on ABC and *As the World Turns* on CBS. C: Wink Martindale, Peggy Connelly, Katie Gran, Bob Marlot, Dan Minter, Pat Henderson, Jack Quigley. P: Armand Grant, Howard Felsher. D: Lou Tedesco.

The Most Deadly Game

Detective Drama. Ran on ABC Saturdays 9:30–10:30 P.M. Oct. 10, 1970–Jan. 16, 1971, opposite *The Mary Tyler Moore Show* and *Mannix* on CBS and movies on NBC. C: George Maharis (as Jonathan Croft), Yvette Mimeux (as Vanessa Smith), Ralph Bellamy (as Mr. Ethan Arcane). EP: Aaron Spelling. P: Joan Harrison.

San Francisco International Airport

Drama. Ran on NBC Wednesdays 10–11 P.M. Oct. 28, 1970–Aug. 25, 1971, opposite *Dan August* (through Jan. 6), *The Young Lawyers* (from Jan. 20 to May 5) and *The Immortal* (from May 12) and *NFL Action* (from May 12) and *Hawaii Five-O* on CBS. C: Lloyd Bridges (as Jim Conrad), Clu Gulager (as Bob Hatten), Barbara Werle (as June), Barbara Sigel (as Suzie Conrad). EP: Richard Irving. P: William Read Woodfield, Allen Balter. D: John Llewellyn Moxie, Boris Sagal.

The New Andy Griffith Show

Sitcom. Ran on CBS Fridays 8:30–9 P.M. Jan. 8–May 21, 1971, opposite *The Partridge Family* on ABC and *The Name of the Game* on NBC. C: Andy Griffith (as Mayor Andy Sawyer), Lee Meriwether (as Lee Sawyer), Lori Ann Rutherford (as Lori Sawyer), Ann Morgan Guilbert (as Nora), Marty McCall (as T.J. Sawyer), Glen Ash (as Buff MacKnight), Susan Davis (as Verline MacKnight). EP: Richard O. Linke. P: Aaron Ruben.

Strange Report

Drama. Ran on NBC Fridays 10–11 P.M. Jan. 8–Sept. 10, 1971, opposite *Love American Style* on ABC and movies on CBS. C: Anthony Quayle (as Adam Strange), Kaz Garas (as Hamlyn Gynt), Anneke Willis (as Evelyn McLean). EP: Norman Felton. P: Buzz Berger. D: Roy Ward Baker, Peter Medaak, Charles Crichton.

Even though it's virtually forgotten today, *Strange Report* marks a considerable milestone as the last series from the United Kingdom to air nighttime on an American network. The trend kicked off in the fall of 1955 when CBS imported *The Adventures of Robin Hood* to America and received a top 20 hit in the 1955-56 season for the move. That led to 15 years of occasional entries on all three networks, some moderately successful (*The Saint, The Avengers*) but most not. By the end of the 1960s most of the series brought from overseas were just variety series that aired as summer replacements (e.g., *The Picadilly Palace* in 1967, *Dean Martin Presents the Golddiggers in London* in 1970). Indeed, *The Val Doonican Show* was the only other English series on a network in 1970-71 apart from *Strange Report*.

Strange Report did boast of starring an Oscar-nominated performer, Anthony Quayle, who got his nomination for Best Supporting Actor in 1969 for *Anne of the Thousand Days*. Here Quayle played Adam Strange, a modern-day Sherlock Holmes whose ability to solve cases Scotland Yard could not crack earned him worldwide fame. He resided in an unpretentious flat in London by himself. Adam's wife had died, but there were intimations of a possible relationship with his neighbor Evelyn McLean, a model who often found herself in the thick of Strange's investigations.

Also assisting Strange was Hamlyn Gynt, known commonly as "Ham." A Rhodes scholar who served as a researcher at a museum, Ham was Strange's aide and did footwork for the expert. Ham also was said to be an American. Interestingly, the actor portraying him, Kaz Garas, was born in Lithunia.

In a letter to me, executive producer Norman Felton, an American, wrote that NBC blamed the locale for its failure to best its competition. "We filmed in England, and the stories had a fine actor in the lead, but after a short run (33 episodes), the network felt that lower ratings occurred because people did not like the British accents," he wrote.

Actually, NBC showed only half of the episodes produced — 16, to be exact — and repeated them. *Strange Report* was a replacement for the faltering *Bracken's World*, a melodrama involving a movie studio which had ended midseason following a year-and-a-half run (it was on from Sept. 19, 1969–Dec. 25, 1970). And the networks still offered a few productions for Anglophiles in the form of miniseries or limited run series, such as *The Search for the Nile* on NBC from Jan. 29 to Feb. 25, 1972, and *The Strauss Family* on ABC from May 5 to June 16, 1973.

NBC filled the *Strange Report* time slot in the fall of 1971 with a movie series that ended at 10:30 P.M., except for every fourth Friday of the month, when a newsmagazine called *Chronolog* filled the 9–11 P.M. period.

The Reel Game

Game. Ran on ABC Mondays 8:30–9 P.M. Jan. 18–May 3, 1971, opposite *Here's Lucy* on CBS and *Rowan and Martin's Laugh-In* on NBC. C: Jack Barry. P: Ken Johnson, John J. Macker. D: Marty Pasetta.

The Pearl Bailey Show

Musical Variety. Ran on ABC Saturdays 8:30–9:30 P.M. Jan. 23–May 8, 1971, opposite *My Three Sons* and *Arnie* on CBS and movies on NBC. C: Pearl Bailey, the Allan Davies Singers, the Robert Sidney Dancers, Louis Bellson and his Orchestra. P: Bob Finkel. D: Dean Whitmore. W: Bill Angelos, Buz Kohan, Pearl Bailey.

Outspoken, exuberant Pearl Bailey had been a rarity on TV for much of the 1940s through 1960s — a black female entertainer who managed to appear frequently on variety and talk shows. She was overdue to have her own variety series when it hit the air in 1971, and when it did, she managed to snag some top-name guests to appear.

The debut featured Lucille Ball. Later shows featured mostly singers ranging from Bing Crosby to Louis Armstrong (in one of his last TV appearances before he died on July 6, 1971). "She got everybody she wanted. Nobody would turn her down," said the show's producer Bob Finkel. "They all loved Pearl."

Ah, but did the show's staff have the same feeling? Well, according to Finkel, yes and no. "She was extremely difficult. She hated to use a script. She would ad lib. It was difficult for other performers to keep up with her in their scripts. But she cooked meals for the staff at the end of the series' run, and she constantly gave me gifts from Cartier and Tiffany."

Beside writing for her show, Bailey also had her husband since 1952, drummer Louis Bellson, serve as her orchestra conductor. "He was one of the great drummers," Finkel said.

Finkel points to Bailey going to ABC officials with her suggestions and complaints about the show as the main reason why it wilted. "She had no compunctions about going to the executives. And she truly harassed them to the point that they thought twice about renewing her. She was a brilliant performer, but they couldn't take it." That approach, plus the fact that her competition of *My Three Sons* and NBC's Saturday night movies easily swamped her in the ratings, led to the show ending within four months.

However, the show's guest list has made it a sought-after property among many fans of them and Bailey and documentary producers. "I get calls periodically to look at *The Pearl Bailey Show*," Finkel acknowledged. Most of these came after Bailey died in 1990, and so he consulted with her widower, Louis Bellson, to see if he knew what happened to the tapes. Unfortunately, Bailey misunderstood what she needed to do to preserve them. As Bellson told him, "Bob, when she left, she took all the shows from them. They told her to keep them cold. Bob, she put them in her freezer." The frost generated by putting the tapes there rather than in a cool room damaged them, ergo there are none that have survived, unfortunately.

The Psychiatrist

Drama. Ran on NBC Wednesdays 10–11 P.M. Feb. 3–Sept. 1, 1971, opposite *The Young Lawyers* (through May 5) and *The Immortal* and *NFL Action* (from May 12 to Sept. 1) on ABC and *Hawaii Five-O* on CBS. C: Roy Thinnes (as Dr. James Whitman); Luther Adler (as Dr. Bernard Altman). EP: Norman Felton. P/D/W: Jerrold Freedman.

Cecil Smith, TV critic for *The Los Angeles Times*, wrote in 1971 that *The Psychiatrist* was the closest to a personal statement on television one could get, crediting its producer and sometime writer and director Jerrold Freedman. But Freedman noted many others contributed to the final product.

"Norman Felton had signed a deal with Universal [Studios] shortly before this, and decided to do a show about contemporary psychiatry," Freedman said. Writers Richard Levinson and William Link read an article about drug use and built a script on it to serve as a pilot for Felton's concept. But, Freedman said, "I think they were involved in some other things too and couldn't work on it." Universal officials went to one of their producers, Jack Laird, to ask what writers he knew could flesh out the script. "For one reason or another, none were available, so he offered me a crack at it."

The two men had produced *The Protectors*

(q.v.) in 1969-70, but Freedman was shocked by Laird's offer. "I had produced and directed one episode of *The Protectors*, but I had never written anything," he said. Over a weekend he cranked out a script which Sid Sheinberg, vice president in charge of television at Universal, liked. So did NBC. "They were bedazzled by the pilot." It aired with the subtitle *God Bless the Child* as a TV-movie on Dec. 14, 1970, with Roy Thinnes and Luther Adler as doctors treating the drug addiction of junkie Casey Pope (played by Peter Deuel). Two months later the show aired as part of an umbrella or "wheel" series titled *Four in One*.

"The way the other wheels worked was not like this one," Freedman noted. Here the elements aired six shows of the same series, then six of the next, and so on, before rotating all four weekly in reruns in the late spring and summer. *McCloud*, *San Francisco International Airport* (q.v.) and *Night Gallery* all aired their six shows before *The Psychiatrist* debuted. "They put us on last, which killed us," said Freedman, feeling that the setup did not endear itself to audiences.

Still, Freedman did like doing the show. "We wanted a really bold, ass-kicking show, different from what was on television," he said. "There were times we had scripts and they'd say, 'This is awfully tough,' but Sid would back me over the network." Freedman wrote only one of the series' scripts but acknowledged the rest came from "friends of mine" who freelanced on the show.

As far as directing, a standout appears in retrospect. "To a certain extent, I was [Steven] Spielberg's mentor," Freedman said. Although Spielberg had directed one story in the TV-movie pilot for *Night Gallery*, the director scarcely worked on other projects after that. "He wasn't doing very well. Beau May, the associate producer, wrote a show called 'The Private World of Martin Dalton' which involved kids. Steven directed it and did a really good job, and then came another episode. From that point, he really took off."

And though he blames the scheduling, Freedman said, "I think it was the kind of show that wouldn't be popular at that time. Today it could make it. You have so much more freedom to deal with impotency and topics which turned off NBC." Don't expect Freedman to be the one to do it, however; he now works mostly

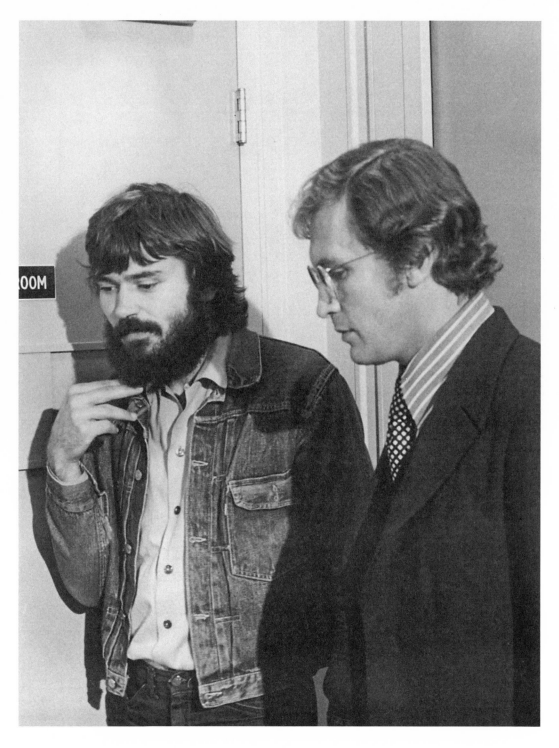

Bearded Pete Deuel played ex–drug addict Casey Poe, a patient assisted by Roy Thinnes' Dr. James Whitman, on both the TV-movie pilot and April 14, 1971, episode of *The Psychiatrist*. Less than a year after the episode aired, Deuel died from a self-inflicted gunshot wound.

Stewardess Millicent Martin examines a vase with pal and colleague Pat Finley sitting nearby during
an episode of *From a Bird's Eye View*.

as a novelist, with six books to his credit since 1994, and he has no interest at present to return to TV.

Joe Garagiola's Memory Game

Game. Ran on NBC Mondays through Fridays 1:30–2 P.M. Feb. 15–July 30, 1971, opposite *Let's Make a Deal* on ABC and *As the World Turns* on CBS. C: Joe Garagiola. EP: John Tobyansen. P: Robert Rubin, Les Roberts. D: Jeff Goldstein.

From a Bird's Eye View

Sitcom. Ran on NBC Mondays 7:30–8 P.M. March 29–Aug. 16, 1971, opposite *Let's Make a Deal* on ABC and *Gunsmoke* on CBS. C: Millicent Martin (as Millie Grover); Pat Finley (as Maggie Ralston); Peter Jones (as Mr. Clive Beauchamp); Robert Cawdron (as Uncle Bert Quigley); Noel Hood (as Miss Fosdyke). P/D: Ralph Levy.

For a director thinking about getting away from Hollywood, as was Ralph Levy, *From a Bird's Eye View* was the perfect ticket. "It was shot in England," he said. "Sir Lew Grade owned the show."

The cast was all British except for American Pat Finley, who would have a longer run playing Bob Newhart's sister Ellen on *The Bob Newhart Show* from 1974 to 1976. Millicent Martin, however, worked considerably in America as well as her native land. The two played flight attendants with the International Airline company, with Millie being a dotty, well-meaning type who got into misadventures which Maggie invariably had to assist in extri-

cating her from the mess. Mr. Beauchamp was the airline personnel director, Miss Fosdyke his secretary, and Uncle Bert a relative of Millie's.

The idea of doing a show seen on American TV in England was a novelty at the time, but, as Levy explained, "Those were the days when everybody was trying to get the transatlantic hit." The growing popularity of *All in the Family*, which was based on the British hit *Till Death Do Us Part*, convinced NBC executives that a British series with some American involvement would have appeal with U.S. viewers too.

From a Bird's Eye View replaced the faltering *Red Skelton Show*, which came back on Sunday evenings in the summer of 1971 before vanishing network television after a 20-year run. It ran only five months against *Gunsmoke*, but Levy was not willing to say competition from that show, which finished in the top five that year, was the reason for the failure of *From a Bird's Eye View*. "I don't think you know," he said. "You just go along and hope it gets going."

While the series ended fairly quickly, Levy did get some mileage out of it. "I stayed in London quite a while," he said. "I think I was there a few years." He did direct another series seen in America, *Shirley's World* (q.v.), but had only faint memories of the program. He retired from directing in 1981. Twenty years later he was happily retired in New Mexico. Most of the cast of *From a Bird's Eye View* was inactive in show business as well by that time, with Peter Jones dying in 2000 and Noel Hood passing away in 1979.

1971-72

Longstreet

Crime Drama. Ran on ABC Thursdays 9–10 P.M. Sept. 9, 1971–Aug. 10, 1972 opposite *Nichols* (through Nov. 18) and *Ironside* (from Nov. 25) on NBC and *The CBS Thursday Night Movies* on CBS. C: James Franciscus (as Mike Longstreet), Marlyn Mason (as Nikki Bell), Peter Mark Richman (as Duke Paige), Ann Doran (as Mrs. Kingston). EP/W: Stirling Silliphant. P: Joel Rogosin.

Longstreet was TV's first blind detective — correct that, insurance investigator. The job title did not thrill producer Joel Rogosin. "I didn't like that," he said. "I thought we would have had a lot more latitude had he been a private eye."

But Rogosin did not create Mike Longstreet. Veteran movie and TV writer Stirling Silliphant came up with the character and cast

James Franciscus in the lead. "Stirling Silliphant and the network agreed on that," Rogosin said. "I came into the show after the pilot. We cast the supporting cast for the series separate from the pilot." The 90-minute TV-movie, also titled *Longstreet*, aired on ABC on Feb. 23, 1971, with the characters of his girl Friday, Nikki Bell, and employer Duke Paige being in place too.

Arriving as a series in the fall of 1971, *Longstreet* added the character of housekeeper Mrs. Kingston while keeping the New Orleans locale. "I think that was a strong factor," Rogosin said of the latter. "We shot the bulk of the show in Los Angeles. We had a terrific art director who designed a set virtually the same as the New Orleans exteriors filmed by the second unit. The set, to this day, was one of the best in Hollywood."

The setup for the show's lead did not meet with similar acclaim. "There was a lot of controversy by blind people about whether he could do what Longstreet could do," Rogosin acknowledged. The producer was a friend of blind actor/pianist Tom Sullivan and feels what the character did was within the realm of possibility. The plot lines were not some wild fancy of Silliphant's, either. Although *Longstreet* was Silliphant's concept, Rogosin said, "A lot of the writing was freelance."

One other element remembered about *Longstreet* were some appearances by kung fu superstar Bruce Lee as Longstreet's defense instructor, Li Tsung. "Stirling Silliphant was interested in martial arts, and he liked Bruce Lee, who was a terrific guy," Rogosin said. "He was into features, so we could only make a few shows with him."

Longstreet did fine its first few months until NBC replaced its competition in the time slot with *Ironside*, a top 10 hit at the time — and a show which Rogosin had served as producer. "*Ironside* I did for three or four years," he said. "It was not good news."

Aware of their iffy status for renewal, the producers and star of *Longstreet* made a pitch for a second season. "Stirling and Jim and I went to New York when the pickup looked like it was marginal," Rogosin said. "It was a very close call. We were prepared to make some adjustments." One was to lose Nikki Bell's solicitous nature about Longstreet and his blindness while fighting criminals. "I thought it was

a one-note joke and we had played it out," Rogosin said.

Their presentation did not sway ABC, so *Longstreet* became history. Rogosin returned next season with *Ghost Story* (q.v.), while Franciscus came back in 1974 with *Doc Elliot* (q.v.).

Barrier Reef

Adventure. Ran on NBC Saturdays 10–10:30 A.M. Sept. 11–Dec. 25, 1971, opposite *Bewitched* reruns on ABC and *Pebbles and Bamm Bamm* on CBS, then NBC Saturdays 10:30–11 A.M. Jan. 8–Sept. 2, 1972, opposite *Lidsville* on ABC and *Archie's TV Funnies* on CBS. C: Joe Jones (as Captain Ted King), Rowena Wallace (as Tracey Deane), George Assana (as Jack Meuranki), Ellie Maclure (as Diana Parker), Ihab Nafa (as Dr. Elizabeth Hanna), Harold Hopkins (as Steve Goba), Ken James (as Kip King). EP: John McCullum, Bob Austin.

The Funny Side

Comedy Variety. Ran on NBC Tuesdays 9:30–10:30 P.M. Sept. 14–Nov. 16, 1971, opposite movies and *Marcus Welby, M.D.* on ABC and *Cannon* on CBS, then NBC Tuesdays 8:30–9:30 P.M. Nov. 30–Dec. 7, 1971, opposite movies on NBC and *Hawaii Five-O* on CBS. C: Gene Kelly, John Amos, Warren Berlinger, Dick Clair, Pat Finley, Teresa Graves, Michael Lembeck, Jenna McMahon, Burt Mustin, Queenie Smith, Cindy Williams. P/W: Bill Persky, Sam Denoff. D: Clark Jones.

Originally planned as a special for NBC, *The Funny Side* became a series anticipated to do well thanks to producers Bill Persky and Sam Denoff securing Gene Kelly as its host. They had known Kelly for nearly a decade prior to the show. The men came to Hollywood in 1961 to write for *The Steve Allen Show* on ABC, and head writer Leonard Stern recommended that they do the script for the entertainment of the ABC affiliates meeting in 1962. One new show that fall was *Going My Way* (q.v.) starring Kelly, and they had to work up a routine for him.

"We were nervous," Denoff remembered. "Here we were, meeting this legend at his home." In the spirit of the Catholic setting for *Going My Way*, the two wrote "a whole bunch of priest and nun jokes, and Gene loved them." But ahead of the affair, Kelly thought the jokes might be too hip for the room and suggested, "Why don't I [pretend to] talk to my Irish

Smile for the camera and pretend you're having fun: Four couples from *The Funny Side* mug it up in this picture. They are, from left, Dick Clair, Jenna McMahon, Warren Berlinger, Pat Finley, Burt Mustin, Queenie Smith, John Amos and Teresa Graves. Not pictured are Michael Lembeck, Cindy Williams and host Gene Kelly.

mother in Chicago, like the way George Jessel used to do?" He did so, it went over well, and though they had little to do with the final product, Kelly called the producers on stage and credited them for writing it. "What a generous guy!" Denoff said.

Kelly told the producers he'd work with them anytime. In 1971, with his career in a downturn, they held him to his word to host *The Funny Side*. "With this show, we said, 'We can't think of anybody better,'" Denoff said. Beside Kelly's musical comedy background, the fact that he was a "name" performer among a largely unknown cast (at the time) was considered a plus too.

As for the format, Denoff said, "Each show we'd do the funny side of money, the funny side of newspapers and so on. There was a new revue every week." Playlets and music about each topic took place among five married couples—newlywed (Michael Lembeck and Cindy Williams), longtime wed (Burt Mustin and Queenie Smith), rich (Dick Clair and Jenna McMahon), working class (Warren Berlinger and Pat Finley) and minority (John Amos and Teresa Graves).

For the special "the other Ray Charles" (the white arranger, not the black singer) created original tunes but was busy when it became a series, so David Fishberg replaced him. "It might have been better parodying popular songs than coming up with original ones every week," Denoff said in retrospect. He felt viewers did not care to hear new, unfamiliar material versus ones they already knew. But he did not feel that led to its short run, blaming it more on its tough competition in two different time slots, with all the ABC and CBS series against it being in the top 30.

One NBC executive told Denoff at the time, "This is the finest show we've ever cancelled." But cancelled it was. Much of the cast and crew went on to other TV series work (e.g., Williams as star on *Laverne & Shirley*, Amos as star on *Good Times*, Lembeck as an actor and director, Clair and McMahon as writers for *The Carol Burnett Show* and more), but Kelly never did another TV series after the disappointment of this and *Going My Way*.

Shirley's World

Sitcom. Ran on ABC Wednesdays 9:30–10 P.M. Sept. 15, 1971–Jan. 5, 1972, opposite *Medical Center* on CBS and *The NBC Mystery Movie* on NBC. C: Shirley MacLaine (as Shirley Logan), John Gregson (as Dennis Croft). EP: Sheldon Leonard, Ronald Rubin. P: Barry Delmaine, Ray Austin. D: Ray Austin, Charles Crichton.

The Man and the City

Drama. Ran on ABC Wednesdays 10–11 P.M. Sept. 15, 1971–Jan. 5, 1972, opposite *Mannix* on CBS and *Night Gallery* on NBC. C: Anthony Quinn (as Mayor Thomas Jefferson Alcala), Mike Farrell (as Andy Hays), Mala Powers (as Marian Crane), Carmen Zapata (as Josefina). EP: David Victor. P: Stanley Rubin. D: Fernando Lamas, Lee Philips, Jeannot Szwarc, Paul Henreid.

Veteran actor Anthony Quinn's only regular series cast him as the mayor of Albuquerque, New Mexico. His character first appeared in a TV-movie pilot called *The City* that aired on May 17, 1971. None of the regulars apart from Quinn appeared in the pilot. In the series, Mayor Alcala appeared at work with his aide Andy Hays, who did not like the personal attention Alcala provided his constituents despite it winning him 16 years in office; and his secretary, Marian Crane. Greeting Quinn's character at home was Josefina.

"I played his housekeeper," said actress Carmen Zapata. "He was wonderful to work with. An amazing actor. However, he was not happy with the material."

Specifically, Quinn did not feel the scripts did an adequate job of conveying the story. "He was always complaining about something with the writing, and usually he was right," she said. She remembered there were many rewrites done on the spot to accommodate the actor's wishes.

Amid the waiting, Zapata found that Quinn liked to unwind with her. "We used to play chess on the set," she said. "He was very fond of me, because I could ad lib, and we did that in some scenes."

But much money and time was being lost by the large amounts of rewrites Quinn requested, and Zapata claims that is what ended the series after 13 episodes. "The cost of the show got out of hand, and they just decided not to continue because of that," she said. She emphasized it was not due to shooting on location at all. Though some sources say the series was filmed at Albuquerque, Zapata said it was not so: "The pilot was filmed there, but they brought it to Universal Studios for the series."

Actually, it could have been the fact that *The Man and the City* ran a constant third place in the ratings opposite *Mannix* and *Night Gallery* that led to its disappearance. In any event, after failing with this series and a year earlier with *The Interns* (see 1970-71), Mike Farrell returned to series TV three years later with a winner as B.J. Hunnicut on *M*A*S*H*, a role he held until 1983. Zapata also returned to doing a regular program in the 1975-76 season, but she was not as fortunate as Farrell; see *Viva Valdez*.

As for Quinn, he seldom acted on TV afterward, making a rare appearance in the pilot for *Hercules: The Legendary Journeys* in 1994. He gained more notoriety for his personal life in later years (including fathering a child as a septuagenarian) before he died in 2001.

Bearcats

Adventure. Ran on CBS Thursdays 8–9 P.M. Sept. 16–Dec. 30, 1971, opposite *Alias Smith and Jones* on ABC and *The Flip Wilson Show* on NBC. C: Rod Taylor (as Hank Brackett), Dennis Cole (as Johnny Reach). EP: Douglas Heyes. P: David Friedkin, Morton Fine.

Nichols (a/k/a James Garner as Nichols)

Western. Ran on NBC Thursdays 9–10 P.M. Sept. 16–Nov. 18, 1971, opposite *Longstreet* on ABC and movies on CBS, then NBC Tuesdays 9:30–10:30 P.M. Nov. 30, 1971–Aug. 1, 1972, opposite movies and *Marcus Welby, M.D.* on ABC and *Cannon* on CBS. C: James Garner (as Nichols), Neva Patterson (as "Ma" Sara Ketcham), John Beck (as Ketcham), Stuart Margolin (as Mitch), Margot Kidder (as Ruth), Alice Ghostley (as Bertha). EP: Meta Rosenberg. P: Frank Pierson. D: Gerd Oswald.

The Chicago Teddy Bears

Sitcom. Ran on CBS Fridays 8–8:30 P.M. Sept. 17–Dec. 17, 1971, opposite *The Brady Bunch* on ABC and *The D.A.* on NBC. C: Dean Jones (as Linc McCray), Art Metrano (as Nick Marr), Mar-

vin Kaplan (as Marvin), Mickey Shaughnessy (as Duke), Jamie Farr (as Lefty), Mike Mazurki (as Julius), Huntz Hall (as Dutch), John Banner (as Uncle Latzi). P: Jerry Thorpe. D: Norman Tokar.

The D.A.

Drama. Ran on NBC Fridays 8–8:30 P.M. Sept. 17, 1971–Jan. 7, 1972, opposite *The Chicago Teddy Bears* (through Dec. 17) and *O'Hara, U.S. Treasury* (from Jan. 7) on CBS and *The Brady Bunch* on ABC. C: Robert Conrad (as Deputy D.A. Paul Ryan), Harry Morgan (as Chief Deputy D.A. H.M. "Staff" Stafford), Ned Romero (as D.A. Investigator Ned Romero), Julie Cobb (as Public Defender Katherine Benson). EP/D: Jack Webb. P: Robert H. Forward. D: Harry Morgan, Ozzie Nelson, Alan Crosland, Jr.

O'Hara, U.S. Treasury

Drama. Ran on CBS Fridays 8:30–9 P.M. Sept. 17–Dec. 17, 1971, opposite *The Partridge Family* and *Room 222* on ABC and movies on NBC, then CBS Fridays 8–9 P.M. Jan. 7–Sept. 8, 1972, opposite *The Brady Bunch* and *The Partridge Family* on ABC and *The D.A.* (through Jan. 7) and *Sanford and Son* (from Jan. 14) and movies on NBC. C: David Janssen (as Jim O'Hara). EP: Jack Webb. P: Leonard B. Kaufman. D: Lawrence Dobkin, Alan Crosland, Jr., Paul Landers.

Getting Together

Sitcom. Ran on ABC Saturdays 8–8:30 P.M. Sept. 18, 1971–Jan. 8, 1972, opposite *All in the Family* on CBS and *The Partners* on NBC. C: Bobby Sherman (as Bobby Conway), Wes Stern (as Lionel Poindexter), Susan Neher (as Jennifer Conway), Jack Burns (as Officer Rudy Colcheck), Pat Carroll (as Rita Simon). EP: Bob Claver. P: Paul Junger Witt. D: Roger Duchowney.

The Partners

Sitcom. Ran on NBC Saturdays 8–8:30 P.M. Sept. 18, 1971–Jan. 8, 1972, opposite *Getting Together* on ABC and *All in the Family* on CBS, then NBC Fridays 8–8:30 P.M. July 28–Sept. 8, 1972, opposite *The Brady Bunch* on ABC and *O'Hara, U.S. Treasury* on CBS. C: Don Adams (as Det. Lennie Crooke), Rupert Crosse (as Det. George Robinson), John Doucette (as Capt. Aaron Williams Andrews), Dick Van Patten (as Sgt. Nelson Higgenbottom), Robert Karvelas (as Freddie Butler). EP/D: Don Adams. P: Arne Sultan. D: Christian Nyby, Earl Bellamy.

The Good Life

Sitcom. Ran on NBC Saturdays 8:30–9 P.M. Sept. 18, 1971–Jan. 8, 1972, opposite movies on ABC and *Funny Face* (through Dec. 11) and *The Mary Tyler Moore Show* (from Dec. 18) on CBS. C: Larry Hagman (as Albert Miller), Donna Mills (as Jane Miller), David Wayne (as Charles Dutton), Hermione Baddeley (as Grace Dutton), Danny Goldman (as Nick Dutton). EP: Lee Rich. P/D: Claudio Guzman.

Funny Face

Sitcom. Ran on CBS Saturdays 8:30–9 P.M. Sept. 18–Dec. 11, 1971, opposite movies on ABC and *The Good Life* on NBC. C: Sandy Duncan (as Sandy Stockton), Valorie Armstrong (as Alice McRaven), Kathleen Freeman (as Kate Harwell), Henry Beckman (as Pat Harwell). EP: Jerry Davis. P: Carl Kleinschmitt. D: Hal Cooper. W: Bob Rodgers.

The Persuaders

Adventure. Ran on ABC Saturdays 10–11 P.M. Sept. 18, 1971–Dec. 25, 1972, opposite *Mission: Impossible* on CBS and movies on NBC, then ABC Wednesdays 9:30–10:30 P.M. Jan. 12–June 14, 1972, opposite *Medical Center* and *Mannix* on CBS and *The NBC Mystery Movie* and *Night Gallery* on NBC. C: Tony Curtis (as Danny Wilde), Roger Moore (as Lord Brett Sinclair), Laurence Naismith (as Judge Fulton). P: Robert S. Baker. D: Roy Ward Baker, Roger Moore, Val Guest.

The Jimmy Stewart Show

Sitcom. Ran on NBC Sundays 8:30–9 P.M. Sept. 19, 1971–Aug. 27, 1972, opposite *The F.B.I.* on ABC and movies on CBS. C: Jimmy Stewart (as Prof. James K. Howard), Julie Adams (as Martha Howard), Jonathan Daly (as Peter Howard), Ellen Geer (as Wendy Howard), John McGiver (as Dr. Luther Quince), Kirby Furlong (as Jake Howard), Dennis Larson (as Teddy Howard). P/D: Hal Kanter.

Cade's County

Police Drama. Ran on CBS Sundays 9:30–10:30 P.M. Sept. 19, 1971–Aug. 6, 1972, opposite movies on ABC and *Bonanza* and *The Bold Ones* on NBC, then CBS Mondays 10–11 P.M. Aug. 7–Sept. 4, 1972, opposite movies on ABC and baseball on NBC. C: Glenn Ford (as Sheriff Sam Cade), Edgar Buchanan (as J.J. Jackson), Taylor Lacher (as Arlo Pritchard), Victor Campos (as Rudy Davillo),

Peter Ford (as Pete), Betty Ann Carr (as Betty Ann Sundown), Sandra Ego (as Joannie Little Bird; 1971). EP: David Gerber. P: Charles Larson.

Sarge

Drama. Ran on NBC Tuesdays 8:30–9:30 P.M. Sept. 21–Nov. 23, 1971, opposite movies on ABC and *Hawaii Five-O* on CBS, then NBC Tuesdays 7:30–8:30 P.M. Nov. 30, 1971–Jan. 11, 1972, opposite *The Mod Squad* on ABC and *The Glen Campbell Goodtime Hour* on CBS. C: George Kennedy (as Father "Sarge" Samuel Cavanaugh), Sallie Shockley (as Valerie), Harold Sakata (as Kenji Takichi), Ramon Bieri (as Barney Verick). EP: David Levy. P: David Levinson. D: John Badham, Richard A. Colla, Jeannot Szwarc.

The ABC Comedy Hour

Comedy Variety. Ran on ABC Wednesdays 8:30–9:30 P.M. Jan. 12–April 5, 1972, opposite *The Carol Burnett Show* and *Medical Center* on CBS and *The NBC Mystery Movie* on NBC, then ABC Wednesdays 9:30–10:30 P.M. opposite *Medical Center* and *Mannix* on CBS and *The NBC Mystery Movie* and *Night Gallery* on NBC. C: Frank Gorshin, George Kirby, Rich Little, Marilyn Michaels, Joe Baker, Charlie Callas, Fred Travalena. P: Dwight Hemion, Gary Smith. D: Dwight Hemion. W: Frank Peppiatt, Jay Burton, Jack Burns, John Aylesworth, Bryan Blackburn, Tony Hawes.

The ABC Comedy Hour is a borderline entry for this book. Mostly a collection of humorous specials, the show did feature prominently during its run roughly every other week a regular cast of impersonators in comedy sketches, thus allowing its inclusion. The called themselves *The Kopycats*, and it was under that subtitle that the shows actually secured some business in repeats in syndication in the 1970s.

"It was fun," said producer/director Dwight Hemion. "That was a good show. We did that mostly in England. The network there, ATV, had a deal with ABC to do specials over there." When pressed, Hemion admitted there was one thing about the show that bothered him — "Strange bookings."

Some of the guests made sense. Debbie Reynolds, who did a clever Zsa Zsa Gabor and other ladies, fit in fine, as did the genius casting of bringing Ed Sullivan on along with the man who made his career by impersonating him, Will Jordan. Hemion remembered liking Steve Lawrence. "He had a great sense of humor, did impressions of Tony Bennett," he said.

But then there were head scratchers like bland Robert Young, probably enlisted due to the fact that his series, *Marcus Welby, M.D.*, was the top-rated series on ABC at the time, and bombastic Raymond Burr, who reportedly did variety shows like these to convince TV viewers of the period he was not paralyzed from the waist down like his character on the hit *Ironside*.

Among the cast were the top names of impressionists in America at the time — Frank Gorshin, Rich Little and George Kirby (whose best known character might have been Pearl Bailey, of all people; he would return to TV later in the fall of 1972 with his syndicated series *Half the George Kirby Comedy Hour*). Marilyn Michaels was the sole female of the group and did a solid Dinah Shore, among other women. After three shows, Fred Travalena replaced Callas.

"We used them all, but not each week, depending on their schedules," Hemion said of the regulars. "Travalena's thing was doing Sinatra, but he wasn't that great, in my opinion."

While doing impressions can be a somewhat limiting field of comedy, Hemion said his writing staff had no trouble coming up with sketches for the shows. "They were good guys," he said. "It wasn't hard to put them together, rather easy in fact."

The biweekly airing of the shows between specials might have hurt *The Kopycats* from going into a second season. Then again, the fact that it ran against *The Carol Burnett Show*, *Medical Center* and *The NBC Mystery Movie*, all top 25 shows in the 1971-72 season, didn't help it either. ABC reran just The Kopycats segments in the summer of 1972 before moving onto other offerings.

Me and the Chimp

Sitcom. Ran on CBS Thursdays 8–8:30 P.M. Jan. 13–May 18, 1972, opposite *Alias Smith and Jones* on ABC and *The Flip Wilson Show* on NBC. C: Ted Bessell (as Mike Reynolds), Anita Gillette (as Liz Reynolds), Scott Kolden (as Scott Reynolds), Kami Cotler (as Kitty Reynolds). EP/D/W: Garry Marshall. P/D: Alan Rafkin. D: Oscar Rudolph, Roger Duchowny, Ted Bessell, Richard Kinon. W: Gordon Farr, Frank Buxton, Larry Markes.

The Don Rickles Show

Sitcom. Ran on CBS Fridays 10:30–11 P.M. Jan. 14–May 26, 1972, opposite *Love, American Style* on ABC. C: Don Rickles (as Don Robinson), Louise Sorel (as Barbara Robinson), Erin Moran (as Janie Robinson), Robert Hogan (as Tyler Benedict), Joyce Van Patten (as Jean Benedict), Judy Cassmore (as Audrey), Barry Gordon (as Conrad Musk). EP: Sheldon Leonard, Sam Denoff. D: Hy Averback.

Though it ran just four months, *The Don Rickles Show* was a happy memory for its producer, Sam Denoff. "This was a show that my partner on it was Sheldon Leonard," Denoff said. "He was my god, the best there was." Denoff had worked together with Leonard since the days when Denoff wrote *The Dick Van Dyke Show* in the 1960s while Leonard produced it.

Denoff also said he enjoyed working with the star of the show. "Don was a joy to work with. Truly a professional. Don was always so deferential and caring. He wanted everybody to be happy."

If that doesn't sound like the insulting style most people associate with Rickles, don't worry. The show's format had "the Merchant of Venom" as the head of a Long Island, New York, household with a wife and daughter who let off steam there after coming home from his high-pressure job at the advertising firm of Kingston, Cohen & Vanderpool. Don's co-worker was Conrad Musk, and his secretary was Audrey. The Benedicts were friends of the Robinson family.

With all that talent in front of and behind the camera, *The Don Rickles Show* looked like a winner. But Denoff felt there was one major problem, and that came from CBS's nighttime programmer. "Freddy Silverman didn't like it," Denoff said. Denoff said that Silverman essentially "buried" the show on the schedule.

When the series debuted in January 1972, it did not take the 8–8:30 P.M. slot vacated by the departure of *The Chicago Teddy Bears* (q.v.). Instead, CBS moved *O'Hara, U.S. Treasury* up a half hour from its previous start of 8:30 P.M. and put *The Don Rickles Show* on at 10:30 P.M. following movies on CBS. There it faced competition from the second half hour of *Love, American Style* and whatever programs NBC affiliates installed at the time (the network gave the slot in 1971-72 to its stations to make up for starting programs a half hour earlier on

If photographs could talk: Don Rickles looks ready to make a snippy remark after the anniversary present he and Louise Sorel (center, as his wife) bought for their friends the Benedicts is superfluous because the latter duo has separated. Joyce Van Patten (left) guest starred as Tyler's estranged wife Jean on the episode, which ran February 18, 1972.

Tuesdays at 7:30 P.M. rather than 8 P.M. like most weeknights). Sitcoms typically never do well from the 10–11 P.M. slot, and coming near the end of the night before the news, *The Don Rickles Show* bombed.

Some have blamed Rickles' insult humor as too tough for viewers to take on a weekly basis. Denoff disagreed and pointed to *C.P.O. Sharkey*, a later sitcom starring Rickles. "That show worked," Denoff said, although with only a year-and-a-half run on NBC from 1976 to 1978, one could argue it didn't really click. His later series efforts were similarly unimpressive; he co-hosted another year-and-a-half series, *Foul-Ups, Bleeps & Blunders*, on ABC from 1984 to 1985 and then spent just two months on the Fox schedule in 1993 with the sitcom *Daddy Dearest* opposite Richard Lewis. He fared much better as a frequent and favored guest on talk shows into the 21st century.

The Sixth Sense

Supernatural Drama. Ran on ABC Saturdays 10–11 P.M. Jan. 15–Dec. 30, 1972 (off summer months), opposite *Mission: Impossible* (through Dec. 9) and *The Carol Burnett Show* (from Dec. 16) on CBS and movies on NBC. C: Gary Collins (as Dr. Michael Rhodes), Catherine Ferrar (as Nancy Murphy; January–May only). P: Stan Sheptner. AP: Robert F. O'Neill. D: John Newland, John Badham, Earl Bellamy. W: Nancy Lawrence, Harlan Ellison, Dorothy C. Fantana.

The Amateur's Guide to Love

Game. Ran on CBS Mondays through Fridays 4–4:30 P.M. March 27–June 23, 1972, opposite *Love, American Style* reruns on ABC and *Somerset* on NBC. C: Gene Rayburn. EP: Merrill Heatter, Bob Quigley. P: Robert Noah, Art Alisi. D: Jerome Shaw.

The Marty Feldman Comedy Machine

Comedy Variety. Ran on ABC Wednesdays 9–9:30 P.M. April 12–Aug. 16, 1972, opposite *Medical Cen-* *ter* on CBS and *The NBC Mystery Movie* on NBC. C: Marty Feldman, Barbara Feldon, Spike Milligan, Lenny Schultz, Fred Smoot, Thelma Houston, Orson Welles.

1972-73

Runaround

Children's Game. Ran on NBC Saturdays 11:30 A.M.–Noon Sept. 9, 1972–Sept. 1, 1973, opposite *Kid Power* on ABC and *The Flintstones Comedy Hour* on CBS. C: Paul Winchell. EP: Merrill Heatter, Bob Quigley. P: Les Roberts, Art Alisi. D: Jerome Shaw.

The New Bill Cosby Show

Comedy Variety. Ran on CBS Mondays 10–11 P.M. Sept. 11, 1972–May 7, 1973, opposite football (through Jan. 1) and movies (from Jan. 8) on ABC and movies on NBC. C: Bill Cosby, Foster Brooks, Oscar DeGruy, Mike Elias, Lola Falana, Ronny Graham, Ray Jessel, Pat McCormick, Stan Ross, Frank Shaw, Susan Tolsky, the Quincy Jones Orchestra. P: George Schlatter. D: Mark Warren. W: Pat McCormick, Stanley Ralph Ross, Jerry Mayer, Ronny Graham, Gene Perrett.

The Paul Lynde Show

Sitcom. Ran on ABC Wednesday 8–8:30 P.M. Sept. 13, 1972–May 30, 1973, opposite *The Carol Burnett Show* (through Nov. 29) and *The Sonny and Cher Comedy Hour* (from Dec. 16) on CBS and *Adam-12* on NBC, then ABC Saturdays 8:30–9 P.M. June 30–Sept. 8, 1973, opposite *Bridget Loves Bernie* on CBS and *Emergency!* on NBC. C: Paul Lynde (as Paul Simms), Elizabeth Allen (as Martha Simms), John Calvin (as Howie Dickerson), Jane Actman (as Barbara Simms Dickerson), Pamelyn Ferdin (as Sally Simms), Jerry Stiller (as Barney Dickerson), Anne Meara (as Grace Dickerson), Herb Voland (as T.J. McNish), James Gregory (as T.R. Scott), Allison McKay (as Alice). EP: Harry Ackerman. P/D: William Asher. D: George Tyne, Ernest Losso, Jack Donohue. W: S.A. Long, Robert Fisher, Arthur Marx, Ed Jurist, Phil Sharp, Ron Clark, Sam Bobrick.

Opening dialogue from the debut of *The Paul Lynde Show*:

PAUL SIMMS (PAUL LYNDE, with his characteristic sniggering delivery): Martha! Quick, my dry martini! …
MARTHA SIMMS (ELIZABETH ALLEN): Hello, dear. How goes the rat race?
PAUL: The rats are winning!

The Paul Lynde Show came about because of an unusual deal set up with Bill Asher and ABC due to the former's clout with the network's most popular show of the 1960s, *Bewitched*. The network stipulated that *Bewitched* would run through 1974, or the network would have to accept two, not just one, series produced by Asher. So when Asher's wife, Elizabeth Montgomery, decided in 1972 she had enough of eight years playing a witch, Asher was able to return that fall with two sitcom series—*Temperatures Rising* and *The Paul Lynde Show*.

Lynde, as any *Bewitched* fan can tell you, was a favorite on that show as mischievous Uncle Arthur in occasional appearances from 1965 to 1971. He also was a top guest star on other comedies and variety shows in the 1960s and early 1970s, and was the regular star "center square" on the top-rated daytime game show *The Hollywood Squares* since 1968. Yet despite his popularity, he starred in at least four TV pilots for series that never came to fruition until *The Paul Lynde Show*.

"I did two of his pilots with him and they didn't get on," Asher said, referring to 1962's *Howie* and 1966's *Sedgewick Hawk-Styles*. "I loved the man."

The Paul Lynde Show was an updated version of the *Howie* pilot. Paul Simms was the

The idea of someone spraining an ankle hardly seems funny, but that's what's happening to Jerry Siller here on the September 27, 1972, installment of *The Paul Lynde Show*, with (from left to right) his daughter-in-law Barbara (Jane Actman), son Howie (John Calvin) and wife, Grace (Stiller's real-life wife Anne Meara) assisting him. Lynde and his TV wife, Elizabeth Allen, seated at right, grin because they think the mishap may reconcile Stiller and Meara, their fellow in-laws. Don't ask me why or how that worked out.

frustrated father-in-law of Howie Dickerson, a well-meaning blond hunk with a high IQ but low common sense. Paul seemed to dislike him from the first episode, wherein Howie and Paul's daughter Sally got married in the Simms' backyard pool (an unusual permanent set for a series filmed in front of a studio audience) and came to live with the Simms in their home in Ocean Grove, Calif., while Howie tried to find a job. Adding to Paul's headaches were his other daughter, teenager Sally, who was already dating; the overbearing fellow in-laws the Dickersons; and his law partners McNish and Scott. Alice was Mr. McNish's secretary.

The series did moderately well against strong competition, though some felt Lynde was better as a supporting comic than as a star. "I think they might have felt that," Asher said. "I don't agree with that, though."

In fact, Asher thought the show and *Temperatures Rising* would have long runs, but ABC

executives had a different idea. "Both of them were good, had reasonably good ratings. But they wanted to take Paul Lynde and put him in *Temperatures Rising* and thought they'd get a big hit." They were wrong; Lynde's addition to *Temperatures Rising* in the fall of 1973 did not raise the ratings, and the show aired its last episode on Aug. 29, 1974. Lynde would have no other regular TV jobs apart from *The Hollywood Squares* until his death in 1982.

The Julie Andrews Hour

Musical Variety. Ran on ABC Wednesdays 10–11 P.M. Sept. 13, 1972–Jan. 10, 1973, opposite *Cannon* on CBS and *Search* on NBC, then ABC Saturdays 9–10 P.M. Jan. 20–April 28, 1973, opposite *The Mary Tyler Moore Show* and *The Bob Newhart Show* on CBS and movies on NBC. C: Julie Andrews, Rich Little, Alice Ghostley, The Tony Charmoli Dancers, The Dick Williams Singers, The Nelson Riddle Orchestra. P: Nick Vanoff,

William Hardac. D: Bill Davis. W: John Aylesworth, Larry Klein, Lila Garrett, others.

One of the greatest musical comedy stars ever of Broadway and cinema, Julie Andrews had starred in some 1950s and 1960s American TV specials before her faltering films in the early 1970s convinced her to give a series a go. With her wholesome appeal and terrific voice, Andrews looked to be a winner as a regular TV attraction. Unfortunately, ABC executives forgot that many of her fans were children when they scheduled the show.

"I always thought we did excellent shows," said Tony Charmoli. "I just thought that the time slot was terrible. We were on at 10 o'clock at night, and most of the principal audience was in bed. She did do an 8 o'clock Thanksgiving special that season, and she had a sky-high rating."

Charmoli had choreographed *The Dinah Shore Chevy Show* in the 1950s and *The Danny Kaye Show* in the 1960s before doing the same for *The Julie Andrews Hour.* He got involved with the series because "I knew the producer Nick Vanoff." As the show's choreographer, Charmoli staged numbers with Julie, guest stars like Donald O'Connor and Sammy Davis, Jr., and his regular dance troupe of men.

"I think I had maybe eight male dancers, and we would augment that depending on the number," he said. "Since Julie's fairly tall, we needed fairly tall dancers with her. We would have an orchestral rehearsal, but daily rehearsal would be piano and drum."

Charmoli would alter his routine somewhat if the number involved Andrews rather than just his dancers. "I'd often work out the dance numbers without her," he said. "She was out working on vocals so the arrangements could be done." Regarding Andrews as a talent, he said, "She's a very good musical performer. Not a great dancer, but she liked to move and dance, especially where there was a storyline where she could move."

Despite Andrews' husband Blake Edwards' background as a TV producer (e.g., *Peter Gunn*), Charmoli said, "He was not terribly involved. He just left it to Nick Vanoff and Sir Lew Grade [the head of the series' production company]. He just said, 'Just keep it in good taste. I don't care how much it costs.'"

Edwards may not have worried about the show's finances, but ABC did as *Cannon* regularly beat Andrews' show on Wednesday. Incredibly, they switched her mid-season to compete opposite TV's sweetheart of the time, Mary Tyler Moore. It was no contest. The show left the air three months after the change, albeit with Emmys for Outstanding Variety Musical Series and Outstanding Directorial Achievement in Variety or Music (for Bill Davis for an episode where Julie reprised her Eliza Doolittle character from the Broadway hit *My Fair Lady* and her starring role in the movie *Mary Poppins*).

Andrews would not do another series until nearly 20 years later. Ironically, on the sitcom *Julie* she played a hit variety show hostess. The feeble program wasted her talents and ran even shorter than her first show, airing from just May 30–July 4, 1992 on ABC.

Search

Adventure. Ran on NBC Wednesdays 10–11 P.M. Sept. 13, 1972–Aug. 29, 1973, opposite *The Julie Andrews Hour* (through Jan. 10) and *Owen Marshall, Attorney at Law* (from Jan. 17) on ABC and *Cannon* on CBS. C: Hugh O'Brian (as Hugh Lockwood), Tony Franciosa (as Nick Bianco), Doug McClure (as C.R. Grover), Burgess Meredith (as Cameron), Angel Tompkins (as Gloria Harding), Ford Rainey (as Dr. Barnett; 1972), Keith Andes (as Dr. Barnett; 1973), Ginny Golden (as Miss Keach; 1972), Tony De Costa (as Ramos), Byron Chung (as Kuroda), Albert Popwell (as Griffin), Ron Castro (as Carlos), Amy Farrell (as Murdock), Tom Hallick (as Harris; 1973), Pamela Jones (as Miss James; 1973). EP: Leslie Stevens. P: Robert J. Justman. D: Barry Shear, William Wiard, Marc Daniels, George McCowan.

Ghost Story (a/k/a Circle of Fear)

Supernatural Drama. Ran on NBC Fridays 9–10 P.M. Sept. 15, 1972–June 22, 1973, opposite *Room 222* and *The Odd Couple* on ABC and movies on CBS. C: Sebastian Cabot (as Winston Essex). EP: William Castle. P: Joel Rogosin. D, Story Consultant: Jimmy Sangster.

Ghost Story is the great neglected network TV horror series. For example, it does not appear in Stephen King's study of horror portrayals in the media *Danse Macabre* (1979, Everest House), or even the autobiography of the show's executive producer William Castle, *Step Right Up! I'm Gonna Scare the Pants Off America* (1976, Putnam).

But story consultant Jimmy Sangster did discuss it in his autobiography, *Do You Want It Good or Tuesday?* (1997, Midnight Marquee). After writing more than 30 British horror films, Sangster did the show because he wanted to work in Hollywood. He supervised the scripts and wrote and directed each show's introductions and epilogues delivered by Sebastian Cabot. Cabot played Winston Essex, operator of the hotel Mansfield House. Sangster summed up his feeling about *Ghost Story* as "It deserved a better fate. It was a good show with good people involved."

One of those "good people" was William Castle, the veteran horror movie producer who hit big in 1968 with *Rosemary's Baby*. His reputation helped Screen Gems, then the TV arm of Columbia Pictures, sell the series to NBC. Castle had produced only one other series, the syndicated *Men of Annapolis* in 1956, but had veteran TV producer Joel Rogosin to help him.

"Bill and I put the show together conceptually," said Rogosin. "He hired the writers and the actors." As for Sebastian Cabot as host, he noted, "I think they looked around for someone who had some stature and significance. He was terrific."

A strong slate of guest stars appeared on the show, among them Patricia Neal and Jason Robards. "The network provided us with a large budget," Rogosin said. "It was good money for them."

Most script ideas Rogosin and Castle hashed out in meetings with writers. Rogosin recalled once he and Castle improvised a tale on a 10-minute ride from the studio to NBC's Burbank headquarters for a meeting. "There were guys digging up the street and I said, 'What would happen if one of those guys dug something up?' And Bill said, 'What if it was a chest?'" The two men kept improvising until they came out with a story of a toy horse inside the chest which grew in size and terrorized a young couple whose husband found the chest at work.

But the tales concocted did not bring the ratings NBC wanted, and on Jan. 5, 1973, the show was retitled *Circle of Fear* and Cabot was dropped. Rogosian called that decision "very painful" and added "I think they could've done

more with Sebastian. We talked about involving him more in the stories, but it didn't happen." *Circle of Fear* ended five months later.

Rogosin blamed the show's short run on a lack of faith by NBC to give it a fair chance. "Anthologies, they're tough nuts to crack," he said. "It's demonstrated time and again that they take time to catch on." The producer went on to do other series, including one that became a real-life horror story for him behind the scenes; see *The Blue Knight*.

The Men

Umbrella title for three rotating adventure series that ran ABC Thursdays 9–10 P.M. Sept. 21–Jan. 4, 1973, opposite movies on CBS and *Ironside* on NBC, then ABC Saturdays 10–11 P.M. Jan. 13–Sept. 1, 1973, opposite *The Carol Burnett Show* (through May 12) and *Mission: Impossible* (from May 26) on CBS and movies on NBC. Components were as follows:

Assignment: Vienna

C: Robert Conrad (as Jake Webster), Charles Cioffi (as Maj. Bernard Caldwell), Anton Diffring (as Inspector Hoffman). EP: Robert H. Justman. P: Jerry Ludwig, Eric Berovich.

The Delphi Bureau

C: Laurence Luckinbill (as Glenn Garth Gregory), Anne Jeffreys (as Sybil Van Loween). P: Sam Rolfe.

Jigsaw

C: James Wainwright (as Lt. Frank Dain). P: Stanley Kallis, Harry Tatelman. D: Stephen J. Cannell, Calvin Clements, Marc Daniels. W: David Friedkin, Thomas Drake, Herb Bermann.

Banyon

Crime Drama. Ran on NBC Fridays 10–11 P.M. Sept. 15, 1972–Jan. 12, 1973, opposite *Love American Style* on ABC and movies on CBS. C: Robert Forster (as Miles C. Banyon), Joan Blondell (as Peggy Revere), Richard Jaeckel (as Lt. Pete McNeil), Julie Gregg (as Abby Graham). EP: Richard Alan Simmons, Quinn Martin. P: Ed Adamson. D: Robert Day, Reza S. Badiyi, Theodore J. Flicker.

Bridget Loves Bernie

Sitcom. Ran on CBS Saturdays 8:30–9 P.M. Sept. 16, 1972–Sept. 8, 1973, opposite *Alias Smith and Jones* (through Jan. 13), *A Touch of Grace* (from Jan. 20 to June 16) and *The Paul Lynde Show* (from June 30) on ABC and *Emergency!* on NBC. C: Meredith Baxter (as Bridget Fitzgerald Steinberg), David Birney (as Bernie Steinberg), Harold J. Stone (as Sam Steinberg), Bibi Osterwald (as Sophie Steinberg), Audra Lindley (as Amy Fitzgerald), David Doyle (as Walt Fitzgerald), Ned Glass (as Uncle Moe Plotnick), Robert Sampson (as Father Mike Fitzgerald), William Elliott (as Otis Foster), Ivor Barry (as Charles). EP: Douglas S. Cramer. P: Arthur Alsberg, Don Nelson.

Anna and the King

Sitcom. Ran on CBS Sundays 7:30–8 P.M. Sept. 17–Dec. 31, 1972, opposite *Walt Disney* on NBC. C: Yul Brynner (as the King of Siam), Samantha Eggar (as Anna Owens), Keye Luke (as Kralahome), Eric Shea (as Louis Owens), Brian Tochi (as Crown Prince Chulalongkorn) Lisa Lu (as Lady Thiang). P/W: Bill Idelson. D: Gene Reynolds, William Wiard. W: Jim Fritzell, Gerald Mayer, Harvey Miller.

We have CBS President Fred Silverman to thank for the odd notion of adapting *The King and I* into a weekly sitcom. Silverman loved the property and thought it had potential, and word about that got out to Bill Idelson and Harvey Miller, who had a deal to write a pilot for CBS. "We thought, 'Hell, Freddy Silverman wants to do it, it'll get on the air,'" said Idelson.

So they made the pilot, which he admitted borrowed heavily from the 1950s Broadway musical and movie. The King of Siam, accustomed to lording over his household in 1862, found himself at odds with the methods of newcomer Anna Owens, an American widow who arrived with her 12-year-old son Louis to teach the royal family. Observing the conflicts between the ways of the East and West were the King's aid Kralahome, the Crown Prince Chulalongkorn, and Lady Thiang, the King's number-one wife out of who knows how many.

Yul Brynner had almost as many actresses play Anna opposite him as the King of Siam had wives. Samantha Eggar took the part for the ill-fated 1972 sitcom version.

After the pilot sold, Miller stayed as a writer/producer on *The Odd Couple*, which was entering its third season in the fall of 1972, so he could not do the series. Idelson handled the jobs solo. He learned his biggest problem would be his lead actor. Yul Brynner came to fame playing the King in the 1950s and rarely did TV, but with his career slumping in the early 1970s he agreed to be the one person to reprise his role from the film and Broadway versions, with Brynner getting a small percentage ownership of the series. According to Idelson, the actor gave the impression he owned and knew everything about the series.

"He was so egotistical," Idelson said. "Everybody was scared around him." In addition, for some unexplained reason Brynner did not like the scripts of Gerald Mayer, who Idelson felt wrote wonderfully for the show. "Good scripts were hard to find because of the locale and so on," he noted.

So one time Idelson presented a script of Mayer's to Brynner without giving the author's name. Brynner praised it to the hilt. When he learned it was by Mayer, Brynner sniffed, "He still doesn't have the King right."

Given this situation, Idelson did not fret when *Anna and the King* ended after 13 episodes. "We'd run out of ideas for the king, and Yul Brynner was a bastard," he said. "We took a sledgehammer and broke up all the Buddhas on the set." (A side note: Apart from Brynner, the rest of the Asian characters on the show were played by Asians, something that had not always been done in the past. "They made us hire real Asians," noted Idelson.)

Idelson said the show did remain popular overseas for a time. "When they took it to Europe, it ran everywhere," he said. "We were living in England, and they reran it twice." Apparently Brynner couldn't escape the King either. After a few more movie and stage roles, the actor went back to doing Broadway and touring in *The King and I* for eight years until his death in 1985, playing the role more than 4,500 times.

The Sandy Duncan Show

Sitcom. Ran on CBS Sundays 8:30–9 P.M. Sept. 17–Dec. 31, 1972, opposite *The F.B.I.* on ABC and *The NBC Sunday Mystery Movie* on NBC. C: Sandy Duncan (as Sandy Stockton), Tom Bosley

(as Bert Quinn), Marian Mercer (as Kay Fox), M. Emmet Walsh (as Alex Lembeck), Pam Zarit (as Hilary), Eric Christmas (as Ben Hampton). EP: Arne Sultan. P: Earl Barrett.

Cool Million

Adventure Drama. Ran on NBC Wednesdays 8:30–10 P.M. Oct. 25, 1972–July 11, 1973, opposite movies on ABC and *The Carol Burnett Show* (through Nov. 29) and *The Sonny and Cher Comedy Hour* (from Dec. 16) and *Medical Center* on CBS. C: James Farentino (as Jefferson Keyes), Adele Mara (as Elena), Ed Bernard (as Tony Baylor). EP: Roy Huggins. P: Jo Swerling, Jr. D: Daryl Duke, John Badham, Barry Shear, Charles S. Dubin.

"I guess I have to take the blame for *Cool Million*, even though I didn't create it," said executive producer Roy Huggins about his entry in the *NBC Wednesday Mystery Movie*, an umbrella title for *Cool Million*, *Banacek* and *Madigan* series, which each one appearing every third week. Huggins said the show's premise came from a NBC executive, whose name he could not recall, who pitched him the notion of doing a series where the lead detective charges $1 million per client, hence the title.

Huggins thought to himself, "Well, it's kind of screwy, but it'll put me in cases above what I'm used to, and into the area of [mystery writer] Raymond Chandler. I saw him as the way to do a private eye story among the wealthy." So Huggins gave the initial concept a go.

However, the situation already was in motion at Universal Studios, where a TV-movie pilot was made featuring James Farentino as Jefferson Keyes, a detective who handled cases anywhere in the world for the aforementioned amount. The TV-movie aired a week before the series debut, on Oct. 16, 1972, but by that time Huggins added several elements to the program. Keyes would have his own private jet flown by a regular pilot, Tony Baylor. He also would run his operation out of Lincoln, Nebraska, at the home of a woman named Elena, who relayed messages to him via a special phone line. Playing Elena was Huggins' wife in real life, actress Adele Mara. Oh, and let's not forget that Keyes had a 100 percent money-back guarantee should he fail to solve anyone's mystery.

Huggins thought the setup alone promised the show an early exit. "I think maybe people were bored with the idea of a guy making $1 million a case," he said. "I don't think anyone believed it."

Yet one could argue another reason. *Cool Million* came on last as part of *The NBC Wednesday Mystery Movie*, and by that time *Banacek* had appeared three times. That series also featured a wealthy, urbane investigator, albeit one who received a percentage of the amount of stolen property he recovered in his cases. The income the title character on *Banacek* received was more realistic, and the show had him solve crimes in the manner of *Columbo*—the most successful series under *The NBC Wednesday Mystery Movie* before it, *McCloud* and *McMillan and Wife* moved to Sundays in the fall of 1972 to let *Cool Million*, *Banacek* and *Madigan* take over Wednesdays. The differences were enough that viewers favored *Banacek* considerably more than *Cool Million*, leading NBC to renew *Banacek* and *Madigan* for a second (and final) season while canning *Cool Million*.

After this season, with the exception of *Quincy, M.E.*, all the future entries on any *NBC Mystery Movie* lasted a year or less. The flops were *Faraday & Company*, *Tenafly* and *The Snoop Sisters* in 1973-74; *Amy Prentiss* in 1974-75; *McCoy* in 1975-76; and *Lanigan's Rabbi* in 1976-77.

The Vin Scully Show

Talk. Ran on CBS Mondays through Fridays 4–4:30 P.M. Jan. 15–March 23, 1973, opposite *Love, American Style* reruns on ABC and *Somerset* on NBC. C: Vin Scully. P: Paul W. Keyes, Armand Grant. D: Bill Foster. W: Bob Howard, Sidney Reznick, Bruce Taylor, Brad Lachman.

The Bobby Darin Show

Musical Variety. Ran on NBC Fridays 10–11 P.M. Jan. 19–April 27, 1973, opposite *Love, American Style* on ABC and movies on CBS. C: Bobby Darin, Dick Bakalyn, Geoff Edwards, Tommy Amato. P/W: Saul Ilson, Ernest Chambers. D: Gordon Wiles. W: Sidney Miller, Jack Hanrahan, Sol Weinstein, Alan Thicke.

Here We Go Again

Sitcom. Ran on ABC Saturdays 8–8:30 P.M. Jan. 20–June 16, 1973, opposite *All in the Family* on CBS and *Emergency!* on NBC. C: Larry Hagman (as Richard Evans), Diane Baker (as Susan Evans), Dick Gautier (as Jerry Standish), Nita Talbot (as Judy Evans), Chris Beaumont (as Jeff), Leslie Graves (as Cindy), Kim Richards (as Jan). EP: Charles Fries. P: Robert Kaufman, Stan Schwimmer. P: Marc Daniels, Jerry London, Bill Persky, Alan Rafkin, Jay Sandrich, Mel Stuart. W: Gordon Garr, Austin and Irma Kalish, Arnold Kane, Steve Pritzker, Milt Rosen.

A Touch of Grace

Sitcom. Ran on ABC Saturdays 8:30–9 P.M. Jan. 20–June 16, 1973, opposite *Bridget Loves Bernie* on CBS and *Emergency!* on NBC. C: Shirley Booth (as Grace Simpson), J. Pat O'Malley (as Herbert Morrison), Warren Berlinger (as Walter Bradley), Marian Mercer (as Myra Bradley). P: Saul Turteltaub, Bernie Orenstein. D: Carl Reiner.

The Wizard of Odds

Game. Ran on NBC Mondays through Fridays 11–11:30 A.M. July 17, 1973–June 28, 1974, opposite *Gambit* on CBS. C: Alex Trebek. EP: Burt Sugarman. P: Perry Cross, Alan Thicke, Neal Marshall. D: Terry Kyne.

1973-74

Lotsa Luck

Sitcom. Ran on NBC Mondays 8–8:30 P.M. Sept. 10, 1973–Jan. 7, 1974, opposite *The Rookies* on ABC and *Gunsmoke* on CBS, then NBC Fridays 8:30–9 P.M. Jan. 11–May 24, 1974, opposite *The Six Million Dollar Man* on ABC and *Good Times* on CBS. C: Dom DeLuise (as Stanley Belmont), Kathleen Freeman (as Mrs. Belmont), Wynn Irwin (as Arthur Swann), Beverly Sanders (as Olive Swann), Jack Knight (as Bummy). EP: Bill Persky, Sam Denoff. P/W: Norman Barasch, Carroll Moore, Don Van Atta. W: Carl Reiner.

Here it is, the infamous toilet-buying debut of *Lotsa Luck*. Checking out the merchandise with rather interesting attitudes are, from left, Beverly Sanders, Wynn Irwin, Dom DeLuise and Kathleen Freeman.

NBC executives asked Sam Denoff and partner Bill Persky to adapt the English sitcom *On the Buses* in the hopes of generating another transatlantic translation hit in the manner of when the British comedy *Till Death Do Us Part* became *All in the Family*. They used the same premise of the show of a bachelor employee of a bus company who lived with his nagging mother, his sister and his mooching brother-in-law. Denoff said the main change was locating the show in Brooklyn "because [lead actor Dom] DeLuise talked like that."

For the opening show, producers Norman Barasch and Carroll Moore wove a plot involving Stanley Belmont deciding to get his sister Olive Swann a new toilet for her birthday. Stanley and his pal Bummy planned to install it in time for her birthday party, but chaos erupted as they learned the door wouldn't close when the toilet was installed. "We finished the pilot. Oh boy, we loved it," Denoff said. So

did NBC executives who saw it — until it aired Sept. 10, 1973.

"The following morning, we were in our office with Barasch and Carroll Moore, when an NBC executive said, 'Listen, we got a lot of calls from the Bible Belt [the Southern states]. The station owners down there got very angry about us showing a toilet when children were watching.' We said, 'What?' And a whole bunch of affiliates dropped the show," Denoff said. He couldn't believe it, but it was true. Because few shows in 1973 even mentioned commodes, and the show aired in the early evening, it was considered a shocking program to some of the more easily offended conservative viewers of the time.

The dropping of the show by some stations just for that episode stunned Denoff, who thought the scenario was funny and not in poor taste. "The audience roared watching it," he recalled. But the network in general stood behind the show, and while it floundered on Monday nights opposite *Gunsmoke* and *The Rookies*, NBC switched it mid-season to air after its biggest hit at the time, *Sanford and Son*. Unfortunately, the big audience for that show did not stay to watch *Lotsa Luck*. Despite scripts from writers who would go on to later success, including Steve Gordon, who wrote the 1981 hit Dudley Moore comedy film *Arthur*, *Lotsa Luck* had little fortune in the ratings and expired after eight months.

As Denoff put it after ended his musing of the show, "You never know why it doesn't connect."

Diana

Sitcom. Ran on NBC Mondays 8:30–9 P.M. Sept. 10, 1973–Jan. 7, 1974, opposite *The Rookies* on ABC and *Gunsmoke* on CBS. C: Diana Rigg (as Diana Smythe), David Sheiner (as Norman Brodnik), Barbara Barrie (as Norma Brodnik), Richard B. Shull (as Howard Tolbrook), Robert Moore (as Marshall Tyler), Carol Androsky (as Holly Green), Richard Mulligan (as Jeff Harmon), Liam Dunn (as Smitty the bellboy). EP/D: Leonard Stern.

"In retrospect, that may have been one of my biggest regrets," Leonard Stern said of *Diana*. The sitcom starred Diana Rigg, the classy actress of the theater who wowed audiences with her martial arts antics on the TV series *The Avengers* (seen on American TV from 1966 to 1969), and tamed James Bond into marrying her in the 1971 film *On Her Majesty's Secret Service*. But there was nothing she could do to defend herself from the lousy scripts she received on *Diana*.

The show's setup was a knockoff of *The Mary Tyler Moore Show*. Here British career gal Diana Smythe moved into her brother Roger's New York City apartment after her divorce, only to find that her brother, now working in Ecuador, left keys to the place with many of his friends who felt no need to knock before

walking in on Diana. If that wasn't enough, at work as a fashion coordinator in a department store, she faced a cranky boss, Mr. Brodnik, the store president; his wife Norma, who was in charge of the merchandising department; Howard Tolbrook, a copywriter who liked to play poker; and Marshall Tyler, a "temperamental window dresser" (1973 TV's way of saying "token gay"). Comforting her through all the stress were her pals mystery writer Jeff Harmon and model Holly Green.

"After the pilot, we were never able to duplicate what we wanted to do," Stern said. "I felt we had done her [Diana Rigg] a disservice. Originally, the concept was to be that she was to be the boss, the woman in charge, and if any woman could do that, it was she."

Stern said that he and his writers "lost the initial thrust" of the series and gave her pedestrian material. "We couldn't find writers at the

Barbara Barrie tells some news that shocks Diana Rigg on the latter's sitcom *Diana*. Could it be the scripts, or the ratings?

time equal to the talent," he said. Rigg could have complained, and Stern said she would have been justified if she did, but instead she acted as a professional and went about doing as well as she could with what scripts she received. "She said, 'I'm paid to say the words,' and she did her job," he said.

The show ended after four months. Stern took responsibility for its short life, choosing not to blame the show's lead-in, *Lotsa Luck* (q.v.), or its competition. "To me, it's always in the material," he said. "Here, I don't think we did enough to encourage the audience to return."

Rigg did not do another American TV series after *Diana*, but she did host the public television British series *Mystery!* for more than a decade starting in 1989. She also continued to act occasionally in TV-movies and miniseries, and won her first Emmy in 1997 for a supporting role in the public television presentation of *Rebecca* as Mrs. Danvers.

Chase

Adventure. Ran on NBC Tuesdays 8–9 P.M. Sept. 11, 1973–Jan. 8, 1974, opposite *Temperatures Rising* and movies on ABC and *Maude* and *Hawaii Five-O* on CBS, then NBC Wednesdays 8–9 P.M. Jan. 16–Aug. 28, 1974, opposite *The Cowboys* and movies on ABC and *The Sonny and Cher Comedy Hour* (through May 29), *The Bobbie Gentry Show* (from June 5 to June 26) and *Tony Orlando and Dawn* (from July 3 to July 24) on CBS. C: Mitchell Ryan (as Capt. Chase Reddick), Reid Smith (as Officer Norm Hamilton), Michael Richardson (as Officer Steve Baker), Brian Fong (as Officer Fred Sing), Wayne Maunder (as Sgt. Sam MacCray), Albert Reed (as Inspector Frank Dawson), Gary Crosby (as Officer Ed Rice), Craig Gardner (as Officer Tom Wilson). EP: Robert A. Cinader. P: William Stark, David Friedkin, Jack Webb. D: Jack Webb, Stephen J. Cannell, Christian Nyby, Christian I. Nyby II.

NBC Follies

Comedy Variety. Ran on NBC Thursdays 10–11 P.M. Sept. 13–Dec. 27, 1973, opposite *The Streets of San Francisco* on ABC and movies on CBS. C: Sammy Davis, Jr., Mickey Rooney, the Carl Jablonski Dancers, the Harper MacKay Orchestra. EP: Sy Marsh. P/D: Bob Wynn. W: Bob Becker, Sol Weinstein, Jack Raymond, Milt Rosen, Howard Albrecht, Hal Goldman, Al Gordon, George Foster.

Calucci's Department

Sitcom. Ran on CBS Fridays 8–8:30 P.M. Sept. 14–Dec. 28, 1973, opposite *The Brady Bunch* on ABC and *Sanford and Son* on NBC. C: James Coco (as Joe Calucci), Candy Azzara (as Shirley Balukis), Jose Perez (as Ramon Gonzales), Jack Fletcher (as Oscar Cosgrove), Peggy Pope (as Elaine Fusco), Bill Lazarus (as Jack Woods), Bernard Wexler (as Walter Frohler), Rosetta LeNoire (as Mitzi Gordon). EP: Robert H. Precht. P: Howard Gottfried. D: Burt Brinkerhoff.

The Girl with Something Extra

Sitcom. Ran on NBC Fridays 8:30–9 P.M. Sept. 14–Dec. 21, 1973, opposite *The Odd Couple* on ABC and *Roll Out!* on CBS, then NBC Fridays 9–9:30 P.M. Jan.–May 24, 1974, opposite *The Six Million Dollar Man* on ABC and movies on CBS. C: Sally Field (as Sally Burton), John Davidson (as John Burton), Zohra Lampert (as Anne), Jack Sheldon (as Jerry Burton), Henry Jones (as Owen Metcalf), William Windom (as Stuart Kline), Stephanie Edwards (as Angela). EP: Bob Claver. P: Mel Swope.

Adam's Rib

Sitcom. Ran on ABC Fridays 9:30–10 P.M. Sept. 14–Dec. 28, 1973, opposite movies on CBS and *The Brian Keith Show* on NBC. C: Ken Howard (as Adam Bonner); Blythe Danner (as Amanda Bonner); Dena Dietrich (as Gracie Peterson); Ron Rifkin (as Asst. D.A. Roy Mendelsohn); Edward Winter (as Kip Kipple); Norman Bartold (as D.A. Francis Donahue). P: Peter H. Hunt, William Froug. D: Peter H. Hunt, Gary Nelson. W: Peter Stone.

Though credited as creator of *Adam's Rib* in *The Complete Directory to Prime Time Network and Cable TV Shows*, producer/director Peter H. Hunt said the honor should go to another man. "It actually started with Peter Stone, the writer of it," Hunt said. "We just finished the movie *1776* [in 1972; Stone wrote the book for the Broadway musical and its screenplay, while Hunt directed both the Broadway and movie versions of the show]. Peter talked to Garson Kanin, who wrote the screenplay with Ruth Gordon [his wife], about making the movie into a TV series, and he said do it."

The 1949 film *Adam's Rib* starred Katherine Hepburn and Spencer Tracy as a married couple on opposite sides of a fence during a trial. For TV, Hunt came up with the idea of

Ken Howard and Blythe Danner playing the wedded lawyers. "It was a great group of people basically stealing, if you will, from a classic motion picture and taking it into the present time," Hunt said.

Part of the updating included more feminist themes in the plots, such as the disparity in pay between males and females. "We had decided to usher in women's rights, and it was way ahead of its time," Hunt said. "That was its strength and weakness."

However, before anyone considers this a true "women's lib" program, keep in mind that Hunt noted "It was mostly written by men. [The industry] was still very male dominated. The men who wrote our scripts were committed to the idea of equal rights for women, but there was a level of reserve so that it wasn't a polemic."

Nonetheless, Hunt recalled ABC executives objected to many of the concepts advanced in the scripts. "I had a weekly fight with the network," he said. "They said, 'The public will not accept this,' and so they took them in front of sample audience to view. Each time the number went through the ceiling [meaning the audience enjoyed what they saw]. The audience was way ahead of them."

Weary of fighting a series that could not beat movies on CBS, ABC canned *Adam's Rib* after 16 weeks (in contrast, the shows that respectively preceded and followed it, *Room 222* and *Love, American Style*, aired two more episodes each before ending on Jan. 11, 1974). Hunt said he is proud of the show as well as two others he later directed — *The Wizard*, a fantasy series airing from 1986 to 1987 starring David Rappaport that despite its short run in America nearly was revived in France due to overwhelming popularity there until Rappaport committed suicide in 1990, and *Touched By an Angel*, the hit religious drama starring Roma Downey that started in 1994. "It's about trying to make life a little better," he said of *Touched by an Angel*. "That's why I like that show."

The New Perry Mason

Law Drama. Ran on CBS Sundays 7:30–8:30 P.M. Sept. 16, 1973–Jan. 27, 1974, opposite *The F.B.I.* on ABC and *The Wonderful World of Disney* on NBC. C: Monte Markham (as Perry Mason), Sharon Acker (as Della Street), Albert Stratton (as Paul Drake), Dane Clark (as Lt. Arthur Tragg), Harry Guardino (as Hamilton Burger), Brett Somers (as Gertrude Lade). EP: Conwall Jackson. P: Ernie Frankel, Art Seid.

Needles and Pins

Sitcom. Ran on NBC Fridays 9–9:30 P.M. Sept. 21–Dec. 28, 1973, opposite *Room 222* on ABC and movies on CBS. C: Deidre Lenihan (as Wendy Nelson), Norman Fell (as Nathan Davidson), Louis Nye (as Harry Karp), Bernie Kopell (as Charlie Miller), Larry Gelman (as Max), Alex Henteloff (as Myron Russo), Milton Selzer (as Julius Singer), Sandra Deel (as Sonia Baker). EP: David Gerber. P/D: Hy Averback.

Bob & Carol & Ted & Alice

Sitcom. Ran on ABC Wednesdays 8–8:30 P.M. Sept. 26–Nov. 7, 1973, opposite *The Sonny and Cher Comedy Hour* on CBS and *Adam-12* on NBC. C: Robert Urich (as Bob Sanders), Anne Archer (as Carol Sanders), David Speilberg (as Ted Henderson), Anita Gillette (as Alice Henderson), Brad Savage (as Sean Sanders), Jodie Foster (as Elizabeth Henderson). EP: M.J. Frankovich. P: Jim Henderson.

Faraday and Company

Detective Drama. Ran on NBC Wednesdays 8:30–10 P.M. Sept. 26, 1973–Jan. 9, 1974, opposite movies on ABC and *The Sonny and Cher Comedy Hour* and *Cannon* on CBS, then NBC Tuesdays 8:30–10 P.M. April 30–Aug. 30, 1974, opposite movies on ABC and *Hawaii Five-O* and movies, *Shaft* and *Hawkins* on CBS. C: Dan Dailey (as Frank Faraday), James Naughton (as Steve Faraday), Sharon Gless (as Holly Barrett), Geraldine Brooks (as Lou Carson). EP: Leonard Stern. P: Stanley Kallis. D: Reza S. Badiyi, Jimmy Sangster, Richard L. Bare.

Griff

Detective Drama. Ran on ABC Saturdays 10–11 P.M. Sept. 29, 1973–Jan. 5, 1974, opposite *The Carol Burnett Show* on CBS and movies on ABC. C: Lorne Greene (as Wade Griffin), Ben Murphy (as S. Michael Murdoch), Patricia Stich (as Gracie Newcombe), Vic Tayback (as Capt. Barney Marcus). EP: David Victor. P: Steven Bochco. D: Edward Abroms, Lou Antonio, Boris Sagal.

The Magician

Adventure/Crime Drama. Ran on NBC Tuesdays 9–10 P.M. Oct. 2, 1973–Jan. 8, 1974, opposite movies on ABC and *Hawaii Five-O* and movies, *Shaft* and *Hawkins* on CBS, then NBC Mondays 8–9 P.M. Jan. 14–May 20, 1974, opposite *The Rookies* on ABC and *Gunsmoke* on CBS. C: Bill Bixby (as Anthony Blake), Keene Curtis (as Max Pomeroy), Todd Crespi (as Dennis Pomeroy), Jim Watkins (as Jerry Wallace), Joseph Sirola (as Dominick). EP: Laurence Heath. P: Barry Crane. D: Marvin Chomsky, Barry Crane, Alexander Singer.

Shaft

Adventure/Crime Drama. Ran on CBS Tuesdays 9:30–11 P.M. alternating with movies and *Hawkins* Oct. 9, 1973–Aug. 20, 1974, opposite movies and *Marcus Welby, M.D.* on ABC and *The Magician* (through Jan. 8) and *The NBC Tuesday Mystery Movie* (from Jan. 15) and *Police Story* on NBC. C: Richard Roundtree (as John Shaft), Ed Barth (as Lt. Al Rossi). EP: William Reed Woodfield, Allan Balter. D: John Llewellyn Moxey, Ivan Dixon, Alexander Singer.

Tenafly

Detective Drama. Ran on NBC Wednesdays 8:30–10 P.M. Oct. 2, 1973–Jan. 2, 1974, opposite movies on ABC and *The Sonny and Cher Comedy Hour* and *Cannon* on CBS, then NBC Tuesdays 8:30–10 P.M. April 30–Aug. 6, 1974, opposite movies on ABC and *Hawaii Five-O* and movies, *Shaft* and *Hawkins* on CBS. C: James McEachin (as Harry Tenafly), Lillian Lehman (as Ruth Tenafly), Paul Jackson (as Herb Tenafly), Rosanna Huffman (as Lorrie), David Huddleston (as Lt. Sam Church). P: Richard Link, William Levinson. D: Robert Day, Richard A. Colla, Jud Taylor.

Hawkins

Drama. Ran on CBS Tuesdays 9:30–11 P.M. Oct. 2, 1973–Sept. 3, 1974, opposite movies and *Marcus Welby, M.D.* on ABC and *The Magician* (through Jan. 8) and *NBC Tuesday Mystery Movie* (from Jan. 15) and *Police Story* on NBC. C: Jimmy Stewart (as Billy Jim Hawkins), Strother Martin (as R.J. Hawkins). EP: Norman Felton. P: David Karp. D: Jeff Corey, Jud Taylor.

After decades of being one of the best-loved and respected actors of the cinema, Jimmy Stewart took two stabs at TV series in the 1970s. (Note: According to Lee Goldberg's *Unsold Television Pilots 1955 Through 1989*, pro-

ducer Aaron Spelling tried to sell a pilot in 1963 called *Luxury Liner* wherein Stewart would introduce the dramatic adventures on a cruise ship. Spelling later added comedy to the mix and made *The Love Boat*.) The first came in the 1971-72, when *The Jimmy Stewart Show* (q.v.) ran one year. The sitcom featured Stewart as a patriarch whose 29-year-old son moved his family into his parents' house while Stewart and wife Julie Adams tried to raise their other son, an 8-year-old.

After taking a season off, Stewart ventured a second time into TV series with *Hawkins*. Playing a cagey small-town lawyer in the series gave Stewart a role not unlike his Oscar-nominated lead role in 1959's *Anatomy of a Murder*. Billy Jim Hawkins formerly was a deputy district attorney before he set up shop to defend those accused of crimes in Beauville, West Virginia. But like Andy Griffith's later character of Ben Matlock, Hawkins established a track record so solid in his defendants being found not guilty that people from out of state often sought his help. His cousin B.J. Hawkins did much of the sleuthing to uncover who really committed the dastardly deeds. Playing B.J. was veteran character actor Strother Martin, whose only previous regular series role was on *Hotel De Paree* in 1959-60 (q.v.)

The character of Hawkins first showed up in a TV-movie pilot that aired March 13, 1973, titled *Hawkins on Murder*. Stewart, Martin, and virtually the main top production people stayed with the project when it became a series nearly seven months later. Stewart and Martin had been in several movies prior to their collaboration here, including *Strategic Air Command* (1955), *The Man Who Shot Liberty Valance* (1962), and *Shenandoah* (1965).

Hawkins aired every three weeks, rotating with a TV version of *Shaft* (q.v.) and movies. This setup may have been a contributing factor to why it didn't get a regular large audience, but one participant said the reason for *Hawkins* lasting only a season was something else.

"With Jimmy Stewart in the lead, and a fine cast, we expected a hit series," executive producer Norman Felton wrote to me in a letter. "But Jimmy was becoming tired, and it was beginning to show. He knew it, and asked us to stop. He was right."

Whatever the reason, *Hawkins* would be Stewart's last regular series effort. CBS filled its slot the following season with *Hawaii Five-O* and *Barnaby Jones*.

Toma

Crime Drama. Ran on ABC Thursdays 8–9 P.M. Oct. 4, 1973–Jan. 3, 1974, opposite *The Waltons* on CBS and *The Flip Wilson Show* on NBC, then on ABC Fridays 10–11 P.M. Jan. 18, 1974–Sept. 6, 1974, opposite movies on CBS and *The Dean Martin Show* (through May 24) and then movies on NBC. C: Tony Musante (as David Toma), Simon Oakland (as Inspector Spooner), Sean Manning (as Jimmy Toma), Michelle Livingston (as Donna Toma). EP: Roy Huggins. P: Stephen J. Cannell. D: Alex Grasshoff.

Had Tony Musante been so inclined, he could have kept *Toma* from being a one-season series eligible for this book. ABC wanted the program back for a second year, but the actor declined to play the lead role any further. "He just got a little tired of it," said director Alex Grasshoff, who oversaw the filming of four episodes of *Toma*. "He's a funny fellow. The show was very successful, and he got tired of it."

To be truthful, *Toma* was not exactly "very successful," finishing at best second to its competition in each of its two time slots in 1973-74, but it was enough for ABC to offer it a renewal. The series began as a TV-movie pilot on ABC on March 21, 1973, with Musante as Newark, New Jersey, undercover detective David Toma, Susan Strasberg as his wife, Patty, and Simon Oakland as his irritable boss, Inspector Spooner. All three returned when the series debuted seven months later, as well as two juvenile actors playing the Tomas' children. The main character existed in real life; David Toma played some bit parts in the pilot and series.

Coming along for the ride on the series was Grasshoff, who particularly liked directing the scripts from the show's producer, Stephen J. Cannell. "Steve, I thought, was the best," he said. "He would go home at nights and write a script ready to be filmed the next day. I said to him, 'I want to direct only your scripts.'"

The stories were not the only element appealing to Grasshoff. "The ambience of the set I enjoyed," said. "Everybody got along."

But all of this could not keep the show on the air as Musante decided to leave the show after a year. "I just thought he was crazy," Grasshoff said. "I said, 'Look at the money

you're making.' I was totally amazed. I would've continued working on it [had he stayed]."

Musante could not be swayed, but Cannell, determined not to let a potential hit idea die, refashioned it without the Toma family (or any of the cast, for that matter) into *Baretta*, which debuted on ABC in the fall of 1975. Cannell convinced Grasshoff that despite the director's pleasure in working with him on *Toma*, he should not do the same on *Baretta* due to the volatile nature of its star, Robert Blake. "He said, 'You don't want to work with that other guy,'" Grasshoff said. "I was controlling, and he was controlling. It was a good idea."

Baretta ran three years while Grasshoff went on to do other series. As for Musante, he's stayed true to his word, and as of this writing has not been a regular on a TV series since *Toma*.

Roll Out!

Sitcom. Ran on CBS Fridays 8:30–9 P.M. Oct. 5, 1973–Jan. 4, 1974 (Friday 8–8:30 P.M. last show), opposite *The Odd Couple* on ABC and *The Girl with Something Extra* on NBC. C: Stu Gilliam (as Capt. Carter "Sweet" Williams), Hilly Hicks (as Pfc. Jed Brooks), Mel Stewart (as Sgt. B.J. Bryant), Val Bisoglio (as Capt. Rocco Calvelli), Ed Begley, Jr. (as Lt. Robert W. Chapman), Garrett Morris (as Wheels Dawson), Darrow Igus (as Jersey Hampton), Rod Gist (as Phone Booth), Theodore Wilson (as High Strung), Penny Santon (as Madame Delacourt). P: Gene Reynolds, Larry Gelbart. D: Gene Reynolds, William Wiard.

Dick Clark Presents the Rock and Roll Years

Music. Ran on ABC Wednesdays 8–8:30 P.M. Nov. 28, 1973–Jan. 9, 1974, opposite *The Sonny and Cher Comedy Hour* on CBS and *Adam-12* on NBC. C/EP: Dick Clark. P: Bill Lee. D: Mark Warren.

The Snoop Sisters

Mystery Drama. Ran on NBC Wednesday 8:30–10 P.M. Dec. 19, 1973, opposite movies on ABC and *The Sonny and Cher Comedy Hour* and *Cannon* on CBS, then NBC Tuesdays 8:30–10 P.M. Jan. 29–Aug. 20, 1974, opposite movies on ABC and *Hawaii Five-O* and movies on CBS. C: Helen Hayes (as Ernesta Snoop), Mildred Natwick (as Gwen Snoop), Lou Antonio (as Barney), Bert

Convy (as Lt. Steve Ostrowski). EP/D: Leonard B. Stern. P: Tony Barrett. D: Boris Sagal, David Friedkin, Leonard J. Horn.

Helen Hayes, the esteemed actress dubbed "the First Lady of American Theater," did her first and only regular TV series role in *The Snoop Sisters*, though it took considerable effort to persuade her to do so. "We were in pursuit of Miss Hayes," said the show's executive producer, Leonard Stern. Unfortunately for him, while he was on vacation in Europe, she received the original copy and then the first rewrite of the script for the show, neither of which met with his nor with Miss Hayes' satisfaction. She didn't care to do or hear of the project after seeing those scripts.

Stern prevailed upon her and gave her his rewrite to examine. Reading the third time around, Hayes changed her tune and agreed to do the show's pilot. "This is a rewrite that works," she told Stern. "I don't know if the show will be good, but I like this."

Hayes played one of a pair of senior citizen sisters (the other played by Mildred Natwick in her first and only regular TV series role as well) who not only wrote crime novels but investigated mysteries as well, thus anticipating Angela Lansbury's role on *Murder, She Wrote* by more than a decade. Their nephew Steve Ostrowski was a lieutenant who reluctantly worked with them on their cases. He hired Barney to act as their bodyguard and chauffeur while they checked out murders. The pilot for *The Snoop Sisters* aired on Dec. 18, 1972, with Art Carney as Barney and Lawrence Pressman as Ostrowski.

All looked well as NBC installed the show as part of its rotating *Tuesday Mystery Movie* series designed to emulate the success of *The Sunday Mystery Movie* series with *Columbo*, *McMillan and Wife* and *McCloud*. But the other three series with which *The Snoop Sisters* alternated — *Banacek*, *Faraday and Company* (q.v.) and *Tenafly* (q.v.) — were far less successful than the Sunday edition, and the show moved Tuesday a month after *The Snoop Sisters* debuted. "I don't think it was a great time slot," Stern noted, pointing to how the series started in the middle of two top 10 shows on CBS, *The Sonny and Cher Comedy Hour* on Wednesdays and then *Hawaii Five-O* on Tuesdays. (A writers strike held up the series from debuting until December.)

However, Stern did admire the stamina and professionalism of Hayes and Natwick, who were 73 and 65, respectively, at the time the series was in production. "Those two women were so respectful of each other," he said. "Remarkable rapport. If one would be acting alone on stage, the other would watch." To accommodate them, the show's production schedule ran from 10 to 14 working days, longer than most other TV series, although airing the show just monthly did help in setting up the schedule. They competed against each other in the 1974 Emmy awards for Outstanding Actress in a Limited Series, with Natwick winning.

Both Hayes and Natwick continued acting on TV in guest roles and TV-movies through the mid–1980s. Hayes died in 1993, and Natwick passed away in 1994.

Dirty Sally

Western. Ran on CBS Fridays 8–8:30 P.M. Jan. 11–July 19, 1974, opposite *The Brady Bunch* on ABC and *Sanford and Son* on NBC. C: Jeanette Nolan (as Sally Fergus), Dack Rambo (as Cyrus Pike). EP: John Mantley. P: Leonard Katzman.

Chopper One

Police Drama. Ran on ABC Thursdays 8–8:30 P.M. Jan. 17–July 11, 1974, opposite *The Waltons* on CBS and *The Flip Wilson Show* (through June 27) and *The Mac Davis Show* (July 11 only) on NBC. C: Jim McMullan (as Officer Don Burdick), Dirk Benedict (as Officer Gil Foley), Ted Hartley (as Capt. Ted McKeegan), Lou Frizzel (as Mitch). EP: Aaron Spelling, Leonard Goldberg. P: Ronald Austin, James David Buchanan.

Firehouse

Adventure. Ran on ABC Thursdays 8:30–9 P.M. Jan. 17–July 11, 1974, opposite *The Waltons* on CBS and *The Flip Wilson Show* (through June 27) and *The Mac Davis Show* (from July 11) on NBC. C: James Drury (as Capt. Spike Ryerson), Richard Jaeckel (as Hank Myers), Michael Delano (as Sonny Caputo), Brad David (as Billy Dalzell), Bill Overton (as Cal Dakin), Scott Smith (as Scotty Smith). EP: Aaron Spelling, Leonard Goldberg, Dick Berg. P: Ronald Austin, James David Buchanan, Joe Manduke.

Doc Elliot

Drama. Ran on ABC Wednesdays 10–11 P.M. Jan. 23–Aug. 14, 1974, opposite *Kojak* on CBS and movies on NBC. C: James Franciscus (as Dr. Benjamin Elliot), Neva Patterson (as Margaret "Mags" Brimble), Noah Beery (as Barney Weeks), Bo Hopkins (as Eldred McCoy). EP: Lee Rich. P: Sandor Stern, M.D. D: Robert Totten, Edward Abroms, Harry Harris.

The Cowboys

Western. Ran on ABC Wednesdays 8–8:30 P.M. Feb. 7–Aug. 14, 1974, opposite *Chase* on NBC and *The Sonny and Cher Comedy Hour* (through May 29), *The Bobbie Gentry Show* (from June 5 to June 26) and *Tony Orlando and Dawn* (from July 3 to July 24) on CBS. C: Moses Gunn (as Jebediah Nightlinger), Diana Douglas (as Mrs. Annie Anderson), Jim Davis (as U.S. Marshal Bill Winter), A Martinez (as Cimarron), Robert Carradine (as Slim), Sean Kelly (as Jimmy), Kerry MacLane (as Homer), Clint Howard (as Steve), Mitch Brown (as Hardy), Clay O'Brien (as Weedy). EP: David Dortort. P: John Hawkins.

Apple's Way

Drama. Ran on CBS Sundays 7:30–8:30 P.M. Feb. 10, 1974–Jan. 12, 1975, opposite *The F.B.I.* (through Sept. 8), *The Sonny Comedy Revue* (from Sept. 22 to Dec. 29) and *The Six Million Dollar Man* (from Jan. 19) on ABC and *The Wonderful World of Disney* on NBC. C: Ronny Cox (as George Apple), Lee McCain (as Barbara Apple), Vincent Van Patten (as Paul Apple), Patti Cohoon (as Cathy Apple), Franny Michel (as Patricia Apple; 1974), Kristy McNichol (as Patricia Apple; 1974–75), Eric Olson (as Steven Apple), Malcolm Atterbury (as Grandfather Aldon Apple). EP: Lee Rich, Earl Hamner. P/W: John Furia, Jr. D: Hal Cooper, Marc Daniels, David Moessinger, Ivan Dixon. W: Joseph Bonaduce, David Moessinger, Austin and Irma Kalish.

Winning Streak

Game. Ran on NBC Mondays through Fridays 10:30–11 A.M. July 1, 1974–Jan. 3, 1975, opposite *Gambit* on CBS. C: Bill Cullen. EP: Bob Stewart. D: Michael Gargiulo.

After nearly three years together on the daily game show *Three on a Match*, moderator Bill Cullen, executive producer Bob Stewart and director Michael Gargiulo went from that show's cancellation on June 28, 1974,

and returned on the NBC lineup just three days later in a time slot three hours earlier than the previous show. *Winning Streak* did not live up to its name; it ended in just six months.

However, the title was appropriate in describing the friendship between Stewart and Gargiulo. As Gargiulo explained, "Bob has been a favorite of mine for many, many years, going back before the '60s. He created *The Price Is Right*." He also came up with *To Tell the Truth* and *Password*, all of which were hits for the Mark Goodson–Bill Todman production company. Wanting a bigger share of game show riches, Bob Stewart left the company in 1964.

Gargiulo wanted to follow him. "Bob is a family man, and I was a family man, and Bob was going out on his own. But I was under contract." Gargiulo stayed on with Goodson-Todman until the cancellation of *The Match Game* in 1969. "I left to do a show called *Sale of the Century*, and I was kind of bored," he said. When Stewart finally had an opening for him to direct *Three on a Match* when it started in 1971, Gargiulo took up the offer.

Like *Three on a Match*, *Winning Streak* involved general-knowledge questions, but here once one of two players gave a right answer, they won one of 16 letters from the alphabet seen on a board. The first player to form a word from his or her letters played a bonus round involving 12 hidden letters where he or she tried to make a word out of each letter as they appeared. The player could stop at any point and collect whatever money was attached to the exposed letters if he or she felt the next letter would not allow for the creation of a successful word using all letters currently on the board.

"It never really worked," Gargiulo said of the show. "Sometimes you see something, a game is an amusing incident you're interested in a few minutes, and you move on. But to be interesting, you have to be able to summarize it. That show, you had to sit down and explain it, and nobody really got it."

Gargiulo stayed with Stewart to do a few other shows, including *Shoot for the Stars* (see 1976-77) and *Pass the Buck* (see 1977-78), both of which he felt were like *Winning Streak*— word games that did not play well on stage. He now directs game shows in Italy. Given the dropoff in game show production in America since its 1970s heyday (*The Price Is Right* has been the only daily network game show since 1993), he was philosophical, noting that "There comes a point in a genre where you have to say 'Good night.' We did that with the westerns, and we did it here."

1974-75

Korg: 70,000 B.C.

Children's Adventure. Ran on ABC Saturdays 10:30–11 A.M. Sept. 7, 1974–Jan. 25, 1975, opposite *Shazam* on CBS and *Sigmund and the Sea Monsters* on NBC, then Sundays 10:30–11 A.M. Feb. 2–Aug. 31, 1975, opposite *Look Up and Live* on CBS. C: Jim Malinda (as Korg), Naomi Pollack (as Mara), Bill Ewing (as Bok), Christopher Man (as Tone), Charles Morteo (as Tor), Janelle Pransky (as Ree), Burgess Meredith (as narrator). EP: William Hanna, Joseph Barbera. P: Richard L. O'Connor, Fred Freiberger. D: Irving J. Moore, Christian Nyby.

The first totally live action series from veteran cartoon producers William Hanna and Joseph Barbera, *Korg, 70,000 B.C.* dramatized the life of the title character, his wife, Mara, and their four children in prehistoric times. Playing Korg was Jim Malinda, whose agent sent him for an interview for the series in the spring of 1974. He thought little of it as he went to France for the Cannes Film Festival and enjoyed it so much he considered relocating to Paris to do European films. Then his agent called.

"She told me, 'They want you for the *Korg* show. You only have a couple of minutes to make up your mind.'" he said. "My whole life passed before my eyes, because I had spent 12 years in acting without getting on a series." Malinda decided he would rather be a star on American television than in foreign films, so he returned home.

Hanna-Barbera held high hopes for the series too, but their working conditions were not lavish. The crew shot two episodes a week, mainly on location around southern California. Griffith Park provided the Korg clan's cave. "There was a rock quarry dug out there, and that served as our home," Malinda said.

Malinda spent two and a half hours each morning having stringy body hair and other makeup applied to himself. "Most of the stunts I did myself," he said, adding that he once fell and injured his shoulder doing one. He also noted that "I didn't have a day off throughout the whole shoot. It was rough."

As far as content, Malinda said, "It was a pretty accurate show from what we know about Neanderthal man." However, to let children understand the plots better, the characters spoke English. Malinda did not like another decision. "They were afraid to let Korg do anything they thought would hurt animals," he said. "It ruined the show." Even with that, Malinda said, some groups deemed the show "too violent."

What hurt more in his opinion was ABC's scheduling. "We had a hit show for the first few months, and then football started pre-empting us on ABC," he said. College football games starting at noon Eastern time pushed *Korg: 70,000 B.C.* off Saturday mornings on the West Coast, and ratings dropped so much that ABC moved the show to Sunday mornings in January, which virtually guaranteed the show would not get renewed for a second season.

Despite its short run, Malinda remained fond of Korg and proposed a few years later to Hanna-Barbera the idea of "bringing Korg back to modern-day Hollywood." That notion did not fly, but Malinda's ties to the producers remained strong. He was on the American Television Academy of Arts and Sciences Board of Governors and lobbied for them to receive the prestigious Governors Award for their lifetime work in 1988. "They were more excited about their Governors Award Emmy than all their Oscars," he said.

Finally, Malinda has four *Korg* shows on

tape and is collecting the merchandising done for the shows, including a board game and dolls, which he regrets he did not do earlier. In fact, he ruefully noted, "I had to buy the lunch pails in New Orleans, where I was born and raised!"

Born Free

Drama. Ran on NBC Mondays 8–9 P.M. Sept. 9–Dec. 12, 1974, opposite *The Rookies* on ABC and *Gunsmoke* on CBS. C: Gary Collins (as George Adamson), Diana Muldaur (as Joy Adamson), Hal Frederick (as Makedde), Peter Lukoye (as Nuru), Nelson Kajuna (as Awaru), Joseph De Craft (as Joe Kanini). EP: David Gerber. P: Paul Radin.

Sons and Daughters

Drama. Ran on CBS Wednesdays 8–9 P.M. Sept. 11–Nov. 6, 1974, opposite *That's My Mama* and movies on ABC and *Little House on the Prairie* on NBC. C: Gary Frank (as Jeff Reed), Glynnis O'-Connor (as Anita Cramer), Jay W. Macintosh (as Lucille Reed), John S. Ragin (as Walter Cramer), Jan Shutan (as Ruth Cramer), Michael Morgan (as Danny Reed), Scott Colomby (as Stash Melnyck), Barry Livingston (as Murray "Moose" Kerner), Laura Siegel (as Mary Anne), Lionel Johnston (as Charlie Riddel), Debralee Scott (as Evie Martinson), Christopher Nelson (as Cody). EP: David Levinson. P: Michael Gleason.

Lucas Tanner

Drama. Ran on NBC Wednesdays 9–10 P.M. Sept. 11, 1974–Aug. 20, 1975, opposite movies on ABC and *Cannon* on CBS. C: David Hartman (as Lucas Tanner), Rosemary Murphy (as Margaret Blumenthal; 1974–January 1975), Robbie Rist (as Glendon Farrell), Alan Abelew (as Jaytee Drumm), Trish Soodik (as Cindy Damon), Kimberly Beck (as Terry Kiltsner), Michael Dwight-Smith (as Wally Moore), John Randolph (as John Hamilton; 1975). EP: David Victor. P/D: Charles S. Dubin, Jay Benson. D: Paul Krasney, Jerry London, Leo Penn, Richard Donner, Randal Kleiser.

Get Christie Love!

Police Drama. Ran on ABC Wednesdays 10–11 P.M. Sept. 11, 1974–March 1975, opposite *The Manhunter* on CBS and *Petrocelli* on NBC, then ABC Fridays 10–11 P.M. April–July 18, 1975, opposite movies on CBS and *Police Woman* on NBC. C: Teresa Graves (as Christie Love), Charles Cioffi (as Lt. Matt Reardon; 1974), Jack Kelly (as Capt.

Arthur P. Ryan; 1975), Andy Romano (as Det. Joe Caruso; 1974), Dennis Rucker (as Det. Steve Belmont), Scott Peters (as Det. Valencia; 1975), Michael Pataki (as Sgt. Pete Gallagher; 1975). EP: David Wolper. P: Paul Mason, Glen A. Larson, Ron Satlof. AP: Mervin Dayan. D: Mark Warren, Gene Nelson. W: Olga Ford, Calvin Clements, Brad Radnitz.

Get Christie Love! first emerged as a TV-movie of the same name on ABC on Jan. 22, 1974. Christie was a character TV had never seen—a karate-chopping black female cop. Based on the novel *The Ledger* by Dorothy Uhnak, the TV-movie generated enough ratings for ABC to make it a series. Creators Peter Nelson and George Kirgo, who served as producer and writer, respectively, of the TV-movie, left the series in the hands of others. The only TV-movie actors to do the series were Teresa Graves and Andy Romano (a sergeant in the TV-movie, but a detective in the series).

One person who saw the TV-movie was Det. Olga Ford with the New York Police Department. "A friend of mine and myself were talking about it," she said. When she heard it was going to be a series, she said, "I called the producer and said, 'I'm a black policewoman, and maybe I can help you.'"

Ford joined the crew in Hollywood as a technical advisor and writer of a few episodes. "I was really at the beginning of the show," she said. "I had to go back to New York City, because I was still working." But she became appalled at what she saw at the start.

"Even when we were writing it, I thought it was a little bit much," she said. "I thought they presented a very strange picture of a policewoman." For example, once in every show Christie told the suspects she captured, "You're under arrest, sugar!" "No policewoman on earth of any color would say that!" Ford said.

She felt the constant antagonistic nature between Christie and her boss, Lt. Reardon, was contrived too. "I worked in units where I was the only woman," she noted. "If you did your job, the men accepted you."

But given her limited role, Ford found no one listened to her complaints about these inaccuracies. "I didn't think in any way I helped them make her character," she said.

The crew did have to listen to Teresa Graves, formerly a bikini-wearing regular on *Rowan and Martin's Laugh-In*. She had become a Jehovah's Witness, and her contract for the show included having religious advisors available for consultation on the scripts. "I wasn't there, but I heard about them from Paul Mason [the show's producer]," said Ford. "They were on the set, approving what she would and wouldn't do. I don't think they did a good job."

It didn't matter in the end. *Get Christie Love!* suffered ratings trouble quickly. In 1975 Glen A. Larson and Ron Satlof replaced Mason as producer, and installed virtually a new crew of supporting police officers, mostly Caucasians as before (the show was set in Los Angeles). Ford didn't get upset when it ended after a 10-month run. Graves died in a fire in 2002. She was 54.

Asked if any TV series have presented female cops realistically, Ford said in 2001, "Currently, some of the shows do. *Law & Order: Special Victims Unit*— I like the woman in that. I liked *Cagney and Lacey*. We have reached the point where women are integrated in these shows."

The Manhunter

Detective Drama. Ran on CBS Wednesdays 10–11 P.M. Sept. 11, 1974–April 9, 1975, opposite *Get Christie Love* on ABC and *Petrocelli* on NBC. C: Ken Howard (as Dave Barrett), Robert Hogan (as Sheriff Paul Tate), Hilary Thompson (as Lizabeth Barrett), Ford Rainey (as James Barrett), Claudia Bryar (as Mary Barrett). EP: Quinn Martin. P: Sam Rolfe. D: Lawrence Dobkin, Bernard McEveety, Walter Grauman.

Paper Moon

Sitcom. Ran on ABC Thursdays 8:30–9 P.M. Sept. 12, 1974–Jan. 2, 1974, opposite *The Waltons* on CBS and *Sierra* (through Dec. 12) on NBC. C: Christopher Connelly (as Moses Pray), Jody Foster (as Addie Pray). EP: Anthony Wilson. P: Robert Stambler.

Sierra

Adventure. Ran on NBC Thursdays 8–9 P.M. Sept. 12–Dec. 12, 1974, opposite *The Odd Couple* and *Paper Moon* on ABC and *The Waltons* on CBS. C: James G. Richardson (as Ranger Tim Cassidy), Ernest Thompson (as Ranger Matt Harper), Jack Hogan (as Chief Ranger Jack Moore), Mike Warren (as Ranger P.J. Lewis), Susan Foster (as Ranger Julie Beck). EP: Robert A. Cinader. P: Bruce Johnson, Edwin Self.

Kodiak

Police Drama. Ran on ABC Fridays 8–8:30 P.M. Sept. 13–Oct. 11, 1974, opposite *Planet of the Apes* on CBS and *Sanford and Son* on ABC. C: Clint Walker (as Cal "Kodiak" McKay), Abner Biberman (as Abraham Lincoln Imhook), Maggie Blye (as Mandy). P: Stan Sheptner. D: William Witney.

Planet of the Apes

Science Fiction. Ran on CBS Fridays 8–9 P.M. Sept. 13–Dec. 27, 1974, opposite *Kodiak* (through Oct. 11) and *The Six Million Dollar Man* (through Oct.) on ABC and *Sanford and Son* and *Chico and the Man* on NBC. C: Roddy McDowall (as Galen), Ron Harper (as Alan Virdon), James Naughton (as Pete Burke), Mark Lenard (as Urko), Booth Colman (as Dr. Zaius). EP: Herbert Hirschman. P: Stan Hough. D: Don McDougall, Bernard McEveety. W: Art Wallace, Robert W. Lenski.

The Texas Wheelers

Sitcom. Ran on ABC Fridays 9:30–10 P.M. Sept. 13–Oct. 4, 1974, opposite movies on CBS and *The Rockford Files* on NBC, then ABC Thursdays 8:30–9 P.M. June 26–July 24, 1975, opposite *The Waltons* on CBS and *The Gladys Knight and the Pips Show* (from July 10) on NBC. C: Jack Elam (as Zack Wheeler), Gary Busey (as Truckie Wheeler), Mark Hamill (as Doobie Wheeler), Karen Oberdiear (as Boo Wheeler), Tony Becker (as T.J. Wheeler), Lisa Eilbacher (as Sally), Dennis Burkley (as Bud), Bruce Kimball (as Lyle). EP: Dale McRaven. P: Chris Hayward. D: Jackie Cooper, Bob Claver.

Kolchak: The Night Stalker

Supernatural Drama. Ran on ABC Fridays 10–11 P.M. Sept. 13–Dececember 1974, opposite movies on CBS and *Police Woman* on NBC, then ABC Fridays 8–9 P.M. Jan.–July 1975, opposite *Khan* (from Feb. 7 to 28) and *The Friday Comedy Special* (from March 14 to May 23) and *We'll Get By* (from March 14 to May 23) on CBS and *Sanford & Son* and *Chico and the Man* on NBC, and then ABC Saturdays 8–9 P.M. Aug. 30, 1975, opposite *Big Eddie* (from Aug. 23) on CBS and *Emergency!* on NBC. C: Darren McGavin (as Carl Kolchak), Simon Oakland (as Tony Vincenzo), Jack Grinnage (as Ron Updyke), Ruth McDevitt (as Edith Cowles). EP: Darren McGavin. P: Paul Playdon (first two shows), Cy Chermak (last 18 shows). D: Allen Baron, Alex Grasshoff, Dan McDougall, Don Weis. W: Rudolph Borchert, David Chase, L. Ford Neale, John Huff.

Kojak, Kodiak, Kolchak—the similarity of lead characters' names in the fall of 1974 provoked some mirth among critics about the unoriginality of television producers and programmers. But there was little mistaking Kolchak from the other two law enforcement figures, for he was the one who went chasing after ghosts, witches, vampires and other supernatural beings in Chicago. Quite different, indeed.

Actually, Kolchak was on the air before the other soundalikes, as a top-rated TV-movie called *The Night Stalker* on ABC on Jan. 11, 1972, where Darren McGavin played the dogged Carl Kolchak who fought a vampire while tailing a story to the disbelief of his cranky editor, Tony Vincenzo, played by Simon Oakland. The two returned again for another well-received TV-movie, *The Night Strangler*, about an apparently immortal killer, on Jan. 16, 1973, prompting the call for the property to become a series.

Joining them for the series were fellow Independent News Service employees Jack Grinnage, a laidback reporter, and elderly Edith Cowles, a "Dear Abby"–type advice columnist. However, the real stars were the monsters the show had Kolchak face every week, ranging from a zombie controlled by voodoo to a headless motorcyclist. It was preposterous to some, but not to one participant.

"I worked 18 hours a day on it and I loved it," said Alex Grasshoff, who directed three episodes. "We shot at night, long, long hours. I remember once we went way over, way over budget, and the staff said, 'Don't worry about it, Alex.'" The crew didn't report him for violating their work hours nor ask him for extra overtime—something rarely done in Hollywood.

While Grasshoff liked the show, he left when one monster he was given in a script was impossible for him to imagine doing within the program's production schedule. "They wanted me to do an underwater thing, and I said, 'How in hell are we going to do that?'"

The show eventually ran short of money for costumes and effects, forcing the production company to cut corners and use wind machines toward the end to indicate monsters. The series also only made 20 episodes, fewer than the 24 normally done each season, to save money as well. Had *Kolchak: The Night Stalker*

been renewed, it would have been interesting to see how they would have done a second season under the show's circumstances.

Kolchak: The Night Stalker has retained a small cult following despite its one-season run. CBS repeated the show to surprisingly good ratings as part of its late night lineup Fridays in 1979 and 1981. More recently, *The X-Files* creator Chris Carter has listed the show as an inspiration for his series, and even hired McGavin to act on a few episodes in the late 1990s as Agent Arthur Dukes.

The New Land

Drama. Ran on ABC Saturdays 8–9 P.M. Sept. 14–Oct. 19, 1974, opposite *All in the Family* and *Paul Sand in Friends and Lovers* on CBS and *Emergency!* on NBC. C: Bonnie Bedelia (as Anna Larsen), Scott Thomas (as Christian Larsen), Todd Lookinland (as Tuliff Larsen), Debbie Lytton (as Anneliese Larson), Kurt Russell (as Bo Larsen), Donald Moffat (as Rev. Lundstrom), Gwen Arner (as Molly Lundstrom), Lou Frizzel (as Mr. Murdock). EP: William Blinn. P/D: Philip Leacock. D: John Erman.

Paul Sand in Friends and Lovers

Sitcom. Ran on CBS Saturdays 8:30–9 P.M. Sept. 14, 1974–Jan. 4, 1975, opposite *The New Land* (through Oct. 19) and on ABC and *Emergency!* on NBC. C: Paul Sand (as Robert Dreyfuss), Michael Pataki (as Charlie Dreyfuss), Penny Marshall (as Janice Dreyfuss), Dick Wesson (as Jack Riordan), Steve Landesberg (as Fred Meyerbach), Craig Richard Nelson (as Mason Woodruff), Jack Gilford (as Ben Dreyfuss). EP: James L. Brooks, Allan Burns. P/W: Steve Pritzker. D: Jay Sandrich, Robert Moore, Alan Rafkin, Peter Bonerz. W: Gordon Farr, Phil Mishkin, Lowell Ganz, Steve Gordon, David Pollock.

Paul Sand in Friends and Lovers had its roots in an early episode of *The Mary Tyler Moore Show* that first aired on Nov. 28, 1970. "When we were doing *The Mary Tyler Moore Show*, David Davis and Lorenzo Music wrote Bob Newhart a part as an auditor who comes over to Mary's and falls in love with her," director Jay Sandrich explained. "At the last minute, Bob couldn't do it. Paul was a pal of Valerie Harper's [who played Rhoda on *The Mary Tyler Moore Show*], and they brought him on, and loved him."

The MTM production company remained

How urbanites looked on television in 1974: Michael Pataki, Penny Marshall and Paul Sand look askance offstage in this photograph from the debut of *Paul Sand in Friends and Lovers.*

high on Sands thereafter but never could hammer out the right series idea for the curly-haired actor with the rubbery face. He did a few other TV guest spots and a 1973 pilot called *Lady Luck* for Universal before the creative minds at MTM sold him on doing a series where he played a harried bass violinist who on the debut episode won a prime spot after auditioning for the Boston Symphony Orchestra.

But his character, Robert Dreyfuss, found that while professionally he was on top of the world, socially he was in distress, having to deal with his rather pushy brother Charlie and Charlie's snappy wife, Janice, both of whom felt he was a loser when it came to dating. Other characters were the orchestra's manager, Jack Riordan; fellow symphony violinist Fred Meyerbach; orchestra conductor Mason Woodruff; and Robert and Charlie's dad, Ben.

Sandrich directed the pilot and felt that the magic on it was not quite duplicated afterward. "Sometime pilots work and the series doesn't, and I think that's the case here," he said, noting that he came back to do one more show. He did not blame it on any particular element of the show, just that it did not click as expected. He thought Sand was a serviceable lead for the show, though he did note that when it came to rehearsal, "He was not someone who would take lines and do them as written. He needed a couple of days to do them right."

Though the series finished at #25 for the season, a hit by the usual standards, the fact that it aired between *All in the Family* and *The Mary Tyler Moore Show* and they had much bigger audiences (they were #1 and #11 in the 1974-75 season ratings) made the show look like a relative disappointment, so it ended midseason. Taking its place was the much more successful *All in the Family* spinoff, *The Jeffersons*, which ran from 1975 to 1985.

While co-star Penny Marshall would go on to TV fame the next season starring in *Laverne & Shirley*, Paul Sand was not as fortunate in the medium. He acted infrequently and to date has had only two other regular roles, as Dr. Michael Ridley on *St. Elsewhere* from 1983 to 1984 and as Marty on *Gimme a Break* from 1986 to 1987.

Nakia

Police Drama. Ran on ABC Saturdays 10–11 P.M. Sept. 21–Dec. 28, 1974, opposite *The Carol Burnett Show* on CBS and movies on NBC. C: Robert Forster (as Deputy Nakia Parker), Arthur Kennedy (as Sheriff Sam Jericho), Gloria De-Haven (as Irene James), Taylor Lacher (as Deputy Hubbel Martin), John Tenorio, Jr. (as Half Cub). EP: Quinn Martin, Charles Larson. P: Ernest Losso, George Sunga.

The Sonny Comedy Revue

Comedy Variety. Ran on ABC Sundays 8–9 P.M. Sept. 22–Dec. 29, 1974, opposite *Apple's Way* and *Kojak* on CBS and *The Wonderful World of Disney* and *The NBC Mystery Movie* on NBC. C: Sonny Bono, Peter Cullen, Teri Garr, Freeman King, Murray Langston, Billy Van, Ted Zeigler, the Lex DeAzevedo Orchestra. P/W: Allen Blye, Chris Bearde. D: Art Fisher. W: George Burditt, Paul Wayne, Coslough Johnson, Bob Arnott, David Panich, Ronny Graham, Bob Einstein.

The Sonny and Cher Comedy Hour without Cher would be an apt alternate title for this series. It carried over almost all the same personnel, onstage and offstage, as the hit *Sonny and Cher Comedy Hour* had in its last season on CBS in 1973-74, save for the presence of Cher and her daughter with Sonny, Chastity Bono. However, during that season, Sonny and Cher went through a divorce that left them unwilling to continue the series together, even though it was doing better than it ever had since debuting as a summer series on Aug. 1, 1971, finishing at #7 in the season ratings.

Figuring the name was still hot, ABC signed Sonny and crew to continue the show. Some critics said by picking Sonny over Cher, who had more hit records as a solo artist by this time than her husband, ABC was showing why it was still in third place in the network ratings. Still, most of the hit show's personnel followed suit and went with Sonny to ABC, including writer George Burditt.

"My partner Paul Wayne and I, we used to write the opening monologues for Sonny and Cher," Burditt said. "We attempted to do the same for Sonny without Cher. It didn't quite work without the stingers from Cher." The show tried to use guest stars such as Ken Berry to joke about Sonny's flat singing voice and other supposed flaws, but it did not come off as well as on the previous show.

In fact, Burditt believed the image of Sonny as sort of a loser that *The Sonny and Cher Comedy Hour* perpetuated in the monologues and sketches hurt his appeal as a solo host. "A lot of people judged him on the bumbling character he played at the time, but he was savvy," he said. "He was pretty good. His persona as a performer was nothing like him as a person."

Shortly into doing *The Sonny Comedy Revue*, the cast and crew realized it was not going to be the same success that Sonny and Cher were. They plundered ahead until the inevitable cancellation notice after 13 weeks, but regarding the show's atmosphere, Burditt said, "It seemed like a lost cause at the time." After went it off, Cher's show went on in the same time slot on CBS two months later; see *Cher* in this section.

Bono later made a successful transition to politics that included him becoming the Republican congressman for Palm Springs, California, in the House of Representatives in 1994. He still held that post when he died hitting a tree in a skiing accident in January 1998. He was a month shy of his 63rd birthday. Incidentally, in his 1991 autobiography, *And the Beat Goes On*, he barely mentioned *The Sonny Comedy Revue*.

Amy Prentiss

Detective Drama. Ran on NBC Sundays 8:30–10:30 P.M. Dec. 1, 1974–July 6, 1975, opposite *The Sonny Comedy Revue* (through Dec. 29) and movies on ABC and *Kojak* and *Mannix* on CBS. C: Jessica Walter (as Amy Prentiss), Art Metrano (as Det. Rod Pena), Steve Sandor (as Det. Tony Russell), Johnny Seven (as Det. Contreras), Helen Hunt (as Jill Prentiss), Gwenn Mitchell (as Joan Carter). P: Cy Chermak. D: Boris Sagal, Lou Antonio.

The Big Showdown

Game. Ran on ABC Mondays through Fridays 2:30–3 P.M. Dec. 23, 1974–July 4, 1975, opposite

The Edge of Night on CBS and *The Doctors* on NBC. C: Jim Peck. EP: Ron Greenberg, Don Lipp. P: Shelley Dobbins. D: Dick Schneider.

The Moneymaze

Game. Ran on ABC Mondays through Fridays 4–4:30 P.M. Dec. 23, 1974–July 4, 1975, opposite *Tattletales* (through June 13) and *Musical Chairs* (from June 16) on CBS and *Somerset* on NBC. C: Nick Clooney. EP: Don Lipp. P: Don Segall. D: Arthur Forrest.

Blank Check

Game. Ran on NBC Mondays through Fridays 12:30–1 P.M. Jan. 6–July 4, 1975, opposite *Split Second* on ABC and *Search for Tomorrow* on CBS. C: Art James. EP: Jack Barry. P: Mike Metzger. D: Richard Kline.

After flopping with *Fractured Phrases* (see 1965-66) and *Temptation* (see 1967-68), Art James hosted a hit daytime game show, *The Who What or Where Game*, on NBC from Dec. 29, 1969–Jan. 4, 1974. A year after that show ended, James returned in the same time slot against the same competition *The Who What or Where Game* faced a year earlier, but *Blank Check* was worthless in his view.

"The crew used to call it *Blank Mind*," he said. "It was kind of a no-brainer. It was dumb luck, a guessing game."

Six contestants played for a week, with one designated as a "check writer." That person picked one of five numbers on display. The other players competed to be the first to answer a riddle successfully and get to guess what number the check writer chose. A hit led that player to become the new check writer and select from a new group of five numbers; a miss meant that the number guessed became the first digit in the check writer's "blank check" and the guesser was out of that round. The procedure continued until either someone knocked off the check writer or it reached the fourth guess, wherein a member of the studio audience had to determine which of the two remaining numbers was the check writer's choice. A wrong guess won the check writer the amount listed on his blank check.

Somehow this concoction did well enough in the ratings to run more than one of the normal 13-week cycles most flops had, plus knocked off the competing game show *Split*

Second on June 27, 1975, after a three-year run on ABC. Otherwise, the show deserves comment only for its backstage antics.

Blank Check was the first game show Jack Barry sold to NBC after being dismissed by the network in disgrace in 1958 along with his packager partner, Dan Enright, for their rigging the big-money game show *Twenty-One* and a few other productions. James had worked for them as the announcer for the daytime game show *Concentration* in 1958 before they had to relinquish control of their creation.

"Jack was not a very convivial person to work with," James said. "He and Dan were kind of tight-fisted." NBC apparently was not impressed with their return; the two men never packaged another game show for the network after *Blank Check*.

More significantly for James, as *Blank Check* stumbled toward its Independence Day closing, he managed to return three days later on the following Monday hosting another game show, *The Magnificent Marble Machine* (q.v.). As he explained, "The candidates they had were not working out, a weatherman from Chicago or something. [NBC Vice President of Daytime Programming] Lin Bolen talked to me about it. I remember talking to her, offering my services. It wasn't a direct pitch on my part." But it did the trick, and James stayed alive and kicking while *Blank Check* was null and void after six months on the air.

Hot L Baltimore

Sitcom. Ran on ABC Fridays 9–9:30 P.M. Jan. 24–June 6, 1975, opposite movies on CBS and *The Rockford Files* on NBC. C: James Cromwell (as Bill Lewis), Richard Masur (as Clifford Ainsley), Conchata Ferrell (as April Green), Al Freeman, Jr. (as Charles Bingham), Jeannie Linero (as Suzy Marta Rocket), Gloria Le Roy (as Millie), Robin Wilson (as Jackie), Stan Gottlieb (as Mr. Winthrop Morse), Lee Bergere (as George), Henry Calvert (as Gordon), Charlotte Rae (as Mrs. Esmee Bellotti). EP: Rod Parker. P: Norman Lear. D: Bob La-Hendro.

Karen

Sitcom. Ran on ABC Thursdays 8:30–9 P.M. Jan. 30–June 19, 1975, opposite *The Waltons* on CBS and *The Bob Crane Show* (from March 6) on NBC. C: Karen Valentine (as Karen Angelo), Charles Lane (as Dale Busch), Dena Dietrich (as Dena Madison), Aldine King (as Cissy Peterson), Will Seltzer (as Adam Cooperman), Oliver Clark (as Jerry Siegel), Alix Elias (as Cheryl Siegel). EP/D: Gene Reynolds. P: Burt Metcalfe. W: Larry Gelbart.

After the sitcom *Room 222* ended a four-and-a-half year run on ABC on Jan. 11, 1974, the network remained hot on signing its supporting actress Karen Valentine, who played teacher Alice Johnson, for her own TV show. The pert, perky brunette won an Emmy for her role in 1970 and proved to be a popular draw in light TV-movie comedies like *Coffee, Tea or Me?* and *The Girl Who Came Gift Wrapped*, as well as a semiregular on *The Hollywood Squares*. Her first effort, *The Karen Valentine Show*, was a sitcom pilot ABC rejected for its fall 1974 lineup, but the network gave the green light in midseason to *Karen*.

The series had Valentine play a lobbyist in Washington, D.C., for the fictional organization Open America. Dale Busch was her boss (played by Denver Pyle in the pilot) and Dena and Adam were co-workers. Karen resided in Georgetown with her roommate Cissy. But the office activities did not seem to work out in the first few shows, so *Karen* added two cast members.

"*Karen* was a series already going when I went into it," said Alix Elias. "They decided to beef up the house situation and downplay the office." She and Oliver Clark ("A very nice guy," said Elias) played the Siegels, neighbors to Karen and Cissy.

Elias thought the show's problems stemmed from the producers' inability to define what kind of character the lead actress was portraying. "They didn't have a bead on what they wanted her to do," Elias said. "I think what they had in Karen was a caring, sweet person, but not a particularly strong person."

Although the show's producers, Gene Reynolds and Burt Metcalfe, had done the same on the *M*A*S*H* TV series, Elias felt they were not seeing eye to eye on the concept for *Karen*. "Those shows that are most successful have a strong person in the middle, one person who's creatively in charge and has a vision and sticks to that vision. That wasn't the case here," she said.

She noted another *M*A*S*H* producer and writer contributed to *Karen* to little effect. "We actually had Larry Gelbart as one of our writers," she said. "It just seems they should've known better. It just kind of never jelled."

Karen followed another new sitcom, *Barney Miller*, on ABC's Thursday night lineup in early 1975. Though neither provided any challenge to *The Waltons* (a top 10 series that season), ABC felt *Barney Miller* had more potential, and indeed it stayed on the network through 1982. By that time, Karen returned to TV after leaving the medium in 1978 to star in a grittier role in the TV-movie *Muggable Mary: Street Cop*. She did one more series, hosting the summertime nostalgia variety show for baby boomers *Our Time* in 1985, after which she became an object of nostalgia too as her TV role grew smaller and more fleeting.

Elias had a quicker return to TV series acting when in the 1975-76 season she joined *Grady* (q.v.) — as another next-door neighbor.

Archer

Crime Drama. Ran on NBC Thursdays 9–10 P.M. Jan. 30–March 13, 1975, opposite *The Streets of San Francisco* on ABC and movies on CBS. C: Brian Keith (as Lew Archer), John P. Ryan (as Lt. Barney Brighton). EP: David Karp. P: Jack Miller, Leonard B. Kaufman.

Khan

Crime Drama. Ran on CBS Fridays 8–9 P.M. Feb. 7–Feb. 28, 1975, opposite *Kolchak: the Night Stalker* on ABC and *Sanford and Son* and *Chico and the Man* on NBC. C: Khigh Dhiegh (as Khan), Irene Yah-Ling Sun (as Anna Khan), Evan Kim (as Kim Khan), Vic Tayback (as Lt. Gubbins). P: Laurence Heath, Joseph Henry. D: Ivan Dixon, Bill Derwin.

Cher

Variety. Ran on CBS Sundays 7:30–8:30 P.M. Feb. 16–June 1975, opposite *The Six Million Dollar Man* on ABC and *The Wonderful World of Disney* on NBC, then September 1975–Jan. 4, 1976, opposite *The Six Million Dollar Man* on ABC and *The Family Holvak* (through Oct. 12) and *Ellery Queen* on NBC. C: Cher, Gailard Sartain, The Tony Charmoli Dancers (1975), The Anita Mann Dancers (1975-76), The Jimmy Dale Orchestra (1975), The Jack Eskew Orchestra (1975-76). EP/W: George Schlatter. P: Lee Miller, Alan Katz, Don Miller.

D: Bill Davis, Art Fisher. W: Digby Wolfe, Don Reo, Alan Katz, Iris Rainer, David Panich, Ron Pearlman, Nick Arnold, John Boni, Ray Taylor.

After seeing ex-husband Sonny Bono fail on ABC (see *The Sonny Comedy Revue* this season), Cher came out in her splashy solo variety replete with navel-baring costumes which caused quite a stir at the time. She began each show singing with a spotlight just on her face, then belting out the tune after a few bars to signal the entire stage to be lighted to display the orchestra around her as she walked the runway for a dramatic entrance. The introduction gained such notoriety that Carol Burnett spoofed it in her show, wearing a long black wig and a fat suit showing a huge belly sticking out from a spangled outfit.

"That was a trippy show to do," remembered choreographer Tony Charmoli. He recalled especially the debut with the impressive guest lineup of Elton John, Bette Midler and Flip Wilson amid flashy set production numbers and costumes. "I remember we did a finale with white balloons coming down," he said.

Charmoli said he worked considerably with Cher's costume designer, Bob Mackie, on coming up with her show's dance sequences. "Bob Mackie and I had done many shows together, and he'd show us her clothing and we'd work from that," he said.

The choreographer was impressed by the ability of the series' star, generally known for just her singing ability. "Cher can move," he said. But after three shows with her, he received an offer which was so enticing he left the show. "I went on to do a special with Shirley MacLaine," he said. "Shirley was going to do an all-dance special, *Gypsy in My Soul*, and I wanted to get in on that." It aired six days after *Cher* ended, on Jan. 10, 1976, and won Charmoli an Emmy for Best Choreography.

Also winning Emmys were Jack Albertson and Cloris Leachman in 1975 for their guest appearances on *Cher*. The series also received an Emmy nomination as Best Comedy-Variety or Music Series, losing to *The Carol Burnett Show*. But all the acclaim could not hide the fact that most viewers were tuning out the series. *Cher* lasted less than a year before drooping ratings convinced all involved that Sonny and Cher needed to be back on the air together. *The Sonny and Cher Show* returned to the air four weeks after *Cher* ended.

Writer George Burditt wrote many of the monologues for Sonny and Cher on their earlier (1971–74) series but declined to do new ones for the reunited duo. "I never really cared for her show, and I didn't think their show would work," he said. He was right; the professional but not personal reunion of two divorcées lasted only a year and a half, petering out on Aug. 29, 1977. They would perform together on TV only rarely afterward until Bono's death in 1998.

Caribe

Crime Drama. Ran on ABC Mondays 10–11 P.M. Feb. 17–Aug. 11, 1975, opposite *Medical Center* on CBS and movies on NBC. C: Stacy Keach (as Lt. Ben Logan), Carl Franklin (as Sgt. Mark Walters), Robert Mandan (as Deputy Commissioner Ed Rawlings). EP: Quinn Martin. P: Anthony Spinner. D: Virgil W. Vogel, Barry Crane.

Sunshine

Sitcom. Ran on NBC Thursdays 8–8:30 P.M. March 6–June 19, 1975, opposite *Barney Miller* on ABC and *The Waltons* on CBS. C: Cliff DeYoung (as Sam Hayden), Elizabeth Cheshire (as Jill Hayden), Billy Mumy (as Billy Weaver), Corey Fischer (as Corey Givits), Meg Foster (as Nora). P: George Eckstein. D: Daniel Haller.

The Bob Crane Show

Sitcom. Ran on NBC Thursdays 8:30–9 P.M. March 6–June 19, 1975, opposite *Karen* on ABC and *The Waltons* on CBS. C: Bob Crane (as Bob Wilcox), Patricia Harty (as Ellie Wilcox), Todd Susman (as Marvin Susman), Jack Fletcher (as Dean Lyle Ingersoll), Ronny Graham (as Mr. Ernest Busso), Erica Petal (as Pam Wilcox), James Sutorius (as Jerry Mallory). P: Martin Cohen, Norman S. Powell. D: Norman S. Powell, Buddy Tyne.

We'll Get By

Sitcom. Ran on CBS Fridays 8:30–9 P.M. March 14–May 30, 1975, opposite *Kolchak: The Night Stalker* on ABC and *Chico and the Man* on NBC. C: Paul Sorvino (as George Platt), Mitzi Hoag (as Liz Platt), Jerry Houser (as Muff Platt), Willie Aames (as Kenny Platt), Devon Scott (as Andrea Platt). EP: Marc Merson, Alan Alda. P: Allan Katz, Don Reo. D: Jack Shea, Jay Sandrich. W: Alan Alda.

Blankety Blanks

Game. Ran on ABC Mondays through Fridays 11:30 A.M.–Noon April 21–June 27, 1975, opposite *Love of Life* and news on CBS and *The Hollywood Squares* on NBC. C: Bill Cullen. EP: Bob Stewart. P: Anne Marie Schmidt, Donald Epstein. D: Michael Gargiulo.

When I informed director Michael Gargiulo that I remembered watching *Blankety Blanks*, he laughed and said, "So you're the one!" *Blankety Blanks* ran just 10 weeks, and to make matters more embarrassing, the show that took its slot was the one *Blankety Blanks* came on the air to replace — reruns of *The Brady Bunch*.

That process was not unprecedented. *The Clear Horizon* (see 1959-60) came back after *Your Surprise Package* went off in 1962, although *Your Surprise Package* had moved to start a half hour later than its original slot during its run. And later, in 1988, *The $25,000 Pyramid* (which had the same executive producer as *Blankety Blanks*, Bob Stewart) re-emerged on CBS four months after the collapse of the unremarkable *Blackout* game show.

But the now-you-see-it, now-you-don't appearance of *Blankety Blanks* came when game shows were at their apex on the daytime network lineups. With the exception of the 1–1:30 P.M. time block, which CBS and NBC gave to local affiliates while ABC aired the soap *All My Children*, it was possible to watch network game shows from 10 A.M.–4:30 P.M., with three and a half of those hours offering at least two networks with game shows on simultaneously. Gargiulo agreed that the quick rejection of *Blankety Blank* simply could have been because viewers in 1975 had more than their fill of the genre's bright lights and noisy effects.

Blankety Blanks was not as gimmicky as some of its brethren, although the rotating circle placed at an elevated angle to the right of host Bill Cullen was a rather flashy method to pick a player for the game. Cullen inserted an encoded card chosen at random from that circle, and a machine determined which of four players (divided into two teams, each with a celebrity and a contestant) would try to identify a mystery subject, and how much money he or she would get, starting from $10 to up to 10 times that amount. If correct, he or she then had to solve a "Blankety Blank," or a phrase with a pun with the key word(s) missing, to double the amount already won. The object was to be the first duo to amass $2,000. Guest celebrities included *M*A*S*H* co-stars Loretta Swit and Larry Linville for one week.

Beyond the issue of game show overkill, Gargiulo thought the concept of *Blankety Blanks* came up short. "First of all, puns are very difficult. Not everybody gets it. And for something to be successful, everybody has to get it."

For the record, *The Brady Bunch* reruns lasted from July 1973 to April 18, 1975, and then resumed June 30, 1975–August 1975 after *Blankety Blanks* drew a blank. ABC replaced it with reruns of another nighttime sitcom, *Happy Days*, until it moved *Family Feud* into the slot on April 25, 1977, where it ran for three years — the longest any show had spent in that period since ABC began programming there.

Musical Chairs

Game. Ran on CBS Mondays through Fridays 4–4:30 P.M. June 16–Oct. 31, 1975, opposite *You Don't Say* on ABC and *Somerset* on NBC. C: Adam Wade. EP: Jerome Schnur, Don Kirshner. P: Bill Chastain. D: Lynwood King.

Eighteen years before *The Late Show with David Letterman* took residence in it, the Ed Sullivan Theater in New York played host to the game show *Musical Chairs*, connected in name only with a 1955 summer series of the same name. This *Musical Chairs* lived up to its name by progressively eliminating the poorest performing of initially four contestants through pulling them and their chairs back through panels, making for rather dramatic exits.

"It took four stagehands to get them in," said director Lynwood King of the process, which also involved slotting the chairs so that the stagehands could slide a player back or push them into place (as was done when introducing the contestants on air) in one fell swoop. It was not easy for the stagehands to do but, noted King, "If they're on your side, they'll break their asses for you. And they did."

King got the job after having directed the game show *Concentration* on NBC until its cancellation in 1973. Bud Grant, president of CBS daytime programming after having been at NBC, remembered King when *Musical Chairs* was undergoing production. "I got the call from him, and he said, 'Why don't you go over and talk to a guy named Jerry Schnur, because he wants to do a musical game show?'" King did, and he and host Adam Wade recognized each other from when Wade was a guest on the King-directed series *Saturday Prom* (see 1960-61). Wade, a singer with several hits in the early 1960s (e.g., "Take Good Care of Her"), hit it off with King and vice versa ("Adam was just lovely"), so King became the show's director.

"The whole gimmick of the show was projecting lyrics on the lines, and you had to guess the lines," King said. Specifically, Wade or guest vocalists sang a tune and stopped at a point where three possible lyrics appeared on a screen. Each player won money for each correct lyric he or she picked ($50 for round one, $75 for round two, $100 for round three), with three songs played per round. In round three, the lowest scoring players were eliminated one by one per each game until one was left and named the winner.

King said the hardest part of the series was planning the presentation of the songs. "We would rehearse something like 60 songs in an afternoon," he said. Because of the large amount of live music presented, "We only did two shows a day for the first week and a half, and then decided they'd have to accelerate it, so we then taped three shows a day."

Nevertheless, King liked doing the series. "It was very fun, because most union musicians were jazz-oriented, and I love music." He got a kick in noting that Gordon MacRae, his wife, Sheila, and his daughter Meredith all sang on the show.

Others didn't share the same enthusiasm, and CBS stopped playing *Musical Chairs* within five months. The network replaced it by moving its hit *Tattletales* into the slot, where it ran for two years.

Spin-Off

Game. Ran on CBS Mondays through Fridays 10–10:30 A.M. June 16–Sept. 5, 1975, opposite *Celebrity Sweepstakes* on NBC. C: Jim Lange. EP: Nick Nicholson, E. Roger Muir, Barbara Horn. P: Willie Stein. D: Bob Schwartz.

Showoffs

Game. Ran on ABC Mondays through Fridays Noon–12:30 P.M. June 30–Dec. 26, 1975, opposite *The Young and the Restless* on CBS and *Jackpot* (through July 4) and *The Magnificent Marble Machine* (from July 7) on NBC. C: Bobby Van. P: Howard Felsher. D: Paul Alter.

Showoffs kicked off on a somber note as the series planned to have Larry Blyden as its host. Blyden's TV acting career had been a disappointment — his last regular TV acting role was on *Harry's Girls* (see 1963-64) — but he excelled as a game show moderator, scoring hits with *Personality* from 1967 to 1969 and the syndicated *What's My Line?* from 1972 to 1975. The latter show had ended production when Blyden was announced to do *Showoffs*. Unfortunately, he died from the aftereffects of a car accident in Morocco on June 6, 1975, 17 days before what would have been his 50th birthday and 24 days before *Showoffs* was to begin.

Forced to come up with a last-minute host, the production company of Mark Goodson and Bill Todman selected former song-and-dance man Bobby Van. Van's career had a new lease on life in the early 1970s starring in a Broadway revival of *No, No, Nanette*, and that led him to more guest appearances, including guest shots on Goodson-Todman's *Match Game*. *Showoffs* became the first game show he hosted, not to mention his first regular TV series job.

"Larry Blyden was perfect for it," said director Paul Alter. "We built the show around him. Bobby Van was very good, but not as good as Larry would've been."

The rules of the game were that two teams, each with a pair of celebrities and one contestant, competed to see who could identify the most words or phrases by charades. Two members of each team had a minute to give the remaining partner clues for the items, and the team with the highest tally after both played won that round. The first team to win two rounds got to play a bonus game involving more identifications by one player from the other teammates' charades, with prize amounts sometimes totaling up to $10,000.

If the charades aspect sounded similar to an earlier game show, Alter said that was intentional. "This was an expanded version of *Pantomime Quiz*, and possibly overproduced," he said. "We weren't the first to copy it."

After six unimpressive months, ABC dropped *Showoffs* from its lineup. Somewhat surprisingly, Van returned as a game show host six months later on NBC's daily concoction *The Fun Factory*, but it lasted just 13 weeks (see 1975-76). He had yet another short-lived game show, 1979's *Make Me Laugh*, before he too died too young on July 31, 1980, at age 51. As for Alter, he went on to direct other game shows, and for the last 14 years, he has been the director for *The Price Is Right*.

A modified revival of the *Showoffs* concept appeared on CBS nearly a decade later. *Body Language*, hosted by Tom Kennedy, had three times as long a run as *Showoffs*; it was on the daytime lineup from June 3, 1984 to Jan. 3, 1986.

The Magnificent Marble Machine

Game. Ran on NBC Mondays through Fridays Noon–12:30 P.M. July 7, 1975–June 11, 1976, opposite *Showoffs* (through Dec. 26) and *Let's Make a Deal* (from Dec. 29) on ABC and *The Young and the Restless* on CBS. C: Art James. EP: Merrill Heatter, Bob Quigley, Robert Noah. P: Bob Synes, Art Alisi. D: Jerome Shaw, Lou Fusari.

"Anybody want to buy a 50-foot pinball machine?" joked host Art James about his most notorious game show, *The Magnificent Marble Machine*. The oversized contraption made contestants feel almost as small as the silver ball which they played in the bonus game to try to light up seven bumpers within a minute's worth of play. James noted that "The tour groups that came to visit NBC [in Burbank, Calif.] always came to ask about the machine."

Still, the gimmick was both the appeal and downfall of *The Magnificent Marble Machine*. As James explained, whenever the gadget was in action with players operating the machine's flippers, "The noise level in the studio was tremendous. With the noise of the effects and the music, it never involved the viewer… Watching somebody operate a machine did not engender involvement on the show."

The machine playing occurred after one of two teams, each composed of a celebrity and a contestant, won a word guessing game. Clues rolled out left to right on an electronic screen, followed by spaces covering the mystery word(s). If no one could guess the word from the clue, the spaces covering the word(s) would reveal the letters one by one. It took five correct guesses for a team to get a chance to play the machine, launch the silver ball with a plunger and win money and prizes, depending on which of the seven bumpers were hit. A team that hit all seven got to play a gold-colored ball for another minute for a shot at additional loot.

The word game sometimes had unintended hilarity. For example, the clue "Athletic Supporter" rolled out followed by the concealed three-letter answer, which was "Fan." "David Brenner buzzed in and said 'Jock,'" James remembered. "I asked him if he thought 'jock' was a three-letter word. He explained to me that 'In my gym class, nobody wore a fan!'"

The Magnificent Marble Machine was able to score better than its ABC competition *Showoffs* (q.v.), but it trailed *The Young and the Restless* on CBS considerably, so to goose its appeal the show had only pairs of celebrities compete for members of the studio audience starting in January 1976. The change did not help, and *The Magnificent Marble Machine* went off in mid–1976.

Like most Heatter-Quigley game shows, most tapes of the shows no longer exist. But one clip featuring Joan Rivers as a player did make it into the 1979 movie *The China Syndrome*, on a monitor showing the regular programming at a TV station before an emergency at a nuclear plant took place.

"I've been getting residual checks because of that one television set," James said of the movie. "I've probably received 100 checks, but they total about one dollar."

James remained active on game shows through the 1980s. Now based in Minnesota, he is working on his autobiography and is available for personal appearances as an emcee. However, don't expect him to bring an enormous pinball machine if you get him.

Rhyme and Reason

Game. Ran on ABC Mondays through Fridays 2:30–3 P.M. July 7, 1975–Dec. 26, 1975, opposite *The Edge of Night* on CBS and *The Doctors* on NBC, then ABC Mondays through Fridays 1:30–2 P.M. Dec. 29, 1975–July 9, 1976, opposite *As the World Turns* on CBS and *Days of Our Lives* on NBC. C: Bob Eubanks. EP: Steve Friedman. P: Walt Case. D: John Dorsey.

1975-76

Big Eddie

Sitcom. Ran on CBS Aug. 23–Sept. 6, 1975, Saturdays 8:30–9 P.M. opposite *Kolchak: The Night Stalker* (through Aug. 30) and on ABC and *Emergency!* on NBC, then Fridays 8–8:30 P.M. Sept. 19–Nov. 7, 1975, opposite *Mobile One* on ABC and *Sanford and Son* on NBC. C: Sheldon Leonard (as "Big Eddie" Smith), Sheree North (as Honey Smith), Quinn Cummings (as Ginger Smith), Billy Sands (as Monte "Bang Bang" Valentine), Alan Oppenheimer (as Jessie Smith), Ralph Wilcox (as Raymond McKay). EP/W: Bill Persky, Sam Denoff. P/D: Hy Averback.

Sam Denoff has the highest regard for Sheldon Leonard, the star of *Big Eddie*. "He was my god, my mentor, the best there was," Denoff said. He and his partner, Bill Persky, worked for Leonard first on *The Dick Van Dyke Show* in the 1960s, where Leonard was the show's executive producer along with Carl Reiner. Leonard popped up on that show and a few others in the 1960s as an actor too, which he was when he broke into movies in 1939, but had been mostly absent on screen for nearly a decade before Denoff and Persky brought him back into the spotlight with *Big Eddie*.

Written expressly with Leonard in mind as the lead, *Big Eddie* played off the image he had in many movies and often on *The Jack Benny Program* in the 1940s and 1950s, that of a New York City native with a shady background. Big Eddie Smith was once a hardcore gambler but attempted to redeem his ways as the head man at his Big E Sports Arena. He loved his family, which included his wife, Honey, granddaughter Ginger and brother Jessie, Big Eddie's business partner. Other regulars were Eddie's cook, Bang Bang, and employee Raymond.

According to Denoff, Leonard loved the idea, and so did Leonard's wife. "She loved to see him act," he said. "Producing didn't impress her." CBS also was high on the show too, Denoff said, but maybe too confident. The network first decided to give the series a "sneak preview" airing before the 1975 fall season officially began and in late August put it on Saturday evenings after repeats of *All in the Family*. Those three shows received high ratings, no doubt helped by its lead-in, and Denoff and company felt they had a hit on their hand.

But then CBS decided to give that slot to *Doc*, a sitcom starring Bernard Hughes, and move *Big Eddie* to Friday nights opposite *Sanford and Son*, the #1 series on NBC. "And that was it," Denoff noted. Within two months *Big Eddie* was history. *Doc* did not do much better. Its ratings were nowhere near that of the programs which preceded and followed it (*The Jeffersons* and *The Mary Tyler Moore Show*, respectively), and CBS dumped it two months into its second year with a revamped cast.

Leonard went on to make occasional TV acting appearances the rest of the 1970s until his death in 1997 while producing as well. His first guest job after *Big Eddie* was a part on — *Sanford and Son*.

Beacon Hill

Soap Opera. Ran on CBS Monday 9–11 P.M. Aug. 25, 1975, opposite movie on ABC and baseball on NBC, then CBS Tuesdays 10–11 P.M. Sept. 3–Nov. 4, 1975, opposite *Marcus Welby, M.D.* on ABC and *Joe Forrester* on NBC. C: David Dukes (as Robert Lassiter), Stephen Elliott (as Benjamin Lassiter), Roy Cooper (as Trevor Bullock), Nancy Marchand (as Mary Lassiter), Edward Herrmann (as Richard Palmer), George Rose (as Mr. Hacker), Beatrice Straight (as Mrs. Emmaline Hacker), David Rounds (as Terence O'Hara), Maeve McGuire (as Maude Palmer), Deann Mears (as Emily Bullock), Linda Purl (as Betsy Bullock), Michael Nouri (as Giorgio Bellonci), Paul Rudd (as Brian Mallory), Kathryn Walker (as Fawn Lassiter), Holland Taylor (as Marilyn Gardiner), Kitty Winn (as Rosamond Lassiter). EP: Beryl Vertue. P: Jacqueline Babbin. D: Fielder Cook, Jay Sandrich, Mel Ferber. W: Sidney Carroll.

The Montefuscos

Sitcom. Ran on NBC Thursdays 8–8:30 P.M. Sept. 4–Oct. 16, 1975, opposite *Barney Miller* on ABC and *The Waltons* on CBS. C: Joe Sirola (as Tony Montefusco), Naomi Stevens (as Rose Montefusco), Ron Carey (as Frankie Montefusco), John Aprea (as Joseph Montefusco), Phoebe Dorin (as Theresa Montefusco), Linda Dano (as Angela Montefusco Cooney), Bill Cort (as Jim Cooney),

Sal Viscuso (as Nunzio Montefusco), Jeffrey Palladini (as Anthony Carmine Montefusco), Robby Paris (as Jerome Montefusco), Dominique Pinassi (as Gina Montefusco), Damon Ruskin (as Anthony Patrick Cooney). EP: Bill Persky, Sam Denoff. P: Tom Van Atta, Bill Idelson. D: Bill Persky, Don Richardson.

The Montefuscos grew out of memories creators Sam Denoff and Bill Persky had from their childhoods living in the Northeast. Each man grew up in houses where all the members of the extended family—brothers, sisters, aunts, uncles, nieces, nephews and so on—convened on the last night of the weekend for a meal and conversation. They thought this situation had great appeal as a TV series with the same setting.

"It was originally titled The Sunday Dinner, because that was when our families would get together," Denoff said. But network honchos objected to the title. Denoff re-enacted the conversation starting on the other side. " 'You can't call it Sunday Dinner!' 'Why not?' we asked. 'Because it's airing on Thursday nights, and people will get confused!' they said."

Denoff and Persky were not happy about the news that it would air on Thursdays rather than Sundays, but there was nothing they could do about it. They could choose their producer, however, and one of them was Bill Idelson, who had to decide whether to do this series or Big Eddie for the duo. "They called me in and said, 'Watch both of these pilots and tell us which one you want to produce,'" Idelson said. Frankly, neither impressed him, but not wanting to displease the men who offered him a job, Idelson found The Montefuscos "less bad" and went with that show.

Making up Denoff and Persky's TV family were a cast of little-known or unknown actors playing the Italian family the Montefuscos. Tony and Rose were mom and pop of Frankie, Joseph, Angela and Nunzio. Joseph and Nunzio were unmarried men (Joseph had to be, since he was a priest!), while Angela lived with her husband, Jim, and their son Anthony Patrick, and Frankie and Theresa were the parents of Carmine, Jerome and Gina. The 12 regulars ate, talked, argued and reconciled at their weekly supper at Tony's house in Connecticut.

But The Montefuscos were not The Waltons, and most of America preferred CBS's Depression-era drama over the "ethnic" comedy.

The Montefuscos vanished after two months. Much of the mostly obscure cast stayed that way, with one exception: Linda Dano joined the NBC daytime soap Another World in 1983 as Felicia Gallant and stayed with it until its cancellation in 1999, then went to ABC as a recurring character in its daytime soaps.

Fay

Sitcom. Ran on NBC Thursdays 8:30–9 P.M. Sept. 4–Oct. 28, 1975, opposite On the Rocks on ABC and The Waltons on CBS, then NBC Wednesdays 9:30–10 P.M. May 19–June 2, 1976, opposite Baretta on ABC and Cannon on CBS. C: Lee Grant (as Fay Stewart), Audra Lindley (as Lillian), Joe Silver (as Jack Stewart), Margaret Willock (as Linda Stewart Baines), Stewart Moss (as Dr. Elliott Baines), Bill Gerber (as Danny Messina), Norman Alden (as Al Cassidy), Lillian Lehman (as Letty Gilmore). EP: Paul Junger Witt. P: Jerry Mayer, Tony Thomas. D: Richard Kinon, James Burrows, Alan Arkin.

Say you're at NBC in 1975 trying to fill the half hour following your new family comedy The Montefuscos, and you're also having to fulfill the new "family hour" pledge this season by the networks to air shows children could tolerate between 8 and 9 P.M. What could be a more perfect fit than Fay, a comedy about a newly liberated middle-aged feminist fresh off a divorce? Probably anything else, that's what.

Created by Susan Harris, who later created Soap and The Golden Girls, Fay told of a lady who divorced her roving husband, Jack, got a job with lawyers Danny Messina and Al Cassidy, and generally planned to enjoy life as a bachelorette, much to the dismay of her straight-laced daughter Linda and son-in-law Jack. Her best pal was her married, envious neighbor Lillian.

"Everybody loved it, but it was the first time they saw a divorced woman dating and going out," actor Norman Alden said of the show's pilot. "CBS started taking it, and then it didn't go."

When it got on NBC, plans by Harris and others to explore Fay's blossoming sex life and other controversial issues went up in smoke in favor of less weighty situations due to its time slot. Lee Grant, who took the role as her first regular TV job since being blacklisted in the 1950s, was not thrilled by the change but stuck with it, and Alden said it still remained a strong comedy. "There was nothing about the show in any way offensive to anyone or anybody," he said. "We had huge yocks on the shows."

Less affected by all this was Alden's role as Cassidy. "I played her boss," he said. "She was a legal secretary. I had a partner in the firm. We had two secretaries. Lillian [Lehman] was my secretary too." He also did the audience warm-ups before the tapings of each show.

But even Alden allowed the time slot for the sophisticated show was all wrong. NBC programming head Marvin Antonowsky preferred to throw the towel in rather than re-schedule the program after initial low ratings, so he canned *Fay* after three weeks on the air.

His announcement came while Grant was getting ready as a guest on *The Tonight Show with Johnny Carson* to promote her series. "While she was on there, she got the word the show was cancelled," Alden said. "She gave the head of the network 'the [middle] finger' on the show." She also memorably dubbed Antonowsky "the mad programmer."

Fay did return for three episodes in the late spring of 1976, at a later time slot too. The "family hour" concept also died at the end of the 1975-76 season too. Ironically, a little over a month after *Fay* ended, CBS debuted a sitcom starring a divorcée, *One Day at a Time*, and it ran nine years.

Uncle Croc's Block

Children's with Cartoons. Ran on ABC Saturdays 10:30–11:30 A.M. Sept. 6–Oct. 18, 1975, opposite *The Shazam/Isis Hour* and *Far Out Space Nuts* on CBS and *Run, Joe, Run* and *Return to the Planet of the Apes* on NBC, then ABC Saturdays Noon–12:30 P.M. Oct. 25, 1975–Feb. 14, 1976, opposite *Valley of the Dinosaurs* on CBS and *The Jetsons* on ABC. C: Charles Nelson Reilly (as Uncle Croc), Alfie Wise (as Mr. Rabbit Ears), Jonathan Harris (as Basil Bitterbottom), and voices of Alan Oppenheimer, Lennie Weinrib, Robert Ridgely, Kenneth Mars, Allan Melvin. P: Mack Bing, Don Christensen. D: Mack Bing.

Westwind

Adventure. Ran on NBC Saturdays 11:30 A.M.–Noon Sept. 6, 1975–Sept. 4, 1976, opposite *The Oddball Couple* on ABC and *The Ghost Busters* on CBS. C: Van Williams (as Steve Andrews), Niki Dantine (as Kate Andrews), Kimberly Beck (as Robin Andrews), Steve Burns (as Tom Andrews).

EP: Bill D'Angelo. P: Richard Bluel. D: Christian I. Nyby II, Richard L. Bare.

The Family Holvak

Drama. Ran on NBC Sundays 8–9 P.M. Sept. 7–Oct. 12, 1975, opposite *The Six Million Dollar Man* on ABC and *Cher* on CBS, then NBC Monday 8–9 P.M. Oct. 27, 1975, opposite *Mobile One* on ABC and *Rhoda* and *Phyllis* on CBS. C: Glenn Ford (as Rev. Tom Holvak), Julie Harris (as Elizabeth Holvak), Lance Kerwin (as Ramey Holvak), Elizabeth Cheshire (as Julie Mae Holvak), Ted Gehring (as Chester Purdle), Cynthia Howard (as Ida), William McKinney (as Deputy Jim Shanks). EP: Roland Kibbee, Dean Hargrove. P: Richard Collins. D: Alf Kjellin, Ralph Senensky, John Newland.

Give-N-Take

Game. Ran on CBS Mondays through Fridays 10–10:30 A.M. Sept. 8–Nov. 26, 1975, opposite *Celebrity Sweepstakes* on NBC. C: Jim Lange. EP/D: Bill Carruthers. P: Joel Stein. D: John Dorsey.

The Barbary Coast

Fantasy Western. Ran on ABC Mondays 8–9 P.M. Sept. 8–Oct. 20, 1975, opposite *Rhoda* and *Phyllis* on CBS and *The Invisible Man* on NBC, and then ABC Fridays 8–9 P.M. Oct. 31, 1975–Jan. 9, 1976, opposite *Big Eddie* (through Nov. 7) and *M*A*S*H* (through Nov. 28) and movies (from Dec. 19) on CBS and *Sanford & Son* and *Chico and the Man* on NBC. C: William Shatner (as Jeff Cable), Doug McClure (as Cash Conover), Richard Kiel (as Moose Moran), Dave Turner (as Thumbs). EP: Cy Chermak. P: Douglas Hayes. D: Alex Grasshoff, Don McDougall, Bill Bixby, John Florea.

Created by Douglas Heyes, *The Barbary Coast* presented itself as a cross between *The Wild Wild West* TV series and the con movie *The Sting*. Here Jeff Cable, an agent from the governor's office of California, based his operations in San Francisco's rowdy Barbary Coast district in the 1870s. He set up operations at the Golden Gate Casino, operated by Cash Conover, who assisted Cable in his efforts to nab criminals in the area, as did Conover's towering right-hand man, Moose Moran, and the casino's pianist, Thumbs. Cable often wore makeup and went undercover in his duties.

In the TV-movie pilot that aired on May

4, 1975, all the actors reappeared for the series except for Dennis Cole, who played Cash. Doug McClure replaced him and co-starred with William Shatner in what was Shatner's first regular series role since *Star Trek* ended in 1969. There were high expectations *The Barbary Coast* would do well, given the phenomenal appeal Shatner's previous series had in reruns.

"My only problem on that show was Shatner," recalled Alex Grasshoff, who directed four episodes. "He kept asking me why I am doing this and why am I doing that, and I've had this from a lot of actors, wanting to learn how to direct from me." (Shatner later directed the *Star Trek V: The Final Frontier* movie in 1991. He barely mentioned *The Barbary Coast* in his 1994 memoirs, *Star Trek Movie Memories*.)

Actually, Shatner's co-star posed a potential headache for Grasshoff too, but the director managed to work around him. "Doug McClure, he got drunk every night. We had to shoot all of his scenes early in the day because he was drunk."

Even with that situation in mind, the biggest obstacles for *The Barbary Coast* were the comedies that ran against it. On Monday nights, CBS's spinoffs from *The Mary Tyler Moore Show*, *Rhoda* and *Phyllis*, crushed it so thoroughly that ABC moved the series to Fridays, only to see another pair of top 25 sitcom hits, *Sanford & Son* and *Chico and the Man*, do the same.

Yet Grasshoff did not believe it was the competition that doomed the series. "I think *The Barbary Coast* was one of those things that did not relate to the everyday human psyche," he said. "In *The Barbary Coast* you were in a real fantasy world. I couldn't relate to it."

ABC replaced *The Barbara Coast* with an arguably even more unbelievable, unrealistic series— the variety show *Donny and Marie*, starring the brother-and-sister duo of the Osmond family. It ran until 1979. Shatner did not have another series until *T.J. Hooker* in 1982, which was produced until 1986, while McClure was a regular on the syndicated sitcom *Out of This World* from 1987 to 1991 before he died in 1995.

The Invisible Man

Science Fiction. Ran on NBC Mondays 8–9 P.M. Sept. 8, 1975–Jan. 19, 1976, opposite *The Barbary Coast* (through Oct. 20) and *Mobile One* (from Oct. 27 to Dec. 29) on ABC and *Rhoda* and *Phyllis* on CBS. C: David McCallum (as Dr. Daniel Westin), Craig Stevens (as Walter Carlson), Melinda Fee (as Dr. Kate Westin). EP: Harve Bennett. P: Leslie Stevens, Robert F. O'Neill, Frank Telford. D: Alan J. Levi, Sigmund Neufeld, Jr. W: Steven Bochco, Leslie Stevens

Joe and Sons

Sitcom. Ran on CBS Tuesdays 8:30–9 P.M. Sept. 9, 1975–Jan. 13, 1976, opposite *Welcome Back, Kotter* on ABC and *Movin' On* on NBC. C: Richard Castellano (as Joe Vitale), Jerry Stiller (as Gus Duzik), Barry Miller (as Mark Vitale), Jimmy Baio (as Nick Vitale), Florence Stanley (as Aunt Josephine), Bobbi Jordan (as Estelle). EP: Douglas S Cramer. P: Bernie Kukoff, Jeff Harris. D: Peter Baldwin.

"That really was a big favorite of mine," said producer Bernie Kukoff of *Joe and Sons*. "I really felt that show should've run longer. We were up against *Welcome Back, Kotter*, but still we competed with them. Beat them a couple of times."

Joe and Sons was a blue-collar family comedy set up in the Northeast, giving it a certain similarity to *All in the Family*. In fact, Kukoff said he heard some CBS officials say they were thinking about airing *Joe and Sons* following *All in the Family*, but that did not occur. The show centered on Joe Vitale, a very Italian-American living in an apartment in Hoboken, New Jersey, with his sons Mark (the older, curly haired one) and Nick (the chubby one). A widower, Joe relied on the help of his sister Josephine and next-door neighbor Estelle, a cocktail waitress, in raising his boys. Commiserating with him at home was Gus Duzik, his pal and co-worker at the Hoboken Sheet and Tube Company, a sheet metal manufacturer.

"This had kind of an edge to it, and a warmth to it," noted Kukoff. "I thought all the performers did a wonderful job. We did some wonderful shows."

Kukoff thinks the show went off because some important higher-ups at the network disliked Richard Castellano's rather realistic portrayal of an unkempt, beefy lower-class family head struggling to keep his clan fed and upstanding. "We'd get notes like 'Put a sweater on him,'" he said. "I heard [CBS owner William] Paley didn't like the big fat guy."

On that point, Kukoff disagreed, saying he thought Castellano was great, especially in dialogue scenes with Jerry Stiller. "There was a crony quality with him and Jerry," he said.

Castellano had done one series earlier, the 1972 summer sitcom *The Super*. An obese man spouting his native dialect from the Bronx, New York, he obviously was a limited type to cast, and he would have just one more series, the flop 1981 drama *The Gangster Chronicles* as a mob boss, before he died of a heart attack in 1988 at the age of 55.

After *Joe and Sons* ended, Kukoff and partner Jeff Harris went on to create their biggest hit, the sitcom *Diff'rent Strokes*, which ran from Nov. 3, 1978 to Aug. 30, 1986. They ended their professional relationship in 1981. But despite the long run of *Diff'rent Strokes*, Kukoff said, "*Joe and Sons* was probably our favorite situation comedies we wrote and produced."

CBS replaced *Joe and Sons* with another urban ethnic sitcom, *Popi* (q.v.). That lasted only five episodes in the time slot as a week after it debuted. ABC moved *Welcome Back, Kotter* to Thursdays at 8 P.M. to make room for the massive new hit *Laverne and Shirley*. Incidentally, CBS never managed to beat ABC in that time slot until it ended in 1983.

Joe Forrester

Police Drama. Ran on NBC Tuesdays 10–11 P.M. Sept. 9, 1975–Jan. 27, 1976, opposite *Marcus Welby, M.D.* on ABC and *Beacon Hill* (through Nov. 4) and *Switch* (from Dec. 2) on CBS, then NBC Mondays 9–10 P.M. Feb. 2–Aug. 30, 1976, opposite movies on ABC and *All in the Family* and *Maude* on CBS. C: Lloyd Bridges (as Joe Forrester), Patricia Crowley (as Georgia Cameron), Eddie Egan (as Sgt. Bernie Vincent), Dwan Smith (as Jolene Jackson), Taylor Lacher (as Det. Will Carson). EP: David Gerber. P: Mark Rodgers, James H. Brown. D: Alf Kjellin, Alexander Singer, Alvin Ganzer.

When Things Were Rotten

Sitcom. Ran on ABC Wednesdays 8–8:30 P.M. Sept. 10–Dec. 24, 1975, opposite *Tony Orlando and Dawn* on CBS and *Little House on the Prairie* on NBC. C: Dick Gautier (as Robin Hood), Misty Rowe (as Maid Marian), Dick Van Patten (as Friar Tuck), Bernie Kopell (as Alan-a-Dale), Henry Polic II (as Lord Hubert, the Sheriff of Nottingham), Richard Dimitri (as Bertram/Renaldo),

David Sabin (as Little John), Ron Rifkin (as Prince John), Jane A. Johnston (as Princess Isabelle). EP/W: Mel Brooks. P/W: Norman Steinberg. D: Marty Feldman, Jerry Paris, Bruce Bilson. W: John Boni.

Doctors' Hospital

Drama. Ran on NBC Wednesdays 9–10 P.M. Sept. 10, 1975–Jan. 14, 1976, opposite *Baretta* on ABC and *Cannon* on CBS. C: George Peppard (as Dr. Jake Goodwin), Zohra Lampert (as Dr. Norah Purcell), Victor Campos (as Dr. Felipe Ortega), Albert Paulsen (as Dr. Janos Varga), Russ Martin (as Dr. Chaffey), John Larroquette (as Dr. Paul Herman), John Pleshette (as Dr. Danvers), James Almanzar (as Dr. Anson Brooks), Elizabeth Brooks (as Nurse Connie Kimbrough), Adrian Ricard (as Nurse Hester Stanton), Barbara Darrow (as Nurse Forester), Elaine Church (as Nurse Wilson), Susan Franklin (as Nurse Franklin), Larry Watson (as Barney), Maxine Stuart (as Scotty). EP: Matthew Rapf. P: Jack Laird. D: Leo Penn, Robert Abrams, Vincent Sherman.

Kate McShane

Legal Drama. Ran on CBS Wednesdays 10–11 P.M. Sept. 10–Nov. 12, 1975, opposite *Starsky and Hutch* on ABC and *Petrocelli* on NBC. C: Anne Meara (as Kate McShane), Sean McClory (as Pat McShane), Charles Haid (as Ed McShane). EP: E. Jack Neuman. P: Robert Foster, Robert Stambler. D: Marvin Chomsky, Bill Bixby, Robert Scheerer.

On the Rocks

Sitcom. Ran on ABC Thursdays 8:30–9 P.M. Sept. 11, 1975–Jan. 8, 1976, opposite *The Waltons* on CBS and *Fay* on NBC, then ABC Mondays 8–8:30 P.M. Jan. 12–May 17, 1976, opposite *Rhoda* and *Phyllis* on CBS and *The Rich Little Show* (from Feb. 2) on NBC. C: Jose Perez (as Hector Fuentes), Hal Williams (as Lester DeMott), Rick Hurst (as Cleaver), Bobby Sandler (as Nicky Palik), Mel Stewart (as Mr. Gibson), Tom Poston (as Mr. Sullivan), Pat Cranshaw (as Gabby), Logan Ramsey (as Warden Wilbur Poindexter). P: John Rich, H.R. Poindexter. D: John Rich, Dick Clement.

The British Broadcasting Corporation comedy *Porridge* was just one of several 1970s shows adapted for U.S. television, but it arguably had the toughest locale to do humor — a prison. The lead character was Stanley Fletcher, serving five years for robbing a truck, and his interactions with fellow prisoners and officials ran from 1974 to 1977. A year into its run, an Americanized *Porridge* emerged in the form of *On the Rocks* (the original never aired in the States, not even on public television).

Substituting for Stanley in *On the Rocks* was Hector Fuentes, an unusual (for the time) Hispanic lead character. Joining him in the slammer were DeMott, Cleaver, Nicky, and Gabby, who ran the gamut in ethnicities and ages. Keeping an eye over them were Mr. Gibson the corrections officer and the somewhat gullible Mr. Sullivan the guard, who usually was an easy target for the convicts to manipulate. The fictional setting was the Alamesa State Minimum Security Prison.

Playing the ancient Gabby was Pat Cranshaw, whose work in Hollywood almost always had him playing a man much older than himself. "I was just a character-type actor, and I was around 50 when I came back out here from Texas—we left here in '52—but even then I had done a 78-year-old trapper," he said.

Cranshaw recalled Gabby's advanced age was the main source of the character's humor. "He apparently had been in a number of years," he said. Though Cranshaw had trouble remembering specifics, he did know at one point the character was in the hospital for a time with some long-forgotten ailment.

Other than that, Cranshaw knew that he had an enjoyable time doing the series. "*On the Rocks* was a good cast that got along well," he said.

However, not all people thought it was light and good. The National Association for Justice wanted the show stopped in 1975 for giving what it felt was too nice a depiction of prison. That request did not occur, but the show did go off before the end of the season because, in Cranshaw's opinion, the general American public did not warm to the overall concept. "The idea of guys in prison having fun didn't set well with them," he said.

On the Rocks was on the air long enough to allow for a possible spinoff. The episode that aired March 29, 1976, was a pilot for *The Rita Moreno Show* where the titular Oscar/Emmy/Tony/Grammy winner played an aspiring actress who took money from her brother Hector to make it in Hollywood. It didn't make the cut, and Moreno didn't get a regular acting role on TV until the sitcom *9 to 5* from 1982 to 1983.

Ellery Queen

Mystery. Ran on NBC Thursdays 9–10 P.M. Sept. 11–Dec. 25, 1975, opposite *The Streets of San Francisco* on ABC and movies (through Nov. 20) and *Hawaii Five-O* (from Dec. 4) on CBS, then NBC Sundays 8–9 P.M. Jan. 4–Sept. 5, 1976, opposite *The Six Million Dollar Man* on ABC and *The Sonny and Cher Show* on CBS. C: Jim Hutton (as Ellery Queen), David Wayne (as Inspector Richard Queen), Tom Reese (as Sgt. Velie), John Hillerman (as Simon Brimmer), Ken Swofford (as Frank Flannigan). EP: Richard Levinson, William Link. P: Peter S. Fischer, Michael Rhodes. D: Seymour Robbie, David Greene, Jark Arnold.

Mobile One

Adventure. Ran on ABC Fridays 8–9 P.M. Sept. 12–Oct. 17, 1975, opposite *Big Eddie* and *M*A*S*H* on CBS and *Sanford and Son* and *Chico and the Man* on NBC, then ABC Mondays 8–9 P.M. Oct. 27–Dec. 29, 1975, opposite *Rhoda* and *Phyllis* on CBS and *The Invisible Man* on NBC. C: Jackie Cooper (as Peter Campbell), Julie Gregg (as Maggie Spencer), Mark Wheeler (as Doug McKnight). EP: Jack Webb. P: William Bowers. D: David Moessinger, E.W. Swackhamer, Jackie Cooper, Paul Krasny.

Swiss Family Robinson

Adventure. Ran on ABC Sundays 7–8 P.M. Sept. 14, 1975–April 11, 1976, opposite *Three for the Road* (through Nov. 30) and *60 Minutes* (from Dec. 7) on CBS and *The Wonderful World of Disney* on NBC. C: Martin Milner (as Karl Robinson), Pat Delany (as Lotta Robinson), Willie Aames (as Fred Robinson), Eric Olson (as Ernie Robinson), Cameron Mitchell (as Jeremiah Worth), Helen Hunt (as Helga Wagner). EP: Irwin Allen. P: Arthur Weiss,. D: Harry Harris, George Fenady.

Three for the Road

Adventure. Ran on CBS Sundays 7–8 P.M. Sept. 14–Nov. 30, 1975, opposite *Swiss Family Robinson* on ABC and *The Wonderful World of Disney* on NBC. C: Alex Rocco (as Pete Karras), Vincent Van Patten (as John Karras), Leif Garrett (as Endicott "Endy" Karras). EP/W: Jerry McNelly. P: John G. Stephens, William F. Phillips. D: Boris Sagal, Hy Averback, Lou Antonio, Barry Crane. W: Perry Grant, Jack Miller, Sid Dorfman.

Matt Helm

Spy Adventure. Ran on ABC Saturdays 10–11 P.M. Sept. 20, 1975–Jan. 3, 1976, opposite *The Carol Burnett Show* on CBS and movies on NBC. C: Anthony Franciosa (as Matt Helm), Laraine Stephens (as Claire Kronski), Gene Evans (as Sgt. Hanrahan), Jeff Donnell (as Ethel). EP: Irving Allen. P: Buzz Kulick, Ken Pettus, Charles B. Fitzsimons. D: Buzz Kulick, John Newland, Don Weis.

Bronk

Crime Drama. Ran on CBS Sundays 10–11 P.M. Sept. 21, 1975–July 18, 1976, opposite movies on ABC and *The NBC Sunday Mystery Movie* on NBC. C: Jack Palance (as Lt. Alex Bronkov), Joseph Mascolo (as Mayor Pete Santori), Henry Beckman (as Harry Mark), Tony King (as Sgt. John Webber), Dina Ousley (as Ellen Bronkov). EP: Carroll O'Connor, Bruce Geller. P: Leigh Vance. D: Stuart Hagmann, Richard Donner, Sutton Roley, Russ Mayberry.

Three for the Money

Game. Ran on NBC Mondays through Fridays 12:30–12:55 P.M. Sept. 29–Nov. 28, 1975, opposite *All My Children* on ABC and *Search for Tomorrow* on CBS. C: Dick Enberg. P: Stu Billet. D: Hank Behar.

Saturday Night Live with Howard Cosell

Variety. Ran on ABC Saturdays 8–9 P.M. Sept. 20, 1975–Jan. 17, 1976, opposite *The Jeffersons* and *Doc* on CBS and *Emergency!* on NBC. C: Howard Cosell, the Elliot Lawrence Orchestra. EP: Roone Arledge. P: Rubert Hitzig. D: Don Mischer.

McCoy

Detective Drama. Ran on NBC Sundays 9–11 P.M. Oct. 5, 1975–March 28, 1976, alternating as part of *The NBC Sunday Mystery Movie*, opposite movies on ABC and *Kojak* and *Bronk* on CBS. C: Tony Curtis (as McCoy), Roscoe Lee Browne (as Gideon Gibbs). P: Roland Kibbee. D: Richard Quine, Stan Dragoti.

Grady

Sitcom. Ran on NBC Thursdays 8–8:30 P.M. Dec. 4–Dec. 25, 1975, and then NBC Thursdays 8:30–9 P.M. Jan. 8–March 4, 1976, both times opposite *Barney Miller* on ABC and *The Waltons* on CBS.

C: Whitman Mayo (as Grady Wilson), Carol Cole (as Ellie Wilson Marshall), Joe Morton (as Hal Marshall), Roseanne Katan (as Laurie Marshall), Haywood Nelson (as Haywood Marshall), Alix Elias (as Rose Kosinski), Jack Fletcher (as Mr. Pratt). EP: Saul Turteltaub, Bernie Orenstein. P: Jerry Ross, Howard Leeds. D: Gerren Keith.

After four seasons of being NBC's top sitcom from 1972 to 1975, *Sanford and Son* finally merited a spinoff in 1975. *Grady* had Fred Sanford's bearded, easygoing pal Grady Wilson stop visiting the Sanford junkyard to live in a more upscale Santa Monica, Calif., neighborhood at his daughter Ellie's home along with his son-in-law Hal and grandchildren Laurie and Haywood.

Stopping by were the Marshalls' Caucasian landlord, Mr. Pratt, and neighbors the Kosinskis, or at least that was the original plan for the latter. Alix Elias, who played Rose Kosinski, said George Dzundza signed with the show to play her husband but soon hated his role. "After the second episode, he left," she said. "He basically said it was a piece of shit and left."

With Elias still under contract, "They essentially made me a single white woman next door," she said. No reference was made to her husband again. Unfortunately, someone at NBC decided to run the pilot as the third episode, thus confusing viewers who saw two Kosinskis moving into a neighborhood where only one had already been seen. This was only one of the show's confusing elements, in Elias's opinion.

Elias believed executive producers Saul Turteltaub and Bernie Orenstein, who produced *Sanford and Son*, did not put as much thought as needed into creating the spinoff. "They really didn't have a point of view," she said. "They didn't know who those characters were and how to make the audience fall in love with them."

Part of the problem she thought was with Whitman Mayo, who it was hoped would be as big as Redd Foxx was starring on *Sanford and Son*. "Whitman had been an agent in New York providing a lot of actors for [*Sanford and Son*] before he joined it [in 1973]," she said. "He didn't really have as much of a performing background as Redd did.

"Essentially, he had a clear-cut character on *Sanford and Son*, and then they took him

"At this point, Fred Sanford would be telling me to shut up…": Whitman Mayo explains to his grand-daughter Roseanne Katan what he's learned from a black history course he's taken on the January 8, 1976, installment of *Grady*. One wonders if the show's writers ever took a similar class in coming up with this and other storylines.

without knowing what that character was. They basically wanted to make him into a middle-class Jew."

Emphasizing she is not anti–Semitic, Elias noted that "The closest thing we had to a black person backstage — we had a black stage manager, and that was it. The male, white Jewish creators there really had no idea what went on in a black family. They just didn't know. And anything the cast tried to offer was seen as creative encroachment."

She added that her character could be as hard to accept too due to the scripts. "I'd walk into people's houses unannounced, which would seem unlikely. They just kind of ignored the racial overtones," she said.

Summing up *Grady*, Elias said, "They were so anxious not to have a point of view. They wanted to keep their options open as much as possible. It's kind of being safe, so you end up with nothing."

Mayo returned to *Sanford and Son*, but the show ended a year later when Redd Foxx left to do a variety show (see *Redd Foxx*). Mayo stayed on for a second spinoff from *Sanford and Son* which ended even quicker than *Grady* (see *The Sanford Arms*). He died in 2001 at age 70.

The Cop and the Kid

Sitcom. Ran on NBC Thursdays 8:30–9 P.M. Dec. 4–Dec. 25, 1975, opposite *On the Rocks* on ABC and *The Waltons* on CBS, then NBC Thursdays 8–8:30 P.M. Jan. 8–March 4, 1976, opposite *Welcome Back, Kotter* on ABC and *The Waltons* on CBS. C: Charles Durning (as Officer Frank Murphy), Tierre Turner (as Lucas Adams), Patsy Kelly (as Mrs. Brigid Murphy), Sharon Spelman (as Mary Goodhew), Curtiz Willis (as Shortstuff),

Eric Laneuville (as Mouse), William Pierson (as Sgt. Zimmerman). EP: Jerry Davis. P: Ben Joelson, Art Baer. D: Alexander March, Gary Nelson.

The Blue Knight

Police Drama. Ran on CBS Wednesdays 10–11 P.M. Dec. 17, 1975–July 28, 1976, and Sept. 22–Oct. 27, 1976, opposite *Starsky and Hutch* (through July 28) and *Charlie's Angels* (from Sept. 22) on ABC and *Petrocelli* (through July 28) and *The Quest* (from Sept. 22) on NBC. C: George Kennedy (as William "Bumper" Morgan), Phillip Pine (as Sgt. Newman), Charles Siebert (as Sgt. Cabe), Lin McCarthy (as Lt. Hauser). EP: Lee Rich, Phil Capice. P: Joel Rogosin.

Cop turned writer Joseph Wambaugh scored a double success on TV in the fall of 1973, first with creating the series *Police Story*, which ran four years, and then with *The Blue Knight*, a miniseries based on his best-selling novel of the same name which aired on NBC from Nov. 13 to 16, 1973. William Holden played somewhat weary veteran lawman Bumper Morgan in the miniseries, but when it became a series on CBS two years later, George Kennedy inherited the role. "I thought he played the role beautifully," said producer Joel Rogosin of Kennedy's work. "I thought he was perfect."

However, Wambaugh, who was part of the TV series' backstage staff, prompted different feelings from Rogosin. "He was very actively involved in reading the stories and scripts and provided vitriolic feedback," said Rogosin. "The bottom line is Joe wanted a much darker, grittier show than the network wanted at the time." Wambaugh wanted something akin to what *Hill Street Blues* would pioneer later when it debuted in 1981, according to Rogosin.

Rogosin sympathized with Wambaugh's goals to an extent. "He was trouble because he wanted the best," he said. But he found the ex-policeman's objections wearing himself down as well as network honchos. For example, Rogosin said, "I wanted to give Bumper a personal life, so we built a set for his home life. I thought it was rather modest, especially in comparison with other sets you saw on television at the time. Wambaugh thought it was too upscale."

The frustration of dealing with Wambaugh's demands versus those of the network and other members of the production staff grew on Rogosin ("It was war," he noted). CBS re-newed the midseason replacement after an OK if unspectacular few months of finishing second opposite the top 20 hit *Starsky and Hutch* on ABC, but Rogosin wanted no part of handling Wambaugh anymore.

"I didn't do the second year," he said. "It was too tough. His desire to translate [his novel] to TV wasn't practical."

As it turned out, *The Blue Knight* would have an abbreviated second season which ended after just six episodes after it returned from a summer hiatus (CBS aired movies in its time slot in that period). The addition of two new characters, Lt. Hauser and Sgt. Cabe, produced little interest against its new competition. Thoroughly walloping the show in the ratings was the hit *Charlie's Angels*, a program whose glamorous portrayal of law enforcement was the antithesis from the realism of *The Blue Knight*. One only can wonder what Wambaugh's reaction was when he learned his baby was knocked off the air by *that*. Incidentally, the author did no other TV series after *The Blue Knight*.

The Neighbors

Game. Ran on ABC Mondays through Fridays 2:30–3 P.M. Dec. 29, 1975–April 9, 1976, opposite *Guiding Light* on CBS and *The Doctors* on NBC. C: Regis Philbin. EP: Bill Carruthers. P: Joel Stein. D: John Dorsey.

Popi

Sitcom. Ran on CBS Tuesdays 8:30–9 P.M. Jan. 20–March 2, 1976, opposite *Laverne & Shirley* on ABC and *Movin' On* on NBC, then CBS Tuesdays 8–8:30 P.M. July 20–Aug. 24, 1976, opposite *Happy Days* on ABC and *Movin' On* on NBC. C: Hector Elizondo (as Abraham Rodriguez), Edith Diaz (as Lupe), Anthony Perez (as Abraham Rodriguez, Jr.), Dennis Vasquez (as Luis Rodriguez), Lou Criscuolo (as Angelo Maggio). EP: Herbert B. Leonard, Arne Sultan. P: Nick Anderson, A.J. Nelson. D: Hy Averback, E.W. Swackhamer.

The Dumplings

Sitcom. Ran on NBC Wednesdays 9:30–10 P.M. Jan. 28–March 24, 1976, opposite *Baretta* on ABC and *Cannon* on CBS. C: James Coco (as Joe Dumpling), Geraldine Brooks (as Angela Dumpling), George S. Irving (as Charles Sweetzer), George Furth (as Frederic Steele), Marcia Rodd (as Stephanie), Mort Marshall (as Cully), Jane Cannell (as Bridget McKenna), Wil Albert (as the prude). EP/W: Don Nicholl, Michael Ross, Bernie West. P: George Sunga. D: Paul Bogart, Hal Cooper, Bernie West.

The devoted middle-aged couple of Angela and Joe were obese and had the surname of Dumpling—can't get any cuter than that for a sitcom, can you? They spent much of their time near food running the Dudley's Take-Out restaurant in a Manhattan skyscraper with a cashier named Cully. The regulars there included the fictional Bristol Oil Company executive vice president Charles Sweetzer and his secretary, Ms. McKenna, both of whom worked in the complex; their landlord, Frederic Steele; and Angela's sister Stephanie.

The concept of a fat couple being the star of a sitcom seems odd, especially today, given how image-conscious television executive and actors, but actress Jane Connell said that in 1976, everyone involved thought it had possible merit. "They figured the audience would be more comfortable with the ones like them," she said.

As with most of the cast, Connell was better known for her stage work than for television, and considered them all pals from her days on Broadway. Despite that distinction, and the show's locale of New York City, it actually was recorded in Los Angeles. As Connell joked about getting her role, "We were living in California at the time. I knew everybody associated with the show. They finally put me on as low man on the totem pole."

A sad fact hidden from most of the viewers at the time was the condition of the show's female lead. "Geraldine was very ill," Connell said. "She was dying of cancer." She would die of the disease on June 19, 1977, at the age of 51, but Connell emphasized she didn't think this was a reason the show was cancelled, since Brooks managed to act without showing external symptoms of her condition.

Connell declined to speculate on why *The Dumplings* perished so quickly, but a glance at the schedule indicates the lead-in program was part of the problem. NBC thought its hit show *Chico and the Man* would prove just as popular a draw on Wednesdays nights against crime shows on ABC and CBS as it had been following *Sanford and Son* on Friday nights. Unfortunately, many viewers didn't go along with the move, and the former #3 program in the 1974-75 season ratings dropped out of the top 20 and ended up trailing its competition *Baretta* by the end of the 1975-76 season. With that weakened appeal, *The Dumplings* had less of an audience to draw coming on in the middle of the crime shows, so after just nine weeks, it was history.

The Practice

Sitcom. Ran on NBC Fridays 8:30–9 P.M. Jan. 30–Aug. 6, 1976, opposite *Donny and Marie* on ABC and *Sara* on CBS, then NBC Wednesdays 8–8:30 P.M. Oct. 13–Nov. 3, 1976, opposite *The Bionic Woman* on ABC and *Good Times* on CBS, then NBC Wednesdays 9:30–10 P.M. Dec. 1, 1976–Jan. 26, 1977, opposite *Baretta* on ABC and movies on CBS. C: Danny Thomas (as Dr. Jules Bedford), Dena Dietrich (as Molly Gibbons), Shelley Fabares (as Jenny Bradford), David Spielberg (as Dr. David Bradford), Didi Conn (as Helen), Allen Price (as Paul Bedford), Damon Raskin (as Tony Bedford), John Byner (as Dr. Roland Caine), Sam Laws (as Nate), Mike Evans (as Lenny). EP: Danny Thomas, Paul Junger Witt. P: Steve Gordon, Tony Thomas. D: Lee Philips, Noam Pitlik, Bill Persky. W: Sam Denoff, Dale McCraven.

The Rich Little Show

Comedy Variety. Ran on NBC Mondays 8–9 P.M. Feb. 2–July 19, 1976 (except from May 24 to June 14), opposite *On the Rocks* (through May 17) and *Viva Valdez* (from June 21) and *Good Heavens* (through April 5) and baseball (from April 12) on ABC and *Rhoda* and *Phyllis* on CBS. C: Rich Little, Charlotte Rae, Julie McWhirter, R.G. Brown, Mel Bishop, Joe Baker, the Robert E. Hughes Orchestra. EP: Jerry Goldstein. P: Rich Eustis, Al Rogers. D: Lee Bernhardi, Walter C. Miller. W: Rudy DeLuca, Ray Jessell, Barry Levinson, Ron Clark.

Jigsaw John

Police Drama. Ran on NBC Mondays 10–11 P.M. Feb. 2–Sept. 6, 1976, opposite movies (through April 5) and baseball (from April 12) on ABC and *Medical Center* on CBS. C: Jack Warden (as John St. "Jigsaw" John), Alan Feinstein (as Sam Donner), Pippa Scott (as Maggie Hearn), James Hong (as Frank Chen). P: Ronald Austin, James David Buchanan. D: Reza S. Badiyi, Paul Krasny, Charles R. Rondeau.

City of Angels

Mystery Drama. Ran on NBC Tuesdays 10–11 P.M. Feb. 3–Aug. 10, 1976, opposite *Family* on ABC and *Switch* on CBS. C: Wayne Rogers (as Jake Axminster), Elaine Joyce (as Marsha), Clifton James (as Lt. Murray Quint), Philip Sterling (as Michael Brimm). EP: Jo Swerling, Jr. P: Roy Huggins. D: Don Medford, Douglas Heyes, Barry Shear, Ralph Senesky.

With *City of Angels*, producer Roy Huggins had the chance to emulate the kind of stories told by one of his favorite authors, Raymond Chandler. Unfortunately for him, what he wanted to do and how others involved in the series thought it should be were considerably different perspectives, and Huggins came out on the losing end of the arguments, as did the series ultimately.

Recalled Huggins: "I was in New York on television business, and the head of programming for NBC [Marvin Antonowsky of *Fay* (q.v.) infamy] took me to the Russian Tea Room, and he sat me down and said, 'Roy, we want to do a private eye in the style of Chandler and set in the 1930s.'"

Huggins contemplated the thought, then realized a large problem would lie in following that setup faithfully. The show's lead character, he said, would be "a basically cynical man who makes his living as a private eye, and Chandler wrote his stories as a comment on the current society. Chandler wrote them in the 1930s, and that was the current social situation in urban America. The points he was making about corruption and so on lacked punch. They were history."

After explaining this to Antonowsky, Huggins nevertheless conceded and did the show ("He begged me to do it," Huggins said). But he warned Antonowsky that "I will have fun with it. But the audience will not enjoy it."

Actually, it was Huggins who did not like what happened next. The show's production company set up a condition with NBC executives that he did not realize nor approve when putting the series together. "They agreed to put us on the air without a pilot if we would accept Wayne Rogers as the lead," Huggins said. Rogers was a hot name, having left a co-starring role on the hit sitcom *M*A*S*H* in 1975 over the terms of his contract. But the curly-haired actor's fame rested on being a witty light comic actor, not a gritty, moody detective as envisioned for *City of Angels*.

"He certainly isn't right for a private eye," Huggins said. "And certainly his career has proved me right. He loved to change dialogue and thought he was producing the show."

For the record, the other regulars on the series were Marsha, Jake's secretary as well as operator for an answering service for call girls (!), Lt. Quint, and Jake's lawyer Michael Brimm. As the title indicated, the action took place in Los Angeles, the "city of angels." Though it was set in the Depression era, there was no mistaking this for the rural family struggles of *The Waltons* then on the air at the same time.

When *City of Angels* went off after six months, the network moved the anthology *Police Story* into its time slot. That show spent its fourth and final year there.

Sara

Western. Ran on CBS Fridays 8–9 P.M. Feb. 13–July 30, 1976, opposite *Donny and Marie* on ABC and *Sanford and Son* and *The Practice* on NBC. C: Brenda Vaccaro (as Sara Yarnell), Bert Kramer (as Emmet Ferguson), Albert Stratton (as Martin Pope), William Wintersole (as George Bailey), Mariclare Costello (as Julia Bailey), William Phipps (as Mayor Claude Barstow), Louise Latham (as Martha Higgins), Kraig Metzinger (as Georgie Bailey), Debbie Lytton (as Debbie Higgins), Hallie Morgan (as Emma Higgins). EP: George Eckstein. P: Richard Collins.

Schoolteacher Sara Yarnell left Philadelphia in the 1870s to venture out west and live in Independence, Colorado. As the town's only instructor for children, she faced constant scrutiny from school board members Emmet Ferguson, Mayor Claude Barstow and George Bailey. George's wife, Julia, liked Sara, however, as did Julia's son Georgie. His classmates Debbie and Emma Higgins were the daughters of Sara's landlady, Martha Higgins, while Martin Pope published the town's newspaper *The Bulletin* and generally endorsed Sara's efforts over the narrow-minded school board. The series was based on a book by Marian Cockrell.

Playing Georgie was Kraig Metzinger. In an e-mail to me, Metzinger recalled how he got the role: "I was on the Universal lot one day looping sound [matching a vocal track to a film] for a character in a TV-movie. The producer of that movie was George Eckstein, and after I finished in the green room, I was asked to come and see him for an interview for the role of Georgie. I went over to Mr. Eckstein's office, read for the part and got the job on the spot."

Metzinger did not recall any particular plots, but noted that "Brenda Vaccaro was very nice to us kids on the show and one day invited us to her dressing room. Her jeweler was there. She told us to pick out whatever we wanted, and I picked out a beautiful gold bracelet that I still have today." He also recalled two top juvenile actors of the period, Lance Kerwin and Kristy McNichol, guested on the show.

He did not speculate on why the show did not last long, but did mention his post–*Sara* acting career, which included playing Beatrice Arthur's grandson Philip on the last season of *Maude* (1977-78). "The cast and writers were all great people. Bill Macy [as Maude's husband, Walter] would make faces during filming to try and crack me up. I worked one show with Dana Plato, and remember Conrad Bain asking for advice from the cast on a show he was considering with a funny little black kid — Gary Coleman." Plato, Bain and Coleman went on to do *Diff'rent Strokes* from 1978 to 1986.

Then came high school. "I lettered in varsity golf at Granada Hills High School, and I snapped the football to John Elway [future quarterback for the Denver Broncos] during summer practice for the football team. Some things came up here and there, but I really lost interest in acting at that time and decided to commit to high school and my neighborhood friends."

When he e-mailed me, Metzinger was based in Houston and had spent 17 years working for Continental Airlines. "I have traveled all over the world, and I mean all over, for work and pleasure, and still get back to L.A. frequently to see family and friends. It amazes me that people still ask me about things that happened nearly 30 years ago, and by the way, I just got another residual check from *Maude* the other day. Pays for dinner, anyway."

Bert D'Angelo/Superstar

Crime Drama. Ran on ABC Saturdays 10–11 P.M. Feb. 21–July 10, 1976, opposite *The Carol Burnett Show* (through May 29) and *Dinah and Her New*

Best Friends (from June 5) on CBS and movies on NBC. C: Paul Sorvino (as Sgt. Bert D'Angelo), Robert Pine (as Inspector Larry Johnson), Dennis Patrick (as Capt. Jack Breen). EP: Quinn Martin. P: Mort Fine. D: David Friedkin, Bill Bixby, William Wiard.

Good Heavens

Sitcom. Ran on ABC Mondays 8:30–9 P.M. March 8–April 5, 1976, opposite *Phyllis* on CBS and *The Rich Little Show* on NBC, then ABC Saturdays 8–8:30 P.M. May–June 26, 1976, opposite *Doc* on CBS and *Emergency!* on NBC. C/EP: Carl Reiner (as Mr. Angel). P: Mel Swope, Austin and Irma Kalish. D: Carl Reiner, Mel Swope, Peter Bonerz.

Viva Valdez

Sitcom. Ran on ABC Mondays 8–8:30 P.M. May 31–Sept. 6, 1976, opposite *Rhoda* on CBS and *The John Davidson Show* (through June 14) and *Comedy Theatre* (from July 26) on NBC. C: Rodolfo Hoyos (as Luis Valdez), Carmen Zapata (as Sophia Valdez), James Victor (as Victor Valdez), Nelson D. Cuevas (as Ernesto Valdez), Lisa Mordente (as Connie Valdez; May 31–June), Teresa Hoyos (as Connie Valdez; July–Sept. 6), Claudio Martinez (as Pepe Valdez), Jorge Cervera, Jr. (as Jerry Ramirez). EP: Bernard Rothman, Stan Jacobson, Jack Wohl. D: Alan Rafkin.

TV's first sitcom — or drama, for that matter — to be set amid a Latin family was *Viva Valdez*. The Valdezes lived in East Los Angeles, with Rodolfo Hoyos as the head of the family.

"It was the first series that portrayed a Mexican family fairly," said actress Carmen Zapata. "He was a plumber, I was his wife, and we had a daughter and two sons. We [actors] were thrilled because it was the first for our community. They weren't using us except as maids." James Victor played the oldest son, Claudio Martinez the youngest one, and Lisa Mordente (replaced by Teresa Hoyos) the daughter in the middle. Also joining in the clan were cousin Jerry Ramirez from Mexico, played by Jorge Rivera, Jr.

But unfortunately for them, the Latin influence on the show did not stretch very far. Asked how many Latino writers the program had, Zapata said, "Not a one. The cast were the only ones who were Hispanic."

Zapata believed the cultural gap between the scripters and the actors helped sink the show. "I thought it would be a hit," she said.

What would a sitcom be without a happy ending? On the July 5, 1976, episode of *Viva Valdez*, Victor (James Victor) kissed Mama Sophia (Carmen Zapata) after being made a partner in dad Luis' plumbing business. Observing contentedly from left are Nelson D. Cuevas as Ernesto, Claudio Martinez as Pepe, Teresa Hoyos as Connie and Rodolfo Hoyos as Luis.

"But we had writers coming out of the Catskills of New York. I definitely think there were missed opportunities and the writing was not what was needed."

There also may have been some under-counting of Latin households by the ratings services at the time that did not account for all the viewers of *Viva Valdez*, in Zapata's view. As it stood, however, she said. "They pulled it after 13 weeks, saying we weren't having the ratings."

Interestingly, Zapata also starred at the same time on *Villa Allegra*, a public television series for children where she played the mayor of the town. "I thought that show was wonderful for children," said Zapata, noting how it used both English and Spanish and allowed them to see Spanish-speaking people in non-stereotyped roles. Unfortunately, that 1970s show was the exception to the rule of much of what was— and is— on American national television.

In fact, 25 years after *Viva Valdez*, network TV still had no regular drama or comedy centering around Hispanics, even though the 2000 Census showed they were the largest growing minority in the country. Zapata, who has operated a theater for Hispanic actors in Los Angeles for nearly three decades, remains doubtful that many will appear anytime soon. "Certainly not in my lifetime, I don't think so," she said. "We have a long way to go. We haven't developed writers who know the community and understand the community."

The Fun Factory

Game. Ran on NBC Mondays through Fridays Noon–12:30 P.M. June 14–Oct. 1, 1976, opposite *Let's Make a Deal* (through July 9) and *Hot Seat* (from July 12) on ABC and *The Young and the Restless* on CBS. C: EP: Ed Fishman, Randall Freer. P: David Fishman, Mort Green. D: Walter C. Miller, Tom Trbovich.

The Jacksons

Musical Variety. Ran on CBS Wednesdays 8–8:30 P.M. June 16–July 7, 1976, opposite *The Bionic Woman* on ABC and *Little House on the Prairie* on NBC, then CBS Wednesdays 8:30–9 P.M. Jan. 26–March 9, 1977, opposite *The Bionic Woman* on ABC and *The Life and Times of Grizzly Adams* on NBC. C: The Jacksons (Michael, Jackie, Tito, Marlon, Randy), LaToya Jackson, Maureen "Rebie" Jackson, Janet Jackson, Jim Samuels (1976), Marty Cohen (1976), Emmett Ashford (1977), Tom Biener (1977), Johnny Dark (1977), Biff Manard (1977). EP: Joe Jackson, Richard Arons. P: Bill Davis, Arnie Hogen, Bonnie Burns, Ray Jessell. D: Bill Davis. W: Biff Manard, James Tisdale, David Smilow, Wayne Kline.

Hot Seat

Game. Ran on ABC Mondays through Fridays Noon–12:30 P.M. July 12–Oct. 22, 1976, opposite *The Young and the Restless* on CBS and *The Fun Factory* (through Oct. 1) and *50 Grand Slam* (from Oct. 4) on NBC. C: Jim Peck. EP: Merrill Heatter, Bob Quigley, Robert Noah. P: Bob Synes. D: Jerome Shaw.

1976-77

Delvecchio

Police Drama. Ran on CBS Thursday 9–10 P.M. Sept. 9, 1976, opposite *The Streets of San Francisco* on ABC and movies on NBC, then CBS Sundays 10–11 P.M. Sept. 26, 1976–July 17, 1977, opposite movies on ABC and NBC. C: Judd Hirsch (as Sgt. Dominick Delvecchio), Charles Haid (as Sgt. Paul Shonski), Michael Conrad (as Lt. Macavan), Mario Gallo (as Tomaso Delvecchio), Jay Varela (as Sgt. Rivera), George Wyner (as Asst. D.A. Dorfman). EP: William Sackheim. P: Michael Rhodes. D: Lou Antonio, Walter Doniger, Ivan Nagy.

McDuff, the Talking Dog

Sitcom. Ran on NBC Saturdays 10–10:30 A.M. Sept. 11–Nov. 20, 1976, opposite *The Scooby-Doo/Dynomutt Hour* on ABC and *The Shazam/Isis Hour* (through Oct. 30) and *Tarzan, Lord of the Jungle* (from Nov. 6) on CBS. C: Jack Lester (as voice of McDuff), Walter Willson (as Dr. Calvin Campbell), Gordon Jump (as Amos Ferguson), Monty Margetts (as Mrs. Osgood), Johnnie Collins III (as Squeaky), Michelle Stacy (as Kimmy Campbell). EP: William P. D'Angelo, Ray Allen, Harvey Bullock. P: Victor Paul. D: Gordon Wiles, James Sheldon, William P. D'Angelo.

Monster Squad

Sitcom. Ran on NBC Saturdays 10:30–11 A.M. Sept. 11, 1976–Sept. 3, 1977, opposite *The Krofft Supershow* on ABC and *The Shazam/Isis Hour* on CBS. C: Fred Grandy (as Walter), Michael Lane (as Frankenstein monster), Henry Polic II (as Dracula), Buck Kartalian (as Bruce Wolfman). EP: Bill D'Angelo, Harvey Bullock, Ray Allen. P: Michael McLean. D: Herman Hoffman, James Sheldon.

Veteran character actor Buck Kartalian found himself in a dream situation when he met with longtime TV producer Bill D'Angelo about the latter's new TV series in 1976. "I had worked for him [as a guest] on *No Time for Sergeants* and *The Gallant Men*, about three or four things," Kartalian said. "I went into his office with Fred Grandy and the others. He told each of us which parts he wanted us for, and we asked him, 'Do we read for you?' He looked at me, and said, 'Buck, you guys got it if you want it.'" And so the cast of *Monster Squad* was born on the spot.

The series starred Grandy as caretaker of a wax museum who accidentally brings to life with his computer three horrific creatures. The three decide to fight crime under Grandy rather than attack him or other people, each week facing a villain as bizarre as they are. Kartalian considered the show "quite clever" but admitted as far as being a Saturday morning sitcom, "In some ways, it was a little sophisticated for the little ones. Like in one episode, we used a Ronald Ray-Gun."

There were 13 episodes shot. The series was low budget, and Kartalian did his part by

Not to be confused with *The Mod Squad*: Frankenstein (Michael Lane), Bruce Werewolf (Bruce Kartalian) and Dracula (Henry Polic II) get ready to fight crime on *The Monster Squad*.

having his own beard to lessen the number of appliances needed to make him as a werewolf. While it took him more than three hours to be made up as the simian Julius, keeper of the cages, in the 1968 movie *Planet of the Apes*, *Monster Squad* took "20 minutes, half an hour at the most."

Kartalian blamed the one season run of *Monster Squad* on a lack of publicity by the network and D'Angelo. "We never really got a lot of PR on it," he noted. He said the cast urged D'Angelo to let them ride in character in the Hollywood Christmas parade, but the producer turned them down. The result was that all went on to other projects in 1977, with Grandy getting the best offer to become Gopher on *The Love Boat* for nine years, followed by a term as a Republican congressman from Iowa in the U.S. House of Representatives. The latter job did not surprise Kartalian. "He was always talking about politics between takes," he said.

As for Kartalian, he remained active as an occasional actor into the 21st century. Some fans still ask him about *Monster Squad* and if it will ever return in reruns. He's asked D'Angelo about doing so, and the latter has shrugged him off by saying, "I've got everything locked up in a vault."

Obviously the producer does not share the same warm sentiments of Kartalian for the show. "It was fun doing the show," Kartalian said. "I really enjoyed it."

Big John, Little John

Sitcom. Ran on NBC Saturdays 11:30 A.M.–Noon Sept. 11, 1976–Sept. 3, 1977, opposite *The Krofft Supershow* (through Nov. 27) and *Super Friends* (from Dec. 4) on ABC and *Clue Club* (through Oct. 30) and *The Shazam/Isis Hour* (from Nov. 6) on CBS. C: Herb Edelman (as "Big" John Martin), Robbie Rist (as "Little" John Martin), Joyce Bulifant (as Marjorie Martin), Mike Darnell (as Ricky Martin), Olive Dunbar (as Miss Bertha Bottomly). EP: Sherwood Schwartz. P: Lloyd Schwartz. D: Gordon Wiles, Wes Kenney, Ross Bowan.

The Kids from C.A.P.E.R.

Sitcom. Ran on NBC Saturdays Noon–12:30 P.M. Sept. 11–Nov. 20, 1976, opposite *Junior Almost Anything Goes* on ABC and *Fat Albert and the Cosby Kids* on CBS, then NBC Saturdays 12:30–1

P.M. April 16–Sept. 3, 1977, opposite *American Bandstand* on ABC and *Ark II* on CBS. C: Steve Bonimo (as P.T.), Cosie Costa (as Bugs), John Lansing (as Doc), Biff Warren (as Doomsday), Robert Emhardt (as Chief Vinton), Robert Lussier (as Klintsinger). EP: Alan Landsburg, Don Kirshner. P/D/W: Stanley Z. Cherry.

The Kids from C.A.P.E.R. was one sitcom which had many wacky antics in front of and behind the cameras, according to its creator Stanley Z. Cherry. "There's an example of a show that was bought to be an animated cartoon," he said. But the costs of cartoons in 1976 were rising and NBC favored live action shows for its Saturday morning lineup, so the kids went from being drawn to being cast. But child labor laws crimped the number of hours youngsters could work on this tightly scheduled show, so now the "kids" became teenagers— or rather, actors playing teenagers. "One of them was 42 years old," laughed Cherry, referring to actor Cosie Costa.

On the show P.T., Bugs, Doc and Doomsday were part of C.A.P.E.R. (Civilian Authority for the Protection of Everyone, Regardless), which reported to Chief Vinton in the town of Northeast Southwestern. They sang, did goofy gags and were trailed by the reporter Klintsinger, who hoped to get a scoop on their latest cases. Any resemblance to reality was purely coincidental.

"We were doing the Three Stooges," Cherry said. "We'd make it up as we sent along, threw the script out the window." He said the production schedule dictated the knockabout atmosphere. "We made two of those shows a week. We made next to nothing, yet we worked two months and got rich because there was no time to spend it."

A few future stars guested too, such as Rita Wilson, later to be Mrs. Tom Hanks. "Deborah Winger appeared on the show when she had just arrived from Arizona," Cherry said.

The series did not click with children, who favored the cartoon *Fat Albert and the Cosby Kids*. NBC canned the show after 11 weeks, then ran repeats in 1977. Cherry blamed it on the rushed circumstances to create the shows. "It was an ensemble show that wasn't an ensemble on screen," he said.

Yet even after its failure, Cherry liked the program enough that he dreamt up a reunion show. "I tried to get everybody back," he said.

"I had an idea about these four whose careers never went anywhere, so they got back together." But a hitch stalled his vision. "We couldn't get the rights," he said. "A company then owned the film and wasn't interested in being involved in it."

What really happened to the show's cast seems more improbable than anything Cherry could've scripted. Costa and Steve Bonimo continued low-key acting careers, John Lansing became a producer of the Chuck Norris police drama *Walker, Texas Ranger* (1993–2001), and Biff Warren died of AIDS in 1993 at the age of 38. Robert Emhardt, a character actor whose TV appearances from the 1940s through 1980s probably outnumbered the rest of the cast combined, died in 1994, while Robert Lussier left acting to become a priest.

As for Cherry, he left the grind of directing and producing TV shows for writing shortly after doing *The Kids from C.A.P.E.R.* "That was the most fun I had working in television, because I didn't care anymore," he said.

Muggsy

Children's Drama. Ran on NBC Saturdays 12:30–1 P.M. Sept. 11, 1976–April 2, 1977, opposite *American Bandstand* on ABC and *Way Out Games* (through Feb. 5) and *Ark II* (from Feb. 12) on CBS. C: Sarah McDonnell (as Margaret "Muggsy" Malloy), Ben Masters (as Nick Malloy), Star-Shemah (as Clytemnestra), Danny Cooper (as T.P.), Jimmy McCann (as Li'l Man), Paul Michael (as Gus Gardician). EP: George Heinemann. P: Joseph F. Gallo. D: Sidney Smith, Bert Saltzman, J. Philip Miller.

"It was one of the first children's series shot on location," recalled director Sidney Smith of *Muggsy*. The series, videotaped in Bridgeport, Connecticut, was the brainchild of ex– NBC children's programming head George Heinemann, who Smith said "pushed it on NBC."

Heinemann may have secured a slot on NBC for the show, but Smith admitted the producer gave him only the barest bones of a budget. Most of the cast were unknown, pay was low, and shooting schedules were tight, with much work done outside on the streets. "We would rehearse in a hotel," Smith said.

Still, Smith said the production crew nonetheless radiated with optimism. "It had a great staff of young writers, production designers and so on," he said. It also had a predominantly young cast, including Sarah McDonnell, who played the title character. Child labor laws limited how much time she could be in front of the cameras.

"I think they kind of carried a tutor on the scene," Smith said. "You'd work with her from 8 to 10 in the morning, then she'd go to school, and after lunch you'd shoot with her. If you had night scenes, you could start later in the day."

McDonnell's character Muggsy, the 13-year-old, lived a tough life. With her parents being deceased, she had to live with her half-brother Nick Malloy the cabbie as her guardian. The two of them made a truck behind Gus Gardician's garage. She hung around with her pals Clytemnestra, T.P. and Li'l Man while coping with the social issues of the day. In effect, the show attempted to offer preadolescents and teenagers basic lessons in life in an entertaining, if somewhat somber, format.

"We had a lot of fun," Smith said about the crew involved on the show, given the show's limitations in time and budget. But the drama could not dislodge the longtime leader in the time period, *American Bandstand*, and so NBC dropped it after seven months. Actually, the 1976-77 season was tough for any series on NBC Saturdays before 1 P.M., with all series except *The Pink Panther* being cancelled (and even that show found itself cut from 90 to 30 minutes in length).

Most of the cast disappeared from view once *Muggsy* left the airwaves, save for Ben Masters, who played Nick. The actor appeared in several miniseries and TV-movies in the 1980s and 1990s before getting a regular role on the daytime soap opera *Passions* from 1999 up through this writing.

Way Out Games

Children's Game. Ran on CBS Saturdays 12:30–1 P.M. Sept. 11, 1976–Feb. 5, 1977, opposite *American Bandstand* on ABC and *Muggsy* on NBC, then CBS Saturdays 1–1:30 P.M. Feb. 12–April 2, 1977, opposite *American Bandstand* on ABC, then CBS Sundays 9–9:30 A.M. April 10–Sept. 4, 1977. C: Sonny Fox. EP: Jack Barry, Dan Enright. D: Richard S. Kline.

Snip

Sitcom. Was to run on NBC Thursday evenings for half an hour starting Sept. 30, 1976, but was

A rare shot from the set of *Snip*, with star David Brenner on the phone while Lesley Ann Warren listens. The outfits, the set design, and the hair all obviously scream 1976.

canceled before any episode aired. C: David Brenner (as David); Lesley Ann Warren (as Beverly); Hope Summers (as Aunt Polly); Kim Soloman (as David and Lesley's daughter); Walter Wanderman (as Michael); Bebe Drake-Hooks (as Daffney). EP/Creator: James Komack. P/W: Stan Coner.

"It was touted as the comedy hit of the new season," David Brenner recalled of *Snip*. Indeed, the show seemed like it couldn't miss. Brenner was a favorite 1970s talk show guest and talked up the series frequently in the summer of 1976, including appearances on *The Hol-*

lywood Squares. His co-star was the beautiful Lesley Ann Warren. Its creator, James Komack, made hit shows for comedians such as *Chico and the Man* for Freddie Prinze and *Welcome Back, Kotter* for Gabe Kaplan. How and why was this show slotted on NBC's lineup, then pulled so late that *TV Guide* did not have time to remove a feature on the show in its Fall Preview issue of Sept. 18–24, 1976?

Let's start at the beginning. Brenner working with Komack was payback for what Brenner provided the producer a few years earlier. "I had gotten Freddie Prinze booked on *The Tonight Show,* and he grabbed Freddie for *Chico and the Man,*" Brenner said. "Then Freddie hosted *The Mike Douglas Show,* and I was a guest, and he grabbed me."

Komack gave Brenner the role of a divorced hairdresser. "It was a takeoff of the movie *Shampoo,*" Brenner said. His ex-wife (Lesley Ann Warren), daughter and aunt found themselves living with him at their home in Cape Cod, Massachusetts, while the former husband and wife also worked in the same beauty salon with Michael, a gay man, and Daffney, a black woman. "I'm on the pretext of being there to help her out [at the salon], but really to get her back," Brenner said.

The programs were shot live before a studio audience with one unusual provision. "We weren't allowed to use a laugh track. It was in my contract," he said. He disliked the phony "sweetening" done with laugh tracks, and beside, he said, they didn't need it because "It was brilliantly funny."

So what went wrong? Brenner said it was homophobia. "Before we were to debut, NBC got cold feet because we had a gay character on the show," Brenner said. Gay groups who screened the show did not complain about Michael, but NBC felt uneasy nevertheless because, Brenner said sarcastically, "In 1976, there were no gay people in America."

This was the closest to a last-minute decision ever made about a network TV series, as it already was in full production when the announcement to drop it occurred. "We had filmed seven, five of them were edited clean, ready to be aired, and we were working on the eighth when word came down," he said. "Everybody was crushed."

The only place the series aired was in Australia, where Komack gave them the five completed shows which aired during one work week. "It was the highest rated show in Australian history," Brenner said. They asked for more, but Komack told them they had no more finished.

Yet strangely *Snip* benefited Brenner, thanks to the publicity he had done on TV during the summer pushing the show making him an in-demand name. "When I was on the road after that show was cancelled, my career exploded," he said. "That's when I became a star." And NBC, seeing that the man who they had under contract as a guest host for *The Tonight Show* when Johnny Carson was on vacation was a top draw in personal appearances, booked him even more to do the show. "When *Snip* was snipped — they only care about money — I was such a draw in Johnny's place, they kept putting me on it," he said.

Twenty-five years after *Snip* snapped, Brenner remained a popular guest and touring stage comedian and is glad he pursued these outlets in entertainment. "*Snip* really soured me on sitcoms," he said, not to mention make him sensitive to prejudices which are still around among network executives concerning minorities (one told him not too long ago that he was "too Jewish" for one project they considered). While admitting that "I would jump out of my seat to get a talk show," he said that "I really prefer live performing." For anyone who cares to see a clip of *Snip,* Brenner said Komack donated the five episodes to the Museum of Television and Radio in Beverly Hills, Calif.

Spencer's Pilots

Adventure. Ran on CBS Fridays 8–9 P.M. Sept. 17–Nov. 19, 1976, opposite *Donny and Marie* on ABC and *Sanford and Son* and *Chico and the Man* on NBC. C: Christopher Stone (as Cass Garrett), Todd Sussman (as Stan Lewis), Gene Evans (as Spencer Parish), Margaret Impert (as Linda Dann), Britt Leach (as Mickey "Wig" Wiggins). EP: Bob Sweeney, Edward H. Feldman. P: Larry Rosen. D: Bill Bixby, Don Weis, Ernest Pintoff.

Cos

Children's Variety. Ran on ABC Sundays 7–8 P.M. Sept. 19–Nov. 7, 1976, opposite *60 Minutes* on CBS and *The Wonderful World of Disney* on NBC. C: Bill Cosby, Jeff Altman, Tim Thomerson, Marion

Ramsey, Buzzy Linhart, Willie Bobo, Mauricio Jarrin. P: Chris Bearde, Alan Thicke. D: Jeff Margolis. W: Larry Markes, Tony Geiss, Tom Meehan, June Reisner.

The Captain and Tennille

Comedy Variety. Ran on ABC Mondays 8–9 P.M. Sept. 20, 1976–March 14, 1977, opposite *Rhoda* (through Jan. 10) and *Phyllis* (through Jan. 10) and *The Jeffersons* (from Jan. 17) and *Busting Loose* (from Jan. 17) on CBS and *Little House on the Prairie* on NBC. C: Daryl Dragon ("the Captain"), Toni Tennille. EP: Alan Bernard, Dick Clark, Mace Neufeld. P/D: Bob Henry. D: Tony Charmoli. W: Thad Mumford, Ray Jessel, John Boni, Lennie Ripps, Stephen Spears, Norman Stiles.

All's Fair

Sitcom. Ran on CBS Mondays 9:30–10 P.M. Sept. 20, 1976–Aug. 15, 1977, opposite football (through January), *Most Wanted* (from March to April 25) and baseball (from May) on ABC and movies on NBC. C: Richard Crenna (as Richard C. Barrington III), Bernadette Peters (as Charlotte "Charley" Drake), Lee Chamberlain (as Lucy Daniels), J.A. Preston (as Allen Brooks), Judy Kahan (as Ginger Livingston), Jack Dodson (as Sen. Wayne Joplin), Michael Keaton (as Lanny Wolf; 1977). EP: Rod Parker. P: Bob Weiskopf, Bob Schiller, Michael Elias. D: Hal Cooper, Bob Claver.

Executive Suite

Soap Opera. Ran on CBS Mondays 10–11 P.M. Sept. 20, 1976–January 1977, opposite football on ABC and *Van Dyke and Company* (Sept. 20 only) and movies on NBC, then CBS Fridays 10–11 P.M. January–Feb. 11, 1977, opposite movies on ABC and *Serpico* (through Jan. 28) and on NBC. C: Mitchell Ryan (as Don Walling), Stephen Elliott (as Howell Rutledge), Sharon Acker (as Helen Walling), Leigh McCloskey (as Brian Walling), Richard Cox (as Mark Desmond), Gwyda DonHowe (as Astrid Rutledge), Wendy Phillips (as Stacey Walling), Trisha Noble (as Yvonne Holland), Madlyn Rhue (as Hilary Madison), Paul Lamber (as Tom Dalessio), Carl Weintraub (as Harry Ragin), Brenda Sykes (as Summer Johnson), Percy Rodrigues (as Malcolm Gibson), William Smithers (as Anderson Galt), Byron Morrow (as Pearce Newberry). EP: Norman Felton, Stanley Rubin, Rita Lakin. P: Don Brinkley, Buck Houghton. D: Joseph Hardy, Vincent Sherman, John Newland.

Van Dyke and Company

Comedy Variety. Ran on NBC Monday 10–11 P.M. Sept. 20, 1976, opposite football on ABC and *Executive Suite* on CBS, then NBC Thursdays 10–11 P.M. Oct. 7–Oct. 28, 1976, opposite *The Streets of San Francisco* on ABC and *Barnaby Jones* on CBS, and then NBC Thursdays 8–9 P.M. Nov. 4–Dec. 30, 1976, opposite *Welcome Back Kotter* and *Barney Miller* (through Dec. 23) and *What's Happening!!* (Dec. 30 only) on ABC and *The Waltons* on CBS. C: Dick Van Dyke, Andy Kaufman, Marilyn Sokol, Pat Proft, Bob Einstein, Richard Kiel, Chuck McCann, the L.A. Mime Company. EP: Byron Paul. P: Allan Blye, Bob Einstein. D: John Moffitt. W: Bob Einstein, George Burditt.

Ball Four

Sitcom. Ran on CBS Wednesdays 8:30–9 P.M. Sept. 22–Oct. 27, 1976, opposite *The Bionic Woman* on ABC and *The NBC Mystery Movie* on NBC. C: Jim Bouton (as Jim Barton), Jack Somack (as "Cap" Capogrosso), David-James Carroll (as Bill Westlake), Ben Davidson (as Benjamin "Rhino" Rhinelander), Bill McCutcheon (as Coach Harold "Pinky" Pinkney), Lenny Schultz (as Lenny "Birdman" Siegel), Marco St. John (as Rayford Plunkett), Jaime Tirelli (as Orlando Walter Lopez), Sam Wright (as C.B. Travis). P: Don Segall. D: Jay Sandrich, Nick Havinga, Peter Lewis.

The Quest

Western. Ran on NBC Wednesdays 10–11 P.M. Sept. 22–Dec. 29, 1976, opposite *Charlie's Angels* on ABC and *The Blue Knight* (through Oct. 27) and movies (from Nov. 3) on CBS. C: Kurt Russell (as Morgan Beaudine), Tim Matheson (as Quentin Beaudine). EP: David Gerber. P: Mark Rogers, James H. Brown. D: Micheal O'Herlihy, Earl Bellamy, Corey Allen.

Gemini Man

Science Fiction/Adventure. Ran on NBC Thursdays 8–9 P.M. Sept. 23–Oct. 28, 1976, opposite *Welcome Back, Kotter* and *Barney Miller* on ABC and *The Waltons* on CBS. C: Ben Murphy (as Sam Casey), Katherine Crawford (as Abby Lawrence), William Sylvester (as Leonard Driscoll). EP: Harve Bennett. P: Leslie Stevens, Robert F. O'Neill, Frank Telford. D: Alan J. Levi. W: Frank Telford, Steven de Souza.

Serpico

Police Drama. Ran on NBC Fridays 10–11 P.M. Sept. 24, 1976–Jan. 28, 1977, opposite movies on

ABC and CBS. C: David Birney (as Officer Frank Serpico), Tom Atkins (as Lt. Tom Sullivan). EP: Emmet G. Larvey, Jr. P: Dan Ingalls, Barry Oringer. D: Reza S. Badiyi, Paul Stanley, Michael Caffey.

Holmes and Yoyo

Sitcom. Ran on ABC Saturdays 8–8:30 P.M. Sept. 25–Dec. 11, 1976, opposite *The Jeffersons* (through October) and *The Mary Tyler Moore Show* (from October) on CBS and *Emergency* on NBC. C: Richard B. Shull (as Det. Alexander Holmes), John Schuck (as Gregory "Yoyo" Yoyonovich), Bruce Kirby (as Capt. Harry Sedford), Andrea Howard (as Officer Maxine Moon). EP: Leonard B. Stern. P: Arne Sultan. D: Leonard B. Stern, Reza S. Badiyi, Noam Pitlik.

Producer Leonard Stern took supporting actors John Schuck from his long-running hit *McMillan and Wife*, where he played the none-too-bright Sgt. Charles Enright from 1971 to 1976, and Richard B. Shull from his disastrous 1973-74 sitcom *Diana* (q.v.), and starred them in *Holmes and Yoyo*, a series emphasizing them as a physical comedy team.

"I liked them as performers, and John Schuck and I spent all those years together on *McMillan and Wife*, and he became a personal friend," said Stern. "I thought Shull was a great 'reactor' like [Jackie] Gleason."

Stern did not create the series (Jack Sher and Lee Hewitt did so), but he did endorse the concept when it was pitched to him simply because "I always love physical comedy." The show's setup allowed him to indulge in that fondness freely. Schuck played a robot created to team up with Det. Holmes, a cop who had trouble holding onto his partners since he was clumsy and often wound up hurting them unintentionally. The android, named after its creator, Dr. Yoyonovich, had a variety of features which gave him advantages over regular humans, such as the ability to take pictures, develop them and print them out of his shirt pocket. Unfortunately, he also tended to have disasters with his circuitry while working cases with Holmes, like having to run backwards to corral a suspect. Holmes found out about his partner's true identity inadvertently, but kept it hidden from the rest of the force, leading to additional humor as Officer Maxine Moon made unsuccessful, misunderstood passes to "Yoyo."

To test how well Schuck acted as a robot, a little experiment occurred unbeknownst to Jackie Cooper, who was to direct the show's pilot. "John Schuck behaved in an odd way throughout the whole meeting and then 'malfunctioned,'" laughed Stern. It took Cooper by surprise, but it convinced the director and others the viability of the concept.

Still, Stern believed the show erred in one overall plot element which prevented it from being as funny as it could have been. "The great debate was, would it have been better if the Richard B. Shull character did not know the John Schuck character was a robot? I now say in retrospect, maybe it would've been better if he didn't know," said Stern.

The antics of *Holmes and Yoyo* lasted less than three months. ABC replaced it with *Wonder Woman*, which ran two months in the Saturday 8–9 P.M. slot before yielding to the short-lived *Blansky's Beauties* (q.v.), then replacing that show in the summer of 1977 before *Wonder Woman* moved over to CBS for an additional two-year run. Before the end of that series, Schuck had another short-lived sitcom role even more outrageous than being a robot. He played a woman trapped inside a man's body on *Turnabout*, which aired on NBC from Jan. 26 to March 23, 1979.

Mr. T and Tina

Sitcom. Ran on ABC Saturdays 8:30–9 P.M. Sept. 25–Oct. 30, 1976, opposite *Doc* on CBS and *Emergency!* on NBC. C: Pat Morita (as Taro Takahashi), Susan Blanchard (as Tina Kelly), Pat Suzuki (as Michi), Ted Lange (as Harvard), Miriam Byrd-Nethery (as Miss Llewellyn), "Jerry" Hatsuo Fujikawa (as Uncle Matsu), June Angela (as Sachi), Gene Profanato (as Aki). EP: James Komack. P: Madelyn Davis, Bob Carroll, Jr. D: James Komack, James Sheldon, Rick Edelstein.

The Nancy Walker Show

Sitcom. Ran on ABC Thursdays 9:30–10 P.M. Sept. 30–Dec. 23, 1976, opposite *Hawaii Five-O* on CBS and *NBC's Best Sellers* on NBC. C: Nancy Walker (as Nancy Kitteridge), William Daniels (as Lt. Cdr. Kenneth Kitteridge), Ken Olfson (as Terry Folson), Beverly Archer (as Lorraine), James Cromwell (as Glen), Sparky Marcus (as Michael Futterman), William Schallert (as Teddy Futterman). EP: Norman Lear. P: Rod Parker. D: Alan Rafkin, Hal Cooper.

Stumpers

Game. Ran on NBC Mondays through Fridays 11:30 A.M.–Noon Oct. 4–Dec. 31, 1976, opposite *Happy Days* reruns on ABC and *Love of Life* and news on CBS. C: Allen Ludden. EP: Lin Bolen. P: Walt Case. D: Marty Pasetta, Jeff Goldstein.

50 Grand Slam

Game. Ran on NBC Mondays through Fridays Noon–12:30 P.M. Oct. 4–Dec. 31, 1976, opposite *The Don Ho Show* on ABC and *The Young and the Restless* on CBS. C: Tom Kennedy. EP: Ralph Andrews. P: George Vosburgh. D: Dick McDonough.

Most Wanted

Crime Drama. Ran on ABC Saturdays 10–11 P.M. Oct. 16, 1976–February 1977, opposite *The Carol Burnett Show* on CBS and movies on NBC, then ABC Mondays 9–10 P.M. March–April 25, 1977, opposite *Maude* and *All's Fair* on CBS and movies on NBC. C: Robert Stack (as Capt. Linc Evers), Shelly Novack (as Sgt. Charlie Benson), Jo Ann Harris (as Officer Kate Manners), Hari Rhodes (as Mayor Don Stoddard). EP: Quinn Martin, John Wilder, Paul King. P: Harold Gast. D: Virgil W. Vogel, William Wiard, Walter Grauman.

The Don Ho Show

Variety. Ran on ABC Mondays through Fridays Noon–12:30 P.M. Oct. 25, 1976–March 4, 1977, opposite *The Young and the Restless* on CBS and *50 Grand Slam* (through Dec. 31) and *Name That Tune* (from Jan. 3). C: Don Ho. EP: Bob Banner. P: Brad Lachman. D: Jack Regas, Jeff Margolis.

Gibbsville

Drama. Ran on NBC Thursdays 10–11 P.M. Nov. 11–Dec. 30, 1976, opposite *The Streets of San Francisco* on ABC and *Barnaby Jones* on CBS. C: John Savage (as Jim Malloy), Gig Young (as Ray Whitehead), Biff McGuire (as Dr. Michael Malloy), Peggy McCay (as Mrs. Malloy), Bert Remsen (as Pell). EP: David Gerber. P: John Furia, Jr. D: Alexander Singer, Alf Kjellin, Marc Daniels.

The McLean Stevenson Show

Sitcom. Ran on NBC Wednesdays 8:30–9 P.M. Dec. 1, 1976–January 1977, opposite *The Bionic Woman* on ABC and *The Jeffersons* on CBS, then NBC Wednesdays 9:30–10 P.M. February 1977–March 3, 1977, opposite *Baretta* on ABC and movies on CBS. C: McLean Stevenson (as Mac Ferguson), Barbara Stuart (as Peggy Ferguson), Madge West (as Grandma Muriel), Ayn Ruymen (as Janet), Steve Nevil (as Chris), David Hollander (as David), Jason Whitney (as Jason). EP: Monty Hall. P: Arnold Margolin, Don Van Atta. D: Alan Myerson, Bill Hobin.

Sirota's Court

Sitcom. Ran on NBC Wednesdays 9–9:30 P.M. Dec. 1, 1976–January 1977, opposite *Baretta* on ABC and movies on CBS, then NBC Wednesdays 9:30–10 P.M. April–April 13, 1977, opposite *Baretta* on ABC and movies on CBS. C: Michael Constantine (as Matthew J. Sirota), Cynthia Harris (as Maureen O'Connor), Kathleen Miller (as Gail Goodman), Fred Willard (as Bud Nugent), Ted Ross (as Sawyer Dabney), Owen Bush (as Bailiff John Bellson). EP: Harvey Miller, Peter Engel. D: Mel Ferber.

Was the long-running NBC sitcom *Night Court* (1984–92) actually a ripoff of *Sirota's Court*, a sitcom that aired nearly a decade earlier? Well, consider the similar plotlines: Both had a judge viewed as an offbeat justice of the peace who favored negotiation between parties over jail time. Both judges had a more than platonic relationship with their court clerks. And in their courts were egotistical lawyers from the district attorney's office and bailiffs who thought highly of their judges. Hmmm...

Mel Ferber, the director for most of the episodes of *Sirota's Court*, said he can't make a judgment call one way or the other. "My viewing of *Night Court* is not enough," he said. " I really don't know."

What Ferber does know is that he got the job as the series' director thanks to his work on *The Odd Couple*. Harvey Miller, a co-executive producer of *Sirota's Court*, held the same title on *The Odd Couple* and remembered Ferber's direction of a few shows there, so he offered the job to Ferber.

The cast included Michael Constantine as the title judge character, Cynthia Harris as the clerk court, Kathleen Miller as the public defender, Fred Willard as the D.A. and Ted Ross as a lawyer. "The atmosphere was good," Ferber said of the show's cast and crew. He remembered especially Harris ("She was really very talented") and Willard ("He's funny"), and remarked that the scripts did not talk down to its audience, making it a rather intelligent sitcom, in his view.

"It was a difficult kind of show," Ferber said. "Maybe that's why it didn't catch on. I thought it was funny."

The Feather and Father Gang

Adventure and Crime Drama. Ran from Dec. 6, 1976–July 30, 1977. Ran on ABC Mondays 10–11 P.M. March 7–April 1977, opposite *The Andros Targets* on CBS and movies on NBC, then ABC Saturdays 10–11 P.M. May–Aug. 6, 1977, opposite *Switch* on CBS and movies on NBC. C: Stefanie Powers (as Toni "Feather" Danton), Harold Gould (as Harry Danton), Frank Delfino (as Enzo), Joan Shawlee (as Margo), Monte Landis (as Michael), Lewis Charles (as Lou). EP: Larry White. P: Robert Mintz, Bill Driscoll, Buzz Kulick. D: Seymour Robbie, Buzz Kulick, Jerry London.

"It was a joy to do that show," said director Seymour Robbie. "I knew it wasn't going to go anyplace, but I loved doing it." Asked to explain how he knew it would fail, Robbie said, "I don't know. When you get so involved in a show, it's just something you sense. I didn't think it would be a popularity winner."

Double Dare

Game. Ran on CBS Mondays through Fridays 11–11:30 A.M. Dec. 13, 1976–April 29, 1977, opposite *Happy Days* reruns (from April 25 to 29) on ABC and *Wheel of Fortune* on NBC. C: Alex Trebek. EP: Jay Wolpert. P: Jonathan Goodson. D: Marc Breslow, Paul Alter.

Shoot for the Stars

Game. Ran on NBC Mondays through Fridays 11:30 A.M.–Noon Jan. 3–June 10, 1977, opposite *Happy Days* reruns (through April 22) and *Family Feud* (from April 25) on ABC and *Love of Life* and news on CBS, then NBC Mondays through Fridays Noon–12:30 P.M. June 13–Sept. 30, 1977, opposite *Second Chance* (through July 15) and *The Better Sex* (from July 18) on ABC and *The Young and the Restless* on CBS. C: Geoff Edwards. EP: Bob Stewart. P: Bruce Burmester. D: Mike Garguilo.

Busting Loose

Sitcom. Ran on CBS Mondays 8:30–9 P.M. Jan. 17–May 9, 1977, opposite *The Captain and Tennille* (through March 14) and baseball (from March 21) on ABC and *Little House on the Prairie*

on NBC, then CBS Wednesdays 8:30–9 P.M. July 27–Nov. 16, 1977, opposite *Donny and Marie* (through Aug. 3) and *Eight is Enough* (from Aug. 10) on ABC and *The Life and Times of Grizzly Adams* on NBC. C: Adam Arkin (as Lenny Markowitz), Barbara Rhoades (as Melody Feebeck), Jack Kruschen (as Sam Markowitz), Pat Carroll (as Pearl Markowitz), Danny Goldman (as Lester Bellman), Steve Nathan (as Allan Simmonds), Greg Antonacci (as Vinnie Mordabito), Paul Sylvan (as Woody Warshaw), Paul B. Price (as Ralph Cabell), Ralph Wilcox (as Raymond St. Williams), Louise Williams (as Jackie Gleason). EP: Lowell Ganz, Mark Rothman. P: Lawrence Kasha, John Thomas Lenox. D: James Burrows, Tony Mordente, John Thomas Lenox.

Code R

Adventure. Ran on CBS Fridays 8–9 P.M. Jan. 21–June 10, 1977, opposite *Donny and Marie* on ABC and *Sanford and Son* and *Chico and the Man* on NBC. C: James Houghton (as Rick Wilson), Martin Kove (as George Baker), Tom Simcox (as Walt Robinson), Susanne Reed (as Suzy), Ben Davidson (as Ted Milbank), Robbie Rundle (as Bobby Robinson), W.T. Zacha (as Harry). P: Edwin Self. D: Richard Benedict, Gruce Kessler, Andrew McLaglen.

Lanigan's Rabbi

Mystery Drama. Ran on NBC Sundays at different times (generally 8–9:30 P.M.) Jan. 30–July 3, 1977, opposite *The Six Million Dollar Man* and movies on ABC and *Kojak* on CBS. C: Art Carney (as Chief Paul Lanigan), Bruce Solomon (as Rabbi David Small), Janis Paige (as Kate Lanigan), Janet Margolin (as Miriam Small), Barbara Carney (as Bobbie Whitaker), Robert Doyle (as Lt. Osgood). EP: Leonard Stern.

Of all the idiotic comments Leonard Stern received from network executives, one stands out in particular to him. "On *Lanigan's Rabbi*, I got a memo saying, 'Could you make the rabbi less Jewish?' I just ignored it," he said. The sad thing is that Stern will admit network pressure about the show's religious angle did get to him and the show, and probably helped lead to its early end.

Crimesolving Rabbi David Small was the creation of author Harry Kemelman, who kicked off a series of successful novels involving the character starting with *Friday the Rabbi Slept Late*. Hollywood producers took note of the property, and according to Stern at one point Dustin Hoffman was set to play the character in a movie. But that plan fell apart, and Stern won the rights instead.

Stern created a TV-movie based on the first novel that starred Stuart Margolin as Rabbi Small and Art Carney as his Irish contact on the Cameron, California, police department. He was quite pleased with Margolin's job as the rabbi. "He played it with a certain mischief and madness, as well as conviction," Stern said. But when NBC decided the TV-movie, which aired on June 17, 1976, would become a series, Margolin could not do the job because of his regular supporting role as Angel the con man on *The Rockford Files*, so Bruce Solomon took his place.

All the others who would be regulars on the TV series were in the TV-movie, including the actresses who played the wives, and Art Carney's daughter Barbara, who played a snooping newswoman. Stern called the senior Carney "A delight. I worked with Art on *The Honeymooners* for four years [as a writer in the 1950s]. A consummate actor, a non-complainer and a great after-hours piano player."

But Stern faced a stiff battle against network pressure on the show. "At that time, you were really moving into creative interference," Stern sighed. NBC officials were skittish over featuring an obviously Jewish lead character on a series, so *Lanigan's Rabbi* the series stressed the investigative work of Lanigan over what his rabbi found out—in essence, destroying the setup of Kemelman's book series.

"We took the police chief and made him the head," Stern said. "And from that point, Mr. Kemelman was disenchanted, and rightfully so. I think we were a disappointment to him."

Kemelman wasn't the only one unhappy with *Lanigan's Rabbi* on TV. The show rotated as part of *The NBC Sunday Mystery Movie* with *Columbo*, *McCloud* and *McMillan* (without the *and Wife* since Susan St. James left the series in 1976), but by the 1976-77 the series were all on their last legs, having aired since 1971. *Lanigan's Rabbi* replaced *Quincy, M.E.* in the middle of the season. The latter got the chance to become a regular series away from *The NBC Sunday Mystery Movie* and ran through 1983; *Lanigan's Rabbi* went off along with other aging dramas in the summer of 1977 after five months.

The Andros Targets

Drama. Ran on CBS Mondays 10–11 P.M. Jan. 31–May 1977, opposite *The Feather and Father Gang* (through March 14) and baseball (from March 21) on ABC and movies on NBC, then Saturdays 10–11 P.M. July 2 and 9, 1977 opposite *The Feather and Father Gang* on ABC and movies on NBC. C: James Sutorius (as Mike Andros), Pamela Reed (as Sandi Farrell), Roy Poole (as Chet Reynolds), Ted Beniades (as Wayne Hillman), Alan Mixon (as Norman Kale), Jordan Charney (as Ted Bergman). Creator: Jerome Coopersmith. EP: Bob Sweeney, Larry Rosen. P: Edward H. Feldman. D: Bob Sweeney.

Anyone who mentioned in early 1977 that the new series *The Andros Targets* dealt with an investigative reporter probably immediately thought of Bob Woodward and Carl Bernstein, the two writers with *The Washington Post* who uncovered the Watergate scandal and whose story was dramatized in the 1976 film *All the President's Men*. But neither was the real inspiration for the series. "It was based on *The New York Times*' Nicholas Cagle," said Ted Beniades.

For the series neither Cagle's name nor his paper were used. Instead, the lead's name was Mike Andros, a muckraking journalist with *The New York Forum*. His aide was Sandi Farrell, while the rest of the cast were various editors at the paper. "I was the city editor," Beniades said. "I sent them out [for stories], and they came back to me." This being television, Mike and Sandi always managed to find something illicit wherever they looked in the Big Apple.

A midseason replacement for *Executive Suite* (q.v.), *The Andros Targets* was something of a rarity in the 1970s, a TV show shot in New York City. "It was done in New York, and right above us filming at the same time was *Kojak*," Beniades noted. Except for James Sutorius, previously a regular on *The Bob Crane Show* (q.v.), it was the first regular nighttime series role for each cast member. Pamela Reed was a newcomer, while Roy Poole and Jordan Charney were veterans of daytime soap operas. Charney played Sam Lucas on *Another World* from 1967 to 1970 and then on its spinoff *Somerset* from 1970 to 1973, followed by two years on *One Life to Live* as Vince Wolek before doing *The Andros Targets*. Poole starred as Al Skerba/Driscoll on *A Time for Us* from 1964 to 1966. As for Beniades' involvement, he said, "I was sent by my agent to audition. I was doing a summer stock audition from Boston."

While the lack of name actors may have hurt the show's appeal, Beniades though the title was more at fault. "I thought the name was inappropriate," Beniades said. "*The Andros Targets*— such a strange title for a newspaper-oriented show. It seemed better for a police show."

Nevertheless, Beniades declined to speculate on exactly why *The Andros Targets* was shot down. "You never know. They certainly had the backing from CBS, a lot of good New York directors and producers. But it just didn't go."

The Andros Targets was the swan song for regular nighttime network TV roles for much of the cast except Reed, who starred in three failed sitcoms in the 1990s—*Grand* (1990), *Family Album* (1993) and *The Home Court* (1995–96). Poole died in 1986, and Mixon passed away in 1997. Sutorius pursued stage acting on Broadway and other venues, while Beniades said he is now retired in New York state after 50 years of being an actor.

The Fantastic Journey

Science Fiction. Ran on NBC Thursdays 8–9 P.M. Feb. 3–April 13, 1977, opposite *Welcome Back, Kotter* and *What's Happening!!* on ABC and *The Waltons* on CBS. C: Jared Martin (as Varian), Carl Franklin (as Dr. Fred Walters), Ike Eisenmann (as Scott Jordan), Katie Saylor (as Liana), Roddy McDowall (as Dr. Jonathan Willaway). EP: Bruce Lansbury. P/W: Leonard Katzman. D: Vincent McEveety, Victor French. W: Michael Michaelian, Kathryn Michaelian-Powers.

Blansky's Beauties

Sitcom. Ran on ABC Saturdays 8–8:30 P.M. Feb. 12–May 21, 1977, opposite *The Mary Tyler Moore Show* on CBS and *Emergency* on NBC. C: Nancy Walker (as Nancy Blansky), Caren Kaye (as Bambi Benton), Lynda Goodfriend (as Ethel "Sunshine" Akalino), Eddie Mekka (as Joey DeLuca), Scott Baio (as Anthony DeLuca), George Pentecost (as Horace "Stubbs" Wilmington), Johnny Desmond (as Emilio), Taaffe O'Connell (as Hillary S. Prentiss), Rhonda Bates (as Arkansas), Bond Gideon (as Lovely Carson), Gerri Reddick (as Jackie Outlaw), Shirley Kirkes (as Gladys "Cochise" Littlefeather), Antoinette Yuskis (as Sylvia Silver), Jill Owens (as Misty Karamazov), Elaine Bolton (as Bridget Muldoon), Pat Morita (as Arnold). EP:

Garry Marshall, Edward Milkis, Thomas Miller. P: Bruce Johnson, Nick Abdo, Tony Marshall. D: Jerry Paris, Garry Marshall, Alan Rafkin.

Nancy Blansky first appeared at the end of an episode of *Happy Days*, where Howard Cunningham (played by Tom Bosley) stated that Nancy was his cousin working in Las Vegas supervising showgirls at the Oasis Hotel. Shortly thereafter *Blansky's Beauties* debuted, and showing up along with Nancy was Arnold the coffee shop operator, a dead ringer for Arnold the drive-in restaurant operator from *Happy Days*, played by the same actor. What a coincidence.

Blansky's Beauties also featured an actor from another production by Garry Marshall— Eddie Mekka, who played Carmine Ragusa on *Laverne & Shirley* but here was Nancy's nephew Joey DeLuca the choreographer. Playing his leering pre-adolescent brother Anthony was Scott Baio, who in the fall of 1977 would become Chachi's, Fonzie's cousin on *Happy Days*. At the same time, actress Lynda Goodfriend joined *Happy Days* as Richie Cunningham's girlfriend and later wife Lori Beth, except from Sept. 22–Dec. 15, 1978, when she and Baio, along with another *Blansky's Beauties* alumnus, Caren Kaye, starred in the Garry Marshall–produced sitcom *Who's Watching the Kids?*, which like *Blansky's Beauties* dealt with Las Vegas showgirls. Wow!

Let's forget this roundelay and talk to actor George Pentecost, who played Horace "Stubbs" Wilmington, Nancy's boss and manager of the hotel under never-seen owner Major Putnam. "I was sort of a nebbishy henchman, this character who had to be tough and was just a weakling," he said. He was the only other male regular apart from Johnny Desmond, who played Nancy's boyfriend Emilio, a maitre d' at Oasis. (The rest of the cast were showgirls, naturally.)

Pentecost got the role very easily. "I came out to LA in '76. I had done a *Barney Miller* a week before, my first job out here, then I got the role because Nancy Walker was an old chum of mine on the New York stage in the Sixties. I never had to audition. Isn't that wonderful?"

His only problem was learning he did not have to project himself in a studio the way he did on stage. "Television was new to me," he said. "I just found that less is more."

Blansky's Beauties was Walker's second sitcom on ABC in 1976-77 following the flop of *The Nancy Walker Show*. But, as Pentecost said, "Fred Silverman was running ABC, and she was running the show. She had carte blanche on what she wanted to do."

With that clout, why did *Blansky's Beauties* run just three months? "I really don't know," Pentecost said. "At the time, I was sold on it. I thought it was the best and wanted the steady income. It was the most money I'd made in my life." He never had another regular TV role, and when he was diagnosed with multiple sclerosis in 1995, he decided to retire from acting.

Walker did two other series before she died in 1992, *Mama's Boy* (1987-88) and *True Colors* (1990-92). Pentecost praised her to the hilt. "She was a great, great dame and a great comic," he said.

Hunter

Spy Drama. Ran on CBS Fridays 10–11 P.M. Feb. 18–May 27, 1977, opposite movies on ABC and *Quincy, M.E.* on NBC. C: James Franciscus (as James Hunter), Linda Evans (as Marty Shaw), Ralph Bellamy (as Gen. Harold Baker). EP: Lee Rich, Philip Capice. P: Christopher Morgan. D: Bruce Bilson, Harry Harris, Gary Nelson.

Dog and Cat

Crime Drama. Ran on ABC Saturdays 10–11 P.M. March 5–May 14, 1977, opposite *The Carol Burnett Show* on CBS and movies on NBC. C: Lou Antonio (as Det. Sgt. Jack Ramsey), Kim Basinger (as Officer J.Z. Kane), Matt Clark (as Lt. Arthur Kipling). EP: Lawrence Gordon. P: Robert Singer. D: Paul Stanley, Robert Davis.

Second Chance

Game. Ran on ABC Mondays through Fridays Noon–12:30 P.M. March 7–July 15, 1977, opposite *The Young and the Restless* on CBS and *Name That Tune* (through June 10) and *Shoot for the Stars* (from June 13) on NBC. C: Jim Peck. EP: Bill Carruthers. P: Joel Stein. D: Chris Darley.

Westside Medical

Medical Drama. Ran on ABC Thursdays 10–11 P.M. March 15–Aug. 25, 1977, opposite *Barnaby Jones* on CBS and movies on NBC. C: James Sloyan (as Dr. Sam Lanagan), Linda Carlson (as Dr. Janet Cottrell), Ernest Thompson (as Dr. Philip Parker), Alice Nunn (as Carrie). EP: Martin Starger. P: Alan A. Armer. D: Leo Penn, Ralph Senensky, Vincent Sherman.

Loves Me, Loves Me Not

Sitcom. Ran on CBS Sunday 10:30–11 P.M. March 20, 1977, opposite movies on ABC and NBC, then CBS Wednesdays 8:30–9 P.M. March–April 27, 1977, opposite *The Bionic Woman* on ABC and *The Life and Times of Grizzly Adams* on NBC. C: Susan Dey (as Jane Benson), Kenneth Gilman (as Dick Phillips), Art Metrano (as Tom), Phyllis Glick (as Sue). EP: Paul Junger Witt, Tony Thomas. P: Susan Harris, Ernest Losso. D: Jay Sandrich, Noam Pitlik.

Kingston: Confidential

Drama. Ran on NBC Wednesdays 10–11 P.M. March 23–Aug. 10, 1977, opposite *Charlie's Angels* on ABC and movies on CBS. C: Raymond Burr (as R.B. Kingston), Art Hindle (as Tony Marino), Pamela Hensley (as Beth Kelly), Nancy Olson (as Jessica Frazier). EP: David Victor. P: James Hirsch, Don Ingalls, Joe L. Cramer, Don Nicholl. D: Don Weis, Robert Day, Harvey Laidman.

Nashville 99

Police Drama. Ran on CBS Fridays 8–9 P.M. April 1–April 22, 1977, opposite *Donny and Marie* on ABC and *Sanford and Son* and *Chico and the Man* on NBC. C: Claude Akins (as Det. Lt. Stonewall Jackson "Stoney" Huff), Jerry Reed (as Det. Trace Mayne), Lucille Benson (as Birdie Huff). EP: Ernie Frankel. D: Don McDougall, Lawrence Dobkin, George Sherman.

It's Anybody Guess

Game. Ran on NBC Mondays through Fridays 11:30 A.M.–Noon June 13–Sept. 30, 1977, opposite *Family Feud* on ABC and *Love of Life* and news on CBS. C: Monty Hall. EP: Stu Billet, Stefan Hatos. P: Steve Feke. D: Joe Behar.

Shields and Yarnell

Comedy Variety. Ran on CBS Mondays 8:30–9 P.M. June 13–July 25, 1977, opposite baseball on ABC and *Little House on the Prairie* on NBC, then CBS Tuesdays 8:30–9 P.M. Jan. 31–March 28, 1978, opposite *Laverne and Shirley* on ABC and *The Man from Atlantis* (through Jan. 10) and *The*

Chuck Barris Rah Show (from Feb. 28) on NBC. C: Robert Shields, Lorene Yarnell, Ted Zeigler (1977), Joanna Cassidy (1977), Gailard Sartain (1978), Flip Reade (1978), the Norman Maney Orchestra. EP/D: Steve Binder. P: Frank Peppiatt.

The Better Sex

Game Show. Ran on ABC Mondays through Fridays Noon–12:30 P.M. July 18, 1977–Jan. 13, 1978, opposite *The Young and the Restless* on CBS and *Shoot for the Stars* (through Sept. 30) and *To Say the Least* (from Oct. 3) on NBC. C: Bill Anderson, Sarah Purcell. EP: Ira Skutch. P: Robert Sherman. D: Paul Alter.

Ira Skutch first worked for the game show production empire of Mark Goodson and Bill Todman in 1957 as producer/director of *Two for the Money*. He moved into other hits for the company as a producer, director or producer/director, including being producer on *Match Game* from 1973 to 1982. Though credited as executive producer for *The Better Sex*, he did not create the program initially.

"That show came from an idea from Howard Felsher," said Skutch. Felsher also was a producer for Goodson-Todman, including handling the 1971–75 edition of *Password*. "He said, 'What is the fundamental thing about human beings? Competition. Suppose we carry that on to the extent of getting rid of people on the show?' It was a really radical concept at the time."

Staff members of Goodson-Todman discussed what would be the most successful way to do the show. "Creatively, it evolved where it was played with two teams where you would 'knock out' people," Skutch said. "For awhile, the show was called *Knockout* [not to be confused with the 1977-78 series of the same name]."

But it took the company head to nail the series' essential gimmick. "Goodson came in and said, 'You've got to be able to tell the contestants apart in relation to those teams,'" Skutch said. "He came up with the men against women setup." In the final version, a male and a female sextet competed. With each question asked, at least two members of each team were up for elimination from the initial game. The one with at least one member left standing faced 30 members of the opposite sex in the studio audience for a bonus game that could

net the sextet $5,000 if they outlasted the audience members through six questions.

Goodson also suggested having a male and female host. Only a few women had hosted game shows, all of them in the 1940s and 1950s, so this was a major new enterprise in 1977. "We had a very hard time finding her," said Skutch. He thought Stephanie Edwards, a hostess seen on several syndicated series in the 1970s and 1980s, was very good, but they decided ultimately on Sarah Purcell, who hosted a local talk show in Hollywood called *A.M. Los Angeles* before doing this, her first network series. "She got *Real People* [a nighttime comedy series from 1979 to 1984 she hosted] because of this show," Skutch said.

As for her co-host, Bill Anderson was primarily a country music singer. "His manager was a friend of Howard's and mine, and we tried him out on *Match Game*," Skutch said. "At the time, we were looking for new people."

Yet even with the refining and adding of new talent, *The Better Sex* ran only six months. Asked if he could pinpoint any reasons why it failed, Skutch said, "Nope. I never understood that with my shows."

Skutch left Goodson-Todman, and television work, in 1983 to become a writer. For an entertaining read about TV history, check out his 1989 memoir, *I Remember Television*.

Szysznyk

Sitcom. Ran on CBS Mondays 8:30–9 P.M. Aug. 1–Aug. 29, 1977, opposite baseball on ABC and *Little House on the Prairie* on NBC, then CBS Wednesdays 8:30–9 P.M. Dec. 7, 1977–Jan. 25, 1978, opposite *Eight is Enough* on ABC and *The Life and Times of Grizzly Adams* on NBC. C: Ned Beatty (as Nick Szysznyk), Olivia Cole (as Ms. Harrison), Leonard Barr (as Leonard Kriegler), Thomas Carter (as Ray Gun), Scott Colomby (as Tony La Placa), Barry Miller (as Bernard Fortwengler), Jarrod Johnson (as Ralph), Susan Lanier (as Susan Chandler; August only). EP: Jerry Weintraub. P: Rich Eustis, Michael Elias. D: Peter Bonerz, James Burrows. W: Jim Mulligan, Ron Landry.

Sugar Time!

Sitcom. Ran on ABC Saturdays 8:30–9 P.M. Aug. 13–Sept. 3, 1977, opposite *The Bob Newhart Show* on CBS and *Emergency!* on NBC, then ABC Mondays 8–8:30 P.M. April 10–May 29, 1978, opposite

The Jeffersons on CBS and *Little House on the Prairie* on NBC. C: Barbi Benton (as Maxx Douglas), Marianne Black (as Maggie Barton), Did Carr (as Diane Zuckerman), Wynn Irwin (as Al Marks), Mark Winkworth (as Paul Landson), Charles Fleischer (as Lightning Jack Rappaport). EP: James Komack. P: Hank Bradford, Martin Cohan, Gary Belkin. D: Bill Hobin, Howard Storm, Bill Foster.

1977-78

The Fitzpatricks

Drama. Ran on CBS Monday 9–10 P.M. Sept. 5, 1977, opposite football on ABC and movies on NBC, then CBS Tuesdays 8–9 P.M. Sept. 20, 1977–Jan. 10, 1978, opposite *Happy Days* and *Laverne & Shirley* on ABC and *The Richard Pryor Show* (through Oct. 4) and *The Man from Atlantis* (from Oct. 11) on NBC. C: Bert Kramer (as Mike Fitzpatrick), Mariclare Costello (as Maggie Fitzpatrick), Clark Brandon (as Sean Fitzpatrick), James Vincent McNichol (as Jack Fitzpatrick), Michele Tobin (as Maureen "Mo" Fitzpatrick), Sean Marshall (as Max Fitzpatrick), Derek Wells (as R.J.), Helen Hunt (as Kerry Gerardi). EP: Philip Mandelker. P: John Cutts. D: Gene Reynolds, Peter Tewksbury, Stuart Margolin.

Rafferty

Medical Drama. Ran on CBS Mondays 10–11 P.M. Sept. 5–Nov. 28, 1977, opposite football on ABC and movies on NBC. C: Patrick McGoohan (as Dr. Sidney Rafferty), Millie Slavin (as Nurse Vera Wales), John Getz (as Dr. Daniel Gentry), Joan Pringle (as Nurse Beryl Keynes), David Clennon (as Dr. Calvin). EP/D: Jerry Thorpe. P: James Lee, Norman S. Powell, Robert Van Scoyk. D: Patrick McGoohan, Barry Crane, Alexander Singer.

Search and Rescue: The Alpha Team

Adventure. Ran on NBC Saturdays 11:30 A.M.– Noon Sept. 10, 1977–Jan. 28, 1978, opposite *The Krofft Supershow* on ABC and *The Batman/Tarzan Adventure Hour* on CBS. C: EP: Seymour Burns, Will Lorin. P: Lew Lehman. D: Peter Carter.

Thunder

Children's Adventure. Ran on NBC Saturdays 11–11:30 A.M. Sept. 10, 1977–Sept. 2, 1978. C: Melora Hardin (as Cindy Prescott), Clint Ritchie (as Bill Prescott), Melissa Converse (as Anne Prescott), Justin Randi (as Willie Williams). P: Irving Cummings, Jr., Charles Marion. D: William Beaudine, Jr., Sigmund Neufeld, Jr.

If the synopsis for *Thunder*, "A family takes care of an intelligent animal as a pet," sounds similar to that of the *Lassie* TV series, it should come as little surprise that a director of several episodes of the latter program did the same task on *Thunder*. William Beaudine, Jr., son of the director of the same name, produced as well as directed many episodes of *Lassie* in the 1950s and 1960s, and he said that directing Thunder the black stallion was the same to him as directing the famous collie Lassie.

"When I first got a chance to direct on the *Lassie* show, the key is you cannot expect animals to be directed like humans," Beaudine said. "You bring them in, get the shot and stop. You have to be patient." Beaudine would go over all the shots he had of the animals' movements in the editing room to create a final product where the creature appeared to be moving fluidly with the camera. "You did it in little cuts, and then you pasted it together," he said.

To hear Beaudine tell it, he had a simpler time handling Thunder the horse than Melora Hardin the star juvenile, who played Thunder's 8-year-old owner, Cindy, daughter of Bill and Anne Prescott. (Cindy's pal was Willie, who rode a mule.) Recalling one particular moment in filming, Beaudine noted, "One of my worries was she was not paying attention when I was talking with her, so I was stern. I yelled at her. Suddenly the teacher on the set said 'You shouldn't have said that' and her parents were nearby. So I apologized to her parents."

Despite his outburst, Beaudine said that overall Hardin was not as professional as other child actors he had handled. "She wasn't paying attention," he said. "She was a little problematic."

Beaudine got his gig on *Thunder* thanks to industry connections. "Irving Cummings, Jr., was the producer of the show, and he had known me and wanted me," Beaudine said. Cummings also produced *Fury* back in the 1950s, another equine-centered children's show which invited comparisons with *Thunder*.

But whereas *Fury* ran 11 years on NBC (eight of them in the same time slot as *Thunder*), Cummings' later series ran only a year. Apart from having married parents and a girl rather than a boy as the lead, both shows were quite similar. Cummings and crew were going for the same approach leavened with the long-running appeal of *Lassie*, which Beaudine credited as "It showed an animal as being lovable, intelligent and protective, and it taught young people lessons." Yet that sort of success was not to be with *Thunder*.

Nevertheless, Beaudine has a soft spot for *Thunder*, even if it did nothing for his career the way *Lassie* did. "A quick and a very nice assignment," he said of the series. "I enjoyed it."

The Red Hand Gang

Adventure. Ran on NBC Saturdays 12:30–1 P.M. Sept. 10, 1977–Jan. 28, 1978, opposite *American Bandstand* on ABC and *Fat Albert and the Cosby Kids* on CBS. C: Matthew Laborteaux (as Frankie), J.E. Miller (as J.R.), Jolie Newman (as Joanne), James Bond III (as Doc), John Brogna (as Li'l Bill). EP: William P. D'Angelo, Ray Allen, Harvey Bullock. D: William P. D'Angelo, Charles R. Rondeau.

The Betty White Show

Sitcom. Ran on CBS Mondays 9–9:30 P.M. Sept. 12–Nov. 28, 1977, then CBS Mondays 9:30–10 P.M. Dec. 5, 1977–Jan. 9, 1978, both times opposite football (through December) and movies (from December) on ABC and movies on NBC. C: Betty White (as Joyce Whitman), John Hillerman (as John Elliot), Georgia Engel (as Mitzi Maloney), Caren Kaye (as Tracy Garrett), Alex Henteloff (as Doug Porterfield), Barney Phillips (as Fletcher Huff), Charles Cyphers (as Hugo Muncy). EP: Ed Weinberger, Stan Daniels. P: Bob Ellison, Dale McRaven. D: James Burrows, Noam Pitlik.

Young Dan'l Boone

Western. Ran on CBS Mondays 8–9 P.M. Sept. 12–Sept. 26, 1977, opposite *The San Pedro Beach Bums* on ABC and *Little House on the Prairie* on NBC, then CBS Tuesday 8–9 P.M. Oct. 4, 1977, opposite *Happy Days* and *Laverne & Shirley* on ABC and *The Richard Pryor Show* on NBC. C: Rick Moses (as Daniel Boone), Devon Ericson (as Rebecca Bryan), Ji-Tu Cumbuka (as Hawk), John Joseph Thomas (as Peter Dawes), Eloy Phil Casados (as Tsiskwa). EP: Ernie Frankel. P: Jimmy Sangster. D: Earl Bellamy, Ernest Pintoff, Don McDougall, Arthur Marks.

The Richard Pryor Show

Comedy Variety. Ran on NBC Tuesdays 8–9 P.M. Sept. 13–Oct. 20, 1977, opposite *Happy Days* and *Laverne & Shirley* on ABC and *The Fitzpatricks* on CBS. C: Richard Pryor, Allegra Allison, David Banks, Sandra Bernhard, Victor Dunlop, Argus Hamilton, Jimmy Martinez, Paul Mooney, Tim Reid, Marsha Warfield, Robin Williams, "Detroit" John Witherspoon. EP: Burt Sugarman. P: Rocco Urbisci. D: John Moffitt.

"Unless you're over 45, you cannot fathom how popular Richard Pryor was at his height," noted comedian Argus Hamilton about the man who had him in his TV series comedy troupe. Hamilton said Pryor was at the right time doing his racially-tinged humor in the 1970s when, as he put it bluntly, "A black man could tell 'nigger jokes' at the expense of telling white folks the truth."

That doesn't sound like humor appropriate for the early evening hours on TV, however. Hamilton agreed. "It made absolutely no sense," he said of the scheduling. He felt the time slot killed the show and said it been later in the evening, given Pryor's popularity in concerts and movies in 1977, "It could've been the cult hit of all time."

Hamilton got cast on the program via comedian Paul Mooney, whom he credited for "shepherding" Pryor from his non-controversial comic approach in the 1960s to edgier efforts in the 1970s. "At the Comedy Store [a club in Los Angeles], Paul Mooney was and still is a major force," said Hamilton. "Mooney and I developed a Huck and Jim relationship, because I was a white Southerner and he was black. I was also extremely hip. He picked me up to give Richard a Southern man to bounce off of."

The rest of the cast were relatively unknowns at the time. "Richard just wanted people around him he knew," said Hamilton. "There was about eight or nine of us. Richard spotted Robin [Williams] right away. Robin's talent was just all over the place."

Hamilton said the newcomers felt like kids in a candy store on the series. "We were all kids in our early twenties. We used the entire NBC makeup crew. We were just having the time of our lives."

They also had a political point of view in their comedy. "All the sketches really meant something," Hamilton said. That often disturbed the network brass. Hamilton recalled that when he watched NBC executive Dick Ebersol review the cast and crew at work, "You could see the sweat coming down the sides of his face." Hamilton estimated that there were at least two hours' worth of profanity-laced bits that could not be used for the show, which no doubt did not endear the show among NBC officials.

Still, some that made it to air had sting in them. Hamilton recalled one time when Pryor played America's first black president at a press conference. When Hamilton introduced himself as a reporter for the fictional *Mississippi Journal*, Pryor yelled "Sit down! Sit down!" in obvious reference to that state's segregationist history.

After *The Richard Pryor Show* ended, Hamilton went back to comedy clubs and wrote a syndicated humor column. The show's star eventually mellowed in humor and his approach to life after a near-death experience in 1980 doing cocaine. He even hosted a children's show called *Pryor's Place* from 1984 to 1985. Unfortunately, in the 1990s he suffered from multiple sclerosis. The disease's degenerative effect on his body has allowed him to perform on TV rarely.

Redd Foxx

Comedy Variety. Ran on ABC Thursdays 10–11 P.M. Sept. 15, 1977–Jan. 26, 1978, opposite *Barnaby Jones* on CBS and *Rosetti and Ryan* (through Nov. 10) and *What Really Happened to the Class of '65?* (from Dec. 8) on NBC. C: Redd Foxx, the Gerald Wilson Orchestra. P: Allan Blye, Bob Einstein. D: Donald Davis.

The Sanford Arms

Sitcom. Ran on NBC Fridays 8–8:30 P.M. Sept. 16–Oct. 14, 1977, opposite *Donny and Marie* on ABC and *Wonder Woman* on CBS. C: Theodore Wilson (as Phil Wheeler), LaWanda Page (as Esther Anderson), Bebe Drake-Hooks (as Jeannie), Whitman Mayo (as Grady Wilson), Norma Miller (as Dolly Wilson), Don Bexley (as Bubba Hoover), Raymond Allen (as Woody Anderson), Tina Andrews (as Angie Wheeler), John Earl (as Nat Wheeler). EP: Bud Yorkin, Saul Turteltaub, Bernie Orenstein. P: Woody Kling.

Logan's Run

Science Fiction. Ran on CBS Fridays 9–10 P.M. Sept. 16–Sept. 30, 1977, opposite movies on ABC and *The Rockford Files* on NBC, then CBS Mondays 8–9 P.M. Oct. 3, 1977–Jan. 16, 1978, opposite *The San Pedro Beach Bums* (through Dec. 19) and *Lucan* (from Dec. 26) on ABC and *Little House on the Prairie* on NBC. C: Gregory Harrison (as Logan 5), Heather Menzies (as Jessica 6), Randy Powell (as Francis 7), Donald Moffat (as Rem). EP: Ivan Goff, Ben Roberts. P: Leonard Katzman. D: Paul Krasny, Nicholas Colasanto. W: D.C. Fontana, Harlan Ellison.

Wacko

Comedy Variety. Ran on CBS Saturdays Noon–12:30 P.M. Sept. 17–Oct. 8, 1977, opposite *The ABC Weekend Special* monthly on ABC and *Baggy Pants and the Nitwits* on NBC, then CBS Saturdays 1–1:30 P.M. Oct. 15–Nov. 12, 1977, opposite *American Bandstand* on ABC, and then CBS Sundays 9:30–10 A.M. Nov. 20, 1977–Sept. 3, 1978. C: Charles Fleischer, Bo Kaprall, Julie McWhirter, Bob Comfort, Doug Cox, Millicent Crisp, Rick Kellard, the Sylvers (occasional). EP: Bob Wood, Chris Bearde. P: Coslough Johnson, Richard Adamson, Kathe Connolly. D: Stanley Dorfman. Animation D: John Wilson.

The San Pedro Beach Bums

Sitcom. Ran on ABC Mondays 8–9 P.M. Sept. 19–Dec. 19, 1977, opposite *Young Dan'l Boone* (through Sept. 26) and *Logan's Run* (from Oct. 3) on CBS and *Little House on the Prairie* on NBC. C: Christopher Murney (as Buddy Binder), Stuart Pankin (as Anthony "Stuf" Danelli), John Mark Robinson (as Edward "Dancer" McClory), Darryl McCullough (as Moose Maslosky), Christopher DeRose (as Boychick), Louis Hoven (as Louise), Susan Mullen (as Suzi Camelli), Lisa Reeves (as Margie), Nancy Morgan (as Julie),

Kristoff St. John (as Ralphie Walker). EP: Aaron Spelling, Douglas S. Cramer. P: E. Duke Vincent, Earl Barrett, Simon Muntner. D: Barry Shear, Don Weis, Gene Nelson.

The Oregon Trail

Western. Ran on NBC Wednesdays 9–10 P.M. Sept. 21–Oct. 26, 1977, opposite *Charlie's Angels* on ABC and movies on CBS. C: Rod Taylor (as Even Thorpe), Darleen Carr (as Margaret Devlin), Charles Napier (as Luther Sprague), Andrew Stevens (as Andrew Thorpe), Tony Becker (as William Thorpe), Gina Marie Smika (as Rachel Thorpe). EP: Michael Gleason. P: Richard Collins, Carl Vitale. D: Virgil W. Vogel, Hollingsworth Morse, Bill Bixby.

Big Hawaii

Soap Opera. Ran on NBC Wednesdays 10–11 P.M. Sept. 21–Nov. 16, 1977, opposite *Baretta* on ABC and movies on CBS. C: Cliff Potts (as Mitch Fears), John Dehner (as Barrett Fears), Lucia Stralser (as Karen "Keke" Fears), Bill Lucking (as Oscar Kalahani), Elizabeth Smith (as Big Lulu Kalahani), Moe Keale (as Garfield Kalahani), Remi Abellira (as Kimo Kalahani). EP: Perry Lafferty. P: William Wood, William Finnegan. D: Seymour Robbie.

"I loved that show," said director Seymour Robbie of *Big Hawaii.* "That show I felt should've been a hit. Why it wasn't, I don't know."

But executive producer Perry Lafferty offered a few reasons why. "It was just exactly like *Dallas* or *Knots Landing* initially," he said. Yet the idea of carrying over storylines every week unnerved NBC officials, who preferred the more traditional way of ending individual episodes. *Big Hawaii* could have started the trend that blossomed the next year with *Dallas* in doing nighttime soap opera. This was one big mistake, in Lafferty's view.

He felt another was the melodrama's setup. Set at Paradise Ranch in, yes, Hawaii, it detailed an often stormy relationship between ranch operator Barrett Fears and his independent-minded son Mitch over work and life issues. Keke Fears was Barrett's niece, while the other regulars were family maid Big Lulu Kalahani and her three sons, Oscar, Garfield and Kimo, who all assisted in running the ranch.

"There was no detective, no doctor, just people running around on a ranch," Lafferty

said. "Everyone was starting on ground zero every week." That was another strike.

Yet the show's pilot, which aired as a TV-movie titled *Danger in Paradise* on May 12, 1977, with a slightly different angle (Mitch fought his stepmother for control of his sick dad's ranch), did generate enough interest to make into a series. It had all the series cast except Remi Abellira. Lafferty ruefully noted that the pilot and series' lead boiled down to two actors—Cliff Potts and Christopher Reeve. "We put a hold on Chris Reeves for 72 hours before we got an OK from Cliff," he said.

Lafferty conceded that Potts did a fine job, as did the show's frequent director Seymour Robbie. Robbie noted that "It was fun shooting in Hawaii. Difficult as hell, though." The outdoor set was hard to position some equipment, while the indoor stage had echoes that made it difficult to do sound properly. "They hadn't anticipated everything," he said. (The producers were not the same ones who did *Hawaii Five-O,* filming concurrently that season during its 12-year run from 1968 to 1980. Robbie did a few episodes of that series too.)

And there was one script whose writer apparently forgot where the series took place. "Everything was shot inside!" Robbie said. He yelled for a rewrite to get a least a few shots done outdoors to display the tropic island's beauty. Otherwise, Robbie said, "I had a very good time doing that show."

Lafferty said what really killed the show was NBC's weird scheduling. "They preempted its second and fourth weeks," he said. Obviously the network was less than sold on the property even against weak competition (*Baretta* would go off at the end of the season), and they said aloha to *Big Hawaii* after a total of six shows even though they had ordered 13 episodes. For those interested, Lafferty noted that "I have seven films of *Big Hawaii* never played."

The Man from Atlantis

Science Fiction/Adventure. Ran on NBC Thursdays 9–10 P.M. Sept. 22 and 29, 1977, opposite *Barney Miller* and *Carter Country* on ABC and *Hawaii Five-O* on CBS, then NBC Tuesdays 8–9 P.M. Oct. 11–Jan. 10, 1978 and April 18–July 25, 1978, opposite *Happy Days* and *Laverne & Shirley* on ABC and *The Fitzpatricks* (through Jan. 10) on CBS. C: Patrick Duffy (as Mark Harris), Alan Fudge (as

C.W. Crawford), Victor Buono (as Mr. Schubert; 1977), Robert Lussier (as Brent; 1977), Richard Williams (as Jomo), J. Victor Lopez (as Chuey), Jean Marie Hon (as Jane), Anson Downes (as Alan). EP: Herbert F. Solow. P: Herman Miller, Robert Lewin. D: Virgil W. Vogel, David Moessinger. W: Stephen Kandel, Michael Wagner., Herman Miller, Larry Alexander.

Lee H. Katzin directed the TV-movie pilot for *The Man from Atlantis*, but beyond that he emphasized he had no connection to the series. As he put it, "Herb Solow [the show's executive producer] and I are still good friends, but it was made into a joke."

The pilot, which aired March 4, 1977, told of a malelike species who washed ashore near the Foundation for Oceanic Research in southern California. Dr. Elizabeth Merrill of the foundation dubbed him "Mark Harris" but thought he may not be a human but rather a creature from the fabled lost city of Atlantis, given his webbed feet and hands and other abilities more suited for aquatic than land life. He joined forces with Dr. Merrill to learn about himself and help her with her studies.

By the time the series began, the two were part of the crew along with Jomo, Chuey, Jane and Alan on the submarine *Cetacean*. C.W. Crawford was the foundation's director, while Mark's recurring enemies were blustery Mr. Schubert and his assistant Brent, who planned to take over the world in some manner involving the seas. The latter two were written out midseason so that Mark faced even more ridiculous obstacles, including once where an undersea time warp landed him in the 1300s amid Romeo and Juliet, depicted as real people. Is there any wonder why this show lasted less than a year?

Auditioning to play Mark were some interesting applicants. As with *Big Hawaii* (q.v.), Christopher Reeve was a candidate for the lead. "We interviewed him, but he said he didn't want to wear anything on his hands," Katzin said, referring to the "webbing" makeup. "And we even interviewed Sylvester Stallone." (The TV-movie was in production before *Rocky* became a hit movie for Stallone in late 1976.)

In the end, Patrick Duffy won out. "Patrick was wonderful," Katzin said. "He was the very last person we met. We were at the end of our testing day. He was great, had a wonderful sense of humor. Patrick also had this otherworldly quality."

The production team was so eager to hire him that they forgot initially to see if he was a swimmer, as would be needed for the role. They tested his abilities in Katzin's pool and were amazed. "He could hold his breath for two minutes," Katzin said.

In fact, Duffy adapted to his aquatic scenes better than his makeup did. "If you'll notice, he closed his hands a lot," Katzin said. "They couldn't hold up in the water."

Katzin added a few touches to the pilot that stayed in the series that emphasized Mark's amphibious nature. "It was my idea for the dolphin strokes, and also to jump in the air like a dolphin to get the fish," he said. But as he said before, he had nothing else to do with the series. Neither did Duffy after a few months, who luckily got a regular job on the nighttime soap opera *Dallas* from 1978 to 1991 and escaped what could have been a career-crippling part.

Rosetti and Ryan

Law Drama. Ran on NBC Thursdays 10–11 P.M. Sept. 22–Nov. 10, 1977, opposite *The Redd Foxx Show* on ABC and *Barnaby Jones* on CBS. C: Tony Roberts (as Joseph Rosetti), Squire Fridell (as Frank Ryan), Jane Elliot (as Asst. D.A. Jessica Hornesby), Dick O'Neill (as Judge Praetor Hardcastle), William Marshall (as Judge Marcus T. Black). EP: Leonard B. Stern. P: Jerry Davis. D: John Astin, Harry Falk, Richard Crenna.

There was no mistaking *Rosetti and Ryan* with *Perry Mason* or *The Defenders*. While those TV lawyers were dead serious in their intent to win cases in the courtroom, Rosetti and Ryan were much more the prototypical 1970s swinging bachelors off the job and not as earnest during trials. Rosetti was the curly-haired dandy who loved fine food, while Ryan was a former policeman who did more of the legwork in defending their clients. They got the job done despite disapproval from their constant adversary, Asst. D.A. Hornesby, and tough Judge Hardcastle, both of whom disliked their freewheeling style on and off work.

"It was our attempt to be sophisticated and stylish and present lawyers less in the courtroom and move out in the streets solving crimes," said executive producer Leonard B. Stern of the series. The show began as a TV-movie pilot titled *Rosetti and Ryan: Men Who Love Women* on May 23, 1977, with all the parts

On the debut of *Rosetti and Ryan*, Julie Cobb played an odd TV star accused of shooting at a football star who enlisted the help of Rosetti (Tony Roberts, right) and Ryan (Squire Fridell).

in the series being played by the same actors in the TV-movie.

Befitting its premise, Stern drew as his leads two actors with rather dissimilar backgrounds. Tony Roberts primarily performed in movies and theater, with his only regular role on TV prior to *Rosetti and Ryan* being Lee Pollock on the daytime serial *The Edge of Night* from 1965 to 1967. Stern worked with him on a sitcom pilot for NBC called *Snafu* which aired on Aug. 23, 1976, and kept him in mind for the new project. As for Fridell, Stern said, "I'd seen him in endless commercials." Fridell later wrote a book about performing in commercials.

But hanging over any chance for a show to present lawyers in a slightly irreverent fashion was the nervousness of NBC management at the time. As with *Big Hawaii* (q.v.), the network did not really seem to get behind the show and aired just six episodes before canceling it in less than two months as it flagged behind *Barnaby Jones* (a top 25 show at the time). "It did not have that immediate following," Stern allowed, and that was what NBC, desperate for a hit after having become the #3 network behind ABC and CBS, wanted at the time.

Stern has remained active in television since *Rosetti and Ryan*. The multiple Emmy winner (for writing *The Phil Silvers Show* in the 1950s and *Get Smart!* in the 1960s) thinks that his professional field in which he's toiled for decades is constantly improving. "When you have shows such as *The West Wing, Law & Order* and *The Practice*, you've got literate, well-written shows," he said. "I think it's going to become a wiser, mature medium. I see it not revolutionary, but evolutionary. And I think it'll be better."

We've Got Each Other

Sitcom. Ran on CBS Saturdays 8:30–9 P.M. Oct. 1, 1977–Jan. 14, 1978, opposite *Operation Petticoat* on ABC and *The Bionic Woman* on NBC. C: Oliver Clark (as Stuart Hibbard), Beverly Archer (as Judy Hibbard), Tom Poston (as Damon Jerome), Joan Van Ark (as Dee Dee Baldwin), Ren Woods (as Donna), Martin Kove (as Ken Redford). EP: Tom Patchett, Jay Tarses. P: Jack Burns. D: James Burrows, Will MacKenzie.

Knockout

Game. Ran on NBC Mondays through Fridays 11:30 A.M.–Noon Oct. 3, 1977–April 21, 1978, opposite *Family Feud* on ABC and *Love of Life* and news on CBS. C: Arte Johnson. EP: Ralph Edwards. P: Bruce Belland, Mark Maxwell-Smith. D: Arthur Forrest.

To Say the Least

Game. Ran on NBC Mondays through Fridays Noon–12:30 P.M. Oct. 3, 1977–April 21, 1978, opposite *The Better Sex* (through Jan. 13) and *The $20,000 Pyramid* (from Jan. 16) on ABC and *The*

Young and the Restless on CBS. C: Tom Kennedy. EP: Merrill Heatter, Bob Quigley. P: Robert Noah. D: Jerome Shaw.

On Our Own

Sitcom. Ran on CBS Sundays 8:30–9 P.M. Oct. 9, 1977–Aug. 20, 1978, opposite *The Six Million Dollar Man* (through Jan. 30, 1978), *How the West Was Won* (from Feb. 12–May 1978 and then from July–Aug. 27, 1978), and *Lucan* (from June to July 1978) on ABC and *The Wonderful World of Disney* and *Project U.F.O.* (from Feb. 19) on NBC. C: Bess Armstrong (as Julia Peters), Lynnie Greene (as Maria Teresa Bonino), Gretchen Wyler (as Toni McBain), Dixie Carter (as April Baxter), Dan Resin (as Craig Boatwright), John Christopher Jones (as Eddie Barnes), Bob Randall (as J.M. Bedford). EP: David Susskind. P: Sam Denoff.

On Our Own was the series that brought veteran TV producer Sam Denoff back from the West Coast to his old working days in New York City through a somewhat circuitous route. "The pilot was written by a guy named Bob Randall, who was a playwright," Denoff said. Randall also appeared occasionally on the show as J.M. Bedford, board chairman of the Bedford Advertising Agency. Randall did the show for Talent Associates, the production company for TV producer and talk show host David Susskind. Susskind had little experience doing sitcoms, whereas Denoff had done plenty of them since the 1960s, so Denoff received an offer to do the show, which would be taped in Manhattan rather than Denoff's base of Los Angeles.

"I thought, 'Gee boy, I'd like to go back to New York,'" Denoff said. So he packed up his family and moved them to Central Park South in late June. The glamour of the city wore off soon. In October, shortly after the series debuted, he went to his dry cleaner and told him he was doing the new TV show *On Our Own*. As frank as a New Yorker could be, the dry cleaner told him, "That's a piece of shit. My daughter and my wife like it, but I think it's a piece of shit."

Naturally, Denoff disagreed and had positive feelings for the show except for dealing with Susskind. "He was tough," Denoff said. "He was too tough as a partner." Denoff preferred to dwell on the cast, which included Dixie Carter nearly a decade before starring in the series *Designing Women* playing a copy-

The spirited *On Our Own* cast consisted of, from left, John Christopher Jones, Lynnie Greene, Bess Armstrong, Dan Resin, Gretchen Wyler and Dixie Carter.

writer who was just as confident and outspoken as was her later character Julia Sugarbaker. "Dixie Carter was the ultimate pro," Denoff said.

But Carter was not the star of *On Our Own*. Bess Armstrong and Lynnie Greene played two upcoming single girls at the Bedford Advertising Agency (a copywriter and art director, respectively), whose escapades on and off the job concerned most of the plots. Their stylish boss was Toni McBain, while Eddie Barnes produced the agency's TV commercials and Craig Boatwright was a salesman. Among guest stars for the show, Denoff remembered hiring Danny Aiello. "I gave him his first shot on TV," Denoff said. "I think he played a priest."

The odd thing about *On Our Own* was that it ran just a year opposite fairly weak and changing competition on ABC and NBC. "We were cancelled but with a very high rating," Denoff said. Well, finishing #29 for the season in the Nielson ratings may not be "very high," but still respectable, and not too far behind its

most successful competitor, *Project U.F.O.*, which landed at #19. Denoff learned several years later that CBS canned it because Susskind constantly bothered network officials with matters regarding the show to the point of complete irritation. "And with it being a borderline hit, the network cancelled us," Denoff said.

Denoff went back to Hollywood, and Greene and Armstrong went there too. Greene appeared a few times on *The Golden Girls* in flashbacks as Bea Arthur's character Dorothy, while Armstrong starred in several failed yet interesting series, including playing the mother of Clair Danes in the drama *My So-Called Life* from 1994 to 1995. Oddly, that same season another unrelated sitcom called *On Our Own* aired on ABC. Dealing with a family of six kids leaving without their parents, it lasted off and on the network from Sept. 13, 1994–April 14, 1995.

Mulligan's Stew

Comedy Drama. Ran on NBC Tuesdays 9–10 P.M. Oct. 25–Dec. 13, 1977, opposite *Three's*

Company and *Soap* on ABC and *M*A*S*H* and *One Day at a Time* on CBS. C: Lawrence Pressman (as Michael Mulligan), Elinor Donahue (as Jane Mulligan), Johnny Doran (as Mark Mulligan), Julie Anne Haddock (as Melinda Mulligan), K.C. Martel (as Jimmy Mulligan), Chris Ciampa (as Adam Friedman), Suzanne Crough (as Stevie Friedman), Sunshine Lee (as Kimmy Friedman), Lory Kochheim (as Polly Friedman), Jaime Alba (as Polo Polocheck). P: Joanna Lee. D: Hollingsworth Morse, Curtis Harrington, Leslie H. Martinson.

James at 15

Drama. Ran on NBC Thursday 9–10 P.M. Oct. 27, 1977–March 16, 1978, and June 1–July 27, 1978, opposite *Barney Miller* and *Carter Country* (through March 16) and movies (from June 1) on ABC and *Hawaii Five-O* on CBS. C: Lance Kerwin (as James Hunter), Linden Chiles (as Alan Hunter), Lynn Carlin (as Meg Hunter), David Hubbard (as Sly "Ludwig" Hazeltine), Kim Richards (as Sandy Hunter), Diedre Berthrong (as Kathy Hunter), Susan Myers (as Marlene Mahoney). EP: Martin Manulis, Joseph Hardy. P: Ernest Losso, Ronald Rubin. D: Joseph Hardy, Ernest Losso, James Sheldon, Marc Daniels. W: Dan Wakefield.

When journalist Dan Wakefield presented his proposal of a drama centering on a teenage boy's life based on a novel he wrote, he found a willing audience with veteran executive producer Martin Manulis. "I loved his writing," he said. "I came back to television to do it." Manulis was director of the western branch of the American Film Institute when he received Wakefield's presentation.

First done as a TV-movie pilot which aired Sept. 5, 1977, *James at 15* told the story of young James Hunter going through the pains of adolescence, starting with his unhappiness of his family relocating to Boston from Oregon and forcing him to leave his girlfriend. The middle child of Alan and Meg Hunter (Sandy was younger than him, Kathy older) eventually got used to living in Boston with the help of his hip (for 1977) black pal Sly and platonic girl friend Marlene. All the actors playing the Hunter family also were in the TV-movie.

"It was a charming show. We had a nice family group. The young man was excellent," Manulis said, referring to actor Lance Kerwin, whom Manulis picked for the role.

Though the show often dramatized James' flights of fancy in lighter moments, to give it a semblance of reality Wakefield plan to age his character one year every season. Thus, on the episode aired Feb. 9, 1978, *James at 15* became *James at 16*. However, Wakefield also planned for James to sleep with his girlfriend at the time of his birthday on the episode, and his script about it upset network executives.

"Their idea of censorship at NBC, it was when James had to lose his virginity, or rather we decided he would. He was having a date with this girl, and he stopped at a drug store. You didn't hear what he said. You saw the hand of the pharmacist graze the hand of James." The implication, of course, was that James bought a condom to use for sex.

"The network absolutely refused to have that, but then they didn't mind he had sex with her *without* the use of anything," Manulis said. (Remember, this was prior to the spread of AIDS, when condoms implied more about sexual activity than safe sex.) When informed of this decision, Wakefield said, "I think this is the most peculiar morality I've ever known" and left the show. Manulis was similarly distressed and noted that "I must say it's one of the reasons why I never did a series afterward."

Without Wakefield at the helm, and no noticeable improvement in ratings despite the much-publicized brouhaha, NBC gave up on the series a month later, returning it in the summer to burn off a few extra episodes. Kerwin, a promising actor, wound up in bit roles by the 1980s as drug abuse took a toll on him. He resurfaced in the late 1990s as a substance abuse counselor in California at a Christian ranch called U-Turn for Christ and said he had no plans to return to acting.

Razzmatazz

Children's. Ran on CBS Saturdays once a month 1:30–2 P.M. Nov. 5, 1977–June 8, 1978, opposite college football on ABC (through Nov. 26). C: Barry Bostwick.

Tabitha

Sitcom. Ran on ABC Saturdays 8–8:30 P.M. Nov. 12, 1977–Jan. 14, 1978, opposite *The Bob Newhart Show* on CBS and *The Bionic Woman* on NBC. C: Lisa Hartman (as Tabitha Stephens), Robert Urich (as Paul Thurston), Mel Stewart (as Marvin

Decker), David Ankrum (as Adam Stephens), Karen Morrow (as Aunt Minerva). EP: Jerry Mayer. P: George Yanok. D: Charles R. Rondeau, Murray Golden, George Tyne.

What Really Happened to the Class of '65?

Drama. Ran on NBC Thursdays 10–11 P.M. Dec. 8, 1977–July 27, 1978, opposite *Redd Foxx* (through Jan. 26) and *Baretta* (from Feb. 2) on ABC and *Barnaby Jones* on CBS. C: Tony Bill (as Sam Ashley). EP/D: Richard Irving. P: Jack Laird, Jules Irving. D: Leo Penn, Ron Satlof, Jules Irving, Jack Starrett.

Baby, I'm Back

Sitcom. Ran on CBS Mondays 8:30–9 P.M. Jan. 30–Aug. 12, 1978, opposite *The Six Million Dollar Man* (through March 6) and baseball (from March 13) on ABC and *Little House on the Prairie* on NBC. C: Demond Wilson (as Raymond Ellis), Denise Nicholas (as Olivia Ellis), Helen Martin (as Luzelle Carter), Kim Fields (as Angie Ellis), Tony Holmes (as Jordan Ellis), Ed Hall (as Col. Wallace Dickey). EP: Charles Fries, Sandy Krinski. P: Lila Garrett. D: Asaad Kelada, Mark Warren, Nick Havinga.

Quark

Sitcom. Ran on NBC Fridays 8–8:30 P.M. Feb. 24–April 24, 1978, opposite *Donny and Marie* on ABC and *Wonder Woman* on CBS. C: Richard Benjamin (as Adam Quark), Tim Thomerson (as Gene/Jean), Richard Kelton (as Ficus), Tricia Barnstable (as Betty I), Cyb Barnstable (as Betty II), Bobby Porter (as Andy the Robot), Conrad Janis (as Otto Palindrome), Alan Caillou (as The Head). EP: David Gerber. P: Mace Neufeld, Bruce Johnson. D: Hy Averback, Bruce Bilson.

The Chuck Barris Rah Rah Show

Variety. Ran on NBC Tuesdays 8–9 P.M. Feb. 25–April 11, 1978, opposite *Happy Days* and *Laverne & Shirley* on ABC and *Celebrity Challenge of the Sexes* (through Feb. 28) and *Sam* (from March 14) and *Shields and Yarnell* (through March 28) on CBS. C: Chuck Barris, Jaye P. Morgan, the Milton Delugg Orchestra. EP: Chuck Barris. P: Gene Banks. D: John Dorse.

Husbands, Wives and Lovers

Sitcom. Ran on CBS Fridays 10–11 P.M. March 10–June 30, 1978, opposite movies on ABC and *Quincy, M.E.* on NBC. C: Ron Rifkin (as Ron Willis), Jesse Welles (as Helene Willis), Stephen Pearlman (as Murray Zuckerman), Cynthia Harris (as Paula Zuckerman), Eddie Barth (as Harry Bellini), Lynne Marie Stewart (as Joy Bellini), Mark Lonow (as Lennie Bellini), Randee Heller (as Rita DeLatorre), Charles Siebert (as Dixon Carter Fielding), Claudette Nivens (as Courtney Fielding). EP: Hal Dresner, Edgar Rosenberg. P: Don Van Atta. D: Marc Daniels, Bill Persky, James Burrows.

Sam

Adventure. Ran on CBS Tuesdays 8–8:30 P.M. March 14–April 18, 1978, opposite *Happy Days* on ABC and *The Chuck Barris Rah Rah Show* on NBC. C: Mark Harmon (as Officer Mike Breen), Len Wayland (as Captain Tom Clagett). EP: Jack Webb, Paul Donnelly. P: James Doherty, Leonard B. Kaufman. D: Jack Webb, John Florea.

Richie Brockelman, Private Eye

Crime Drama. Ran on NBC Fridays 9–10 P.M. March 17–April 14, 1978, opposite movies on ABC and *The Incredible Hulk* on CBS, then NBC Thursdays 9–10 P.M. Aug. 10–Aug. 24, 1978, opposite *Barney Miller* and movies on ABC and *Hawaii Five-O* on CBS. C: Dennis Dugan (as Richie Brockelman), Robert Hogan (as Sgt. Ted Coopersmith), Barbara Bosson (as Sharon Deterson). EP: Stephen J. Cannell, Steven Bochco. P: Peter S. Fischer. D: Hy Averback.

A.E.S. Hudson Street

Sitcom. Ran on ABC Thursdays 9:30–10 P.M. March 23–April 20, 1978, opposite *Hawaii Five-O* on CBS and *James at 15* on NBC. C: Gregory Sierra (as Dr. Antonio "Tony" Menzies), Rosana DeSoto (as Nurse Rose Santiago), Stefan Gierasch (as J. Powell Karbo), Susan Peretz (as Foshko), Ralph Manza (as Stanke), Ray Steward (as Nurse Newton), Bill Cort (as Dr. Jerry Mackler), Allan Miller (as Dr. Glick). EP: Danny Arnold. P: Roland Kibbee. D: Noam Pitlik.

The Amazing Spider-Man

Adventure. Ran on CBS Wednesdays 8–9 P.M. April 5–May 3, 1978, opposite *Eight Is Enough* on

ABC and *The Life and Times of Grizzly Adams* on NBC. C: Nicholas Hammond (as Peter Parker/ Spider-Man), Michael Pataki (as Capt. Barbera), Robert F. Simon (as J. Jonah Jameson), Chip Fields (as Rita Conway). EP: Charles Fries, Daniel R. Goodman. P: Robert Janes, Ron Satlof, Lionel E. Siegel. D: Ron Satlof, Fernando Lamas. W: Robert Janes.

The Ted Knight Show

Sitcom. Ran on CBS Saturdays 8:30–9 P.M. April 8–May 13, 1978, opposite *Operation Petticoat* on ABC and *The Bionic Woman* on NBC. C: Ted Knight (as Roger Dennis), Normann Burton (as Burt Dennis), Iris Adrian (as Dottie), Thomas Leopold (as Winston Dennis), Cissy Colpitts (as Graziella), Fawne Harriman (as Honey), Ellen Regan (as Irma), Tanya Boyd (as Philadelphia Phil Brown), Janice Kent (as Cheryl), Deborah Harmon (as Joy), Claude Stroud (as Hobart Nalven). EP: Mark Rothman, Lowell Ganz. P: Martin Cohan, David W. Dulcon. D: Martin Cohan, Joel Zwick, Howard Storm.

Another Day

Sitcom. Ran on CBS Saturdays 9–9:30 P.M. April 8–April 29, 1978, opposite *The Love Boat* on ABC and movies on NBC. C: David Groh (as Don Gardner), Joan Hackett (as Ginny Gardner), Hope Summers (as Olive Gardner), Lisa Lindgren (as Kelly Gardner), Al Eisenmann (as Mark Gardner). EP/D: James Komack. P: Paul Mason, George Kirgo. D: Burt Brinkerhoff, Nick Havinga.

The Roller Girls

Sitcom. Ran on NBC Mondays 8–8:30 P.M. April 24–May 1, 1978, opposite *Sugar Time!* on ABC and *The Jeffersons* on CBS, then NBC Wednesday 8–8:30 P.M. May 10, 1978, opposite *Eight is Enough* on ABC and on CBS. C: Terry Kiser (as Don Mitchell), Rhonda Bates (as "Mongo" Sue Lampert), Candy Ann Brown (as J.B. Johnson), Joanna Cassidy (as Selma "Books" Cassidy), Marcy Hanson (as Honey Bee Novak), Marilyn Tokuda (as Shana "Pipeline" Akira), James Murtaugh (as Howie Devine). EP: James Komack, Stan Cutler, George Tricker. P: Tom Cherones. D: James Komack, Burt Brinkerhoff.

Joe and Valerie

Sitcom. Ran on NBC Mondays 8:30–9 P.M. April 24–May 10, 1978, opposite baseball on ABC and *Baby, I'm Back* on CBS, then NBC Fridays 8:30–9 P.M. Jan. 5–Jan. 19, 1979, opposite *Donny and Marie* on ABC and *Wonder Woman* on CBS. C: Paul Regina (as Joe Pizo), Char Fontane (as Valerie Sweetzer), David Elliott (as Paulie Barone), Donna Ponterotto (as Thelma Medina), Robert Constanza (as Vincent Pizo), Bill Beyers (as Frank Berganski; 1978), Lloyd Alann (as Frank Berganski; 1979), Pat Benson (as Stella Sweetzer; 1978), Arlene Golonka (as Stella Sweetzer; 1979). EP: Linda Hope. P: Bernie Kahn (1978), Frank Badami (1979). D: Bill Persky, Bob Claver.

Operation: Runaway

Drama. Ran on NBC Thursdays 9–10 P.M. April 27–May 18, 1978, opposite *Barney Miller* and movies on ABC and *Hawaii Five-O* on CBS, then NBC Thursdays 10–11 P.M. Aug. 10–Aug. 31, 1978, opposite movies on ABC and *Barnaby Jones* on CBS, and then NBC Tuesdays 8–9 P.M. May 29–Sept. 4, 1979, opposite *Happy Days* and *Laverne & Shirley* (through July 24) and *Detective School* (from July 31–Aug. 14) on ABC and *The Paper Chase* (through July 17) and *Wonder Woman* (from July 24) on CBS. C: Robert Reed (as David McKay; 1978), Karen Machon (as Karen Wingate), Michael Biehn (as Mark Johnson), Ruth Cox (as Susan Donovan; 1978), Alan Feinstein (as Steve Arizzio; 1979), Patti Cohoon (as Debbie Shaw; 1979), James Callahan (as Sgt. Hal Grady; 1979). EP: William Robert Yates. P: Mark Rodgers (1978), Andy White (1979). D: William Wiard, Walter Grauman, Kenneth Gilbert.

America Alive

Informational/Talk. Ran on NBC Mondays through Fridays Noon–1 P.M. July 24, 1978–Jan. 5, 1979, opposite *The $20,000 Pyramid* and *Ryan's Hope* on ABC and *The Young and the Restless* and *Search for Tomorrow* on CBS. C: Jack Linkletter, Bruce Jenner, Janet Langhart, David Horowitz, David Sheehan, Dr. William Masters and Virginia Johnson, Dick Orkin and Bert Berdis, Virginia Graham (1978). EP: Woody Fraser. P: Susan Winston, Kenny Price, Marty Berman, Joan Auritt. D: Don King, Bob Coudin.

One of the more ambitious daily series of the 1970s, *America Alive* meant to show that the networks could program more than just game shows and soap opera in the afternoon hours. Unfortunately for the series, it was those types of shows which outrated it and knocked it off the air. The format was a somewhat unsettled mix of news, interviews, informational pieces and comedy bits presided over by host Jack

Linkletter live (as the title implied) with a studio audience from New York. Guests also appeared, either in taped segments or live in the studio or via satellite from another location (one of the first shows to do so, though not the first, as some of its ads implied).

Former Olympic decathlon champion Bruce Jenner and female reporters Pat Mitchell and Janet Langhart alternated in filing news stories from outside the studio at the start of each show. They were followed by different segments involving regular contributors David Horowitz (consumer news), David Sheehan (Hollywood entertainment news and reviews), Masters and Johnson (sex advice), Virginia Graham (gossip, or as her segment was billed, "People Talk") and Dick Orkin and Bert Berdis (humorous routines).

The latter duo, who gained national fame for funny radio commercials they produced and delivered on air, came onto the program in a fortuitous manner. "We were just in the process of moving from Chicago to L.A.," recalled Berdis. "They gave us the 'Dick and Bert Corner' to do our kind of humor three times a week."

Berdis forgot exactly what bits he and Orkin did. "It's odd. I've saved some tapes of us from a lot of shows, but not that one." But, he noted "They certainly were commenting on the times. Woody [Fraser, the show's executive producer] was terrific, he let us do whatever we wanted us to do."

Apart from their sketches, Berdis and Orkin had nothing to do with *America Alive*, whose progress was anything but a laughing matter at NBC. Midway through its run, with ratings low and costs high, the series dropped Graham and a few other segments. But the changes did not lead to bigger audiences. "It was just not getting what NBC wanted," Berdis said. NBC replaced it with revivals of two old game shows—*Jeopardy!* and *Password Plus*.

Most of the regulars on *America Alive* continued with long broadcasting careers afterward despite the show's failure, except for sex experts Masters and Johnson, who preferred to remain in their field of study. Berdis and Orkin became regulars on *The Tim Conway Comedy Hour* in 1980, then continued doing radio advertisements. In 1990 the men went their separate ways, with Berdis now supervising his own production company that creates some 500–600 radio ads per year, with half of them being read or acted by Berdis. "The only performing I do now is as a voiceover actor," he said.

APPENDIX:
THE SHORTEST OF THE
SHORTEST-LIVED SHOWS
1948–1978

Cancelled Prior to Debut

Snip: September 1976*

One Week Only

1. *Who's Whose*: June 25, 1951
2. *You're in the Picture*: Jan. 20, 1961*
3. *Turn On*: Feb. 5, 1969*

Two Weeks Only

1. *Joey Faye's Frolics*: April 5–12, 1950
2. *Ranger Ranch Roundup*: April 16–23, 1950
3. *Guess Again*: June 14–21, 1951
4. *Tag the Gag*: Aug. 13–20, 1951

Three Weeks Only

1. *Doc Corkle*: Oct. 5–19, 1952*
2. *100 Grand*: Sept. 15–29, 1963*

Four Weeks Only

1. *Buzzy Wuzzy*: Nov. 17–Dec. 8, 1948
2. *Draw Me a Laugh*: Jan. 15–Feb. 5, 1949*
3. *Rendezvous*: Feb. 13–March 5, 1952
4. *Breakfast in Hollywood*: Jan. 11–Feb. 5, 1954 (daily show)
5. *The World at Home*: Aug. 22–Sept. 9, 1955 (daily show)
6. *The Tammy Grimes Show*: Sept. 8–29, 1966
7. *Khan*: Feb. 7–28, 1975
8. *Nashville 99*: April 1–22, 1977
9. *Young Dan'l Boone*: Sept. 12–Oct. 4, 1977
10. *The Roller Girls*: April 24–May 10, 1978

* Profiled in depth in this book

BIBLIOGRAPHY

Books

Andrews, Bart, with Brad Dunning. *The Worst TV Shows Ever.* New York: E.P. Dutton, 1980.

Brooks, Tim. *The Complete Directory to Prime Time TV Stars 1946–Present.* New York: Ballantine, 1987.

_____, and Earle Marsh. *The Complete Directory to Prime Time Network and Cable TV Shows 1946–Present.* (7th Edition). New York: Ballantine, 1999.

Castleman, Harry, and Walter J. Podrazik. *The TV Schedule Book.* New York: McGraw-Hill, 1984.

Dunning, John. *On the Air: The Encyclopedia of Old-Time Radio.* New York: Oxford University, 1998.

Goldberg, Lee. *Unsold Television Pilots, 1955 Through 1989.* Jefferson, N.C.: McFarland, 1990.

Hyatt, Wesley. *The Encyclopedia of Daytime Television.* New York: Billboard, 1997.

Kaplan, Mike (ed.). *Variety Presents the Complete Book of Major U.S. Show Business Awards.* New York: Garland, 1985.

Kisseloff, Jeff. *The Box: An Oral History of Television, 1920–1961.* New York: Viking, 1995.

LaGuardia, Robert. *Soap World.* New York: Arbor House, 1983.

Marill, Alvin H. *Movies Made for Television: The Telefeature and the Mini-Series 1964–1984.* New York: Zoetrope, 1984.

McNeil, Alex. *Total Television: The Comprehensive Guide to Programming from 1948 to the Present, Fourth Edition.* New York: Penguin, 1996.

Phillips, Mark, and Frank Garcia. *Science Fiction Television Series.* Jefferson, N.C.: McFarland, 1996.

Schemering, Christopher. *The Soap Opera Encyclopedia.* New York: Ballantine Books, 1985.

Schwartz, David, Steve Ryan and Fred Wostbrook. *The Encyclopedia of TV Game Shows.* 3rd ed. New York: Facts on File, 1999.

Terrace, Vincent. *Television 1970–1980.* San Diego: A.S. Barnes, 1981.

_____. *Encyclopedia of Television Series, Pilots and Specials 1937–1973.* New York: Zoetrope, 1986.

Whitburn, Joel. *Pop Memories 1890–1954.* Menomonee Falls, WI; Record Research, Inc., 1986.

Wicking, Christopher, and Tise Vahimagi. *The American Vein: Directors and Directions in Television.* New York: E.P. Dutton, 1979.

Woolery, George W. *Children's Television: The First Thirty-Five Years.* Metuchen, N.J.: Scarecrow, 1985 (Part II).

Periodicals

Billboard. 1948–1956 (TV reviews).
Variety. 1948–1978 (TV reviews).
TV Guide. 1954–1978 (TV listings).
The New York Times. 1948–1963 (TV listings).

Internet Sites

www.imdb.com (Internet Movie Database)
www.tvparty.com

INDEX

Series titles in *bold italics* indicate a reference to a main entry in the book (a **bold** number indicates the page of that series' main entry). Other series titles are in *italics*.

281